WIN

BLOOD

Religion, Culture, and Public Life

Series Editor: Karen Barkey

The resurgence of religion calls for careful analysis and constructive criticism of new forms of intolerance, as well as new approaches to tolerance, respect, mutual understanding, and accommodation. To promote serious scholarship and informed debate, the Institute for Religion, Culture, and Public Life and Columbia University Press are sponsoring a book series devoted to the investigation of the role of religion in society and culture today. This series includes works by scholars in religious studies, political science, history, cultural anthropology, economics, social psychology, and other allied fields whose work sustains multidisciplinary and comparative as well as transnational analyses of historical and contemporary issues. The series focuses on issues related to questions of difference, identity, and practice within local, national, and international contexts. Special attention is paid to the ways in which religious traditions encourage conflict, violence, and intolerance and also support human rights, ecumenical values, and mutual understanding. By mediating alternative methodologies and different religious, social, and cultural traditions, books published in this series will open channels of communication that facilitate critical analysis.

After Pluralism: Reimagining Religious Engagement,
edited by Courtney Bender and Pamela E. Klassen

Religion and International Relations Theory, edited by Jack Snyder

Religion in America: A Political History, Denis Lacorne

Democracy, Islam, and Secularism in Turkey,
edited by Ahmet T. Kuru and Alfred Stepan

Refiguring the Spiritual: Beuys, Barney, Turrell, Goldsworthy, Mark C. Taylor

Tolerance, Democracy, and Sufis in Senegal, edited by Mamadou Diouf

*Rewiring the Real: In Conversation with William Gaddis, Richard Powers,
Mark Danielewski, and Don DeLillo*, Mark C. Taylor

Democracy and Islam in Indonesia, edited by Mirjam Künkler and Alfred Stepan

Religion, the Secular, and the Politics of Sexual Difference,
edited by Linell E. Cady and Tracy Fessenden

BLOOD

A CRITIQUE OF CHRISTIANITY

Gil Anidjar

COLUMBIA UNIVERSITY PRESS

NEW YORK

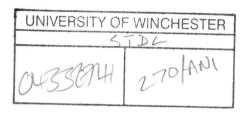

Columbia University Press
Publishers Since 1893
New York   Chichester, West Sussex
cup.columbia.edu

Copyright © 2014 Columbia University Press
Paperback edition, 2016

Library of Congress Cataloging-in-Publication Data
Anidjar, Gil.
Blood : a critique of Christianity / Gil Anidjar.
pages cm. — (Religion, culture, and public life)
Includes bibliographical references and index.
ISBN 978-0-231-16720-8 (cloth : alk. paper)—ISBN 978-0-231-16721-5 (pbk. : alk. paper)—
ISBN 978-0-231-53725-4 (e-book)
1. Blood—Religious aspects—Christianity.   2. Christianity—Essence, genius, nature.
3. Blood—Miscellanea.   I. Title.
BR115.B57A55 2014
230—dc23
2013040714

Columbia University Press books are printed on permanent and durable acid-free paper.
Printed in the United States of America
c 10 9 8 7 6 5 4 3 2
p 10 9 8 7 6 5 4 3 2 1

Cover design: David Drummond

CONTENTS

PREFACE: WHY I AM
SUCH A GOOD CHRISTIAN

IS THERE SUCH a thing as "the Christian Question"?[1]

What would it mean to ask it? What could it mean today to attend to "the *enormous question mark* called Christianity" and to ask, for instance, *what* Christianity is?[2] The answer—so obvious, so unremarkable, and so resilient—is, of course, religion. Christianity is a religion.[3] A religion like any other, then? Not by any means. Yet the claim, common to the point of banality, for the singularity of Christianity out of the fabled sources of theological reason ("theologians and everything with theologian blood in its veins," as Nietzsche phrased it) could have led to a more strenuous interrogation, one not grounded in the tautological form: *vera religio* is—a religion.[4] Before suggesting that Christianity might have persisted, is persisting still, as something else entirely than what it has called itself for some time now (belatedly and grudgingly extending the favor to others)[5]; before proposing that "the essence of Christianity" might not be reducible to its theological or religious dimensions nor indeed be so stable, so *essentially* identical to itself, as to answer to that term, *religion*, for the entire duration of its tumultuous, contested, and admittedly transformative history; before or aside from all that, there is the task of measuring or marking the boundaries and limits of Christianity.[6] How far does Christianity go? How wide does it spread, and what depths does it reach? What divisions does it establish or undo, within and between? This is not merely a spatial or geographic matter—besides, only Western Christendom will be at stake here.[7] The question is one of assignation and integration, of inner realms and outer regions, of distribution and motion, of measure, indeed, and limits.

As I read and survey these limits, seeking to gauge the growth and expanse of oddly chartered domains, I shall have occasion to reiterate (interrogate and elaborate on) the following formulation, blatantly plagiarized from Carl Schmitt, which I offer here as a partial summary for the book that follows: *All significant concepts of the history of the modern world are* liquidated *theological concepts. This is so not only because of their historical development—in which they circulated between theology and the operations of the modern world, whereby, for example, the blood of Christ became the flow of capital—but also because of their systematic fluidity, the recognition of which is necessary for a political consideration of these concepts.* Three of these concepts will occupy me in particular. They are nation, state, and capital, more precisely, what Kojin Karatani magisterially—and transcritically—describes as "the trinity of Capital-Nation-State," a trinity indeed, a conceptual triad that moves and circulates, derives and grows.[8] It is an incomplete but significant triad, one that, to be precise, has rather ebbed and flowed, moved and morphed. It has been distributed and divided. It has traveled perhaps because of its form, a liquid and fluid shape in and through which each of the three concepts acquired a systematic if highly plastic and fluctuating structure and import. With these motions and circulations, through an impressive and effective capacity for change and transformation (of the person, for example, as "flesh and blood"), nay, for transubstantiation, nation, state, and capital become what they have been, *hematological* and *hematopoietic*, and for long enough, which is to say not always, I hope (and fear too). Liquidated, therefore: liquefied and dissolved and finally absolved. "Christ's presence transmutes liquids," writes Michel Serres cannily, but "the cycle loops back upon itself."[9] A political consideration of these concepts, the irresolute condition for comprehending, contesting, or opposing them, has little to do with "the new atheism," God forbid; it is rather tantamount to a recognition that "the worst witness to truth," blood flows still—in, under, and through these concepts. It is by way of blood, Christian blood, that these concepts have become available, sustainable, and readable in their multifarious structure and historical development, in their endurance, too, and cathected significance.[10] A scholarly and, let us say, critical exploration of those concepts, the blood that runs through them, shall have to follow closely and fluently their motion and their flows. It shall adhere to blood, stick to it, heed to the presence of blood and to its absences, to its making and its fashioning, and to its differences (in philosophy and in medicine, from ancient Greece to Melville; in love and in melancholia; in poetry, history, and on TV; from economy to science; and from Jesus to Freud and beyond). For blood not only suffuses these concepts, regions, and more; it constitutes each as a clotted version of its currents.

Not so long ago, one might have asserted that blood is a myth ("the Christian myth") rather than a symbol—another commonplace of the alleged universal—incarnate and manifest as it is in its variable versions, discourses, or concepts.[11] Blood is minimally mytheme, and it is meme, too. Blood is, at any rate, iterated and reiterated in and through these, with and beyond them. Blood functions as a mark, a citation, and a repetition. It moves, operates, and circulates to the extent that it is inscribed, co-agitated, repeated.[12] And "in so doing it can break with every given context, engendering an infinity of new contexts in a manner which is absolutely illimitable."[13] It *can* so break and might therefore *engender* new contexts; it has, in the form of new notions of kinship and of race or of novel, massive, and massively hailed and barely interrogated practices (circulation, donation, and transfusion, for instance).[14] Whether and how it has done so, whether or not the resilience and persistence of this mark—blood—testifies to change, novelty, or indeed repetition: such is what is at stake here. The reading I offer, the argument I ultimately propose, is that between presence and absence, blood is the *element* of Christianity, its voluminous mark (citation, context). It is the way in which and upon which Christianity made its mark. More broadly, a consideration of what blood reflects, produces, and sustains, what it engenders, must take—as one adopts—the form of a critique of Christianity.

ELEMENT, *N.*

Etymology: < Old French element, *< Latin* elementum, *a word of which the etymology and primary meaning are uncertain, but which was employed as translation of Greek στοιχεῖον in the various senses < a component unit of a series; a constituent part of a complex whole (hence the "four elements"); a member of the planetary system; a letter of the alphabet; a fundamental principle of a science.*
A component part of a complex whole. . . .
* of material things.
1. One of the simple substances of which all material bodies are compounded.
†a. In ancient and mediaeval philosophy these were believed to be: Earth, water, air, and fire.
†b. In pre-scientific chemistry the supposed "elements" were variously enumerated, the usual number being about five or six.
†c. In modern chemistry applied to those substances (of which well over one hundred are now known) which have hitherto resisted analysis, and which are provisionally supposed to be simple bodies. . . .
2. In wider sense: One of the relatively simple substances of which a complex substance is composed; in pl. the "raw material" of which a thing is made. . . .

3. *The bread and wine used in the Sacrament of the Eucharist. Chiefly pl.*
[The word elementa *is used in late Latin in the sense of "articles of food and drink,*
the solid and liquid portions of a meal" (see Du Cange); but in the ecclesiastical
use there is probably a reference to the philosophical sense of mere "matter" as apart
from "form"; the "form," by virtue of which the "elements" became Christ's body and
blood, being believed to be imparted by the act of consecration.] . . .
** *of non-material things.*
5.

a. A constituent portion of an immaterial whole, as of a concept, character, state
of things, community, etc.
b. Often followed by of = "consisting of". . . .
6. *One of the facts or conditions which "enter into" or determine the result of a*
process, calculation, deliberation, or inquiry. Also with of (cf. 5b). . . .
II. *The "four elements."*
9. *a. Used as a general name for earth, water, air, and fire; originally in sense 1, to*
which many of the earlier instances have explicit reference; now merely as a matter
of traditional custom. . . .
12. *That one of the "four elements" which is the natural abode of any particular*
class of living beings; said chiefly of air and water. Hence transf. and fig. (a person's)
ordinary range of activity, the surroundings in which one feels at home; the
appropriate sphere of operation of any agency. Phrases, in, out of (one's) element. . . .
III.
13. *Primordial principle, source of origin. rare. . . .*
IV.
14. *a. pl. †The letters of the alphabet (obs.). Hence, the rudiments of learning, the*
"A, B, C"; also, the first principles of an art or science.
—*OXFORD ENGLISH DICTIONARY*

Thus this book offers no explanation. And certainly no *historical* explanation. After all, Pablo Neruda already explained a few things (*algunas cosas*), enough things, and blood is still running in the streets.[15] A different exercise in resignation, the pages that follow laboriously linger in uncertain viscosity, contending instead with the fact that explanations are, if not a thing of the past, then a peculiar and peculiarly constricted struggle with finitude. "We do not seek to explain why things persist," writes William Connolly, least of all ourselves, we scholars.[16] Indeed, to acknowledge the finitude of the scholarly enterprise in confronting perdurance as well as transience could well mean welcoming its ends, one of which would be the irremediable failure (not just belatedness or irrelevance) of explanation. There is no history lesson, one might translate, no lesson learned, not from the victors.[17] And there is no meta-image, which means that it is no longer clear, if it ever was, which is the medium and which the message (which the Christian, which the Jew), or whether an explanation would be forthcoming or even possible, let alone believable. The time of explanation may not be completely over—what ever is?—but explanations, particularly scholarly explanations, have no doubt reached a limit (they have an end somewhere, as Wittgenstein had it). Having proliferated further than every Ockhamian edge, they are past repair and beyond hope. Call it digital nihilism or obstinate retardation, "the last gasp of a dying discipline"[18]; call it speculative realism or negative pedagogy ("the teaching of language is not explaining," Wittgenstein went on); or call it, as Sheldon Pollock did, "the death of Sanskrit."[19] But the recourse to name calling is here analogous to alleging that resoluteness in being toward death—with "the evening redness in the West" (or perhaps it is *Twilight*), is it not time?—can only be glossed as testifying to a suicidal inclination or to an apocalyptic imagination, as if these were what? This, in any case, is not to say that thought, learning, or reflection are at their end (although that *is* a distinct possibility), but that we are past sensing the futility of writing a scholarly book, doing it *by* the book (as if the book could do it, just do it; as if this was not the end of the book in the age of the world tweet-ure). Especially now, "when the history of the world has so terribly and so untidily expanded its endless successiveness."[20] The sheer weight of accumulation, fifty shades of clay and mountains of waste (not to mention, *horribile dictu*, footnotes), among other expansions and past all counts, nonetheless counts for something, that is, for nothing, if only because it accounts for and testifies to the victory of the quantitative—by attrition. Was it ever otherwise? This may or may not be a reason to stop writing books (though I suspect it is). Cunningly endorsing Marx's take on the "gnawing criticism of the mice," Lacan suggests somewhere that praise might be in order when producing a *worst-seller*.

Have I not called this a book? Is it not one after all? To the extent that my opinion matters (having been exposed, just like anybody by now, to an inordinate number of opinions, I am less and less persuaded I should have or add any, much less that I am *capable* or in fact *entitled* to an opinion of my own), I will merely assert that I did not wish for this to be a book. Instead, one could imagine the whole thing as restless and otherwise bound, neither new science nor archaeology, but rather partaking of a different, older tradition of *disputation*—in its initial and final stages a reading, a measuring of the adversary, among whom one lives and whom one invariably emulates, however grudgingly. Think of it as an unfinished project of some premodernity. Early on, at any rate, the growing number of meandering pages now lying ahead impressed themselves upon me (no, seriously) as plausible candidates for a gathered volume, though I would have preferred otherwise. Like much else, the uptake is hardly mine—my fear is that I am but "full of goodwill, a devoted local government worker who has not earned the right to responsibility"—which is why worn caveats blissfully apply, regarding propriety, property, and indeed responsibility, the legal and financial kind in particular (going public, with block if not stock quotes).[21] That being said, I beg you, please, delicate and obsolete monster, *mon lecteur, ma soeur*, copyleft and rearrange at will. Dispute and destroy.

One late night, this story goes, a man is pacing under a streetlight. Another comes along. "Have you lost something?" "Yes," answers the first, "my keys." They search together for a while. "Are you sure you lost them here?" "Oh, no, no. I dropped them over there, but here is where the light is." In the spirit of *Witz*, then, past the enlightenment and through a scanner darkly, blood illuminates, if nothing else, the chapters ahead. Blood, described by Wallace Stevens as "the more than human commonplace of blood / The breath that gushes upward and is gone," marks a more specific trail, delineates a contained if expanding domain, and signals limits. A long way from here, out of sources that—neither Greek nor Jew, not quite, thankfully— bring the trail of repetitive iterations to a provisional end, an answer beckons (ah, but for the question!). All of which signals but another series of negations: blood is not found here as an object, nor is it a subject. It is neither a thing nor an idea. And blood is not a concept. It is not an operator, neither actor nor agent. Blood mobilizes and condenses, it singles out and constitutes, a shifting *perspective* (ebbing and flowing, later circulating) like one of those images and forms—elements, again, or complexes of culture—that fill the material imagination, of which Gaston Bachelard wrote in *Water and Dreams*.[22] Blood could promisingly have served the function of a "signature," which, Giorgio Agamben insists, is not a concept but "something that in a sign or concept marks and exceeds such a sign or concept referring it back to a determinate interpretation or field, without for this reason leaving the semiotic to constitute a new meaning or a new concept."[23] Blood is better intuited, I said, as an element. Part or whole, in any case, blood does not, cannot refer back to any privileged field, *not even to theology*, coming as it does to seize, occupy, and linger in and across regions, dissolving between and beyond signs. The extracts I use from the *Oxford English Dictionary* begin to delineate this spread and proliferation of blood through multiple fields and meanings that, clotted or liquidated, speak to its place and instantiations as the element of Christianity. Blood is not, I repeat, an explanation, though it may be so misunderstood—what ever has not? Blood has no identity to speak of, and *its* integrity or agency, its "internal consistency," is not what I am after.[24] There will be bloods, in other words, but more precisely, multiple iterations of blood—medical and anthropological, juridical and theological, political and economic, rhetorical and philosophical, in disorder of appearance and disappearance. Like other marks, like other signatures or events, these iterations engender, as I have said, a context (or contexts, but the very notion of context silently undoes the significance of this plurality). And therein lies the issue. For I have also been forced to acknowledge that, along with a widespread dissemination and series of distinctions (bloods rather than blood), a definite coagulation in "the restricted permeability of global culture,"[25] a special and spatial concentration, the marking of a fluid but integrated domain, all have taken place and settled in a definite somewhere ("we seek rather to increase knowledge of how things stabilize in a world of becoming," concludes Connolly). Think of *politics*, Dotan Leshem suggests, the transformations and distortions of that Greek word in its rapport to *economics* and beyond, the pertinacity of its framing and stabilizing effects.[26] Think of the Latin *religion* if you will (a different and more opaque history on the margins of which much of this book is written). And then think of blood. There will be bloods, then, but also and finally, retroprospectively, blood.[27] And this precisely *because* what has left us with no alternative to speak of these days seamlessly and relentlessly moves on to and around the plural form. "To pluralize," Derrida pointed out, "is always to provide oneself with an emergency exit, up until the moment when it's the plural that kills you."[28] Or, as the case often is, someone else. For now, and until then, everything remains as if nothing existed as long as unity and oneness can be disproved and dismissed (they can, always). A strange assumption as the plural (histories, modernities, capitalisms, races) is hardly the mark of nothingness or the foundering of integration: only a sign of "misdescription," a problem of "compositeness [*Zusammensetzung*]" (Wittgenstein again), a missing and shrunken perspective on, say, the West, which, Talal Asad reminds us, long consisted of "many faces at home" while presenting "a single face abroad."[29] Who is the subject, then? "Who is the subject? None other than the circulation. None other than the object of this circulation. None other than the cup that circulates and the very object that is drunk. The wine, object, is the subject. The blood of the body's circulation has become, for one moment, unanimous, the blood of a new subject—eternal, doubtless, like the bonds uniting the group. Through circulation and the rupture of the *principium individuationis* the object becomes subject, the wine becomes blood, personality becomes unanimity, and death immortality. Constitution of a unanimous body."[30] Blood for bloods, in other words, and vice versa; no explanation but critique, as my title advertises—blood ebbing, Kant's dove flying—the marking of limits (expansion and depth, divisions and transformations), the acknowledgment of boundaries (for people "do not construct their walls in the same places as do their counterparts. . . . They draw incongruent border lines around their respective communities and establish different kinds of barriers along these borders because they imagine the proper social order in fundamentally different ways"), and inevitably perhaps the policing of borders and flows, at the very least the writing on the wall.[31] But remember, there is no hope for the hopeless, and music says it best: "Blood is worthless." That, at least, is how Life in a Blender stays away from "blood music" (and "blood makes noise," as Suzanne Vega shows), and the point from which we might extend our imagination—or something.[32] I mean by this that *blood is nothing*, nothing much really, and that, reading blood, "we will discover a burden unsuspected and even actively excluded . . . that blood does not matter at all, and to think otherwise is to think like a vampire."[33] And no, not everyone is like that.

ACKNOWLEDGMENTS

SOME SECTIONS AND segments of part 1 were published in different iterations. They were first presented at lectures, seminars, and conferences, for which I thank organizers and audiences and publishers, too. I started speaking about some of this material while a fellow at Wissenschaftkolleg at a conference on "cultural mobility" (I thank Ines Zupanov and Heike Paul for the invitation). Also at WiKo, Pascal Grosse kindly put me in touch with Mariacarla Gadebusch Bondio, which resulted in an early formulation of the argument published as "Lines of Blood: *Limpieza de Sangre* as Political Theology," in *Blood in History and Blood Histories*, Micrologus Library 13, ed. Mariacarla Gadebusch Bondio (Florence: Sismel—Edizioni del Galluzzo, 2005), 119–36. The following year, Yehuda Elkana granted me the possibility of working some of it out during a short stay at Central European University, Budapest, as did Aziz al-Azmeh and Nadia al-Baghdadi for "Theologies of Empire" at Collegium Budapest. Around that time, I also gave a version of "Christians and Money (The Economic Enemy)" at a conference held at the university of Tilburg honoring Egidius Berns (subsequently published in *Ethical Perspectives: Journal of the European Ethics Network* 12, no. 4 [2005]); I had reworked it quite a bit by the time I accepted Rodolphe Gasché's invitation at the Department of Comparative Literature, University of Buffalo, in October 2011. "We Have Never Been Jewish" is the result of a conference on "Jewish Blood" organized by Mitch Hart at the University of Florida, Gainesville, February 2007, subsequently published in *Jewish Blood: Reality and Metaphor in History, Religion, and Culture*, ed. Mitchell B. Hart (New York: Routledge, 2009). I used the same title for the Twenty-Seventh

Annual Hayward Keniston Lecture, Department of Romance Languages and Literatures, University of Michigan, Ann Arbor, February 2008 (I thank my host Jarrod Hayes and his colleagues in the department). "The Blood of Freedom" was delivered, at the invitation of Shaul Bassi and Annalisa Oboe, at "Try Freedom: Rewriting Rights in/through Postcolonial Cultures," EACLALS Triennial Conference at Venice International University, March 2008. It was published in *Experiences of Freedom in Postcolonial Literatures and Cultures*, ed. Annalisa Oboe and Shaul Bassi (New York: Routledge, 2011). Peggy Kamuf asked me to contribute to a special issue of the *Oxford Literary Review* on "Words of War," which became the occasion for "Blutgewalt" (*OLR* 31, no. 2 [December 2009]: 153–74). A segment of "Bleeding and Melancholia" was presented at "Postcolonial Melancholia," organized by Elliot Colla and Nauman Naqvi, Department of Comparative Literature, Brown University, March 2009. Under the heading "Blood," I condensed some of the arguments of "The Vampire State" at "Reworking Political Concepts: A Lexicon in Formation" at the New School for Social Research, December 2010 (my gratitude to Hagar Kotef, Ann Stoler, and Adi Ophir), published online at www.politicalconcepts.org/issue1/blood/. Nina Caputo and Hannah Johnson encouraged me to present some finalized reflections on blood and the Inquisition at their workshop on "The Middle Ages and the Holocaust: Medieval Anti-Judaism in the Crucible of Modern Thought" at the University of Pittsburgh in April 2012. Kriss Ravetto and Mario Biagioli invited me to the program in Cultural Studies, Cinema and Technocultural Studies, and the Center for Science and Innovation Studies, University of California, Davis, to present "Leviathan and the Blood-Pump" (January 2013). Finally, Pleshette DeArmitt gave me the opportunity to try to be just with Freud's Jesus. I am grateful to Emily Zakin for her thoughtful response and to all the participants at the annual Spindel conference at the University of Memphis, the proceedings of which are now published in the *Southern Journal of Philosophy* ("Jesus and Monotheism," *The Southern Journal of Philosophy* vol. 51, Spindel Supplement [2013] 158–183).

Institutions and individuals, faculty and staff, readers and listeners (and listeners some more), hosts and guests, teachers and colleagues, friends, families; days, months, or years (lunar, solar, saturnine, and mercurial); support and comfort, gifts, debts and hyperbolic debts, incommensurate asymmetries. Wissenschaftskolleg zu Berlin; Institute for Advanced Study, Princeton—the members of the "Secularism" seminar; Fakultet za Medije i Komunikacije, Belgrade; Makerere Institute of Social Research, Kampala; at Columbia, the Department of Religion, the Department of Middle Eastern, South Asian, and African Studies, and the Institute for Religion, Culture, and Public Life; at Columbia University Press, Wendy Lochner, Jennifer Crewe, and Christine Dunbar; at Cenveo, Ben Kolstad and Chris Curioli;

elsewhere through time and space, Colette and Raphael Anidjar, 'Eylam and Niv Orent Anidjar, Amnon Raz-Krakotzkin, Ronit Chacham, Marc Nichanian, Ani Garmiryan, Talal and Tanya Asad, Mayanthi Fernando (beyond duty and friendship), Nina Caputo, Mitch Hart, Mark C. Taylor, Joan W. Scott, Elisabeth Weber, Stathis Gourgouris, Neni Panourgiá, Obrad Savić, Dušan Djordjević Mileusnić, Dušan Bjelić, Nada Popović Perišić, Jelisaveta Blagojević, Jovan Cekić, Ruth Tsoffar, Dominique Pestre, Nadia Abu el-Haj, Mahmood Mamdani, Hagar Kotef, Sanjay Reddy, Courtney Bender, Jonathan Schorsch, Claudia Baracchi, Partha Chatterjee, Shaul Bassi, Rebecca Herzig, Quentin Skinner, Isabelle Nicou, Sarah Cole, Martin Harries, Peter Szendy, Laura Odello, George Hoffman, Nauman Naqvi. And Nermeen Shaikh, life itself.

BLOOD

Introduction RED MYTHOLOGY

IF WALTER BENJAMIN'S "Critique of Violence" is also a critique of war—martial or "military violence [*kriegerischen Gewalt*] . . . being primordial and paradigmatic of all violence used for natural ends"—it is far from obvious how the brief and opaque remarks on blood found therein could add, much less contribute, to that critique.[1] Besides, expounding the relations of blood to war and justice hardly seems compelling as a pressing epistemo-critical task of political import. Here too, here especially, Benjamin's essay is likely to fall "short of providing an incisive difference between just and unjust uses of violence, and therefore, in the final analysis, of offering a credible critique of violence."[2] Credible critique indeed—for it must be granted that Benjamin's enigmatic argument reaches singular heights, a culminating intensification of its opacity at the precise juncture where blood appears (under the heading of a "mythical violence" contrasted with divine, "bloodless" violence).[3] There is, moreover, no apparent reason to think that tending to these "bloody" remarks would bring about a better understanding of war or violence; that it would in any way augment the strength of critique or its credibility (notwithstanding the fact that war and violence have proved quite resilient, not to say oblivious, in the face of critique, "and let us not forget," as Jacques Derrida reminds us in his own reading of Benjamin, "if we do not wish to sink into ridicule or indecency, that we are comfortably installed here on Fifth Avenue" or thereabout, "only a few blocks away from the inferno of injustice," where wars of many kinds are conducted and fostered, and where they rage on indeed).[4] Still, by the time Benjamin concludes and evokes "true war" as a privileged instance of "divine violence," the stakes have been raised somehow higher. "One cannot help," Stathis Gourgouris pointedly writes, "but pose the question in brutal literalness: What is violence without blood?"[5]

A second supposition. If, otherwise than as the symbol Benjamin says it is ("for blood is the symbol of mere life" [250]), blood were provisionally taken as a cipher of opacity, as an opportunity for reading or interpreting (war, for example), then the daunting wealth of commentaries generated by "Critique of Violence"—each of them invaluable—could then be summarily organized along a more or less continuous line. Does not "the voice of the blood [*die Stimme des Blutes*] come from the fundamental mood of the human being?"[6] Taking up, or passing on, the opportunity to answer that voice and its question would be those who have nothing, and certainly nothing explicit, to say about blood in Benjamin (Habermas, Marcuse, Hamacher, Agamben, Düttmann, Avelar, Mack, de Wilde); those who take note of blood and offer a quick, if at times pained, gloss on it (LaCapra, Menke, Azoulay, McCall, Hanssen, Gourgouris, Butler); and finally those who view the remarks on blood as a moment of major import in Benjamin's argument (Derrida, Haverkamp, and, more recently, Greenberg).[7]

Whether blood is a cipher, a metaphor or a metonymy (Benjamin, to repeat, calls it a symbol), or indeed "the key to his political-theological thinking,"[8] even the most cursory account must acknowledge it as very much a part of the image drawn by Benjamin of divine violence (the latter being, as Giorgio Agamben has it, "the central problem of every interpretation of the essay").[9] It is at any rate in reference to this precise "problem" that, Derrida writes, "blood would make all the difference."[10] This is not to say that this "thought of blood" is a comforting or even helping thought. It is simply to highlight that it is "as troubling, despite certain dissonances, in Benjamin as it is in Rosenzweig" (288). Why? Because there emerges the no less enigmatic but terrifying possibility that this thought of blood, this notion of a "bloodless violence," constitutes an "allusion to an extermination that would be expiatory because bloodless." Thus, it "must cause one to shudder. One is terrified at the idea of an interpretation that would make of the holocaust an expiation and an indecipherable signature of the just and violent anger of God" (298).

Now, any evaluation of Derrida's reading (or of his alarm) would have to confront the charge or significance carried by blood in "Force of Law."[11] But it is of course with regard to Benjamin's own text that this injunction must first be heeded.[12] For upon such an inquiry, as I attempt to conduct it in this introduction, some steps might be taken, and with some measure of cogency, toward a critique of war (to begin with, as it were) and its relation to a critique of blood.

One more preliminary remark. If a critique of war entails a critique of blood, then what of it? Before getting to blood, Benjamin famously made his critique of violence (juridical, military, social, linguistic, and so forth) contingent on a suspension of the realm of ends and on the ability (or at least the need) to "discriminate within the sphere of means themselves, without regards for the ends they serve."[13] It has long been impossible to un-hear echoes of Clausewitz here, along with its ensuing transpositions. Accordingly, a critique of war after Benjamin would have to suspend both the notion that "war is the continuation of politics by other means" and its now equally famous, and inverted, rendering, namely, that "politics is the continuation of war by other means."[14] But if Benjamin's critique of violence is notoriously obscure, the adoption of his perspective with regard to blood—whatever this perspective is—may very well be entirely unfathomable. The exercise (the exclusion of the realm of ends from the limits of the inquiry) seems nonetheless appealing, and particularly so when one considers that the relation between war and blood has most certainly been naturalized, albeit in still shrouded ways, along the lines of means and ends. Minimally, a rudimentary acquaintance with history would seem to support a narrative whereby it used to be the case that war *followed* blood. War was a consequence of blood and its logical end. It was conducted for blood motives (family and tribe, lust and revenge). It maintained and reproduced itself as the culmination of innumerable and massive instances of blood feuds.[15] Then—according to enduring lines of assumption, yet without more assurance that this would be of relevance to our present—war came to *result* in blood. War was followed by blood rather than preceded by it—and thankfully so (or so we might think). Blood followed war where it could not be avoided. It was the unavoidable end for which war was the means (one could phrase this another way and say that, anticipating the regrettable event of collateral spillage, the blood banks, the blood supply, were sent ahead of time to prepare for war).

Shifting registers ever so slightly to underscore the link between blood and war, one might emphasize that the two further share a certain historicity. Like war, blood seems a thing of the past. It has "faded out as a symbol in the age of the police and self-contained administration."[16] One no longer goes to war (bear with me here), not for blood at least. Similarly, war, if it must be waged, must be conducted so as to shed the least amount of blood. War strives toward bloodlessness (on our side at least, where God is). In this context, "No Blood for Oil" is an exemplary slogan that testifies to a proximate, if perhaps mistaken, assumption, namely, that war is still about motives; that blood is still shed for a reason: means to an approaching end, even peaceful ends—eternally peaceful, as Benjamin wryly remarks echoing Kant. No doubt, the phrase could only cynically be read as intending to promote the shedding of blood—as if there were other and better reasons to go to war, to let out the proverbial rivers of blood. Whatever the motives (oil), there are here consequences (blood), the unwanted or unanticipated product or result of war, and possibly the last hurdle to a war to end all wars. And though the equation is precisely what is resisted, the conflation seems inevitable in any number of configurations: Oil can be substituted for blood (and vice versa) in a broad arc of "metaphoric" figurations. More important, and on a most *literal* plane (an attribute that should be anything but secure, as we shall repeatedly see, and particularly when it comes to blood), what if war were "simply" blood? Is it not equal to, even identical with, blood? What could be more obvious, more natural than this after all?[17] Alternatively, what are the effects of relinquishing to an alleged empiricity, which may well be outdated, the equation of war (and murder) with bloodshed? War is blood and blood is war. In this realm of impure means, war and blood no longer serve any purpose. There they remain, nonetheless, confined to what Agamben would call their "indistinction."

🗺 🗺 🗺

Is it at all feasible, then, desirable or even *useful* to try to disentangle and decouple war from blood? It cannot be doubted that this is quite precisely what Benjamin proposes to do.

> Just as in all spheres God opposes myth, mythic violence is confronted by the divine [*so tritt der mythischen Gewalt die göttliche entgegen*]. And the latter constitutes its antithesis in all respects. If mythic violence is lawmaking, divine violence is law-destroying; if the former sets boundaries, the latter boundlessly destroys them; if mythic violence brings at once guilt and retribution, divine power only expiates; if the former threatens, the latter strikes; if the former is bloody, the latter is lethal without spilling blood. (249/G199)

Much of our understanding of the complex divisions lined up in this passage hangs on what Benjamin means by "antithesis [*Gegensatz*]." It is as if war were already raging between two opposite sides, defined asymmetrically by way of blood and culminating with it. One is unlikely, for instance, to miss echoes of familiar oppositions, which would associate myth with flesh and blood and the divine with an abstract or idealized instance. A more erudite version might associate the mythical with the historical, opposing both to the divine as their interruption (the question being, as Benjamin says, "of a pure immediate violence that might be able to call a halt to mythical violence" [249]). In these perspectives and in others too, blood has been taken to stand for the literal, for the concrete, and even for the biological.[18] But this would be forgetting that violence is on both sides of the equation and that the asymmetry of the two sides must reside in the kinds of violence here discussed. Gourgouris's question still stands, in other words: "what is violence without blood?"

As tempting as the identification between blood and the biological might be, it would also have to contend with what Benjamin writes in the lines that follow, and therefore with the distinction between "life," and more precisely "mere life," on the one hand and "the living" on the other. It seems quite difficult, at any rate, to distinguish between the two on the basis of a biological understanding that would be confined to one side only. Violence without blood may be one thing, but what of living beings without life? By emphasizing a biological or physiologic understanding, moreover, and without necessarily adjudicating on the alleged Jewishness of this text, one ends up ignoring the force of the biblical citations that intervene in quite an exacting manner on the very question of "life" and its relation to blood.[19] After all, Benjamin leaves no doubt that "mere life" is fundamentally related to "the doctrine of the sanctity of life," and he links both to blood (250). Notwithstanding his debate with vitalism or with Darwinism and other forms of scientism, it is here that Benjamin makes multiple, unmitigated appeals to a "religious" or "theological" source—the Bible.[20] What it precisely is, however, that he does with the Bible has yet to attract much attention.

Among Benjamin's readers, and particularly those interested in his Jewishness or in his alleged affinities with Gershom Scholem's stakes on modern and premodern Jewish thought,[21] few are those who have sought to disentangle the Jewish from the Christian in the essay at hand.[22] For overdetermined reasons, no doubt, the focus has remained on Greek myth as a significant, opposite or apposite figure, contrasted with whatever Benjamin himself alludes to or designates as "Jewish."[23] Gourgouris has rightly noted that there might be something like "a monotheistic conception of myth" and a "paradigmatic monotheistic conception of law" at work in Benjamin's text, but he does not linger on how this implicit opposition of Athens and Jerusalem casts or recasts figures of *internal* dissension in that not-so monological monotheism.[24] True, Benjamin himself opposes Niobe to Korah, and the lexical registers he deploys with regard to mythical violence (law, blood, guilt, sacrifice) and to "the sanctity of life" could easily be identified with Athens (or, for that matter, and assuming the famous opposition stands, with Jerusalem). This identification, though, has notably been dismissed by Giorgio Agamben, who has made a series of remarkable contributions to these debates, beginning, of course, with his uptake of the notion of "bare life." Agamben writes that

[T]he principle of the sacredness of life has become so familiar to us that we seem to forget that classical Greece, to which we owe most of our ethico-political concepts, not only ignored this principle but did not even possess a term to express the complex semantic sphere that we indicate with the single term "life." Decisive as it is for the origin of Western politics, the opposition between *zoe* and *bios* . . . contains nothing to make one assign a privilege or a sacredness to life as such.[25]

The important thing to note is that, unless we accuse him of caricatural misunderstanding, Benjamin is deploying a language of conflict that has little to do with classical Greece (or again, with biology), for which the latter is ultimately no more than a cipher. Following Agamben's suggestion that "life became sacred only through a series of rituals whose aim was precisely to separate life from its profane context," I want to argue that Benjamin offered a little-noticed answer to Agamben's question "when and in what way did a human life first come to be considered sacred in itself?"[26] It is an answer that traverses, and cuttingly so, any Judeo-Christian *entente* or *détente* (and let us remember that being a text about war, "Critique of Violence" itself can hardly be read as anything less than "polemical through and through," anything less than a declaration of war), that is, not merely with the Judaism now cherished by countless readers, but with Christianity as well.[27] This is so, at least in part, because as one of Benjamin's sharpest commentators, Jacob Taubes, eloquently points out, this is a time in which the "Jewish–Christian controversy" was in fact raging in Germany, involving public figures like Buber, Rosenzweig, and others.[28] Moreover, as Brian Britt explains, "if Benjamin's project were simply to describe Western culture, the Christian emphasis would come as no surprise," even if few bothered to take notice. Yet, "the deeper problem lies in sorting out Benjamin's interpretive standpoint toward Christian sources."[29] Indeed, in "Critique of Violence," Benjamin repeatedly returns to the Old Testament not so much to take sides (this will come in due time) as much as to articulate a standpoint that would enable him to illustrate an opposition between mythical and divine violence. With these illustrations (if illustrations they are—one might speak with more accuracy of "fighting words" or indeed of "fighting images"), Benjamin sets the stage for a conflict. And it is precisely in this "Judeo-Christian" context (what Benjamin calls "contemporary European conditions" [238]) and not with regard to Greek material (or an awkwardly isolated "Judaism") that blood emerges as a major element—the very *Kampfplatz*—that sustains the warring distinction between a violence associated with law (whether lawmaking or law-preserving) and a violence associated with justice. There is something here that, as Britt has it, "goes beyond critical method to the heart of Benjamin's project." And it raises a fundamental, and for us guiding, question: "Would there be room for a critique of Christendom and its modern legacy . . . by means of a tradition shared by Christianity and Judaism?"[30] It is a dispute over the soul as well, quite literally so, a Jewish–Christian dispute. But we have yet to secure a better ground to stand (and fight) on as we seek to make sense of Benjamin's critique of blood and war. Or of Christianity.

On the one hand, by calling blood "the symbol of mere life," Benjamin is unequivocally alluding to biblical commonplaces that articulate or legitimate the interdiction to eat blood and identify it with life: "Only you shall not eat flesh with its life, that is, its blood."[31] This equation cum injunction is repeated later in its canonical formulation: "For the life of the flesh is in the blood."[32] There is little room, therefore, to doubt that, for the Bible more than for classical Greece, blood is a symbol of life, of mere life, and indeed of the flesh. On the other hand, the question is, of course, which Bible?

At first, the Hebrew text (whose pertinence belongs perhaps to no more than the history of translation) appears to bring more confusion, and particularly so when one considers that, having placed blood on the side of mythical violence and "mere life" (that is, it would paradoxically seem, on the side of the Bible as well), Benjamin turns to the soul as a singular marker of divine violence. "It is justifiable," he writes, "to call this violence, too, annihilating; but it is so only relatively, with regard to goods, right, life, and suchlike; never absolutely with regard to *the soul of the living* [*die Seele des Lebendigen*]" (250/G200; emphasis added). Before proceeding further, it might be important to recall that Benjamin expects this statement "to provoke, particularly today, the most violent reactions." What exactly is Benjamin saying? Let me just suggest that it is difficult to think that he would have been unaware of a crucial difference between the Hebrew text and its (mostly) Christian translations. I say this with little philological ground to stand on (it's there, though, I promise) except for the fact that Benjamin is opposing blood and soul (sounds like flesh and spirit, doesn't it? but wait for it!) as a kind of interlinear translation. What may clarify the matter, at least to some extent, is that the Hebrew text happens never to mention this little thing called "life." More precisely, the term that is insistently translated as "life" in European languages is the Hebrew *nefeš*, which should otherwise be translated as "soul" (the Arabic cognate is *nafs*).[33] To the extent that "life" has been perceived as implicit in the text, it has been understood alternatively as blood (which is then either associated with the flesh or opposed to it) or indeed as the soul (with many commentators identifying this soul with blood, and both with life, that is, ultimately, the life of a flesh that can hardly be isolated, and leaving little room to disentangle the threads).[34] Interestingly enough, with the word *anima*, Jerome's Vulgate follows the Septuagint's *psyche* and thus renders both Genesis 9:4 and Leviticus 17:11 ("quia anima carnis in sanguine est") more "accurately" or at least equally plausibly. Nor should it be surprising that what has become a modern, Judeo-Christian commonplace and consensus (a consensus with Luther!) should have been broken once, and once only, by none others than those Jacob Taubes identified as Benjamin's partners in dispute, Martin Buber and Franz Rosensweig: "doch Fleisch mit seiner Seele," they write, "seinem Blut sollt ihr nicht essen."[35]

If all this is beginning to look like an exegetical and theological dispute, which only yesterday elicited "the most violent reactions," it is because it is, of course. It involves an understanding of life and indeed of "mere life," as well as the lines separating it—or not—from its "attributes" ("goods, right, life, and suchlike" as Benjamin writes [250]). And it involves a contest over blood, as well as over the proper bearers of "souls."[36] It is at any rate no accident that Christian interpreters (John Chrysostom and Bede, for example) have understood the soul and the blood mentioned here as being *human* privileges (as if only human life were sacred, as if only human blood had life), rather than the indisputable attribute of all creatures, of "the living" (later, as Shylock famously discovered, they would pile upon this yet another difference *between bloods*).[37] Now, I have already suggested that all this—with blood at the center—would unavoidably have to be called the Jewish–Christian dispute (some might call it a war, after all), and though it may be said to have mostly ended around the sixteenth century, one may wonder whether Benjamin was not in the process of rekindling it.[38]

What the aforementioned issues of translation should make manifest is the war in the text, in the Bible (or, one should say, Bibles, *ta biblia*, "the books") and in Benjamin's own text. This is not another statement about Benjamin's so-called Jewishness, much less about the Bible's (which itself knows of Hebrews and Israelites, but hardly of any "Jews"). It is rather about the wars and contests that occur between the flesh and the spirit, the blood and the soul, the text and its translations. And do recall that "the Bible and its translation are not mere facts but central philosophical categories for Benjamin."[39] Yet not only are the protagonists far from playing the roles we would expect them to play ("carnal Israel" and all that), but also they appear to follow a set of agonistic displacements that play and replay a war that has blood as one of its major keys or vehicles. Where has this war, these contests, gone? A number of studies have recently underscored the significance of blood at the center of Jewish–Christian polemics, and they contribute much, albeit indirectly, to our understanding of Benjamin and of blood.[40] It should be noted, however, that they have proposed a perspective that is predicated on a certain symmetry.[41] Blood, they point out, no doubt correctly, is a thing of the past, and even then it was something of a shared substance, a shared symbol, of life. Perhaps also of death. By inserting and indeed staging a conflict anew and depicting a *fundamental asymmetry* between divine and mythical violence, today still, Benjamin calls our attention to a different understanding of blood—and of war. It is not that there would be or could be war, or violence, without blood (Gourgouris's question); it is rather that blood testifies to a singular understanding of war.[42] Whatever blood is, it cannot be understood as a biological substance (whatever this reductionism might mean). Nor can "life," sacred life, which falsely appears to have become the common inheritance of Christians and Jews finally at peace—eternal peace?—in their biblical translations. For "peace is the continuation of war by other means," Benjamin knew well—and guess who the victor was? Not even the dead will be safe, he reiterates, calling our attention to the difference between annihilation and destruction, between blood and soul. There is a "theological" battle, then, that has everything to do with "life" and that Benjamin clearly thought should be fought (and thought) anew. Like war, indeed, *in* war, blood must be understood as a theological matter, and a rhetorical one too. (Was it ever otherwise? The historicity of "biology"—or lack thereof—continues to puzzle in this context.) Through it, mere life has devastatingly come about, tied to a singular understanding of the profane and of the sacred. And what Benjamin explains is that, along with life, blood became sacred through a series of rituals whose aim was precisely to separate blood into different kinds.[43] Thus, some bloods are more sacred than others, as are some lives. It is this particular understanding that Benjamin associates with mythical violence—and with Christianity. And it is against them that he goes to war.

Benjamin might as well have been screaming bloody murder. As a matter of fact, he kind of did. It is precisely with regard to murder that he deploys a logic that has become somehow familiar to his readers through "The Task of the Translator," another 1921 text. There, Benjamin famously writes: "In the appreciation of a work of art or an art form, consideration of the receiver never proves fruitful. . . . No poem is intended for the reader, no picture for the beholder, no symphony for the audience."[44] And it is in the same precise fashion that he explains how, in the appreciation (the judgment or evaluation) of a murder—or of a war—consideration of the receiver must be suspended as well. No killing, in other words, is ever intended for its victim. War is always collateral damage.

This should not come as a surprise. If the ends of war are, as Clausewitz famously had it, who wrote of "the art of war [*Kriegskunst*]," "the destruction of the enemy's physical and psychic force"; if war is "an act of force [*ein Akt der Gewalt*]" intended "to compel our enemy to do our will," then the enemy is clearly pegged as the "end" toward which means are put to work, the intended receiver of this horrid, but definite, "work of art."[45] When Benjamin explains that "the realm of ends" must be "excluded for the time being from this study"; when he argues that distinct kinds of violence must be attended to "independently of cases of their application" (237), he is therefore being entirely consistent—and impeccably clear. "The reason for the commandment" not to kill must *not* be sought "in *what the deed does to the victim, but in what it does to God and to the doer*" (251; emphasis added).

Before attending to the meaning of these assertions, it is important to repeat that they are essential to an understanding of divine violence. It is not, to be sure, that divine violence is indifferent to (its) victims. Rather, divine violence, as Benjamin explains it, never wavers on justice. It maintains its attention on the nature of the deed and points to the limits of the victim's perspective (the "addressee" of the violence). One can find well-known parallels to this unpopular view, which are hardly coincidental in their relation to Benjamin. In Hannah Arendt's take, for instance, what should have become clear to the Jerusalem court sitting in judgment of Adolf Eichmann is that "the supreme crime it was confronted with, the physical extermination of the Jewish people, was a crime against humanity, perpetrated upon the body of the Jewish people, and that only the choice of the victims, not the nature of the crime, could be derived from the long history of Jew-hatred and anti-Semitism."[46] "It is apparent," adds Arendt a few pages later, "that this sort of killing can be directed against any given group, that is, that the principle of selection is dependent only upon circumstantial factors" (288). Arendt's position has of course nothing to do with an affirmation of the humanism of international law. It constitutes rather a strict reiteration of Benjamin's crucial suggestion: In the understanding of a crime, of "the nature of the crime," considerations of the receiver, of the victim, never prove fruitful.[47] What must be understood is what the deed does to the doer. And to God.

Elias Canetti pursues the very same line of thought, I think, when he reflects on "the image of him whose death Christians have lamented for nearly two thousand years."[48] Canetti explains that this image "has become part of the consciousness of mankind," and so much so, in fact, that "there is no-one who suffers persecution, for whatever reason, who does not in part of his mind see himself as Christ." What is crucial here is that Christ is at once "the dying man and the man who ought not to die." His "divinity has become less important" with secularization, "but he remains as an individual, suffering and dying." Canetti describes this process as one in which "the value of the individual has become not less, but more." Yet, what he implies is also a shift of value whereby "the one who in the end proves weaker can see himself as the better . . . the dying itself makes him significant." It is impossible not to see in this "significance" the precise opposite of what Benjamin is proposing. It is the significance of the victim (Canetti calls him "the survivor [*der über-lebende*]") over the doer of the deed—and even of God. This further explains why "the secret admiration of the public" for the great criminal results "not from his deed but only from the violence to which it bears witness" (239). It makes it easier to understand why Benjamin's attention never wavers from such "doers" (although, as Werner Hamacher has made clear, we should be able to hear in this word something else than an active or productive dimension).[49] For "the violence of an action can be assessed *no more from its effects than from its ends*, but only from the law of its means" (246; emphasis added)—which is to say from the perspective of "the care of the self."[50] To judge otherwise is to take the side of blood, as we will soon recall, and adopt the perspective of the state and of state power (*Staatsgewalt*), "which has eyes only for effects" (246/G195). It is to abandon all consideration of violence as belonging to a realm of pure means and focuses instead on its end or ends, which, like faith, justifies. Tom McCall makes this perfectly clear when he invokes in this precise context key Christian theologemes (note however that McCall otherwise follows the dominant interpretive line by drawing on Greek mythology).

> Signs tell stories. Like the scar of Odysseus, which encapsulates the whole story of this first boyhood adventure, blood or bloodshed, which Benjamin would have tell us the story of a certain mythical transformation: how a singular act of violence, making a singular bloody mark upon a (momentary, singular) body, magically *transubstantiates its own evanescent act into an indelible mark*, thereby memorializing that act with the psychological scars of trauma and the lasting inscriptions of bodily scars.[51]

There is no better way, I think, to explain what blood symbolizes; no better way, that is, to illustrate why Canetti would write (and Benjamin imply) that it is precisely in this indelible, bloody mark (Gr. *stigma*, pl., *stigmata*), which puts the victim at the center of history, that "the legacy of Christianity . . . is inexhaustible."[52]

❈ ❈ ❈

It is time to return to Taubes and to his claim that "the Christian religion in general, and the body of the Christian church in particular, is of no *religious* relevance to the Jewish faith . . . Christian history can have no religious significance of any kind for the Jewish creed."[53] For it highlights the kind of asymmetric war that has been described as the Jewish–Christian dispute and that Benjamin himself is engaged in when he puts blood on one side—and on one side only—of the *Kampfplatz* he draws.[54] This much should now be clear as well: The asymmetry of blood has little to do with the presence or absence of some physiologic substance. It has everything to do with the association between blood, "the sanctity of life," the primacy of the victim over the doer and "the nature of the crime."[55] It constitutes, in other words, a particular kind of violence, which Benjamin calls "mythical," from which blood cannot be abstracted or ignored. One might perhaps think of it as a tradition of power, a political tradition (at the polar opposite of what he will later evoke under the notion of "the tradition of the oppressed"), which gathers "all the forms of violence permitted by both natural law and positive law," not one of which is "free of the gravely problematic nature . . . of all legal violence" (247). It is also a tradition of law, therefore, and more important, a tradition of war. Today still, it is what either "regards violence as a natural datum" or seeks "the justification of certain means that constitute violence" (237) but in either case governs and rules over the modern state.[56] It is the very rule of the state and that of the police (most devastating in *democracies* where its existence "bears witness to the greatest conceivable degeneration of violence"; where it "intervenes for 'security reasons' in countless cases where no clear legal situation exists, when they are not merely, without the slightest relation to legal ends, accompanying the citizen as a brutal encumbrance through a life regulated by ordinances, or simply supervising him" [243]).[57] It is the militarism of the modern state ("Militarism is the compulsory, universal use of violence as a means to the end of the state" [241]) and its "higher orders," the "common interests" that "threaten to overwhelm equally victor and vanquished" but are "hidden from the feelings of most, and from the intelligence of almost all" (245). It takes the form of "the modern economy," which, "seen as a whole, resembles much less a machine that stands idle when abandoned by its stoker than a beast that goes berserk as soon as its tamer turns his back" (246).[58] It sustains "the stubborn prevailing habit of conceiving . . . just ends as ends of a possible law—that is, not only as generally valid (which follows analytically from the nature of justice) but also as *universalisable* [*verallgemeinerungsfähig*], which as could be shown, contradicts the nature of justice" (247/G196; emphasis added).[59] It extends its universal reach by spreading its peculiar benevolence far and wide ("Poor and rich are equally forbidden to spend the night under the bridges," as Anatole France had it), by building walls and establishing frontiers, at once internal and external, which is to say that "when frontiers are decided, the adversary is not simply annihilated; indeed, he is accorded rights, even when the victor's superiority is complete. And these are, in a demonically ambiguous way, 'equal' rights" (249). It is a system that "strives to limit by legal ends even those areas in which natural ends are admitted in principle within wide boundaries, like that of education" (238).[60] This tradition of violence, finally, is a "philosophy of history" that rests on "the proposition that existence stands higher than a just existence," that "existence" ultimately "is to mean nothing other than mere life." It finds its origin in "the dogma of the sacredness of life," which makes "man" coincide "with the mere life in him . . . including even the uniqueness of his bodily person," the "bodily life vulnerable to injury by his fellow man" (as I suggested above, Canetti called this "the survivor," thereby warning us that today *homo sacer* is Christ as Everyman) (251). It is a tradition of violence, the legal tradition Benjamin describes, that is ruled by the intention to preserve itself—and God knows it has. Today still; today especially. It is a tradition that,

Benjamin makes clear, is defined or distinguished by blood, that rests on blood (and recall that its critique should no longer call our attention to "what the deed does to the victim," that is, to the latter's blood, but rather to "what it does to God and the doer"). It is against this tradition of violence, this tradition of war, that Benjamin articulates his own critique of war (the paradoxical task of which is therefore "ceaselessly to try to interrupt the working of the machine that is leading the West toward global civil war") and appeals to a "true war."[61]

Now, as many have underscored, Benjamin refers to that very tradition under the heading of "mythical violence." What seems to have escaped the attention of translators and interpreters, however, is that he gives it another, much more telling name. It is one simple word or perhaps indeed a proper name that gathers, with utmost conciseness and clarity, everything that "divine violence" (and Benjamin himself) opposes, the tradition of violence and power that we are still confronted with: *Blutgewalt*.[62]

THE FORCE OF BLOOD

Let us pause and retrace our steps, after a fashion, and examine anew what has brought us closer to the grounds and reasons for a critique of blood, a critique of the force of blood and of power as blood. Now, "for power to be free to flow," writes Zygmunt Bauman in 1999, "the world must be free of fences, barriers, fortified borders and checkpoints."[63] Bauman speaks to a different register than Benjamin, yet it is remarkable that, whether manifest or covert in its exercise of violence and whether to posit, affirm, or criticize it, power has here and elsewhere come to be figured as *flow*.[64] Befitting "liquid modernity" and the nature of "cultures of circulation"—for though recent, such cultures would be many—power now *circulates*.[65] Inversely related to the availability of usable water on the planet, power, what Michel Foucault strikingly referred to as "the *capillary* functioning of power," has now joined the novel abundance of fluxes and flows, celebrated or berated but recognized by all.[66] Along with information (which itself would be "a kind of bodiless fluid that could flow between different substrates without loss of meaning or form"),[67] the arbitrary signs of postmodern fame, and numerous other currencies, power flows and floats freely. In the circulatory logic that emphasizes motion and speed as well as growth and expansion, the freedom of power is the freedom of a world that is vitally free and open to flows. Nature itself became "a global network of networks through which the currents that sustain life constantly circulate."[68] *Naturally*, then, the freedom of flow—the rhetoric of liquidity and the affirmation of fluidity—is invoked by Bauman as a contrast with "the practice of feverish

nation-and-nation-state building," which "put the 'soil' firmly above the 'blood' "
(12). There is nothing radically surprising in this. "The Sea is History" and the association of freedom (or its semblance, as Bauman makes clear) with motion and
circulation, and more precisely with the liquidity of the sea and with circulation, as
opposed to the attachment to territory and soil and the fencing constraints of the
solid ground—this association is an ancient one, even if it has not always registered
on even scales of significance.[69] Nietzsche knew this well, who wrote of our having "forsaken the land and gone to sea."[70] For Bauman, the liquidity of modernity
breaks with past models and only recently extends to social and economic relations. Bauman joins others in considering this "mobile modernity" or "modernity
at sea" to be a novel development.[71] Earlier, Carl Schmitt had written of similar
matters, liquid matters, and though he acknowledges a considerable measure of
change, Schmitt points out that the sea has *always* been a space of exchange, of
war and commerce. What is for Bauman a qualitative change—lines of flight as it
were broken by the walls of (modern) history—is, for Schmitt, an extension and a
generalization across a continuous and circulatory geographic and historical space.
In both versions, however, liquidity and flow are maintained as figures, if paradoxical ones (for what is the shape or form—what is the *figure*—of liquid?). In both it
is implied that it is the sea, and not the wasteland, that grows. Before engaging in
some detail these proliferating tropes of flow and circulation and what they carry
for the contemporary imagination (political and otherwise), I want to linger on
the sheer expanse and expansion of liquidity.

Shifting or widening the issue to the realm of (international) law, and from
power back to violence and hostility, Schmitt describes the extension of flows, the
growth, as it were, of the sea. Notably, and though he engages ancient concerns,
Schmitt writes in the future, adopting a quasi-prophetic rather than descriptive
tone for his assertions ("it may very well be [*es mag sein*]," he writes, "that traditional distinctions . . . which up until now legitimized the international opposition
of land and sea, will one day be dissolved in the melting-pot of industrial-technical
progress [*im Schmelztiegel des industriell-technischen Fortschritts einfach zerge-
hen*]").[72] At stake, for him, in this dissolution-to-come is the emergence and advent
of a "transformation of space [*Raumveränderung*]" (17/G31). This includes the creation of new spaces—insides and outsides—by way of technological advances, and
mostly through the modern occurrence of partisan warfare, something we might
place more readily today under the heading of the emergence of network cultures
and "netwars," or of "the war on terror."[73] Here too power—legal, technological,
and military power, of course, but not exclusively so—circulates and flows through
a new "theater of war [*Kriegsschauplatz*]" that is redefined as a "complex structure,
a new space of operations" in which the partisan "forces his enemy into another

space [*einen anderen Raum*]" (49/G72). It is this "other space" that invites the comparison between land and sea and that provides the occasion for the collapse of their distinction. For what the partisan testifies to is a generalized dissolution, a *liquefaction* of territory (it is probably not an accident that, for Schmitt, the very concept of "partisan," which provides a significant occasion for Schmitt's reflections, is itself already in "dissolution [*Auflösung*]" (12/G24), and that what remains of this and other similar concepts is "still unclear and floating [*noch unklar und schwankend*]" [15/G29]). In *The Nomos of the Earth*, Schmitt goes on to recall the "hazardous wager" of the pirate who goes further than sailing "into the open sea." Yet, it is as if everyone were called upon "to test, to try, to risk," to roam the unchartered space of the high seas, where power flows freely and there are "no limits, no boundaries, no consecrated rites, no sacred orientations, no law, and no property."[74] All this partakes of a slow transformation that involves the very concept of law in its rapport to territory—and to liquidity. Hence, the pirate is only one among many actors in a state of affairs that generalizes the sea space and its liquidity. There are others, "who manage to keep their own actions unbound, norm-free and so unpredictable," who have the "capacity to escape, to disengage, to 'be elsewhere,' and the right to decide the speed with which all that is done."[75] Like the pirate and the partisan, they belong to an expanse that has everything to do with law precisely because it remains outside the law, il-legalized, neither legal nor juridical. This space in which those willing and able to undertake the crossing move and circulate is a space without walls and without borders, whence they rule and govern. As a figure of this free-flowing power, the pirate is of course an outlaw, but he participates with others in a practice that Schmitt calls "sea-appropriations" (which he attributes to the great sea empires, beginning with England in its competition with Spain).[76] There, law seizes upon the sea as if it were a territory that one could divide, separate and partition, one upon which one could impart order.

According to Schmitt, medieval European law had ignored all non-European spaces and, more precisely, all sea spaces. With the conquest of the New World and the extension of a legality in transformation, there began a definition and a tracing of "great areas of freedom" that were "designated as conflict zones in the struggle over the distribution of a new world."[77] The consequence of such a partition enabled the "bracketing of European wars." With the establishment of amity lines, there explicitly emerged zones outside the law and defined as such. Such definition of spaces outside the law is once again linked by Schmitt to the space of exception created by the state of emergency and by martial law. The very notion of "amity line," Schmitt writes, is that of a "designated zone of free and empty space [*rechtleerer Raum*]" ("The English construction of a state of exception, of so-called martial law, obviously is analogous to the idea of a designated zone of free and empty space") (98). It is precisely the New World that will be defined in a privileged manner as "free space" (a space where war and commerce govern, outside the law—and which will be only strengthened, Schmitt explains, with the instituted distinction between commercial law and international law), but also from which the rest of the world (European and non-European) will be transformed. The history of this transformation, as Schmitt traces it, is long and complex, and little would be gained from entering into its details here. For now, I only wish to recall the singular role Schmitt grants to America in general and to the United States in particular. Here too, one could say that everything begins in 1492. The conquest of the New World defined entire stretches of territorial spaces as "free space," defining them, in other words, as sea spaces. This "liquefaction" of land came to an end with the conclusion of land appropriations on the North American continent. "Until then, the old boundaries separating settled from free land, i.e., unsettled open land free for appropriation, still had existed. . . . This freedom ended when there was no more free soil" (293). At that historical crossroad, Schmitt explains, nostalgia emerges for a "free space," a space outside the law that will continue to determine American law as well as American foreign policy. This space will have to be maintained as a space of "freedom." It will ultimately signify the pursuit of the abolition of a well-established, if waning, distinction between land and sea. Finally, it will continue to be determined and governed by a maritime logic, that is to say, as a space of freedom and conquest, of war and commerce. In less than a century, this conception of the world, save the United States, as "free," sea space, will become doctrine and, ultimately, law. Later on, with the institutionalization of the notion of "Western Hemisphere," major changes are finalized that extend the space of the land mass toward a "security zone" and as a limit to the "free sea as a theater of war." From now on, "the borders of America were drawn also on the sea" (283). But such a transformation of the world space also constitutes a change in the very status of the United States and of its security (territory/terror). Schmitt quotes the American scholar of international law, Philip S. Jessup, who wrote in 1940: "Today the dimensions change rapidly, and the interest we had in Cuba in 1860 corresponds to our interest today in Hawaii; perhaps the argument of self-defense will lead the United States one day to pursue war on the Yangtze, the Volga, or the Congo."[78] Or the Euphrates. But it is 1950 as Schmitt writes this, and he is describing the operations of American policy long before World War II (the Monroe doctrine, and later the efforts of President Woodrow Wilson). Still, he insists that what is being shaped at that time is truly "a new spatial order of the earth," an order that seeks to separate "a sphere of guaranteed peace and freedom from a sphere of despotism and corruption." Thus, "only on American soil did conditions exist whereby meaningful attitudes and habits, law and freedom were possible as a normal situation"

(289). The rest of the world—which still means, for the time being, Europe, the Old Europe ("Like old Asia and old Africa before her, old Europe had become the past"), where abnormal conditions reign, without peace—the rest of the world, then, has now become a free space, a space outside the law (290). An ocean of freedom.

Beyond international law, but inscribed within the same periodization, it was perhaps political economy that most visibly deployed ideas and figures of flow, expanding the reach of the sea's "attributes," namely, war and commerce. We shall repeatedly return to the fact that, quickly following Harvey's discovery of the circulation of blood (1628) and its deployment by Hobbes (who invokes the term *sanguification*, of still recent coinage), the word *circulation* acquired the general meaning and the semantic range now attributed to it only in the seventeenth century.[79] We may recall for now that, after the Physiocrats and the mercantilists, by way of whom "circulation becomes one of the fundamental categories of analysis,"[80] it was probably Karl Marx who raised circulation to the level of a concept, "the general concept of circulation."[81] With Marx, circulation achieved its general, modern and even postmodern, importance, if also by wavering and oscillating. It is as if, for Marx, circulation itself were circulating in terms of its scope, function, and relevance. Thus, "circulation itself [is] merely a specific moment of exchange or [it is] also exchange regarded in its totality" (98).[82] "A totality of the social process," circulation "is also the first form in which the social relation appears as something independent of the individuals . . . extending to the whole of the social movement itself" (197).[83] The circularity of this system clearly does not preclude its openness. It seems in fact to demand it.[84] And indeed, Bauman's description extends further still than social circulation and the seas of exchange. Bauman also returns us to the notion that the expanse and freedom of the sea (as opposed to the narrow rigidity of the soil) has affinities with the liquidity of the blood. Marx had invoked blood in a proximate context, reinscribing, as well as interrogating and redirecting, the relevance of blood and the relation between blood and circulation. "The circulation of capital," he writes, "is at the same time its becoming, its growth, its vital process. If anything needed to be compared with the circulation of the blood, it was not the formal circulation of money, but the content filled circulation of capital" (517).[85] Hobbes would not have said it better. For now, consider that, in *Capital*, Marx prophetically confirms Bauman's description of a world without walls, a sea world. Marx famously writes: "the circulation of capital has . . . no limits."[86] As I have already suggested, similar statements can be elicited today from a variety of sources, and most strikingly perhaps from those attending to the complexities of "biocapital."[87] Mark Taylor engages the tail end of this circulatory and open-ended process when he writes, like Bauman, of "the absence of walls."[88] Thus, "with the ostensible triumph of multinational, informational, or digital capitalism, walls, which once seemed secure, become permeable screens that allow diverse flows to become global" (20). The erection of walls, ostensibly following the writing of these lines, does not contradict the logic of flows. Both have long been in place, and Wendy Brown is right therefore to point out that walls are "built to regulate, rather than impede flows."[89]

Few have explored the covert or overt role of blood in this loose configuration, the puzzling link of blood and flow, of sea and circulation, and the erection (or abolition) of walls. Fewer still have done so as strikingly as Italo Calvino, who, in "Blood, Sea [*Il sangue, il mare*]," sheds a difficult and equally ancient-new light on the matter (that is, on the bloody, circulating matter).[90] Indeed, the entire story, down to its tragic and bloody end in a road accident, could be read as a condensed commentary on one of the restricted senses of *circolazione*—the traffic of vehicles on modern highways. Somehow more serenely, it is to our liquid origins that the narrative brings us. And these would not be found, not exclusively at least, in "water and dreams" as Bachelard suggested. Instead, Calvino informs us half in jest, the primal soup would already testify to a *generalized hematology*. "The primordial wave" of the oceans "continues to flow in the arteries," forming "a system of blood circulation [*un sistema di circolazione sanguigna*]."[91] Our blood, Calvino continues, "in fact has a chemical composition analogous to that of the sea of our origins, from which the first living cells and the first multicellular beings derived the oxygen and the other elements necessary to life" (39–40/I185). Grounded in the rhetoric of scientificity rather than in law or political economy, Calvino's sea shares the principal features with which we have begun to get acquainted. His sea of blood is at once infinite and striated by walls, although these seem to be different from Bauman's modern "fences, barriers, fortified borders and checkpoints." Blood, at any rate, "a kind of general pulsation [*una specie di pulsazione generale*]" and the free flow of power (43/I188), blood is a sign and a remembrance of the sea—inside us, enclosed within us. Calvino writes: "the sea where living creatures were at one time immersed is now enclosed within their bodies" (40). Thus blood more readily evokes the ancient, primordial seas than it does the future, the boundless and prospective anticipation that is our modernity at sea. Yet, across the span of time of our entire history, we may be led to imagine the vast and hematologic expanse of "a combustion chamber of infinite volume as the sea appeared infinite to us, or rather the ocean, in which we were immersed" (44). By blood, we would be fated to perceive the past into the future, the future of the past, and thereby to "repeat the pulsing of the ocean now buried inside us, of the red ocean that was once without shores, under the sun" (44). The world, it would seem, is a beating heart, filled with blood. It is natural enough, therefore, to think of the free flow or pulsing of the sea as having a "piston effect" (I will later argue that, before Calvino, Herman Melville offered us a rich series of insights into the global mechanics of this "blood pump"). After Bauman and Calvino, we also have "to imagine a piston without walls [*uno stantuffo senza pareti*]" (43/I189). Oceans without shores, power without borders, blood without walls—such would be the unfinished project, not of modernity perhaps, but of our oceanic history. "The sea-blood would have become one with us, that is, all blood would finally be our blood [*tutto il sangue sarebbe stato finalmente il nostro sangue*]" (47/I192). Calvino's famous narrator, *old Qfwfq*, sums up what we have seen so far with a kind of warning that would be inherent to the history of blood, to the uncertain, progressive motion and the circulatory development of the blood of freedom.[92]

> Thus far everything may seem clear: however, you must bear in mind that to make it clear I have so simplified things that I'm not sure whether the step forward I've made is really a step forward. Because from the moment when blood becomes "our blood," the relationship between us and blood changes, that is, what counts is the blood insofar as it is "ours," and all the rest, us included, counts less. (49).

Blood counts—and then there are bloods that count less. Within the expansive logic of circulation and flow, there occurs, or recurs, *a difference between bloods*. This essential, seemingly natural and universal feature brings us back to the question of walls and separation. It should become increasingly evident that this difference between bloods—blood as the site of difference—is constitutive of the history of blood that occupies me throughout this book. One question thereby raised is that if the blood that counts is the blood that freely flows, the blood of freedom—what then of the blood of others? Well, "let's start talking right now about the others, those who are not I," as *Qfwfq* puts it in "Blood, Sea." They are, after all, "our neighbor," and "we know our neighbor exists because he's outside, agreed?" (40–41). Pursuing his reflections out of the flow of power and within its freedom, *Qfwfq* acknowledges that, already on the inside, there is a demographic threat—the obscene beauty of that phrase—that runs along bloodlines. For, along with his prospective partner, *Qfwfq* too is "willing to multiply our presence in the sea-blood so that there would be more and more of us to profit from it . . . , so that our presence would increase in both absolute number and in percentage" (47). Majority rule! *O poca nostra nobiltà di sangue!*[93] Such, at least, "was the dream, the virtual obsession that gripped me—a minority that would become smaller and smaller, insignificant, zero point zero zero etc."[94] Along with his prospective partner, *Qfwfq* is thus less the surviving witness of a prophesied hecatomb than he is the hematoid, dissolute embodiment, himself the red tide, of a demographic threat. ("For the organism the inside is nothing other than the outside. The organism itself is simply this border-line which relates to itself as its own other.")[95] And it is as such that he understands the freedom of power to flow in terms that are at once reminiscent of and markedly distinct from Bauman's. *Qfwfq* ("he is in his own blood," Greg Bear could have written of him as well)[96] reminds us that the most common way to deal with the neighbor, with these unseemly minorities, has long been to engage in a pedagogy of sorts, to teach them something about the difference between inside and outside, the difference between bloods. It is, at any rate, "the best way to separate [them] from the blood-sea when the blood [is] in fact the sea, when our present inside was outside and our outside, inside" (48). Keeping in mind the distinction between inside and outside certainly makes it easier to imagine the free flow of power. It makes it easier to imagine oceans without shores, power without borders, blood without walls. And yet it would be careless to ignore the attempts to contain and wall in, precisely, to shape and figure the flows that grow.[97] It would, moreover, be a gross simplification to suggest that since Bauman made his own prediction on the "new technique of power" and the forthcoming liquidation of fences, barriers, fortified borders, and checkpoints, walls have been proliferating. Walls have been doing more than that, and earlier too. They have been *circulating*. And growing. Virtual walls and firewalls, but also less abstract, rather concrete walls and, well, concrete walls surrounded by barbed wire and electronic sensors, prison walls and security fences and more—these have been exponentially growing, along with the carceral state.[98] And though the tendency seems to either universalize this condition or place September 11 at its origin, the fact is that we seem to be back at having to imagine the freedom of the sea and the flow of power as contradictory. Once again (but who is really counting?), it would appear that the solidity of the soil has merged and seized control over—it has injected itself into—the liquidity of the blood, the blood of freedom. Not much has changed.

> Basically not much has changed: I swim, I continue swimming in the same warm sea,—*Qfwfq said,*—or rather, the inside isn't changed, what was formerly the outside, where I used to swim under the sun, and where I now swim in darkness, is inside; what's changed is the outside, the present outside, which was the inside before, that's changed alright; however, it doesn't matter very much. I say it doesn't matter very much and you promptly reply: What do you mean, the outside doesn't matter very much? What I mean is that if you look at it more closely, from the point of view of the old outside, that is from the present inside, what is the present outside? It's simply where it's dry, where there is no flux or reflux, and as far as mattering goes, of course, that matters too, inasmuch as it's

the outside, since it's been on the outside, since that outside has been outside, and people believe it's more deserving of consideration than the inside. When all is said and done, however, even when it was inside it mattered, though in a more restricted range or so it seemed then. This is then what I mean: less deserving of consideration. (40)

This ongoing event whereby "not much has changed" does articulate a "sense of complexity and mobility [that] carries over from outside to inside . . . creating an interplay of interiority and exteriority that simultaneously dissolves and maintains the walls."[99] These are "circulatory circuits" in which everything is as if "the flow of the space follows the swirling eddies and turbulent whirlpools" of what *Qfwfq* calls "the sea-blood [*il mare-sangue*]."[100] In this space, there are those who circulate ("the currents of the Universal Being circulate through me" wrote Emerson), and there are those who do not matter very much, those less deserving of consideration that appear to be lazing outside the liquid loop.[101] We can gather a surer sense of them by way of the following, and highly pertinent, rendering of William Harvey's discovery.

> Medicine took a great leap forward when William Harvey discovered the way in which this precious substance circulated and recirculated through the body of the living individual. Unlike the wealth of a miser, which accumulates without its doing any useful work, the value of blood can be exploited only if it is kept ceaselessly on the move. It is useless when stationary, but it is beyond price as long as it visits and revisits every part of the body. How does this treasure work? In what currency are its transactions conducted? What are its denominations? Such questions would have made no sense to Harvey, for the value of blood was self-evident, and since he regarded it as indivisible the very suggestion that it might have denominations would have seemed absurd.[102]

So much, then, for the free liquidity of the sea, its walls or lack thereof, and the importance of circulation. So much for the metaphorics of blood. But why return to and insist on this—if such is what it is—metaphor? Why, among elemental markers, privilege the liquid? And why, among all bodily metaphors (assuming that figures and metaphors are what this is all about), single out blood and circulation? Although it comes with a number of local variations, the answer appears to be as obvious as it is (or said to be) universal. "Here is blood," writes Arlette Farge, "indispensable fluid, companion of the human adventure in all its dimensions, physical, ideological and even spiritual."[103] Leaving aside the matter and means of identifying the human (and the human only) on the basis of blood, this implies that there are no other companions. But what about water? What about skin or bones? Mark Taylor (who has much to say about water in *After God*) reminds us that, similarly rich in material and symbolic force (what Farge refers to as "physical, ideological and even spiritual" dimensions), their significance widespread across cultures, these metonymies (bones, water) do not seem to carry a comparable burden. They have not been the kind of figurative contender that blood has been. Surely, the question—"Is the veneration of bones a thing of the past? Do bones still have stories to tell and lessons to teach?"[104]—resonates differently here, although this says nothing yet about blood. Does blood "itself" insist, then? And if so, what is the nature of this insistence? Are we to believe not that "the being of Spirit is a bone," but that everything solid has melted into blood?[105] Why revive and reactivate what seems like an odd archaism—a limited reserve of figurative material—marked with occult echoes and disturbing political associations? What—aside from the compelling moment of Italo Calvino's hematography or the elemental, evocative force that blood shares perhaps most closely with fire—justifies the rhetoric of sanguification I have adopted, the general iteration of prophecies of blood? Blood is a thing of the past, is it not? To ask "whose past?" however suggests that one could contain blood in a particular historical or cultural realm. Across oceans (of space or time), there would be, once again, differences *between* bloods. Seemingly and mostly confined today to medical discourse and to "tissue economies," blood, whether one or many, seems remote and distant: an archaism and a remnant of antiquated thought. Minimally, blood is so far gone for us that it no longer holds even the memory of a promise of "the elixir of long life that would make it possible to recover time gone by and consumed years."[106] The time of this blood is itself gone by. If it belongs anywhere—and who would want to revive a politics of belonging predicated on blood?—it is to what Piero Camporesi calls "the bygone culture of blood." (28). In a way, blood today marks the passing of time, as if it were a remnant of a foreign past. "The taste of blood permeated yesterday's violent, cruel, immoderate society" (27). It testifies to "a logic of life that we have no more" (28). Foucault has already described the way in which "the old partners of the spectacle of punishment, the body and the blood, gave way."[107] Foucault further concurs with Camporesi when, in the *History of Sexuality*, he persistently writes of blood in the past tense, assuring us that "the blood relation long remained an important element in the mechanisms of power."[108] Over the course of that long gone period, blood "constituted [and note, again, the use of the past tense] one of the fundamental values." This was then, this is now. And so it is that, in the distant past, "power *spoke* through blood." If "blood was a reality," then it was so because it had "a symbolic function." At the time, society was, or it could become, "a society of blood." And though "the passage from one to the other did not come about without overlapping, interactions, and echoes," it is nonetheless clear that something "caused our societies to go from *a symbolics of blood* to *an analytics of sexuality*."[109] All this is not to say that blood must simply be overturned to become a figure of our future. Nazi associations notwithstanding (not that anybody writing on blood will let us forget that blood is forever linked to Germany, something that does not seem to diminish its alleged universal and otherwise uncontested appeal),[110] it does seem harder to perceive blood as a figure of the future, of our present even, harder at least than to imagine oceans without shores, power without borders, blood without walls.

Is blood a thing of the past, then? If blood was ever a thing (Hegel seems to suggest that though bone might be a thing, blood is not, or not quite), then it seems accurate to say that it has passed and run its course. Yet, while no doubt marginal, the sanguification of rhetoric—what Susan Gillman calls "bloodtalk"—appears to linger and operate still among us. (Indeed, the very notion of a collective us—whether familial, tribal, national, or racial—lingers with blood still. Or blood lingers with it.) If blood speaks still, what of blood in our present, in our liquid modernity? I remain unsure about the evidence—unsure as to what would qualify as such; unsure that there could be an ordeal of blood, a blood test or blood proof—but let me review some of the parameters, major or minor, that will recur in the book. As I suggested earlier, the enduring force of the recurring call "no blood for oil!" operates so as to recast, and presumably escape, older preoccupations with "blood and soil" raising again the lingering specter of Nazi or proximate ideologies. Or consider the AIDS crisis and the innumerable cases of contaminated blood, which shook what had otherwise become a well-established and internationalized practice of social responsibility and of individual and collective generosity: the gift of blood. (Douglas Starr's history of blood narrates this "metamorphosis" of blood, its transformation "from a magical substance to a component of human anatomy" and into "the basis for a global industry"; Kieran Healy importantly adds, in this context, that "donation" is less significant than circulation: collection and procurement.[111]) And then there is the way in which there would remain, again and at any rate (or price), a difference between bloods. "The community of race, nation, nature, language and culture transmitted by blood and kinship never disappeared from popular racialism in the United States" even if "this bonding has not been meaningfully sustained by the biological sciences for half a century."[112] Instructively suspending the language of flow, Donna Haraway reminds us in this context of "the fungal web of nature, nation, sex, race, and blood in U.S. history" (214). Throughout race discourse, of course, the figure and invocation of blood imprinted a seemingly inescapable logic, a circulatory logic, on human (or inhuman) affairs. Blood itself—as if there were such a thing—"proved a very expansible and inclusive fluid" at the very time it was slicing the social body (232). More recently, the title of a Hollywood movie makes ever more explicit what the dominant object of cinematic promise has become by announcing that "there will be blood." In countless ways, Hollywood graphically enacts, and seems at least to confirm, the force of blood in popular culture, an otherwise unaccounted and bloody investment in "the Passion of the Christ" and in "the juice of life"—or vampiric death. Academic scholarship and artistic production have also seen periodic surges of interest in blood, much (but hardly all) of which takes its departure from the "discovery" of the Eucharist and its importance in medieval culture.[113] But the difference between bloods therefore partakes of the distinction between past and present, religion and economy, kinship, politics, and race, culture and technology. It is in this sense as well that we must attend to the difference between bloods.

It seems appropriate to consider a distinct if proximate phenomenon to what I have been referring to as a rhetoric of sanguification. Samuel Weber guides us in this direction when he describes "the militarization of thinking" to which we are currently witness. Now, Walter Benjamin already taught us that there is something more to this plausible analogy than the mere association of blood and war. It is a matter of words, of course, and of their historical circulation, their overt and covert advance and endurance. And Weber explains that "although the history of words is rarely simple or transparent, it is almost always symptomatic, which is to say, significant, though often in a dissimulating mode."[114] But pursuing this thought on the liquid terrain that has become ours would also suggest that blood, the word and flow of blood, is equally symptomatic and along similar if distinctly dissimulated lines. Militarization, in other words, would be a late instance of sanguification. For it is not so much how blood functions that matters here, but rather the mere fact that it does, and the distinct and distinguished extent to which it does. Along numerous divided lines, one should not be surprised to find if not the history of blood, at least a singular love of blood. Call it perhaps *hemophilia*. But what does the word *hemophilia* have to do with dissimulation? I would argue that it is, in this context, quite precisely and revealingly symptomatic—historically and otherwise—and further that it testifies to the wide sanguification of rhetoric and of thinking that, simultaneously exposed and dissimulated on the surface of our own oceans, marks our historical location but has yet to be lingered upon. I admit that here too I remain uncertain with regard to its precise meaning (and indeed function), but it strikes me as significant that in 1828, Johann Lukas Schönlein, a German physician, first coined the German word *hämophilie* in order to name a pathologic condition that hardly seems to signify a love of blood. (I am sure some might volunteer and donate a justification for this peculiar choice of words, but I urge them to refrain and consider the sheer absurdity of suggesting that the people affected with a dire blood condition signal in whatever way some form of vampiric existence.) Regardless of such minor, semantic obstacles, the word did rapidly spread through other European medical lexicons, and it has remained confined to medical, professional vocabularies. If sanguification demands our attention, it does not seem far-fetched to suggest that the word *hemophilia* has functioned as part of a containment apparatus, channeling a more general—and singular—flow of blood, a generalized love of blood, which it seized and confined to, which it *dissimulated* in, this medical vocabulary. Naming a particular condition may have obscured a phenomenon of much broader import—economic, scientific, and political—and one that resonates with *Qfwfq*'s wish that "all blood would finally be our blood" (47).

The history of *that* phenomenon—in a dissimulated mode, as Weber suggests—whereby blood becomes one and the world evolves and expands into "a sea of common blood" may be further traceable through the translations of a famous biblical passage: Acts 17:26. It emerges in the momentous distance that separates the Vulgate from Luther and filiation from blood. Indeed, the difference between old and new, between Latin and German, is precisely reversed in the notes of the New Revised Standard Version ("From one ancestor he made all nations to inhabit the whole earth," following Jerome's Latin, which has "fecitque ex uno omne genus hominum inhabitare super universam faciem terrae"), where the more recent variant is attributed to "ancient authorities": "from one blood" (as in the King James version, "And hath made of one blood all nations of men for to dwell on all the face of the earth," just as Luther's German offers, "Und er hat gemacht, daß von einem Blut aller Menschen Geschlechter auf dem ganzen Erdboden wohnen"). We shall often turn and return back to the United States, where the continued relevance of Acts 17:26 in nineteenth-century American "blood talk," for example, has been compellingly demonstrated by Paul Goodman and by Susan Gilman.[115] Gilman, in particular, shows how blood increasingly pervades the discourses of science and spiritualism and underscores the systemic links of a liquid regime, where walls and flows operate together. There one can read the tensions and cooperations between efforts at keeping bloods separate ("Strange it is that our bloods, / Of colour, weight, and heat, poured all together, / Would quite confound distinction, yet stands of / In differences so mighty" is the way Shakespeare puts it in *All's Well that Ends Well*) and the universal humanist dream of one world, one blood: from the one-drop rule to the one-blood world. Either way, as *Qfwfq* puts it, "not much has changed: I swim, I continue swimming in the same warm sea." Blood counts and blood rules, if in a peculiarly ambivalent way. As Gilman herself writes, in the United States of America, "the uses of blood do not add up: both literal and figurative, *blood* remains both a stubborn biologism and a vision of interracial harmony."[116] This, along with what can only be called "the hematological style in American politics," is another reason why we will have to read Melville as well.

Blood counts, then, even if it does not add up. It remains, or so I want to argue, a dissimulated keyword of a culture and society in which hemophilia—the love of blood—is a general, but not universal, condition. Blood is, again, a word that implicates much more than medieval preoccupations or Nazi phantasmagoria. Blood is a word, but it is more than a word from the past, much more of our present, infusing the order of things in ways that we have yet to recognize. Like *Qfwfq*, we live in a red ocean and we are traversed by hematologies—at once more contained and more expansive formations of a biopolitical nature. I do not mean by this to provoke (or essentialize) sanguinary instincts, only to take seriously *Qfwfq*'s own assertion as to their dissimulation. Such instinct, what can only be referred to once again as *hemophilia*, occurs, *Qfwfq* says, "in all secrecy, given my constant mien as a civil, polite person just like the rest of you." Still, it is this sanguinary instinct that remains "connected to the meaning of blood as 'our blood' which I bear in me just as you do, civilly and politely."[117] There is therefore nothing said here that intends to reiterate the uncontroversial claim that "blood is one of the most powerful and ubiquitous of human symbols," that "the way we understand this 'special juice' shapes the way in which we conduct our lives, choose our partners, structure our institutions, and express our culture."[118] Instead, I wish to get to the heart of things and argue that though *we* swim in a sea of blood, it has not been the case that blood has flown just everywhere, in the presence or absence of walls. Indeed, neither law nor politics, neither science nor kinship, not theology or literature are *universally* or *naturally* determined by or predicated on blood, on a figuration or an understanding of blood. It makes as little sense, in other words, to claim that blood is a universal than to say, after Foucault, that sexuality is a universal. At stake is rather the peculiar way in which blood circulates, the way it speaks and is spoken, the way it governs and rules over us—beginning perhaps with the very fact that the conception of a collective body, whether familial, tribal, national, or racial, is, in the Christian West and its historical avatars, massively conceived or figured as *consanguinity* by way of blood. How did blood turn into an ocean of blood? How did walls come to striate and divide this ocean at the same time as blood became generalized and universalized? The relation between blood and the distinct realms—the wall-divided seas—that define a particular civilizational area (what Cormac McCarthy singles out as "the evening redness in the West") does not simply separate one red ocean from another. Instead, the articulation of this separation on the basis of one "element," the very idea that there are walls between bloods amidst an ocean of blood, the ideal of distinct bloods in the world, as well as distinct blood realms—all this testifies to a highly developed *hematopoietic* capacity, a sanguification, which cannot be understood by flattening and diluting the rivers of blood that otherwise seem to run through it. "Because from the moment when blood becomes 'our blood,'" *Qfwfq* explains, "the relationship between us and blood changes, that is, what counts is the blood insofar as it is 'ours,' and all the rest, us included, counts less."[119]

THE FORGETTING OF BLOOD

Since "Shakespeare's *Severall Degrees in Bloud*," Marlowe's *Faustus* and Goethe's *Faust*, at least, by way of Dante and through Baudelaire's "Fountain of Blood" (in *Les fleurs du mal*) and Melville's *Moby-Dick* and Stoker's *Dracula*, all the way to Calvino and McCarthy, blood also courses through and irrigates literature and philosophy.[120] Adam Smith, for one, considered something he called "the force of blood" to "exist no-where but in tragedies and romances."[121] Nietzsche disagreed and famously spoke, and forcefully so, "of writing in blood, telling us that of everything written, his Zarathustra 'loves' only 'what one has written with one's blood. Write with blood and you will learn that blood is spirit.'"[122] Commenting on this well-known *topos*, Babette Babich insists that we must take Nietzsche at his word and read the hard and bloody letter of his words (29). Although it is not entirely clear that what Babich refers to here is, in fact, the blood that Nietzsche insists on inscribing, she does suggest that the matter is of greater import. Blood implicates others. Babich writes, "words in blood express the passion that for Heidegger belongs to philosophy at its inception" (vii). Earlier, Spinoza would hardly have disagreed, who, we will see, offered the image of "a little worm" that "would live in the blood, in the same way as we live in the universe."[123] Nor would Hegel himself dispute the matter when, in a prefiguration of Calvino's universe, he proposes that "the absolute Notion [*der absolute Begriff*] may be called the simple essence of life, the soul of the world, the universal blood [*das allgemeine Blut*], whose omnipresence is neither disturbed nor interrupted by any difference, but rather is itself every difference, as also their supersession; it pulsates within itself [*in sich pulsiert*] but does not move, inwardly vibrates, yet is at rest. It is *self-identical*, for the differences are tautological; they are differences that are none."[124] Blood, "this universal flux" (106), is and is not difference, yet pulsating, vibrating, blood would make all the difference. And the difference it makes fills and overflows the philosophical seas. "The endless restlessness of the Infinite is the eternal pulse of life."[125] Ultimately, blood breaks down the uncertain walls of fiction, figuration, and speculation and becomes part and parcel of politics, *blood politics*. This too is indicative of the red ocean flooding modernity such as Thomas Hobbes invented it.

As we have begun to consider and will have to review from a number of angles, Hobbes was the first to introduce William Harvey's new discovery, the circulation of the blood, into political philosophy and political economy. Hobbes—who himself credited Harvey for being, in fact, the first to initiate the true science of man's body—definitely started a trend when he wrote of "the Sanguification of the Commonwealth" ("For Natural Bloud is in like manner made of the fruits of the Earth; and circulating, nourisheth by the way, every Member of the Body of Man").[126] Hobbes thereby announces the demographic threat associated with the foreign blood of the multitude ("Blood, it seems, is a population" writes Jonathan Miller).[127] Giambattista Vico put this discovery to good scientific use, perhaps sealing the sanguification of rhetoric in and as "the study methods of our time." "We shall arrange our discourse," Vico writes, "and discuss first the instruments, then the aids to our method of study. As for the aim, it should circulate like a blood stream, through the entire body of the learning process. Consequently, just as the blood's pulsation may best be studied at the spot where the arterial beat is most perceptible, so the aim of our study methods shall be treated at the point where it assumes the greatest prominence."[128] Vico's "new science" is thus recast as the science of blood, a *hematology*, and it functions always as a political science, soon to rely on demographics (as Foucault and Calvino show). Blood endures, as I have said, or rather, it flows on and on, not only through modern politics, but also circulating like a blood stream through the streets and through the entirety of the body politic, from kinship to nation, and from tribe to race, accounting for the fact that to this day "the [U.S.] federal government through the Bureau of Indian Affairs (BIA) continues to use blood quantum as both a metaphor and measure of 'Indian' identity. . . . Not quite a century ago, blood degree varied among tribal members from 'full-blood' to 1/256. Today the range is far greater—from full-blood to 1/2048."[129] Majority rule, indeed. And don't forget "the one-drop rule" and its continuing effects as well as what Anne Norton has referred to as the "Bloodrites of the Post-Structuralists."[130] Finding the sources of these rites in the early modern period, Norton explains that "blood flows . . . not only on the battlefield but between men and women in sex, between the mother and the child in her womb and at her breast, between one generation and the next."[131] Yes, affirms Luce Irigaray, "woman is the keeper of the blood," whence Irigaray's proposal to think "a metaphysics generated from feminine desire . . . [which] might conceptualize being as fluid rather than as solid substances, or things. Fluids, unlike objects, have no definite borders; they are unstable which does not mean that they are without pattern. Fluids surge and move."[132] Oceans without shores, power without borders, blood without walls. Irigaray takes us back to Bauman and to Calvino, to law and to literature, and to the gendering of blood, the difference, again, between bloods. As Peggy McCracken describes it, while insisting on the modernity of this medievalism, "the gendering of blood in literature does not simply reflect medical, religious, or popular views of sexual difference. Rather, in their appropriation and modification of cultural views about men's blood and women's blood, literary texts expose the gender systems that these views construct."[133] Between literature and politics, between words and blood (a division that hardly does justice to the circulation of blood through distinct linguistic and institutional realms but testifies to the peculiar hematology I am trying to identify), between words and blood, then, most modern states—vampire states—have come to deploy and maintain a legal notion of citizenship that is predicated on variations or articulations of *jus sanguinis*. Blood is in the law; blood is the law, the force of law and its violence, which Derrida reads, after Walter Benjamin, around the force of blood (and bloodlessness). Derrida himself goes so far as to plug deconstruction into the history of blood and the history of its future. "For what remains to come of or from deconstruction," Derrida writes, "I believe that something else runs through its veins, perhaps without filiation, an entirely different blood or rather something else entirely than blood, be it the most fraternal blood." Such an "impure genealogy" will perhaps refrain from creating "a law that makes blood flow and exacts blood as payment."[134] Perhaps. By way of law, kinship and race science, political economy and international (and personal) relations, and most prominently through the history of medicine, blood seems to be at the heart of things. It is at the heart of economics and of what Douglas Starr has called "an epic history of medicine and commerce."[135] From Harvey's discovery, which I have already mentioned, to Marx's concern for "the living blood of labor," and all the way to Richard Titmuss's groundbreaking study of "the gift relationship" which takes us "from human blood to social policy," the centrality of blood to political economy and "tissue economies," as well as its formative role in the market in human goods, what Kaushik Sunder Rajan calls "biocapital," is impossible to miss or deny.[136] Thus, referring to the international system of blood donation and the complex technical apparatuses that sustain it, Catherine Waldby and Robert Mitchell underscore the social dimension of "blood economy" as they echo Qfwfq and lament the fact that "rather than a form of circulation that includes all citizens and revivifies the body politic, it has become a form of circulation that divides populations precisely because it links them . . . the power of the gift to circulate tissues potentially vitiates rather than augments the body politic."[137] Speaking more generally of the use of "human goods" (the expression is Kieran Healy's), they reveal "the extent to which strategies of appropriation once reserved for the third world—for example, the perceived right to appropriate *terra nullius* (empty land)—are being extended to the citizenry of first-world countries."[138] What Bruno Latour has called, after Vico's fashion perhaps, "science's blood flow" ("by following the ways in which facts circulate, we will be able to reconstruct, blood vessel after blood vessel, the whole circulatory system of science") expands the red tide at the same time as it demands that we locate the "blood meridian."[139] From science and law back to literature, as T. S. Eliot vividly and triumphantly illustrates. Eliot famously asks "What Is a Classic?" and deploys the figure and *topoi* of the body politic along with the concept of circulation. "We need to remind ourselves," writes Eliot, "that, as Europe is a whole (and still, in its progressive mutilation and disfigurement, the organism out of which any greater world harmony must develop), so European literature is a whole, the several members of which cannot flourish, if the same blood-stream does not circulate throughout the whole body. The blood-stream of European literature is Latin and Greek—not as two systems of circulation, but one . . ."[140]

Literature and philosophy, law and politics, colonialism and race science, political economy, medicine, and social policy—the sanguification of rhetoric cuts through all these realms. It bleeds from one into the other. It divides and unites them, testifying to something more than the sheer distinction between bloods upon which it depends. It repeats and maintains the enigma of blood as a site of difference, a universal difference that matters and matters not. It speaks, at any rate, of our relationship to blood, to *Blutgewalt*, as Benjamin calls it, and to our generalized hemophilia. But I have simplified things, no doubt. And like Calvino's narrator, whom I have already cited at length, "I'm not sure whether the step forward I've made is really a step forward. Because from the moment when blood becomes 'our blood,' the relationship between us and blood changes, that is, what counts is the blood insofar as it is 'ours,' and all the rest, us included, counts less."[141] All the rest—everything really. Everything but blood; and blood in everything. Eduardo Galeano thus recounts that "a Grenadian economist, Davison Budhoo, resigned from the International Monetary Fund. In his farewell letter he wrote: 'The blood is too much, you know, it runs in rivers. It dries up too; it cakes all over me; sometimes I feel there is not enough soap in the whole world to cleanse me from the things that I did do in your name.'"[142] Indeed, everything is as if we were merely repeating "the pulsing of the ocean now buried inside us, of the red ocean that was once without shores, under the sun."[143] How far does this red ocean reach? I have said that, hardly universal, it may still be general, even global—a generalized hematology, and a growing hemophilia—but the sanguification of rhetoric has yet to produce a world of oceans without shores, power without borders, blood without walls.

Part One

THE VAMPIRE STATE

BLOOD IS DIVIDED into two parts, each one comprising three chapters. In this first part, three central concepts of modernity (nation, state, capital) are examined anew in terms of their rapport to blood: the community of blood, the bloodless body-politic, and the blood of economic thought. Underlying the argument are my reservations with regard to the theory of figuration that sustains much of the massive body of literature devoted to blood. We shall repeatedly see that the distribution of blood between realms and spheres, including the distinction between literal (or "real") blood and figurative (or "symbolic") blood, is an essential mechanism for the distribution and operations of blood in Christianity. The "political hematology" of Christianity, its *hemophilia*, implicates the nonpolitical dimensions of blood as well, while the specificity of blood found with increased frequency in its different spheres (economy, law, science, and so forth) does not permit the rising to primacy of any of these spheres. Blood, therefore, was never a physiologic or medical substance *first,* which would *later* have acquired symbolic dimensions. Instead, blood merges and evolves, it spreads or circulates through the three concepts here at play: nation, state, capital.

The community of blood—"Jesus' Kin"—is predicated on the notion, erroneously presumed to be ancient and universal, that communities partake, or understand themselves to partake, of one substance. In the first chapter, I propose to reverse the temporality of that claim and argue that the sharing of blood fostered by the Eucharist gave rise to the community of blood, from which was extrapolated a universal anthropology. Accordingly, the perceived exceptionality of a community discriminating and excluding on the basis of blood (the *limpieza de sangre* of medieval Spain, the Nazi race laws) must be reconsidered in light of the rule, the constitution of the community of blood shared by all Christians in the Middle Ages and thereafter. Blood is accordingly at the center of the "papal revolution," the disciplinary revolution that recasts and refigures first the body mystical as the visible body of the church's members; second, the earthly authority of the pope (the Crusades); and third, the community of Christians as united in the pure blood of Christ. Blood is where the origin of both nation and race must be explored—at the very least. Incidentally, the striking absence of Jesus' pure blood from scholarly theorizations of race testifies to the vanishing of Christianity from critical attention.

At the center of the community of blood, there is a political hematology as well as a hematocentric embryology, a conception of kinship based on consanguinity. In the second chapter (subtitled "The Vampire State"), I explore the historical reach of these drenched notions and conceptions along with their significance, which exceeds any recognizable "religious" dimension, while testifying to the extraordinary diffusion of blood throughout Western Christendom. I proceed toward the remarkable *absence* of blood, in the Middle Ages and since, from most reflections and explicit representations of the body politic. I say remarkable because of the contrast this constitutes with the spread of blood I just mentioned. Like Christianity—indeed, as Christianity in its constitutive attributes and dimensions—blood is therefore at once essential and absent, only to be found again, crucial again, in Hobbes's *Leviathan* and thereafter. The friend and pupil of William Harvey, who identified the circulation of blood, Hobbes deployed the discovery of the blood pump (which preceded Boyle's air pump, documented by Shapin and Shaffer) and sedimented the liberal political imagination with streams of blood. The place of blood in this political and legal tradition can be followed from the founding texts of modern political thought to the vicissitudes of blood in the Americas, down to the infamous "one-drop rule" and beyond.

Finally, in the third chapter (subtitled "Christians and Money"), economic thought is seen to have eagerly embraced Harvey's re-coining of the term *circulation* by way of an ancient, albeit persistent and renewed, association of blood and money (deployed in a novel way by Hobbes and increasingly popularized after him, and not only by the Physiocrats). Marx was more than instrumental in linking capitalism and Christianity, finance and vampirism, money and blood, but I elaborate on a detail much less remarked upon in an otherwise foundational text, Shakespeare's *Merchant of Venice*, where Shylock is barred access to "Christian blood," a ban that is also the means by which he is *graciously* stripped of his financial assets. The centrality of the concern with the purity and immunity of Christian blood here mixes with economic conceptions, where liquidity confirms the operations of capital while replicating social and political—as well as racial and theological—hierarchies.

One NATION (JESUS' KIN)

WHAT IS THE community made of?

It is a strange enough question to ask. Yet, and stranger still, it appears to have been routinely *answered*. Under cover of a universalism that—from Aristotle to Maine presumably—asserts this very fact and simultaneously claims emancipation from it, the community has been held to be *made of one shared substance*. Some confusion may arise, no doubt, as to the meaning of the verb *made* in this context. For if the community (the family or the clan, the tribe or the nation, even) is in fact made of one substance, it could imply that the community is, as it were, *given*. In this perspective, to say that the community is made means that the community simply *is*, it exists as contemporaneous and coextensive with the substance of which it is always already formed and which its members a priori share. Alternatively, the verb *made* can imply that the community is produced, that it is made *into* what it is; that rather than given, its substance is the emancipatory outcome of a collective action, magical, ritualistic, or otherwise laborious—later, say, legal or contractual—that *results* in the common as substance (not necessarily as essence) and brings forth that substance along with, or as, itself. In Peter Fitzpatrick's formulation, which summarizes centuries of political and anthropological thought, "the deed creates society but a society was already created so as to perform the deed."[1] Between being and acting, the granted and the produced, the community could always be given or, indeed, made.

One might go a step further and recall, with Roberto Esposito, that the term *given* (and its cognates) has undergone in this precise context a transformation of sorts, a translation of its own. In earlier versions, the assertion that the community was given had not yet acquired its later meaning. Simply put, what was given did not initially refer to a common or shared substance, much less to a shared possession. As he traces the etymology of the word *community* to the Latin *munus*, Esposito explains by elaborating on an earlier meaning of the notion of "gift."

> Although produced by a benefit that was previously received, the *munus* indicates only the gift that one gives, not what one receives. All of the *munus* is projected onto the transitive act of giving. It doesn't by any means imply the stability of a possession and even less the acquisitive dynamic of something earned, but loss, subtraction, transfer. It is a "pledge" or a "tribute" that one pays in an obligatory form. The *munus* is the obligation that is contracted with respect to the other and that invites a suitable release from the obligation.[2]

Neither made nor strictly speaking shared or common, the community is rather a site of expropriation with no prior propriety. It is a loss and a subtraction, a transfer.[3] The momentous "misunderstanding" can hardly be underestimated, therefore, whereby the community comes to be conceived of as a gift or given, seeing itself as a possession in common, rather than as an obligation due. It is a misunderstanding because the community is neither property nor appropriation. To repeat: The community is neither given nor made; it expropriates. As Esposito puts it, "it is precisely the no-thing of the thing that is our common ground" (8).

Now, Esposito is quite clear that this misunderstanding constitutes a modern development. He places Hobbes at the origin of a vector that favors *immunitas* (and the protection and preservation of what one has and owns) over *communitas*. The terms are obviously linked as different relations to the *munus*, and the error of the (modern) ways is therefore comprehensible. But it is also, as it were, reprehensible. And so the question naturally arises: What went wrong?

"If we are to complete the categorical and semantic frame that functions as the presupposition for the communitarian genealogy under examination here," Esposito writes, "we need to turn for a moment to the Christian conception of community" (9). It is only a brief detour, then, but it is an important one, for what Esposito describes as an early instance of the parting of ways (Esposito writes of a "double move") has everything to do with what he will only later attribute to Hobbes and to modern politics, namely, the emphasis on property and appropriation and from there to preservation and protection. Starting from the early centuries of Christianity, as it turns out, there are already two vectors that can be distinguished within it, the first "historical-institutional" and the second "theological-philosophical" (9).

The first vector would seem to follow an itinerary of the increasing erasure of the originary ancipital character of the *munus* in the direction of that "appropriating" drift in meaning to which the *lectio difficilior* of *communitas* is still sacrificed. In all of the medieval lexicons, in fact, the lemma *communitas* is associated with the concept of "belonging," in its contemporary subjective and objective meaning: the community is that which belongs to a collective and is that to which it belongs as its own properly essential type [*genere*]: *communitas entis*. Over time, however, the particular [*localistico*] character of this totality always takes on the shape of a fixed territory, as emerges in the nearness of usage between the concept of *communitas* and those of *civitas* and *castrum*; the latter having an obvious military inflection, signifying the defense of proper borders. (9)

The second vector remains closer to the proper understanding of the *munus* (which is to say that it is, strictly speaking, "im-proper" as the *munus* is neither owned nor proper) as that of which one partakes, from which one is expropriated. Following Paul on the body of Christ—the community of Christians—Esposito describes it as what divides and separates across "the infinite heterogeneity of substance" (10), "having nothing, yet possessing everything," as Paul has it in 2 Corinthians 6:10. Esposito then goes on to attend to the history of translation and explains—or restores—the link between "participation" (as partaking and taking part) and the expropriating gift (*munus*) of the community (Gr. *koinonia*).

> This gift-giving [*donativo*] inflection of "participation" restores to the Christian *koinonia* all of the expropriating drama of the ancient *munus*; what one participates in isn't the glory of the Resurrection but the suffering and the blood of the Cross (1 Corinthians 10:16; Philemon 3:10). Any possibility of appropriation is diminished; "taking part in" means everything except "to take"; on the contrary, it means losing something, to be weakened, to share the fate of the servant, not of the master (Philemon 3:10–11). His death. The gift of life, offered in the communitarian archetype of the Last Supper. (11)

Although he describes two vectors, Esposito is, I think, clear on the restorative dimension of his own interpretation. That is perhaps why he does not attend to Christianity in its historical-institutional dimensions. More precisely, to the extent that Christianity is historical and institutional, it constitutes a vector (the first, appropriating vector Esposito described) that must be distinguished from the second, theological-philosophical vector or aspect of the same Christianity. It is this second aspect, at any rate, that Esposito restores in the passage I have just quoted, and it is on this aspect as well that he relies in order to assert the *historical* break performed by the moderns, by modern political thought, beginning with Hobbes. It is, to be sure, a difficult break to ascertain. Consider, for instance, that Augustine has a number of relevant things to say, some of which, Esposito writes, introduce "us into the modern, Hobbesian, perception of community" (11). There are, in other words, lines of continuity, or minimally nonlinear lines of confusion. That confusion, one with which we started concerning what the community is made of, is now revealed as having a longer history that may go back to Augustine. It does not divide history (between modern and premodern, say), but rather divides between history and theology, philosophy and institutions. One could go so far as to say that between the abstract and the concrete, the spirit and the flesh, the confusion fails to achieve a precise divide among the three distinct answers it formulates to the question: What is the community made of? It is made of being (or substance), by fiat (act or making), or of nothing (it is expropriating). As far as Esposito's account is concerned, the only historical precedent to the misunderstanding that identifies community with the given of a proprietary substance is therefore found in the very tradition on which he relies in order to argue against it, in order to argue that *communitas* must be properly understood as expropriation. Somewhere along the line, a thing came of nothing. This is what went wrong. The community of Christians came to understand itself as a community of substance, as partaking of, which is to say *as sharing rather than dividing*, some thing.

Does it matter what that thing or substance is? As I have already suggested, the conception according to which the community is made of a shared substance, powerfully recapitulated by Freud in *Totem and Taboo*, is held to be ancient, found in most, if not all, collective entities around the globe and throughout history. Yet one cannot but wonder whether the detour proposed by Esposito toward a genealogy of community, a detour that takes us back to Christianity in its effective and singular history, is not deserving of a closer examination for the light it sheds on that universal conception and its spread. For the only historical precedent Esposito offers us, after all, in order to reflect on the misunderstanding of the community is what occurred in Western Christian political thought and practice. And one could easily think of a number of good reasons why this particular history is deserving of greater attention. But be that as it may, whatever is the nature of the break that translates the synchronic "double move" of Christianity (historical-institutional and theological-philosophical) into a diachronic rupture to modernity as historico-philosophical (empirico-transcendental), it is part of a "communitarian genealogy" of the Christian West. Recall that "over time . . . the particular character of this totality always takes on the shape of a fixed territory" and that what "emerges" there and only there, *localistico*, is "the nearness of usage between the concept of *communitas* and those of *civitas* and *castrum*, the latter having an obvious military inflection, signifying the defense of proper borders" (9). Ultimately, the path of transformation is laid, the erroneous translation of the *munus* and of community is confirmed, the tradition sedimented. "Those *communia* that before signified a simple rural or urban collection now begin to acquire the increasingly formal traits of a true juridical-political institution, until *communia* designates, from the twelfth century on, the features that autonomous cities possess both factually and legally, which is to say, they are the proprietors of themselves" (9).

From the twelfth century onward, the path of the Christian community in its effective history is traced as a true juridico-political institution that factually and legally (one might say historically and philosophically) grants itself autonomy and secure and militarized borders and appropriates for itself the shared substance it sees itself as given and as being made of: "they are the proprietors of themselves." Thus men (that is, Christian men, later self-made men, men of "flesh and blood," as the expression goes) own and make their history. Or at least their own community.

And what is this community made of?

Arguably, Hume's answer was "fear and hope." Esposito generally agrees, I think, although in a passage I have already cited he refers more specifically to the "suffering and the blood of the Cross." This brings us back (or around), with slightly more insistence, to the Middle Ages and to Christianity. And consider the possibility that "this is Christianity not as a source of religious doctrine but as a form of understanding of self and community."[4]

※ ※ ※

The argument I wish to advance in this chapter is this: Christianity simultaneously invented the community of substance as the community of blood. Beginning with its conception of the human as "flesh and blood," it became the first community ever to understand and conceive of itself as a community of blood. And if the first shall be the last, then this should tell us something about "the permanence of the theologico-political" and about our so-called modernity.[5] It minimally recasts, at any rate, the figures or metaphors, symbols and incarnations that have been asserted, recognized, or projected by way of collective imaginings. For Christianity may have been "imaginable largely through the medium of a sacred language and written script," but it congealed deeper and longer in the element of blood.[6] One could think of the process whereby this transformation came about as a particular development in the history of religions, a shift more modest than was brought about by the Axial age, but a massive one nonetheless. One could think of it as a momentous revolution that took place in multiple bursts, layers and sites, practices and doctrines, individuals and institutions. This would be the papal revolution, the reach of which needs perhaps to be rethought and expanded, and to which I shall return in more detail later on.[7] Or one could think of it as a public relation campaign (no newspapers or print press at first, but a regulated calendar and set of rituals, habits, practices, and meanings, and an informational infrastructure, an architecture too, all well ordered and regimented), and we will see that much work, many "early techniques of mass social operation," had to be deployed in order to instill in fact the love of blood—*hemophilia*—in the hearts and minds of Christians, as it were on their flesh.[8] I will try to demonstrate that it was, at the very least, a disciplinary revolution, which reshaped the body of individuals ("flesh and blood"), the collective bodies of families and classes, ultimately of nations and races.[9] As well, this revolution famously, all too famously, affected the rapport to others (the spilling of the infidel's blood, the blood libel, the Inquisition), but I want to underscore that it involved above all an inner and inward-directed activity, a collective self-fashioning rather than primarily a construction of alterity (I speak here of hermeneutical primacy and do not pronounce on ontological entanglements). Indeed, one of this revolution's major effects and lingering symptoms, identified by Claude Meillassoux as the "ideology of consanguinity," was almost entirely "internal" and concerned kinship, genealogy, and lineage.[10] Over the course of time, it went so far as to erase the distinction between blood and kinship, so much so that the emergence and spread of a lexicon of blood—among the nobility, for instance, and a number of other collectives as well—has been seen as both singular and banal, thus becoming quite challenging to locate and identify in historical terms.[11] We speak this language still. Thus, rather than an exact dating (yet another stab at periodization), it has seemed more important to trace some of the essential steps in the massive enterprise of "social disciplining" that got under way around the formation of the "eucharistic matrix," which took the "flesh and blood" individual and the community (later, communities) as its aims and refashioned them in hematological terms. Everywhere in Western Christendom (and its later national divisions), blood became an essential element investing (and invested by) embryology and genealogy, belief and ritual, laws and habits, persons and collectives, the state and the church. Blood became a governing center of Christian life. Such is our enduring legacy, such our Christianity.

Accordingly, neither this chapter nor the next will be content to treat blood as a *material* or physiologic substance, as a *symbolic* repository into which social energies are merely poured, or as a *metaphorical* marker that inherently structures the understanding.[12] These are all significant and active registers in their own right, of course, even if their disaggregation seems increasingly arduous.[13] But blood will here serve as a peculiar, multifarious, and ubiquitous prism through which one might reexamine the so-called Middle Ages. Such an *asymmetric hematology* seeks therefore to recognize the flow and distribution of blood *as if there were different bloods*, the strict disciplinary division that separates, say, medicine from religion and rhetoric (or "symbology" as Dan Brown would have it), as well as the rigid periodization that maintains the medieval period as principally different from modern times.[14] For the path of blood is tortuous and its time unhurried. Blood surfaces over time, yes, and it slowly comes to saturate and to persist as a crucial and expanding element, which marks and underscores the contours and the endurance of Christianity, indeed, the persistence of the Christian question. The rest of the book will attend to this slow expansion and to this endurance with a view toward the Christian exception (or rather its rule), but this chapter is more immediately dedicated to reclaiming formative moments of Western Christendom as it gains its relative integrity—in, by, and through blood. And ultimately pure blood.

BLOOD: A USEFUL CATEGORY OF HISTORICAL ANALYSIS

Somewhere between the "eucharistic matrix" and the Inquisition, the Middle Ages stand out as exceptional.[15] On the one hand, "the eucharist wafer was constructed as a symbol for which over hundreds of years, and all over Europe, people lived and died, armies marched, bodies were tormented or controlled by a self-imposed asceticism."[16] On the other hand, there is "the myth of *The Inquisition*," a myth that refers to "procedures, personnel, and institutions" that operated in Western Europe in the Middle Ages and the perception of which was expanded and darkened with time. The myth, the Black Legend, was then "universalized in series of great artistic works into an indictment, by a modern world, of an earlier Europe for its crushing of the human spirit."[17] But why relate between the Eucharist and the Inquisition? Between law and love? And why speak of exception? More important, why blood? It is quite evident that blood plays a crucial role in the Eucharist, even if the measure, depth, and meaning of that role have yet to be fully fathomed, as I will seek to establish. With regard to the Inquisition, however, blood might appear to be a mere accident, an aggregate or a supplement, perhaps a metaphorical addition, which nonetheless colors, more or less insistently, our perception of the Inquisition's courts as bloody and cruel ("the Black Legend"), no doubt one among "the various forms of Spain's [cultural] 'belatedness' " described by Ernst Curtius and others.[18] As will become clear, what interests me most "in" the Inquisition is something that its own courts and jurisdictions, indeed, the church as a whole, took some time to accept and were late endorsing, but is no less important for all that. I refer to the 1449 Statutes on the Purity of Blood (*estatutos de limpieza de sangre*), the institutionalized perception whereby Christians were deemed hematologically distinct from converts, the latter having failed to achieve Christianization by reason of their tainted blood. Earlier already, infidels had begun to be seen as being of different blood.[19] This seems a curious notion, a revolution of sorts, one that demands an explanation or at least a reckoning.[20] That is where the Eucharist comes in, of course—"the cult which became the central symbol of a culture," and indeed a matrix of signification and of rule.[21] For something had to be done, or given, some operation or ritual had to take place that could make Christians (and not only Spaniards) believe that their blood was different from the blood of others, that there were different kinds of bloods. And believe they did, practiced it too, although to my knowledge the unprecedented appearance of and widespread belief in a pure blood (the pure and glorious blood of Christ), a blood claimed and shared by Christians for centuries, has never been considered for its contributing role in blood-based, racial or proto-racial thought—"Spanish" or "Semitic" blood thirst or alleged ancient concerns with "blood purity" did not get away so easy.[22] The matter is vastly more complicated, of course, and it cannot be reduced to "the invention of racism."[23] As I shall repeatedly emphasize, blood is about much more than race, more than the outward forces of othering. A patient mapping—the purpose of this chapter—is therefore required, of the bounded but far from trivial expansion of our hematological horizon to the formation and transformation of the community of blood, a community that defines Western Christendom and is found in its later (national, racial) projections and congealments. It is, to be sure, a new community, a *communia* that, in Esposito's terms (and according to the periodization he follows), comes to belong to itself, sharing with itself a common property and a common substance that defines it, rather than experience that substance as expropriating *munus*.

But why exception? The association of blood with the Middle Ages is after all so obviously manifest and well recognized as to appear banal rather than exceptional. But precisely therein lies *the exceptionality of the Middle Ages*. As Piero Camporesi puts it, "the tale of blood permeated yesterday's violent, cruel, immoderate society."[24] It is *then* that blood was a banality, then and not now.[25] First, therefore, is the matter of periodization (the Middle Ages, the modern period), the exception constituted by periodization.[26] Attending specifically to "the making of the Middle Ages" in literary, historical, and juridico-political consciousness,[27] Kathleen Davis compellingly argued that periodization "functions as sovereign *decision*."[28] This means that, along with the sovereignty it buttresses (sovereignty itself being a concept and an institution grounded in the supreme right to spill and draw blood, the nature of which is at once material, symbolic, and rhetorical),[29] periodization

also bears the structure of the exception, literally maintaining the "epistemological boundaries" of each period and primarily supporting the claims of modernity.[30] And if this is true of the Middle Ages at large, it is even more acutely so when it comes to blood, which powerfully signifies the troubled march of the "civilizing process," the distance that separates us from our archaic past.[31] As Ferdinand Tönnies renders that widespread and recurring, if not always linear, narrative, what was once "community by blood, indicating primal unity of existence, develops more specifically into community of place, which is expressed first of all as living in close proximity to one another. This in turn becomes community of spirit, working together for the same end and purpose."[32] Between blood and spirit, out of blood and soil, "medieval blood" is, to this extent, a pleonastic phrase, for blood *makes* the Middle Ages into the period it has become.[33]

There is of course a tension that, confirming the exception, operates from within the multifarious streams of medieval blood while sedimenting and exceeding the association of blood with the Middle Ages. Peggy McCracken importantly refers to that tension as "the curse of Eve, the wound of the hero," but it can be recast or at least observed in other ways and locations.[34] From the (numerous) crusades to torture practices ("getting medieval"),[35] from the blood libel and indeed to the Inquisition, blood is distant from us. It seems a distant curse, as it were.[36] In a different manner, the blood of the Eucharist, the potent and healing virtues of "royal blood,"[37] the sacrificial marker of communal gathering—these feel proximate still, intimate even, participating as they do in the formation of "our" Middle Ages and reminiscent of much more. They constitute, at any rate, a powerful matrix of answers to the putatively perennial question: What is the community made of? Defined by the proliferation, the persistence, and the insistence of blood, distant and exceptional blood, the Middle Ages constitute an included exclusion, an exception. They bespeak a Christian exceptionalism, its endurance, and its semblances. Ultimately, the exceptionality of blood in the Middle Ages has everything to do with the emergence, in ways that are both manifest and hidden, of a singular collective, a community of blood seemingly bound by time and, indeed, by historical periodization. Consider, at any rate, that both the Eucharist and the Inquisition are about collective existence, the construction—imaginative or fictional, ritual and institutional—of a community. They each constitute a "moment of powerful, elevated articulations of Christian community as universal, transcendent *ecclesia*."[38]

These two "moments," Eucharist and Inquisition, are also exceptional in their relation (or lack thereof) to each other. For there is hardly even a contradiction operating between them. In fact, they are as distant and distinct as two historical paths, an internal parting of ways within Christianity and its understandings (the rule and the exception), marking its relation to the modern world—or to Jews and others.[39] True to the very image of community they each sustain, the Eucharist and the Inquisition signify unity and division, communion and persecution, inwardness and outwardness, continuity and rupture, transformation and revolution. One could go further and map, with varying degrees of accuracy and agreement, other key signifiers onto that relation, which is not one. Between Eucharist and Inquisition, in other words, one might trace a "blood hyphen" and attend most obviously to love and to law (even to good and evil), to North and South (England vs. Spain), or to past and present (the Catholic Church vs. the Reformation, medieval and modern), and of course to religion and race—divisions that are securely inscribed in most of the scholarly works on blood to which I refer throughout. Volumes upon volumes treat the Eucharist without mentioning Spain or the Inquisition.[40] Nor, again, is the collective identification with the pure and purifying blood of Jesus ever mentioned as a probable cause for "the consolidation of Spanish identity around notions of timeless Christianity and pure blood,"[41] its role in the establishment of "the persecuting society," much less in the emergence of the Statutes on the Purity of Blood, the special blood of the nobility, or the rise of nationalism and of (so-called biological or scientific) racism.[42] The matter could be traced further into academic traditions and habits, to the founding of modern disciplines as ever so respectful, incidentally, of national boundaries. One might finally turn to two of the monumental figures of the American scholarly enterprise, the first who founds anthropology as the science of kinship on the basis of a eucharistic "community of blood" (Lewis Henry Morgan); the second who dedicates his life to historiography and to the "bloody Inquisition" (Henry Charles Lea). Rarely the twain shall meet, although one may suspect that they would have both agreed to take distance from "the severity of the Hebrew law-giver" while congratulating themselves for having "fortunately inherited the noble ideals of the School of Hillel, broadened and deepened and rendered applicable to all mankind by the teachings of Christ."[43] In and through these Christo-Christian moments and *figurae*, by way of such persistent divisions, blood remains exceptional, indeed, a marker of exceptionality. Race or religion? To add to the paradox, and as I shall elaborate in the next chapter, blood is also seen as universal, as if all communities had to have been made of one substance, as it were, analogous to blood (this is said of the family, the class, the tribe and the race, and the nation too, except for the evolved or civilized ones that have emancipated themselves from blood).[44] For now, let us content ourselves with the curious fact that blood is omnipresent, yet it does not define or determine its coordinates. It remains extraneous to the sites it otherwise drenches, as if exceptionally. There is, then, *a difference between bloods*. That is how blood remains, in numerous lingering ways, the very mark of (past or collective) exceptionality: the blood of Christ, the blood of kings, the blood of the nobility, the blood of the community, and ultimately (that is, primarily) the blood of Christians.[45]

There remains nevertheless ample reason and ground to interrogate the logic of the exception, beginning with its characterization as a separating cut or decision, and more basically with its very nature *as* exception.[46] For what after all is the rule? The veracity of the claim of exceptionality, with regard to blood, matters only to a limited extent. What concerns me here are the markers or attributes of exceptionality that have attached themselves to historical configurations and to communal aggregations, which I am summarizing as "Eucharist and Inquisition," and beyond these to the relative hardening of historical and political collectives, of entire periods and realms. Periodization and sovereignty, as Kathleen Davis aptly has it, partake of an exception that does not conform to, nor confirm, just any rule. And neither does blood. Insofar as it singularizes and exceptionalizes, insofar as it quietly governs or rules over and across the unbridged opposition of Eucharist and Inquisition, insofar as it constitutes one of the earliest and most massive instances of "social disciplining," blood may well be a rule we have yet to contend with.[47] Blood is what the Christian community is made of, how the community comes to be and understand itself as what is either given or made from one substance. But blood is, to repeat, much more than a material or symbolic element to be included in or restored to the historical or anthropological record. Blood must become a category of historical analysis.

FLESH AND BONE

Has the community not been made of blood always?

In a later chapter, I will attend to ancient Greece in its plausible or likely status as an originary, or alternative and non-Christian, source of answers to this question. There, I shall also point out the disconcerting asymmetry, when it comes to blood, between "the Jew and the Greek," and what might be revealed by considering it anew. Here, I adhere to this asymmetry and to the widely perceived biblical, or better yet, "Semitic" origins of Christianity's investment with blood.[48] For it is surely not difficult to grant that the Bible accords significant importance to murder and to sacrifice, nor could one deny the overdetermined association, albeit one that is neither obvious nor natural, between these keywords and blood.[49] By no means do I therefore seek to diminish the constitutive role of violence and sacrifice in the formation, regulation, and preservation of the community and of its internal and external boundaries—and consider that the temporality I have already described, whereby blood signifies the primal and the archaic, remains identical in this instance as well. In the words of one of the foremost interpreters of biblical sacrifice, "blood sacrificial religions are disappearing as modern industrial production, the world market, democracy, and science expand. Blood sacrifice does not even make sense in contemporary industrial society, where separate individuals, joined in temporary voluntary association, are thought of as the basic units of society."[50] Yet, what seems crucial to point out, at this early stage, is the striking absence of blood from the sources, and from the explicit assertions having to do with the communal bond of the ancient Hebrews. Although there may be a deep link between sacrifice and kinship, indeed, between blood and covenant, it is simply a fact that for the Old Testament, flesh and bone—never flesh and blood—signify the basis of the elementary communal bond.[51] Note that this does not easily translate into a "community of substance," not even after the establishment of the (sacrificial) covenant by way of blood rituals.[52] As a matter of fact, rather than some general, proprietary, and enduring substance, flesh and bone signify a provisional and limited relation or kinship, perhaps a limiting one as well, not obviously extendable or indeed extended to the larger group.[53] Prior to being markers of continuity and inheritance, moreover, flesh and bone do not differentiate but rather signal contiguity and contemporaneity, the ephemeral "given" of a community under probation by means of covenantal deed, a literal and carnal repetition of the divine creative act and, as it were, a becoming-carnal. "This," famously says the human creature after woman is taken from its side, "this at last is bone of my bones and flesh of my flesh [*zot ha-pa'am 'etzem me-'atzmi u-vasar mi-besari*]" (Genesis 2:23) and thus "man leaves his father and his mother and clings to his wife, and they become one flesh [*ve-hayu le-basar ehad*]" (Genesis 2:24). Such logic is reiterated some generations later, when Laban reassures Jacob with regard to his word, the assertion of his bond and the formulation of the given as made: "Surely, you are my bone and my flesh [*akh 'atzmi u-besari ata*]" (Genesis 29:14). The same lateral kinship is repeated again when Judah convinces his brothers to refrain from killing Joseph: "Come, let us sell him to the Ishmaelites, and not lay our hands on him, for he is our brother, our own flesh [*ki ahinu, besarenu hu*]" (Genesis 37:27), or when Abimelech vying for leadership after the death of Gideon will ask the lords of Shechem to "Remember that I am also your bone and flesh," to which they eagerly reply: "He is our brother" (Judges 9:2–3).

First and foremost, then, "flesh and bone" mark contemporaneity rather than form the substrate of a link between and across the generations. They are also the result of a contractual deed that can also be made or rather pronounced collectively around the monarch.[54] Indeed, the sign of public and political recognition of, and allegiance to, David's claim for the crown occurs when "all the tribes of Israel came to David at Hebron, and said: 'Look, we are your bone and flesh'" (2 Samuel 5:1).

Later on, when David's standing becomes more precarious, he attempts to gather legitimacy and support by turning to the elders of Judah and recalling flesh and bone as a precise reminder (2 Samuel 19:13): "You are my brothers [*ahayi atem*], you are my bone and my flesh; why then should you be the last to bring back the king?" Flesh is a sign of horizontal contiguity. It further constitutes an argument that works against hierarchical distinctions. It is a marker of contemporaneous equality, which has implications with regard to the next generation, but is not identical with continuity across generations ("Now our flesh is the same as that of our brothers; our children are the same as their children [*ki-basar aheinu besarenu ki-beneihem baneinu*], and yet we are forcing our sons and daughters to be slaves"; Nehemiah 5:5).[55]

Obviously, none of this should be taken to mean that the Old Testament is not concerned with lineage and genealogical continuities or with hierarchical distinctions, social and other. (After gender hierarchy, the priestly line comes perhaps most readily to mind, even if historical antiquity is something of a nonissue: Unlike many ancient peoples, the Hebrews did not see themselves as the original humans. They were a young people, late on the historical scene.[56]) Nor is this a claim that blood is not massively important in the Bible, in sacrificial and covenantal acts (the story of Abraham testifies to this repeatedly) or even with relation to community building, in the rapport to the divine. The question is where and whether in the body (or indeed in the blood) or beyond it does the Bible locate the preservation or continuity of genealogy, the material, substantive, or imaginary bond of the community?[57] And the answer is clear: Not only does the Old Testament not adhere to the equation routinely ascribed to it between blood and life (as we have already seen), but also biblical genealogical thought simply does not partake of blood. Neither in its embryology (to the extent that we have access to it) nor in the apparatus of its communal relations does blood figure in a recognizable manner. Put another way, "Semitic religion," as Robertson Smith called it, does not provide any evidence of a "blood based kinship," identifying itself and appropriating for itself a bloody substance or potentially differentiating between collectives on the basis of blood. And regardless of whether this state of affairs is perpetuated in postbiblical practice and doctrine,[58] it is more than sufficient to provide a notable alternative to the conception that blood is the "natural" sign and carrier of genealogy, the substance of the community. It is not. Indeed, blood is only one term among many in an economy of locutions and symbols—"natural" or not—that have appealed to the collective imagination. "The official and explicit myth of conception in rabbinic texts" illustrates this quite clearly in the case of reproduction. What is there "is a partnership of three in that the father supplies the white parts of the body: bones, teeth, the white of the eye, brain matter; the mother the red parts: blood, muscle, hair, the pupil of the eye; and God supplies the intelligence, the spirit, the soul, eyesight, motion of the limbs, and the radiance of the face."[59] But note that the Talmud, "the invention of the rabbinic science of blood,"[60] is partly inheriting—and, indeed, reconstructing—a biblical conception that, to repeat, never once invoked the phrase "flesh and blood" and in which kinship was void of blood, functioning instead as the unity (or temporary unification) of "flesh and bones." The Bible's enduring presence therefore makes for a convenient measure, a marker of the distance that could separate us from blood, and for the historico-hematological shift that takes place once blood does become the privileged and hegemonic sign or matter of filiation. Close to this shift, we may be better equipped to contend with the significance of later translations, which equate blood with life. There will be other such instances.

A few more words on blood in the Old Testament. For the biblical text does make a link, if a negative one, between flesh and blood (although I must once again underscore the fact that the expression "flesh and blood" itself does not appear in the entire text of the Hebrew Bible). It is a negative link because the Bible establishes in fact a crucial, normative distinction between flesh and blood, whereby the latter is the interruption or disruption of the former. Not only is blood not a figure of continuity (or, like flesh, of contiguity), blood rather figures as a site of interruption, invoking mainly images of violence, death, and contamination.[61] Again, we have seen earlier that blood is not the life it is massively taken to be. Blood may be proximate to life, but it is not identical with it. Instead, blood is the soul of the creature (human or not). It is a great equalizer, ultimately closer to death. Blood is, at any rate, what must be excluded from consumption, and does not in any way pass on. Even its cleansing or "purifying" role follows this logic of interruption. Accordingly, examples of aberrant behavior must include the suggestion of blood consumption, as in 2 Samuel 23:17 where David exclaims: "Shall I drink the blood of the men that went in jeopardy of their lives?"[62] Blood is also a necessity of course (albeit one that is, again, revealed in death), and as such it is tied to the singular, living individual (human or animal) who lives by it. Typical of the blood of the dead (or later of "innocent blood"), blood speaks therefore, but not before being spilled (even its innocence is thus postmortem). It voices the cause of Earth's blame, which has swallowed it, and it demands vengeance (Genesis 4:10–15). And, as in most vengeance schemes, blood can only be redeemed by the blood of another, by contiguity. Blood, in other words, is the voice of the dead.[63] By way of this association with death, it also functions, and repeatedly so, as an apotropaic sign (of the covenant; Exodus 24:8), and if not quite a positive sign, at least a protective one. Thus in Egypt before the last plague (Exodus 12:13). For the most part, though, blood is a bad sign, especially if it is "upon one's head," which is why it must always be washed (although by that point, it may well be too late).[64] God sometimes does it himself (Isaiah 4:4, Ezekiel 16:9), and overall, water is best, which works for menstrual blood as well as for sacrificial blood (but sometimes a sacred place is needed as in Leviticus 6:20; and one may also have to wait). This is also why the turning of water into blood, rendered famous by the Ten Plagues, is a very bad thing in the Old Testament. Yet, whereas some instances of blood running are considered contaminating ("the contrast between menstrual blood, which is contaminating, and the blood of circumcision or sacrifice, which is positively marked, indicates that only some kinds of blood are contaminating"), it is unequivocally clear that these are effects of blood (tied to the function and location of blood) and that they "have nothing to do with an inherent quality of blood." More generally, blood is endowed with a wide range of significance, that is to say, with numerous effects in the Bible: "blood has different meanings depending upon how it originates and from whence it comes."[65]

Blood is also a site of substitution because of the symbolic and possibly material equality it signifies. Blood must be spilled to substitute for spilled blood (e.g., Numbers 35:33), and spilled blood may also prevent additional spilling (as in the Exodus narrative, again).[66] This belongs to, or rather, it includes the logic of sacrifice and atonement, which necessitate other forms of spilling such as sprinkling, pouring, or draining blood. It is as sacrificial that one may understand the blood of the covenant (of which circumcision may be the major site).[67] Blood, as I have said, must always be washed, and though it may redeem (as in, again, sacrificial substitution), blood itself never washes nor does it purify *as such* (though it might be part of a work of purification in a paramedical sense, as in the ritual purification of a house from disease; Leviticus 14:49–57). Blood is therefore proximate to, but not equated with, life ("In your blood, live!" Ezekiel 16:6). It is rather more closely associated with death (or rather, with murder as in Cain and Abel) and, by another contiguity, with purity and danger (to invoke Mary Douglas). It is rare but possible to read that, by being spilled or sprinkled—never consumed— blood either soils or redeems, both soils and redeems (Douglas insists, as is well known, that place is the determining factor regarding the purity or defilement value of most elements).[68] Redemption, which can also be called purification,[69] may at any rate be a consequence of an activity involving blood (which procreation never appears to be), but there is no sign that blood "itself" could ever be said to be "pure" or "clean." [70] Under no circumstances is it to be eaten. Nor does it ever appear as a part of genealogy or as being passed on in a line of genealogical descent. Blood is not community, although it partakes of the community's making (in a manner markedly derivative of God's command, should this need to be said) as a great equalizer between human and animal. Not only is there no distinction of the community—much less between communities—on the basis of blood, but also there is *no difference between bloods*. Blood is blood and is thus affected by its place and usage. But all creatures, insofar as they are created, "have" blood. Blood is not property and only doubtfully substance. Like death, it is a great leveler.[71]

To conclude for now. The Bible clearly "knows" blood and suffuses it with multifarious meanings, and though many of these meanings invest blood with a powerful charge (ritual, symbolic, and other), none suggest that blood could ever be what the community is made of, a measure of difference or of distinction, let alone running pure in anyone's veins. Most significantly for our understanding of community and the substance it allegedly shares, none of the meanings associated with blood have anything to do with kinship and generation.[72] Fundamentally, kinship appears to be asserted linguistically in the Bible. As in many ancient societies, kinship is a slow process of acquisition, not the acknowledgment of a given. It is also a matter of memory, which etymologically links masculinity to remembrance. (The male seed—seed, not blood—does have an important, if not exclusive, role to play therefore. Sometimes it needs to be "erected" for one's brother; Genesis 38:8.) The materiality of kinship, as opposed to sacrificial and covenantal rituals, is neither of blood nor of flesh but of names, memory, and genealogical lists. And so with the community, which is constantly mediated by the command of God. In neither case can one witness the emergence of a ground, the appearance of a community of substance, or the claims of a community of blood.[73]

FLESH AND BLOOD

For the Old Testament, then, there are neither communities nor hierarchies of blood. To be sure, the text does make some difference between Hebrew and Gentile, a difference that has much to do with gods and worship and with occasional marriage restrictions (although these do not seem to have stopped anybody, nor was the matter of children and their status or belonging a primary concern).

There is also reason to doubt that even the ancient Greeks, often invoked in this context, ever held a model that would be consistent with what was learned (or imagined to have been learned) from them. We will, as I mentioned, revisit this in a later chapter, but suffice to say for now that the blood that is there said to run in the veins of relatives (as if one could generalize from Oedipus!) hardly provides evidence for the kind of medico-legal and political conception that came later to be held, to the effect that kinship (and beyond kinship, collective identity) "is" blood. True, "Laius' *haima*, his blood, runs in Oedipus' veins." But that blood cannot simply be identified as the sign—much less, the fact—of filiation. Indeed, at stake here "is Oedipus' blood, *as well as* the blood Oedipus spills, and it is this blood that needs to be avenged in order to lift the plague ruining the city of Thebes."[74] This makes clear that here at least blood as kinship and filiation cannot be isolated from blood as murder, something that further undercuts any evidence for the claim that kinship has always been (called) blood. Indeed, to assert that the different tragic characters are related "by blood" would be precisely like saying that siblings are "related by murder," as clearly murder is the foregrounded content of the relation of those other, paradigmatic brothers, Cain and Abel.[75] And the argument can be generalized to other tragedies and ancient sources.[76] Closer to the time that occupies us in this chapter, for instance, "the Arthurian romances tell us that the blood relation between father and son cannot be recognized in itself, as they produce the most horrifying kinds of murder, murders of one's own blood: infanticide and parricide."[77] As we will see in more detail, the matter is further complicated by taking into consideration the medical tradition, the divergence of opinions having to do with the number of seeds involved in procreation ("the well-known Aristotle versus Galen match"),[78] the place of blood among the humors or apart from them, pangenesis versus hematogenesis ("according to Hippocratic theories of generation, the embryo is indeed formed by the intermingling of the male and female spermatic humors"), and so forth.[79]

Recall, for example, that if Aristotle did hold the view that male ejaculation is derivative of blood, he would have laughed at the claim that what the father (indeed, *the* genitor) passes on is blood. "The ejaculate, he makes absolutely explicit, was but the vehicle for the efficient cause, for the sperma, which worked its magic like an invisible streak of lightning."[80] And what about the mother's blood? It turns out that "the female, the material, contribution to generation is only slightly more material and thus recognizable by the physical properties of menstrual blood. Aristotle is at pains to point out that catamenia, the menstrual residue itself, is not to be equated with the actual blood that one sees: 'the greater part of the menstrual flow is useless, being fluid.' "[81] In medieval times, at any rate, there was a "lack of clarity about the female fluid or fluids involved in procreation," something that remained "a persistent problem—and eventually an issue—in late medieval discussions of reproductive roles."[82] From reproduction to lineage and heredity, and to blood as the common substance shared by kin and nation, the line is far from obvious or necessary and its connection to ancient Greek physiology more than tenuous.[83] Nor is it free from errors, and particularly not from "errors [that] arose from misinterpretations of Galen or from efforts to combine the teachings of Galen and Aristotle."[84] At this juncture, my argument is not that blood was or was not really there (whatever this might mean historically), but rather to document the ways in which blood appears and functions, the ways it is deployed and invoked, given and made, and the ways it is not.[85]

By the time the New Testament is written in a Greco-Roman cultural and legal environment, the very fact of "flesh and blood" as the appellation and conception of the human, the understanding of genealogy by way of blood, are barely beginning to come about. The phrase "flesh and blood" now appears explicitly in the text, although only in Paul's letters. Still, even there, blood has yet to become the substance of the community.

In this context, it is perhaps the meaning of life itself that is most radically changing in the New Testament, which is why Paul states that "flesh and blood cannot inherit the kingdom of God, nor does the perishable inherit the imperishable" (1 Corinthians 15:50).[86] Thus, for Paul, neither flesh nor blood are sites of desirable continuity or contiguity. They do not signify memory in the manner flesh and bone had. Nor is it necessary to insist on the well-known writings of Paul as denying "the relevance of descent in determining membership or social standing," his claims that "one's genealogy would not guarantee salvation."[87] Paul certainly advocated a different kind of genealogy, a kinship of the spirit rather than of the flesh. Yet here too the link with genealogy has yet to be made explicit or consistent. "Not all flesh is alike, but there is one flesh for human beings, another for animals, another for birds, and another for fish. There are both heavenly bodies and earthly bodies, but the glory of the heavenly is one thing, and that of the earthly is another" (1 Corinthians 15:39–40). On the basis of emerging new distinctions (flesh and blood on the one hand and spirit on the other, but also distinct kinds of flesh), Paul proclaims a new (kind of) genealogy and kinship, and he does so by diminishing the relevance of physical descent. Doing so, he inscribes that descent in blood, in the difference between bloods. One is henceforth *justified* by Christ's blood, rather than by one's "own" (Romans 5:9).[88]

As numerous interpreters have pointed out,[89] there is a strong conception of the body in Paul and in the Gospels, but it is a body that ultimately matters less than the spirit. (Later on, it is this very difference between body and spirit that will be used by advocates of the Statutes on the Purity of Blood to argue that what is at issue in Paul's *adiaphora* is spirit and belief, even if belief in the blood of Christ; Romans 3:25.) Matter—the matter of blood and blood as matter, if that is what it is—cannot be invoked therefore as a site of identity; it is preemptively dismissed as what could "gather" potential or future converts into the church of Christ. Howard Eilberg-Schwartz describes the consequences of this conception of the body upon the construction of ritual cleansing and purity, citing as a striking example the famous episode in which a woman is cured of bleeding by touching Jesus' coat, the implication apparently being that contact with her could not be polluting and would no longer be seen in such terms.[90] In this context, the idea that blood as such could be either purifying or contaminating still makes little sense. And yet blood *can* differentiate; it is slowly becoming the site of a difference. There will be bloods.

Parallel to the general disparaging of blood, at any rate, to the production of blood as disparaged, we find the unique elevation of Jesus' blood.[91] There are different versions of Jesus repeatedly offering his blood ("Drink ye all of it; for this is my blood of the new testament which is shed for many for the remission of sins"; Matthew 26:27–28). At times, it is not so clear whether that blood is supposed to be actually drunk (Luke 22:20), but the confusion is cleared up later: "Verily, verily, I say unto you, Except ye eat the flesh of the Son of Man, and drink his blood, ye have no life in you. . . . For my flesh is meat indeed, and my blood is drink indeed. He that eateth my flesh, and drinketh my blood, dwelleth in me, and I in him" (John 6:53–56). Slowly but surely, *this* blood is becoming life. And not just any life. John's first epistle makes even more explicit and obvious the contrast with the earlier, biblical conception of flesh and blood: "If we say that we have fellowship with him, and walk in darkness, we lie and do not tell the truth: but if we walk in the light, as he is in the light, we have fellowship one with another, and the blood of Jesus Christ his Son cleanseth us from all sin" (1 John 1:6–7). Rendering difficult his own emphasis on spiritual kinship, Paul is thus inscribed along a line that will give exegetes and laymen and women much to ponder, but it announces in no uncertain terms the community of substance, the community of flesh and blood: "The cup of blessing which we bless, is it not the communion of the blood of Christ? The bread which we break, is it not the communion of the body of Christ? For we being many are one bread and one body: for we are all partakers of that one bread" (1 Corinthians 10:16–17).[92]

Judas too is intimately associated with Jesus and with blood. He admits that he has sinned and that he betrayed "the innocent blood." The money he gained for it, which he tries to dispose of at the temple, is considered "the price of blood," and when the priests decide to use that money to buy a field for future burial, that field becomes known as "the field of blood" (Matthew 27:4–8). Pilate, in contrast, declares himself "innocent of the blood of this just person," doing so after having symbolically, and cautiously, washed his hands. The people there assembled appear to have no qualms in establishing a peculiar continuity of blood (recall that in the Bible, having blood upon one's head is definitely a bad sign). Embracing the peculiar equation that links murder and kinship, they enthusiastically place Jesus' blood upon their own heads as well as upon their children's: "His blood be on us, and on our children" (Matthew 27:24–25). There is no possibility of reading here an assertion of a differential analytic of blood, and yet it is important to underscore that the blood that is placed on the head of the next generation(s) is figured as innocent and pure. Peter's first epistle provides what is perhaps the strongest image of Christ's blood as a site or image of purity when he writes of "the precious blood of Christ, as of a lamb without blemish and without spot" (1 Peter 1:19). With regard to the community of blood—as something that remains at once distant and proximate—the ambivalence is maintained in the Gospel According to John, where after asserting that the word was made flesh, John explains that "to all who received him, who believed in his name, he gave power to become children of God, who were born, not of blood or of the will of the flesh or of the will of man, but of God." (John 1:12–13). There is blood and there is blood, good blood and bad blood. And then there is (pure) blood.

The innovations are, it seems to me, straightforward enough, and they constitute the essential building blocks of a singular and peculiar history that will require a few more centuries to reach a completion of sorts, fully to coagulate, as it were. It is this history that culminates when an entire society "in which blood is thick with magical significations, mystical claims, pharmacological prodigies, alchemistical dreams" and where "the torments of Christ, along with the cult of his body and blood" all become "a collective *passio*"; where, finally, "the blood of the divine Lamb becomes the exemplar and instrument of purity."[93]

THE EUCHARISTIC MATRIX

What happens then is—literally—a *wonderful* story. More precisely, this is the history of the rise of a "wonderful blood." I shall be brief in summarizing it, for it has been well researched and depicted from a number of perspectives. Writing of medieval Christianity, Carolyn Walker Bynum concludes *Wonderful Blood*, her essential contribution to the study of medieval blood, by stating that "rather than interpreting blood as merely one among many objects in a struggle for control or one among many themes in an extravagantly emotional religiosity, we should see in blood the central symbol and central cult object of late medieval devotion—and perhaps the central problem as well."[94] This is to say that blood is not merely a part of medieval Christianity. It is rather its very fabric. Bynum nonetheless isolates part from whole (explicitly and implicitly, synecdoche, *pars pro toto*, is a significant device in the apparatus she deploys). She differentiates, in other words, between bloods. On the one hand, she writes of blood in "theology and practice in late medieval northern Germany and beyond." She describes a blood cult and a blood devotion and thereby adds to the growing scholarly understanding of blood in this specific period.[95] On the other hand, she also makes clear that she is attending to something much larger, a longer period as it were, and a wider if still contained issue. Bynum clearly says that she is writing about "religion" ("if we are to understand why themes such as bleeding become prominent at a particular moment in the history of a religion, we must (the point is an obvious one!) look at the whole of that religion: pious prayers and practices, local shrines, artistic commissions, theological debates, accounts of visions and miracles, ecclesiastical politics, and the context of all this in regional and national strife").[96] And although it is not the place to debate with Bynum's understanding of the term *religion* or to wonder about the viability of the category in that particular historical context,[97] I do wish to underscore that blood as fabric covers, in her own descriptions, a much more expansive domain than *religion* (as Bynum herself defines it). The evidence extends further and suggests, for example, "that blood relics were politically, financially, and religiously desirable" (58). Ultimately, "it was blood to which kings, clergy, and common people voyaged, blood that filled the hearts of penitents and the coffers of merchants, blood over which theologians fought, blood that inspired imitation and competition from churches and monasteries" (32). Blood, in other words, is everywhere. It flows and overflows, and it covers theological, cultic, and devotional matters, but also—and in a novel way—politics and economy, kinship and community. "The behavior of blood is described in these texts as people believed blood was wont to behave. Dividing, it remained forever whole; and its distribution created filiation and community" (72). Parts and wholes at once, blood surges and flows to include and to divide, to determine finally a wider conception of the collective, of the community it singles out, the community of blood. For what Bynum ultimately shows is that medieval debates and practices in Western Christendom did not take place merely "over proper Eucharistic piety or the authenticity and veneration of relics. Rather, it was, on the one hand, a matter of the relation of the body and blood of Christ to each other and to his person, and on the other hand, a question of how Christians gain access to the *sanguis Christi* that saves" (110). The distinct particles, parts, and bodies found in the fabric of blood would soon be meeting with others. They would collide or be repulsed and communicate with each other. Which body, which blood? Individuals and collectives were being conceived anew, reconceptualized around and within blood ("Aquinas, basing himself on Albertus Magnus, held that blood is the seat of life, and, indeed, of the whole body *in potentia*" [162]). In the final analysis, the issue turned out to be at once "physiological, philosophical, theological, and finally what we might even call sociological" (121). As well, "the blood is more than sexual and social or marital status; it is more even than the bearer of ethical status, that is purity or impurity. It is as if the body is only a mold into which blood as animating force or soul or self is poured" (163).[98] And medieval theologians could thus explain the nature of the collective change Western Christendom was undergoing: "we eat God not so that he changes into us but so that we change into him."[99] Indeed, what "theologians were really debating when they debated the possibility of blood relics and miracle hosts was the nature of identity" (145). And "in all this, what is stressed is the immediacy and physicality of *sanguis Christi*. Warm and alive itself, it warms and liquefies the blood of sinners who have grown cold, hard, dried, and dead in selfishness and alienation. It restores life to the *imago Dei* within the self, as liquid warmth softens hard wax. But it goes further. It fuses with—becomes—the blood of the self" (170).[100] It is not difficult, therefore, to see that Christians were changing indeed in their very substance, purity, and property, and not only in the north of Europe, not only in the fifteenth century. Christians were becoming a community of blood. Understandably—but also historically—they "equated their own blood with Christ's" (244). "You will not change me into you, as you do with the food of your body," Augustine had explained, ventriloquizing Jesus, "Instead you will be changed into me."[101] Henri de Lubac elaborates, pointing out that "the natural symbolism of food is reversed," and quoting William of St. Thierry, "those eating are transformed into the nature of the food they eat." Indeed, "this is because the Eucharistic bread is no ordinary bread," and the eucharistic wine no ordinary wine: "it is the Life in which all living beings participate. 'When Christ is eaten, Life is eaten.' He transforms into himself those whom he nourishes with his substance. He himself is the body whose food those who eat it become."[102] That is what made blood into the fabric it became (for what else is transubstantiation?). "In this sort of piety ... the blood *is* Christ" (180).

But perhaps I have been misquoting. Using and abusing the words of the historians, I have taken some parts, at my convenience, and made them stand for the whole. After all, not all Christians have thought or lived along the coordinates I have begun to draw. And besides, blood does not only gather and unify. It also separates and discriminates. Bynum dedicates an entire chapter, in fact, to precisely this, to "Blood as Separated and Shed," to "blood as separation" (173). Why unify, then, where there is division? Why take the parts for the whole? Surprisingly enough, Bynum herself seems to answer this important question when she deploys the beginnings of an explanation for "why blood?" Why the prominence of blood at this particular (broad but limited) historical juncture. What Bynum calls "natural blood" (as opposed to "symbolic" blood) operates as a crucial part of the explanation. And the explanation is, well, natural enough. "Natural blood is the ultimate synecdoche: the human part that *is* the human and the social whole" (187). (Later, Bynum will insist that "blood was, moreover, a particular apt image for retribution and satisfaction"—for economy, that is—"for arousal, and for the synecdoche implied in incorporation" [209].) "This late medieval habit of understanding part to be whole, instance to be *in* exemplar, made it possible to think not only of humans subsumed in the *humanitas* of Christ but also of relatives, neighbors, even heretics as subsumed into one's own suffering in a union that was more participation than substitution" (203). Parts for the whole, sociology (along with history, anthropology, and biology to boot) has become, *naturally enough*, Christology. Or vice versa. And Christology is hematology; it is the fabric of our lives. It raises "new questions about family, society, and politics" (256). For it is indeed a fact that "not all religions give meaning by such stark, simultaneous assertion of life and death as does medieval Christianity" (255). Simply put, not all religions (but what is "religion"? and are there really many within this asymmetric hematology?) give meaning, whether theological, political, anthropological and familial, legal and economic—eventually *natural*—by way of blood.

✠ ✠ ✠

The ubiquitous link in the Christian West between blood and community— the Eucharist or the language of "blood ties" spoken through family, tribe, class, nation, or race—which is to say, the notion that blood is the substance, site, and marker of collective identity in its many existential dimensions, is a late and *contingent* link that binds us still to the "Middle Ages." Far from universal, this link must be unsettled and de-sedimented, recognized for its processual advent and for its endurance. We have begun to consider that neither the Bible nor the rabbis ever thought of genealogy and kinship as being a matter of blood, that the phrase "flesh and blood" as a descriptive and as a signifier of identity or of genealogical continuity is either absent or, and so only later, at the very least reductive (for much more than blood is involved in identity and in transmission, unless blood is everything),[103] and that even the New Testament is remote from "the ideology of consanguinity." Again, though, nothing is said here to diminish the multiple and heavy symbolic charges often carried by blood (murder and sacrifice, menstruation and birth) or of its multilayered role in collective practices of whatever kind—pure, dangerous, and other.[104]

How, then, did the community of blood emerge? How were blood ties created? How did "natural blood" become "a particular apt image" and "the ultimate synecdoche" ("the human part that *is* the human and the social whole")? How did blood come to trickle and flow within all these? More precisely perhaps, how did family ties, communal ties, come to be called by the name of blood? In a groundbreaking study to which I have already alluded, Gianna Pomata has pointed out that "historians have not asked which ideas about blood shaped the legal notion of consanguinity. What was meant by blood in the legal usage of *consanguinitas*? How were blood ties created, according to the law? And whose blood are we talking about?"[105] Pomata clarifies that the matter is not—was never—primarily physiologic or indeed natural. Medical discourse, at any rate, although intervening and participating in the articulation of the matter, was neither exclusively adjudicating on it nor was it particularly pressing toward a universalization of blood. In Roman law and culture, *consanguinitas* was a restricted juridical matter and a political one as well. And so blood was never quite what allegedly, or "simply," runs in the veins, never exclusively so. To the extent that blood did partake of the making of kinship, it did so by way of a radical asymmetry not between families and communities, but *within* them. Blood was the peculiar site of sexual difference in that it belonged exclusively to the father. "The notion of *consanguinitas* tells us that the tie between father and children is twofold: part of it derives from the father's power and part of it derives from the father's blood." In other words, "the natural relationship between a father and his children creates *consanguinitas*; that between a mother and her children does not."[106]

We may be beginning to gain a better sense of time—and of contingency— when it comes to blood as the name of kinship (and more precisely, as the juridico-medical name for what relates father to child). For what has been called "the hematogenic theory of semen," the notion that semen is the father's blood, only "became dominant, after the fourth century BC, in both philosophical and medical discourse, superseding other ancient theories—still current, for example, in the Hippocratic texts—where semen was seen as derived from the brain (via the spinal marrow) or from all the parts of the body . . . [T]he hematogenic view was established as the unchallenged theory of semen in European culture long after antiquity: in fact, surprising as it might seem, the theory persisted into the eighteenth century."[107] But recall that, as Pomata demonstrates, blood is the site of a division—not a constitution—of the community, and that too along gender lines.[108] In Roman law, blood (that is, *consanguinitas*) did not mean that there were different bloods. It was simply a notion that defined the matter of property, "matters of inheritance and succession," and was thereby favoring a segment of the male progeny.[109] Another essential element, then, will have to contribute its part. This is what can be found exemplarily and explicitly in Tertullian, for whom "the blood of Christians is seed [*semen est sanguis Christianorum*]," an assertion that must be understood simultaneously as medical, political, and theological, the three "domains," within which it radically intervenes and ultimately transforms.[110] Fundamentally, then, the recognizable configuration, "the coinciding dependency" that will come to unite medicine and law, family and politics, along with economics, cannot be understood as merely theological or "religious."[111] It is however and definitely *Christian*—dividing and linking each of these domains. Indeed, well after Tertullian and Isidore of Seville, it is only with canon law, finally, that the notion of blood is expanded, redistributed, and translated into the realm of marriage.[112]

From then on, that is, from the Christian Middle Ages on (and recall that "the first liturgical rituals of marriage appeared in northern France around 1100"),[113] the notion that the child receives the blood of *both* father and mother becomes accepted, at first *against reigning medical conceptions* and around them, in order to determine kinship, in order, that is, for the church to authorize or forbid alliances.[114] "Even the naturalistic justifications that sometimes found their way into the legal and political discourse," in other words, "the justification of the inclusion of affines under incest regulations by the 'unity of flesh and blood' supposedly instituted by marriage . . . were not, as far as we can see, immediately reflected in medical or philosophical accounts of generation."[115] Canon law figures the couple as *unitas carnis*, the "figure of the non-dissolvable union between Christ and its Church," thereby including father and mother into what had otherwise become reserved for brothers as "blood brothers."[116] Accordingly, along with the rise of the Eucharist cult and the dissemination of bleeding relics, the very notion of the church as the "mystical body of Christ" also changes. It no longer signifies the *invisible* body of Christ mysteriously found in the sacrament and distinct from other, material, bodies, but rather embodies the visible members (the flesh and blood) of the community.[117] It is within this transformative framework—a generalized hematology that involves a "new notion of consanguinity" and weaves a fabric at once medical and juridical, theological and political—that the nobility too could be invented as a "social category" grounded in blood as genealogy or lineage, along with others.[118] Consanguinity, in other words, has a history, and it is briefer, more contained and specific, than commonly supposed. It corresponds to a particular distribution (not yet a circulation) of blood within Western Christendom.[119] Which means that we can more or less establish "the coinciding dependency with respect to the . . . historical situation," the dissemination of the notion, at once legal, medical, and political, of the community of blood.[120] It is time to relate what we have learned so far—the eucharistic matrix—to the Inquisition.

EXPECTING THE SPANISH INQUISITION

With "a history much older than the term itself," the Black Legend has always been displayed under the sign of blood.[121] It testifies to "the contemporary madness of blood purity," the "Spanish hysteria over the improper mixing of bloods,"[122] and signifies "Spain's colonial brutality in the Americas during the sixteenth and seventeenth centuries," sustaining "the characterization of Spain by other Europeans as a backward country of ignorance, superstition, and religious fanaticism that was unable to become a modern nation."[123] But as I have been arguing, it is not really difficult to see that this does not constitute a major deviation, much less an exception, from medieval history. For the entire "Middle Ages" is carrying a red tide of "wonderful" and not so wonderful blood.[124] Still, some spots are bloodier than others, some bloods appear more distressing than others. The blood of persecution (and of menstruation) seems more troubling therefore than the blood of Christ: the curse of Eve, the wound of the hero, as McCracken describes this structure. Spain is alleged to have been a bloodier empire than England, and Catholics are said to have displayed more cruelty, more bloodiness, than Protestants. My argument, however, is that one cannot maintain a strict distinction between the two bloods (although their very distinction, the *difference between bloods*, will prove to be an essential factor), between the blood of the Eucharist and the blood of the Inquisition. One should have expected the Spanish Inquisition, in other words, for blood is on every side of the divide it otherwise marks—and the historical divide too. Far from exceptional, then, blood is in fact the rule.

The prominence and equivocation of blood, its relative invisibility too, constitute no more than one cluster of reasons why the difficulties that continue to plague inquiries about the Inquisition are so massive. Has "the Inquisition come out of its ghetto"? Is it no longer an unquestioned exception, "no longer a marginal institution of peripheral states engaging in activities that are on the side of the main current of European history?"[125] Minimally, the Inquisition itself appears to be something of a divisive issue. Like blood, and like the histories of blood in which it strangely fails to appear, the Inquisition divides—and is divided—along historical and disciplinary lines: Is the Inquisition medieval or modern? And to what history does it, in fact, belong? Religious history? Political history? Does it prevent or foster, say, the development of modern individualism or modern legalism? Upon what lines, in what areas should one look for continuities or interruptions? How to think the end of the Inquisition? And where is its impact to be witnessed? Is the Inquisition its own contemporary, or is its significance to be looked for in its later effects? The "mythological" uses to which it is put or the belated ways in which it affected its victims? The Inquisition also divides along national and colonial lines: Is there much sense, for example, in speaking of one Inquisition? And whether or not there is, what can one learn by comparing the Italian (and earlier French) as well as Spanish and Portuguese Inquisitions? Given the unification of Western Christendom occurring in the late Middle Ages, its spreading to the New World (as well as to other colonial spaces), is it possible to ignore the extended geographies and the common traits of the after all unique "Holy Office," the seat of which was found in Rome? What relations are there, then, between the lands covered by the Inquisition (within Europe and outside of it) and those that remained outside of its jurisdiction? There are indeed geographic lines at stake: Given that most Inquisitorial courts were located in Spain and Portugal, what are we to make of the Inquisition in the Americas, in the Indian subcontinent? And, are there links, other than conjectural, between the Inquisition and the Spanish and Portuguese Empires? The Inquisition divides along gender lines as well: The differential impact on men and women has led to the increased recognition that without a gendered analysis, no adequate understanding of the Inquisition and its effects could be forthcoming. Finally, what are the discursive realms according to which we are to understand the Inquisition? If political history, does the Inquisition testify to the emergence of the modern state or rather to the slow collapse of medieval forms of sovereignty? Is it to be understood as a bastion of conservative resistance to political modernity? Does it foster or hinder the accession of Spain into the European and even international community of nations? If legal history, where does the Inquisition play its role? Does it elaborate modern juridical procedures or does it testify to the endurance of medieval anachronism? What is its role in "social disciplining"? What mechanisms of power did the Inquisition put in place, if any? How are we to understand the role of the Inquisition in the treatment of minorities, the relation of papacy to monarchy, the acquisition of territory, and the constitution of political communities in the colonies? The Inquisition also belongs, of course, to the history of race as it applied or implemented, or simply authorized, in one way or another and even if reluctantly, the famous Statutes on the Purity of Blood (*estatutos de limpieza de sangre*). More practically, perhaps, debates rage as to the function of the Inquisition in matters of race and of religion: Was it repressive or productive? Did the Inquisition "invent" the *conversos*, did it "make Christians into Jews" as some critics put it, or did it find and arrest them? Finally—and here might be a crux of the questions and distinctions I have just recalled—how does the Inquisition affect our understanding of religion? Was it a religious institution? A religious aberration? Is it one kind among many, and can it be found among other "religions"? Was it an instrument of political (read: secular) power or was it an effect of religious motivations, even religious fanaticism? To the history of which religion does it properly belong? Should it be understood in terms of its victims, or does it testify to seen and unseen changes in the dominant society, in the very community in which and out of which its apparatuses were deployed? Is the Inquisition more or less, finally, than the distorting mirror unavoidably produced by the bias of its enormous archives? Prior to these questions, perhaps, is once again the persistent issue of whether the Spanish Inquisition is exceptional, the singular and aberrant doing of a society gone awry in the extremity of its pursuits. Is the Inquisition another sign—if such was needed—of Spain's cultural belatedness, of Spanish (or Catholic) exceptionalism?

I have no intention of answering these all too numerous questions, which may require adjudicating on the integrity, the exceptionality, or lack thereof, of an object—the Inquisition—as if its integrity was not always in question, as if one could so adjudicate (quite unlike the Inquisition itself, in fact) in isolation from secondary, contextual conditions and effects of allegedly minor significance.[126] What I do want to do, however, is suggest that stepping aside from such questions (while keeping them in mind nonetheless) might bring about an unexpected clarity regarding the formative role the Inquisition has played, its contribution to the emergence, indeed, to the integrity, of the community of blood. The alternative, adjacent point of perspective I offer is perhaps not so minor, and it is found in the element that is accompanying us throughout, the significance of which colors more than the whole affair, incidentally, while consistently if partially withdrawing from critical attention. The separations between Eucharist and Inquisition, between self and other, and religion and race; between the "Spanish" obsession with blood and with blood purity and modern racism or nationalism; between "medieval blood" and the growth and proliferation, the endurance, of the community of blood throughout Western Christendom—these are what I seek to bridge and somehow remedy. For this purpose, I will from here on be guided by the Statutes on the Purity of Blood, which in themselves have of course attracted substantial scholarly attention, although strikingly none that take blood as a point of focalization.[127]

According to the current consensus, the Statutes on the Purity of Blood were first proclaimed in 1449 in Toledo, Spain. We have begun to see that they institute—or rather confirm—a hematological difference, locating purity in the blood of Christians. The explicitness of the statutes no doubt explains why they are credited by most scholars as historically significant, even crucial. Among the historians themselves, the statutes constitute a divided point of origin, the historical and contentious beginning around which comes to be articulated what we have come to call "modern racism."[128] Whether they are included in the history of modern racism as its radical beginning or excluded from it by way of adamant distinctions (much of which invested on both sides with the added weight of eager comparisons linking late medieval Spain to Nazi Germany), the statutes themselves are deemed exceptional and originary, exceptional *as* originary.[129] They have no explanation per se, certainly no simple history, except perhaps for a kind of discontinuous psycho-history (cognates of the word "anxiety" are ubiquitous) and the limited sociological considerations that usually attend to generalities on interactions between majority and minority, integration and exclusion, and, finally, Spanish exceptionalism or even hematological universalism. ("Many medieval Christians believed, as so many other societies have done, that the transition from 'other' to 'self'—in this case, from infidel and alien to Christian and kin—would culminate in sexual union";

"the discourse of collective sexual honor [which] functioned to stabilize 'the cohesion, standing, regularity, and furtherance of the life processes' of the Christian community"; "heightened fears about pollution and the coherence of the body social"; "interfaith sexual panic"; "In the Iberian Peninsula more than in many other regions of Europe, medieval Christians defined themselves sociologically, as well as theologically, against the Jews. Individually and collectively, they asserted their honor as members of God's privileged people by contrasting themselves to the dishonored Jew"; and ultimately "the actions of a society anxious about the biological reproduction of religious identity."[130]) The Statutes on the Purity of Blood, and the very idea of a purity of blood, thus seem to present us with the eruption of a singularity, the sudden invention of a mechanism of exclusion and social control on the basis of blood (the *figurative* status of which remaining, as I have said earlier, under suspended interrogation), and possibly the onset of an ominous and bloody history that is with us still, though, as David Nirenberg puts it, "the walls with which societies divide themselves need rebuilding by each generation's hands."[131]

As an object of scholarly interest, racism is paradigmatic of the narrative of secularization,[132] as is, for the most part, nationalism. Both are seen as the result of ruptures, as governed by secular (secularizing and secularized) conceptions and developments. More precisely put, their history constitutes a striking chapter illustrating the strange success of the enduring fiction secularization is. At stake for me here, however, is less a definition of the changes occurring in the sixteenth century (periodization, again) than an attempt to consider the multidimensionality of these changes in order to interrogate their construction. Whatever "modernity" might be when it comes to the history of racism, the narrative of secularization (from religion to race) fails to describe it, as the very distinction between race and religion is an *effect* of the historical movements we are still trying to grasp. The situation remains that, whether discussing the distinction between anti-Judaism and anti-Semitism, for instance, or simply the distinction between "religious" exclusion and modern racism, historians have held on to a long-established consensus. This consensus is only broken by asserting at best that there are, at times, links and conjunctions between race and religion. Clearly, by the time the categories emerge as categories, they can be dissociated and distinguished. They can function to refer to distinct phenomena, even different orders of existence, which can be subsequently associated. The argument I am trying to invoke, however, is that race and religion, nation and religion, emerge as co-constitutive *in their distinctiveness.*

By exploring, as I do here, the community of blood, the notion of purity of blood, I do not mean therefore to engage in chronological or periodizing claims relating to the origin of racism or of nationalism. Rather, I am trying to interrogate the construction of the origin or of the exception as a mechanism of power that displaces and separates, distinguishes and purifies, as it were, a particular site of power (race, nation) from its alleged other (religion). I begin, then, with a different question: How and when did blood become the carrier of genealogy, of race, and finally of nation? Valuable studies locate the origin of biological racism in decisively "secular" historical lines. This is where the Inquisition (though not the Eucharist) slowly comes in, gaining its place in secular modernity.

Ann Stoler, for instance, reiterates the crucial argument that race is "one of the central conceptual inventions of modernity."[133] Stoler thus joins scholars who argue for an early start, signaling toward "the rise of individualism and the decline of monarchy" as prompting "new theories about 'how individuals might be linked together by their natural character.' "[134] She underscores as well the role of sexuality (as foregrounded by Foucault) and the importance of colonial conquest and rule (mostly ignored by Foucault). Accordingly, Stoler locates the beginnings of racism in a wider history and a more expansive geography, tracing it to colonial practices of discrimination at the hands of the Dutch, the French, and, of course, the British over the course of the seventeenth century.[135] Attending to the recurring obsession she identifies with "purity of blood," Stoler shows that the idea may have had multiple origins, all European, though its presence is subsequently attested in a large number of contexts. Still, the earliest evidence appears to point to the Spanish and Portuguese empires, where purity of blood served in "the forging of 'cleansed' Spanish identity 'that referred both to national unity and to the overseas empire,' " whereas in colonial Latin America, "the notion of 'purity of blood acquired new force *as it lost any religious connotation*, becoming a clearly racial notion' by the beginning of the eighteenth century."[136] So it is that, although some mention is made, if in passing, of "religious" antecedents, the dominant purpose Stoler pursues is "to underscore the fact that the racial lexicons of the nineteenth century have complex colonial etymologies," rather than Christian ones. Such complexity, crucial as it is to recognize, does narrow down, however, and finally points to yet another turn, a surprising beginning in the sixteenth century, at which point it is *through* that social complexity that "aristocratic discourses on 'purity of blood' were replayed and transformed" (52). A few pages later, Stoler lists a number of scholars and thinkers who all "grappled with the same conversion of the idea of race from an aristocratic political weapon into its more pervasive bourgeois form" (58). Finally, in a later footnote documenting the emergence of the idea of race in debates opposing the nobility to the bourgeoisie in seventeenth-century France, Stoler mentions the work of Albert Sicroff, still the major scholarly authority on the Statutes on the Purity of Blood, and asserts that in this case too, the nobility protected itself by way of racial arguments emphasizing the purity of its blood (67–68, n. 14).[137] In his famous study of nationalism, Benedict Anderson concisely endorses this narrative and, a bit strangely perhaps, confirms it. Anderson underscores the element of "divinity," which is, to a large extent, what has been occupying us throughout. When it comes to racism, however, Anderson writes that "the dreams of racism actually have their origin in ideologies of *class*, rather than in those of nation: above all in claims to divinity among rulers and to 'blue' or 'white' blood and 'breeding' among aristocracies."[138] The community of blood is first and foremost the (aristocratic) class. Foucault's periodization is perfectly *laïcard*. Another, no less impressive scholarly endeavor, that of Giorgio Agamben, directs us toward Roman law (and, implicitly, to Greek medicine), which, Agamben says, determined political belonging in terms of "blood and soil," *jus solis* and *jus sanguinis*.[139] To put it briefly, then, the scholarly consensus is that the bio-political is ostensibly *not* the theologico-political.[140]

Working along similar lines, scholars of the *limpieza* generally agree in emphasizing the novelty of the statutes and assert that, prior to their proclamation, "we must assume that in this period the Jews were not the object of a racist animus. For now at least, it was not their race that distinguished them, but their religion."[141] To be sure, the paradigmatic status of the Jews has not fully translated into a consensus among historians and theoreticians of racism. There are even harsh disagreements. And yet, by considering the way in which they relate to and constitute this particular and early object, it is possible to group a large number of scholars as sharing more than has perhaps been apparent (including those who, like Benzion Netanyahu, claim that racial anti-Semitism or anti-Judaism are ultimately *perennial*). In this perspective, even someone like Gavin Langmuir, who has compellingly asked us to reconsider our definitions of anti-Semitism (which he spells "antisemitism"), is part of the large group of historians and theoreticians I am gathering here, whom I would describe as subscribing in one way or another to the narrative of secularization, understood as the (relative) autonomy of nation (or race) from religion, be it along temporal, existential, or simply analytical lines.[142] Allow me to conclude this brief survey by proposing that we take a nonsecular view of the *limpieza* (which is to say that we treat the Inquisition as nonexceptional and reject the quasi-hermetic division of race from religion). For if we do so, most of the daunting edifice of distinctions and divisions to which the Inquisition, as a historical object, bears witness and most of the questions I have listed earlier appear to vanish.[143] To put it as briefly as I can: The Inquisition—and with it, the *limpieza de sangre*—makes sense. Not because it becomes thereby more (or less) comparable to modern racism, Nazi or other, but because its occurrence is no longer *sui generis*: neither an aberration nor an exception. The factors that lead to its emergence—and the statutes do *precede* the establishment of the Spanish, and more specifically Castilian, Inquisition (1478), much as they are opposed by it (1580–1632) and will, subsequently, outlast it (1865)—these factors, then, become significantly clearer, and the specific efficacy of the Inquisition upon minorities from the time of its establishment becomes less relevant than it seemed.[144] Spain is no longer an exception, nor is it isolated from the rest of Europe (not to mention the Christian world, old and new). It can gain its place as part of a larger history of the development of the modern state as well as that of colonialism, a history that must be refigured as less modern and less secular than still usually thought. Not that the Inquisition is simply modern, then. But, as we shall see in more detail in the next chapter, neither is the modern state (or nationalism), as it continues to be conceived of and largely operative still.[145] Whether we consider the nation-state as completing the Reformation (with the French Revolution), as changing the structure of social classes (the emergence of the bourgeoisie, the democratization or at least generalization of aristocratic privileges, modes and standards of behavior, and manners), as grounded in a prepolitical community called the "people" or "nation" (the invention of nationalism), or as the sign of a shift from sovereignty to discipline, as Foucault had it (from the theologico-political to the bio-political, as he also suggests, or from political theology to "politische Biologie");[146] whether we see the state, finally, as the result of a process of secularization whereby religion, fundamentally altered, is now subsumed under the state's territorial authority; and whether we want to document, in a historically precise way, the developments undergone by the slowly evolving notion of race as a concept and as an ensemble of social mechanisms of marginalization, classification, and exclusion—whatever all these cases may be, we will see that the Inquisition articulates an essential moment of the history of Europe, a history whereby, to invoke Walter Benjamin again, the exception has become the rule.[147] More modestly, however, by attending to the conditions of possibility of the *limpieza*, the necessary, enabling conditions without which it could not have emerged and of which it is an integral part, I hope to show that the pervasive distinction of (modern) nation and (medieval) religion is not only regrettable and inaccurate but also answers to (and complies with) disciplinary and governing mechanisms and to long-standing biases, which continue to affect and even structure our historical understanding, our understanding of the present.[148] When I argue that the Statutes on the Purity of Blood make sense, then, I mean that they are part of a theologico-political history that has further produced the *necessary* (if, perhaps, not sufficient) conditions of what we call nationalism (or racism) and of much more—what the community is made of. Clearly, distinctions can be made (between nation and religion, political and theological, and so forth), although it is doubtful that the categories apply just as they do today. Just like race and religion, then, nation and religion may be distinguishable, but that is precisely because, in the Christian European context, they are co-constitutive and contemporaneous.[149]

As the opponents of the statutes understood very well, however, what was at stake (as well as endangered) was the community of blood; that is, Christian political theology, the nature and unity of the mystical body of Christ ("the blood is Christ") and of the church understood as a *spiritual* union from above.[150] With the rise of blood, of the community of blood, political theology was being invented and reinvented, fashioned and refashioned: the community as a community unified in, by, and as blood, with blood understood as (endangered and vulnerable) property and possession. What I seek to underscore, then, is the general, indeed massive, emergence of blood as the site—figurative as it may at times be—of the collective bond, of which the Inquisition is but a small if significant part. It is the rise of a new theologico-political thought and form. For with this new material and rhetorical link unifying it, the community no longer depends on a transcendental condition or external, indeed expropriating, order. Grounded in its own materiality, in its own unified existence qua community, the community no longer awaits unification, no longer needs to *perform* its unity. It no longer gives itself away, nor does it need to be gathered (from above or from below).[151] It *is* already one in blood; it is the general kinship of blood. Paradoxically, not so much displaced as replaced, and given a new depth, the social bond becomes one among a set of layers, spheres, or dimensions to be fully distinguished in subsequent reflections. It can already be refigured as contingent, contractual or negotiable, collective or individual. It can also be thought as being in dissolution on the basis of the new "natural" ground that, always already there, at once unifies and divides the community. To put the matter more clearly, if slightly in jest, perhaps: God divides and rules upon a humanity awaiting its unification, but blood unifies and divides, while leaving the question of rule suspended, the seat of the ruler empty. By then, it is only a matter of time before the head falls, having already been discarded as contingent, rather than as the locus of life and death ("The king is dead. Long live the king!").[152] The community of blood is also the community of the heart. The unity of its members being granted by blood, its dismemberment (decapitation) renders the body latent or artificial. "When society can no longer be represented as a body and is no longer embodied in the figure of the prince [i.e., the head], it is true that people, state and nation acquire a new force and become the major poles by which social identity and social communality can be signified. But to assert, in order to extol it, that a new religious belief takes shape is to forget that this identity and this community remain indefinable."[153] The indefinite and invisible element is, of course, blood, which orients the community toward immanence and immunity (protection and preservation), toward the national revolution and "the time of a people, of the people who await their incarnation, who are in a sense always invisible, but who reveal themselves for one moment in history."[154] The community identifies itself with, it appropriates for itself, the substance it takes itself to be: The blood of Christ, blood pure and proper.

To inquire anew into the enabling conditions of the very idea of a purity of blood, to locate them within a theologico-political history, thus means to take seriously the notion that the community of blood was engaged in *self-fashioning*. Less invested in alterity than otherwise appears, the community of Christians was reinventing itself as the community of blood. Paradoxically perhaps, this ultimately means that we must shift our attention away from racism and exclusion (outward projections) and ask about inward-oriented practices, the formation and fashioning of the community that constitutes itself as a community of blood, a *socius sanguis*, and only subsequently supplements this self-referential gesture with the exclusion of those whose blood, by logical deduction and historical consequence, is deemed impure or tainted. As it becomes the marker, ultimately the substance, of the community, blood redefines and internally refashions the community—and the difference between communities. It bounds and defines an inside as if autonomously, independently. What emerges, at any rate, is a new community: a new notion of the community as appropriated substance, and a community that identifies itself by way of blood, within which identification, belonging, and property are defined by blood. Ultimately, the subsequent difference between communities will be a difference *between bloods*. Then, and only then, will this defining difference slowly spread to class and to clan, to religion and to nation. First of all, however, it applies inwardly and primarily to Christians. This is why, as we embark on this part of our inquiry, we should suspend the philologically correct appellation of "Old Christians" (as opposed to converts, or *conversos,* deemed "New Christians"). Instead, we must recognize that what is being fashioned is indeed a new kind of Christian, in fact, many different kinds of "New Christians." And among them, the most important are the so-called Old Christians.

1449

It is along the frontier of blood—on the red line between pure and impure—that the inexhaustible drama between the sacred and the profane is played out: between the history of the divine, and the history of the human element that would struggle free of the human.

—CAMPORESI, *JUICE OF LIFE,* 121

On June 5, 1449, the governing body of the city of Toledo, Spain, seems to have reached that very conclusion. Its members, at any rate, had little to say by way of a direct comment upon the purity or impurity of the blood of others (apart from claiming that these were at war, "con mano armada de sangre y fuego," against the church and the city of Toledo). Rather, they officially and emphatically asserted *about themselves* that they were "old, pure Christians," *christianos viejos lindos*, thus claiming that their antiquity (as well as their own purity) was to be viewed anew as a basis for privilege, as a source of symbolic capital.[155] The religion of the "Good News" was thus becoming oddly similar to "la ley vieja," the old law, which was being condemned again in order to protect "las casas antiguas e faciendas de los christianos viejos." The religion that asserted its own youth and novelty was transforming itself on the basis of a transvalued sense of antiquity.[156] More significantly, the site of this antiquity was lineage and, more specifically, blood. As Benzion Netanyahu describes it,

> Three times does the term *lindos* (pure) appear in the *Sentencia* as a title of *christianos viejos*, emphasizing no doubt, that in its authors' view, the "purity" which characterizes the Old Christians emanates from their "pure" origin, just as the corruption of the New Christians emanates from their impure, "perverted" source—i.e., the "stock and breed of the Jews."[157]

What is once again critical to understand is the emphatic self-fashioning at work in the constitution of the New Christian (by which I mean, again, and in distinction from common usage, the "Old Christian," that is to say, the hereby newly invented "Old Christian"). As Netanyahu well recognizes, though he does not elaborate on it further, the novelty by no means lies in the emphasis on genealogy. Rather, it has to do with blood itself and with its purity. By the time such a notion of "purity of blood" emerges, a number of factors will necessarily have to have been in place. As we have been seeing, each of these factors testifies to a growing concern with, and a growing investment in, blood.

1. The notion that lineage and kinship are signaled and carried, whether physiologically, legally, or figuratively, by blood.
2. The notion that there are different kinds of blood.
3. The notion that beyond the family, blood is also constitutive of the larger community such that blood functions dominantly to unify that community around it, regardless of leadership or government. Based, moreover, on the notion that there are different kinds of blood, there are also different kinds of communities, even "within" the larger community.
4. The notion that blood can purify, that the blood of a human being can be pure, but also that it is vulnerable to defilement, and that such is the case not only for individuals but indeed for the community at large.

Each of these recast, in a manner that should be obvious by now, the biblical and neo-testamental antecedents, along with the quick history of medicine and the transformations of Roman law I have briefly traced. And one must of course add the discovery of the story of the Holy Grail and, much more significantly, the widely disseminated narratives, conceptions, and ritual practices involving the blood of Jesus as holy, worthy of adoration, and indeed, as pure and purifying. All of this leads to a number of remarkable consequences: the identification of each and every Christian individual with Jesus' flesh and blood and the incorporation of those individuals in that flesh and blood[158]; an active and collective participation in the novel community that emerged through the Eucharist[159]; the particularly charged status of blood, which, in eucharistic practice, was quickly deemed so vulnerable that it could no longer be tasted by the community of laymen and laywomen; and the repeated association of Jews with blood (as Christ-killers and repeat offenders in the blood-libel narratives or as host-desecrators in need of Christian blood, as renowned physicians, or, more often, as blood merchants, found in constant and dangerous proximity to blood relics). All of this points to a refiguration of the Christian community (that is to say, of the community *as* Christian) and the Christian individual ("flesh and blood") as determined by blood and, more strikingly, as a vulnerable community of pure blood.[160] One could thus say about blood what Lee Palmer Wander astutely asserts about Christianity; namely, that it "surrounded and permeated every European's life."[161] The pure blood of Christ, as well as Christian blood—which could not but be seen as partaking of that purity, by virtue of the *corpus mysticum* doctrine, but also because of its figuration as the innocent and pure blood of children, as victims of blood sacrifices—the blood of Christians, then, was under constant and growing attack.[162] And it was worth every drop. From the twelfth century at least, Christians developed a passion for blood.[163] They thus sought to "protect" themselves and their blood everywhere in Western Christendom. A logic of containment and contamination, of infection (the Black Death) and separation, of purity and purification, governed by blood logic and by a passion for blood was to be found everywhere. The paradigm of immunity, which Roberto Esposito attributes to Hobbes and to modernity, is contemporary with the emergence of blood as vulnerable property, the shared substance of the community of Christians.

Clearly, the statutes were about lineage and genealogy, but it is one thing to relate oneself to ancestors, and another to locate that relation in blood, and yet another to consider that blood to be not only pure and cleansing but, finally, vulnerable to contamination and desecration.[164] As David Nirenberg has underscored, "anxieties" about and regulations of intercourse between communities are practically universal. They testify, at any rate, to the widespread practice of what

Nirenberg calls a "sexual logic." Such policing of borders may even expand and enter the space of "reproductive strategies" (whereby sexual proximity endangers, as Nirenberg puts it, "the future by corrupting the 'breeding stock' ").[165] Yet they do not and cannot account for the prominence of blood—whether as a figure or as an actual, bodily fluid—in said policing.

According to the famous and prominent *converso* Pablo de Santa Maria, however, one already had to applaud the massacres and conversions of 1391 because the blood of Christ was thus avenged.[166] By 1553, a few years after the statutes were endorsed by a wide number of institutions, Juan Arce de Otalora could explicitly assert that because of their crime against Christ, the blood of the Jews had become "infected" and that this blood infection was hereditary.[167] More directly relevant perhaps to the new centrality of fluids in Christian culture is the fact well perceived by opponents of the statutes; namely, that Jewish blood was now considered to interrupt the purifying flow of baptismal waters. This was the theological scandal as well as the theological revolution: Baptism was no longer efficient.[168]

If, then, it is correct to assert as Edward Peters does that "there emerged a new view of the ethnic character of the Old Christians," that such Christians had "heroically preserved their pure . . . blood from contamination by the blood of inferior races," if the identity of these Old Christians was indeed "grounded in ethnic purity,"[169] it is fundamentally incorrect to consider this novelty as restricted to the Iberian Peninsula. As José Antonio Maravall rightly points out (although he focuses on one limited historical period), "at that time all of Europe still [*sic*] based itself on this principle, which in the Spanish baroque was again and again articulated as the constitutive principle of the social order. Nature operates through the blood of one's lineage and, behind nature, God. The hierarchized societies of baroque Europe were based on this scale."[170] One must therefore recognize that the true "New Christians" were precisely the Old Christians, those now convinced, for exclusively and overdetermined theological reasons, that they were a community of blood, of pure blood, a community brought together by the bonds of blood that would come to define kinship and group identity, as well as citizenship in the modern state on the basis of blood and soil (or, as Roman law never had it, *jus solis* and *jus sanguinis*). The adoption of this novel way of thinking and living by the Christian community vastly exceeds the Inquisition. It exceeds the exceptionality of Spain and its particular "obsession," "madness," and "hysteria" with blood. Incidentally, the notion of *limpieza*, which was introduced *before* the Spanish Inquisition, also outlasted it. The last official statement abolishing the practice of demanding proofs of purity is dated May 16, 1865.[171]

None of this should be taken to reiterate any notion of Spanish exceptionalism, quite the contrary. As we have begun to consider, the spread of blood goes well

beyond Spain to the heart, as it were, of Christianity. And consider that scholars have also started to document one of the most pointed legacies of the Inquisition outside of Spain, a legacy *converso* communities carried with them when they
"returned to Judaism." This legacy had everything to do with blood and purity, and
it is this dual understanding of lineage as a pure bloodline by a number of these
"Judios Nuevos"—as some referred to them—that determines one of the essential
traits of their Christian heritage (one that will later be identified as "Semitic").
Already in 1492, "a *converso* from the environs of Cuenca was reported to have
said 'that the blood of the Jews was good and pure, and that they were of royal
blood . . . and moreover, because the Jews were of such pure blood, God has chosen
our lady for his incarnation.'"[172] What was beginning to be articulated then were
"notions of Jewish 'purity of blood'" that were to have quite a resonance in centuries to come, and particularly with regard to "Semitic" religions. Among the New
Christians, some "did not hesitate to make generous use of the Iberian terminology of the days of the Statutes of Purity of Blood."[173] Isaac Cardozo, the famous
seventeenth-century *converso* and Jewish apologist, transparently phrases such a
notion regarding the *nação,* the "Hebrew nation." "The Hebrews are of the most
noble blood, and their family tree is extremely ancient. . . . Because of the antiquity,
their election, their purity, and their isolation, the Jews are the most noble nation
on the face of the earth."[174]

More than the race, the nation is of course the ultimate community of blood.
Menasseh ben Israel, arguing for the admission of Jews to England, wrote of the
"nobleness and purity of their blood."[175] Consequently, the Portuguese community of Amsterdam adopted stringent rules that redefined allegiances along
national (not to say ethnic or racial) borders that were seen as transcending the
legal and religious allegiances to which they also bound themselves. Marriage, as
well as social and financial support to the needy, and business transactions, too,
were shaped according to a network of relations and loyalties based on a kinship
that, often articulated in terms of blood, famously excluded Ashkenazi Jews. "Our
nation" was not to welcome individuals that did not belong to it.[176] In the process,
of course, and as with the new "Old Christians," it was religion "itself" that was
being defined, along with nation and race: all communities of blood. And by that
point, there was no doubt that flesh and bones had little to do with it. It was all
about blood and all in the blood. Modern medicine would promptly confirm the
diagnostic. But that is another story to which we shall attend later. For now, let us
go back again to around 1449.

In 1450, Fray Alonso de Oropesa decided to publish his *Lumen ad Revelationem
Gentium,* a treatise he wrote against the statutes as well. Doing so, Fray Alonso
used a strategy that was deployed by numerous Christian writers and that testifies

to the hegemony of blood as a determining element of identity and community. He himself had no Jewish ancestors, he claimed, and was therefore of pure blood. However, he would have been proud of belonging to the "race of Abraham," from which Christ himself came. Fray Alonso would even have rejoiced in this lineage had the Apostles not forbidden such pride.[177] In 1459, Alonso de Espina composed his *Fortalitium Fidei* in which he lists all the accusations launched at Jews at the time. These accusations are well known and they are common to all of Europe as well, of course, as to Spain where Espina writes.[178] Although, as I have mentioned, Spain is rarely mentioned in the enormous body of scholarship that engaged the issue of blood libel, host desecration, lust for blood, and medical and ritual poisoning commonly attributed to the Jews (one erudite scholar going as far as to claim that "a preoccupation with blood was unusual for the Mediterranean world during the late Middle Ages"!),[179] it is clear that these "traditional" accusations were all recent effects of theological and ritualistic developments of Western Christendom, effects that were shared by medieval Christians as well as by their Spaniard brethren in blood. Here, too, and beginning with the New Testament verses we considered earlier, it has long become clear to countless scholars that an enormous shift occurred in Christian consciousness with the dissemination of the Eucharist and the feast of Corpus Christi. Along with Carolyn Walker Bynum, Miri Rubin has brought the "eucharistic matrix" to a strikingly sharp light.

> As the juxtaposition of Jew and Eucharist became more laden with meaning throughout the thirteenth century, narratives increasingly came to include the host as the object of Jewish abuse, as bearing the tenderness of a child within it. . . . The world of the Eucharist was that of promise, but also of punishment. Its truths were taught as much by rules of belief and practice—the belief in transubstantiation, the communion in a state of purity—as by exemplary instruction on infringement and its dire consequences. This process of forging a Christian identity depended on the articulation of perceptible differences, and it occurs in this period through the use of a variety of types—heretic, Jew, woman, incontinent, priest—and with the deadliest of consequences to the Jew.[180]

Bynum has further argued that, in addition to the Eucharist, what she calls "blood piety" was also fostered by "a noneucharistic blood tradition in Europe."[181] Like other examples of this new and massive phenomenon that Bynum herself documents in her previous work, this second tradition, "the devotion to the blood relics of Christ" (691), accompanying and sustaining narratives and representations of the Holy Grail, constituted itself in the thirteenth and fourteenth centuries as a veritable industry, the hugely popular production of "objects that accuse and threaten by bleeding" (690, n. 17). The "theology of the blood of Christ competed with, absorbed, and influenced eucharistic theology and imagery" (692) and "blood relics then streamed into Europe" (693). "In this conflation of types of blood," Bynum continues, "we see one of the most sinister aspects of blood-cult. Whether Christ himself, the consecrated host, or a devotional object, the victim is increasingly in the years around 1300 seen as violated by Jews" (694). These are not the "rare charges of ritual murder but the quite frequent charge (sometimes also directed against Christian women and criminals) that an effort at magical manipulation became a kind of crucifixion of Christ in the host" (695).

But Bynum unwittingly brings us back to 1449 as well. She documents how, on August 19 (that is, just a month before he disavowed the Statutes on the Purity of Blood), Pope Nicolas V "permitted blood veneration." Another papal bull followed in 1464 (entitled *Ineffabilis summi providentia Patris*), which confirmed said veneration but "forbade further discussion of the status of the blood (divided or undivided) after the Passion" (698, n. 49). But the question of how exactly Christ's blood could be in so many sites at once, how it could have been so from the beginning and what divisions and hierarchies could affect it, the question of the "status of the blood," did linger, if elsewhere. Be that as it may, blood, blood, everywhere, and "the blood that springs into the churchyard to save the poor souls," that blood "also accused the Jewish faces that clustered around in the conventional *arma Christi*. And, as Gerhard of Cologne wrote, Christians are the new Jews. Their sins daily kill God. Medieval blood devotion was a piety of horror, accusation, and self-accusation as well as of encounter with God" (714). Christians are New Jews, and Jews are New Christians. With the advent of novelty, we witness in fact the New Christian who emerges throughout Europe, if not out of nothing, certainly out of pure blood.

In the year 1449 as well, Don Alonso de Cartagena, bishop of Burgos and son of Don Pablo de Santa Maria, published his *Defensorium Unitatis Christianae*, which formed the basis of the anti-statutes argument for the next two centuries.[182] The *Defensorium* seeks to return to a biblical logic whereby "flesh" is understood as the primary unity of humanity (43). Yet, it is notable that the book has long surrendered to the notion that lineage is neither flesh nor bones but blood. Hence, affirming the unity of humanity will have to be settled with the notion that blood *differentiates*. There are different bloods. It is only because the blood of one is different from the blood of another that it is worth emphasizing that in Jesus' own veins flowed the blood of Rahab of Jericho and that of Ruth the Moabite (47). Similarly, the purifying flow of baptism may well wash away all differences, as Paul had made clear, but social rank was far from abolished. The *Defensorium* has yet to endorse the novel and evolving conception of aristocracy as race, but it does lay the ground for a kind of bracketing effect of the sacraments. Their efficiency is revealed here to be finite: social rank is immune to it (48). This does not place nobility outside of theology, nor is it a secularization of theological notions. Rather, nobility is justified theologically by distinguishing, in fact, between theological, moral, and political nobility (50). The finitude of the sacrament of baptism is precisely what the *Defensorium* is trying to counter by affirming the infinite power of both holy water and holy blood. "The waters of baptism purify all men from all sins. Whoever has been redeemed by baptism and denies that very redemption to another individual, claiming that there remains in the latter traces of sin, also claims that there are sins so grave that even the *blood* of Christ could not wash them. From this follows that Christ would have died in vain," which is clearly scandalous (51).[183]

In 1449, and, more precisely, on September 24, Pope Nicolas V answered the call that the *Defensorium* was articulating by publishing a bull bearing the "significant title *Humani Generis Inimicus* (Enemy of the Human Race) in which he denounced the idea of excluding Christians from office simply because of their blood origins."[184] What was at stake, as we have begun to see, was the unity of the mystical body of the church. The integrity and unity of Christ's body along with the unity of the church was, in fact, at the center of the controversy over the statutes, linking them, once again, to the Eucharist. There is more at stake here than the symbols by which a community imagines itself. What the Eucharist inaugurated was a new community, a new political thought. More precisely, the Eucharist was at the center of medieval political theology. This political theology was grounded in the practice of Christians throughout Western Christendom. It was also grounded in theological doctrine, aesthetic representations, and philosophical and political reflections. Beginning in the twelfth century with John of Salisbury's *Policraticus* (who generously, if fictionally, attributed the idea to Plutarch) and confirmed in the fourteenth century, among others by Christine de Pizan (in her *The Book of the Body Politic*), the political community came to be "described as a body, with king as head, soldiers and administrative officers as the hands and the peasants at the feet."[185] De Pizan thus bases social hierarchies on an organic conception that, thoroughly grounded in theology—first and foremost in Paul's representation of the church—as well as in theological developments, nonetheless leaves this theological ground unspoken, rendering it invisible. De Pizan imagines a society made of three "estates," a body that is apparently and pointedly void of heart and blood; a body and a society that appear completely worldly and secular, free, as it were, of a church or even of a God. The "body politic," an invention of medieval political theology, would thus already signal toward a community so organically linked, so immanent to itself, that it is no longer dependent on any exteriority, nor even on any one of its elements. Rather, it is fully constituted by all of them. Emphatically justifying hierarchy, medieval political theology nonetheless announces its end, the end of transcendence and the demise of all hierarchies by making all its limbs equally essential (and perhaps even inessential) to its very life.[186]

> These three types of estate ought to be one polity like a living body according to the words of Plutarch who in a letter which he sent to the Emperor Trajan compared the polity to a body having life. There the prince and princes hold the place of the head inasmuch as they are or should be sovereign and from them ought to come particular institutions just as from the mind of a person springs forth the external deeds that the limbs achieve. The knights and nobles take the place of the hands and arms. Just as a person's arms have to be strong in order to endure labor, so they have the burden of defending the law of the prince and the polity. They are also the hands because, just as the hands push aside harmful things, so they ought push all harmful and useless things aside. The other kinds of people are like the belly, the feet, and the legs. Just as the belly receives all that the head and the limbs prepare for it, so, too, the activity of the prince and nobles ought to return to the public good, as will be better explained later. Just as the legs and feet sustain the human body, so, too, the laborers sustain all the other estates.[187]

Newly faced with the prospect of their own contingency, the "hands" of the community will soon find themselves immersed in blood and occupied with the question of their own blood purity.

❧ ❧ ❧

The notion that communities are communities of proprietary substance first became accepted and instituted with the advent of the community of blood. The first nation (or is it the first race?) of distinct blood is the Christian nation. In its trace, and along with the related refiguration of kinship, communities of blood became, in fact, a standard point of reference.[188] Nation (*populus Christianus*), class (the nobility), and, by way of further genealogical, juridical, and medical thought and practice, race. This was established by the Eucharist in its theologico-political and bio-political implications. It was also reinforced and confirmed by and culminated in the Inquisition. There is no exception therefore. Instead, there is the spread of a politics of substance, a continuum of blood. The impact and legacy of Spanish and Portuguese rule on the Americas, from conceptions regarding the humanity (or inhumanity) of the "Indians" and that of the slaves all the way to the "one drop" rule of the nineteenth and twentieth century, is well if not sufficiently attested.[189]

Studies that consider both Spain and the New World have noted the significance of the notion of blood purity in the history of the (mostly South) American continent, but more on this in the next chapter. The origins in and impact on Europe as a whole, Christian Europe, is even less discussed; it is at once visible and invisible.

As I conclude, I want to return to the question that I evoked earlier; namely, the role of the nobility in the dissemination of novel conceptions of race and bloodlines (and, by implication, the social and secular rather than theological history of racism). Here, I want to underscore that blood and the "contamination" by it with which Spain was, we continue to be told, exceptionally and singularly obsessed, did have its own infectious consequences. Blood (which is to say, Christian blood) is the main legacy of the Inquisition, but the legacy of a history of blood belongs to Western Europe and to Western Christendom as a whole. We have seen earlier the way in which the New Jews of Amsterdam adopted and adapted conceptions of blood purity. More interesting, perhaps, is the fact that Spain itself became a figure of contamination from which other kingdoms were to protect themselves. *Their* blood purity, implicit or explicit, could thus be taken for granted. Outside of Spain, and throughout Europe, Spaniards were often called "marranos," and "Portuguese" quickly became a synonym for "Jew."[190] In sixteenth-century France, Antoine Arnaud advocated against any Spanish interference in French affairs on the basis of such blood impurity.[191]

Most significant in the general emergence of the New Christian throughout Western Europe is, therefore, the dissemination of the notion that lineage *is* blood, that different bloodlines had greater worth than others based on their purity and their antiquity. Far from inventing the notion, the aristocracy *adopted* and participated in what was already an existing, widespread discourse. Part of a mechanism of "social disciplining," every individual came to see himself or herself as part of a bloodline and to value it with different degrees of worth. This was, indeed, the beginning of "race," to the extent that race is, historically at least, insistently tied to blood. More generally, it was the beginning of the community of blood, soon to be called "the nation." And it was a theological beginning, much as its conditions and subsequent dissemination were produced and effected by the church. Every Christian individual and, ultimately, every individual came to this conception. Exemplary of this new individual and of this New Christian is the founder of the Jesuit Order, Ignatius of Loyola. I single him out because of his importance and the importance of the Jesuits for an understanding of early modern Europe, but also because the scholarly consensus is that, whether because of his brush with the Inquisition (while a student at Alcalá in 1527) or for other reasons, "Ignatius had managed to free himself from one of the major social prejudices in Spain."[192]

Ignatius was by no means "racist," nor was he anti-Jewish. Aside from his exemplary and tireless opposition to the statutes, there are stories that testify to the fact that he held the Jews in great respect.[193] It was while dining with friends, in fact, that he declared "he would have considered it a divine favor to be descended from Jews. When asked his reason for saying this, he protested, 'What! To be related to Christ Our Lord and to Our Lady the glorious Virgin Mary?'"[194] The New Christian, as opposed to the Old, pre-eucharistic one, would take pride in a lineage linking him directly with Jesus and Mary. He is Jesus' kin. And with him, the community of Christians, newly spanning the whole of Christian history, and all generations of Christians, now locates itself in the flesh and, indeed, in the blood. In the individual bloodline that establishes worth, distinction, and nobility, the New Christian renounces the novelty the Spirit had brought to the flesh and reinvents himself as Old, and as Jesus' kin. By blood.

The spread of this conception (and we ought to remember that there is a strong consensus as to the source of the statutes and of their persistence until the nineteenth century: it is to be found in the will of the people, in the sheer popularity of blood and blood purity) is what provided every Spaniard with a title of nobility.[195] Thus, "many individuals who could not pretend to nobility found cause for pride in an ancestry purer than that of many aristocrats, whose genealogy was not without a few dark patches."[196] If purity of blood, that is to say, the conception of an ancient and uncontaminated lineage, is a sign of true nobility, then nobility had truly become democratized.[197] Indeed, it is as a result of what Albert Sicroff calls a "social revolution"[198] (one that took place, if in other guises, elsewhere in Europe, where women, beguines and mystics, and countless others were clamoring for blood, complaining about the withholding of the blood of Christ from the laity during the Eucharist ceremony, the exclusive and elitist monopole claimed by the church "nobility," the priesthood in the consumption of said blood, and so forth) that there appeared uncounted instances of complaints of the following sort: "In Spain we esteem a common person who is *limpio* more than a hidalgo who is not *limpio*."[199] It is, in other words, because the people claimed to be of "pure blood" that they could "recognize" (and on that basis as well as others—always others—attack) Jews and nobles as lacking it.[200] And we can now better understand the striking analogies that were offered with horses and their blood, race (*raza*), and breeding.[201] On another level, it is in this context as well that we can understand the "social disciplining" (from "below") at work from the Eucharist and all the way to the accusations of ritual murder, the denunciations by neighbor and kin, and the general, panoptical scrutiny produced and maintained around Christian blood, for and by the masses. As demonstrated by the paradigmatic figure of Archbishop Juan Martínez Silíceo of Toledo, under whose authority the statutes were first established, it is the Christian people, the newly discovered *christianos viejos* (and Silíceo claimed in fact to be defending the unity of the church, to protect the mystical body of Christ, its head and members, as well as to prevent the "Old Christians" from lowering the *nobility* of their blood), who launched a social, indeed, theologico-political, revolution against the Jews and the nobility.[202] If the nobility claimed privileges and advantages, it would have to *justify* itself. By blood. That it did (and the fact that it could and could not, thanks to scrupulous archives and hagiographies, often served only to buttress the "purity" of the masses who had "only" their memory and no written documentation, and therefore no embarrassing proof of contamination—except for ill-intending or grudge-bearing, that is, "honest" and duly denunciating neighbors or family members, of course), and it is at this point that it apparently gave the idea to the entire European aristocracy. According to the *Oxford English Dictionary*, in fact, the very phrase "blue blood" is a sixteenth-century translation of the Spanish "sangre azul." But the Spanish people did not invent the association of blood and lineage, nor did they invent the notion of pure blood as a source of worth and glorious lineage. In the passion for blood they shared with the whole of Western Christendom, the people did not invent religion and race, religion as race. Nor did the aristocracy. Nor, finally, did Spain. The church—the *corpus mysticum* of the church, heads, hands, and feet, head over heels in its passion for blood—did.

Clearly, Jews and the nobility were associated in the popular mind (because they were associated, period), but whereas Jews (and *conversos*) could be stripped of their privileges and could be isolated and eradicated from the social structure, it was not so with nobles. Yet, the masses had to see themselves as entitled to privilege in the first place, as worthy and pure. Substantively so. The Eucharist and the passion for blood that was spreading throughout Europe, the compulsive notion that the pure blood of Christians was at risk, provided the governing and enabling logic for such radical transvaluation. And whereas the other kingdoms of Europe avoided the intensity of the mounting crisis by expelling their Jews, Spain was, in fact, late. This may be Spain's only "belatedness," then. By refraining from expelling the Jews until the end of the fifteenth century, and by converting them, it lit the fuse that was waiting to explode a barrel that had been constituted and filled by the eucharistic matrix. It is the "pure blood" filling this barrel that was passionately boiling—and it was awaiting as a theologico-political revolution. It had overwhelmingly become the substance of which the community is made, a gift and a given.

Two STATE (THE VAMPIRE STATE)

A WORM WITH A VIEW

"LET US IMAGINE," writes Benedict de Spinoza in a letter to Oldenburg, "let us imagine, with your permission, a little worm living in the blood [*vermiculum in sanguine vivere*], able to distinguish by sight the particles of blood, lymph, &c. . . . That little worm would live in the blood, in the same way as we live in a part of the universe, and would consider each particle of blood, not as a part, but as whole."[1] With this striking image, Spinoza puts blood at the center of our reflections on the place of bodies in the universe. Blood would serve as a medium and a comparative term, a *tertium quid*, whereby, here at least, Spinoza "altogether relativized the distinction between bodies natural and artificial; the state and its institutions, much as any physical compound," all of which "are nothing but a balance of forces."[2] To be sure, writing just a few years before Locke discussed property, inheritance, and the "next of blood" in *The Fundamental Constitutions of Carolina*, Spinoza is not explicitly engaging with state politics.[3] He is not engaging with Hobbes either, not with "the Body Naturall" or the "Artificiall," with which Hobbes famously opened *Leviathan*.[4] Still, blood is for him a "physical compound," one among many, which must be understood, therefore, as a body verging on the distinction between natural and artificial, individual and collective, medical and political. Spinoza's worm, the sight and perspective it offers, puts us at the center of a flow that irrigates the distinctions constituting our universe, part and whole. It will lead us, at disparate velocities, to the state and to law, to kinship and to science, and to the difference, if there is a difference, *between bloods*.

Spinoza seems at once to take William Harvey's lead and to depart from it to offer his own version of the motion and circulation of the blood.[5] Spinoza is also pursuing his reflections on bodies and "the association of parts" in nature and lays the ground for a kind of grand unified theory of the universe as a social whole, minimally a theory of bodily ensembles and collectives. In this universe, "each body, insofar as it exists as modified in a particular manner, must be considered as a part of the whole universe, as agreeing with the whole, and associated with the remaining parts [*ut partem totius universi, considerari debere, cum suo toto convenire, & cum reliquis cohaerere*]."[6] Elaborating on the relation between individual and collective—the relevance and irrelevance of blood—Spinoza takes us on a somehow vertiginous ride in and around the bloodstream, simultaneously adopting and rejecting the discriminating perspective, literally the "sight [*visu*]," of a worm who lives in the blood "in the same way as we live in a part of the universe [*ut nos in hac parte universi*]." Is blood a part or a whole? This is one question that Spinoza proposes to explore, although by underscoring the difficulties involved in doing so he raises a different issue altogether, namely, how did blood become the figure for a collective, a part for the (social) whole? It is an enduring truism that "all those who descend from one and the same stock . . . are, consequently, of the same blood,"[7] that kin, class, and nation emerge as communities of blood (literal or metaphoric, imagined or not), and that Blackness and Indianness, Whiteness even, run in the blood.[8] "There is only one community," writes Franz Rosenzweig about the Jews, articulating a historical commonplace rather than a doctrinal particularity, "a community of blood [*eine Gemeinschaft des Bluts*]." This, which "holds true in general of peoples as the union of blood-families, as opposed to all the communities of spirit, holds true as well, and particularly, of ours."[9]

According to Spinoza, at any rate, we live—we are—like every other body or body part in the universe. And we too may be "agreeing with the whole." It is remarkable, however, that out of this particular and strange instance—a worm in the blood—Spinoza figures that general agreement as a swirling and chaotic scene. He deploys, indeed, almost upholds as ideal and exemplary something that can only be described as the turbulent surge of an unruly stream. For this, the newly discovered, circulatory bloodstream is where the worm must be able "to reflect on the manner in which each particle [*particula*] on meeting with another particle, either is repulsed, or communicates a portion of its own motion." And everything is as if the motion of the blood was also, as the ancients had it, an oscillation— ebbing and flowing—between constant flux and a kind of hardening of the fluid into parts and wholes, a multiplicity of bloody waterways. In the midst of such intense traffic and circulation, it is understood that the view is an uncertain one. This flow which is not one translates therefore the impossibility of a stable perspective on parts and wholes, motion and motionlessness. One the one hand, the worm is "able to distinguish by sight" the different "particles," which suggests that he discriminates and sees them as precisely that: parts that collide and interrupt or communicate their motion. But on the other hand, and somehow surprisingly, Spinoza insists that the worm fails to see these parts as anything but a whole. So it is that the worm looks at "each particle of blood, not as a part, but as a whole [*ut totum, non vero ut partem*]." He is therefore "unable to determine how all the parts are modified by the general nature of blood [*quomodo partes omnes ab universali natura sanguis moderantur*]." Seeing only wholes and not parts, and, paradoxically, the particular as opposed to the general, the worm fails to perceive change, and not only change but fixity as well. He is unable to determine how the parts "are compelled by it [i.e., by the general nature of blood] to adapt themselves, so as to stand in a fixed relation to one another." Parts and whole, motion and stasis—these bloody parts are treacherous to navigate. And were we to adopt, like the worm, an internal perspective, dismissing those "causes external to the blood, which could communicate fresh movement to it;" were we to imagine no bodies other than these particles of blood that "could communicate their motion," then "it is certain that the blood would always remain in the same state, and its particles would undergo no modifications." What is less clear, however, is whether the flow of motion is ultimately affected by the imagination or lack thereof ("for if we imagine that there are no causes external to the blood . . . it is certain that the blood would always remain in the same state . . ." the sentence reads) or whether the hypothetical cause for the interruption of the blood flow is to be searched for elsewhere. What is indubitable is that the failure to imagine blood in its relation to an outside is related—by lack of relation—to a kind of interruption of the flow, an immobility that further determines the relation between part and whole. "The blood," in the perspective of such impoverished imagination, "would then always have to be considered as a whole, not as a part [*ut totum non vero ut partem consideraret*]." And that would assuredly be a mistake. Indeed, it seems obvious that the proper perspective is rather for the blood "to be regarded as a part, not as whole [*hoc modo sanguis rationem partis, non vero totius habet*]."

We could rest here and interrupt the stream of our own considerations, bring our blood tests and analyses to an end. It would be easier to do so had Spinoza not demonstrated that the partial perspective we have reached enables and even forces us to properly perceive—perhaps with the worm to partake of—the motion of blood, unavoidably taking us back on the worm's dizzying ride, where particles glide and collide, and onward toward other motions and flows. There will be no rest, therefore, no pause or interruption. And it does turn out, as a matter of fact, that to perceive the blood as a part, not as whole, means that the oscillation continues. We must perceive blood at once from within *and* from without, that is to say, as *both part and whole*. Spinoza explains:

> But as there exist, as a matter of fact, very many causes which modify, in a given manner, the nature of the blood, and are, in turn, modified thereby, it follows that other motions and other relations arise in the blood, springing not from the mutual relations of its parts only, but from the mutual relations between the blood as a whole and external causes [*quae consequuntur non a sola ratione motus ejus partium ad invicem, sed a ratione motus, sanguinis, & causarum externarum simul ad invicem*].

It is at this point—anything but a fixed point, obviously—that Spinoza, who has just underscored both the parts of the whole as well as a whole that exceeds its internal parts, concludes that the whole is and must be regarded as a part. "Thus the blood comes to be regarded as a part, not as whole. So much for the whole and the part [*hoc modo sanguis rationem partis, non vero totius habet. De toto, & parte modo dixi*]." Indeed.

Blood might appear as a mere example here; it functions as such, if perhaps differently, as a part for the whole—another synecdoche of unknown measures. We will not be able to escape the question, at any rate, the oscillating and surging perspective, of part and whole.[10] As I have already suggested, it is mainly this rhetorical and political issue that has Spinoza raise the question of blood, the question of the rapport of blood to a body that is always already collective, part for the whole. Yet, seen from within and perhaps from without—if one can still call this a view— blood, the collective of particles, indeed, the community as such, also appears *falsely* as a whole (which would not even be the sum of its parts). There is, then, in Spinoza, a perspective that is not one, but whereby one can acknowledge that there are parts in the whole and in this manner arrest a motion that makes *both* the whole *and* its parts. Flow no longer occurs, motion fails to be imagined, unless one considers "the mutual relations between the blood *as a whole* and external causes," unless one considers that there is and there is not a whole ("thus the blood comes to be regarded as a part, not as whole"). Like any collective entity, blood may be at once more and less than the sum of its parts, which includes its own being-a-part, being-apart. Blood comes to be regarded as what distinguishes and discriminates between parts and wholes, what moves parts and wholes, and as one of the key signifiers for a collective so conceived. How could it have been otherwise for Spinoza? Unlike his worm, he was able "to determine how all the parts are modified by the general nature of blood, and are compelled by it to adapt themselves, so as to stand in a fixed relation to one another." He thus testifies to an obvious *moment* in the history of blood, a moment whereby blood becomes part for the whole, and comes to dominate the whole, as a privileged example, a generalized synecdoche. This is the turbulent and raging moment—an extended one, but still only a moment—whereby a collective (family or tribe, clan or nation) can be isolated, separated and singled out, taken as a part and taken apart, by way of blood.[11] Spinoza testifies to a people apart, a people of a particular kind. He testifies to the community of blood. He illustrates, if implicitly, how one has come to speak of other bloods: Jewish or Christian, Black or Indian, blood.

But can one really speak of distinct bloods? It is precisely to the extent that one indisputably has[12] that I wish here to consider further what made this possible. Perhaps one will then be able to argue "against" Jewish, Black, or Indian blood, or at least to interrogate the meaning and endurance of a notion of blood as the figure of these and other collectives. Such an endeavor will have to be conducted against the grain and against the tide—like a worm fighting the flow of the bloodstream, as it were—which has *naturalized* (and not merely *biologized*) the figurative relation between part and whole, between blood and collective, making blood the ground and figure of family and genealogy, community and ethnicity, nation and race. At once unifying and distinguishing, at any rate, blood is a figure of the community. But before there could be a different and specific blood, a blood that, rather than serve as an attribute of all living creatures,[13] would distinguish a family, a class or a community, a nation or later a race, blood had to be seen as a particular kind of part or particle [*particula*], one that stands in a privileged—or merely plausible—relation to *any* whole or body, any collective whole or body, *whether kin or community, nation or race*.[14] It is the motion whereby this striking figure (in technical terms, a synecdoche) appeared and disappeared, *circulated* and *coagulated* in and as the so-called modern state that I want to explore in this chapter. For through it and with it, blood also proliferates. It grows in its power, seizing and fashioning, even making the state, which thereby furthers itself as a Christian state (as if we did not know that, as if Marx had not taught us that). Note however that having attended to the power of blood and to the Christianity of blood, I am less concerned in what follows with a direct demonstration of this Christianity of blood. Besides, such is the task of this book as a whole. Instead, and for reasons that are essentially related to appearance and to disappearance, to presence and to absence (of blood, of Christianity) in the body politic, I propose here to draw a general map, anatomic, geographic, and, predominantly, political, in effect, bio-theologico-political, in its dimensions, a map of the "redness of the West," as Cormac McCarthy has it, of the pervasiveness, the singular force and power of blood.[15] *Blutgewalt*.

HEMO POLITICUS

And yet the formal inclusion of blood in a lexicon of political concepts would seem to require the removal of two quite formidable obstacles. First, blood is not a concept. And second, blood is not, strictly speaking, political.[16] I will return to the first obstacle, but I should begin by deferring to understandable reservations with regard to the removal of the second. For who, after all, would want to make blood political, tear down the wall and close the gap that separates blood from politics? Who would wish together to have and to hold in unholy matrimony blood and politics? Are not the worst perversions, the worst *exceptions*, of our global political history conjured easily enough by this ominous apposition? At the most basal, as the most basal, blood functions as a liminal marker, the potent sign of politics at its recalcitrant limits. Blood operates, or shall we say circulates, at the outer extremes of politics, there where the shedding of blood signifies sovereignty and the ultimate exercise of power (*ius gladii* and all that), as well as the undoing of the community that descends into violence. As Martin Luther limpidly puts it, "Let no one think that the world can be ruled without blood; the sword of the ruler must be red and bloody; for the world will and must be evil, and the sword is God's rod and vengeance upon it."[17] Accordingly, blood figures that which, from past to present, female to male, and status to contract, politics transcends, manages, or excludes; what it should, at any rate, exclude: the archaism of blood feuds, the threat of cruel and unusual punishment—or of menstruation—and the pertinacity of kinship, of tribalism, and finally of race. Like Diderot, we still "are filled with indignation at the cruelties, either civil or religious, of our ferocious ancestors, and we turn away our eyes from those ages of horror and blood."[18] In this broad perspective, the inclusion of blood in a lexicon of political concepts—the removal of the two obstacles I have mentioned—smacks of a strange revivalism, of fundamentalism even, minimally an archaism of sorts. "To what extent have we escaped," Alain Brossat recently wondered with justifiable unease, "the archaic and obscure dramaturgy of blood, this political dramaturgy evoked by Foucault?"[19] The question should be answered slowly, the inquiry conducted with the utmost care, for they demand the exertion of the same protective vigilance that has sought to keep the floodgates closed, which haltingly prevented blood from engulfing our political existence.

A distinct kind of exertion would perhaps be demanded by a simpler and antipodal acknowledgment, namely, that blood has played (and continues to play) a central role in, been a constitutive factor or element of, whatever we conceive politics to be. This means, I think, that blood is not the exception. Blood might very well be the rule. Granted, blood did not become a concept, though Hegel—who else?—did propose, in *The Phenomenology of Spirit*, that the "absolute notion,

der absolute Begriff" may well be called "the universal blood," suggestively inti-
mating that blood may be *the very name* of the concept.[20] But what of it? Blood
never became a *political* concept, nor one of the foundations of modern political
thought, yet its universality—its rule—is hardly diminished thereby.[21] It is merely
of a different order, a different register. Indeed, as Hegel himself makes clear, what
could be more universal than blood? The phrase "flesh and blood," which has long
defined the legal person (or its normative horizon) is everywhere (well, almost).[22]
But beyond—and above—it, who would deny the force of blood, the determining
and general power of blood? Famously attending, as we saw, to a worm with a view,
Spinoza opined that "all the bodies in Nature can and should be conceived in the
same way as we have here conceived the blood."[23] Everything is therefore as if, but
for the realm of concepts, the realm of political concepts in particular, blood were
ubiquitous and omnipresent, locally and even globally.

The emerging paradox, if it is one, should therefore be clear. Blood is at once
very much present, universally so, *and* absent—or absented—from politics. Its presence is both exceptional (racism, Nazism) and normal, universal. Has the exception
become, yet again, the rule? Whereas it might lead us to "question the rationality of
the norm itself," of which blood is the center, a reigning universalism, one capable
of finding political theologies at every corner of the globe, partakes of the sedimentation of this paradox, while claiming to resolve it.[24] It would have us accept that
blood is everywhere and *therefore* that politics must be shielded from it. Rendered
in a familiar declension: where blood was, there politics shall be. What I will argue,
however, in the course of this chapter is that blood irrigates a *particular* conception
of politics and defines a momentous political tradition that, unacknowledged as
such—that is, in terms of its rapport to blood—may well claim universal status (with
the means to prove and enforce it too) but has yet fully to achieve this status, at least
reflectively and conceptually. In *this* tradition, which is of course not exhausted but
rather distinguished by this singular feature, blood is never a concept, but it exer-
cises, across time, a peculiar and not inconstant dominion. Blood makes and marks
difference, an allegedly universal difference inscribed *between bloods*. Considered in
this manner, blood quietly traces the contours, the external and internal limits in
fact, of a unique circulatory system, a system of different bloods. Law and science,
race and economics, war and the culture of peace, along with the apparatuses of
the so-called modern state, all deploy their "own" blood, while concealing blood's
governing or defining role *across* these realms. But the argument, I suggested at the
beginning of this book, may perhaps be phrased more clearly. *All significant concepts
of the history of the modern world are* liquidated *theological concepts. This is so not only
because of their historical development but also because of their systematic fluidity, the
recognition of which is necessary for a political consideration of these concepts.*[25]

Such is, at any rate, the formulation I propose with this slow meditation on politics and on the state, where blood and politics insistently mix and merge, the vampire state. The phrasing I just offered is short and, to repeat, clearly plagiarized from Carl Schmitt, recognizably memorable therefore. It should assist us as we attempt to take the measure of what connects us to, and distances us from, a concept of blood, from blood as a political concept. But allow me one preliminary remark before I engage on what can only be, at this stage, an abbreviated exposition toward a "sociological consideration" of our political concepts—concepts such as nation and emancipation, kinship and race, law and capital, sovereign and citizen, property, inheritance, and freedom, all of which are connected by blood. I will admit it is a rather futile engagement, meant merely to make the obvious manifest, the simple fact that, far from having "an invisible influence" as Daniel Defoe once surmised, blood rather ostensibly suffuses and unites the political life of the West.[26] In a manner that is at once unique and undeniable, blood distinguishes our political imagination—and the political institutions we insist on calling modern—and so perhaps to the precise extent that blood never comes to mind as an idea or concept. Not only has blood not been evacuated from politics, therefore, but the ominous apposition with which I began is better understood, in fact, as a simple equation. In the Christian West, blood is politics and politics is blood. Our *political hematology*.

A preliminary remark, then, on a matter that bears revisiting. When it comes to blood, to an understanding of blood, the distinction between literal and figurative must be suspended and rethought. Blood must be denaturalized. For what we mean by blood has never been abstracted from what is said and done about, with and to, blood. More than that, the very distinction between literal and figurative blood is part and parcel of the peculiar and enduring dominion of blood, enabling the dissemination of blood across seemingly distinct realms, which it covertly unifies. The absence of a concept of blood, at any rate, makes it impossible to assert with any assurance that the blood of kinship, for instance, is metaphorically *derivative* with regard to the presumed literal, allegedly primary, blood of physiology or medicine (this is why blood is not a signature, in Agamben's sense, as it cannot be referred back to a field to which it would primarily belong). The impossibility might be illustrated by way of a rich account, compellingly extensive, which brings together "the ancient belief that sperm is comprised of blood," the fact that "kinship ties were imagined as ties of shared blood," the transformation whereby the European nobility came to understand itself by way of "its genealogical records of the 'blood' ties of lineal kinship," and the sedimentation of "the rhetoric of blood" as "the means used to naturalize the role of reproduction and procreation."[27] While not inaccurate in the vectors that it reveals, and most notably, as we will see, in the connection it makes between kinship and race, this description nonetheless implies that a primeval physiologic conviction becomes the object of a "naturalization," which otherwise seems to have been universally given, firmly and originally in place beforehand. The argument, in other words, is that a bodily fluid is in fact a metaphor that continues, by mistake or by design, to be understood literally, which it incidentally always was. Minimally, as Gail Paster rightly emphasizes, "blood's lexical unwieldiness should not distract us from noticing a significant correlation between the scientific account of blood," its juridical, genealogical, and political accounts as well, and the "hierarchies in which blood figures as a key signifier."[28] It is the singularity of blood's locations and its expansion, along with its persistence across realms and discourses that, prior to any received division into literal and figurative, will have to be confronted as a rhetorical problem.

Otherwise put, and to remain within the narrow bounds of the political imagination, no community was ever a "community of blood"—the phrase was famously deployed by Henry Lewis Morgan—that did not deploy an insistent and expansive rhetoric of blood, that did not speak of blood as the substance of community, even if, especially if, to take its distance from it, as if metaphorizing it. How do we know this? As we have had the occasion to observe, the Old Testament for one never uses the phrase "flesh and blood," nor would it imagine blood as the attribute of a particular grouping or community, as a site of difference or distinction between creatures of any kind. Christian translators and exegetes, however, insisted that blood was the life of God's creatures rather than their soul (*nefeš, psyche, anima*) and erroneously came to imagine humankind—and even then, only those admitted in it—as being "of one blood."[29] The universalization of blood and of its truth, as well as the transformation of blood into a marker of specificity, was on its way (and recall that "to the mediaeval mind," at least, "the destiny and preordained end of Christendom was always identical with that of mankind at large").[30] Ludwig Feuerbach, to take but one instance, partly but effectively summarizes the matter. "As the truth of personality is unity, and as the truth of unity is reality, so the truth of real personality is—*blood*."[31] Still, by what translation could the ancient Israelites, or other occupants of "the savage slot" as Michel-Rolph Trouillot called it, ever be included in this anthropotheistic schema, understood, as they famously were by Ernest Renan and countless others, as a community of blood?[32] Like other aggregates of the *hemophilic* kind—recall that I mean this term in its strictest technical, that is, etymological and nonmedical, sense—the translations of blood remain unremarked and unreflected. The postulated universality of blood grounds our political hematology, our political *hemophilia*. Our politics are drenched in blood. The love of blood.

"When several families are united," Aristotle famously said, "and the association aims at something more than the supply of daily needs, then comes into existence the village." Aristotle goes on to clarify the structure of the early political unit, the Greek city-state governed, he says, by kings. "Every family is ruled by the eldest, and therefore in the colonies of the family the kingly form of government prevailed *because they were of the same blood*."[33] From Aristotle to Henry James Sumner Maine and to William Robertson Smith, blood would have been the undisputed and primary ground, "the sole possible ground," of the political (incidentally, despotic) community.[34] In Maine's formulation, "the history of political ideas begins, in fact, with the assumption that kinship in blood is the sole possible ground of community in political functions."[35] Do we not believe it still? Do we not cling, as Alain Brossat does, to a model of political emancipation that at once affirms and denies blood? "I am sick to death of bonding through kinship and 'the family,'" writes Donna Haraway poignantly enough, and proceeds to toe the expected hematological line by asserting that "ties through blood—including blood recast in the coin of genes and information—have been bloody enough already."[36]

Of course, no conceptualization of blood as political can avoid the matter of race, which might otherwise be thought as the *intensification* of blood in the post-Reformation era. This will occupy us at length here. It is becoming increasingly evident, however, that there are deep and intricate connections between race and kinship—that other discourse of blood. What Alys Weinbaum refers to as "the race/reproduction bind"[37] constitutes in fact "a privileged, but still rather little-explored, way of grasping dimensions of race, ethnicity and nationality" together.[38] More generally, one can point to the "too few conscientious efforts made to examine the continuities between cultural constructions of kinship and those of other categorical distinctions such as race, nation, and caste."[39] And indeed, very few are those who have devoted their attention to the peculiarities of the "European cognatic kinship systems," and more precisely to what, in them, "allows for a clearer understanding of certain dimensions of racist contexts."[40] As one scholar uncharacteristically puts it, "an important component of our identity is determined by the very act of generation, defined in terms of the consubstantiability contained in the blood, which at least from Christian times has been the major symbol of our kinship system."[41] What should be underscored once again is the contingency, and the persistence, the unique rhetorical, and cultural, configuration, that has long equated blood and kinship, indeed, blood and community, in race thinking and well beyond it. It is at any rate no accident that Emile Benveniste's justly celebrated compendium of our inherited lexicon deploys the language of blood without ever treating blood as a technical term, much less as a concept.[42]

After Foucault (who significantly came to describe modern governmentality as the persistence, and extension, of "pastoral power")[43] and also against him, Ann Stoler has already asked us to widen our hematological horizons, alerting us to the limitations of Foucault's diagnostic and of his quite orthodox periodization, whereby history would have moved from one stage to the next, from "a symbolics of blood" to "an analytics of sexuality."[44] Here again, where blood was, there (modern) politics shall be. Stoler underscores that, after the Reformation, no blood was left behind.[45] Far from disappearing into the dark recesses of history, blood came *increasingly* to govern the political imagination in its social and national registers. From kinship to colonialism, by way of the nation-state and the "global color line," Stoler suggests that the very notion of a community of blood not only persists beyond its so-called premodern origins, but far exceeds the discourse and practices of nation and race. Blood rather moves through the *capillaries of power*—this remarkable phrase that resonates with the concept of *circulation*, the resignification and dissemination of which we owe William Harvey, and upon which Foucault also insisted. From the theorists of just war to the canon lawyers, from the doctrine of the sacraments to the philosophy of property and wealth ("inheritable blood," "corruption of the blood"), from the head of the sovereign to the sacred heart, the perdurance of blood, of the community of blood, marks and shapes a massive, albeit heterogenous, political tradition. It also accounts for the laws that regulate kinship, citizenship, and ownership—and international law.[46] Essential to the canonical figurations of the body politic, that "continually renewed dream, of community as a body united by some principle of life," which since John of Salisbury have been strangely devoid of it, blood shapes and defines the channels and motions that carry the family, the class, and the race, the nation and the economy too.[47] "There is, indeed," as Adriana Cavarero points out, "a sort of embryology of the body politic."[48] Thus, following his mercantilist predecessors, and building on the work of Harvey, Hobbes writes of the "concoction" and the "sanguification of the commonwealth," the money and wealth that is the nourishment, the blood of the state (colonies, incidentally, were of a proximate metabolic order for Hobbes, that of reproduction).[49] Moses Hess well understood, and Marx also confirmed (both were redeploying an earlier claim made by Huldrych Zwingli) that the political and economic machine was feeding on the blood of the workers.[50] Not so distant from such exploitative hematologics, Hume suggested that "animals have little or no sense of virtue or vice; they quickly lose sight of the relations of blood; and are incapable of that of right and property."[51] A more recent formulation strikingly crosses metaphorical lines and thus captures the matter exemplarily. After September 11, say Catherine Waldby and Robert Mitchell, "the excessive desire to give blood was perhaps driven by a sense that the body politic was itself wounded in the attacks."[52]

Thus filling a strange conceptual vacuum in the body politic, communities of blood have served and free-refilled, at different times supplemented, fashioned, and preserved, the competing forms of our political hematology. Referring to one instance of this phenomenon, Foucault writes that "in these rituals in which blood flowed, society found new vigor and formed for a moment a single great body."[53] But one could evoke as well the adoption of variants of *jus sanguinis* in the modern state, along with the fiction of its Roman filiation, and its essential relation to race and genealogical thinking.[54] At once widespread and historically contingent, blood defines a vision of politics that has yet to be recognized in its relative integrity. But contrary to the narrative (and faulty translation) I have cited above, its history does not go back to Aristotle or to a proverbial—and obviously stereotypical—Semitic bloodthirstiness, nor does it correspond to some universal, archaic drive. It does not hark back to Roman political notions, and even less to the otherwise obvious candidate, the concept of *consanguinitas*, which was originally deployed, we have seen, in Roman law. In fact, the Latin notion of consanguinity only began to define the "community of blood" around the twelfth century, at the time when Aristotelian embryology was beginning to compete with Galenic theories.[55] This extraordinary development—at once juridical and medical—involves a well-known redefinition of the family, and it has been more or less fully translated into the modern codes of law that have taken over the planet—as if by miracle.[56] At the receiving end, I mentioned earlier, Claude Meillassoux paid singular attention to the lingering effects of this hematocentrism and argued that critiques and dismissals notwithstanding, blood continues to inform the anthropological study of kinship.[57]

As we saw in the previous chapter, the emergence of the community of blood coincides—but this is no mere co-incidence—with the first "disciplinary revolution,"[58] whereby each and every Christian was transformed into a vessel of Christ's blood, a blood the devout were given to drink *en masse*, if I may be forgiven the interlingual pun, in a sacramental practice that was theologically sealed in 1215 and fully canonized in 1280. The community of blood, the *corpus mysticum* (an expression that "passed from the Eucharist to the Church" and came to designate the *visible* body of the church, instead of the ritualized, direct and mysterious action of the sacrament) was not only growing but also hardening in a peculiar manner.[59] As theologians were reminding Christians of doctrinal subtleties—that "we eat God not so that he changes into us but so that we change into him," for instance[60]— it was becoming clearer to many that Christian blood was not quite the same as other bloods. Ernst Kantorowicz described in quite meticulous detail the historical (and physiologic) transformation whereby a fundamental difference *between bloods* emerges, although he puzzled over its origins and strangely confined it to the sole body, that is, the sole *two* bodies, of the king. Having underscored the role of God (and not of blood, not explicitly) in royal birth, Kantorowicz goes on to highlight a process whereby ritual could ultimately be abandoned, as the essential difference it made had now become innate. "The Holy Spirit, which in former days was manifested by the voting of the electors, while his gifts were conferred by the anointment, now was *seated in the royal blood itself*, as it were, *natura et gratia*, by nature and by grace—indeed, 'by nature' as well; for the royal blood now appeared as a somewhat mysterious fluid."[61] What happened then was that "one began to combine the dynastic idea with philosophical doctrines implying a belief in certain royal qualities and potencies dwelling in the blood of kings and creating, so to speak, *a royal species of man*" (331; emphasis added). We have just seen, of course, that there was another ritual that could, and would, confer on a larger group of individuals a new kind of blood, "a somewhat mysterious fluid" indeed, and the status of a novel species of man.[62]

There ensued a peculiar history of Christian theophagy[63] and of sacrifice, accusations of ritual murder, *limpieza de sangre*, projections of blood thirst onto Jews, witches, and savages, and of course mass murder, the long and short of it, all of which ensured further coagulation. In Esposito's terms, we have seen, the *communitas* was being misunderstood. No longer an obligation and a subtraction, the giving of what one does not own or have, blood became (a) property, a having and a being simultaneously, *res publica christiana*.[64] One could have "Christian blood" or be of it. Christian blood, at any rate, would become completely distinct, completely good, and, more importantly, completely pure—if also vulnerable to all kinds of attacks and contaminations ("If thou dost shed / One drop of Christian blood . . ." warns fair Portia Shylock).[65] One could then make peace, finally—in the year 1648 for example—in order to stop another "effusion of Christian blood" (as the Treaty of Westphalia describes it).[66] From there, at any rate, the community of blood moved rapidly ahead, toward the modern nation, with all due respect to Benedict Anderson's puzzling claim that "from the start the nation was conceived in language, not in blood, and that one could be 'invited into' the imagined community."[67] Contributing to what should remain a baffling development, Thomas Hobbes and James Harrington had incurred their debt to William Harvey, "the revolution of blood" was pushing through the emergence of liberal—and illiberal—political thought.[68] Perhaps because his "early work with Boyle was on the human blood," Locke expressed doubts about the role blood played in succession and inheritance or about the ability of power to purify blood.[69] He did think that "if language be capable of expressing any thing distinctly and clearly, that of kindred, and the several degrees of nearness of blood, is one."[70] The revolution of blood was easing other judgments, blood judgments, by way of reasonable doubt, and making its way to Rousseau's "ties of blood,"[71] to blood quantums, the "one-drop rule," race science and eugenics,[72] and the "blood feuds" of the AIDS crisis.[73] Blood lies at the foundation of the modern state and, though it is obviously not the only such foundation, it continues to irrigate the state. As Edmund Burke aptly put it, "we have given to our frame of polity the image of a relation in blood."[74] And this "image" (Auden called it "a cement of blood" without which, he said, "no secular wall" would "safely stand")[75] was fast moving forward still, toward what David Schneider described as "American Kinship."[76] One could argue (as I shall shortly) that Richard Hofstadter should have expounded here on "the hematological style in American politics." But due considerations force me to acknowledge that when it comes to blood (and to national anthems), the United States is hardly exceptional or paradigmatic. It is merely exemplary.[77]

Now, in her remarkable book Kathleen Davis demonstrates the intricacies according to which periodization became among the most effective and unacknowledged technologies of rule.[78] Davis shows this by way of the concept of feudalism, which was essential to a double distancing that, always political, always juridico-political, separates the modern from the medieval, and the metropole from the colonial.[79] Medievalism is colonialism, Davis compellingly argues. And vice versa. Key to her argument is the grounding of modern sovereignty—the legitimacy of the modern age—not only in time and space but more precisely in a radical rupture that leaves it as if suspended in "radical newness" (94). The medieval/modern periodization, otherwise known as the narrative of secularization, can thus serve "as a substitute for this absent foundation of sovereignty, and thereby installs certain characteristics of the 'modern' in the place of the sovereign. In this sense, periodization functions as sovereign *decision*" (80). Leaving aside the role and function of blood in sovereignty ("Do you not feel sovereignty coursing through your veins?" asked a French revolutionary,[80] and recall Luther on the "red and bloody" sword of the ruler), it should be clear from what I have said so far that blood—the paradox of blood I laid out at the beginning of this chapter—partakes of this very cut and structure: where blood was, there politics shall be. And so by turning, as I do throughout, to the so-called Middle Ages (or to America), I do not at all mean to produce another iteration of this periodizing narrative, another *exception* or excising decision that would "sustain the 'cloak-and-dagger' drama of 'secularization'" (82). I wish rather to document a remarkable circularity in the way rupture—or shall we say, supersession—is articulated, the way in which blood operates as a site of decision and distinction, an index of sovereignty and community that is at once social, territorial, and temporal, ultimately legal as well. Stuttered otherwise, blood is through and through political, which is to say that Western politics, Christian politics, must be rethought in its hematological registers.

HOW TO DO THINGS WITH BLOOD

But what is meant by blood? Is it the word or the thing?[81]

Let us change register again and take, after Spinoza perhaps, a different perspective on parts and wholes, indeed, on words and things. Since the term *invention* has replaced the term *construction*, everything appears as if we have learned our historical lesson. And it has been a magisterial and impressive lesson, having to do with agency in history as much as with the novelty of words—and of things. Where would we be, for example, had we not learned that the word *homosexual* was invented before the word *heterosexual* and that both date from the end of the nineteenth century? What if Raymond Williams (and Norbert Elias before him) had not explained to us how *culture* recently came to occupy such a prominent place in our vocabulary?[82] Even more recently, what if Leo Marx had not alerted us to the emergence of that "hazardous concept" that is *technology*?[83] New words for old things, but also for new things ("I must also draw attention to a number of other words which are either new, or acquired new meanings," writes Williams), artifacts and products, signs no longer taken for wonder but performed and made—there are by now too many inventions to count, and too many constructions to even need to make the argument anew.[84] And the argument is essentially related to notions of agency and making, to construction, and to self-fashioning.[85] At its basis, the claim is that the new has occurred, that we have made it happen (that we could, therefore, *undo* it along with everything that precedes it), that we have been—that we are, in fact—modern. This is one of the reasons why an entire era could be renamed "the Early Modern period" (during which blood came to signify something closer to "race").[86] And that is also why for every modern "invention," a number of historians or historically minded medievalists and Late Antiquity scholars fight acrimoniously in arguing that they've seen it all before, that the new had occurred earlier, and that the invention, if it was one, was already there and theirs. Bruno Latour did try to explain that the argument is futile, insisting instead that "we have never been modern."[87] By this, Latour meant that the distinction between the given and the made was never operative or secured. But doing so, he may have underestimated the constant and necessary possibility of undoing (precisely) the "seamless fabric of nature-culture," the possibility for "our fabric" to be "no longer seamless," to come asunder across time and space, across history.[88] Nowhere is this more visible than in the habit—at once historical and antihistorical—of marking the distinction between fact and fiction, between the historical (the modern, the new) and the unhistorical. Hence, we continue to distinguish between Vico's famous principle, according to which "men make their own history" (that is to say that what they make is historical), and its inevitable corollary: that what they have not made has no history.[89] Again, Latour's lesson (although I am by no means suggesting that his is the only one) would require that we recognize the fabric that seamlessly connects the historical with the nonhistorical, discourse with reality, or if you will, nature with culture. The provision for this continuous fabric, according to Latour, is that everything in it must be recognized as an agent (*actant*). The generalization of action and of agency goes well beyond "the new, *ergetic* ideal of knowing" by expanding it.[90] It is historical through and through in that everything—not only knowing—becomes a doing or a making.[91] Everything, even relations, *works* and *labors* and, better yet, *produces*. History is truly the history of the conditions and modes of production. And of reproduction. Take blood, for example.

Blood is hardly a modern invention, of course. And indeed, what would it mean to say that blood has a history? As a "natural" object, blood (the thing, I suppose) has always been around, and we have neither made nor invented it. Yet blood *does* have a history, and there is no particular cause for amazement at that idea. Blood even has histories. A few of them have been recently published; some of the most impressive among them consist of thick chapters in a longer and wider history of blood.[92] That is because blood too is constructed and made. And the history of blood (the history of the word, as it were) is the history of beliefs and conceptions, usages and practices, that have surrounded blood, the history of interpretations— in the widest possible sense of the term *interpretation*—of blood.[93] Although it is a fact and a given that *precedes* interpretation (even history as making has its limits), blood was always seized within the fabric, of which Latour speaks. At no point, that is, was blood "not simultaneously real, social and narrated."[94] To be perfectly Latourean then, it is not simply the case that we "make" blood (in the sense that we "construct" and interpret it, invent it, as it were). It is also that blood "makes" us as well (as we discover it anew). And what could be more natural (if also cultural) than to acknowledge that blood makes us who we are?

We? But who, we?

If one ignores, but for a moment, Latour's advice, if one grants that "our fabric" (for it is *our* fabric that Latour describes) is "no longer seamless," then the distinction between the real and the social will be seen as having already expanded, opened, and overflowed (that expansion was operating already in the sharp distinction between "blood" and its "interpretations," the thing and the word—but I simplify). This may well be necessary and inevitable. Still, and if only because we are continuing to consider—like a worm, part of and apart from the collective— the question of different bloods, we will need to linger on the coming apart, precisely, of the social, something that will also bleed into the narrative dimension that Latour describes. It will concern, more specifically, the kind of narratives we have been telling ourselves, as if for all eternity (historical thinking at its limits, again).

For what, finally, is the relation between blood and the social? Between blood as a part and the collective as the whole?

Again, nothing seems to be more obvious. Collective identity, beginning with family and kinship, has always been a matter of blood and blood ties (Spinoza was nothing new, the historians will say). In Frederick Engels's words, and precisely as a recognition that "systems of consanguinity" have changed throughout history, "the whole subsequent development of the family presupposes the existence of the consanguine family as a necessary preparatory stage." And the family (that is "the descendants of a single pair") is grounded in blood. It is the fact of blood ties and of "blood relatives."[95] By extension, communities ("ethnic" communities, but within and around them "classes" as well) have always gathered around blood, found their unity in blood. Nations and states have debated the wisdom and adequacy of "jus sanguinis" as the basis for citizenship policies. Everything is as if consanguinity *as such* (as opposed to "systems of consanguinity") had no history. Which is to say that once again, historical thinking reaches here its limits.

Blood, then—but is it the word or the thing?

As I suggested earlier, one astute anthropologist, who has done extensive work to help us rethink the distinction between nature and culture, explains (or at least illustrates) the matter quite clearly. "The idiom of kinship, the content of kinship, the web of kinship, the kin-based society all depend in large part on the idea of kinship itself."[96] Kinship, in other words, is "an idea." Like the community, it is imagined—constructed or invented.[97] It is an interpretation of blood, a series of conceptions and practices that build upon, or derive from, blood: the fact of blood. To put the matter succinctly, as Schneider does, "the *ideas* about kinship are distinct from the *facts* of blood relationship. . . . The facts of blood relationships are that they constitute bonds, feelings of kindred, instinctive affection."[98] Blood here appears to be a thing, the given upon which a word is based. But that word is not "blood." Rather, "kinship" is. That is to say that if blood is the thing, then kinship is the word.[99] Blood makes kinship. Or alternatively, kinship derives from blood. It is made out of blood—and this time, blood is the thing.

But of course it is not. And we know that very well. Blood too is a word. It is merely a name, here a figure, a metonymy. It is no more than the name we give to something else, and for some other thing. What is that thing, then? Let me abbreviate and rush toward a provisional conclusion. That which blood (the word) names, after having been named by kinship as its origin, is what we call today "biology." (But "biology" too is a modern "invention"! Minimally, it is a particular mode of knowing that, found in ancient times—as a thing, if not as a word—adopted a series of peculiar dispositions of a highly historical nature, dispositions that include but also exceed the physiologic.[100]) Did our ancestors not understand the physiologic connections that link parent to child? Clearly, the question is not operating with a very subtle understanding of "understanding" (or knowledge). It moreover presupposes the kind of isolation of bodies (and peculiar bodies at that) that Spinoza warns us against, even as he showed us its inevitability. Blood is here isolated, as are bodies of knowledge. Indeed, as Claude Meillassoux has brilliantly demonstrated, it does appear that "the biological knowledge of the mode of human reproduction is not general," which is to say that it is not universal, neither cross-culturally nor, more obviously, transhistorically. Moreover, "even when this knowledge is present, *it does not necessarily give rise to an ideology of consanguinity*."[101] It is not just that being "cultural" (i.e., "made"), kinship transcends the "fact" of (so-called) natural "blood" bonds. It is also that in many instances, those bonds, which have nothing to do with blood in the first place, are not even named "blood."[102] That which kinship is and names as its presupposition—assuming, of course, that it does—is thus not always blood (nor is it always physiology, much less biology—but that too is another story, and Meillassoux tells it well). And why should it? Blood is only one name among many in an economy of terms and symbols—"natural" or not—that have appealed to the collective imagination. We have seen that rabbinic texts describe "a partnership of three in that the father supplies the white parts of the body: bones, teeth, the white of the eye, brain matter; the mother the red parts: blood, muscle, hair, the pupil of the eye; and God supplies the intelligence, the spirit, the soul, eyesight, motion of the limbs, and the radiance of the face."[103] We have also considered how, in addition to partaking of Greek science, the Talmud, "the invention of the rabbinic science of blood,"[104] is partly inheriting—and indeed, reconstructing—a biblical conception that never once invoked the phrase "flesh and blood," and in which kinship was void of blood, functioning instead as the unity (or union) of "flesh and bones."

We now know that blood is merely the *name* that was sometimes given, the name we still give today, to the "idea" of kinship; we also know that kinship is not blood (because it is not "really" blood; because it is not "natural"; because the physiology of reproduction and the practices of kinship far exceed the matter of blood; but also because all this was not always understood as, much less called, "consanguinity" or "blood". We nonetheless persist in naming, and referring to, kinship and family relations as "blood." So do anthropologists, and historians too, sometimes going so far as to project it (as if translating it) onto other cultures and other times.[105] Our collective imagination remains bloody, as does the fabric that seamlessly relates the real and the social, blood and community. We narrate ourselves by invoking the same central, if fluid and evasive, "character." Along with the notion of consanguinity, blood continues to support a particular conception of the social and of the political, of the community.

Here as well, I do not particularly seek to identify agency behind blood nor to assert that the community of blood was, or was not, a modern (or ancient) invention. A precise chronology does not interest me either. We have more than ample evidence that shows how both kinship and class have been predicated on (remember now: the word) blood before modern anthropology and before "race science"—assuming there is between them a significant difference.[106] But it is equally clear that the relation between blood and community far exceeds the modern question of "race" and precisely because the former may have enabled the latter. Blood far exceeds the domain of nature and of biology—and there is a crucial difference between these two as well.[107] Hence, what is important for me to show has to do with the edges of a fabric (in which race and biology are ultimately of limited significance by comparison) that covers kinship and politics, theology and anthropology, law and science, and economics too, along with its seamless expansion—a generalized hematology.[108] For what remains the case is that the conjunction of blood with the social has become seamless, that it has survived the discredit of race science and the various undoings of the nature–culture binary (the nature of this survival, beyond its obvious rhetorical dimension, remains to be understood, of course).[109] At the same time, blood—that "hazardous concept"—has served to establish and sediment (or simply, to name) an enduring distinction *between* collectives (family, communities, races, nations) and between the very realms among and across which blood is divided and over which it rules. The significance of these questions and issues with regard to "different" bloods, to the multiplicity of blood, can hardly be overstated. What I seek to understand, then, is the fabric of blood, and blood as fabric (textile or text), the vampire state. That is the fabric that must lead us to interrogate alleged rents in the fabric, rents that would separate religion from politics, law from science, medicine from theology, and later too religion from race. Interdisciplinary *avant la lettre*, blood supports and enables the question that occupies me throughout. Blood must be read, in other words, for it has become a question and a figure for a collective (it has become an object, as historians of science and philosophers might say), as word and thing at once—the fabric of our lives. Blood is always already hematology.

THE HEMATOLOGICAL STYLE
IN AMERICAN POLITICS

From kinship to nation and to race, this brief history of blood, and of the vampire state, must begin again with America. Why must America write itself as bloodied?[110] For it has had, spilled, claimed, or claimed to have through its history numerous bloods: kindred, mingled, and other bloods. But this is to assert no more than a banality, of course, as "the enormously powerful symbolic role of blood in American culture and politics" has been well recognized.[111] It may well be, moreover, that the banality extends further, that America is merely illustrative of a more general condition, the structure of which Benjamin laid out under the notion of "mythical violence"—and *Blutgewalt*—and which I have described as a generalized hematology. At this point, rather than provide an occasion for dismissal or, for that matter, scholarly engagement on grounds of a rhetorical accident, structural parallels, or the universal persistence of a symbolic resource, such banality might prove to demand a reckoning of sorts, as blood illuminates, that is, singularly suffuses and joins, a wide and peculiar range of fields, regions, and realms that extend across America.

I refer first of all and throughout to an equally anticipated, albeit unfortunate, banality, the obvious and relentless grounds of race, spanning the cruel vagaries and strange intricacies of blood quantum—the "blood politics" long associated with Native Americans and operative to this day in federal law; as well as "Hawaiian blood," which played a determining role "as the criterion for Hawaiian land leasing eligibility within the context of U.S. colonial land appropriation."[112] I refer ultimately to the one-drop rule, which has tragically and singularly affected African Americans and those identified as "Negroes" or "Black" over the course of a long history.[113] And although these three specific instances are manifestly linked by blood, their joined and internal operations on that distinct, fluid plane remain very much unattended.[114] But there is yet more blood. There is, for instance, the *ab uno sanguine* of the abolitionists, the shared discourse of blood that reaches across the divides of the racial debate[115]; there is what Orlando Patterson has powerfully described as "rituals of blood" and their enduring effects.[116] There is, in other words, everything that Susan Gilman persuasively calls "blood talk" in American culture.[117]

By invoking many bloods, however, I also mean to signal beyond and elsewhere than race, in order to move toward a recognition that the blood of race is derivative of a larger preoccupation with blood. More generally, for now, I want to point toward the law, toward the "madness of law," that is, the "madness of American law,"[118] whence and into which flow rivers of blood, from the birth of the jury trial out of the sources of "judgments of blood,"[119] to the "corruption of the blood" that sanctions treason in the U.S. Constitution.[120] With and beyond law, I seek to evoke "the sanguinary empire" (as Keally McBride has it), the myths and operations of a "regeneration through violence," murders and mass murders, in cold blood and otherwise, legally and illegally allowed or authorized by way of the "harsh justice" of the death penalty, the "bloodletting" of punishment, cruel, unusual, or pedagogical, that is, legally civilizing.[121] Echoing Benjamin, Robert Cover recalls that "law is that which licenses in blood certain transformations, while authorizing others only by unanimous consent."[122]

And then there are the bloods of kinship, American kinship this time, perhaps one of the most insistent and resilient sites where the law has systematically inscribed blood, where it "created an autonomous legal regime of 'blood'" and where the "general judicial tendency . . . to hypostasize legal concepts" participated in "creating formalistic legal doctrines which were segregated from their factual and political context."[123] As Abraham Lincoln pertinently put it, "Let every man remember that to violate the law, is to trample on the blood of his father."[124] As we have seen, kinship goes beyond the law, but the connections are deep, and covert still, between law, kinship, and race, and "the race/reproduction bind" I mentioned earlier.[125] American kinship, at any rate, relates to, feeds into, but also extends beyond, race. Michael Rogin demonstrated that it lies at the very foundations of the nation.[126] It extends further than the law into culture and to anthropology, to the systems of consanguinity, the "communities of blood" painstakingly constructed, invented, by Lewis Henry Morgan, that have long been naturalized, taken more or less for granted, and increasingly so since David Schneider simultaneously reinscribed and dismissed them. ("It is a fundamental premise of the American kinship," Schneider writes, "that blood is a substance." He goes on to add that "the category of blood . . . not only means the red stuff which courses through the veins, but also that combination of substance and code for conduct which those who share the red stuff, the blood relatives, should have. In one sense its meaning is reserved to that of substance, in the other, it includes both substance and law."[127])

It is only a short step (or perhaps it is a giant one) from here to the bloods of science and of technology, the bloods of medicine, or the making of blood into a national concern, "blood safety and surveillance," as a recent volume has it.[128] This too includes race while going greatly beyond it. Documenting "the rise of an independent hematological sensibility" in the United States, Keith Wailoo argues that "even with the increasing specialization of medicine, blood study continued to have metaphorical appeal, offering the practitioner," that is, the hematologist, "a role as a 'secret agent'—producer of both specific and generalized knowledge."[129] And note that the word *metaphorical* may find new meaning here, closer to fictional even, as "despite its diagnostic flaws, hematology played a crucial role in the identification and control of disease, in the regulation of the hospital and the factory, and in the arbitration of blame in disputes over worker compensation" (96). Turning to a broader field of scientific practice in an essay entitled "Science's Blood Flow," Bruno Latour suggests in turn that "by following the ways in which facts circulate, we will be able to reconstruct, blood vessel after blood vessel, the whole circulatory system of science. The notion of a science isolated from the rest of the society will become as meaningless as the idea of a system of arteries disconnected from the system of veins."[130] Thomas Kuhn did learn much of what he paradigmatically figured out from Ludwik Fleck, whose own *Genesis and Development of a Scientific Fact* is, in fact, an extended reflection on blood.[131] In America, at any rate, the blood flow of science would primarily include the development of anatomy and the establishment of medical schools upon what Michael Sappol calls "a traffic of dead bodies," the labor of grave robbers, the bodies of the slaves and the destitute; the "Tuskegee experiment," sickle cell anemia, and indeed, hematology.[132] In a word, or two, "medical apartheid."[133] Eugenics follows closely, of course, and so does "the first eugenics body in the United States," described by Alexandra Stern. The "Eugenics Committee of the American Breeders' Association" (of which Alexander Graham Bell was a proud member) was established in 1906 to "investigate and report on heredity in the human race, and emphasize the value of superior blood and the menace to society of inferior blood."[134] Whence, in case you were wondering, prenuptial blood tests.[135] By the 1920s, at any rate, the prominence of blood tests (there are 900 of them available today) came to reflect "the supposed relevance of blood work to what many Americans perceived as pressing social concerns—the proper role of women, the health consequences of modern industrial work, professional work relations in the hospital, the rise of the pharmaceutical industry and changing patterns of drug consumption, and the problem of 'Negro blood' and American race relations."[136] Keith Wailoo, whom I have been citing, writes a history of medical technology and the rise of a medical specialization, but he points toward the broader significance of his work when he says that "controversies over the meaning of the blood are everywhere in contemporary American society; they are not merely artifacts of the historian's imagination.... Contemporary Americans [continue to] 'assess' technology" in terms of "contemporary blood beliefs (in the case of bone marrow transplantation and prostate specific antigen). Even with the rising symbolic importance of genes, blood continues to have an appeal for public and professional alike" (194). "By the 1930s," at any rate, "the American Federation of Labor recognized a 'blood seller's union.'"[137]

Much earlier, that is, from the very beginning, some of the towering figures of the American political imagination had begun to show and propagate their bloody concerns, anticipating what would later be called "the blood of government" and deploying a hematological style of their own.[138] Now, in using the expression "hematological style," I obviously mean to recall Richard Hofstadter's famous essay on the "paranoid style in American politics," but unlike Hofstadter, I am not so certain whether I am "speaking in a clinical sense" or "borrowing a clinical term for other purposes." Am I perhaps using the term, as Hofstadter did, the way "a historian of art might speak of the baroque or of the mannerist style"?[139] Such uncertainty is precisely what I am submitting here for examination. And for good reasons, I think, for as Hofstadter puts it, "style has to do with the way in which ideas are believed and advocated rather than with the truth or falsity of their content" (5). Style has to do with the manner in which ideas are imprinted on language, the way language imprints itself on them too, on the collective imagination, and on concrete institutions as well. (And maybe blood does so as well, which Empedocles at least thought was the seat of, well, thought.) Consider at any rate that Tocqueville, to begin somehow arbitrarily with him, ambivalently held onto a notion that might be identified with no more than mitigated assurance as rhetorical or figurative, perhaps even as symbolic. In a remark that was not included in the final version of his celebrated *Democracy in America*, Tocqueville wrote that "the circulation of ideas is to civilization what the circulation of blood is to the human body."[140] No more, nor less than a cliché, one might say. But Tocqueville also wondered "why of all the European races of the New World is the English race the one that has most preserved the purity of its blood and has least mingled with the native races?"[141] How literal was he being then? And what relation is there subsequently between the bloods? Do we measure—and how—the literalization of the metaphor, the concreteness of the symbol, the difference between bloods? What was it, finally, that Tocqueville thought he was saying when he asserted that "*nearly* all the men who inhabit the territory of the Union are born of the same blood."[142] The modifier "nearly" here certainly implies the possibility of measurement, one that, whatever the precise nature of its quantitativeness, appeals to an empiricity, a concreteness and a literality, that is hard to deny, dismiss, or simply resolve. What was it which that South Carolina senator was saying or signaling when a few years later he "boldly promised to drink all the blood that might be shed as a result of the Confederate declaration of independence"? Along with many others, he clearly expected that the confrontation between North and South would be brief.[143] But was he being literal or martial? medical, anthropological, or rhetorical? The very difference in Paster's assertion on early modern English society is once again pertinent here, that "the key social attributes of blood could never be simply symbolic or metaphoric."[144]

Drawing on other, older resources, anatomies and analogies, that may also, and with equal legitimacy (or lack thereof) be filed away as merely metaphorical, John Adams "wrote that a political constitution is like 'the constitution of the human body'; 'certain contextures of the nerves, fibres, and muscles, or certain qualities of the blood and juices' some of which 'may properly be called *stamina vitae*, or essentials and fundamentals of the constitution; parts without which life itself cannot be preserved a moment.'"[145] Incidentally, Adams had been reading James

Harrington's *Oceana* for some time, borrowing from him, at least explicitly, the concept of balance among others. Adams acknowledged balance to be a "political concept" that "was Harrington's discovery ... [who] was as much entitled to credit for it as Harvey was for the discovery of the circulation of the blood."[146] Another founding father, James Madison, was partaking of this hematological tradition. As he turned to his fellow Americans, he was deploying a long-standing custom of interpellating and haranguing, while proceeding seamlessly to move *between* bloods.

> Hearken not to the unnatural voice which tells you that the people of America, knit together as they are by so many chords of affection, can no longer live together as members of the same family; can no longer continue the mutual guardians of their mutual happiness; can no longer be fellow citizens of one great respectable and flourishing empire. Hearken not to the voice which petulantly tells you that the form of government recommended for your adoption is a novelty in the political world; that it has never yet had a place in the theories of the wildest projectors; that it rashly attempts what it is impossible to accomplish. No my countrymen, shut your ears against this unhallowed language. Shut your hearts against the poison which it conveys; the kindred blood which flows in the veins of American citizens, the mingled blood which they have shed in defense of their sacred rights, consecrate their union, and excite horror at the idea of their becoming aliens, rivals, enemies.[147]

Somehow famously (or rather infamously), Jefferson would be hard put to disagree. At any rate, and as Thomas Paine had already opined, "no connection binds like blood." Paine later added, as if prophetically: "I have seen the fine and fertile country of America ravaged and deluged in blood, and the taxes of England enormously increased and multiplied in consequence thereof."[148] Pushing further the limits of that particular rhetoric—if this is, again, what this is—Paine took it upon himself to ventriloquize the voice of women, haranguing in turn the men of the country, "When you offer your blood to the State," his American women would have said, "think that it is ours" (38). Accordingly, Paine elsewhere expressed a proximate concern over "rivers of wasted blood" (74). He also made recurrent use of the phrase "blood and treasure" (e.g., 89), and enthusiastically embraced the view that shall occupy us again, and according to which commerce is the blood of the state, for "like blood, it cannot be taken from any of the parts without being taken from the whole mass in circulation, and all partake of the loss."[149] Somehow more circumspect, John Quincy Adams thought that there was "something akin to the thirst of the tiger for blood ... in the rapacity with which the members of the new states fly at the public lands."[150] Much later, Franklin Delano Roosevelt offered a notably less holistic view, condemning, in a newspaper column, the practice of intermarriage between Japanese and white Americans. "Anyone who has traveled to the Far East," Roosevelt claimed, "knows that the mingling of Asiatic blood with European or American blood produces, in nine cases out of ten, the most unfortunate results. . . . The undesirability of mixing the blood of the two peoples—there can be no quarrel there."[151] Barack Obama, for his part, made clear in his 2009 Inaugural Address that he continues to hold up the bloody torch: "Our Founding Fathers, faced with perils that we can scarcely imagine, drafted a charter to assure the rule of law and the rights of man—a charter expanded by the blood of generations. Those ideals still light the world, and we will not give them up for expedience sake."[152]

I could go on—I really should—and delve further into this "carnival of blood,"[153] into larger and vaster realms of liquidity and bloodletting, specters of the Atlantic and American hieroglyphics, modernity at sea, wolves and men, and the American buffalo too; the white Pacific, Manifest Destiny and the metaphysics of Indian-hating; the science of sacrifice, and the Monroe doctrine.[154] As one popular volume of revolutionary poetry proclaimed in 1778: "Zion is founded; yet means must be us'd. . . . Cursed be he that keeps his sword from blood."[155] Such stages of primitive accumulation—rivers, if not oceans, of blood—can be said to have brought about an ordering or reordering of sorts, the persistence, for instance, of what Kath Weston referred to as "the race/class politics of blood transfusion"[156] and a disciplining of the citizenry, with some fighting "the bloody power of Popery," Mormons worrying about the assimilation of Native Americans to white America serving only "to dilute the 'blood of the children of the covenant,' "[157] and others still, who, with Gobineau, Renan, and Chamberlain, were chiefly preoccupied with the Aryan blood of Jesus (they apparently had lots of admirers in Germany too).[158] Some were "suffering for science," while others were volunteering otherwise, as the growing intricacies of "the gift relationship" expanded, the systems of blood donation analyzed by Richard Titmuss and the ground and basis of our intensive "tissue economies."[159] As Titmuss himself writes, "short of examining humankind itself and the institution of slavery—of men and women as market commodities—blood as a living tissue may now constitute in Western societies one of the ultimate tests of where the 'social' begins and the 'economic' ends."[160] This brings us back to race again, to the segregation enacted by blood banks, among others, during and after World War II, projecting us forward to the AIDS crisis and to some more of the same, the rise of "hemophobia,"[161] which has been lavishly accompanied, for quite a while now, by what might be described as *the bloods of culture*, a phenomenon that, leaving aside perhaps the liquidity of other "blood and gore" genres in literature, film, and video and computer games, manifests itself in a long-standing vampire craze (from *Buffy* to *Twilight*), in what Henry Giroux aptly described as "Zombie Politics and Other Late Modern Monstrosities in the Age of Disposability" in American culture.[162] A recent title, *Abraham Lincoln: Vampire Hunter*, should suffice as a condensed illustration of this growing, even exploding, trend,[163] and we might note that not only vampires but even televised serial killers are now portrayed (it was not obvious enough) as seized by hematological concerns and subtleties—"it starts with blood," says the main character of *Dexter*). One could further evoke the "blood of kindness," the more bucolic glidings of Henry David Thoreau on the Concord and Merrimack rivers, as he marvels at the stream of thoughts, "for there circulates a finer blood than Lavoisier has discovered the law of," he writes, "the blood not of kindred merely, but of kindness, whose pulse still beats at any distance and forever."[164]

And then, of course, there is war.[165]

Offering an alternative of sorts that might prove useful by way of contrast and highlight the vanishing contingency of all this, Mark Taylor, himself an avid reader of Cormac McCarthy's *Blood Meridian*,[166] recently and compellingly suggested that *bones* should have been serious contenders in the fight for our hearts and minds.[167] He makes a good case for them, but it was not to be, at least not yet. Taylor himself cannot be blamed, though in a subsequent book he did move on and along, along these lines that is, and proceed to tell a story of blood. This is a story about his family, a family in which he says "there was no clear line between religion and hunting," but in which "nothing prepared me for the blood involved in this part of the ritual." The sacrificial lamb was a deer, this time, and Taylor goes on to ask: "Does blood sacrifice involve a restricted rather than a general economy?"[168] Taylor does not make the link here, but he evokes it elsewhere, thereby expanding our understanding. "Within such a restricted sacrificial economy," he writes as if in answer to his own question, "all money is blood money."[169] Clarifying the nature of this general, albeit still restricted, economy, Saidiya Hartman pertinently reminds us that "a sea of blood and gold . . . enabled the violent remaking of the nation" after the Civil War. She explains, more broadly, that blood is "the symbol of Christian redemption, national reunion, and immutable and ineradicable differences of race." Blood was "routinely juxtaposed with gold and other treasure expended on behalf of black freedom."[170] Accordingly, and perhaps unsurprisingly, "it was the American physician Bernard Fantus who coined the word 'blood bank' when he opened the first such facility at Chicago's Cook County Hospital in 1937. In an era notable for bank failure and economic collapse, American surgeons became blood 'bankers,' who discussed loans, deposits, and balance sheets."[171] Was blood a *symbol* for money then? Whatever the case, and this one is dubious, it is clear that we have long been transported to the bloods and circulations of political economy, the origins of which have been searchingly traced to England and France by Jonathan Gil Harris.[172] Suffice it to say for now that blood became "the clearest example of a commodity," involving much more than medicine and commerce.[173] Hunting and sacrifice, instant replays of the Great Game, and the blood on our hands, the Bloods and the Crips, "Blood for Oil," torture, and all that—these no doubt deserve special mention, as does perhaps the recently developed practice of shipping blood supplies ahead of the smart bombs, the fleet of drones, and the armored soldiers. "Support our tropes!" Avital Ronell suggested a little while ago—in America, this would still very much mean blood.[174] The circulation of True Blood will be televised. There Will Be Blood.

Academic scholarship, the would-be lifeblood of the American mind, must not be left out of this all-too rapid survey. Within it, the successes of the Black Legend—the *other* empire of blood—are still contended with, or at least inscribed in the mystifying geo-arithmetics of blood and expanded versions of "the myth of southern exceptionalism," whereby "the south" seems always bloodier than "the north."[175] Blood continues to be, at any rate, an ever popular subject, from "the bloodrites of the post-structuralists" theorized by Anne Norton to inquiries into Jewish blood conducted by David Biale and by Mitchell Hart.[176] And consider the phenomenal success of Larry Rickel's "Vampire Lectures" at the University of California Santa Barbara, or the suggestion by Caroline Walker Bynum that Stephen Greenblatt's "New Historicism" is a kind of pandering to an old-new blood cult ("eucharist becomes a way of thinking about everything").[177] But did you know that, in the twentieth century, "hematology had been at the center of almost every medical advance"? And that as the field of "blood studies reached new heights of popular and medical appeal in the immediate post-World War II years, such appeal paradoxically led to the fragmentation of blood studies"?[178] And you should read what Christian presses are publishing on the blood of Christ these days.[179]

All this being, to repeat, no more than another, preliminary report on the banality of evil—I mean the banality of blood in America. But it is a banality the measure and substance of which has failed to register adequately on those charged with the task of interpreting, if not quite changing, the world or at least the nature and operations of the "Redeemer Nation" (in Ernest Lee Tuveson's felicitous phrase).[180] Not least among the reasons for this failure, for the under-theorization of blood, is the strange, even paradoxical, attention the bloods of America have otherwise attracted. Visible and invisible at once, suffusing, as a matter of fact, a dialectic of hypervisibility and utter opacity, blood seems to put an uncanny pressure on our critical abilities. Two random illustrations. The author of *Hellfire Nation*, James Morone, asserts that "unlike the Germans, Americans have no enduring sense of pure blood or culture (despite endless efforts to assert one)."[181] Another distinguished American historian, Francis Jennings, appositely states that "one must somehow contrive to keep a straight face when contemplating the Americans' assumptions of purity of 'blood'; much historical mingling . . . must be blanked out of consciousness."[182] Red, blank, or blue, what is blood anyway? What is it about? Jennings, to be sure, puts blood in quotation marks. Is blood a citation, then? Repeatedly posited, on dubitable grounds, as a universal matter of fact and ultimate concern, and perhaps less spuriously as an equally universal marker of sexual difference, it seems to me that blood—the bloods of America, and of modernity at large—still calls for an understanding that must go beyond the bad infinity of a universal.[183] Such understanding must clearly extend beyond the vast and vastly dominant, if still all too narrow, confines of the history of race, the local associations of blood with science, and ominously, of blood with law and politics. As I already suggested, "the capillary functioning of power" and the distinction Foucault made that has modern politics move from a "symbolics of blood" to an "analytics of sexuality" need to be reconsidered.[184] This is not because Foucault failed to denaturalize sex, but rather because we have yet to denaturalize blood. Or de-periodize and de-universalize it. Or simply confront it. For with all due respect to the imposingly erudite histories of blood that already crowd many a library shelf, what the bloods of America require is the kind of critical work sex has been subjected to: an acknowledgment of excess significance, and a denaturalization.[185] It requires an "analytics of sanguinity," a critical hematology.

Let me conclude these still prefatory remarks by extending the claim I made earlier about banality, and by making explicit my resistance to the notion of an American exceptionalism. This resistance will ambiguously, perhaps paradoxically, accompany my engagement, in the rest of this chapter, with the all-American, and undoubtedly singular, phenomenon referred to as "the one-drop rule," as well as with other dimensions of the vampire state, from law to economics, from kinship to race, and from science to politics. Yet we would do well to recall, once again, the fact that when it comes to blood, we seem to be exclusively confronted with exceptions, numerous as they are, and "national" exceptions in particular, especially so where race is also concerned. We are already familiar with some of them. Spain (the Inquisition), Germany (Nazism), and, to a lesser extent, the United States (slavery) easily—or perhaps queasily—come to mind in this context.[186] I would of course agree that there are many unassailable reasons to uphold the unprecedented, indeed exceptional, exercise of the imagination—in all its practical, juridico-scientifico-institutional, and insistently sanguinary applications—that were brought about since, roughly, 1492. It is however clear that an analytics of blood, the kind of critical hematology I am proposing in this book, will not allow the perdurance of *national* exceptions. The task blood sets in front of us implies rather a general hematology, a reconsideration of race and law, of kinship and science, of politics and culture, and of political economy, which has long been, as Marx recognized early on, an economy of blood. The task blood sets in front of us, I shall argue in more detail, implies a wider, and historically extended, understanding of the mechanisms and institutions of the modern state, a notoriously difficult undertaking, but one that can be considerably eased by turning, and maintaining, our attention resolutely toward blood. To understand the modern state—as body, machine, de-metaphorized polygon, or whatnot—would have to involve the recognition that it finds its uncanny, albeit relative, integrity in blood, in the community of blood. To be sure, there are many kinds of states, many kinds of "magical states," "killing states," or indeed "vampire states."[187] And to each their own hematological style. But whereas for Hofstadter "the single case in modern history in which one might say that the paranoid style has had a consummatory triumph occurred not in the United States but in Germany," it is not clear how these two cases, these two states (and many others as well), could be so neatly distinguished when it comes to their hematological style.[188] I shall refrain at any rate from adding to the citation-fest that surrounds, and obscures, Walter Benjamin's essential argument on the exception that has become the rule, but I do want to be unambiguous on one thing at least. Like Hofstadter, my focus on the United States should by no means be taken as an argument for its exceptionality.[189] To the contrary, and though "it should be noted that ... the Canadian Charter of Rights forbids the use of blood, ethnic, and racial principles for establishing group membership,"[190] I want to repeat and insist that, when it comes to blood, America is merely exemplary.

THE BLOODS OF RACE
(THE BLACK, THE INDIAN)

The one-drop rule has no history.

In this section, I wish to say no more than this: the one-drop rule, this not-infamous-enough institution of Anglo-America, has no history. Such is the enduring hold of the power of blood (ultimately, of bloods). I shall try to render this—no more than this—intelligible, if somehow slowly and sinuously, moving mostly and repeatedly between two of the realms I have been invoking: law and science.

The one-drop rule has no history. This is not a completely accurate statement of course, as books and articles are numerous that attend to some of its historical aspects.[191] Moreover, "many scholars portray the history of race in the United States as the rise of the 'one drop of blood' rule—the legal and cultural norm that any African ancestry makes a person black."[192] And yet, "most legal historians casually describe the rule as the American regime of race without considering its history."[193] This might of course depend on what one means by history, or indeed, by *its* history. In fact, one could very well retort that the one-drop rule has *too many* histories. Scholars have "attempted to trace the rule's origin to the emergence of the cotton economy in the 1830s, the sectional crisis of the 1850s, or Reconstruction. Still others emphasize that most Southern states' legislatures did not formally adopt one-drop racial definitions until the 1910s and 1920s."[194] George Fredrickson, for example, in *Racism: A Short History*, does refer to the rule once (only once), and he does so by underscoring the massive weight it has had, somehow provocatively asserting that "the Nazi definition of a Jew was never as stringent as 'the one-drop rule' that prevailed in the categorization of Negroes in the race-purity laws of the American South."[195] In his acclaimed *Who Is Black? One Nation's Definition*, F. James Davis concurs, at least with regard to the rule's origins, and finds that they indeed lie in the American South. But Davis also notes that the rule was hardly confined to these borders. The one-drop rule, its definition, "emerged from the American South to become the nation's definition, generally accepted by whites and blacks alike."[196] Expanding the geographic reach of the rule, Davis swiftly reinstitutes a logic of containment by underscoring its historical limits. Thus, although he writes that the rule "appeared early," he goes on immediately to add that it would not "become uniformly accepted until during the 1920s" (31). In this narrative or narratives, the focus of which is mostly culture and law, the one-drop rule would therefore constitute a fundamentally modern, even recent, development. Or it would be geographically confined. It would in any case be *exceptional*. Davis himself insists on this singularity, this manifest exceptionality. "Not only does the one-drop rule apply to no other group than American blacks, but apparently the rule is unique in that it is found only in the United States and not in any other nation in the world" (13). I am uncertain as to what can be made of the fact that Davis ignores—in either senses of that verb—the fact that "as early as the Sauk and Fox Treaty of 1830, the federal government had used blood as a basis for racially identifying Native Americans and distinguishing them from the national body," that by "the late nineteenth century, it began to impose a different racial ideology on Native Americans—the eugenic notion that Native-American identity was tied to Indian blood quantum."[197] It is true that the practice of assimilation varied in U.S. law depending on belonging and ancestry among the collectives it singled out.[198] In a way, this is what the one-drop rule is "really" about, of course. It is not *really* about blood but about the law, and about enshrining racial purity in law.[199] That is to say that if blood is a privileged substance for scientific discourse, primarily an object for science (this is a big if, of course), then we can recognize that no scientific theory ever demonstrated that difference was ever *actually* carried by blood, whether Black, Native American, or anything else, with such difference understood in a narrow, physiologic or indeed scientific sense. Still, part of the divide between science and law is precisely about the difference *between* bloods—the blood of African Americans and the blood of Native Americans, the blood of law and the blood of science. Davis, at any rate, does identify earlier antecedents of a quantitative divide, measurements of blood that predate any attempt to advance scientific theories of blood, in the colonies of Maryland and Virginia in the seventeenth century, for example. A recent study reaches a similar historical conclusion and confirms that "the earliest blood-fraction law in British North America was that of 1705 Virginia."[200] This same study also states that one cannot understand the one-drop rule otherwise than as a theory of "invisible blackness"—not as a blood doctrine per se—and that defined in this precise manner it cannot be found in the United States before 1830 (339), incidentally the date at which blood would have become part of the legal definition of Native American belonging. More recently, Peggy Pascoe spreads a different geographic and legal net, and though she begins her account in 1860 and reiterates the "scientific" novelty of miscegenation laws, her argument is that law is at the heart of the matter.[201] Confining herself to Louisiana, Virginia Domínguez also insists on the centrality of law (and of political economy, she adds). She underscores as well that the problem "stems from the existence of widespread assumptions about the properties of blood—that identity is determined by blood; that blood ties, lineally and collaterally, carry social and economic rights and obligations; and that both racial identity and class membership are determined by blood."[202]

Whether distant or close, the origins of the one-drop rule, and its subsequent developments, its very nature even, remain murky, and historical precedents rightly fade from significance. But perhaps it depends on what one understands by significance. If the one-drop rule has a history, so far, it is because it may belong to law and to science, to politics and to culture as well. And it still seems to be distinctly, indeed, exceptionally, an American one, with one *significant* European, forgive me, German, parallel, a modern one.

Most scholars, however, seem to agree on tracing or implicitly associating the history of the one-drop rule to science, and specifically to the emergence of race thinking, the emergence of modern science and of biological racism. Of course, whether such thinking was found in seventeenth-century Virginia may or may not matter, depending here too on what one understands by history, or, for all that, by racism.[203] Be that as it may, those who associate the blood tide that carried (or was carried by) race thinking with science will date the one-drop rule to the late nineteenth or even early twentieth century. The dating of race science would certainly seem to confirm this analysis. To take one typical scholarly assertion:

> By 1850, the concept of race as a valid system of classification was thoroughly established in Europe and the Americas. By this time, not only had race thinking become commonplace, but also the belief that levels of societal development were biologically determined by race had also become commonplace. A position that epitomized this thinking can be found in the writings of anatomist Robert Knox, whom historian Léon Poliakov refers to as the first racist scholar.[204]

But this history of science must contend with earlier sightings and with the scientificity of, say, Médéric Louis Elie Moreau de Saint-Méry (1750–1819), who

> set out with mathematical exactitude in his *Description topographique, physique, civile, politique et historique de la partie française de l'isle Saint-Domingue* (composed between 1776 and 1789 and published in 1797) . . . [and] produced a spectacularly detailed survey of the nuances of colour found among the mixed-race coloureds in what was then the French colony of Saint-Domingue, later to become Haiti. He started with the assumption that a pure white and a pure black was each composed, respectively, of 128 units of white blood or black blood. Between these ranges Saint-Méry traced a complex asymmetric gradation of racial classes composed of varying proportions of white and black blood. A "sacatra," for example, was the class of mixed race which approximated closest to a pure black and was composed of 16 units of white blood, 112 of black; a "griffe" came next with 32 units of white, 96 of black blood; then a "marabou" with 48 units of white, 80 of black; a "mulâtre" with equal shares of 64 units of both white and black blood; next a "quarteron" with 96 units of white, 32 of black; a "métif" with 112 units of white, 16 of black; a "mamelouc" with 120 units of white and 8 of black; then, finally, with infinite care devoted to the detection of the minutest strains of black inheritance, a "sang-mêlé" with 126 units of white and only 2 of black.[205]

And what of this 1828 account, which, formulated by "The Connecticut Colonization Society," still clearly predates the infamous scientific, and allegedly foundational, elaborations of Knox and Gobineau?

> In every part of the United States, there is a broad and impassible line of demarcation between every man who has one drop of African blood in his veins, and every other class in the community. The habits, the feelings, all the prejudices

of society—prejudices which neither refinement, nor argument, nor education, nor religion itself can subdue—mark the people of color, whether bond or free, as the subjects of a degradation inevitable and incurable. The African in this country belongs by birth to the lowest station in society; and from that station he can never rise, be his talents, his enterprise, his virtues what they may.[206]

Is this law, then, or is this science? Is "the blood in [the] veins" that of race or that of kinship? Histories of science are hardly linear, of course, and these citations may show no more than that. It seems to me that they also show that what is meant by science, and by race science in particular, may have to be altered by a more diligent focus on blood science.[207] Minimally, this may provide another route to resolve the question of the novelty (or antiquity) of racial thought and its different manifestations. Indeed, still concerned with the question of race, some scholars have nonetheless insisted on a completely different genealogy of the idea. For them, and Winthrop Jordan is among them, the importance of blood as a distinctive marker of collective identity is hardly exceptional, as it can already be attested in Ancient Greece and in Rome as well.[208] Many recall here the famous assertion attributed by Herodotus to the Athenians, who refer to the "common blood (*homaimon*)" of the Hellenes.[209] Concurring with the line of argumentation, Ivan Hannaford adds to it the complexity of internal transformations. There would have been, in Greece and in Rome, a "transition from kith and kin to polity, from blood relationship to political relationship."[210] The "organizing idea of race" was absent, Hannaford acknowledges, though to be precise, it was perhaps present as an absence, virtually present or indeed "absent so long as the political idea flourished to reconcile the volatile blood relationship (kinship) found in family, tribe, and clan, with the wider demands of the community" (14). Later on, Hannaford reluctantly lights yet another historical path for the idea of race, turning his attention away from the Greeks and toward "the vulgar notion that the origins of race may be traced to these Hebrew teachings about a chosen people of pure blood." This notion, this history, Hannaford rightly calls "erroneous," and so, he says, because "Hebrew piety contains the possibility of conversion of the stranger into the faith" (93). Not the newsflash we were expecting perhaps, nor quite a definitive rejoinder to a view that has gained enough momentum to be quite extensively entertained: that blood racism finds its origin in a "Semitic" ground. Consider that there are those—and the Spanish, philo-Semitic Américo Castro is among them—who have long been arguing that it all began not with some essentialized notion of immutability but precisely with an imperative moment, with the hardness and the harshness of the law, which is to say, I suppose, with "the Hebrew notion of purity of blood."[211] From law to science, by way of philology and culture and back to law.

Now, it is no doubt the case that a responsible history of modern racism (of which the one-drop rule is indisputably a major part) cannot afford to ignore that

> when people used the term "race," they could mean a lot of different things: ideas about "race" did not depend on the new science of biology. From its early days, however, race, like ethnicity today, always involved some idea of physical ancestral descent. Starting with the family line, ancestors and descendants, by the eighteenth century the word "race" was also being used to describe clans, tribes and nations. In all these contexts, race implied a bodily relation that was typically invoked by the word "blood." . . . "Blood" is typical of the discourse of race: it sounds physical and corporeal. Blood suggests a notion of belonging, of one's "own flesh and blood" (even if we now know that actually families may belong to different blood groups). As E. A. Freeman remarked in 1879, "our whole conception of race starts from the idea of community of blood. If the word 'race' does not mean community of blood, it is hard to see what it does mean."[212]

Though contested, much like the idea of blood or of community of blood, the one-drop rule certainly seems singularly unavoidable in raising blood, in bringing us back to blood, ancient and modern blood, whether Greek, Jewish, or African blood. Then again, it may all be an invention of modern race science. As I said, the one-drop rule has no history. Which is to say that it has too many histories.

The overview I am trying to provide would not even be nearing completion without something that has been hinted at and which I have addressed in the previous chapter: yet another possible source, parallel, or analogue for the one-drop rule. I should probably qualify this statement, however, with one caveat, namely, that here again references to this particular source or detail—the establishment of purity of blood statutes in late medieval Spain—are rarely made or deployed, or even alluded to, in existing accounts of the one-drop rule.[213] A recent and impressive volume on *Race, Nation, and Religion in the Americas* does seem to point toward a certain proximity, while it brings a different kind of depth to Robert Young's essential account, which I have just quoted.

> The common preoccupation of nineteenth-century racial discourse with "blood" as a marker of difference and determinant of character probably drew on centuries of *popular speculation about the bodily fluid's magical properties*— speculations that fed the "blood libels" European Christians occasionally leveled against Jews, accusing them of using Christian blood for nefarious purposes. Indeed, the popular perception that "Christian blood" was somehow different from that of Jews and others was codified in the "purity of blood" statutes of

fifteenth- and sixteenth-century Spain—a system of social hierarchy and exclusion targeted not at Jews and Muslims per se but at Christian converts and their descendants.[214]

The one-drop rule would thus have found its origins not so much in the purity of blood statutes but in "centuries of popular speculation about the bodily fluid's magical properties," which themselves gave rise to the statutes. Yet another historical trajectory. So be it. Arguing more forcefully for the historical link between race and religion (rather than race and magic), George Fredrickson and Ann Stoler, whom I mentioned earlier, Etienne Balibar and Immanuel Wallerstein, David Brion Davis, and others too, have joined their voices in underscoring the role of the Spanish statutes (not the blood of Christ) and their contribution to the development of race thinking (and acting).[215] Earlier than most of them, Ronald Sanders had insisted on the shared origins of American racism, at once Spanish and Anglo.[216] Keenly aware of the subtle and not so subtle differences that separate widely (or purely) distinct geographic and historical units, these scholars have been careful neither to essentialize the history of racism and of anti-Semitism nor to claim that anything like "biological racism" had appeared fully formed in the sixteenth century. They insist, nonetheless, that there is a link to be made or explored between certain events, and that the proximate future of this peculiar contribution to the history of "blood politics" lies in social transformations that had to do with class rather than with race (the question being, as I shall ask in a moment, whether these transformations tell us anything about blood). Clearly, we are once again, and most definitely, provided thereby with yet another history, one that adds social distinctions to the scientific or classical trajectories we have explored and could moreover, if incidentally, be said to bring our search to a satisfying albeit abrupt end. For when it comes to "Spain's infamous statues of purity of blood," one scholar recently explained, "their exact origins are still a mystery."[217] But then, I suppose one could always wonder about popular magic, and the nature of the peculiarly bloody imagination manifested by Greeks, Jews, and most of all Spaniards (and let us not forget, Germans). Indeed, one could read one version or another of "the Spanish obsession with blood purity," or the "Spaniard's obsession with clean lineages."[218] Are not Spaniards (and Latinos after them) a people with "blood on their mind" (as Hamlet, a newfound Marrano, would have put it)? Continuing in this direction, one could go on to suggest that, given Spain's legendary and, once again, *exceptional* bloodthirstiness, the Black Legend was always already the Red Legend.

Allow me to recapitulate. If the one-drop rule has no history, it is because it has too many. It is an effect of modern changes, of the advent of modern racism (even though it seems to have preceded the advent of this particular contribution to world history). Or, it finds its sources in American history and in its constraints, an exceptional conception of "miscegenation" (with or without link to slavery per se).[219] Alternatively, it draws from ancient Greek notions of "common blood" and perhaps even from Jewish ("Semitic") conceptions of election. Finally, it could well be related to the medieval Statutes on the Purity of Blood, although, as I have indicated, no scholar I am aware of ever attempts to make, let alone philologically establish, this specific connection.[220] There are to be sure a number of debates that concern themselves with the origins of American racism and racial thought (I always wonder whether there is a difference between these last two), but blood (whether pure or in single drops) does not seem to figure in them.[221] Now, it is not difficult to see, again and again, that the multiplicity (or absence) of history/ies has everything to do with the very strict distinctions—one could almost say, segregations—that carefully construct communities or states of exception; that effectively isolate Jew from Greek, Spain from England (and, more important, the United States), and kinship from polity (or, if you will, and following Benedict Anderson, racism from nationalism), even if for the purpose of ensuing comparison (which presupposes distinction). This historical, or historiographic, predicament may also tell us something about the enduring, if slowly crumbling, division long made between race and magic, I mean, between race and religion (first there was religion, then there was race, goes the well-known narrative).[222] One could, at any rate, easily point to the hermetic barriers that have been erected around the issue simply by invoking the phrase "blood politics," which, like its proximate relative, "blood and soil," never fails to bring up echoes of the occult and the figure of Nazism (with the Spanish Inquisition expected, and by everybody this time, as a close second, and possibly the Old Testament as the next contender. America? Fuhgedaboutit!).[223] It is equally easy, however, to remark that blood—yes, blood—persists and provides a kind of *tertium quid*, something like a general medium, out of which there emerge a relative integrity, a coagulated whole of sorts, thinly striated with a set of analogical links between the series of dichotomous terms that constitute it. A simpler way to say this, I suppose, is that by the time the one-drop rule emerges on the historical or scholarly scene, there is already blood everywhere (as Spinoza showed us), on every side of the comparisons or equations that thus coagulate. It is not so much that there appears a family resemblance, à la Wittgenstein, but more literally that whatever its size, the family, I mean, the community (family, house or clan, tribe, race, nation or commonwealth, empire) has been constituted within and across its frontiers, and with various degrees of literality and reliability, with various degrees of legality and scientificity, as a community of blood.[224] Blood clearly suffuses the Spanish Empire, but blood also flows with equal abundance and alleged integrity at the heart of the British one too, along with its American colonies and after. Blood can be found in kinship (blood ties), in nationalisms (*jus sanguinis*), "blood and iron" and other kinds, and in race, of course. There is "blood talk" everywhere, in other words, at home and abroad, in politics and law, in culture and in science, in economics and in religion too.[225] Or is there? It is at this point that I need to reiterate what I began with, namely, that the one-drop rule has no history. It has no history because none of its histories tell us anything specific about blood. It is as if the matter of blood, blood itself, were as it were secondary, derivative or, for that matter, so originary as to become strangely unexceptional.

To state the problem once again: Either it is the case that, starting in the ancient world, "the original citizens of a commonwealth always believed to be united by kinship in blood and resented a claim to equality of privilege as usurpation of their birthright," and furthermore that "the history of political ideas begins, in fact, with the assumption that kinship in blood is the sole possible ground of community in political functions,"[226] or else, "the idea of a community of race makes its appearance when the frontiers of kinship dissolve at the level of the clan, the neighborhood community, and, theoretically at least, the social class to be imaginarily transferred to the threshold of nationality."[227] Either our collective imagination has always been bloody, or the singularity of "blood obsession," which has been attributed to medieval Spaniards, American Southerners, and Nazi Germans is, in fact, *exceptional* (and even mutually unrelated, to boot). Either blood is old, universal, and omnipresent, or it is modern, newly invented, singular, and, in fact, even rare. To state this in yet another way, I would say that what I want to ask is quite narrowly historical, even if it has not quite become a question for historians. What I continue to ask is this: How did we get into this bloody mess? Or, more politely perhaps, what would a history of the one-drop rule look like—would it be *possible*—if it were written not as a chapter in the history of race but as a chapter in the history of blood instead? Foucault says somewhere that "what enables us to make reality intelligible is simply showing that it was possible; establishing the intelligibility of reality consists in showing its possibility."[228] Toward the becoming intelligible of its reality, I merely want to show *that blood has become possible* and where, with some measure of exacting precision.

❧ ❧ ❧

Now, as I have already made clear, any survey of the expanse of blood in America must rightly and obviously begin with slavery, "the bloody flower," or—and this is to underscore the difficulties that will plague us throughout—with law.[229] This is not necessarily a historical beginning, but an ethical and epistemological one. Slavery is the manifest revelation of the significance of blood, at the same time as it conceals, by containing it, the full range and divisions of the blood realms. Blood is larger than race, though the narrowness of the question notwithstanding, it is by no means useless to ask about history and origins, yes, but also whether blood is a racial—read scientific—category or a legal one. The two are hard to disentangle, nor perhaps should they be disentangled. To the extent, at any rate, that the "problem of slavery," as David Brion Davis calls it, implies and implicates race, slavery is, with equal immediacy, a matter of law.[230] Recall that the first slave law "to give statutory recognition to slavery" is dated 1641 in the Massachusetts colony.[231] The law does not mention blood at this point, much less science, nor would the contested history of race allow an easy identification of racial logic at work—when does it begin, and where is a debated issue that has agitated, of all people, scholars of ancient Greece since Martin Bernal's *Black Athena*.[232] Conversely, it is impossible to narrate the history of law in the United States and ignore the constitutive significance of the law's relation to race and to slavery.[233] Not that this impossibility stops many from trying, of course (alternatively, one could insist on that relation and say little, almost nothing, about blood). What I propose, at any rate, is that by moving away from the minefields of race and its potential anachronisms, and shifting the gaze to blood rather than directly to race (or to the fundamental, though not exclusive, role of law in the making of slavery and segregation), we will be compelled to contend with a different, more expansive set of problems, while some clarity might be gained.

As we just saw, race remains marked as one of the unfortunate contributions, one of the sad legacies, of modern science. It is of course *bad* science.[234] Law, in contrast, the rule of law, is unequivocally held to be a crowning achievement of modernity, hardly stained by those objectionable laws, laws like the laws of slavery (or of property), or those laws that were reproduced or even copied in different settler colonies, and by the Nazi regime. Now, we have read Walter Benjamin on the rapport between blood and power, between blood and the tradition of violence and law he calls *Blutgewalt*. We have begun to reflect on the significance of Robert Cover's assertion with regard to law and blood ("law is that which licenses in blood certain transformations while authorizing others only by unanimous consent"), or the constitutive role played by "judgments of blood" in the emergence of the modern judicial order.[235] We have learned as well that "what is staked out in the defense of legal reason is a legitimacy that belongs to the mythical antiquity of specifically English common law sources and forms, a lineage, a blood, a law whose rationality belongs to the immemorial authority of its source."[236] We recall that, before Solon's intervention, the laws of Draco were, in ancient Athens, written in blood; or that according to Blackstone, "nothing can restore the blood, when once corrupted, if the pardon be not allowed until after attainder, but the high power of parliament,"[237] and we may agree with Otto von Gierke, for whom "the spirit of [Natural] Law can never be extinguished. If it is denied entry into the body of positive law, it flutters about the room like a ghost, and threatens to turn into a vampire which sucks the blood from the body of Law."[238] We might also endorse the work of Pierre Legendre, who places filiation (*le principe de généalogie*) and the ties of blood (*les liens du sang, la descente linéaire du sang*) at the center of the Western juridical tradition, at the core of the Western legal subject.[239] We have minimally been provided with some occasion to reflect on the history of the concept of consanguinity, which Legendre himself sees as unwittingly waning ("nous ne savons pas que nous vivons le déclin précipité de la doctrine généalogique de la consanguinité" [369]). We can think again of the role played by "righteous persecution"—the Inquisition—in the development of modern law.[240] We may know, in other words, of the essential relation between law and blood, and the particular truth, if not quite the extent, of this relation when it comes to "modern" (and not only American) law. We have yet to produce, that is, a sustained reflection on law and blood, on the deployment of blood in law.[241] For the obvious and ancient association of law with blood, the suggestion made by many, as Danielle Allen points out, "that over time a dark Dionysiac and ancient age of mad blood vengeance has ceded to an era of rational, legally based state punishment and Apolline brightness,"[242] may have concealed the singular occurrence and recurrence, the massive deployment of blood in modern law, of blood laws in modernity, and that at least since the Treaty of Westphalia and the attempt to quell the "effusion of Christian blood."[243] From the definition of the person as flesh and blood (or alternatively, to the affirmation or lament that the legal person is *not* flesh and blood),[244] by way of the enduring regulation of kinship on the basis of blood ("blood relations"), the inscription of this same "blood" in the definition of property, to the dialectical use of *jus sanguinis* (vs. *jus solis*) and to the construction of the national collective—or of the race enemy—on the model of the community of blood, all the way to the legal production of blood as commodity: modern law is drenched in blood. If "property served Americans, in the Puritan phrase, as 'the outward and visible sign of inward and spiritual grace,'" one may just as well grant blood the same function.[245] What will ultimately emerge in the remainder of this chapter as the vampire state provides ample occasion to consider the peculiar hemophilia of modern law.

Such is the range of what the one-drop rule should recall for us, even if it gives us no indication that blood would belong "properly" to law (or to science), no definite confirmation as to the realm or discipline in which blood might in fact find its proper place. Is it, finally, law or science, or, as we shall soon see, politics? Or again, as I have said a number of times, all of the above, albeit in an asymmetric manner? Where precisely does "the most commonly used term in racist and racialist

discourse of the nineteenth century"—and perhaps in other centuries as well—
find the ground of its pertinacity?[246] For now, we may have to concede, at the very
least, that although blood is equivocally found in science, even in early race thinking, it does seem to belong to a longer and older history, minimally an American
history of law and culture. I quote from a 1792 Act of the Laws of Virginia, which
itself cites earlier formulas and has, incidentally, nothing directly to do with slavery.

> And, in the cases before mentioned, where the inheritance is directed to pass to
> the ascending and collateral kindred of the intestate, if part of such collaterals
> be of the whole blood to the intestate, and other part of the half blood only,
> those of the half blood shall inherit only half so much as those of the whole
> blood . . .[247]

In law, blood at the very least defines or determines conceptions of both kinship and property.[248] This has long been the case, and the commonplace seems quite
ancient whereby "property is that minor fate which comes (as inheritance or succession) from the father as 'efficient cause,' as blood."[249] To be as precise as possible,
then, located between science and law, blood does not quite belong to either, or not
exclusively so. Nor, I shall reiterate here again, can it be dismissed (or even acknowledged) as a mere metaphor. And the difficulty, the confusion, only increases when
considering the recent increase in scholarship that has sought to recognize and reinscribe race in a longer, theological history. These arguments are more than compelling that demonstrate how race ("science"), law, and religion ("theology") cannot be
hermetically distinguished from one another; that show that we will better understand race if we attend to its theological origins as well, if we linger, that is, with what
Willie James Jennings refers to as "the Christian imagination."[250]

THE VAMPIRE STATE

Recall that the scholarship I have alluded to discusses blood as one element among
many, with the focus of its attention primarily on race. For my part, I have indicated that, although I share the concerns and commitments of race scholars and
activists, not to mention legal historians and philosophers of science, I am primarily interested in blood and in its reach. I have attempted to describe the hematological style in American politics, but above all I have been compelled to ask more
broadly about the nature of blood, the wider multiple fields it irrigates, and the
rhetorical force it assumes or propagates in the so-called modern state. That is why
I am inquiring after the vampire state. This is not to propose a new definition of the

state or to conduct a philosophical inquiry into the concept of the state, nor is it to argue for the homogeneity of the state or to engage in an anthropology of the state, in the kind of "political anatomy" famously evoked by Foucault, which would treat the state as an always already divided whole.[251] Recognizing the long-standing "vigorousness with which states still assert sovereign power,"[252] together with some of the older sources and resources of what Didier Fassin and Mariella Pandolfi have described as "contemporary states of emergency,"[253] what I am trying to formulate is a *political hematology*, an account that attends to the presence (or absence) of blood and its distribution, circulatory or other, through the realms and collectives that have constituted the modern state, from law to society, from economy to class, and from nation to science.

Consider, then, this early instance of the hematological style in American politics, less than twenty-five years after the promulgation of the first slave law in the Massachusetts colony, and very much in the same general area, perhaps the very same city, on the very same hill. Cotton Mather, who famously argued for (and against) the admissibility of "spectral evidence," wished to include "spectral blood" as well.[254] But listen to his father, Increase Mather, who comments, in 1669, on the blood of nations and the purity of the Jews.

> The providence of God hath suffered other nations to have their blood mixed very much, as you know it is with our own nation: there is a mixture of British, Roman, Saxon, Danish, [and] Norman blood. But as for the body of the Jewish nation, it is far otherwise. Let an English family live in Spain for five or six hundred years successively, and they will become Spaniards. But though a Jewish family live in Spain a thousand years, they do not degenerate into Spaniards (for the most part).[255]

And listen, closer still, to Samuel Sewall, who in 1700, initiated a famous debate on slavery.

> Few can endure to hear of a Negro's being made free; and indeed they can seldom use their freedom well; yet their continual aspiring after their forbidden Liberty renders them Unwilling Servants. And there is such a disparity in their Conditions, Color & Hair, that they can never embody with us, and grow up into orderly Families, to the Peopling of the Land, but still remain in our Body Politick as a kind of extravasat Blood.[256]

Both Mather and Sewall are explicitly writing as Christians, of course. Their concern, one could say, is religious or theological, or theologico-racial, to use an awkward and anachronistic construct. Yet the notion of the "extravasat blood" of the body politic—a flow that bursts the proper bounds of its vessels—just years after William Harvey discovered the circulation of the blood, suggests that blood is not exclusively confined to theology, science, nor indeed to "mere" rhetoric. As Tocqueville and Paine already made clear, blood is about all these and more. It is about law and about science, it is about commerce and about religion. More broadly put, blood is about politics, it is about the way "many Americans" have long "developed a strong sense of familial or communal boundaries and feared the intrusion of anyone who was palpably different."[257] It is about a politics writ large, the body politic as a whole, which includes the fields and realms I have just mentioned again. The "heavy judgment of God," for George Lawson, meant that in its recent wars "England gained great skill and experience both by sea and land, yet with the woeful expense of much of her own blood. And how happy had we been," he continues, "if so much valor had been manifested in the ruin of the enemies of Christ and his gospel."[258] As Walter Benjamin made clear for us, blood is about Christian politics. And much as the city of Venice, and Portia's wisdom, sought to protect an already well-defined "Christian blood" from the invading hands of an alien race, the American notion of an extravasat blood of the body politic brings into focus, and with devastating clarity it seems to me, a central problem of the vampire state in its very nature—a fluid one, to be sure.

The hematological style in American politics, of which Mather is an early instance, is therefore crucially related to, and revelatory of, a most expansive history of blood. It is, to be more precise, a testament to the rise of the vampire state, an event or chain of events that, in spite of the contested nature of the very concept of state, can be traced historically with some measure of confidence. As Timothy Mitchell formulated the problem, "it remains difficult to explain exactly what is meant by the concept of the state. There is no shortage of competing definitions. But a definition of the state always depends on distinguishing it from society, and the line between the two is difficult to draw in practice."[259] Yet, it is precisely when this distinction between the social and the political comes to be extensively understood by way of the body, natural or mechanical, that blood emerges as a salient problem. As does the state itself, of course. Indeed, "newer critics find the concept of the modern state looking more and more tired and unreal and unable to cope with the new problems and threats to human survival."[260] At the same time, "the concept has acquired immense institutional power and wide base within global mass culture. It has become an axiomatic part of conventional wisdom or common sense."[261] Now, this paradox, Ashis Nandy argues convincingly, has made it difficult, nay impossible, "to resist the pathologies of the modern state." But are these pathologies so easily discernible? What seems to be needed is a measure of

the unity and relative integrity of the state, which Karl Marx, for one, unequivocally identified as Christian, and precisely across its internal and external divisions
and differences.

This is where blood proves, I think, useful. Indeed, after Carl Schmitt, I have
suggested at the beginning of this book, one might even go so far as to assert that
"all concepts of the modern state are *liquidated* theological concepts." Recalling the multiple senses of "liquidity" (from material and financial liquidities,
through "employee liquidity" and "constant corporate liquidation"[262] all the way
to Zigmunt Bauman's "liquid modernity"), this would mean that the state must
be seen at once as the result of a history of liquefactions, coagulations, and the
consumptive dissolutions of that upon which it depends ("society"). The ensuing, dialectical integrity is what I am calling the vampire state, the hematology
of Christian politics.

In this context, the early representations of the body politic—I refer mostly to
medieval material I have begun to allude to—may acquire some renewed significance. For the concept of the state is articulated upon a dialectic that opposes the
organic to the mechanic, but also around a logic of members and parts, inclusion
and exclusion, inside and outside.[263] It is not just that the state "overawes" the individuals that have relinquished their political power to it, as Hannah Arendt had it
recalling Hobbes. It is rather that the state is indissociable from, and inextricably
dependent on, a community (or set of communities) defined by the imaginative
and organizing force of the Pauline contribution, by the fundamental role played
by Christ's body.[264] Now, to the best of my knowledge, this peculiar feature has not
been commented upon, yet it is striking that Western canonical representations
picture the political body as *bloodless*. Out of this strange vacuum, and at different
levels of explicitness and intentionality, the body of that state reveals and understands itself as empty of blood. As a result, and closer to premodern conceptions
of the body, it should not be surprising that the state engages in various acts of
feeding. Indeed, the state does not merely rule, command, or kill. It rather relies on,
sustains itself, and feeds on—producing and minimally maintaining, sometimes
itself sustaining—a number of "communities of blood." This should suffice to raise
questions with regard to the rhetorical (more precisely, metaphorical) understanding of Leviathan,[265] but note that the sense that links the body politic to a missing
or improperly extraneous ("extravasat") blood is much older, for the state has long
appeared to be suffering from a singular type of blood deficiency—or of excess.
Indeed, the state first emerges as (and along with) a community of blood, a community that, inscribed in the law, supplies it with what it needs or lacks, a community constructed by way of law and by way of ritual—akin to what Dante had
called "a market-place of blood and justice"—and through distinct modalities of

blood relations.[266] At the same time, and true to Sewall's concern with "extravasat blood," there is "the dread of excess blood."[267] The state operates, then, as "a plethoric body."[268] From the "mystical body of Christ" to the canonical notion and calculations of "consanguinitas," of blood as the foundational, legal concept for inheritance, family, and kinship, the medieval state expanded as a theologico-bio-juridical form, later metamorphosing into the modern state.[269] This, I already suggested, was the first disciplinary revolution, the moment when "flesh and blood" began to form, "for the average western Christian of the time, a major constituent of his 'world' or social environment,"[270] and when "families as well as the communal body of the Church were constituted through a shared blood."[271] Henceforward, the vampire state partakes of and refigures money (later political economy) as the blood of the state, the family (and kinship) as a sexual community of blood, the nation as a political community of blood, and race as the theological, later juridico-medical, community of blood. But the distinction between these forms or modalities of the community of blood should be understood, such is my contention, within the complex unity of the vampire state, the blood of which is constituted as an indispensable exteriority ("extravasat"), a set of exteriorities, the sources of its existence and nourishment. Representations of the social as the biological or physiologic (feeding) ground of the administrative (or, to follow Hobbes, the fictional and legal) machinery of the state might find here one of their sources and explanations.[272]

At first sight, the rise of blood to prominence in the life of Christian communities and in the Christian polity can hardly be seen as consistent with the disappearance of blood from its canonical representations in political thought or with the advance of modern history in its march away from blood identified by Foucault. The two moments (prominence and disappearance, visibility and invisibility) participate in the same transformation, a transformation in which blood must be recognized as structurally central, and uniquely so. The change occurs, then, at the very time the conception of the church as a mystical body, a conception inherited of course from Saint Paul, is undergoing a singular development. In this development, the theological metamorphosis of blood, the mystical body becomes the body politic, the visible community of Christians.[273] This is something that has been exceptionally traced and analyzed by Henri de Lubac as well as by Ernst Kantorowicz. But in a parallel, and paradoxical, development, blood remains, as I have said, conspicuously absent from canonical representations of this body politic, representations that, still drawing on Pauline imagery and conceptions, emerged and were disseminated between the twelfth and fifteenth centuries. The contradiction between these two transformations—visibility and invisibility, presence and absence—is only apparent.

There is to my knowledge no account that traces in a systematic way the transformations of the figure of the body politic, of the social and political community as body.[274] There are, of course, innumerable studies of the body, and important chapters have of course been written on the resource it provides and constitutes for social and political thought. More specifically, scholars as diverse as Mary Douglas, Judith Schlanger, Tilman Struve, David George Hale, and Leonard Barkan have long pointed out the importance—and detailed nature—of organic and bodily metaphors in the Western (and non-Western) political imagination, while others have traced the oscillations between organic and mechanical conceptions of the body politic.[275] The turning point constituted by what continues to be called "the Middle Ages" has been effectively analyzed, again, by de Lubac and Kantorowicz and many others since. Later periods have been covered as well, with the French Revolution providing much material, and German philosophy too.[276] Uniquely puzzling, and puzzlingly unique, is John Roger's contention that "at it mid-seventeenth century inception . . . the discourse of liberalism spread to the farthest reaches of cultural expression: like the spirited blood that for Harvey circulated throughout the entire human body, early liberalism labored to distribute itself throughout the whole body of contemporary intellectual practice."[277]

Rogers is not being metaphorical here—blood was "the matter of revolution," the liberal revolution—but he is being quite atypical in his attentiveness to blood (incidentally, the apparent absence of blood from liberal discourse—albeit not from liberal institutions, and not from conceptions of "depoliticized" property— would be deserving of such attentiveness as well).[278] Quentin Skinner, for his part, has compellingly described the moment when the body politic becomes nonorganic and indeed, "artificiall," a moment to which I shall return in a moment.[279] Yet throughout, with Adriana Cavarero as the sole exception I am aware of, little attention has been paid to the changes that, transcending the organic/mechanic distinction, have affected the figure of the body politic, and specifically with regard to what interests me here, namely, the presence, or more massively, the absence, of blood in the canonical instances that run from John of Salisbury and Dante to Christine de Pizan and all the way to Niccolò Machiavelli and Thomas Hobbes.[280] Although they do deploy a rhetoric of blood, "une théologie politique du sang," as Colette Beaune has it (mostly in referring to "bloodlines," to violence, of course, and to the blood of Jesus), none of these writers include blood, much less reflect on it, in their portrayal of the community as body.[281] It is as if, oscillating closer to and farther away from the plethoric body, the body politic was always already empty and devoid of blood as well, anemic and consumptive, one might even say *kenotic*.[282] As the notion and figure of the body politic becomes a widespread commonplace, at any rate, and while the whole of Western Christendom (and first in it, Christian women like Catherine of Sienna) is screaming for blood, ever more thirsting for blood when deprived of it (following well-known changes in the practice of the *eucharist sacrament* that increased the distance between the priest—and the wine cup—and the people)[283]; as the devout are feeling the increased vulnerability of Christian blood while they are gathered anew in the new understanding of the church as *corpus mysticum*[284]; at that very moment, then, we witness a determination of the body politic by blood (a determination that may become fully negative, in the separation or disappearance of blood—its "secularization," as it were).[285] Absent or present, at any rate, blood comes to define the community of Christians, old and new. Inverting the very precise terms that Saint Paul had offered for an understanding of Christian kinship as *spiritual*, the body politic is at once figured as a community (a kinship) of blood and depicted by political writers as bloodless.[286]

In presenting his illuminating account of the "purely artificial person of the state," Quentin Skinner draws the historical and argumentative lines we must follow, and according to which the paradoxical logic of a simultaneous appearance and disappearance of (the community of) blood from representations of the body politic may be understood. Dealing with a later and singular period, Skinner nonetheless locates Hobbes at the culminating point of a history whereby the community—the body politic—grants itself its representation, whereby it is represented as and by a figure that constitutes a different kind of body, a different kind of person.[287] This new body politic that recalls and transforms previous, medieval images of the community as body is the state. Hobbes's originality is not in question here, yet, as Skinner explains elsewhere, Hobbes's endeavor may be situated within a debate that deploys previously existing and indeed different conceptions of community, of sovereignty, as well as reflections on the status of the body politic. In this debate, Hobbes engaged, among others, "the so-called monarchs or king-killers."[288] Adapting "the Roman law theory of corporations," the monarchs were arguing that a people, a community, exists prior to any rule or government over it. In this view, the community lives "in a pre-political condition" in which it always has "the capacity to exercise a single will and make decisions with a single voice."[289] That is how it can proceed at a later stage to give itself a ruler, the existence and legitimacy of whom are clearly derivative. The community is thus already a body, it "can be viewed as a corporation," which may further grant itself a body, an additional *persona*, which, distinct from the people as a legal entity, can only act in its name. Hence, while the monarchs "stress that sovereignty is the property of a legal person, the person whom they treat as the bearer of sovereignty is always the *persona* constituted by the corporate body of the people, never the impersonal body of the *civitas* or *respublica* itself."[290] One could therefore show that the monomarchs considered sovereignty as an attribute that always already belonged to the community. "The body of the people remains at all time the possessor of 'supreme lordship,' and thus remains 'the lord of the commonwealth.' " [291] Sovereignty is immanent to a community that is always already constituted as community. For the monomarchs, the community is, one could say, bodily or *natural*.

Now, "it is precisely this monomarch view of the people as a natural unity capable of acting as one person that Hobbes aims to discredit." As Skinner explains, for Hobbes, the realm of politics is a realm of artifice that leaves nature behind (much as the state of nature is, famously, left behind). For Hobbes, "there is, in short, no natural unity outside the state; unity and community are attained only with the appointment of a representative." [292] There is, then, no transcendent God providing a sacred origin to government ("The state is a wholly human contrivance, not in the least an outcome of God's providence"), [293] nor is there an equally transcendent, if also natural, pre-political community granting itself its own sovereignty. Hobbes adamantly opposes the notion that there would be any kind of "organic community" or any kind of "organic unity" between a community and the will of the sovereign it chooses for itself. Hobbes does seek to maintain a fragile structure of transcendence, better yet, of quasi-transcendence, but it is one whereby the person of the state simply represents (which is to say, artificially or fictionally transcends) the community. Artificial as it is, the state has therefore no existence of its own.

> The state is not a natural person; on the contrary, there is a sense in which it more closely resembles a fictitious person such as Agamemnon in Aeschylus's play of that name. Agamemnon has no existence, except as words on a page, until he is brought to life by the skills of an actor who impersonates him and speaks his lines. The state likewise amounts to little more than a verbal entity in the absence of a sovereign to represent it and play its part in the world. [294]

Recall, then, that the community is no more natural than the state. Indeed, for Hobbes and other absolutists before him, "it is only as a result of submitting to a government that an aggregate of individuals ever becomes converted into a unified body of people." [295] The community neither precedes the state nor is it simply distinct from it. There is no natural union, and there is no natural community. There is, finally, no natural state. Without the state and "without a sovereign, the people are so far from being an *universitas* that they amount to nothing at all." In Hobbes's words, "A Common-wealth, without Sovereign Power, is but a word, without substance, and cannot stand." [296] This is why the community only comes into being at the same time as it grants itself a sovereign. The people, in other words, "only transform themselves into a collective body by way of instituting a sovereign." It makes therefore "no sense to think of them as a collective body setting limits in advance to the exercise of sovereign power."[297]

Unsurprisingly, then, Hobbes stands at a key moment, himself a hinge of sorts,[298] whence "natural philosophy" at once seals and begins a long process of division into realms such as science and politics, as Steven Shapin and Simon Shaffer have famously described, but also medicine and religion, law and culture.[299] Depending on whether we have ever been modern, the status of these divisions remains fragile at best, institutionally powerful and epistemologically misleading at worst—or vice versa, I suppose. But Hobbes establishes another massive chasm, this time between politics and economy, at once laying down the foundations of the modern state and deploying in one of its earliest instances a central concept of economic thought, indeed, a concept that Foucault put at the center of his reflections on political economy, sovereignty (wounded or not), and freedom, the concept of *circulation*.[300] Unsurprisingly, for a friend and disciple of William Harvey, but for reasons, and with a significance, that vastly exceed their personal connection, the crux of the matter, the matter at the crux, is blood. Recall that it is not until chapter 24 of *Leviathan* that Hobbes will finally introduce the blood of Leviathan, thus breaking decisively with the long tradition of bloodlessness I have mentioned earlier. Hobbes introduces blood as a shared substance of sorts, a communal ground or figure of accompaniment, or indeed a commonwealth, a ground or figure of community. The invocation of blood, at any rate, sustains and maintains the general theme of nourishment and of consumption. "By Concoction," writes Hobbes,

> I understand the reducing of all commodities, which are not presently consumed, but reserved for Nourishment in time to come . . . And this is nothing else but Gold, and Silver, and Mony. For Gold and Silver, being (as it happens) almost in all Countries of the world highly valued, is a commodious measure of the value of all things else between Nations; and Mony (of what matter soever coyned by the Soveraign of a Common-wealth,) is a sufficient measure of the value of all things else, between the Subjects of that Common-wealth. By the means of which measures, all commodities, Moveable, and Immoveable, are made to accompany a man, to all places of his resort, within and without the place of his ordinary residence; and the same passeth from Man to Man, within the Common-wealth; and goes round about, Nourishing (as it passeth) every part thereof; In so much as this Concoction, is as it were the Sanguification of the Common-wealth: For natural Bloud is in like manner made of the fruits of the Earth; and circulating, nourisheth by the way, every Member of the Body of Man. . . . And in this also, the Artificiall Man maintains his resemblance with

the Naturall; whose Veins receiving the Bloud from the severall Parts of the Body, carry it to the Heart, where being made Vitall, the Heart by the Arteries sends it out again, to enliven, and enable for motion all the Members of the same.[301]

Following as strictly as possible the difficult logic of this passage, Leviathan at once has and does not have blood. Aside from its delayed appearance in the text, a delay that opens the chasm that haunts us still between politics and economics, blood also oscillates between inside and outside, "within and without the place," passing from man to man and between them, accompanying them, but circulating as well within them, within the body of man, natural and artificial, pushed by the heart, which sends out what is already within every member of the body. Is the blood here deployed always in its place? Can it ever be? Or is it not a blood, always already bloods, that remain, as it were constitutively, in a dual relation of interiority and alterity to the body politic, always already "extravasat blood"? As I suggested earlier, this community that is not one—the community of blood that is a community of gold, the collective fruits of the earth, that are and are not the "common wealth" of mankind—is only one of the communities of blood that are, from Hobbes onward, being instituted. Henceforth, one finds a proliferation of "the extremely common metaphors comparing money, circulating through the nation, to blood circulating through the body." As Michael O'Malley puts it, "Thomas Hobbes understood money as the blood in Leviathan's body, and the metaphor served pro-slavery Southerner John C. Calhoun equally well nearly two hundred years later. 'The currency of a country is to the community,' Calhoun wrote in 1837, 'what the blood is to the body . . . indispensable to all the functions of life.'" And "what is race," pursues O'Malley, "but a theory of purity in blood?"[302]

The vampire state comes into existence with the naturalized institution of a number of plausible and implausible communities of blood: the sexual community of blood, which is also a legal and economic community of blood (kinship and the family; inheritance and property); the social community of blood (the nobility, later the nation); the racial community of blood (the white race, the dark races); and of course the theological community of blood that we explored in the previous chapter. It might become a matter of debate whether the more abstract gathering Hobbes describes (money and commerce as "collectives" making up the blood of Leviathan) can be thought as offering a displaced model of sorts for the others. As we shall see in the next chapter at any rate, the notion will greatly serve political economy all the way to Moses Hess and Karl Marx, who were among the first to recognize the vampiric nature of the modern, capitalist state, what I am referring to here as the vampire state. Note, however, that these different communities—of which Rob Latham's "consuming youth" is but a recent instance—are contingent plausibilities rather than essential necessities.[303] They do mark a need for blood, but in themselves they are by no means necessary elements of the vampire state. They occur as, and proceed from, a widespread and structural inscription of blood, a naturalization of blood, as well as from a concomitant logic of exploitation. This, then, is where necessity lies: the bloodless body of the vampire state rules over, it lives with and feeds on a community of blood, whether that community is the nation it upholds or the races it excoriates, whether the blood is the one it sings, spills, cleanses, or feeds on, or whether it is "the extravasat blood" of the body politic. The American exception, when it comes to race, loses here once and for all its credibility (of which it had little to spare at any rate, when considered historically). For a hematological perspective enables us to observe a more general dependence on a community of blood, a dependence that is more or less exploitative, more or less bloody. It is a question of degrees, in other words, and not of kind. It is a matter of blood quantum, if I may put it that way, a continuum of blood that defines the vampire state. And I do wish to inquire further into this commensurability of the community of blood, later the national or racial community, and to do so precisely in order to demonstrate that its distinction from a theologically founded community of blood is fragile at best, obfuscating at worst, and rather clearly located, at any rate, on a hematological continuum.

ᛝᛝ ᛝᛝ ᛝᛝ

At the beginning of this chapter, I have referred to the rhetorical problem blood constitutes. There is, if I may reiterate it here in this way, a very basic *mistake* that continues to be made when blood is being spoken about. The sheer mention of blood in any context, we are repeatedly told, is a reference (metaphorical as it may be; entirely fictive even) to *biology*, to the most basic physiologic given.[304] Blood would be a name or a metaphor for the physiologic, a natural designation, as it were, for the organic and for the natural—changing or unchanging—but again and again, for the biological. It would be a privileged but recurring—and this for all times, in all places—figure for procreation and for ancestry, as well as the carrier of some or all physiologic traits. Blood is even described as a metaphor for race, the "one metaphor of racial identity [that] has held particular sway with respect to the rights and citizenship of native peoples: race as blood."[305] In one way or another, alternatively, blood would always have belonged to the history of medicine (or to its "magical" antecedents), to it primarily and, finally, *exclusively*. The rest, the rest in its entirety, is mere commentary, and more precisely, mere metaphoric, or allegorical, interpretation (a deviation within which the history of race fits very well, as we have seen). Everywhere, and throughout history, people would have understood blood first and primarily as a material substance that runs through the veins and that conveys some essential information about the person, that defines the person in some determining aspect or measure of who they are. Accessorily, blood would have been the mark and bearer of heredity as well. The only question—if it ever were one—would then be, not what the literal understanding of blood might have been; certainly not ever whether blood in fact partakes of a secure division between the literal and the figurative; and never whether blood might belong to a field or sphere (or to many), one that might be *mediated* in any manner. No, the only question is, again: At what point does blood (always "real blood," of course) *become* a metaphor, and a ruling one at that. But even this question is hardly asked, of course. Most people simply appear to know that if blood is invoked in a way that does not correspond to their expectations, if money is called blood for example, or if roads are said to be the lifeblood of the state, or if blackness is found in one drop of blood—all these are merely "figures of speech."[306] In these cases and more, blood is *not* literal blood, not actual blood, not the material substance that runs in our veins. For this knowledge remains secure. In fact, everything is as if we have always known what blood *really* is, and better yet, what it has always really been. What Spinoza alerted us to, however (which the circulating argument of these pages seeks to confirm), is the contingency of this understanding, along with the arbitrariness of the notion that blood is a figure for the collective—any collective. It is not so much a question of what blood is, then, but rather of what the metonymic link between part and whole in the history of blood is if it turns out not to be contained within the history of medicine or the history of biology, the history of law or that of politics. If we acknowledge this, we might be able to recognize that the history of blood, its secret or covert history, as it were, involves the becoming-fact of a figurative relation between part and whole, such as has been involved in collective understanding.[307] More importantly, we may come to wonder at the selection of this peculiar "part" that blood may or may not be, in order to signify the whole, the family, the clan, the tribe, later, the race, the class, and the nation, along with the processes these operate with (production, circulation, consumption). No history of blood should be able to ignore this. No history of the one-drop rule either. Indeed, even if we go back to Herodotus (as we shall in chapter 4), it should become clear that we have no way of establishing that "blood," "common blood (*homaimon*)," ever served to *distinguish* between the Hellenes and the others. Instead, if we know that the Greeks distinguished themselves from all others on the basis of language and customs, blood—whatever it is in this context—loses a great deal of the significance we have retrospectively attributed to it.[308] It is moreover the fact of a difference, of a distinction *between bloods* that is, I think, essential to consider: not only that blood is a figure for the collective, but also that it is a crucial site of distinction *between* collectives—and between realms like law and science, economy or politics. Only then could the number of drops necessary to make or unmake the difference come to matter at all.

Now, if there is a mistake, a historical error that has been made and that continues to be made, if blood has been deployed for some time now as a privileged signifier for biology or for physicality, as well as for collective references (from family to nation, with much in between), if blood has been found across so many regions of being, the question that emerges is not only whence the source of that error, but also of the reasons for its endurance. More important, it may well be that that error itself tells us about who we are, we who unwittingly insist on exploring it, perpetuating it. I will get to this, of course. Yet, I am not proposing a causal explanation here. I have already indicated that I am rather more concerned with attending to a different, plausibly founding but at any rate telling, moment in the "secret" history of blood. It is secret because it has yet to figure in any of the genealogies of what would later (and without anachronism) be called "racism." Nor does it figure as one of these exceptional moments where an "obsession with blood" would have erupted along with other "ethnic" irrationalities. In another sense, what I am about to discuss is hardly a secret, much less original or unknown, but it has not been enlisted toward a delivering of blood to intelligibility, toward a demonstration of the ways in which blood, like the real, has been possible. It is merely a moment, which I want to propose should be part of our reflections on the one-drop rule, a moment at which blood becomes a practical marker of difference, as well as an unequivocal theologico-political sign and site of a radical asymmetry between collectives.

It should come as no surprise, then, that what I want to conclude with has *nothing* directly to do with race or with biology or even with medicine.[309] Allow me to underscore, however, that it has everything to do with blood. And what I mean by this is that blood can still be understood *literally* without yet having to invoke the rhetorical resources of these overdetermined spheres of existence or science (race, biology, medicine, culture). To the contrary, one *must* understand blood literally and do so precisely outside of these spheres, and with studied indifference to them. As I have been suggesting, in order to perceive the vampire state and its limits, one must rather consider blood, literal blood, material blood, as a theologico-political substance that reaches across and between realms that only appear to have nothing to do with "literal" (that is, narrowly understood) blood. Now, part of me wishes there were not so literal—precisely—an illustration, so bloody an illustration, but as we shall see, it will enable us to make considerable advances on our way toward a history of the one-drop rule, a rule that, over against the current state evidence, has not quite been abolished yet. Nor has its dominion precisely contracted. The empire of blood—the vampire state—is still ahead of us.

I am talking about a revolution. It is a revolution that is usually dated 1058 (or 1075 and even 1122, but allow me to leave the matter of precise dating to the historians), and it sets up the entirety of the theologico-political problem as it has come to persist rather than be resolved. The revolution took place as the empire of blood was coming about. One could even go so far as saying that it took place *as* the empire of blood—period. Harold Berman, at any rate, credits this momentous event with "the formation of the Western legal tradition," explaining that "all the modern Western legal systems originated right in the middle of the Middle Ages."[310] More important, "the Papal Revolution gave birth to the modern Western state" (113). It made Christianity "into a political and legal program" (528). This is no outlandish claim. Gerd Tellenbach, a sober German scholar, described the effects of the Investiture Contest (for that is what our revolution, the papal revolution, is also called) as "a great revolution in world-history," which established a new dominion, indeed an empire, for the church in this earthly world.[311] For Tellenbach, it is "the greatest—from the spiritual point of view perhaps the only—turning point in the history of Catholic Christendom" (164). With it, "the world was drawn into the Church, and the leading spirits of the new age made it their aim to establish the 'right order' in this united Christian world" (164). This was also "the first great age of propaganda in world-history," and it embarked the church, Western Christendom, on the path of the conversion of the world, a world-historical task indeed.[312] What emerges, I hurry to assuage potential concerns, was an accidental empire, of course. None expected or even wished for it as such. It too came about in a fit of absence of mind, in other words. As Tellenbach describes it, it is in fact "astonishing with what suddenness the basic ideas of the Investiture Contest appear" (110). Along with the events, which hastened its development, the ideas that gave rise to them "were insignificant from the standpoint of the contemporary Church and fortuitous from that of the modern historian" (108). And yet, there is no doubt that it was a world-historical revolution, which drastically diminished the theocratic power of the king and emperor, distinguished more powerfully between the Augustinian cities while enabling an ever more active and wide-ranging involvement of one in the other, the ever more active and wide-ranging involvement of the church in this world.

> Thus a new and victorious strength was lent to the old belief in the saving grace of the sacraments and to the hierarchical conceptions based on their administration. Out of this arose the conviction that the Christian peoples of the West formed the true City of God, and as a result the leaders of the Church were able to abandon their ancient aversion from the wickedness of worldly men and to feel themselves called upon to re-order earthly life in accordance with divine precept. (163)

Along with the "age-old Catholic ideas" of righteousness, hierarchy, and the proper standing of everyone before God, many more ideas and movements were here at work. And truly, "it would be incorrect to treat these and related ideas as the personal discoveries of St. Augustine or any other particular individual among the early Fathers, or to attempt to trace out exactly the stages by which [Pope] Gregory [VII] is supposed to have inherited them" (165). What is clear is that the developments in question "would have been impossible if a preexisting community, the *populus christianus*, had not been formed in Europe between the fifth and eleventh centuries."[313] By the time it became fully formed, though, blood—in drops, rivers, or floods—would come to play a significant role. And it is blood, in a nutshell, that brings me to Tomaž Mastnak's groundbreaking, if largely ignored, argument, and to a hitherto less noticed dimension of the papal revolution.[314]

"Traditionally," Mastnak explains, "the Church had been averse to the shedding of blood. *Ecclesia abhorret a sanguine* was a principle ever present in patristic writings and conciliar legislation."[315] What this meant was that killing—shedding blood, in the inherited, biblical parlance—no matter whose and no matter the circumstances, was considered a sin. "Even killing a pagan was homicide," which means that this clearly was an awfully serious rule. Indeed, "from the fourth century to the eleventh century, the Church as a rule imposed disciplinary measures on those who killed in war, or at least recommended that they do penance" (16). One pope had referred to bishops who did engage in warfare as "false priests" because "their hands were 'stained with human blood' "; another referred to "proponents of war" as "sons of the devil" (14). What changed, then? The exception became the rule, and a different rule it was. Talk about a revolution. What happened is that the idea of warfare became licit; that violence and the shedding of blood became *permissible* rather than something impossible to avoid or outright condemned. And Pope Gregory VII, all too easy to blame at this point, the same pope "after whom the Church reform has been called, is [also] held responsible for the profound changes in the Christian attitude toward bearing arms that this idea [of licit warfare] implied" (18). His followers, Alexander II and Urban II, did lend a helping hand. They were accessory to the perfect murder, as it were, and hardly a bloodless one. There were others, of course, who joined the efforts of the emerging *populus christianus*, the Christian people. The most dramatic change at any rate occurred in 1054 (the year of the *filioque* controversy, which hardened the schism between the Eastern and Western churches) in the city of Narbonne.[316] Prior to this "peace council," there had been a rule, which, true to the church's abhorrence of blood, had "prohibited the shedding of human blood." Yet, and to make a long story short, "the councilors of Narbonne substituted, as it were, the word *Christian* for the world *human*."[317] They also declared, for good reiterative measure, that "no

Christian should kill another Christian, for whoever kills a Christian undoubtedly sheds the blood of Christ [*quia qui Christianum occidit, sine dubio Christi sanguinem fundit*]" (37 & 37n215). This was a giant step indeed, if not necessarily for humankind, at least for God. For whereas it had earlier been recognized, as Alexander II wrote, that "God is not pleased by the spilling of blood, nor does he rejoice in the perdition of the evil one," and whereas "all laws, ecclesiastical as well as secular, forbid the shedding of human blood," it was now becoming possible to enact, practice and enforce, for the love of God, a newfound distinction *between bloods*.[318] This great step was in need of only one additional and very light push. Urban II is the one who obliged. It was under his watch that it became "not only permissible but eminently *salutary* to use arms"—against whom? Against the infidel enemy, of course. War "against the enemies of God" quickly became "meritorious," it was "divinely ordered" (50). From there on, things took a rapid and increasingly bloody turn. Heads would soon begin to fall all the way to Jerusalem, where, as one medieval chronicle describes it, "men rode in blood up to their knees and the bridle reins." This is hardly a lone event in history, of course, which may be why the same writer goes on to add its singular dimension in the *longue durée*, namely, "that it was a just and splendid judgment of God, that this place should be filled with the blood of unbelievers, since it had suffered so long from their blasphemies."[319] Thus it was that the Peace of God ("no Christian should kill another Christian, for whoever kills a Christian undoubtedly sheds the blood of Christ") became the occasion for a new and novel notion of interventionism, a Christian interventionism, for the newfound and radical involvement of the church in a world of men newly divided. "Intus Pax, foris terrores" (95). Call it peace as the War on Terror. More important, at least for our purposes, *Christianitas*, which had surely begun to take shape "among the various preconditions of the crusading movement," was now reaching an accomplished stage. It was establishing itself as "*populus Christianus*, the Christian people, united under the supreme authority of the pope . . . bound together as Christendom [in] a common worldly pursuit and a common army . . . fighting for the Christian *res publica*, the common weal" (92–93).

"Like his peacemaking predecessors," Urban II was filled with good intentions. (Incidentally, one reviewer criticized Mastnak, unfairly I think, for refusing to "accept that Westerners associated with the crusades"—allow me to repeat this beautiful turn of phrase: "*Westerners associated with* the crusades were ever well intentioned."[320]) This pope too "condemned fratricidal wars in the West" (94). What was intolerable to him, indeed, unconscionable, was the spilling of Christian blood. Thus was the world divided. "*Effunditur sanguis Christianus, Christi sanguine redemptus* . . . Christian blood, redeemed by the blood of Christ, has been shed," he used to lament. And what he was thereby articulating was, Mastnak says, a new kind of "blood-brotherhood—the founding of Christian unity in blood" (94). This was, let me repeat this too, all well intended, all in the name of love, in other words, if not the love of blood (actually, it now depends *which* blood, doesn't it?). Which is why John of Salisbury wrote that he would refrain from calling those "whose normal occupation it is to shed human blood," those who "wage legitimate war 'men of blood,' since even [King] David was called a man of blood not because he engaged in wars which were legitimate but on account of Uriah, whose blood he criminally shed."[321] You could shed blood in the name of love, therefore, without becoming a man of blood. Or, shedding that blood that is not one (not true blood, that is, not one like Christian blood), you would thereby join in the brotherhood. You could become, you had become, a different man of blood, a man of different blood, as "the substance of that brotherhood was blood, consanguinity in faith. And once faith was filled with blood, it was just a short step to the letting of blood of the unfaithful. Or rather, if faith was in blood, with the shedding of unfaithful blood, unbelief was drained" (126). The church, which had long "considered bloodshed as a source of pollution, now encouraged the shedding of blood—non-Christian blood—as a means to purification. When the reformed Church established its domination over Christendom, Christendom launched a military offensive to establish its domination over the world" (129). Bernard of Clairvaux was yet another, among many others, who decided to join the Christian war effort and brought to it more novelty in the form of his propitious doctrine of *malicidium*, the killing of evil. "The soldier of Christ, Bernard was to repeat, is safe when he kills, even safer when he is killed. If he is killed, it is for his own good; if he kills, he does it for Christ."[322] Others, from Pierre Dubois to Catherine of Sienna, would later support our troops and lend another helping hand. But we ain't seen nothin' yet. This was only the beginning, and the Eucharist, along with the doctrine of transubstantiation, had yet to come. It would take these and a few more additional steps for Christian blood to become fully distinct and distinguished, for it to become pure and "wonderful blood," as Caroline Walker Bynum describes it (though I should mention that Bynum writes about a later period and never refers to Mastnak's work). By then, one would of course come to wonder, with Catherine of Sienna, "how anyone except Christ could save souls by shedding blood, especially the blood of others." In this too, I suppose, there "remained a mystery," one that had been "embedded in the context of the crusade, itself seen as a mystery" (345). One might further wonder how the shedding of blood could ever become the saving of souls—the blood and soul of others too. But of one thing, one could nonetheless be certain. It was that when it came to Christian blood, every drop would count. Christian blood, at any rate, would become completely distinct, completely good, and, more importantly, completely pure—if also vulnerable to all kinds of attacks and contaminations ("If thou dost shed / One drop of Christian blood . . ." warns fair Portia, echoing Bassanio's earlier promise to Antonio: "The Jew shall have my flesh, blood, bones, and all / Ere thou shalt lose for me one drop of blood").[323] As for the blood of others, what can I say? It was indeed on its way to start flowing in rivers and in floods. Alternatively, it was to be weighed and measured, sometimes just in drops: drop by drop. And note, by way of a later example, that "in the early seventeenth century, before slavery was rooted in the British mainland colonies, a person's treatment depended on whether or not he was Christian."[324] By blood then. Nor was this the first or the last time. What would no longer be in doubt by then was that there was a difference between bloods, that there was a blood that was—shall we say, *essentially*?—a different and lesser blood. It had undergone a first and gigantic transformation toward an asymmetric universality, a generalized hematology, an indubitable foundation of Western, which is to say, Christian, politics, and the establishment of the vampire state.

Three CAPITAL
(CHRISTIANS AND MONEY)

"ALL THAT IS solid melts into air, all that is holy is profaned [*Alles Ständische und Stehende verdampft, alles Heilige wird entweiht*]."[1] Among the many striking phrases and slogans of the *Communist Manifesto*, few evoke "the spirit of capitalism" as powerfully as this. I write "spirit" advisedly because, partaking as it does of the "hauntology" Derrida strikingly elaborated, the phrase and its movement from the stable to the vaporous must certainly be read as announcing uncanny abstractions, along with advances in intellectuality, secularization theses, metaphorical versions and conversions, and more Freudian sublimations and their vicissitudes.[2] "All that is solid melts into air, all that is holy is profaned." This divulges new arrangements, "chains of metamorphoses," in a lengthy process that, in Michel Serres's rendering, opens with "the law of fire" and ends with "the law of sublimation."[3] According to the former, "there is no 'naturally' vaporous gas, nor is there an essentially gaseous water vapor. They are both *volatilizations* in which the fundamental element can be discovered by careful observation—whence the law of *sublimation*, namely, direct passage from one limit state to the limit at its farthest remove, from solid to gas without passage through a liquid intermediary."[4] No doubt Deleuze and Guattari were reacting to this excluded middle, to its reversals and elliptical metamorphoses; they were responding to the literal force and topicality of the phrase when they wrote that "we witness a transformation of substances and a dissolution of forms, a passage to the limit or flight from contours in favor of fluid forces, flows, air, light, and matter, such that a body or a word does not end at a precise point."[5] Like all-too numerous specters and spirits, and expansively memorialized in Marshall Berman's book,[6] the phrase crowds, and has come to occupy, if not Wall Street, many an atmosphere with its paradoxical emptiness, "a dissolution of forms," which is ultimately charged with the heaviness of precious and less precious metals, chemicals, and gases that, rising temperatures or not, have long rendered toxic the very air we breathe and the water we drink, while *liquidating* much of our collective existence.[7] In this way, if only in this way, and because of the obvious, albeit novel, cycle it attends to, the *Communist Manifesto* enjoins or warns us to linger and dwell with the spirit and its figures, the famous "spirit of capitalism," and even "the new spirit of capitalism."[8] "All that is solid melts into air, all that is holy is profaned." Stranger still, the phrase may move us yet, not so much away from the ethereal (and what William Connolly aptly calls "the volatility of capitalism") as closer to "the spirit's tidal wave."[9] Goethe's *Faust* (and Alexander Sokurov's too) familiarized us with these damp quarters, with such alchemical descents, moves, and transformations from the lofty air down to the murky realms of liquidity—or vice versa. At their receiving end, Zygmunt Bauman reminds us, "melting the solids" has come to mean by definition "dissolving whatever persists over time and is negligent of its passage or immune to its flow."[10] Surely, the operations of hydraulic systems, the liquidity of "fluid forces" and networks of capitalism, the flows of circulation or indeed of dissolution ("constant revolutionizing of production, uninterrupted disturbance of all social conditions, everlasting uncertainty and agitation . . . all fixed, fast-frozen relations, with their train of ancient and venerable prejudices and opinions, are swept-away, all new-formed ones become antiquated before they can ossify"),[11] none of these should distract us from meditating on hauntology, but they can bring us to focalize on one of its more manifest, if perhaps under-theorized (or over-historicized), dimensions.[12]

Betwixt and between the flesh and the spirit, between solid and subtle by way of liquidity, there would be found capitalism and its spirit or spirits. And in this spirit, indeed, J. K. Graham-Gibson contributes a proximate illustration, highlighting "the seminal fluid of capitalism—finance capital (or money)—which has more traditionally been represented as the lifeblood of the economic system whose free circulation ensures health and growth of the capitalist body. As seminal fluid, however, it periodically breaks its bounds, unleashing uncontrollable gushes of capital that flow every which way, including into self-destruction."[13] Should their liquefactive existence, metaphoric or otherwise, be granted, such representations, such destinations, along with their fluid determinations, are hardly seized in a simple or linear fashion, although Marx himself did suggest we read the writing on the wall, follow the directions, and abide by the literalizing signs. Perhaps evoking a revolutionary replay of the Exodus from Egypt, Marx was warning in 1856 that "all the houses of Europe are now marked with the mysterious red cross" ("History is the judge," he went on to clarify, "its executioner, the proletarian"). At the time, Marx was taking it upon himself to revisit and reframe the revolutions, the "so-called revolutions of 1848."[14] He made a point of describing the bloody events themselves not only in stable, telluric, but also in liquefying, indeed, liquidating terms. For now, Marx wrote, the so-called revolutions, of which there would be more, were "poor incidents—small fractures and fissures in the dry crust of European society. However, they denounced the abyss. Beneath the apparently solid surface, they betrayed oceans of liquid matter, only needing expansion to rend into fragments continents of hard rock."[15] In his unusual attention to "liquid matter," to powerful sources and resources of submerged energy, rising waters turned to blood, Marx was of course looking back to a venerable tradition of "natural metaphors" in economic and political thought.[16] He was also being prescient in more than one way about the future that is now. Consider, for instance, that recently revisiting "the linkages that were constructed between fossil fuels and the forms of mid-twentieth century democracy: the mechanisms that tied together democracy in the West, flows of oil and the value of the US dollar,"[17] Timothy Mitchell harkens back to none other than Marx, as he reminds us of the fluidity of oil and its multiple relevance (some went so far as to describe oil as "a currency in itself"), an essential, indeed tectonic, moment in a long and complex narrative. But the feeders and tributaries are many among the enduring movements of capital, the occurrence and recurrence of revolutions, and the flows of blood.[18] Back in 1843, a Glasgow newspaper columnist had already pointed out that "the temperature of the blood is regulated by the stock exchange barometer."[19] Down the line, and reading along, Norman O. Brown saw with typical clarity that "a need for hemorrhage is built into the system."[20]

Marx's concerns with melted and submerged resources also evokes another register. It is at any rate recognizably related to, perhaps saturated by, his well-known preoccupation with a range of oozing and guzzling beings, melancholy creatures of the occult, although not necessarily, as I have said, in a linear manner. Many have signaled toward the importance of vampires and zombies and their relation to the spirit of capitalism as diagnosed by Marx, what Henry Giroux recently referred to as "Zombie Politics and Other Late Modern Monstrosities in the Age of Disposability."[21] Larry Rickels compellingly attends to some of the inclusive reaches of these links and rhetorical conduits, pointing out that in "Marx's discourse of mixed metaphors, the vampire goes to capital while the werewolf gets assigned the role of capitalist driven to replace living labor with dead labor."[22] Attending to the metaphorical and literal dimensions of what she calls the "market metabolisms" of "animal capital," whereby "animal trimmings, bones, offal, and blood" are repeatedly, nefariously, and multifariously recycled, Nicole Shukin credits Derrida and others for drawing our "attention to a biopolitical violence constituted by the power to keep animal life in a limbo economy of interminable survival, one equal to if not greater than the violence of *liquidating* animal life and extinguishing species."[23] From human to animal and from ghost to vampire, from vampire to werewolf too, trajectories can be detected that take us from gaseous to fluid, and from liquid to telluric and back. Here too, here again, however, between the holy and the profane, the material and the spiritual, the figurative and the spectral, it is not entirely clear where liquid finds its place. And which liquid is this really? What, if any, is its nature? For what interests me here is not, it should already be clear, hydraulics, nor is it quite "somaeconomics," and not even "bioeconomics" (as Catherine Gallagher proposes). It is, in other words, neither the relative solidity of vampires nor the ethereality of ghosts, but rather the fluid and mediatic quality, the insistence and the quiet ubiquity, of a recurring element that "periodically breaks its bounds, unleashing uncontrollable gushes of capital that flow every which way, including into self-destruction" (Graham-Gibson). And one question we might have to begin with is whether this element, blood, in Marx and elsewhere in the discourse and practices of political economy, belongs in any precise manner to a figurative or metaphoric field. Is blood one of Marx's analogies, a "mere" rhetorical moment among "irony, allegory, and capital," such as Jennifer Bajorek identifies, or an affected and contrived reminder that capitalism is, as if we did not know, essentially predatory? Does blood not testify instead to the lasting, if forgotten, impact of William Harvey's discoveries or does it demonstrate the indispensable recourse to literature, the general insertion and mutual reliance of medicine and metaphor in the lexicon of economics?[24] Rickels refers to the complex entanglements of these and other vectors when he writes that "the transformation brought to us by the vampiric blood bond dissolves the uniqueness of an individual life by releasing its social character or caricature, which runs alongside the transformed life, like, keeping up with another one of Marx's analogies, price alongside commodity" (268). Blood would therefore mediate and transform the literal into the figurative, and vice versa. It would signify as well the literal dissolution of individual and social life, the liquidation of animal life. It should therefore be increasingly obvious that the dissolution of which the *Manifesto* speaks cannot be confined to the rhetorical or figurative realm, much less dismissed as a fossilized abstraction.[25] Here too senses and connotations "bleed" into each other.[26] Which is another way to say, as Shukin does, that there are signifiers the "singular mimetic capaciousness" of which "functions as a hinge allowing powerful discourses to flip or vacillate between literal and figurative economies of sense."[27] Minimally, for our purpose here, the devastating flows of capital would be oscillating between animal and spirit, among earth, air, and blood alike, as well as within the figures and things that otherwise attract, abstract, or distract our

attention (the vampires and the werewolves, the individual life and the carica-
tures, social and animal life and their futures).

It is nevertheless remarkable that, however concealed or manifest, blood appears
to be of an altogether different nature in these variously buried or floating accounts.
After all, blood is an element that is simultaneously like and unlike air—or spirit.
Blood must no doubt be perceived or conceived according to rhetorical registers,
and based on the materialist (or idealist) protocols we have implicitly encountered
thus far. Accordingly, we might easily enough come to see blood literally, as it were;
to acknowledge it as that into which all that is solid melts, working along or bringing about the punishing and accelerating flow of time as the flow of capital. Blood
for oil, one might say, and for much else. To this precise extent, though, between
materialism and idealism, blood must be seen at once as an element and a medium
rather than a stable figure. I have begun to suggest, moreover, that blood is transformative as well. It is not merely an end result of the melting process but what
effectuates the dissolving and the transforming. Blood is not only that into which
everything melts, in other words. It is in fact the melting agent. Like money and
capital, like oil and like revolutions, blood circulates and converts everything. Blood
circulates and moves anything—from solid to air, from the holy to the profane. But
blood has a history and it cannot be so easily generalized, much less naturalized.
Its revolutions shall not be metaphorized either, nor will they be secularized, as I
will argue shortly. Rather akin to Hegel's reason, its emergence, ubiquity, and persistence make blood appear as "the fluid universal Substance [*die flüssige allgemeine
Substanz*], as unchangeable simple thinghood, which yet bursts asunder into many
completely independent beings."[28] Found at all stages of the capitalist (and modernization) process, blood is the element and the process. Or, as Hegel again puts it,
blood appears as the "simple infinity, or the absolute Notion [which] may be called
the simple essence of life, the soul of the world, the universal blood [*das allgemeine
Blut*], whose omnipresence is neither disturbed nor interrupted by any difference,
but rather is itself every difference, as also their supersession; it pulsates within itself
but does not move, inwardly vibrates, yet is at rest. It is self-identical, for the differences are tautological; they are differences that are none."[29] Marx was not alone,
then, in suggesting, however indirectly, that all that is solid melts in fact into blood,
that all that is holy is profaned. As he "limns the dismembering drives of capital" and
"underlines the corporeal realities of fetishisation," Marx might have found another
way of saying that there *will* be blood (recall Foucault's periodization).[30] Or perhaps
there will be bloods. In an abbreviated manner, at any rate, and in deceptively recognizable terms, Marx is saying that blood is religion. It is at least one religion. The
spirit of capitalism, therefore, or so I shall find myself compelled to contend, is a
kind of hematology. It is economic theology as hematology.

ECONOMIC THEOLOGY

After Marx, but also before him, have we not heard it said enough that economy is soaked in blood, that "all money is blood money"?[31] This would constitute one reason at least why it is necessary today to turn or return to *economic theology*.[32] Economic theology is the history of blood and money, and it accounts for the long faithful and benevolent credit granted to money, a credit that Egidius Berns has so aptly commented upon in its philosophical and historical, contemporary relevance (*Secrets of the Millionaire Mind* puts it best, no doubt, when it offers the following canticle: "I admire rich people! I bless rich people! I love rich people! And I'm going to be one of those rich people too!")[33] But how did money, "the earning of more and more money," become this *summum bonum*, the natural site of such extreme "devotion to the calling of making money"?[34] To bring peace, perhaps, ever so remote peace or even eternal peace—for which Immanuel Kant believed along with almost everyone else, that what was needed was the power of money, "perhaps the most dependable of all powers included under the state power . . . to promote honorable peace and by mediation to prevent war wherever it threatens to break out."[35] Otherwise put—do we not believe it still, say that we do as if uttering an article of faith?—"the spirit of commerce . . . cannot exist side by side with war."[36] Call it, as Albert Hirschman did, "the passions and the interests." (Bernard Harcourt proposes an adjacent and illuminating version, an internal and domestic formulation, as it were, when he writes of the "exceptional relationship between markets and punishment: natural orderliness in the economic sphere, but government intervention in the penal realm."[37])

No doubt there is more to war (or punishment, capital, and otherwise) than blood, and more to blood than money. And vice versa. There is, in other words, more difference *between bloods*, and as Shakespeare's Salarino suggests to the economic enemy, Shylock, "more between your bloods" than sheer economics.[38] There is also religion. From Shakespeare to Marx, from Weber, Benjamin, and Tawney, to Bataille, Dumont, and, more recently, Lyotard, Shell, Taylor, Goodchild, and Agamben, the link between religion and economics, and more specifically between religion and the exponential growth of modern capitalism, has occupied many a mind.[39] Jesus himself had, after all, uniquely located economics, and more precisely, money, at the center of his political theology, distinguishing between God and Caesar on the face of a silver coin.[40] The related, structural, and perhaps fatal, oscillation between God and mammon was at the center of Marx's early account of "how *money* has become a world power" and how "the Christians have become Jews."[41] Indeed, by "seeking to grasp state and money as a sort of religion," the last of the Schoolmen (in R. H. Tawney's famous phrase) was conducting a scrupulous critique of religion, an analysis of economic theology—otherwise called, "the riddle of the money fetish" as well as "a process of social metabolism." And "he never abandoned this project."[42] By deploying and highlighting the vocabulary of Christian theology (transubstantiation, incarnation, conversion, and, of course, fetishism, thereby underscoring the range of its associations from saving and redeeming to credit and trust, from faith and goods to In God We Trust), Marx reminded us that the critique of political economy is also the critique of religion, that economy *is* religion.[43] Thus, a critique of religion that would not attend to economy or let it continue to expand its dominion—what passes for "secularism" today—would fail to reach its aims. "One might just as well abolish the Pope while leaving Catholicism in existence."[44] Money is religion, then, the "state-capital-Christian complex" as William Connolly has it, and economic theology is the history of religion as political economy.[45]

But Christianity, the true and manifest target of Marx's ire, is evidently not just *any* religion. Nor can it be reduced to "a kind of 'supra-ideology' or universal culture or language in which subcultures or dialects could take up positions more properly termed ideological."[46] Christianity may not be "infinitely malleable," but it must nonetheless be conceived as extending well beyond matters of doctrine and ideology.[47] "Actually existing Christianity," if I may use the expression, is rather better understood as concealing itself within and under this general and generalized term ("Christianity is the religion of all religions," writes Werner Hamacher commenting on Marx, "the religion of religiosity itself, and proves itself as such 'by grouping the most diverse kinds of world views within the form of Christianity—and even more so in that it never demands Christianity from its followers, but just religion in general, whatever religion it may be' ").[48] That is why economic theology can be described as "Cristianismo y Capitalismo," as León Rozitchner and others have proposed, but more aptly so as Christianity qua capitalism, capitalism qua Christianity, each term expanding in a different manner the reach of the other.[49] Economic theology is not just about the right wing, in other words.

Indeed, it is remarkable that the insistence and sharper focus on "right wing" Christianity in much of the otherwise crucial work recently done on "capitalism and Christianity" runs the risk of leaving out "the Christians of the left," as it were (as opposed to "the Deleuzians of the right" invoked by William Connolly) and a longer and more complex history of Christianity, a broad phenomenon, if there ever was one, that Marx and others were contending with.[50] In the last analysis, economic theology is about the state of the world of capital. And one might do worse to understand this than to recast Baudelaire on democracy and say that "we all have the capitalist spirit in our veins, like we have syphilis in our bones. We have all contracted capitalism and syphilis."[51] Thus, economic theology has everything to do with blood, which is why it is more properly understood as the history of what Jacques Derrida has called *mondialatinization* (aptly translated by Sam Weber as "globalatinization").[52] It is the history of a concealed trinity: the translation, transubstantiation, and transvaluation, whereby Christianity became, in fact, "religion," blood became money, and money—faith and works, pace Weber—became what it is all about.[53] Walter Benjamin succinctly describes that history in the following terms: "Capitalism has developed as a parasite of Christianity in the West (this must be shown not just in the case of Calvinism, but in the other orthodox Christian churches), until it reached the point where Christianity's history is essentially that of its parasite—that is to say, of capitalism."[54]

After Shakespeare, and closer to Marx,[55] Moses Hess had said it all, when he pointed out that capitalism was the realization of the "task of Christianity [*die Aufgabe des Christenthums*]" and offered his critique of money as a critique of Christian theology. "Money is the social blood [*Das Geld ist das soziale Blut*]," which is to say that "the mystery of Christ's blood finally appears here as completely revealed [*Das Mysterium des Blutes Christi . . . erscheint hier endlich ganz unverhüllt*]." Mystical theophagy presents itself as the natural history of the social, and bloody, animal kingdom. During the Christian Middle Ages, the cult of blood [*der Blutkultus*]— the task of Christianity—"was theoretically, idealistically, and logically realized, which is to say that one actually consumed the spilled and alienated blood of mankind, while doing the same in imagination only to the blood of the Man-God." Blood, which is to say, money, is the site of anthropophagy (or theophagy) turned economic theology. "The mystery of Judaism and of Christianity," Hess continues, "is revealed in the Judeo-Christian merchant-world [*Krämerwelt*]." Money—blood money—is the true spirit of capitalism made flesh, the incarnation *and* liquefaction of flesh and blood. In a world of delirious consumption and abject poverty, of free competition, unregulated enterprise, and infinite accumulation, speculation, and exploitation, where blood thirst has long driven the money market that is capitalism, Hess insists on testifying to the creation of (rather than the emancipation from) the war of all against all.[56] For such a society, Marx unequivocally concurs, that is, "for a society of commodity producers, whose general social relation of production consists in the fact that they treat their products as commodities, hence as values, and in this material form bring their individual, private labors into relation with each other as homogeneous human labor, Christianity with its religious cult of man in the abstract . . . is the most fitting form of religion."[57]

Clearly, there are nuanced distinctions to be made, discriminating differences to be established, and so, precisely, *between bloods*. "To probe the complex and shifting relations between capitalism and Christianity we need to show how the defining characteristics of capitalism display a degree of indeterminacy, room to be stretched, and evolutionary potential."[58] But we also need to recognize as well that blood is, and how it is, one of its defining characteristics, a crucial element indeed. Today, the transubstantiation of money and its Christian history—the transformation of blood into bloods and back—which was so obvious to the nineteenth century, seems to have become close to invisible ("commerce is peace"). To recapitulate, then. The history of economic theology is also the history of blood groups, the history of race, which we have considered in previous chapters. With the spread of eucharistic practice in the Middle Ages, at any rate, two momentous transformations took place, diametrically opposed yet fully coextensive. One could be described as an extension of a process of incarnation or coagulation, the other as the occurrence of a dissolution or liquefaction. First, then, "the communion wafer often took the form of a stamped coin, which was something like fiat money backed by the priest whose word magically transformed worthless bread into the priceless body of Christ."[59] The word became flesh, and flesh became blood (as the wafer, and no longer the wine, quickly became the only species that Christians were allowed to consume). Clearly, the religious origins of money go back to the very beginnings of history, yet the singular transformation of Christ's blood into an ever more significant object of worship affected the no less ancient association of blood and money. Thus, the "historically momentous change" that takes place with the modern dematerialization of money, the invention of "electric money," can be located on a continuum with that earlier transformation in the history of money and within economic theology, as a series of "processes that moved *Christendom* from the age of electrum coins toward the age of electric money."[60] From the "liquid assets" of medieval Germany so aptly described by Valentin Groebner ("in the fourteenth, fifteenth, and sixteenth century, as in present-day usage, the German verb *schencken* means both to bestow a gift and to pour a liquid")[61] to Luther's "filthy lucre," from William Harvey's circulation, by way of the mercantilist and physiocratic imagination and all the way to Karen Ho's *Liquidated*, the flows of blood in economic thought and practice can hardly be seen as incidental.[62] To the contrary, they tell us much about the importance of the Eucharist in economic history, and all the more so if one recalls, say, the belated appearance of the legend of the Holy Grail ("an influential etymology derives *Holy Grail* (*Saint Graal*) from the 'real/royal blood' (*sang real*) of Jesus").[63] In Marc Shell's pertinent descriptions, Christendom implicitly emerges as the subject of economics, which it became by way of blood. Blood may therefore constitute an intermediary stage in the history of money's dematerialization, its becoming-spirit and its spectralization (as Derrida demonstrates). But it is a fundamentally Christian stage, and it figures Christ's blood before spirit, blood in lieu of spirit (or wine), as the basis of economic theology. That stage—but is it only a stage?—is the liquefaction of money. Incidentally, in French, the word for cash is *liquide* or, eucharistically enough, *espèces*.[64]

The second transformation brought about by the spread of the Eucharist and the surrounding blood cult was the circulation (in the premodern sense) of Christ's blood—historically, the very first pure blood in human history—in the newly conceived, organic and immanent totality of the Christian body politic.[65] Along with the spread of Galenic medicine and the rise of Aristotelian, hematocentric embryological conceptions, the so-called Middle Ages witnessed the conjunction of medical knowledge with genealogical claims made on the basis of blood lines (together with the sedimentation of perceptions of kinship as "blood" ties—as if blood was the natural locus of genealogy), and the seeds of what was to become "scientific" racial thinking. What was occurring was the unification of the entire Christian community into an immanent, organic whole: the community of blood.[66] More directly relevant here is the fact that Christian blood became completely distinct, completely good, and, more importantly, completely pure—if also vulnerable ("If thou dost shed / One drop of Christian blood . . ."). Announcing a similar shift in Christian attitudes toward money, blood—Christian blood—was thus transvalued. Whereas along with flesh and blood (carnal as opposed to spiritual), along with kinship and money, blood had been the object of an explicit taboo, it now became the bearer of a new, positive valuation.[67] Blood became, as it were, the liquid ground or underground upon which would be drawn drastic and radical distinctions between bloods. And "beneath the apparently solid surface, they betrayed oceans of liquid matter, only needing expansion to rend into fragments continents of hard rock."[68] Non-Christians, for their part, became the carriers of impurity, hostile persecutors and defilers of Christian blood. It should therefore come as no surprise that this period, which witnessed an exponential rise of anxiety surrounding Christ's very blood—a blood that was flowing and overflowing in the chalices of Europe as well as on the walls of its churches and out of the eyes of its saints, its statues and other bleeding relics, a blood after which women mystics were vocally hankering—and surrounding Christian blood at large, was the same period that saw the finalized invention of the economic enemy. In both cases, the figure of this double anxiety—blood and money—was, of course, the Jew.[69] There is no need to elaborate further on this well-known constellation, except perhaps to signal the strange absence of inquiry on the significance of its transitive associations. Blood, Jews, and money—these are the three elements that guide the main concerns of this chapter, and together they have sustained the curiosity (or animosity) of countless "inquiries," focusing, for the most part, on anti-Semitic topoi from Judas's blood money to the blood of Christ on Jewish heads and all the way to practices of usury, to Jews as merchants of money, merchants of blood, and, indeed, as inventors of capitalism.[70] Yet, what all these relate is quite simply, and perhaps first of all, an altogether obvious story: the story of another, if hardly more immediate, dyad, namely, Christians and money.[71] The Christian obsession with Jews and usury, with Jews and money, the long history of negative perceptions regarding money within Christian theology, has Christianity as its subject and main protagonist.[72] Otherwise put, Jewish blood was always less important, less significant than Christian blood, no more than a detour to "think" Christian blood. And the history of this detour was doubled over and twice intensified by the new conceptions and practices of blood and blood cult (as well as blood paranoia) such as were circulated most actively between the eleventh and thirteenth centuries and evolved to full-scale ideological structures and embedded practices by the sixteenth century. These beginnings, and the elements thereby gathered, announce the emergence of capitalism as an extended chapter in the history of Christianity, the history of economic theology.

Shakespeare too said it all before of course, whose "immense allegory," *The Merchant of Venice*, "recapitulates the entire history of forgiveness, the entire history between the Jew and the Christian, the entire history of economics."[73] Shakespeare knew that worth and wealth were undergoing a strange liquefaction ("Strange it is that our bloods, / Of colour, weight, and heat, poured all together, / Would quite confound distinction, yet stands of / In differences so mighty" is again the way *All's Well That Ends Well* puts it), quickly becoming, as if naturally, what runs in the veins.[74] And Shakespeare knew that this transformation, this liquefaction, which announced the opening of world banks as blood banks and foreshadowed the main trademarks of modernity, had everything to do with religion, with theology and with its secularization. Secular theology (in Amos Funkenstein's striking phrase) is, in fact, at the origins of William Harvey's discovery of the circulation of blood, his contribution to economic theology and the continuing transvaluation of circulation. Along with the other "natural" sciences, medicine must be seen as a major site of the secularization of theological—and economic—concerns and issues.[75] Harvey himself said as much when he described the beginnings of life as the quasi-divine revelation, more precisely, a dialectic of contraction and revelation, of blood—angels pulsing on a pinhead ("In the midst of the cloudlet in question there was a bloody point so small that it disappeared during the contraction and escaped the sight, but in the relaxation it reappeared again, red and like the point of a pin; so that betwixt the visible and invisible, betwixt being and non-being, as it were, it gave by its pulses a kind of representation of the commencement of life").[76] Furthermore, in his dedication to King Charles I, Harvey explicitly linked theology, politics, and blood as the crux of his discovery—the discovery of blood as the essence of life and of the heart as the center of this life, as the center of the circulatory system, of the political system, and of the divine system.

> The heart of animals is the foundation of their life, the sovereign of everything within them, the sun of their microcosm, that upon which all growth depends, from which all power proceeds. The King, in like manner, is the foundation of his kingdom, the sun of the world around him, the heart of the republic, the fountain whence all power, all grace doth flow. . . . The knowledge of his heart, therefore, will not be useless to a Prince, as embracing a kind of Divine example of his functions,—and it has still been usual with men to compare small things with great. Here, at all events, best of Princes, placed as you are on the pinnacle of human affairs, you may at once contemplate the *prime mover* in the body of man, and the emblem of your own sovereign power.[77]

As is immediately apparent, with Harvey's discovery, all systems are go, which is to say that all systems are closed. From the eucharistic community of blood to Harvey's circulatory system and to the systemic, organic vision of political life: all the basic principles of modern economics, including their natural freedom, had already been put in place well in advance. Harvey—who sent the manuscript of his *Anatomical Disquisition on the Motion of the Heart and Blood in Animals* to another "prime mover," the aptly named president of the Royal College of Physicians, Doctor Argent—left it to his friend Thomas Hobbes to further elaborate on the figure of the state as the body of Leviathan, within whose veins flows none other than *argent*, that is, money and commerce.[78] Harvey's five brothers (and his nephews as well) would have appreciated and even favored the gesture, no doubt, given that they were all merchants "of weights and substance—*magni et copiosi*, trading especially with Turkey or the Levant, then the main channel through which the wealth of the East flowed into Europe."[79] This was only one moment in what was already becoming an unstoppable wave linking state systems to colonial ones, a surging flow and flood of money and blood. But here is Hobbes's version of Harvey's circulation, concoction, and "sanguification."

> By Concoction, I understand the reducing of all commodities which are not presently consumed, but reserved for Nourishment in time to come, to some thing of equal value. . . . And this is nothing else but Gold, and Silver, and Mony. . . . In so much as this Concoction, is as it were the Sanguification of the Commonwealth: For naturall Bloud is in like manner made of the fruits of the Earth; and circulating, nourisheth by the way, every Member of the Body of

Man.... And in this also, the Artificiall Man maintains his resemblance with the Naturall; whose Veins receiving the Bloud from the severall Parts of the Body, carry it to the Heart; where being made Vitall, the Heart by the Arteries sends it out again, to enliven, and enable for motion all the Members of the same.[80]

The circulation of blood is the circulation of money—and "Leviathan is the text" that we are called upon to read on these financial, political, and theological seas.[81] As the famous Scottish financier, mercantilist theoretician, master circulator, inveterate gambler, founder of the first *Banque Royale* and of the *Compagnie d'Occident*—later *Compagnie des Indes*—Comptroller-General of Finances of the Kingdom of France and *nouveau* Catholic, John Law was to put it less than a century later, albeit with a different anatomic emphasis: "Money is the blood of the state and must circulate. Credit is to business what the brain is to the human body."[82] Neither Hume nor Rousseau would disagree, both of them appealing to the same federated reserve of images. Reflecting on this new phenomenon, Eli Hecksher points out, "the comparison of money with blood was current even long before the circulation of blood was discovered and before Hobbes (1651) had made the comparison popular."[83] At the very least, money was beginning to float (a phenomenon that was slowly generalized but only finalized on August 15, 1971).[84] It is on these bloody seas that the economic enemy would come to cut an unforgettable, if no less fluid, figure. As he himself puts it, "ships are but boards, sailors but men. There be land rats and water rats, water thieves and land thieves—I mean pirates—and there is the peril of waters ..."[85]

THE ECONOMIC ENEMY

Elaborating on his reflections on political theology, Carl Schmitt performed a complex, even ambivalent, gesture that located the enemy—and his disappearance—at the center of politics. Two modalities of the enemy effectively vanish from Schmitt's account, a double disappearance that effectively inscribes economic theology on the history of the enemy.[86] On the one hand, Schmitt ostensibly dismisses the significance of the theological tradition when it came to the question of the enemy (hence, in the Gospels according to Schmitt, "no mention is made of the political enemy" and the Bible is said hardly to touch on the political antithesis). Schmitt thus seems to have ignored the theological enemy.[87] On the other hand, conducting a fierce polemics against liberalism and against the modern expansion of the economic domain ("society"), Schmitt unequivocally announces that economics is *the end* of the enemy.

Liberalism in one of its typical dilemmas of intellect and economics has attempted to transform the enemy from the viewpoint of economics into a competitor and from the intellectual viewpoint into a debating adversary. In the domain of economics there are no enemies, only competitors, and in a thoroughly moral and ethical world perhaps only debating adversaries.[88]

Returning to the issue later in the same text, Schmitt continues to lament the disappearance of the enemy but this time suggests that this may be a matter of linguistic obfuscation ("The adversary is thus no longer *called* an enemy but a disturber of peace and is thereby designated to be an outlaw of humanity").[89] Schmitt thus appears to withdraw his earlier assertions when he had unequivocally stated that "economic antagonisms can *become* political." He now considers it evident, at any rate, that "the point of the political may be reached from the economic as well as from any other domain." More pertinently, Schmitt underscores the illusion at work in the view expressed by Kant among others, who, we have seen earlier, conceives of commerce as the condition of peace. Attacking Joseph Schumpeter's version of this conception, Schmitt writes that it is "erroneous to believe that a political position founded on economic superiority is 'essentially unwarlike.'" What is rather "unwarlike," corrects Schmitt now insisting—as often was his wont—on the matter of language, is "the terminology based on the essence of liberal ideology."[90] Strangely adopting a prophetic tone (as if he were talking about the future rather than an all-too current present, one that remains ever more relevant today), Schmitt describes the paradoxical culmination of a development that produced economy and the economic enemy while bringing—or claiming to bring—an end to war.

An imperialism based on pure economic power will naturally attempt to sustain a worldwide condition which enables it to apply and manage, unmolested, its economic means, e.g., terminating credit, embargoing raw materials, destroying the currencies of others, and so on. Every attempt of a people to withdraw itself from the effects of such "peaceful" methods is considered by this imperialism as extra-economic power. Pure economic imperialism will also apply a stronger, but still economic, and therefore (according to this terminology) nonpolitical, essentially peaceful means of force. A 1921 League of Nations resolution enumerates as examples: economic sanctions and severance of the food supply from the civilian population.... For the application of such means, a new and essentially pacifist vocabulary has been created. War is condemned but executions, sanctions, punitive expeditions, pacifications, protection of treaties, international police, and measures to assure peace remain. The adversary is thus no longer called an enemy but a disturber of peace and is thereby designated to be an outlaw of humanity. A war waged to protect or expand economic power must, with the aid of propaganda, turn into a crusade and into the last war of humanity.[91]

By writing of a "crusade" and of the unification of humankind, Schmitt nevertheless reveals his uncanny—indeed, frightening—ability to foresee what has today become ever more obvious. He also brings us back to economic theology. More precisely, Schmitt establishes the basic terms of his later inquiry into the conditions of modernity, an inquiry in which he describes the "dissolution" of state boundaries and the "liquefaction" of space. In *The Nomos of the Earth*, Schmitt attends to the fact that the sea was always located outside of territorial, juridical regulations, defined as a space that enabled and, indeed, linked the very two "practices" that Kant and Schumpeter saw as distinct and even opposite, namely, we saw, war and commerce. In the naval space—where pirates rule—*only* war and commerce take place. And all that is solid melts into blood. Both the dissolution of space (crusade and conquest, which Schmitt identifies with one momentous date: 1492) and the liquefaction of money—its circulation as blood money, under the figure of unification in the blood of Christ—partake of the same logic and of the same transformation.[92] As does the rise of the British empire, for "the commercial expansion of the English nation through international commerce was justified not in terms of the accumulation of value in the embodied form of treasure, but instead in relation to the production of capital through an ongoing process of circulation."[93] And it is again Shakespeare who informs us of that fact, by way of the theological, that is to say, of the economic enemy (as one critic writes, "even Shylock has a friend or two").[94] This too is the history of economic theology.

Remember that *The Merchant of Venice*, like Venice itself, is in a state of dissolution ("all Venice may, like Antonio and Bassanio, have problems with liquidity," is the way Lars Engle puts it).[95] At once wedded to the sea, as the annual *Festa della Sensa* commemorates, and under the constant threat of flood,[96] the city and its merchants are "on the flood," surrounded and obsessed by liquid and liquid wealth. Salarino, who already alerted us to the difference found "between bloods," also explains to Antonio, right at the outset of the play, that his melancholy has everything to do with a state in dissolution. "I know not why I am so sad," Antonio famously complained.

SALARINO
Your mind is tossing on the ocean,
There where your argosies with portly sail,
Like signors and rich burghers on the flood,
Or as it were the pageants of the sea,

Do overpeer the petty traffickers
That curtsy to them, do them reverence,
As they fly by them with their woven wings.[97]

Recalling the liquid world of a closed system—naval or circulatory—and itself ring-like, the play will not close before bringing us back, along with the ships that were lost at sea, and to the ring (incidentally, the very last word of the play). This is a ring that is not unlike the gold band tossed by the Doge into the waters (Portia's invocation of the "virgin tribute paid by howling Troy / To the sea-monster," 3.2.52–7), reaffirming every year the marriage of the city to the sea. Similarly wedded only to the sea, to liquid "life and living," Antonio—"Which is the merchant here, and which the Jew?"—expresses his profuse gratitude to Portia upon her announcing to him, in the last lines of the play, that "three of your argosies / Are richly come to harbour suddenly."

> ANTONIO
> Sweet lady, you have given me life and living,
> For here I read for certain that my ships
> Are safely come to road. (5.1.286–288)

If *The Merchant of Venice* teaches us so much about economic theology, it is first of all because it takes us to the sea—war and commerce—while signaling to us that along with, and in the realm of, money, our minds are "tossing on the ocean," and merchants are "like signors and rich burghers on the flood." It is a hard lesson to learn (Antonio himself insists on forgetting it, carelessly affirming after signing the bond that "in this there can be no dismay: / My ships come home a month before the day," 2.1.177–178), and it takes the whole play for him to learn it. The play is thus not so much framed (for how could liquid frame anything?) as it is flooded and liquefied by it, finding itself—and us with it—in a state of liquefaction, a condition in which liquid assets spill and escape. But the main fluid the play teaches us about is, of course, blood, that is to say, money, I mean, Christian blood.[98]

Not surprisingly, then, Antonio had to be reminded of the fluids surrounding him, as well as of the fact that, in his veins, blood is flowing ("Why should a man, whose blood is warm within, / Sit like his grandsire cut in alabaster"), rather than standing still ("There are a sort of men whose visages / Do cream and mantle like a standing pond, / And do a willful stillness entertain" [1.1.83–90]).[99] Morocco, whose thematic association with Shylock includes not only the attraction to gold but also complexion ("If he have the condition of a saint and the complexion of a devil" announces Portia [1.2.126–127]),[100] takes it upon himself "to prove whose blood is reddest" (2.1.7). Essential to a play that is about "love and friendship, the meaning of Christianity, and a good deal more," bonds of kinship too are repeatedly and insistently located in blood.[101] "Thou art mine own flesh and blood" declares Gobbo to his son Lancelot (2.2.87), while Jessica at once affirms and denies the ties of blood linking her to her father ("But though I am a daughter to his blood, / I am not to his manners," 2.2.18–19), claiming her right to "become a Christian" by wedding one. Shylock calls this as he sees it: "My own flesh and blood to rebel! . . . I say my daughter is my flesh and my blood" (3.1.32, 35) and famously reminds his audience: "do we not bleed?" (3.1.61) as he does the blood curse—Matthew 27:25— that "never fell upon our nation till now; I never felt it till now" (3.1.81–82). Blood is about family and about memory. It is about manners too, about ethics and law. Indeed, "in such an ethically overdetermined discourse, blood and bleeding func- tion as the obvious, indisputable signifiers of natural law, the metonymies of what becomes here a physiology of insistent commonality."[102] Yet, we have also begun to see that there are different kinds of bloods, more difference, in fact, "between . . . bloods than there is between red wine and Rhenish" (3.1.38).[103] There is an "essen- tial difference in blood."[104] And when nothing else speaks, it is blood that does: "Madam," says Bassanio to Portia, "you have bereft me of all words. / Only my blood speaks to you in my veins" (3.2.175–176). Words are bonds and bonds are blood, and what runs in the veins is, therefore, money. Recalling his speechless mouth along with his poverty and his nobility, Bassanio re-circulates the words of his own blood to Portia: "Gentle lady, / When I did first impart my love to you, / I freely told you all the wealth I had / Ran in my veins: I was a gentleman" (3.2.250–253). Words are bonds and words are blood, explains Bassanio, and here is my body ("I once did lend him my body for his wealth," later testifies Antonio [5.1.249]), the body of my friend, here is his wound, bleeding, as blood on paper: "Here is a letter, lady, / The paper as the body of my friend, / And every word in it a gaping wound / Issuing life-blood" (3.2.261–264).[105] Knife-wielding Shylock, we are not surprised to be reminded, is Antonio's "bloody creditor" (3.3.34), and his desires are "wolvish, bloody, starved and ravenous" (4.1.137).[106]

There is more than enough, therefore, to observe the associations of blood with money, along with the circulations of blood and money (there have been specula- tions as to whether Shakespeare could have become familiar with the theories of the other William, although such speculations are of course irrelevant to the play, written earlier than Harvey's discoveries).[107] What needs to be underscored, perhaps, is the figure of Shylock as the economic enemy whose association with blood and money is ultimately interrupted because and by way of blood, and more precisely, because and by way of *Christian* blood. Circulation and exchange reach an end—a literal end, for Shylock—while establishing the supremacy and immunity of Christian blood as well as the victory of Christian commerce and money. The threat constituted by Shylock having access to Antonio's blood, as a substitute for his money, is ultimately defused and dissolved, and money, no longer tainted by Shylock's touch and practices, "droppeth as the gentle rain from heaven" (4.1.182). "The final *deus ex machina* is associated with a reflux of capital, a closure to circulation and exchange as merchant's capital finally returns home," that is, to the Christians.[108] Like "the quality of mercy," then, money ambivalently circulates into the Christian domain. Like Christian blood, however, money is equally barred from access by the Jew. Ultimately, the bond will give the Jew neither blood nor money. Here bonds are not words, no longer words. And no word is blood; blood speaks no word, while money and blood have become entirely interrupted from circulating within reach of the Jew's hands or veins. There has never been more difference *between* bloods.

> PORTIA
> Tarry a little; there is something else.
> This bond doth give thee here no jot of blood;
> The words expressly are "a pound of flesh."
> Take then thy bond. Take thou thy pound of flesh.
> But in the cutting it, if thou dost shed
> One drop of Christian blood, thy lands and goods
> Are by the laws of Venice confiscate
> Unto the state of Venice. (4.1.302–309)

Shylock, of course, knows exactly what is being taken away from him by interrupting all exchange and circulation between Jews and Christians: his blood, that is to say, his money and his life: "Nay, take my life and all! . . . you take my life / When you do take the means whereby I live" (4.1.370, 372–373). Life, and life-blood, can thereby return to Antonio who appropriately thanks Portia for having given him "life and living."

INTERMUNDIA

What requires explanation is not the view that these matters are part of the province of religion, but the view that they are not.
—R. H. TAWNEY

"*Money* has become a world power," wrote Marx, "the Christians have become Jews."[109] It would be difficult to produce a more accurate description of the translation, transubstantiation, and transvaluation that occurs in Shakespeare's *The Merchant of Venice* and, more generally, in the history of economic theology of which Christianity remains the subject and main protagonist. Given Marx's interest in Shakespeare, and his interest in Christianity, it can hardly be considered an accident that "On the Jewish Question"—which makes this uncompromising diagnostic—is remembered, like Shakespeare's play, as an anti-Semitic text more than as an anti-Christian one.[110] Without adjudicating on the play's own controversial place in the history of prejudice, it remains unquestionable that Shakespeare and Marx contributed in a momentous way to a history of economic theology, one that refigures Christianity—Catholic and Protestant, pre- and post-Reformation—as a privileged actor in the transvaluation of blood and money that defines modern capitalism ("It was the economic imperialism of Catholic Portugal and Spain, not the less imposing, if more solid, achievements of the Protestant powers, which impressed contemporaries down to the Armada. It was predominantly Catholic cities which were the commercial capitals of Europe, and Catholic bankers who were its leading financiers," explains R. H. Tawney).[111] By the time Max Weber quotes Benjamin Franklin on the begetting of money and the blood ties of capital, that transvaluation (and the polar sites it connected) had clearly occurred and was already in the process of being forgotten. Weber (who did admit that "the *summum bonum* of this ethic [was] the earning of more and more money") favored a persistent misreading of Marx and emphasized the significance of work over money, of Calvinism over Catholicism.[112] The significance of this history remains, no doubt, as opaque today as it appears to have been for Weber—who could tell whether blood has not already become an antiquated academic topic? This is perhaps an effect of the view upheld by Kant and which persists today in spite of massive evidence to the contrary, to repeat, the view that commerce is the opposite of war, that religion and economics (not to mention politics and economics) are two distinct realms. "Trade is one thing, religion is another."[113] So goes the popular saying. The history of America—since 1492 as Carl Schmitt insisted—is part of the dissolution of such entrenched distinctions, as is the advent of capitalism and the generalization of economics as the free and immanent circulation of money.[114] And of blood. But the liquefaction of space and the new economic theology—the immanence of blood and its valuation in the closed domain of exchange and circulation—had become possible still long before, on the face of a silver coin.

Part Two

HEMATOLOGIES

WHERE ELSE, I anticipate being asked, where else have people accused themselves and others and exonerated themselves clean of, and by, blood? Where else have people drunk the blood of their God, associated their ultimate concern (property above all, money too) with blood, *pure blood*, identified themselves and other collectives too on the basis of blood, of different bloods, and expanded the intricacies of law and medicine to prove it, hierarchize it; inscribed blood in their arts and in their sciences, while transforming blood into a major resource of their political imagination? Where else have the rhetoric of blood, the rituals of blood, and the practices of blood extended to cover or describe almost every human endeavor? Where have technologies been invented and deployed that would make blood transportable, exchangeable, and eminently spillable in quantities that no longer have measure? I have said that this book offers no explanation. It is perhaps time to add that it does not cater much to otherwise plausible contestations (that is, expectedly plausible contestations under the current regime of always already symmetric, two-sides to every story, conversational ethics). Which is to say that blood, blood "itself' as it were, cannot easily serve as a *tertium comparationis,* only as an "internal" marker, a measure of Christianity, of actually existing Christianity out of the sources of its own expanse. I seek a different form of comparison, therefore, a different mode of contestation, a disputation really and a reckoning of sorts with and of Christianity in its unreflected relation to blood, in what it has projected outward and backward. What this requires is a kind of introductory lesson in geography, in hemato-geography, which registers the uneven distribution of blood, pure and innocent blood (and then other bloods), across the planet. There are other "things" that are, for better or for worse, distributed along similar lines, shaping different series no doubt. Like murder for Freud (to which I shall turn in my conclusion), blood heightens the visibility—and invisibility—of these lines and series, the visibility and indivisibility of Christianity. That is why "the problem that now presents itself—and which defines the task of a general history—is," as Foucault had it, "to determine what form of relation may be legitimately described between these different series, what vertical system they are capable of forming; what interplay of correlation and dominance exists between them; what may be the effect of shifts, different temporalities, and various rehandlings; in which distinct totalities certain elements may figure simultaneously."[1]

The second part of this book thus engages the matter of blood and Christianity from a punctually thematic (and textual) perspective rather than from an extended historical one. I begin, however, by entertaining the matter of comparison from an expected site for, an alleged origin of, Christianity's blood investment, namely, ancient Greece, as it itself relates or compares with ancient Judaism. "Odysseus' Blood," visits or revisits the differential place of blood in ancient Greek thought and practice, whether political, philosophical, or medical. Here again, and beginning with Erich Auerbach's own comparison in the famous opening chapter of *Mimesis,* I am guided in part by the responses, the uptake and the translation, of blood in ancient texts (Greek and Hebrew). For as I work my way toward and away from the ancient conceptions, one conclusion becomes inevitable: blood may be a universal concern, but the difference—and the distinct range—of this concern clearly leaves Christianity in a class of its own.

"Bleeding and Melancholia" returns us explicitly to this thread. It reads Freud, Stoker, and, briefly, medieval female mystics, toward a reconsideration of the ancient disease and its vicissitudes, its relation to blood, and particularly the change in the theory of the humors such as it occurred in the Middle Ages. In medicine and in embryology in particular, blood became the dominant humor, much as it was becoming the main carrier of filiation and genealogy. Instead of parsing themselves among four humors (black bile, yellow bile, phlegm, and blood), each of the other three humors became *an attribute of blood*. At the same time, love—love!— became associated with a humoral imbalance, a kind of blood thirst, which produced an image, at times inverted, of vampirism. Renaissance images of Catherine of Sienna, for instance, became the blueprint for modern representations of the mesmerized woman sucking at the side wound of Dracula. In this way, Stoker emerges as the shadow historian of Christianity as the religion of love—the love of blood.

I conclude the second part with the most expansive chapter in its reach. Uniquely described by Charles Olson as "the book of the law of the blood," Melville's *Moby-Dick*, of which I propose a reading, encompasses literature and economy, slavery and science, race and religion, politics and law—indivisible under one blood. My argument is simply enough that Melville wrote an account of Christianity, indeed, a true reckoning of it, probably among the most detailed and extensive, ultimately coming closest to a critique of actually existing Christianity. With Leviathan as its frame and its core, *Moby-Dick* is the most extended and compelling demonstration of the need to rethink Christianity as political hematology.

Four ODYSSEUS' BLOOD

AT THE OUTSET of *Mimesis*, his momentous journey through some of the choicest parts of Western literature, Erich Auerbach famously placed a wound and a scar.[1] True to the conspicuous methodological and thematic choices that have him focus his attention on markedly segmented, textual extracts, this occurs in a way no different from "a newly introduced character, or even a newly appearing object or implement," in countless other passages (5). Yet, Odysseus' scar—a deep and multilayered inscription of ambivalent domestic conditions and identifications and the occasion for an almost Proustian unfolding of memory ("a portion of the hero's boyhood")—singularly and violently calls attention to the matter and manner of parts, cuts, portions, and divisions. Homer himself had sought "to represent phenomena in a fully externalized form, visible and palpable in all their parts [*in allen Teilen tastbar und sichtbar*]" (6/G10).[2] And so here is the scar, here a part or a portion, in what is otherwise a complete and fully illuminated, and seamless, picture. "Here is the scar, which comes up in the course of the narrative; and Homer's feeling simply will not permit him to see it appear out of the darkness of an unilluminated past; it must be set in full light, and with it a portion of the hero's boyhood [*ein Stück Jugendland des Helden*]" (6/G10). Here is a cut, which paradoxically introduces and even constitutes a complete whole. For, as Auerbach insists, everything is as if the text were at once complete and self-sufficient, fully illuminated and free from any concealment, any hidden realm. The reader is thus presented with a demonstration that something greater could be learned

from a wound that is both profound and depthless and that simultaneously signals an unscathed arrangement of wholly present parts: "the syntactical connection between part and part [*die syntaktische Verbindung zwischen ihren Teilen*] is
perfectly clear, no contour is blurred" (3/G7). The scar is the trace of mended parts
that, in the impeccable textual logic of the interpreter, effaces itself there, where it
is inscribed on the sleek surface of the page. "Never a lacuna [*eine Lücke*], never a
gap [*ein Auseinanderklaffen*], never a glimpse of unplumbed depths [*ein Blick in
uneforschte Tiefen*]" (7/G11). There is, as it were, no scar and it conceals nothing. It
is nothing, yet it must be hidden. Everything is present, but something is missing.
Remote and still to come, an edge of potentiality cuts to the quick into the text,
as if regretfully parsing and parting it. If only "the entire story of the scar had been
presented as a recollection which awakens in Odysseus' mind at this particular
moment. It would have been perfectly easy to do; the story of the scar had only to
be inserted two verses earlier, at the first mention of the word scar, where the motifs
'Odysseus' and 'recollection' were already at hand" (7). Such play (or sleight) of the
hand was, alas, not to be. Homer "knows no background" (4). Still, the incision
was made, the intrusive insertion virtually performed. "To the word scar there is
first attached a relative clause . . . ; into this an independent sentence unexpectedly
intrudes . . . which quietly disentangles itself from syntactical subordination" (7).
The complete and self-sufficient text is thus *supplemented*, as if lacking.[3] A severed
part, a portion of a lacerated member and of a past long departed, comes into view
to introduce the possibility and impossibility of depth and absence, of relation and
separation. Was the cut, made or unmade, visible or invisible, bound or unbound?
Did another, supplemental scar form? Will there be blood?

Auerbach was not writing about body parts, of course, not primarily or obviously so. The same might equally be said of Homer himself, although one could
turn with more confidence to the *Odyssey* (as to the *Iliad*) to reflect on the fact
that every part or portion therein is "saturated in blood, a fact which cannot be
hidden or argued away, twist the evidence as one may in a vain attempt to fit
archaic Greek values to a more gentle code of ethics."[4] Nor does any of this suggest that Auerbach wanted to give his readers "a taste of blood," making them
into "spectators of war" (not even a "lettuce war"), as Plato recommended for
the education of children, spectators of blood.[5] Indeed, there is no reason to
think that Auerbach wanted his readers to think about blood at all—if I am
not mistaken the word *blood* never appears in "Odysseus' Scar." Unless, that is,
we consider the possibility that, after the manner of wounds and parts, blood is
left out of the light, as it were excised, hidden, and having lost "almost all 'presentness' " whether or not it is physically present (13), about to be brought back

to the surface; or else it is continuing to operate even as it is confined to one of these "backgrounds," to which Auerbach attributed "fraught" significance. Will there be blood? Is blood a part? If so, which is the part of blood? Can it become, can it be gathered into, a gapless whole? Is it then, and only then, "fraught with background" or consisting in one? And if one were to look into it, cut through it all and into the background, what would one find there? Will there be blood? Where and how far, with what justification, should one look for Odysseus' blood? Will there be, finally, *Greek* blood?

Outside or prior to Christianity, the question of blood emerges here out of the sources of literature. At stake is the matter of an other blood (the blood of the other, here the "Greek" other) and of a difference between bloods, of a different mapping and a different representation, as it were, of the "reality" of blood. It is very much a "Homeric question," in other words.[6] Addressing its emergence will therefore require a few rudimentary steps. First, a recognition that blood is a word (or two). Deployed as it is across a number of rhetorical fields, moreover, it is a figure before it is a concept, by which I mean that blood does not register in any central way on the materialist and physiologic radars of the Presocratic philosophers. This is not to say that there is nothing of blood in philosophy, only that no one ever uttered an "everything is blood" sentence (in contrast with "everything is air," or "everything is fire" or "water").[7] My insistence on the thematic of parts is therefore meant to underscore that blood, wherever it appears, has never been the whole, indeed, a whole of any kind.[8] In this specific instance, blood functions as no more, if also no less than, but at least potentially as, a metonymical figure of sorts. The second thing here required has to do with the related difficulty of properly locating blood in any given body, field, or indeed whole. For however one defines literature—and particularly so in ancient Greece—its contested status vis-à-vis the sciences should suggest that blood is at once within and beyond the regional divisions of the knowable and the known. I have already referred to philosophy, but to begin, as I do here, with blood in literature is not quite to locate blood, but precisely to suspend the question of an allegedly proper or primary belonging of blood to the body (individual or collective), to religion or politics, to medicine or to law. Finally, to read blood out of the sources of literature is to engage in a rhetorical interrogation of the figure of blood, an interrogation that includes the very notion of figure (metonymy, of course, but we will have more occasions to verify that metaphor comes to mind as easily when it comes to blood) as well as that of concept. What kind of word, what kind of thing, is blood? Does it appear, and how? If so, where can it be found? What, if any, is its significance? At bottom, these are the questions the pertinence of which I seek to measure in this chapter.

THE BINDING OF ODYSSEUS

I begin slowly by seizing upon the "motif" of parts, granting the weight that might at last be due to a scar, to try to highlight (by no means to settle) the difference Auerbach seeks and sees between two distinct parts of an increasingly unified whole—let us call it "literary" or better yet "religious"—between Homer and the Bible, Odysseus and Abraham, the Greek and the Hebrew.[9] Engaging rhetorical, psychological, and sociopolitical dimensions, as well as "the irrepressible politico-religious spontaneity of the people" (21), the dispute or divide, if it is one, shows indisputable signs—it is itself a sign—of suture across a complicated temporal terrain and numerous fields or regions. Perhaps oozing still, it takes place at any rate over parts. We ourselves are confronted with two styles, "in their opposition," with "certain parts [*Teile*] brought into high relief, others left obscure" (23). Arguably, on the surface, there is first and foremost "the basic impulse of the Homeric style," which is singularly marked by the attempt "to represent phenomena in a fully externalized form, visible and palpable in all their parts, and completely fixed in their spatial and temporal relations" (6). This would be "the story of a wound," which has already occurred, but now "becomes an independent and exclusive present" (7). In this present, the part becomes the whole. It becomes the (fictitious, but entire) world. "And this 'real' world into which we are lured, exists for itself, contains nothing but itself; the Homeric poems conceal nothing, they contain no teaching and no secret second meaning" (13). Like resistance, interpretation is futile. But the biblical style too, were it left to its own devices, would be exposed (a child is being exposed) to a similar isolation or danger. Unwittingly, the reading—later described as having "disregarded everything that pertains to . . . origins" (23)—reveals any and every text as contingent and severable, tenuously dependent for its existence on an obscure background and on an external, hidden and necessary, authority (but then, the entirety of *Mimesis* would plausibly be accounted for thereby). Bound and abstracted at the same time, a certain autonomy looms. Without that "absolute authority . . . the Biblical stories become ancient legends, and the doctrine they had contained, now dissevered from them, becomes a disembodied image" (16). Legend is what rearranges the parts, of course, the stuff stories are made of. Legend "detaches it [*sie schneidet ihn*, it cuts it] from its contemporary historical context" (19/G25). Thus, instead of providing the reader with a constant awareness "of the universal religio-historical perspective which gives the individual stories their general meaning and purpose" (17), instead of a window into an infinite and unified background, the biblical text itself comes undone, close to being no more than a dissevered part itself, standing for no whole, while appearing as if it were complete still. The background recedes ever further, and we seem to be left with "a local and temporal present which is absolute" (7), a style of narration that "causes what is momentarily being narrated to give the impression that it is the only present, pure and without perspective" (12). Other instances of "presentness" are lost (*fast jede Gegenwart verliert*), perhaps excluded (13/G17). Is it Homer, then, or is it the Bible, Auerbach even, who "excludes all other claims" (14), all other worlds? What is this world—what are the parts—into which we are lured and that exists onto itself? The alternative between Athens and Jerusalem (that is, generically speaking, between epic and epic, as well as epic and tragedy) seems at once striking and exceedingly fragile. Is there more than one world in this world? Parts and whole—these are (found on) both sides, each according to its own, parsed in line with a strict analytic of parts, looking like the whole they are or might be. Each is made of parts, which may or may not have a different relation to a whole that is (or should be) everything and nothing, or at least nothing else. Each of "these two equally ancient and equally epic texts" (11), at any rate, "contains nothing but itself" (13).

Readers of Auerbach have pointed out how seemingly secure distinctions such as those deployed here are on the verge of breaking, and this on more than one occasion: a given sharp object (tusk, spear, or knife) could, as it were, tragically pierce the thinly stitched membrane that separates them.[10] Two worlds confront each other *as they bleed*—and if they bleed—into each other, one providing the depth (the additional part) that is lacking in the first. (The other story is about to begin: Somewhere else, maybe *beneath*, a knife is being raised, suspended in midair. This story too will turn out to be partial, potentially so, waiting to be fulfilled and accomplished, later brought into the light, to be *figuratively* completed on another, and proximate, mountain. Will there be blood?) There is just enough room to wonder whether "the two realms . . . are not only actually unseparated [*ungetrennt*] but basically inseparable [*untrennbar*]" (23/G29). There would be one world, then, one world, perhaps, into which we are lured, which "exists for itself, contains nothing but itself" (13), and in which "the various components all belong [*die einzelnen Stücke gehören alle*] to one concept of universal history" (17). Is blood that concept? Will there be universal blood?[11]

Aside from his cunning, Odysseus' most famous parts or attributes are no doubt his ears and his scar. For the former, we have the Sirens to thank and the recurring, interminable concern for their song or silence on the part of a long line of august listeners and interpreters, beginning with Odysseus himself[12]; for the latter, which calls attention, however faintly, to the blood that occupies me here, we appear to have mostly Auerbach (but I seek to show that his contribution runs *deeper*). Still, it remains far from clear what a part consists of precisely, whether for Auerbach or in Homer's poems, and even more so in the peculiar case of blood.

The question already emerged in Aristotle, who "applies the term *mórion* to all the constituent substances of the body as well as to the limbs and organs," and though we ourselves "should not normally call blood a 'part' . . . for him, blood is one of the *zóon mória*."[13] Let us assume, then, that blood is a part. What does that have to do with Odysseus? Why should *his* blood be of any significance? Or any other blood for that matter (assuming—we are getting there—that there is a difference between Odysseus' blood and the blood of others)? Uncertain of my motivations to raise, much less answer, such questions, I find myself nonetheless compelled to linger in their vicinity, to explore the strange presentness of blood. I am drawn to the manifest and recurring appearance of blood and, to a non-negligible extent, to its disappearance as well, there where everything is "clearly outlined, brightly and uniformly illuminated," where "men and things stand out in a realm where everything is visible"—and perhaps just underneath too. This is about parts, then, and about a different parsing of Homer and the Bible, Abraham and Odysseus, the Hebrew and the Greek. In the thick of it all, in more than one way breaking the sleek surface ("it runs far too smoothly" [19]), Auerbach tells us in what is at once an understated and hyperbolic gesture of foreshadowing that there will be blood, blood and politics. There would be Nazism, in other words: "Let the reader think of the history which we are ourselves witnessing; anyone who, for example, evaluates the behavior of individual men and group of men at the time of the rise of National Socialism in Germany . . . will feel how difficult it is to represent historical themes in general" (19–20). Is this still the same blood? "Look closer," glosses James Porter, "and you will notice that the Jews in that chapter are a little *too Jewish*, while the Greeks are a little too, well, . . . *German*."[14] But the analogy, which is also the difference—between bloods—has everything to do with the invention of democracy, drenched as it is, one could equally say, in bloods. Far beyond the circumstances to which Auerbach was responding, blood evokes and provokes, it constitutes, a figure for politics, a figure of democracy in its ultimate perversion. Blood is its past and its dreaded future, and it provides a language for it. Blood and politics indeed, where the exception that Nazism constitutes oscillates for us still at its dubious sources, interpellating us between the Hebrew (the blood thirst of Semitic monotheism and its infamous intolerance) and the Greek ("the doctrine of Athenian racial purity"),[15] and where, in a manner that has failed to arouse much perplexity, "the Greek text seems more limited and more static in respect to the circle of personages involved in the action and to their political activity" (21). What of Greek blood? As one scholar traced the lines of continuity, "the Athenian people in antiquity believed that they were an indigenous tribe, untroubled by migrations and invasions. . . . For an Athenian, to be earthborn and indigenous was also to be well-born, and so his national pride was tied closely to his sense of inherited personal status: if his city was free of racial impurity, so was he."[16] This is about blood and politics, then, but it is also about divisions and exclusions across realms and collectives. This is about war, hunting, and the nature of worship (sacrifice), the essence of science (biology, embryology, eugenics), and the management of blood ties (kinship). And in the midst of these chronic and anachronistic wholes, everything will revolve, in fact, around the question of *another blood*, and more precisely of a difference that is located in and across blood.[17] To repeat, I am after the visibility (or invisibility) of blood, its dissemination (or lack thereof) across "the divided city," as Nicole Loraux called it, across parts and divisions, beginning still and for now with Odysseus' scar, a wound permanently on the verge of having closed and hardened—coagulated, finally—and that recedes as if into an inexistent background by a trick of blood magic.[18]

Recall that for Eurycleia as well as for the reader, the scar—what remains of a deep and grievous wound—functions metonymically for the body of Odysseus and for the past. If "Philoctetes is a wound which has not healed," Odysseus is one that has.[19] Ultimately, the scar is the means through which he can be recognized in spite of the time lapsed and regardless of the elaborate disguise crafted for him by the goddess Athena ("Surely you are Odysseus, dear child," says Euryclea, "and I did not know you until I had handled all the body of my master").[20] The scar is at once wound and identification, remain and memory, the past and the present of an incident that "makes" Odysseus who he is. During that distant hunt, he had already distinguished himself, first by being wounded, then by killing the animal that wounded him.

> Then first of all Odysseus rushed forward, raising his long spear in his stout hand, eager to stab him; but the boar was too quick for him and struck him above the knee, charging upon him sideways, and with his tusk tore a long gash in the flesh, but did not reach the bone of the man. But Odysseus with sure aim stabbed him in the right shoulder, and clear through went the point of the bright spear, and the boar fell in the dust with a cry, and his life flew from him.[21]

Although it is, I think, noticeable, there is no particular reason to consider strange or suspect the absence of blood from the surface of this passage. Blood does not appear here as a theme, as a "basic unit of content."[22] There is no sacrifice here, and these are definitely not Herodotus' Scythians who "fail to remove all elements of violence" from the sacrificial scene (which had, at any rate, already taken place, just before the hunt)[23]; nor it this yet a tragic scene or a court "where the hand that acts must of necessity be bloody" (the poet does not have to demonstrate Odysseus' agentive energies, his capacities for action).[24] Still, one cannot help but remark on the familiar elements of the description: the proliferation of sharp objects and weapons, the harshness of the encounter and the anatomic precision of its consequences. All this makes somehow ostentatious the fact that, as it is undoubtedly and abundantly flowing from the gaping wound (the *Auseinanderklaffen*, as it were, which Auerbach had earlier denied), blood has here lost a "presentness" we otherwise never would have known it had or lacked.[25] Granting again, perhaps for the last time, "the need of the Homeric style to leave nothing which it mentions half in darkness and unexternalized,"[26] it seems nonetheless plausible to ask: "what should we make of the absence of blood? Is it possible to assign a precise meaning to this absence?"[27] Minimally, the stage is set for a striking contrast and a glorious return. Magical healing will stop the unreadable flow of Odysseus' blood and restore him to health as well as whisk him back—swiftly this time—home.[28] The quasi-miraculous *dénouement* is made all the more expressive because the blood, which returns to the foreground just at the moment its flow has been brought to a stop, has been anything but present or visible. By the time blood appears, in other words, it is really to disappear. Behold, the binding of Odysseus.

> Then the staunch sons of Autolycus busied themselves with the carcass, and the wound of flawless, godlike Odysseus they bound up skillfully, and checked the black blood with a charm, and immediately returned to the house of their staunch father. And when Autolycus and the sons of Autolycus had fully healed him, and had given him glorious gifts, they quickly sent him rejoicing back to his native land, to Ithaca.[29]

This may or may not be Greek literature—or religion—at its best, but the binding of Odysseus ("and the wound of flawless, godlike Odysseus they bound up skillfully") does bring together and condense a number of parts and elements, important attributes of blood that alert us as well to some of its major semantic associations. If what is indeed "striking," among the Greeks, "is, if anything, a certain reticence towards blood magic," we are here made to witness at once reticence and a certain enthusiasm.[30] By the time he tries to conceal his scar, Odysseus, who had proved his own skill in another instance of blood magic, already knows something of this.

Whether it should be seen as evidence that the *Odyssey* too is "fraught with background," the blood we have just encountered carries and reinscribes elements (parts and portions) of an earlier episode, one in which other members of Autolycus' progeny appear, together with blood magic and more revelations regarding the nature of blood. Book 11 of the *Odyssey* is an incontrovertible testament to the power of blood magic, to the wondrous capacity blood is endowed with. Whether human or animal (and perhaps there is no difference, as the biblical text unfathomably suggests), blood can revive the dead whom Odysseus comes to see and interrogate. What takes place then, Pierre Vidal-Naquet explains, is "the opposite of a sacrificial meal, whose purpose is to feed the living."[31] The dead want and need to drink blood, they hanker for it, in order temporarily to revive and know themselves.[32] This time, Odysseus' blood—in this case, the blood he wields from sacrificed animals ("And I myself, drawing my sharp sword from beside my thigh, sat there, and would not allow the strengthless head of the dead to draw near to the blood")[33]—is made to work its magical effects by flowing rather than by stopping. It is a further binding of sorts, which has a similar effect than the one we have just seen, insofar as it brings about another oscillation, a return and a revival ("Whoever of those that are dead and gone you shall allow to approach the blood," explains Tiresias, "he will speak truly to you; but whomever you refuse, he will go back again" [146–49]). It is a partial and indeed temporary revival, to be sure, as "this is the appointed way with mortals, when one dies. For the sinews no longer hold the flesh and the bones together, but the strong force of blazing fire destroys these, as soon as the spirit leaves the white bones, and the ghost like a dream, flutters off and is gone" (218–22). Flesh, bones, and sinews—will there be blood? We are once again confronted with a strange contrast that, although it may not qualify as an absence, does call attention to the visibility and invisibility of blood.

Let us recapitulate what we have garnered (if not necessarily *seen*) so far. In these passages, blood is first and foremost blood magic, though it cannot be fully understood apart from the "bloody rationality" of its crucial correlate, namely, sacrifice.[34] Hunting is there too, but the blood that Odysseus here sheds, whether it is his own or intended for the service of the dead, is a kind of sacrificial blood, which brings together humans and animals, that is, the blood of humans and the blood of animals. Broadly speaking, one could assert, I suppose, that blood is marked as primarily "religious" or cultic, something that scholarly consensus has long confirmed. From a literary or rhetorical perspective, at any rate, blood is made all the more visible, all the more striking in its effectivity, by something that, pace Auerbach, can only be called a play of layers and depth. Blood—but is it the same blood or another blood by the time it flows from a wound?—recedes into the background, there where we would expect it the most (the scene of the hunt and the wound, the bloodless description of death, otherwise complete with flesh, sinews, and bones). Death, magic, and sacrifice—these are most certainly bloody. Or are they? There are more hidden layers that seem to glisten still. And even if we were to ignore the insistence the rest of the narrative of necromancy performs, with its near exclusive focus on (dead) women and the centrality of its genealogical concerns ("and the women came, for august Persephone sent them, all those that had been the wives

and the daughters of chieftains. These flocked in throngs about the dark blood....
I drew my long sword from beside my stout thigh, and would not allow them to
drink the dark blood all at one time. So they drew near, one after the other, and
each declared her birth, and I questioned them all" [226–34]), we would have to
follow the signs pointing at yet another sphere and dimension where blood flows
equally abundantly. Proto-Freudian innuendos aside ("I drew my long sword from
beside my stout thigh"), and beginning with his own mother ("I remained there
steadfastly until my mother came up and drank the dark blood. At once then she
knew me, and with wailing she spoke to me" [152–54]; "My mother, why do you
not stay for me when I wish to clasp you" [210]), Odysseus is repeatedly told about
the sexual and familial life of his informants, something that includes the escapades
of the gods as well ("for not ineffectual are the embraces of a god. Tend and rear
these children" [249–50]). In his "patriarchal hardness," in other words, Odysseus
seems to be reminded of the blood of kinship, whether his own or the blood of
(m)others ("And I saw the mother of Oedipodes, beautiful Epicaste, who did a
monstrous thing in the ignorance of her mind" [271–72]).[35] The blood of kinship?

BLOODLINES

We have been repeatedly turning to the association of blood and kinship implied
in and carried by stock phrases such as "blood ties," "blood relations," "bloodlines,"
and "blood kin" (even "blue blood"!), an utter commonplace that, still very much
in use, has long come under interrogation. Thanks to the work of anthropologists
(David Schneider being among the first usually cited in this context), the reference to blood is now largely understood as metaphorical.[36] The association—and
this is what interests me here—is often enough assumed as having ancient, more
literal, roots: Greek and biblical roots. In fact, everything is as if the symbolic quality of sacrificial blood (the magical and cultic dimensions of blood) authorized the
perception of an alternative, material plane: the blood of kinship. In this second,
particular case, blood would have been devoid of rhetorical or symbolic charge.
And whereas today, the blood of blood ties is admittedly figurative (but figurative
of what precisely? parts and wholes), the blood of kinship, for the Greeks, would
have been simply biological, the physiologic substance transmitted from parent to
child, the concrete carrier of identity and of heredity. As already intimated, blood
(cultic or familial) also becomes the archaic ground from which politics emanates
and emancipates itself, foreshadowing a familiar and repetitive movement, which
throughout history (*Heilsgeschichte*) takes us from flesh to spirit, from exteriority to interiority, and finally, from religion to democracy.[37] My argument here

and throughout is, however, that an understanding of blood must begin with an interrogation of rhetoric, with the distinction, precisely, between the literal and the figurative, which sustains and obfuscates the "making of the disciplines," the division that separates kinship from politics, religion from law, and medicine from philosophy.[38] An understanding of blood must begin with the dissemination of a figure (in the expansive sense whereby *both* literal and figurative values are granted) across its unstable fields of operation. And indeed, when it comes to ancient Greece (and kinship very much included), the "presentness" of blood, the extent of its dissemination, can hardly be taken for granted, much less deemed understood. There is no more than a faint suggestion of its having moved into an uncertain background, along with what is otherwise highlighted as a set of antiquated practices (war, hunting, and, of course, blood sacrifice, "the cornerstone of the state religion"),[39] or a habit of speech, a religious symbol, and even a dead or literary metaphor ("thicker than water"), a medical concern, perhaps. Is blood even part of the Greek revolution, of what it left behind, like a long gone, perhaps discarded, past?[40] By drawing on Odysseus' blood, I have so far sought to demonstrate that the significance (or lack thereof) of this part or substance extends, and withdraws as well, beyond the strictures of whatever one might want to call "religion" (assuming this is where Auerbach has taken us).[41] In what follows, I wish to recast the matter of kinship (and ethnicity), and therefore of politics, in ancient Greece (joining up with Auerbach to expand on his comparative, biblical adventures), later to include, as a corrective of sorts, the all-too ignored implications of medical discourse.

Indeed, a rare scholarly survey of blood and its lexical reach in Homer and beyond explores a larger web of associations of blood with war and hunting, cruelty and skill, and most often injury and death (spilled blood). The survey also traces blood in poetic, philosophical, and scientific representations, engaging as well with "(inherited) blood, race, origin, family."[42] But this last item in particular, and at the very least, should long have brought blood to a heightened foreground—for us moderns, if for no one else. Blood, which particularly and most directly conjures Nazism, as indicated by the references Auerbach made, further raises the specter of other "rituals of blood" and of their antecedents.[43] Attentiveness to blood also underscores (or should underscore) the fact that it is the site of a massive dissymmetry between Homer and the Bible.[44] At the extremes of blood, "Jewgreek" is not "Greekjew." Indeed, National Socialism aside, who would contest upon a closer look that blood is unevenly apportioned, that it is first and foremost a biblical, an "Oriental" or "Semitic" (much more than a Greek) concern?[45] Such is rendered all the more evident when considering the vast literature that, since William Robertson Smith at least and all the way to Mary Douglas, has inquired into the question of blood, presumably real blood, and even pure blood, with regard to the so-called

Semites.[46] Nothing seems easier to imagine, discuss, research, or read about than associations between Jews and blood. And ever more so in a comparative context— that is, in the absence of comparability. "For the Greco-Roman world, no text can be compared to the Bible."[47] Consider the sheer numbers after all: "the Bible mentions blood more than four hundred times."[48] How many times the Greek corpus? There is no comparable "taxonomy of blood in ancient Greece," as there is on that other part of the world.[49] Friedrich Nietzsche himself, hardly squeamish when it comes to blood, and who describes "the Hellene" as "by nature profound and uniquely capable of the most exquisite and most severe suffering," affirming of "the whole flood of suffering and tribulations"—Nietzsche himself remains strangely silent about blood in *The Birth of Tragedy*.[50] Who then would want to speak of Greek blood, of bloods and other bloods?[51] *Greek* bloods? *Other* bloods? The problem of comparison must be transposed to an "internal" space as well, as an equally persistent but more originary dissymmetry puts, for once, women on top. For if Hebrews and Jews have been associated with blood to a larger extent than Greeks, how much more so in the case of women, "the race of women," as the Greeks had it, or, in another register, "menstruation and the origins of culture," argued for by Chris Knight.[52] Hence, Odysseus' blood, not (or not so clearly for now) the blood of Penelope. But are these really different? Are there really different bloods? This is the second part of my current inquiry, and it begins with a sense that this—*different* bloods—might be a strange idea, to say the very least. The Hebrew Bible, for one, does not seem to know about it, conceiving of blood as the equalizing attribute of the living creature as such, whether male or female, human or animal. Odysseus' blood? A different blood? What, if anything, could this be? Can it be singled out and isolated? Upheld, gathered, and recognized? Blood is blood, and it is, is it not, an equal and universal concern, one of these "various components [that] all belong to one concept of universal history."[53] Is blood a concept, then? Or just a part, perhaps? How are we to ascribe significance—if any—to "Greek" blood?

At once omnipresent and conspicuously absent, a paradoxical dialectic seems to govern the terrain, which such unlikely headings (Greek blood, Odysseus' blood) begin to map. Judging on the sources and their circulation (in the nontechnical sense of that loaded word), the assumption might nonetheless be warranted that much of what we know or think we know about blood goes back less to the Bible than to the Greeks; that, quantitatively speaking, at least, we are blessed with much more ancient material on Greek blood, more than on any other blood, which is to say that we have access to a much wider range of sources, and thereby of "attributes," on blood from ancient Greece than we do from ancient Israel.[54] Let us stay away from having to decide, historically or otherwise, between Athens and Jerusalem, and linger instead with the way in which, after hunting and sacrifice, and after magic (we shall come back to "biology" and medicine of course),[55] blood in ancient Greece is also political, or at least domestic and genealogical. Granted we recognize that blood, the blood of kinship, if not the blood of race (whatever these might be in their respective distinctiveness), is "an idea that is not totally alien to classical thought."[56] In this perspective, to be related for the Greeks would be to be related by blood, "having the same blood."[57] And there's nothing wrong with that! One might even go so far as to claim that the presentness of blood is in fact overwhelming in ancient Greek texts—beginning with Homer. Contrast this wealth of material with the singularly uneven image we have of the biblical world or with the way the Hebrew text consistently fails to refer to kinship in terms of "blood ties" (it speaks, we saw, of "flesh and bones").[58] Or to use, as already mentioned, the phrase "flesh and blood"?[59] And what of the fact that the all-too common translation casting blood as "life" is simply an enormous error?[60] Does it make a difference what body part (if a part it is), which "shared substance" (blood, flesh, bones, and so forth), is invoked when describing kinship and kinship systems?[61] Surely, this could hardly provide sufficient ground to dismiss the rich scholarly tradition that has lingered on "Jewish blood" or to dispute well-known arguments about "the central role of blood in the priestly religion of ancient Israel" or the fact that, thank God for Leviticus, "this role is additionally remarkable because blood was evidently less important in other ancient Near Eastern religions."[62] Indeed, by focusing on Odysseus' blood and underscoring the matter of kinship in particular, along with the name given to it (arbitrarily or not), I merely wish to revisit the matter of a scar ("To the word scar there is first attached a relative clause . . . ; into this an independent sentence unexpectedly intrudes . . . , which quietly disentangles itself from syntactical subordination"),[63] and explore the possibility of a hidden, perhaps inexistent, background that sustains, irrigates, or severs the comparison between Homer and the Bible, between Odysseus and Abraham. What is the presentness of Greek blood? What is its expanse? What are its divisions? Is it "unified [*einheitlich*]" or "more obviously pieced together [*viel auffälliger zusammengestückt*]"? Does blood have, or signal toward, parts and components? And if so, do "the various components all belong to one concept of universal history and its interpretation [*die einzelnen Stücke gehören alle in einen weltgeschichtlichen und weltgeschichtsdeutenden Zusammenhang*]"?[64] We have witnessed Odysseus' blood ebbing and flowing, as it were, in and out of a field of visibility that, wider than "religion," spreads over a large array of texts and practices (magic and religion, politics and science—none of which need be taken as secure in its distinctiveness), each drenched in a rhetoric of blood that is at least as rich as, if not richer than, the Bible's.

What is of interest to me, then, is first of all the fact of blood in ancient Greece, and the range of its visibility. Taking Odysseus' blood as my point of departure,

I have begun to suggest that the manifestations of blood, its presence or absence in a variety of spheres, dimensions, or indeed parts and portions, function as a broad equivalence to that dimension of the biblical text, the background of which Auerbach famously saw brimming. There is, then, there would be a kind of bloody background to the works of Homer and to the ancient Greek textual corpus in general. This cannot come as a surprising proposition. Blood occupies that background, and it is teeming with all kinds of significance. Who could fail after all to recognize the importance of blood in epic poems dedicated to war and to its bloody aftermath? Or in the tragedies? But that is precisely why I have been insisting on the *background* and on the invisibility of blood, which must be held and contrasted with its otherwise indisputable visibility. It is these two dimensions, these two parts or portions, which together constitute the "presentness" of blood in ancient Greece, a kind of dialectical motion that has retained its currency for thousands of years. In what follows, I am therefore less preoccupied with kinship per se than I am with blood, which extends to the "field" of kinship, worship, politics, and science. Is it, to ask again, the same blood throughout?

CITIES OF BLOOD

Let us not lose track of Odysseus' blood, then, and particularly of the ways in which it has gone *missing*, remaining either in the background or so remote and severed from relevance as to be plausibly inexistent, as inexistent perhaps as Homer's background. "If in truth you are my son and of our blood [*haímatos*] . . ."[65] Here too, at the very least, here again, everything is as if "what underlies the myth and is implied in the basic structure of the text . . . is, as it were, a logical problem: Blood relations are first overrated then underrated; autochthony is first denied then affirmed."[66] More precisely, the blood of kinship and genealogy, which is in many ways conjured throughout the passages of the *Odyssey* I have already referred to—complete with, for example, ethnographic descriptions of the maternal grandfather's role in the naming of the child Odysseus ("Autolycus, find yourself a name now to give to your child's own child" [19:403–404]) all the way to Oedipus' peculiar family circumstances—is never explicitly mentioned in these passages. To repeat: we know with some degree of certainty that blood is related to fighting and to hunting, to sacrifice and to magic (let us condense all this under the term *religious*, assuming it helps). We know that whether or not blood appears, whether it is expressed and exteriorized, explicitly manifested, matters tremendously to the Greeks (even if they did not quite inherit the Indo-European distinction that, between "inside blood" and "outside blood," left its traces on a number of European and other languages, e.g., the Latin *sanguis* and *cruor*).[67] There are extensive debates about "the blood of the gods" too.[68] And there is of course medicine, about which much has been said and written (the four humors, obviously, but also menstrual blood), and there is law as well (the omnipresent "blood guilt" and the famous *dike homaimon*). Should we not finally wonder at the status or significance of blood with regard to kinship?

In order to ask about the difference blood makes, about what blood is when it makes a difference (perhaps all the difference), and therefore about the possibility of speaking of Odysseus' blood, we will have to linger with the politics of kinship, with kinship as political and with Odysseus' own question, and with what Aeneas refers to as "the lineage amid the blood [*geneēs te kaì haímatos*] wherefrom I avow me sprung."[69] To be sure, this refers to a conception that is not unique to the Greeks, although it is hardly universal (as the Hebrew Bible demonstrates). But we cannot yet relegate it to the strange and, in this case, well-preserved cemetery of dead metaphors.[70] On the contrary, it seems important to note that the equivalence between blood and kinship is far from simple but rather very much dynamic throughout the ancient texts. Even if we confine ourselves to a narrow understanding of this specific matter (by suspending hunting and sacrifice, science, medicine, and magic, even law, at least for the purpose of the argument, as if any of these terms could be strictly disentangled from kinship, and the latter from them), we would have to recognize not only that kinship is a complicated issue (a massive understatement), but also that the terminology of kinship is significantly richer, as well as far more obscure, than generally admitted (beginning with the question of whether blood, in this context, is a referent or itself a technical, indicative term, a figure or a thing). But what would it mean to admit it? When did kinship become blood? Did it in fact? An inquiry into parts.

"The first society to be formed is the village," Aristotle famously explained after having considered how "the compound should always be resolved into the simple elements or least parts of the whole" (these being male and female, on the one hand, and natural ruler and subject, on the other) and having relegated the household to the realm of nature ("The family is the association established by nature for the supply of men's everyday wants").[71] Politics begins, in other words, "when several families are united, and the association aims at something more than the supply of daily needs, the first society to be formed is the village." Aristotle then goes on to clarify the structure of these first political units, which were governed by kings. "Every family is ruled by the eldest, and therefore in the colonies of the family the kingly form of government prevailed *because they were of the same blood*."[72] From Aristotle to Henry James Sumner Maine and to Robertson Smith, blood—identical to, yet also narrower than, kinship—would be the undisputed and primary ground, "the sole possible ground," of the political community.[73] This would certainly suggest something like fraught significance.

But there are too many instances of the word *blood* and its cognates or synonyms appearing in the Greek corpus, as well as too many instances of the word being inserted, as if casually, in scholarly discussions and modern translations, along with numerous references to "blue blood,"[74] and to "blood purity" too (and particularly where, as in the passage from Aristotle I have just quoted, the Greek text says nothing about blood, nothing literal—but recall that much of our concerns revolve around this seemingly minor issue: the literal or the figurative). Too many, that is, for the matter to remain entirely concealed and tucked away in some background. Should blood have become a concept? A technical term at least? "Kinship terms are, after all, linguistic entities: they are more culture-dependent than many, but there is no reason to believe that they will behave in a fundamentally different way than other words."[75] But blood is perhaps an ethics, a mode of comportment in, an attunement of character to, the world[76]; or it is an institution, in the sense Émile Benveniste gave that term ("The term institution is to be understood here in a expanded sense: not only the classical institutions of law, government, and religion, but also the less apparent ones drawn in technologies, ways of life, social relations, the reports of speech and of thought").[77] Was it a common Greek institution?[78] Seemingly unbeknownst to Benveniste and to others, it may well be that blood has so functioned. But be that as it may, should not the boundaries of what the term covers be ascertained with some precision then? Are brothers, for example, always "blood brothers"?[79] What, after all, explains or justifies the extraordinary proliferation of blood terms when it comes to the designation of highly contested designations such as "syngeneia, oikeiotès, philia," but also *genos, anchisteia, phratría, phyle, ethnos,* and more?[80] What precisely is the nature and the extent of the "ideology of consanguinity" when it comes to the Greeks?[81] A massive body of literature and scholarship invokes or deploys a lexicon of blood, partly relying on philological research, linguistic antecedents ("Indo-European" or better yet "Proto-Indo-European"), and drawing on the insistent presence of blood in the Greek texts, but doing so while spending too little energy on the precise linguistic, philological, and interpretive opportunities that are thereby offered.[82] For now, let us agree that even if it were true that every kinship relation could be called "consanguineous" (something that is obviously not the case for reasons that exceed the matter of "fictive kinship," of adoption, and even of marriage, and have to do with the necessarily shifting boundaries of what constitutes the collective, whatever its nature),[83] one would still have to contend with this strange fact: terminological studies do not include "blood" as a technical term or concept worthy of interrogation and even documentation.[84] Nor has blood, otherwise charged with the heavy

burden of ultimate evil (Nazism = blood and politics), become a political concept, a concept whose political import must be scrutinized. For why blood, after
all? Why would kinship be in the blood or named as such? And if that is really the
case, what logic, what *hematologics* sustains this strange arrangement? Once again,
it is less a matter of recognizing whether blood (that is, "blood kinship") is or is not
"structurally primary" than of asking whether, to what extent, and why is kinship
called "blood" in the first place.[85] What are we to make, for example, of the fact
that, although he definitely deploys a blood vocabulary, Homer does not know the
terms *homaimon/homaimos*, "of the same blood," as a designation for siblings?[86]
What is the relation or distance between words like *haíma* and *genos* and their
cognates such as they appear in ancient Greek? How are we to understand the so-
called metaphoric value that is specifically ascribed to the terminology of blood? Is
blood of *any* significance at all? There are also prominent books and studies written
about the Greek family (W. K. Lacey, S. C. Humphreys),[87] Greek religion (E. R.
Dodds, W. K. C. Guthrie, Walter Burkert), or, and assuming there is, once again, a
difference, Greek society and politics (John K. Davies, Moses Finley, Pierre Vidal-
Naquet, Catherine Morgan, Ryan Balot) that hardly make any mention of blood
or expound in any substantial manner on its significance.[88] Indeed, if blood moves,
even disappears, between background and foreground, how can we be certain that
it is ever invested with significance, where, and in what manner? As I have already
said, blood is much more likely to be an object of reflection and inquiry when
it comes to the study of "Semitic" sources. As the bibliography grows on "Jewish
blood," who would think of writing a book on "Greek blood"?[89] Everything seems
as if, when it comes to blood, "Homer knows no background." At least for now.

As we continue to look for Odysseus' blood, we ourselves are bound to think
that it is at once everywhere and nowhere. Nowhere: the absence of blood from key
passages, the dearth of scholarship, or the irrelevance of blood in it. Everywhere
(with complications, of course): Denis Roussel aptly summarizes what remains,
paradoxically perhaps, the scholarly consensus. "The Greek terms that designate
social units in the cities ... evoke groups that are founded on blood ties [*des groupes
fondés sur les liens du sang*]. They seem to send us toward a type of organization
that is ruled by kinship, with no reference to any form of state administration."[90]
Such a view goes back to Maine, as I have already suggested, and to Fustel de Coulanges (e.g., "Thus we see that in the time of Demosthenes, to be a member of a
phratry, one must have been born of a legitimate marriage in one of the families
that composed it; for the religion of the phratry, like that of the family, was transmitted only by blood").[91] Trying to parse the difficult relationships between these
groups, together with the terminology of kinship, M. Miller confidently asserts
that "the *oikoi* are blood-lines within the *genos*."[92] Sensitive to historical shifts,

Walter Donlan explains that for "the aristocratic warriors of the Homeric poems," who were just beginning to identify themselves as a social class ("this process had not advanced far enough"), "there was practically no attempt to prove individual or group superiority on the basis of blood lines."[93] In his own historical study of *Kinship and Politics in Athens*, Robert Littman writes, against all historical sense, that "kinship in its most simple definition is relations between kin, that is, persons related by real, putative, or fictive consanguinity." Fully equating kinship and blood, and oblivious to the dynamic of inclusion, and indeed, of definition implied in the notion of "blood kinship," Littman does grant, of course, that "the notion of real consanguinity is peculiar to each society."[94] Following along in this extraordinary enterprise of cultural translation, a recent collection on "fatherless children" comments on the term *gnésios* found in Homer, that it is "cognate with *genos*, 'family,' and *gonos*, 'seed,' [and] clearly meant at heart 'of the blood.' "[95] And here is another description, which at once troubles and reinscribes the consensus (unless it is the mere rhetorical habit).

> It is therefore necessary to consider afresh what is meant by "tribal" society, and how this may be evaluated against growing bodies of data from early ethne. Disputed and problematic as tribalism is, in essence it involves the use of real or ascribed kinship, age and gender, as the basis for structuring the political community. To some extent this is a question of degree, since kinship is used politically in other forms of society also, but where the majority of roles are defined by other criteria, a system cannot be truly tribal. Hence at least one potential difference between true tribal systems and the "tribes" of states such as Athens, at least from the time of Solon's establishment of economic criteria for political office. Equally, although references to blood ties are pervasive in Greek literature, as for example Herodotos' claim (8.144) that the kinship of all Greeks was as much part of Hellenic identity as shared language and religion, the rhetoric of kinship employed as a means of claiming or reinforcing ethnic ties is not coterminous with the practical ordering of a society.[96]

All this would be to say that, complex as it all might be, there seems to be hardly a sphere of social life that remains untouched, to say the very least, by blood. "La cité dans le sang," is what Giulia Sissa calls it.[97] The texts certainly confirm that this is an accurate moniker, true of the gods even, who proudly claim their blood as the basis of genealogical relations and belonging.

> Zeus verily spake vauntingly among all the gods: "Hearken unto me, all ye gods and goddesses, that I may speak what the heart in my breast biddeth me. This

day shall Eileithyia, the goddess of childbirth, bring to the light a man that shall be the lord of all them that dwell round about, even one of the race of those men who are of me by blood [*haímatos*]."[98]

There is another argument to be made, however, which would advocate a more restricted understanding of the notion of blood (but then, blood would have to be recognized as a notion or signifier, a changing and evolving term, operative within complex referential and differential networks of meaning and sense). Thus, following the passage I quoted earlier on the "first society," Aristotle famously goes on to argue against Plato's "eugenic" program on the ground that "blood kinship" (as some translations have it, referring to those one refers to as "my own") trumps any reinvention of the family as identical to the *polis* as a whole, "for it is better for a boy to be one's own private nephew than one's son in the way described" in the *Republic*. Aristotle does end up invoking blood explicitly when he asserts how "the same person is called 'my son' by one man and 'my brother' by another, and another calls him 'nephew,' or by some other relationship, whether of blood [*haímatos*] or by affinity and marriage, the speaker's own in the first place, or that of his relations."[99] One can claim easy recognition of a hint of patrilineal exclusivity when it comes to blood, a matter that is nevertheless as charged as Pandora's box (blood being also, if perhaps not always, a rife site of sexual difference) and that has thankfully attracted some attention.[100] Elsewhere, in his famous discussion of *philía* among relatives, Aristotle himself suggests that his might be quite precisely a restricted and gender-specific understanding of blood, one that would be confined exclusively to the relation existing between brothers: "brothers love each other as being from the same source, since the identity of their relations to that source identifies them with one another, which is why we speak of 'being of the same blood [*taútòn haíma*]' or 'of the same stock' or the like."[101] What this means is that here too, we should remain attuned to the ways in which blood is invoked and made visible (most notably again in modern translations) and where it remains, as it were, in the background (if at all), invisible even where kinship and lineage are explicitly mentioned. Thus, as I have already pointed out, the key passage with which I began this section, among those sustaining the founding and still operative claim made by Henry Maine ("the history of political ideas begins, in fact, with the assumption that kinship in blood is the sole possible ground of community in political functions"), fails to mention blood in any explicit, much less general, manner.[102] Recall that Aristotle writes: "the village according to the most natural account seems to be a colony from a household, formed of those whom some people speak of as being 'of the same milk [*homogálaktes*],' sons and sons' sons."[103] However one understands the term *homogálaktes*—and Félix Bourriot and

Hans Derks have made compelling arguments against the maternal ("co-uterine") interpretation or the nursing imagery often assumed—it is obviously distinct from blood as well, which barely appears in the discussion of the natural community and scarcely does again in the entire text of Aristotle's *Politics*.[104]

How then does one measure the presentness of blood in familial, social, and political considerations? And what happens if one includes cultic and medical (embryological, and more broadly somatic or physiologic) dimensions? The entire corpus of tragedies would be here to prove that blood and kinship are at once central and crucial (even if we still have to wonder about what it is precisely that is thereby demonstrated).[105] And Herodotus, ever so cited in spite (or perhaps because) of his uniqueness on this front, expanded the circle of blood to its widest definition. As is all-too well known, Herodotus quotes an Athenian call to unity, which claims the "same blood [*hómaimón*]" as one attribute among others for "Greekness."[106] Although mostly found in tragedies,[107] this specific notion resonates shortly thereafter in Plato as well. ("By paying honor and reverence to his kinsfolk, and all who share in the worship of the tribal gods and are sprung from the same blood [*taútoú phúsin haímatos héxousan*], a man will, in proportion to his piety, secure the goodwill of the gods of Birth to bless his own begetting of children"; or "And is it not true that in like manner a leader of the people who, getting control of a docile mob, does not withhold his hand from the shedding of tribal blood [*emphylíou haímatos*], but by the customary unjust accusations brings a citizen into court and assassinates him, blotting out a human life, and with unhallowed tongue and lips that have tasted kindred blood [*phónou syggenoús*: more literally, the murder of kin], banishes and slays and hints at the abolition of debts and the partition of lands—is it not the inevitable consequence and a decree of fate that such a one be either slain by his enemies or become a tyrant and be transformed from a man into a wolf?"[108]) In the *Sophist*, Plato—that is, the itinerant stranger in that dialogue—also suggests that certain intellectual and artistic practices could also be thought of along the lines of "descent and blood."

> The imitative kind of the dissembling part of the art of opinion which is part of the art of contradiction and belongs to the fantastic class of the image-making art, and is not divine, but human, and has been defined in arguments as the juggling part of productive activity—he who says that the true sophist is of this "descent and blood [*geneés te kai haímatos*]" will, in my opinion, speak the exact truth.[109]

Should we say that blood is a metaphor, then?

Before jumping to this popular conclusion, it might be important to consider further what we might want to call "real" or "literal" in this context. ("When metaphor becomes incarnate as social practice," writes Nicole Loraux, "who would be able to distinguish the real from the figurative in this matter? Supposing of course that between the one and the other, the border was not always more virtual than effective."[110]) We may have received a hint of this when considering that "blood" could signify no more than the fraternal relation, plausibly extended to a larger set, which remains mostly defined by patrilineal constraints.[111] But what, for instance, did Plato (that is, Diotima) mean by "blood" in the following passage?

> It is only for a while that each live thing can be described as alive and the same, as a man is said to be the same person from childhood until he is advanced in years: yet though he is called the same he does not at any time possess the same properties; he is continually becoming a new person, and there are things also which he loses, as appears by his hair, his flesh, his bones, and his blood [*haíma*] and body altogether. And observe that not only in his body but in his soul besides we find none of his manners or habits, his opinions, desires, pleasures, pains, or fears, ever abiding the same in his particular self; some things grow in him, while others perish.[112]

Is this a medical or more generally a biological view? A philosophical, religious, or a gendered one? Does it suggest a primordial dimension attributed to blood (as opposed, say, to bones and hair)? If it does in fact refer to a general category of kinship and lineage, the continuity of blood, whether individual or collective, literal or metaphoric, its status as that which is shared across generations, much less its "purity," does not go unquestioned. Plato again:

> And when people sing the praises of lineage [*géne*] and say someone is of noble birth [*gennaîós*], because he can show seven wealthy ancestors, he thinks that such praises betray an altogether dull and narrow vision on the part of those who utter them; because of lack of education they cannot keep their eyes fixed upon the whole and are unable to calculate that every man has had countless thousands of ancestors and progenitors, among whom have been in any instance rich and poor, kings and slaves, barbarians and Greeks. And when people pride themselves on a list of twenty-five ancestors and trace their pedigree back to Heracles, the son of Amphitryon, the pettiness of their ideas seems absurd to him; he laughs at them because they cannot free their silly minds of vanity by calculating that Amphitryon's twenty-fifth ancestor was such as fortune happened to make him, and the fiftieth for that matter.[113]

Perhaps it remains the case that, if blood is anywhere, it is in the family. (But according to which calculations of kinship, and which definitions?) And if it stays anywhere, it is again in the family. (But is it still and always the same blood? And is there then a difference between bloods?) Or so we are told it is or should be by the fervent students of kinship—if only we could define (describe or prescribe) in a secure manner what the family is, precisely. Or its exact relationship to politics.[114] And the same goes for blood, albeit out of a different field as well. Aside from the much-quoted definition by Herodotus, at any rate, we seem to be left with little ground to claim that blood is clearly and explicitly found anywhere else, fully illuminated as it were.[115] Thucydides, if I am not mistaken, does not use the term in the context of kinship. Almost nowhere, blood? Minimally, the blood of kinship, perceived or construed as a pervasive and ever present pre-political or political matter, seems determining to an understanding of the nature of collectives. Then again, from what I am able to gather, blood—again in the sense of kinship and lineage—seems mostly absent from the law.[116] It is not found in the *Athenian Constitution*, and scholars of law appear to have found little use for it.[117] And what about the famous *dike homaimon*? It too hardly enables us to leave the realm of the so-called family, though along with the tragedies that ground our understanding of it, it would seem to confirm, with no less than Hegel, that blood, that is to say kinship, is in tension with the state, the quintessential pre-political substance.[118] A provisional conclusion would have to be that even if we were to suspend the obvious issues, some of which we have begun to consider by way of Odysseus (namely, hunting and sacrifice, healing and magic, as well as war and homicide), it appears undeniable that blood must be contended with. To repeat: I am only derivatively interested in kinship and its definitions, nor do I seek to contribute in a direct manner to the debate over the precise nature of tribes, clans, or even "races."[119] And even though I do wish to register my puzzlement over the arbitrariness of the sign in modern translations (consider, for instance, that in the *Menexenus*, Plato is alleged to have said "we are pure-blooded Greeks, unadulterated by barbarian stock"—or, in French, "nous sommes Grecs authentiques, sans alliage de sang barbare"; yet, the Greek text here again includes no reference to blood terms), what continues to preoccupy me is blood in its presentness, rhetorical and otherwise, across the divided city, and the divisions of its discourse and science.[120] Judging from the literature on ancient Greece, then, blood seems to be everywhere—minimally, as a lexical automatism, an immediately available "metaphor for kinship"—and nowhere.[121] Is it ever literal? And if it is a figure, is it in fact a figure for *all* kinship and lineage? We have seen that this can hardly be taken for granted. But there is tragedy, of course, where the term *homaimoi* rules supreme, and which also accounts for much of the massive use of the word *haîma* in ancient Greek texts, Homer aside.[122] And there is medical science to which I will turn shortly.

HEMATOPOIESIS

So what, to ask again, is blood?[123] What is blood if there are different bloods, blood as and across difference? What if there is, in other words, such a thing as Greek blood? An answer to these questions will begin to emerge, I think, if we continue to adhere to a straightforward, indeed prosaic, principle. In order to understand what significance blood held for the ancient Greeks, we have to suspend our rhetorical habits and perhaps simply grant that blood is never metaphorical. Less hyperbolically, perhaps, we should bracket all assurances with regard to whether blood is ever a metaphor, a metonymy, or, as I have already suggested, a concept. Whatever we have encountered of blood up to this point, the language of blood should continue to be read, and as it were acknowledged, *as if* literally.[124] Along with what we have seen so far, this should make clearer that blood (to take it at its word, so to speak) is what is said and done about it, with it and to it.[125] More precisely, we can begin to see blood such as it is *made*, like history perhaps, in ancient Greece, through a series of rites—cultic, political, medical, and rhetorical. For there are numerous of these "rites that make blood," which need to be explored and explicated.[126] Thus, for example, if "blood is kinship," we will have to consider what it is that has made blood such. Only then will there be room for refinements across a better map of the hematological field; only then will the difference between what we have come to call "blood" and what the Greeks called by the "same" name become apparent. I am not suggesting therefore that one find in the texts a "metaphysics of blood," a system of thought and practice that would be governed and ruled by blood in all its dimensions, each of which being somehow derivative (blood as idea or universal concept). Nor am I intent on maintaining an all-too sedimented and strict division between bloods (the blood of war and the blood of kinship, the blood of sacrifice and the blood of the gods), much less one where the difference between bloods would be at once hierarchical and rhetorical, organized along a scale that spans the literal and the figurative, the biological and the conventional. I have been unable, at any rate, to find any indication that there was such a scale. Nor that blood would be one and the same throughout. Blood may or may not be one. Then again, it does not have to be many. And if blood is a site of difference (if there is such a thing as Greek blood, does it mean that the Persians, say, have a different blood? that they too are defined by the "common blood" they share? or is it rather the case that, much like barbarians do not really have language, blood is a particular feature of the Greeks and of them alone?) or a site of continuity (between parent and child, for instance), how did it come to be so and with what consequences? In what sphere was it so understood? Finally, is a biological or physiologic given operative as the primordial ground upon which other furrows of blood are traced, edifices of blood built?

Returning to the issue of kinship and ethnicity, the argument made or reiterated by scholars is that biological and physiologic conceptions—or better yet, biological and physiologic conditions—explain and sustain the notion of "blood ties" that we now view as metaphorical. What peculiar and contingent sense of life or of nature, what precise meaning of these terms, might be involved seems outside of their considerations. And particularly so when the "biological" is perceived as given and as the primary ground or dimension that must be left behind in its normative aspect, toward a more "cultural" and "political" understanding of the social bond: from kinship to politics, as Maine has it, and from ethnicity to culture, as Jonathan Hall puts it. But this un-interrogated biology or biologism (as if the Greeks had not left us a rich medical literature to be fruitfully consulted) and the alleged hierarchy of which it would be the basis remain operative, determining even, based on unchanging biological facts, which would be known to all, recognized and accepted by all, from Plato to NATO.[127] Thus, when Herodotus mentions "common blood," he is said to operate on the notion that "discrete ethnic groups have a common ancestor, and it looks as if he is referring to descent groups—sharing an ancestor implies biological links, if not the modern idea of race itself."[128] More generally, kinship or, as if in seamless translation, *sungeneia* "is defined by common origin and rests upon the recognition of ties that are considered by the Greeks themselves as natural, upon the transmission, the sharing of corporeal substances."[129] And blood would always be a privileged instance of such corporeal, biological substances. Minimally, it would always have been understood *primordially* as a biological substance, and the meaning of that phrase itself ("biological substance") would be a historical constant, based as it were on empirical common sense. Who, for instance, could ignore that blood is the essential ingredient of procreation?[130] Note, however, that if such is the case, then kinship is *literally* blood, and there is neither need nor ground to invoke metaphor when speaking of the blood of larger collectives.[131] The fact of a common ancestor (whether imagined or real makes no difference when it comes to the biological and hematological understanding and its implications) would mean that, however diluted, his blood is in fact shared by the collective (his blood, and not "blood," as the scare quoters would have it).

It has been a while, of course, that the critique of kinship has sealed the distinction between kinship and biology, and it may very well be that the strange lack of discussion of Greek biological knowledge (or lack thereof) is thereby explained in this context. As C. J. Smith explains, with reference to classical studies, the concept of kinship was being seriously challenged back in the 1970s.

For so long, the connection between kinship and biology had been prominent. Increasingly in the 1970s the social fiction of kinship came to the fore. One's family was more about a set of social choices. Kinship was not about blood. Anthropology moved towards a greater interest in marriage (sometimes described as alliance theory) than in descent. Oddly enough, the radical idea that kinship was really about social choice and not biology (and was therefore more open to be rejected, replaced, and reinvented) might not have worried McLennan, or Maine, who believed in fictions. What it did allow in 1976 was the argument that social entities could be invented, and could be reinvented, and indeed were perhaps of necessity reinvented again and again as larger social and political shifts left old concepts redundant and required or permitted new solutions.[132]

But this critique leaves the matter of blood aside or, more precisely, in place. It does so, moreover, in peculiar circumstances, as the widespread understanding of Greek embryology that the critique of kinship explicitly opposes is radically inaccurate as we shall see, which is to say not that it was "wrong" but that the current perspective on it completely misrepresents ancient Greek understandings of procreation and embryology. To the extent, therefore, that it is constitutive of a biological understanding or constituted by it (and whether or not it is remains in question), blood has been at once dismissed and preserved. To put it briefly, whatever the blood of kinship was (or is), it was never quite supported by the medical— that is, embryological—theories of which we are aware. Who or what, then, is the anthropological argument against blood directed at? This question does not make it necessary to locate medicine, or again, biology, at the source or ground of hematology. On the contrary, it demands that we recognize biology as something else than a historical constant, both in the conceptions it articulates and in its allegedly primordial place on a larger terrain. Blood may be a bodily substance, in other words, a part in and of the body, but that does not mean that that is its primary definition, nor that biology, much less embryology, has a privileged access or dominion over it.

Still, it is undeniably the case that blood plays an important role in the history of Greek biology and embryology, and more generally in what G. E. R. Lloyd calls, with some reservations, "Greek Science."[133] There is much to learn, therefore, from this "field." We should note though, as Lloyd does, that "on the problem of the composition of the seed," the crucial site of speculation and the focus of what will occupy us, "most of the main ideas that were put forward in the late fifth and fourth centuries were supplied by men who were not themselves medical practitioners" (63). This suffices to indicate that the scientific ladder, or rather, the general and hierarchical divisions within which the sciences figure and by which we seem to abide today, was not quite in place. But it is also to remind us of the obvious, namely, that within and without these "scientific" circles, the nature of blood was not, by any means, the same as ours (but this is saying too much about "ours" as well). Thus Socrates could ask "Is it the blood [haímá], or air, or fire by which we think?"[134] whereas Aristotle, who proposed as a definition of anger "a surging of the blood and heat round the heart," also "notes that the thinner and colder the blood, the more conducive to perception and intelligence it is."[135] Odysseus' cunning was already his blood! But I shall remain on the topic of embryology and heredity, as it is most directly relevant to the understanding of kinship upon which I have elaborated so far.

Recall that in Homer, "blood and lineage" are, if not identical, certainly associated in a manner that leaves little doubt that blood is an element, a part that is constitutive of kinship. The question that occupies me, however, is whether this ancient understanding is related in any way to contemporary or near-contemporary medical and, more precisely, embryological views. I have already answered, of course, and said that it is not. But this requires more explanation, which I shall provide by way of a shortcut of sorts, that is, by engaging the matter out of the work of scholars who have, in fact, delved into the complexities of Greek conceptions of embryology and heredity. There are of course serious debates and contested issues, but the broad tripartite division suggested by Erna Lesky has been generally accepted.[136] When it came to the human seed, then, it seems that the ancient practitioner could hold either an encephalomyelic (or cerebrospinal) view, a pangenetic view, or a hematogenic view. Lesky attributes the first to Alcmaeon of Croton (but it is also Plato's view), the second to the Hippocratic corpus (though not unanimously), and the third to Aristotle. There were others, as it were in between, such as the Presocratic Empedocles, who held, as Joseph Needham reports, "that the sinews are formed from a mixture of equal parts of earth and air, that the nails are water congealed, and the bones are formed from a mixture of equal parts of water and earth. Sweat and tears, on the other hand, are made up of four parts of fire to one of water."[137] The related but distinct and, for centuries, hegemonic account (found in Galen as well as in many later treatises from the Talmud to medieval physicians) upholds and illustrates the pangenetic doctrine, whereby the seed, of which, contrary to Aristotle's view, there is one male and one female, is drawn from all parts of the body. The ensuing distributive sketch underscores the important, but also specific and indeed localized, role of blood.

> From the sperm itself are formed the white parts of the body, that is, the brain, the bones, the cartilages, the nerves, the membranes, the ligaments, the veins and the arteries; whereas from the menstrual blood are formed the liver and the other fleshy parts, with the exception of the heart, for this is formed from the blood of the arteries.[138]

All this is quite fascinating and has, as Thomas Laqueur and others showed, multiple consequences for the history of biology, of embryology, and of sexuality.[139] Through it all, blood plays an important function, of course, and menstrual blood most particularly, if not exclusively. And yet, the different theories of embryology tell a different and no less interesting story, which either preceded, or for centuries coexisted with, Aristotle's hematocentrism (about which more anon). According to some scholars, these theories may even have constituted the sole and dominant paradigm until quite late, that is, until Aristotelian hematogenesis "became generally accepted from the twelfth century [CE] onwards."[140] Minimally, what this alternative story tells us in no uncertain terms is that there were different conceptions of conception, of embryology and heredity, many of which did not by any means privilege blood as the signifier (or signified) of transmission or of relation between parent and child, and this at the very time Homer was nonetheless singing of "blood and lineage."[141] There is therefore no reason to think of blood as having occupied a prominent position in medical thinking about embryology, genealogy, and lineage.[142] To the contrary, there is ample and justifiable cause to separate and distinguish blood from embryology because the two adjudicating views are not contemporary (Aristotle's contribution constitutes in fact a *later* development—a serious blow to the claim that the role of blood was always and universally recognized as a biological and primary ground). But there is more, and even more striking, which happens when we take Aristotle at his (emphatically phallocentric) word.

Aristotle held, as I have already said, a hematogenic view (a cardio-hemato-centric view, to be precise).[143] This means that, for him, blood (and not all parts of the whole body, the pangenetic view against which he explicitly argues) is the source and origin of semen, that is, exclusively, of the male seed. As Aristotle puts it, "semen is pretty certainly a residue from that nourishment which is in the form of blood" or "fat is a residue just as semen is, i.e., it is blood that has been concocted, only not in the same way as semen."[144] Aristotle acknowledges the blood of the mother, of course, but he does not think she contributes a seed. More precisely, "the female, though it does not contribute any semen to generation, yet contributes something, viz., the substance constituting the menstrual fluid (or the corresponding substance in bloodless animals)."[145] In other words, in Apollo's infamous words, the mother is not a parent, and heredity is something that happens—that is to say, strictly and correctly—between father and child, not between mother and child (as that would be a sign that the father's seed was not, as it should have been, dominant).

> If the seminal residue in the menstrual fluid is well-concocted, the movement derived from the male will make the shape after its own pattern. . . . So that if

this movement gains the mastery it will make a male and not a female, and a male which takes after its father, not after its mother; if however it fails to gain the mastery, whatever be the 'faculty' in respect to which it has not gained the mastery, in that 'faculty' it makes the offspring deficient.[146]

Put yet another way, "the resemblance between son and father is a fact of nature, the most natural possible," and "the birth of a son that resembles his father is, in a certain way, primary."[147] Leaving aside the question of what is (or rather: what is not) transmitted between mother and child, the crucial question for us is whether Aristotle's assertion can be taken to mean that the father's blood passes from parent to child. I suppose it still depends what one means by blood. One thing is certain, however, regarding the answer to that particular question. Giulia Sissa has impeccably shown that Aristotle held to a strict division of form and matter, which organizes his embryology as well. And as expected, Aristotle left no doubt as to what, of the (higher) form and the (baser) matter, is contributed by whom. "The male provides the 'form' and the 'principle of the movement,' the female provides the body, in other words, the material."[148] Strictly speaking then, as Sissa clarifies, "*nothing* passes from the father's body or from the matter of the semen to the product of generation."[149] That is because, as active partner, the male does not contribute matter, not *any* matter, and certainly not anything that materially remains or persists.[150] It is "the female *qua* female [which] is the passive one," and what she "contributes to the semen of the male will be not semen but material. And this is in fact what we find happening; for the natural substance of the menstrual fluid is to be classed as 'prime matter.' "[151] There is no better or clearer illustration of the fact that the main, nay, the towering figure of hematogenesis (indeed, of hematocentrism) in ancient Greek medicine did not say or think that blood—that is the matter of blood ("the blood, as I have often stated, being the matter for animal organisms," he repeats)—was transmitted from father to offspring.[152] "The seminal fluid is the accidental vector of a completely different kind of heredity."[153] Heredity, the filial bond that connects father to child and, most importantly, father to son; the minimal and uncontested name and referent of the bond between father and son, namely, *consanguinity*; the ground upon which volumes upon volumes of kinship literature have either been constructed or argued against—all that is not blood. Not for Aristotle (and much less for the non-hematogenetic embryological doctrines), and not in any material, substantial, much less literal or even metaphoric, understanding. Which is to say that, as Aristotle puts it, "there is no necessity for any substance to pass from the male; and if any does pass, this does not mean that the offspring is formed from it as from something situated within itself during the process, but as from that which has imparted movement to, or that which is its 'form'" (and that, in case you're wondering, is air, "the warmth of breath," *pneuma*).[154]

But is there not ample evidence—and from Aristotle himself!—that blood is the blood of kinship? That what connects two related persons (minimally, two brothers) is not some generic "shared substance" but is in fact the same blood? If so, and given the state of embryology as we know it, what could this possibly mean?

The answer is beyond simple. But it might help at this point to look elsewhere and recall that, for Aristotle as well as for the Hippocratic corpus and beyond, "blood is first of all nourishment which irrigates the entire body."[155] Before it is kinship (if it is in fact kinship), therefore, blood is food. Here is Plato's scientific opinion, his telling account of the matter, which is worthy of being quoted at some length.

> Moreover, the process of respiration—with which our account commenced—came about, as we previously stated, in this manner and by these means. The fire divides the foods, and rises through the body following after the breath; and as it rises, with the breath it fills the veins from the belly by drawing into them from thence the divided particles. And it is owing to this that in all living creatures the streams of nutriment course in this way through the whole body. And inasmuch as these nutritive particles are freshly divided and derived from kindred substances—some from fruits, and some from cereals, which God planted for us for the express purpose of serving as food—they get all varieties of colors because of their commingling, but red is the color that runs through them most of all, it being a natural product of the action of the fire in dividing the liquid food and imprinting itself thereon. Wherefore the color of the stream, which flows through the body, acquired an appearance such as we have described; and this stream we call "blood," which is the nutriment of the flesh and of the whole body, each part drawing therefrom supplies of fluid and filling up the room of the evacuated matter. And the processes of filling and evacuating take place just as the motion of everything in the Universe takes place, namely, according to the law that every kindred substance moves towards its kind. For the bodies which surround us without are always dissolving us and sending off and distributing to each species of substance what is akin thereto; while the blood-particles, again, being minced up within us and surrounded by the structure of each creature as by a Heaven, are compelled to copy the motion of the whole.[156]

There are countless similar references to this specific understanding of blood ("blood is the ultimate nutrient of the body; blood is composed directly from digested food") throughout Aristotle and elsewhere.[157] We have even seen an instance whereby blood feeds the dead rather than, to be fully precise, revives them.[158] Much less debated than the seed, if at all, this seems in fact to have been the most widespread understanding of blood in any context in Greek antiquity, so much so that the "belief in blood as the agent of nutrition has been correctly described by Solmsen as 'one of the fundamental discoveries of ancient physiology.'"[159] Furthermore, this "theory of digestion/nutrition which assigns a haematopoeic function to the liver . . . subsequently became the most widely accepted theory of digestion in European medicine until the seventeenth century AD."[160] Blood is food, and food is blood. Any discussion of sacrifice (of "religion") could have told us as much, of course, but it does get more complicated since the same goes for menstrual blood ("menstrual blood was thought to be the excess from the diet")[161] and embryology as well, "as the stuff out of which the parts are formed is the same as that from which they derive their growth, namely, the nourishment." Therefore, Aristotle continues, "we should expect each of the parts to be formed out of that sort of material and that sort of residue which it is fitted to receive."[162] Michael Boylan succinctly comments: "for Aristotle, all body parts except the heart are fashioned by blood."[163] This applies to semen as well, which is blood, as we saw, but only because, though "considerably different in character from blood," it is in fact "a residue from that nourishment which is in the form of blood and which, as being the final form of nourishment, is distributed to the various parts of the body."[164] In this process, "the flow of food," that is, the flow of blood, is as Marie-Paule Duminil puts it, "comparable to the flow and deposit of alluvium."[165] Duminil makes clear that all this reaches well beyond embryology. For Aristotle everything is made of blood, because everything is nourished by it, sedimented out of it, and swims within it.[166] The Presocratics were (almost) right after all. Everything is blood. Everything except kinship.[167]

That blood is food is, therefore, a massive commonplace, which is profusely documented throughout the sources, and most vividly perhaps in Homer. For the Greeks, as Jean-Pierre Vernant and others have demonstrated, you really are what you eat.[168] That does not mean that you *are* blood (although Aristotle seems to have been willing to go almost as far), but it does mean that what you eat is transformed into blood, which feeds every part of your body (individual and political). What you eat is what you literally become. Not because you are born with it or into it, having received it from your parents and ancestors, but because you partake of the same diet, which makes the same "kind" of blood. And so, of course, you have to keep eating, as, again, "the supply of blood was conceived as analogous to that of an irrigation system and in an irrigation system the dry earth consumes the water in its runnels. Blood as pure nutriment is similarly consumed by the tissues and organs. It was this widespread and deep-seated belief, then, in the total consumption of the blood which precluded any suggestion of its being recycled"—or preserved across generations.[169] This goes a long way to explaining quite a bit, starting with the famous passage that gave away the name *ichor* to the divine blood (albeit by mistake, it seems)[170] and that suggests that if there is a difference between bloods, for the Greeks, it is not so much because there are different *kinds* of bloods (not because one is born of a different blood at least), but because some have blood, while others do not—depending on what they eat (or don't). Recall that, at this point in the *Iliad* narrative, Aphrodite has just been wounded in battle, and so "forth flowed the immortal blood of the goddess, the *ichor*, such as floweth in the blessed gods; for they eat not bread neither drink flaming wine, wherefore they are bloodless [*anaímonés*], and are called immortals."[171] Blood as food, and food as blood provides the ground upon which we might rethink the nature of those "shared substances" that are said to constitute the stuff of kinship and of ethnicity.[172] After all, it is "the instruments of a way of eating that Herodotus in his accounts of Egypt places at the heart of the difference, the otherness, that the Greeks perceive in themselves with respect to the Egyptians."[173] And the same goes for the Persians.[174] Herodotus' much-cherished phrase about the "common blood" of the Greeks would be a testimony to their eating habits, rather than to some proto-racial or biologically inflected "ethnic" perceptions.

This is hardly a radical idea, but it demands an attention to the dynamic manner in which foreground and background (as Auerbach deploys the terms and such as have occupied me throughout) are distributed across realms and all too often seen as distinct and even separate. Stanley Stowers has made a compelling argument about the "patterns of homology relating cooking (i.e., diet), blood, and procreation to sacrifice." He endorsed the suggestion made by Vernant and others that "Greek sacrifice used food and feasting to produce a system of classifications central to the culture."[175] Stowers speaks in this context of a "ritual control of kinship" (313), whereas I would place a different emphasis (mostly because the procreative power of female blood, on which Stowers insists, are less than compelling and seem to me to be trumped by the nutritive function of all blood, gendered as it remained, throughout all these "rites that make blood").[176] Akin to sacrifice and "the domains and distinctions" it helped to shape, blood also had as much, if not more, to do with the "perception of the human place in the cosmos, gender, descent, kinship, citizenship, civic particularity (e.g., Athenians vs. Spartans), membership and rank in voluntary associations, ethnicity, social status, basic patterns of conviviality, the distribution of food, civic time, life passages, age grading, and civic space" (328). It may not have suffused each of these domains and distinctions quite to the same extent, and it certainly did not do so in the same unified manner. One reason for this might be that blood and sacrifice are not fully contiguous and overlapping "domains" themselves. By taking Odysseus' blood as my point of departure (a point of departure that included sacrifice but was not exhausted by it), I have tried to map out a distinct terrain, which like Stowers and others, acknowledges that "Greek society always rested heavily on kinship, but kinship never merely natural, physiologically determined. Physiology and biology do not create descent groups and patterns of kinship," and neither does blood, unless we recognize that it too means something else altogether (313). Which is to say simply that it *means*. Blood is endowed with significance, already embedded within layers of foreground and background. Indeed, like "the organization of kinship [which] is always political," so blood too (313). It is political, and even ethical, because it is distributed and shared across a variety of spheres, whether somatic, cultic, dietetic, or rhetoric, which are made, not quite out of necessity, bloody ("Politics," writes Claudia Baracchi, "is more architectonic than medicine, for it comprehends the human being as a whole, not merely as a bodily organism, however much ensouled or animated").[177] Blood is one site and object of a collective making, a *poiēsis*. Like children, in fact, which are made and created by a prolonged series of rituals—gestures and actions—literally, by *poiēsis*.[178] As Jean-Pierre Vernant explains, however,

[W]e should like to point out that, in the religious thought of the Greeks, the category of action seems to be defined differently from in our own. Certain actions that run counter to the religious order of the world contain an unpropitious power that quite overwhelms the human agent. The man who commits such deeds is himself caught up in the force that he has unleashed. The action does not so much emanate from the agent as if he were its origin; rather it overwhelms and envelops him, engulfing him in a power that affects not only him but a whole sequence of actions of greater or less duration that are influenced by him.[179]

In the lines that follow, Vernant refers to blood, although he does so in a restricted sense. At the conclusion of our exploration into the matter of Odysseus' blood, it seems to me that blood could easily be identified, albeit in some specific and not all instances, with that force and power Vernant describes, that overwhelming and engulfing power. Like milk, its most directly related nutrient, blood ("Greek" blood) is an agent and a force, and so not only within the sacrificial or cultic, martial and medical contexts.[180] It is also an object or a part that is spilled or stopped, distributed or withheld, consumed, treated, examined, reflected upon, and more. Such actions are not always so active, much less controlled by one's intentions, as Odysseus and a few other famous Greek characters knew. But they do constitute the "rites that make blood" in ancient Greece. And they seem fraught with background indeed.

CODA: WE WHO ARE GREEK, ARE WE GREEKS?

Do we owe our blood (or bloods) to the Hebrews or to the Greeks? Somehow disingenuously, Auerbach would no doubt have answered: both. Yet, this fact alone have I sought to underscore: In contradistinction with the Bible (where blood is juridico-cultic and, derivatively, dietetic), blood mattered to the Greeks across an uncommonly large range of domains, from the scientific to the political, from the cultic to the rhetorical. With Odysseus' blood in its manifestations and disappearances, I have tried to show that blood, for the Greeks, is fraught with background. Blood is itself a fraught background, constituting a "broader fabric of sense into which the human is woven."[181] And yet, I have also been concerned with a demonstration of the dramatic difference between "Greek blood" and Christian blood. For the vastness of domains covered by blood in ancient Greece does not even begin to compare with what has become of blood and Christianity. Most important perhaps, because of the alleged filiation that ties Christianity to "Greekjew" and "Jewgreek," I wanted to underscore the ignorance of the ancients with regard to a "community of blood" in any deep sense comparable with more recent uses and abuses of the term. Whatever the nature of the "sharing" or "unity" made possible by blood in ancient Greece, it is not predicated on kinship or ethnicity in relation to procreation, but rather in relation to food. Thus, and at the very least, "whether a direct line connects 'us' to those who are claimed as 'our' Greek 'forefathers,' whether 'the Greeks' are closer to 'us here' (to the scientific as well as political practices current in Europe and North America today) than other cultures are—this, in a serious sense, remains to be seen."[182] If only because the nature of that line or bloodline of fathers and forefathers, because blood itself, remains indeed to be seen. Or perhaps, toward a generalized hematology, eaten and drunk.

Five BLEEDING AND MELANCHOLIA

MELANCHOLIA,[1] FREUD TELLS us, behaves "like an open wound, *wie eine offene Wunde*."[2] Melancholia acts, it must act, or work, "like a painful wound, *wie eine schmerzhafte Wunde wirken*" (258/G446).[3] Melancholia, in other words, marks or draws blood. This is an old story, which is why melancholia can be said to bear, as Ian Chambers suggests, "interrogations that promote a sense of the unhomely, full of memories that . . . draw blood."[4] Melancholia was always about blood.[5] Which means it was always about *religion*, if we provisionally understand this term in a specific sense, which will have to be borne out in what follows: history and collective psychology, of course, but economy as well, and a generalized hematology too.[6] Within these broad parameters, I restrict myself here to bleeding and melancholia.

Now, even a cursory reading of "Mourning and Melancholia" would reveal that the wound Freud writes of traverses and cuts melancholia itself, which never quite manages to gather into an integral unity. Indeed, melancholia "takes on various clinical forms the grouping together of which into a single unity does not seem to be established with certainty" (243). "Fissured by a crucial ambiguity," melancholia cannot but display "its own internal conceptual self division."[7] Melancholia is a wound that itself suffers from internal cuts, perhaps from internal bleeding.[8] It maintains a wound, hosts and guards it; it preserves *itself* as an open wound that haunts and affects and, one could say, *infects* the subject. The subject too is divided. Freud famously describes this split or cleavage, *Zwiespaltung*, of which Lacan made much in his own elaborations on the subject of psychoanalysis. The division respectively involves and distinguishes "the critical activity of the ego and the ego" (249/G435). Here, as elsewhere, "one part of the ego sets itself over against the other, judges it critically, and, as it were, takes it as its object" (247). Conflict and, most notoriously, *ambivalence* are constitutive of melancholia, the double fate or destiny, the "double vicissitude, *zweifache Schicksal*" (251/G438), which generates a multiplicity of psychic instances, personas of a great tragedy "in which hate and love contend with each other" (256). Freud evokes Hamlet of course. But other tragedies, "countless separate struggles," seem to take place "within" melancholia.[9] Hamlet's "melancholy distraction" along with the conflicts he endured may thus partake of, and even include and incorporate, those "exaggerations of a vital truth about the age in which he lived," as David Scott puts it, but also the truth of other tragic ages, such as one in which there live "conscripts of modernity."[10] To be precise though, with regard to spatial—if not so clearly temporal—coordinates, Freud does insist that "the location of these separate struggles cannot be assigned to any system," but for that famously divided and strictly un-locatable instance that is the unconscious (256). All this should make abundantly clear that melancholia, the bleeding wound of melancholia, has always been a matter of collective psychology, less about "the ego and the id" than about "totem and taboo," "Moses and monotheism," and as promised, finally, religion—call it tragic religion. Everything is as if melancholia provided more than a model for the sedimentations of identification and laid the ground for an understanding of sociability in its many layers, not all of which are psychic or spiritual layers. In "Mourning and Melancholia," at any rate, Freud convincingly drives us in this direction by deploying what can only be described as a rigorous political economy, something like a melancholy ethic in the spirit of capitalism.

THE SPIRIT OF CAPITALISM

I do not need to recall—how could anyone forget?—that melancholia, like mourning, is all about work and no play, indeed, all about work ethics. Melancholia is about "internal work, *innere Arbeit*" (245/G431), "the internal work which is consuming the ego—work which is unknown to us but which is comparable to the work of mourning" (246). Freud willingly testifies, therefore, that "it is tempting to go on," and apparently on, and on, "about the work of mourning and try to give an account of the work of melancholia, *der melancholischen Arbeit*" (255/G443). Himself a legendary workaholic, a melancholy worker of sorts, Freud goes on some more and adds that he wonders where "the work of melancholia, *die Arbeit der Melancolie*, goes on [*vor sich geht*]" and, presumably, on (255/G443). And on. Melancholia is also about accumulation and economics. Its ongoing temporality raises the possibility of diminishing returns and the risk of, well, "becoming poor" (248). Deleuze might have been proud of this downwardly mobile desiring machine, but Freud further insists on "the economics of pain" (244) and "the prominence of the fear of becoming poor" (252) and on the "impoverished" ego that follows the hostile takeovers melancholia conducts (253).[11] Throughout, it is "a matter of general economic experience" and of repeatedly advertised "economic conditions" (254–55, 258), "economic means" (255) and the lack thereof. There are reversals of fortune too, of course—*Queen for a Day* style—such as when "some poor wretch, *ein armer Teufel*, a poor devil by winning a large sum of money, is suddenly relieved from chronic worry about his daily bread" (254/G441). Economy can almost be said to operate as the last instance here, and one could easily go Marxist on Freud, therefore, or at least Weberian. Minimally, Freud (who comes close to lamenting the things that are "not at all easy to explain in terms of economics" [245]) is hardly discreet about his search for "any insight into the economics of the course of events" or better yet, for an "economic understanding, *ökonomische Verständnis*" (253/G439). But let me try to make somehow clearer where this is all going, for it might be time to mention that, as we seek to get closer to the work and to the wound of melancholia, we find ourselves "oriented," as Rebecca Comay beautifully puts it, "toward the viscosity of life-substance."[12] We will continue to remain, that is, in the proximity of what "only slightly quenches the vampire thirst for the living blood of labor."[13]

LE CANNIBALE MÉLANCOLIQUE

Enter the vampire, then. Or, as Larry Rickels puts it, "the melancholic, [who] has . . . shifted down to the biting stage."[14] Freud himself proposed the figure of a "ravenously hungry man, *ein Heißhungriger*" (255/G442), but he had evoked him throughout, by invoking "the oral or cannibalistic phase of libidinal development" (249), "the refusal of nourishment" (250), and the desire to "incorporate" the object "*auf dem Wege des Fressens*," by "devouring it" (250/G436). But "in what, essentially," Joan Copjec asks, "does the phenomenon of vampirism consist? The first thing to note is that it is a matter of an oral relation, of a *jouissance* attained through sucking. One might spontaneously think of the child in its oral-parasitic relation to its mother as the image of vampirism."[15] The equally spontaneous image I am trying to draw here links not just vampirism and anxiety, as Copjec argues ("he fears us; he fear time, he fear want!" explains Van Helsing in his universal English),[16] but also, and perhaps more broadly, bleeding and melancholia ("He have done this alone; all alone! From a ruin tomb in a forgotten land").[17] What should have come to light, in other words, if not quite to sunlight, is the uncanny figure of "deceiving demons,"[18] what Pierre Fédida came to call "the melancholic cannibal, *le cannibale mélancolique*."[19] Such has not really been the case, however, and aside from Tomislav Longinovic's *Vampires Like US* and Larry Rickels breath-taking (and blood-sucking) work in *The Vampire Lectures*, there is, to my knowledge, very little written on vampires (and even, explicitly, on cannibals) as melancholic figures, indeed, as figures of melancholia.[20]

> When mourning shuts down, something like vampirism has already taken its place. The melancholic builds inside himself a crypt where the dead person can be kept alive as undead, and keeps that crypt of preservation secret because all it takes is for someone, an analyst, for example, to open the otherwise unprotected crypt and let in the light and air, and that is the way it goes, what is already dead must again die, now once and for all.[21]

Enter the vampire, then, and the postcolonial melancholia of *Dracula*.[22] It is deeply buried, yet restless, and it bears witness to the good and the holy. "For it is not the least of its terrors," Van Helsing explains, "that this evil thing is rooted deep in all good; in soil barren of holy memories it cannot rest."[23] Call it *collateral damage* under the best of intentions. Or call it, as one scholar has, "vampire religion."[24]

But let me run through some of what I have tried to say so far, if only for the sake of repetition, a compulsive return to the primal scene—or rather, to the primal meal. Melancholia is a wound. Like the uncanny, doubled figure of the vampire— at once alive and dead—melancholia is ambivalently divided, at once internally and externally. Melancholia suffers, in other words, not only from internal wounds and bleeding, but from "balkanization."[25] This provides one important cluster of reasons why we can speak today of postcolonial melancholia in the context of shifting empires, that is, to put it more accurately, one shifty empire ("If America can go on breeding men like that," writes Dr. Seward, "she will be a power in the world indeed." To which the American, Quincey Morris, generously contributes: "I propose that we add Winchesters to our armament. I have a kind of belief in a Winchester when there is any trouble of that sort around").[26] More significantly for my purpose, by reinserting "into colonial historiography the vampires and the phantoms that are often such uninterrogated parts of colonial texts," as Luise White proposes, we might come to acknowledge the overdetermined associations between bleeding and melancholia and better appreciate the moment in which we find ourselves.[27] I did mention the economy—to say nothing of lost ideals and objects: known and unknown ones, or even unknown unknowns. But what, precisely, is this moment of ours? Is it, in fact, ours? And who are we? Is it a historical

epoch? Is it geographically or culturally specific? Local or "glocal"? Before addressing these questions and the answers that a (very quick and somehow allusive) reading of Bram Stoker might offer or suggest, allow me to continue reviewing a few
more well-known things. We do know, for example, that melancholia has long
been associated with the theory of humors of classical medicine. Yet one could
say that its importance (and indeed, the physio-theological investment it occasions) increases substantially with "the Aristotelization of medieval Galenism,"
the growth of Aristotelian hematocentrism.[28] One could moreover say that insofar
as melancholia was always perceived as "melancolia nigra et canina," it was always
already colonial and postcolonial.[29] Persistently associated—and quite literally
so—with the black underdog, melancholia has had something of an underbelly,
which by a strict reversal of logic, may have turned out to be of greater importance.
As I have said, melancholia was always about blood. The wounds, as Mina née Murray (soon to be Harker) puts it, "seem not to have healed. They are still open, and,
if anything, larger than before."[30] That does not necessarily mean that it was always
about race, but we are getting closer to the race wars envisioned and feared by those
who unleash them. "One can roughly divide the nations of the world into the living
and the dying," Lord Salisbury put it a few months after Stoker published *Dracula,*
no doubt in support of helping some of them out of their misery.[31] Incidentally,
or not so incidentally (the precarious status of collateral damages), melancholia
was always about love (and hate), the flight of obsessive spirits, dark and canine
cannibals and blood-thirsty vampires, as well as other frightening visions. By the
sixteenth century, Marsilio Ficino had brought it all together, so to speak, and
explained.

> Wherever the assiduous intentions of the soul bear themselves, there also the
> spirits direct themselves, which are the vehicles or the instruments of the soul.
> The spirits are produced in the heart with the most subtle part of the blood. The
> soul of the lover is pulled toward the image of the beloved written in the imagi-
> nation and toward the beloved itself. Thither are attracted also the spirits, and in
> their obsessive flights, they are exhausted. Because of this a constant refurbish-
> ing of pure blood is necessary to replace the consumed spirits, there where the
> most delicate and transparent particles of blood are exhaled each day in order
> to regenerate the spirits. Because of this, pure and bright blood is dissolved, and
> nothing remains but impure, thick, arid and black blood. Then the body dries
> out and dwindles, and the lovers become melancholic. It is in fact the dry, thick
> and black blood that produces melancholic or black bile, which fills the head
> with its vapors, dries out the brain, and ceaselessly oppresses, day and night, the
> soul with dark and frightening visions.[32]

Everything is already here, and love is all you need—almost everything, bringing us back to Freud on "the intentions of the soul," by way of the associations of melancholia and the open wound, "bloom and blood," blood and melancholia, a blood that, alternatively pure and impure, produces its own antidote, as it were, but is also revealed as the ultimate source of its poisonous double, black bile.[33] As if anticipating the plot so skillfully crafted by Stoker, we are treated to collective psychology—vampire religion—as the religion of love in the "precise sense," as Žižek puts it,[34] and to "the vehicles or the instruments of the soul," without which the modern novel could never have come about.[35] We witness, in other words, "an intensified attachment to things whose prosthetic role is neither countenanced nor entirely denied,"[36] those multiple, technological prostheses and apparatuses that crowd the pages of *Dracula*.[37] With Ficino, we are also given a rigorous description of the grammatological measure of love, along with its telepathic dimensions, whereby "the soul of the lover is pulled toward the image of the beloved written in the imagination." We catch sight, finally, of these exhausted and consumed spirits, the obsessive flight of whom requires "a constant refurbishing of pure blood." Vampires, it seems increasingly obvious, are melancholic cannibals. Or, to put it in the words of another medieval treatise, melancholics are vampires. They are "excessive in lust and without restraint with women . . . their embrace is hateful, twisted, and mortal like that of predatory wolves."[38]

GROUP PSYCHOLOGY

The question of history—postcolonial melancholia—emerges in an uneasy togetherness with the matter of collective psychology.[39] "This entrenched kernel of the unhealed injury, the wound covered with stories of one's greatness perpetuates the work of the historical imagination, which reverberates in the literary and cultural narratives of oppressed [and not so oppressed] peoples like a revenant being of ancient times."[40] Over against a general, self-oriented trend in current discussions, identification, a concept that is central to the vicissitudes (or the "double vicissitude") of melancholia, can remain a matter of individual selves only with extreme difficulty.[41] "Identification," writes Freud at one point, "is the expression of there being something in common, which may signify love" (250). "Identification is always primally grounded and ground up in acts of cannibalism," clarifies Rickels.[42] Such collective acts, totemic meals of sorts, must be equally true of melancholia as well, which always has a social side. For group psychology is, as it were, at work in the very work of melancholia, at the heart of its divisions, and on the edges of its open wound. As Freud has it, we have already seen, melancholia "takes on various clinical forms the grouping together of which into a single unity does not seem to be established with certainty" (243). Sociability itself is therefore at issue. Which is why much could be said about the notions of *Zusammenfassung* (translated as "grouping together") or *Zusammenstellung* (translated as "correlation") in their relation to the economics, and the political economy, I have recalled earlier as being deployed by Freud throughout "Mourning and Melancholia." The very "correlation" between *and within* the two terms is here at stake. Or, as Judith Butler puts it, Freud's "account of melancholy is an account of how psychic and social domains are produced in relation to one another."[43] It may therefore signal some of the vectors we would have to follow to determine the limits of our postcolonial melancholia at once in social and historical terms: history and collective psychology.

THE FUTURE OF CHRISTIANITY

Whose history and whose psychology? Or, as we have been talking about love and about "vampire religion," whose religion?

There are a number of ways to go about answering this. According to Friedrich Kittler, "the race of the Count is the history of Transylvania, his blood a different sort of memory than reference works."[44] But there is a longer and indeed larger history here. One could simply follow Freud's work of incorporation, its Frazerian inspiration or its formulation by Robertson Smith, all the way to Elias Canetti on "the religion of lament" ("The image of him whose death Christians have lamented for nearly two thousand years has become part of the consciousness of mankind").[45] Or at least all the way to the totemic meal, "an act of communion in which the god and his worshippers unite by partaking together of the flesh and blood of a sacred victim."[46] Other scholars—many of them less squeamish than us—have simply referred to this as "a short history of Christian theophagy" or, in other settings, simply as "Cannibalism and Christianity."[47] In a slightly different context, Louis Marin, who knew what he was talking about when he wrote of "food for thought" (in French, *La parole mangée*), invoked "the eucharistic matrix."[48] And do recall that "sucking blood and eating are equated in *Dracula*."[49] The entire language that has been spawned around mourning and melancholia could, in fact, be said to partake of a not so subtle Christian semiology, to be suffused with it: from *incorporation* to the *crypt*, from *economy* to the *work ethic*. No wonder "Christ has continually been accused of being the head of a Jewish cannibal sect."[50] Far from all manifest Christian references, Butler further describes melancholic internalization as "a strategy of magically resuscitating the lost object."[51] Pierre Fédida, for his part, describes cannibalism as "the myth of a killing, *mise à mort*, meant to misrecognize a *difference* [between self and other] and to validate the hope of a possible identity by way of faith in incorporation [*par la croyance en l'incorporation*]."[52] Equally close to Christianity, really very close against it, Larry Rickels suggests, "Dracula strikes back—against the heart of Christianity, and releases the blood inside the cross."[53] That is why we must not be misled, Norman Brown reminds us in his pertinent discussion of "filthy lucre"; "we must not be misled by the flat antinomy of the sacred and the secular, and interpret as 'secularization' what is only a metamorphosis of the sacred."[54] But let me refrain at this juncture from going further on this particular path.

Radically opposed, at least on the surface, would be the alternative assertions to the effect that linking cannibalism (and the melancholic cannibals vampires are) with Christianity is in fact mistaken and misleading. I am not so certain I would want to reduce the argument I am trying to make about "bleeding and melancholia" to an argument about cannibalism, but in the event, our colonial and postcolonial melancholia (along with the difficulty of *zusammenfassen*, with regard to its multiple forms) may have been partly addressed by Gananath Obeyesekere in his discussion of "Cannibal Talk."

> The work of culture can produce all sorts of symbolic variations around this positive form of the sacrifice, the most obvious being the multiple forms of the Christian Eucharist. Hence my reason for rejecting the simplistic view that one could classify the Eucharist as a form of "cannibalism" though it certainly could be brought within the comparative frame of the human sacrifice. God had to become human before he could be sacrificed and eaten in an act of symbolic remove from actual anthropophagy.[55]

Christopher Herbert may have gone equally far, by the way, when he argued that "the breeding ground of the vampire cults and other evils" testify to an "archaic, never uprooted kinship" with their "nominal adversary, Christian faith."[56] Fine, then. Let us agree to content—or discontent—ourselves with a comparative dimension that would leave things off, as it were, in the middle, divided and separated. Freud himself famously concludes by asserting that "the interdependence of the complicated problems of the mind forces us to break off every enquiry before it is completed—till the outcome of some other enquiry can come to its assistance" (258). From enquiry to enquiry—an open wound. Our postcolonial melancholia will always already have failed to come together, especially there, where accusations made against Jews consuming the blood of Christ were deployed at the very time the Eucharist was canonically spreading.[57] By the fifteenth century, "cannibalism was surely a demonic inspiration" and "drinking human blood was a practice the Church frequently attributed to heretics and witches," and of course to Jews.[58] Were we to describe this as a defensive procedure, we might recall that, in *Totem and Taboo*, Freud gave it a technical name: *projection*.[59] And speaking of projection, the body of Christ, because we brought him up, "was the arena for a conflictual and contradictory symbolics . . . a stage-managed spectacle of community . . . the site of an intensive cultivation of identificatory and privatized practice." Indeed, the failure of our coming together around the melancholic cannibal—vampire religion— may be fruitfully compared to "the failure of Christ's body to function as an image of unity, the impossibility of that project" of medieval piety and its "extraordinary preoccupation with the wounds."[60] You might recall Dr. Seward, who movingly asserts that "no man knows till he experiences it, what it is to feel his own lifeblood drawn away into the veins of the woman he loves."[61] You may also recall his description, "how the ruthless hands of the Count had held [Mina Harker] in that terrible and horrid position, with her mouth to the open wound in his breast."[62] It would be hard to deny that "Dracula takes on the role of Christ, offering his own breast and blood to Mina."[63] Let us not part from this without recalling that the image of Christ's wound, an image of wounded attachment if there ever was one, is often an image of "parturition that can never be finished, so that the wounds can stay open."[64] Like the "man of sorrows," like Jesus, "Dracula is a mother."[65] He brings about and sustains the community of blood. "All the characters in Stoker's novel come to be linked together through transfusions, suckings, and nursings within a circle of recycled blood."[66] I could elaborate further here and take you through a minute description of the long tradition of the religion of love as vampire religion. It is after all possible that "the holiest love was the recruiting sergeant for their ghastly ranks."[67] I will restrict myself to quoting a few instances that resonate with Ficino and provide a wider historical frame for the endurance of motifs, which, Ian Chambers suggests in a pertinent context, touch on "the dark heart of the question that has so persistently tortured the fashioning of modern Europe."[68] The first is by the twelfth-century Flemish poet Hadewijch:

> In the anguish of the repose of the madness of love . . . the heart of each devours the other's heart. . . . As he who is Love itself showed us when he gave us himself to eat . . . love's most intimate union is through eating, tasting, and seeing interiorly. He eats us; we think we eat him, and we do eat him, of that we can be certain. But because he remains undevoured . . . each of us remains uneaten by him. . . . As soon as Love thus touches the soul, she eats its flesh and drink its blood.[69]

Another instance dates from the fourteenth century, by the anonymous "monk of Farne."

> Little ones . . . run and throw themselves in their mother's arms . . . Christ our Lord does the same with men. He stretches out his hands to embrace us, bows

down his head to kiss us, and opens his side to give us suck; and though it is blood he offers us to suck we believe that it is health-giving and sweeter than honey and the honey-comb.[70]

By the eighteenth century, John and Charles Wesley were rousing the Methodist imagination with the following hymns.

> Now, Lord, on us Thy flesh bestow
> And let us drink Thy blood,
> Till all our souls are filled below
> With all the life of God.
>
> From Thy blest wounds our life we draw;
> Thy all-atoning blood
> Daily we drink with trembling awe
> Thy flesh our daily food.
>
> We thirst to drink Thy precious blood
> We languish in Thy wounds to rest,
> And hunger for immortal food
> And long on all Thy love to feast.[71]

But it was of course Catherine of Sienna who put it most limpidly, when she urged us to

> drown, then, in the blood of Christ crucified, and bathe in his blood and become drunk with his blood, and sate yourselves with blood and clothe yourselves with blood. And once more I would fain go clad in blood. . . . I will have blood, and in blood have I satisfied and shall satisfy my soul . . . so that in my time of solicitude, I would go washed in blood, and thus I shall find blood and creatures, and I shall drink their affection and love in blood.[72]

CHRISTIANITY AND ITS DISCONTENT

Let me conclude by going yet another route. The melancholic cannibal, I have argued without great effort, is the vampire. And there seem to be some ground to further claim that melancholics, insofar at least as they adhere to the religion of love, also belong to the "vampire religion," to generalized melancholia, if you will. "Take it, then, that the vampire, and the belief in his limitations and his cure, rest for the moment on the same base."[73] Now, I could see how I—or Stoker himself perhaps—might be accused, by no less than Nietzsche himself, of "philosophizing." And Nietzsche did say that, "philosophizing was always a kind of vampirism."[74] I want to return therefore to more explicit considerations of melancholia, considerations that have remained as far as I know little attended to in the particular facets that have concerned me here. I am referring to Walter Benjamin's sparse and, if I may say so, *cryptic* remarks with regard to melancholia and Christianity in *The Origin of the German Tragic Drama*.[75] When gathered together, it seems to me that these remarks state one thing very clearly. Our postcolonial melancholia, Benjamin would say, has only become possible in and through Christianity. "Something new arose," Benjamin writes, and this new thing was "an empty world, *eine leere Welt*."[76] A certain step then became possible, he continues, from Stoic *apatheia* to mourning, "but of course a step which only becomes possible in Christianity" (140). Hamlet brings Benjamin to his conclusion, for "only Shakespeare was capable of striking Christian sparks from the baroque rigidity of the melancholic." That is why it becomes imperative for *Hamlet*, for this drama to be "recognized as the unique spectacle in which . . . things are overcome in the spirit of Christianity, *ihrer überwindung im christlichen Geiste*. It is only in this prince that melancholy's self-absorption attains to Christianity, *kommt die melancholische Versenkung zur Christlichkeit*" (158). Melancholy *attains*, it *comes to*, and, one could say, becomes Christianity. Hegel, whom we have seen referring to "the absolute Notion, *der absolute Begriff*" as "the simple essence of life, the soul of the world, the universal blood, *das einfache Wesen des Lebens, die Seele der Welt, das allgemeine Blut*,"[77] was perhaps trying to convey a similar, if more restricted, sense of Christianity—"that terrible baptism of blood"[78]—when he wrote of the "sadness, *Traurigkeit*" and the "melancholy serenity, *wehmütigen Heiterkeit*" that Christians feel around the Holy Supper.[79]

VAMPIRES 'R' US

Because, like us Christians, secular, suckular, or otherwise, he cannot consume or commune without there being at the same time a sacrifice, a murder, an identification.

—LARRY RICKELS, *VAMPIRE LECTURES*, 328.

I should cut to the quick now, return to Freud, and conclude. You remember Freud's *Moses*, no doubt. We shall return to all this, but try now to recall Freud's

Jesus and his share in mourning or melancholia. He died—Freud underscores this for those who did not notice—yet he lives. We have all killed him, we say in what is no doubt one of the most striking historical instances of self-berating accusations. We have all killed him, yet he is risen. "You, Jews, killed our God," many have somehow tirelessly repeated, and yes, they say, "it is true that we did the same thing, but we *admitted* it, and since then, we have been purified."[80] Like a jury (I almost wrote: "Jewry"), the accusation remains hanging. And this is the case even when religion itself becomes "the abandoned object . . . incorporated into the melancholic self," and the plaint or lament, indeed, "the complaints are directed toward the object that has been incorporated."[81] Secular or postsecular, the wound remains open. The body—"the body as tomb or the omnipotent devouring," as Julia Kristeva describes it—is eaten, sucked dry of its blood, and left as if undigested.[82] Dead and alive. But let the dead bury the dead.[83] Do you not know, asks Paul, "do you not know that all of us who have been baptized into Christ Jesus were baptized unto his death? Therefore we have been buried with him by baptism into death, so that, just as Christ was raised from the dead by the glory of the Father, so we too might walk in newness of life" (Romans 6:3–4). We have been buried and the dead now walk. Can there be mourning in Christianity? Can the crypt, the *empty tomb* (where the dead person is kept alive, where we have come alive, and where the living is preserved as dead *and* risen) be opened to let in the light and air? Is that what Nietzsche did to Christianity?[84] Did he open the tomb? But if that is the way it has gone, as Rickels articulates the matter, and "what is already dead must again die," is it any different now, when keeping and preserving the lost object as *living*,[85] when what is already dead (and risen) must live again?[86] When Paul writes that we are "always carrying in the body the death of Jesus, so that the life of Jesus may also be manifested in our bodies" (2 Corinthians 4:8–10), is it mourning or is it melancholia? "I want you to read the Burial Service," demands Mina, "You must read it over me some day."[87] Is today the day? Is it not everyday? Is this history or collective psychology? Rickels calls it "the double feature of cannibalism and unmourning."[88] I have tried to follow up or simply reiterate, propose that it is bleeding *and* melancholia, the open wound of the vampire religion, the indispensable "arrow in the side of Him who died for man."[89] At least, this would be what happens, Friedrich Kittler explains, "when someone reaches the heart of darkness." They are led "to that point where the power of the Other or Stranger would become decipherable as their own colonialism, if it were not so unbearable to read the writing on the flesh."[90]

And unbearable it is, as Giorgio Agamben also makes clear, reading Gershom Scholem on "the claws and knife-sharp wings" of Klee's angel. Let us try to bear it nonetheless. Let us look at Klee's angel again, "the double figure of the angel" whom Scholem calls "diabolical" and Agamben, well, "love." "There is only one figure that brings together purely angelic characteristics and the demonic traits of claws. This figure," adds Agamben who doth protest, "is not Satan but Eros. According to a descriptive model that we find for the first time in Plutarch (who attributes 'fangs and claws' to Eros) . . . Love is represented as a winged . . . angelic figure with claws."[91] Let us look at Klee's angel again. Is "the angel the chronicler of wreckage, or its agent?"[92] Look at the angel. Look at its wings. Look at its teeth. Is it not the noonday demon? Or perhaps, once "the shadow of the object" falls upon it, the midnight one? Commenting elsewhere on Dürer's melancholy angel, Agamben writes that there is "an authentic minor emblem that holds the key to the larger emblem that contains it."[93] That emblem is the bat. "But why do those superimpositions, those curious, distorting superimpositions of images (there is a frequent overlapping of images which produces a doubling rather than movement) so often assume those wing-like-bat-like-shapes?"[94] Look at Benjamin's angel again. Look carefully. No, it's not a bird, nor is it a plane. It's not Batman either, but the angel of history may well be a bat nonetheless, a big bat "flapping its silent and ghostly way to the west."[95] It is a particular kind of bat, though, full of love—and out for blood. A vampire bat.

Six LEVIATHAN AND
THE BLOOD PUMP

I see vast ocean, like a heart in play,
Pant systole *and* diastole *ev'ry day*
And by unnumber'd venous *streams supply'd*
Up her broad rivers force th' arterial *tide.*
—FRANCIS HOPKINSON

Who well considers the Christian religion, would think that God meant
to keep it in the dark from our understandings, and make it turn upon the
motions of our hearts.
—SAINT EVREMOND

I stand for the heart.
—HERMAN MELVILLE TO NATHANIEL HAWTHORNE, CA. JUNE 1851

I BEGIN[1] BY recasting a title familiar to historians and philosophers of science—
Leviathan and the Air-Pump—in order to allude to another debate, not quite the
one that took place between Thomas Hobbes and Robert Boyle, which divided science (the air pump) from politics (*Leviathan*),[2] but rather the more covert dispute,
"the pitiless war of reading waged between Melville and Hobbes."[3] This debate
would have made visible, had it achieved that status itself, the unity of a larger
system—a circulatory system—that divides and separates between and across multiple realms and domains of which science and politics are only a part.[4] Ultimately,

albeit latently, the debate took place as if within one of these domains, namely, as if contained within the thin but capacious walls of "literature." It unfolded, at any rate, within the precariously bounded pages of Herman Melville's *Moby-Dick*. Leviathan and the blood pump—this, then, refers to *Moby-Dick* as it puts in motion and follows the circulation of blood, an arterial tide forced by broad rivers, from Hobbes to Melville and beyond.[5] For at the center, that is, *at the very heart* of Melville's "total book" (and perhaps in Hobbes's as well), a book expressing "not only a complete human experience but offering itself as the written equivalent of the universe," there is blood.[6] More precisely, throughout the book, and in each of the figures, texts, and debates it stages, cites, incorporates, and engages, blood rushes and circulates—it ebbs and flows too, as premodern medicine had it. True to its numerous meanings and functions, blood distributes and is distributed: It traverses and irrigates all the bodies and domains herein invoked, whether textual or political, physiologic, scientific and technological, or otherwise. At once literal and figurative (but this distinction, once again, will not cease to *liquefy*), blood spills between and within the domains of science and politics, race and religion, literature and economy, and more.[7] Blood is made and remade, as it were, in a new and collective *reading*. Leviathan and the blood pump—this, to do no more than revisit the well-known fact that *Moby-Dick* "has more or less defied classification" (early readers knew it, who described the book as "no mere tale of adventures, but a whole philosophy of life," "neither a novel nor a romance," in which "all the rules which have been hitherto understood to regulate the composition of works of fiction are despised and set at naught")[8]; to explore again the "thematics of form" and "the connection between narrative form and politics,"[9] as well as "literary theory, science and philosophy of science."[10] Leviathan and the blood pump—to draw out an asymmetric cartography of these various realms, domains, and bodies[11]; to read *Moby-Dick* as the striking account and compendium of pervasive inscriptions, a series of testimonies on blood, in short, a writing of blood and in blood: the ultimate *hematography*.

I truly begin, however, with another conjunction between the terms of my title, a slightly different syntax that articulates at once vector and conclusion for everything that follows: Leviathan *is* the blood pump. Like the rivers that run through it—venous streams oozing from a heart at play—I offer this sentence as a summary of *Moby-Dick* and as a guide toward its significance, such as will unfold in the pages of this chapter.[12] At the outset, the sentence is meant to provide an occasion to reiterate C. L. R. James' 1953 assertion that Herman Melville is "the unsurpassed interpreter of the age in which we live, its past, its present and its uncertain future."[13] Ushered in by Hobbes (him again, quoted in *Moby-Dick's* "Extracts" but otherwise quite discreetly operative, if one blissfully ignores the mark he made on the very name of Leviathan), this age in which we live is very much a Christian age. It is the age of Christian blood—its circulation and distribution. In my reading, to put it more precisely, Melville lays out the history of Christianity as the history of blood. And vice versa. For Christianity—and in this resides its singularity, indeed, its integrity—has everything to do with blood, with the massive, distributive presence of blood in and through the modern division of spheres and domains we have been attending to until now. Much as "nature is in fact always another name for writing in Emerson," so blood, for Melville, functions as another name for history and for politics, for the flow and movement of "Christian peoples," which *Moby-Dick* announces, responds to, and enacts.[14] Only a few years before Melville swung open "the great flood gates of the wonderworld," before his account of those "thousands upon thousands of mortal men fixed in ocean reveries," these same peoples had begun to be described in pregnant, foreshadowing terms by Alexis de Tocqueville.[15] "Christian peoples in our day," Tocqueville wrote as if commenting on the book (and on the currents) to come, "appear to me to offer a frightening spectacle; the movement that carries them along is already strong enough that it cannot be suspended, and it is not yet rapid enough to despair of directing it." It is with and in response to this fluid and magnetic movement that, "under the pressure of a sort of religious terror," Tocqueville calls for "a new political science."[16] What he saw as "a world altogether new" demanded a new science, a new politics, and, he made clear, a new literature as well (one that, were it considered within the restricted limits of "literature and religion," would perhaps have to be read while substituting the conjunction "and" to "rather than" in the following: "to reconstitute the discussion on the plane of the hermeneutical rather than the apologetic, the anthropological rather than theological, the broadly humanistic rather than the narrowly doctrinal").[17] And it is this world, whether new or not, that Melville writes in his hematography. Indeed, as the promise and threat of that world's prolonged and no doubt extended conclusion become increasingly evident (and increasingly bloody), national boundaries—the U.S.-centered reading of *Moby-Dick*—must continue to be explored and interrogated, expanded upon and transgressed, from a simultaneously older and newer perspective, and that because "the range, the overreaching, the tremendous energies of this magnificent story of hunting the White Whale *spills over* national, aesthetic, and historical boundaries with massive force."[18] And with massive force too, this "book at odds with itself as a novel . . . sets forth to discover a very old, much-written-about world of the timeless seas," the old-new world of Christianity.[19] For Christianity is old, to be sure, but its new and modern form has become global, extending far beyond the borders of the United States, which it nonetheless uses and buttresses as arterial walls and vessels of asymmetric distribution. Melville compels us to consider this form, to contend with the circulation, the global currents, the constraints and divided domains of the Christian Commonwealth (as Hobbes pointedly called it), which is why one of his major commentators could assert that Melville was the Anti-Christ of that Christian age, or at least that "it was necessary for Melville, because Christianity surrounded him as it surrounds us, to be as Anti-Christ as Ahab was."[20] One could finally say that Melville—whose mind Sophia Hawthorne perceptively described as being in a state of "fluid consciousness"—was a kind of prophet, and that, like another Moses, he "wrote in *Moby-Dick* the Book of the Law of the Blood."[21]

Minimally, by placing Ishmael's "whaling voyage" in the "grand programme of Providence" as a kind of "brief interlude and solo between more extensive performances" and events (a voyage and a performance that, Ishmael says, had a medical, hematological goal, aimed as it was at "driving off the spleen, and regulating the circulation"—in lieu, that is, of "pistol and ball," of following Cato's equally bloody choice, who threw "himself upon his sword" [1: 1]), Melville made a strikingly prophetic—and global—suggestion (1: 7). He became, like Hobbes, a "prophet of the leviathan."[22] Right at the beginning of the book, Melville imagines that the advertising poster for the events Ishmael is about to narrate "must have run something like this."

Grand Contested Election for the Presidency of the United States.
WHALING VOYAGE BY ONE ISHMAEL
BLOODY BATTLE IN AFGHANISTAN (1: 7)

With this uncanny—and at least twice bloody—announcement, which deploys and recasts the modern state and American politics, world economy and the flow of blood, we have already begun our reading of *Moby-Dick*. The following remark will come as no surprise, therefore. Leviathan is the blood pump ("a sort of Golgotha of the heart") because, as Charles Olson first pointed out, whaling oil was the original "blood for oil."[23] From the European Middle Ages to the eighteenth-century establishment of American dominance over the hunting of whales, there was the source of light and of countless other products, what preceded the fuel source that has now taken over the earth—and the sea.[24] Offering thereby a glowing and flowing image of America, Melville himself provides the following description: "It is the land of oil. . . . The streets do not run with milk . . . they have reservoirs of oil in every house, and every night recklessly burn their lengths in spermaceti candles" (6: 32). Having drilled the first local oil well in Pennsylvania in 1859, Edwin Drake made the dynamic parallel between the precious liquids quite clear. "More than any other product," he wrote, "whale oil whetted the human appetite for clean, efficient, and affordable illumination."²⁵ By the mid-nineteenth century, which is to say, by the time Melville wrote *Moby-Dick*, the

> demand for nighttime illumination far exceeded the four million barrels of whale oil produced each year by refineries in New England and New York. It was for this reason that Drake's Connecticut backers sent him to the Oil Creek valley. Journalists and entrepreneurs recognized the continuity. The first oil gushers in Venango County prompted hurrahs akin to seamen's "thar she blows" for the spout of a large sperm whale. In 1861, *Vanity Fair* published a cartoon showing formally attired whales attending a ball honoring Drake's well, pausing to toast the new technology that had spared them.²⁶

Blood for oil thus refers to the "bloody" and "fiery" hunt and chase—"an act of Christian faith," says Robert Zoellner²⁷—and to the "quenchless feud," the relentless hankering for blood shared by "the whalemen as a body" and projected by them onto the whale: "we find some book naturalists ... declaring the Sperm Whale ... to be so incredibly ferocious as continually to be athirst for human blood" (41: 179–81). It is, at any rate, the blood of Leviathan ("he must die the death and be murdered, in order to light the gay bridals and other merry-makings of men, and also to illuminate the solemn churches that preach unconditional inoffensiveness by all to all" [81: 357], or, in Ahab's personal and no less global version, "this is what ye have shipped for, men! to chase that white whale on both sides of land, and over all sides of earth, till he spouts black blood" [36: 163]).²⁸ It further refers to "labor as flood," the streams of blood of "mariners, castaways and renegades," the blood of countless workers and slaves produced and processed by the newly unleashed powers of capitalism and the oil industry.²⁹ More generally, as Eduardo Cadava has strikingly showed, it refers to the blood spilled for the massive fertilization of American soil with "foreign bodies: the seeds that are imported from England, the fertilizer imported from Peru and elsewhere, the bodies and blood of peoples from Africa, Germany, Ireland, Peru, China, and so forth—all of which will become part of the 'American' body ... the black 'blood and tears' that nourish the land."³⁰ Here again, even when writing about America, Melville was always thinking about the world—and about race, which is to say, about blood. That is why he explained that "you cannot spill a drop of American blood without spilling the blood of the whole world. ... Our blood is as the blood of the Amazon, made up of a thousand noble currents all pouring into one."³¹ Or again, as Ishmael poignantly puts it in *Moby-Dick*, addressing a world of ever so avid consumers: "For God's sake, be economical with your lamps and candles! Not a gallon you burn, but at least one drop of man's blood was spilled for it" (45: 206).

By the time Melville writes (but these things started somehow earlier), blood has become an essential element of "the political economy of the sea" and that of the earth.[32] Among the elements, blood irrigates the entire history of industrial capitalism. Like money, it has no odor. This may be a recent development and does not have to be universally true, but in the case at hand, it seems to be the case when blood (that is to say, oil, money, and blood) is found inside the whale. For "the truth is, that living or dead, if but decently treated, whales as a species are by no means creatures of ill odor; nor can whalemen be recognized, as the people of the middle ages affected to detect a Jew in the company, by the nose" (92: 410). Oil for blood, and blood for oil—this is also the history of race and of racism.[33] Along with class and gender—a crew of men and men only, albeit of different provenance and standing—race is the unavoidable horizon of political economy and of a political reading of Melville's "Leviathan."[34] Whether considering the extermination of Native Americans (inscribed in the *Pequod*'s name, and in Ahab's very figure, as Wai-chee Dimock has argued)[35] or the long history of slavery (and its numerous figures and representations throughout Melville's work), American imperialism or the transformations of capitalism (in many ways, the very subject of *Moby-Dick*), it is impossible to ignore that Melville's "uncanny accuracy [regarding] the true political dynamic of his age" is governed by the question of race.[36] Melville, in other words, "saw into the heart of America on the question of race."[37] For what after all is Moby Dick? D. H. Lawrence's answer is unequivocal and impossible to dismiss: "He is the deepest blood-being of the white race. He is our deepest blood-nature."[38] Building on this insight and on the growing body of scholarship dedicated to these issues, it seems important to consider its extensive consequences, namely, that blood traverses, or rather, that blood is distributed, that it circulates, throughout the body of Leviathan, that is, through a vast number of domains that all qualify as natural and as political (theological, economic, medical, and so forth). The blood pump irrigates and constitutes "the image of society in *Moby-Dick*," the constitution of the community, whatever its nature, in the political imagination.[39] This is why, after economy and race, Melville attends to the importance of anatomy (as well as to the counting of bodies and body parts), dissecting and dismembering as he does "the corporeal self" and the world at large ("*Moby-Dick* takes *monster* bodies apart in order to examine of what they are made . . . [It] dismembers the outside world of which the whale is an emblem, with the hope that, as a consequence of the dismemberment, the self could magically take the world—now sufficiently partialized—into its own body").[40] Doing so, Melville is also re-membering the parallels between the collective or mass (and certainly massive) body and the individual body, after the manner of Hobbes and, before him, Saint Paul.[41] In *Moby-Dick*, at any rate, "the whale's body is literally anatomized," whereas at other times the text "anatomizes the human body directly."[42] Fundamentally preoccupied, moreover, with the question of birth, filiation, and kinship (medicalized, racialized, and otherwise), the book "allegorizes the idea of family, enlarges it to embrace the *Pequod*'s crew."[43] Suffice it to say for now that to assert, after Hobbes and with Melville, that "Leviathan is the blood pump" is not simply to renew with the *metaphor* of the body politic as the site of operations of a medical and medicalized thought, nor to revive medicine as the model for political science. Rather, it is to inquire into the addition—perhaps the *supplement*—that blood is or brings: into the function of the presence and circulation of blood, in the constitution of economy and politics, of individual and community, whether national, racial, or familial.

Moby-Dick narrates and describes—and this is, again, Melville's singular contribution—the pervasive presence of blood in every domain. Elements of this story have become manifest at least since Hobbes referred to "the Sanguification of the Commonwealth" (where blood figures the nourishing flow of money and commerce through the state) and perhaps most clearly since *Leviathan and the Air-Pump*, that is, since Steven Shapin and Simon Schaffer meticulously described, in their celebrated book, the debate I alluded to earlier and that opposed Thomas Hobbes to Robert Boyle.[44] This debate certainly engaged all the resources of a culture in flux, highlighting among the domains we have quickly reviewed thus far the scientific realm, its isolation and its transformations. Yet it seems to me that, even in this context, something in "science's blood flow"—essentially related to "the hunting of Leviathan"—has not sufficiently been attended to.[45] Not at least with regard to blood "itself"—literal and metaphoric (and the liquefaction of both). Consider, as we have begun to do, that it is in fact blood that flows and circulates from Hobbes's friend and benefactor, William Harvey, all the way to Herman Melville and beyond. Perhaps more than anything else, it is the circulation of blood—Harvey's discovery—that links Hobbes to Melville and *Leviathan* to "gospel cetology."[46] To be sure, in his 1628 *De Motu Cordis* ("On the Motion of the Heart"), Harvey had not succeeded in fully demonstrating the circulation of blood, but he did prove that the heart is a pump. And within the heart, those "fleshy columns and fibrous bands" that are, Harvey described, "like the elaborate and artful arrangement of ropes in a ship, bracing the heart on every side as it contracts, and so enabling it more effectually and forcibly to expel the charge of blood from its ventricles."[47] After the publication, meteoric dissemination, and acceptance of Harvey's work, further and fundamental questions emerged that would be of extensive significance for the history of science (medicine and anatomy in particular), but also for the enduring history of the "experimental life" and the division between science and politics.[48] In fact, "it was to answer these fundamental questions, and in direct response to Harvey's discovery, that Boyle and Hooke developed the pneumatical air-pump."[49] Before the air pump, then, there was the blood pump.

Like his students and followers, and in a manner that could only with difficulty be described as more literal (perhaps only as more frequently physiologic), Harvey was an anatomist.[50] His "methodology of dissection and experiment became . . . the model procedure for the solution of physiological problems. This experimental imperative, reinforced by the values of experimentalism derived from chemistry and from Bacon's writings, became the dominant methodological theme in the reconstruction of physiology."[51] Following closely in his footsteps, then, there was Boyle who, together with his collaborators, advanced the experimental method and "vigorously promoted Harvey's model of endlessly repeated dissection as the one sure route to understanding the mechanics of respiration."[52] As did Hobbes, who significantly asserted at the opening of his *De Corpore* that

> the science of *man's body*, the most profitable part of our natural science, was first discovered with admirable sagacity by our countryman Doctor Harvey, principal Physician to King James and King Charles, in his books of the *Motion of the Blood* and of the *Generation of Living Creatures*; who is the only man I know, that conquering envy, hath established a new doctrine in his life-time.[53]

Hobbes's theory of bodies in general, his theory of human nature, the psychological principles on which he grounded it, were "predominantly metaphysical," but they grew out of "his materialist metaphysics combined with some of the biological ideas of William Harvey."[54] The blood flow of science can thus literally be said to run in and through the blood vessels of *every* body. This is true with regard to most sciences, but we also know that it is true of political science, and of Hobbes's *scientia civilis* in particular.[55] It is true, in other words, of *Leviathan* and of Leviathan. For "the Artificiall Man maintains his resemblance with the Naturall; whose Veins receiving the Bloud from the severall Parts of the Body, carry it to the Heart; where being made Vitall, the Heart by the Arteries sends it out again to enliven, and enable for motion all the Members of the same."[56] Hobbes did not become systematically cardio-centric, although some commentators consider that he "out-Harveyed Harvey in the supremacy he gave to the heart. He regarded the heart as the controlling organ, not just in the body, but in the whole man"; for him the heart was "the fountain of all sense."[57] More importantly, with the prominence he gave to the heart, and his militant introduction of the image of blood in the body politic, Hobbes played a key role in the sedimentation of Harvey's achievement within political thought and beyond. This is how—if not quite precisely why—Leviathan becomes the blood pump. In the wake of Hobbes and of Harvey,

Melville's *Moby-Dick* condenses and recapitulates—it teaches—the result of this knowledge. It "mixes the discourse of the naturalist with that of political sovereignty," with a knowledge that is at once medical, theological, and political.[58] In all these ways and more, *Moby-Dick* is hematological.

Connecting Hobbes to Melville, the blood pump has everything to do with Melville's science, therefore, and is inextricable from Melville's politics. For although little has been said about the recasting of Hobbes in Melville ("He is lonely Leviathan, not a Hobbes sort. Or is he?" asked a perspicacious D. H. Lawrence), it will be difficult to diminish the significance of the figure of Leviathan as it emerges and reemerges in *Moby-Dick*.[59] Indeed, Melville's own place in the history of science— his participation in establishing a popular genealogy of anatomy—traces and traverses the bodies (whales and men, animal and political) that were dissected from Harvey to Boyle, from John Hunter to Paley's *Natural Theology* (both quoted in the "Extracts"), and all the way to the development of anatomy and the establishment of the medical profession (and of numerous medical schools and universities) through "a traffic of dead bodies" in nineteenth-century America.[60] Melville's debt and contribution to the history of science, his attempt to write "as if to include the whole circle of the sciences" (104: 456), is evident throughout his work.[61] It is almost as if, "by an admirably graduated, growing comprehensiveness," methods and theories had been "thrown into the allegorical fire, till, at length, nothing is left but the all-engendering heart of man."[62] By identifying blood at (and as) the heart of Melville's science, however, I am not arguing for the isolated importance of medicine and of anatomy as privileged sciences (although the importance of these practices and disciplines, as well as their massive development and dissemination after Harvey, and most particularly in the United States in the nineteenth century, can hardly be overstated, as any reader of *Moby-Dick* knows). Rather, I continue to follow Melville in showing how blood, in and through its distributive flow, *governs* the distinct logics of economy ("blood for oil"), of technology and industry, of science (including, but not restricted to, medicine), and of politics ("a good deal of our politics is physiological," as Emerson wrote).[63] We shall have occasion to observe again that blood also governs the notion of kinship (and ever more so within the boundaries of the emerging discourse of anthropology, race science, and kinship studies, and well beyond these boundaries). In short, as "that which bore witness to the displacement of the *theologos* by the *anthropologos*, which is to say, of a visible (and hence resistible) by an invisible and thus virtually irresistible center of authority," blood "enhanced its positive capability of commanding assent," its governing role and function.[64] It will also become apparent that blood governs Melville's writing as well, for "Leviathan is the text" (104: 455, and see also 32: 134– 145).[65] This is something we could continue calling "literature," of course, but only if we ignored what Northrop Frye has already suggested, namely that, along with a few other authors, Melville does not simply write literature, that his must rather be "another form of fiction." Melville, in no way to be thereby diminished in his literary stature, should nonetheless be considered as a writer of *anatomy*.[66] Such is his "total book," at least, the book upon which he looked as if he himself saw "two books . . . being writ . . . the larger book, and the infinitely better, [which] is for [his] own private shelf. That it is, whose unfathomable cravings drink his blood; the other only demands his ink."[67] Melville writes—and doesn't write—Leviathan. "In his remorselessly scientific manner," as C. L. R. James describes it, he pens "a scientific dissection" of Leviathan. Like Hobbes, Melville "does not only anticipate the work of scientists. He is himself a scientist in human relations."[68] He writes, as Charles Olson felicitously puts it, "the Book of the Law of the Blood." Which is to say, finally, that blood also governs Melville's theology, by which I do not mean simply to repeat, as many have done, that Melville's entire oeuvre had a rich, changing, and contested relation to Christianity (and, to a much lesser extent, to other religions). Rather, Christianity is, as it were, the distillate of the logic that Melville reveals and identifies, which delivers and allocates the flow of blood as its element, through the different domains and spheres I have mentioned so far (science and technology, economy and industry, politics and literature). "Leviathan is the blood pump" thus seeks to articulate a most economical formulation for Melville's *Moby-Dick* as an anatomy of Christianity and its distributive blood flow. More precisely, perhaps, it makes clear that Melville writes the only book that could do justice to Christianity as the history of blood. Melville writes, I said, a hematography. And Leviathan is the text—it is the blood pump.

> In most land animals there are certain valves or flood-gates in many of their veins, whereby when wounded, the blood is in some degree at least instantly shut off in certain directions. Not so with the whale; one of whose peculiarities it is, to have an entire non-valvular structure of the blood-vessels, so that when pierced even by so small a point as a harpoon, a deadly strain is at once begun upon his whole arterial system . . . his life may be said to pour from him in incessant streams. Yet so vast is the quantity of blood in him, and so distant and numerous its interior fountains, that he will keep thus bleeding and bleeding for a considerable period; even as in a drought a river will flow, whose source is in the well-springs of far-off and undiscernible hills. (81: 357)

What to make of the doubling of sources—the whale and the book, blood and Christianity—for the unending flow here described? How to read blood and the Christological allusions at work in this passage (flood-gates, piercing, the endless blood flow out of the fountain of life, and so forth), and what of the larger, insistent equation between Christianity and blood? Whence, what Holy Land or Holy Sea, these "well-springs of far-off and undiscernible hills"? Let me reiterate that the errant course of *Moby-Dick*'s narrative, its "narrative flow," provides an explicit, heuristic trajectory—a catechism—for what we have already been learning and reading. Are we not after all, as Queequeg on his whaling voyage, "actuated by a profound desire to learn among the Christians" (12: 56)? Are we not bound to him by old and new ties of blood? Do we not recognize, with him, that "it's a mutual, joint stock world, in all meridians" (13: 62)? If so, has our learning curve not been set already to move us from cannibal to Christian?[69] Let a whale-ship serve as our Yale College and our Harvard! (24: 112) "Was not Saul of Tarsus converted from unbelief by a similar fright?" (45: 207)—for we too, "we cannibals must help these Christians" (13: 62). As members of "the First Congregational Church . . . the same ancient Catholic Church to which you and I, and Captain Peleg there, and Queequeg here, and all of us, and every mother's son and soul of us belong; the great and everlasting First Congregation of this whole worshipping world; we all belong to that . . . in *that* we all join hands" (18: 87–88), and we must therefore acquire a new science—Melville's "gospels in this century" and his contribution to the history of blood. We must attend to a deeper understanding of what it might mean (or simply: be), what kind of learning, what kind of science, whither its "schools and schoolmasters" (88:391–394). "The transition is a keen one, I assure you, from a schoolmaster to a sailor, and requires a strong decoction . . ." (1: 6)

RED TIDE

It is not without irony that the two main characters (and vectors of interpretation for most of the book's readers) are named after biblical figures that live and die under the relentless sign of drought—the radical absence of vital liquids. Recall that Elijah's curse to the ancient Ahab was "there shall be neither dew nor rain these years, except by my word," and that this curse was promptly realized ("there was no rain in the land").[70] The rain does come for Ahab ("look toward the sea," says Elijah to his servant before sending him to Ahab again).[71] But Elijah, alone as Job and his witnesses ("I alone am left"),[72] extends another curse to Ahab, the wicked king who stole Naboth's vineyard and his life. "Thus says the Lord: In the place where dogs licked up the blood of Naboth, dogs will also lick up your blood." And "so the king died" and "the dogs licked up his blood, and the prostitutes washed themselves in it."[73] More or less opposite Ahab—"Ahab, the Arab"—is Ishmael, the son of the slave (but "who ain't a slave?" Ishmael famously asks) and eternal orphan, lost in the wilderness without water.[74] The irony only underscores the citational power of the names and the implied reference to promised lands, faraway hills and deserts—"the great American desert" (1: 4) as well as the hills of the Holy Land, which Captain Bildad's song sweetly evokes ("Sweet fields beyond the swelling flood, Stand dressed in living green. So to the Jews old Canaan stood, While Jordan rolled between" [22: 104]). "Ahab, the Arab," indeed. All this draws our attention to the liquid now drenching the landscape, characters and pages of the book. And so again, "even as in a drought a river will flow, whose sources is in the well-springs of far-off and undiscernible hills," Ahab and Ishmael are surrounded by endless liquid, "their deformities floundering in seas of blood" (81: 357 and 55: 263).

As we have had the opportunity to witness, it is primarily the sea that is brought into relation with (and as) a Hobbesian space of bloody war, a war of all against all, and the primal element of the bond within the animal and human realms and between them as well. War and commerce, as Carl Schmitt explained, and Melville before him—that is the law of the sea.[75] And it is a matter of law, the law of the sea and beyond it, "the fundamentals of all human jurisprudence," for, Ishmael explains at length, "the Temple of the Law . . . has but two props to stand on"—Fast-Fish and Loose-Fish (89: 397). First, Fast-Fish, testimony to what happens when "possession is the whole of the law," and a bloody one at that: "the sinews and souls of Russian serfs and Republican slaves," "the widow's last mite" to "the rapacious landlord," "poor Woebegone, the bankrupt" and his starving family, the money—a "globular 100,000"—seized by the Archbishop of Savesoul from "broken-backed laborers," all the "hereditary towns and hamlets" said to belong to the Duke of Dunder, and more. And then, there is Loose-Fish, which tells us everything we need to know and more about national and international law, conquest and colonies, and economic possession—and the hunting of Leviathan.

> What was America in 1492 but a Loose-Fish, in which Columbus struck the Spanish standard by way of waifing it for his royal master and mistress? What was Poland to the Czar? What Greece to the Turk? What India to England? What at last will Mexico be to the United States? All Loose-Fish. What are the Rights of Man and the Liberties of the World but Loose-Fish? What all men's minds and opinions but a Loose-Fish? What is the principle of religious belief in them but a Loose-Fish? What to the ostentatious smuggling verbalists are the thoughts of thinkers but Loose-Fish? What is the great globe itself but a Loose-Fish? And what are you, reader, but a Loose-Fish and Fast-Fish too? (89: 398)[76]

Leviathan is the blood pump. It is the law of the sea, the Book of the Law of the Blood. In it—and do note that this book is dated with and like America—we read the history of blood, the way in which blood began to flow in a novel way, imbibing law and politics, economics and religion, science and literature.[77] This we learn from *Moby-Dick*, and not only from the endless "bloody hunts" the book graphically evokes, instances and forms of which are mentioned and enacted throughout. We learn it above all from the sea, from its uncanny and threatening attractiveness, its sovereignty and magnetism—qualities that shadow Ahab himself—over the crowds and "more crowds" (1: 4). The sea, the Hobbesian sea, figures again and again the gathering unity of the common and uncommon whale, and that of the commonwealth. In it, the crowds gather. They come to the water and "here they all unite. Tell me, does the magnetic virtue of the needles of the compasses of all those ships attract them thither. . . . There is magic in it." There is also an image in it, painted or imagined, made and artificial, theological and mystical as well ("as if a hermit and a crucifix were within" [1: 4]), spirit or phantom, "it is the image of the ungraspable phantom of life; and this is the key to it all" (1: 5). No wonder that Ishmael, ever anatomically conscious, here recalls his own natural body, being "over conscious of my lungs" (1: 5). But we will also see that the sea—or at least the sailors—can take us *away* from Hobbes's world, offering something like the promise of an alternative, a different kind of composition, if still a melting, or a liquefaction—and more anatomic details. A different dissection will suggest a different kind of social bond, a different blood brotherhood, away, at any rate, from a world repeatedly defined in Hobbesian terms. With Queequeg at least, so Ishmael tells us, "I began to be sensible of strange feelings. I felt melting in me. No more my splintered heart and maddened hand were turned against the wolfish world" (10: 51). For now, though, the world is in the sea, or, more precisely, the world *is* the sea. And like God, the sea is everywhere, "the world's a ship, on its passage out, and not a voyage complete" (8: 40).

This is Father Mapple's early and "pregnant lesson," which he also learns from the sea, and from the reluctant prophet that was Jonah. And we too "feel the floods surging over us; we sound with him to the kelpy bottom of the waters; sea-weed and all the slime of the sea is about us" (9: 42). The world is the sea, and that is why Jonah's attempt was futile, who "sought to flee world-wide from God" (9: 43). Jonah—an allegory for each of us—finds himself "upon the ocean's utmost bones," in "the shuddering cold and blackness of the sea" (9: 47). The sea may be different from the land ("wherein differ the sea and the land, that a miracle upon one is not a miracle upon the other?" [58: 273]), but it is no less bloody, no less "wolfish," no less Hobbesian, than the rest of the world—and perhaps more so. For "not only is the sea such a foe to man who is an alien to it, but it is also a fiend to its own offspring; worse than the Persian host who murdered his own guests; sparing not the creatures which itself hath spawned" (58: 274). The sea is a sacred banquet for the sharks, "a part of the universal problem of all things" (64: 293). Which is why the sharks also need to hear a sermon from old Fleece, the cook (64: 294–297). The sea plays host to a "shark massacre" (66: 301–302). It is itself "a savage tigress," a cruel animal turning against its young, the image of absolute power—rule without rules—in all its might and arbitrariness. "No mercy, no power but its own controls it. Panting and snorting like a mad battle steed that has lost its rider, the masterless ocean overruns the globe" (58: 274). The world is in the sea, it is *governed* by it, inhabited as it is by "most dreaded creatures" and "most remorseless tribes" (58: 274). Sharks rush to "the fresh blood that was spilled" from hunted whales, "thirstily drinking at every new gash" (73: 324) and "as if the now tested reality" was not sufficient, "we find some book naturalists . . . declaring the Sperm Whale not only a consternation to every other creature in the sea, but also to be so incredibly ferocious as continually to be athirst for human blood" (41: 181). The view is fine, but the natives leave much to be desired. Clearly, "the native inhabitants of the seas have ever been regarded with emotions unspeakably unsocial and repelling," and "the most terrific of all mortal disasters have immemorially and indiscriminately befallen tens and hundreds of thousands of those who have gone upon the waters." Regardless of man's bragging about "his science and skill," then, "for ever and for ever, to the crack of doom, the sea will insult and murder him." This is "the full awfulness of the sea," whether or not it is acknowledged or recognized (58: 273). Consider, then, "consider, once more, the universal cannibalism of the sea; all whose creatures prey upon each other, carrying on eternal war since the world began" (58: 274), how "to and fro in the deeps, far down in the bottomless blue, rushed mighty leviathans, sword-fish, and sharks; and these were the strong, troubled murderous thinkings of the masculine sea" (132: 542). Ultimately, it is the sea—"the tiger heart that pants beneath" the ocean's skin, "this velvet paw but conceals a remorseless fang" (114: 491)—that will crucify Ahab, heroic and dejected Ahab, who is "potentially a saint" or at least "a kind of religious hero," at any rate, most Hobbesian—and utterly Christological—among world leaders.[78] "Drive, drive in your nails, oh ye waves! To their uttermost head drive them in!" (135: 567)

The sovereignty of the sea makes it evident that the problem of government, of leadership, rule and consent, in short, of politics (democratic and otherwise), such as it preoccupies Melville at least (as it had Hobbes before him, and obviously countless others), cannot be restricted to the figure of Ahab. Leviathan is the blood pump here means that an understanding of politics must encompass man's relation to the sea, beginning (and ending) with Ahab himself.[79] But it must also include the relations of men among themselves, the creatures and tribes of which we have just read, and the extensive meditations on the nature of the bonds that join ruler and ruled. There is the American presidency—contested as it is—and there are Ishmael's theories, to which we shall return. And then there is the ship, this "one great, predacious *jaw*, expressive of a savagery underlying Christianity which the savages themselves would be hard pressed to emulate," although it unsurprisingly bears the name of one among their exterminated tribes.[80] As an image of the human community (of blood and violence, to be sure, but also of the state and ultimately, perhaps, of the world), the ship is as central as the heart, for which it provides an analogy. Like the whale, like Leviathan, the ship is a space of "explosive economies of power—its disciplinary mechanisms, racial conflicts, nationalist chauvinisms, gendered roles, sexual desires and homophobic anxieties, brutal law enforcements, antinomies of work and leisure, hierarchical subdivisions and distributions of space, the whole multiform dialectic of capital and labor, and the forever impending possibility of mutiny."[81] And still there is—"blood against fire!" (119: 507)—Ahab.

But by considering Ahab himself (or, for that matter, each "character," beginning with the sea) in isolation, I do not mean to erase the unavoidable network of relations that define him—along with everything else. To the contrary, with blood as my guide, it is the *circulatory system* of politics that interests me, the description and inscription of which one finds everywhere in *Moby-Dick*. Melville's hematography—indebted as it is to Hobbes, Boyle, and Harvey, and to their disputed inheritance—is hardly restricted to politics, nor is it restricted to Ahab (although Melville seems to argue that it is restricted to Christianity). More than anyone else, though, more than Hamlet and more even than any *thing* else ("The King Is a Thing"), "Ahab has that that's bloody on his mind" (31: 133). In this, he may not be so different from these other undisputed rulers that sea captains (or "sea kings") are, not so different at least from Captain Bildad and Captain Peleg, the owners of the *Pequod*. Strangely enough, what Ahab shares with them has less to do with qualities of leadership than with blood. Or, if there is a difference, with being a Christian—of that "sect" of Christians that settled in Nantucket, the Quakers (but "Melville makes no nice denominational distinctions," and besides, as Tocqueville pointed out, "all the sects in the United States are within the great Christian unity, and the morality of Christianity is everywhere the same").[82] To this day, Ishmael explains with a heavy irony, the inhabitants of the island "in general retain in an uncommon measure the peculiarities of the Quaker, only variously and anomalously modified by things altogether alien and heterogeneous" (16: 73). No essentialism is discernible here, and even generalizations are hardly made without reservations, or again, without irony. However, as we have yet to be better acquainted with Ahab, it is difficult to ignore the glimpse and foreshadowing we are given, at this particular moment in the book, into his sanguinary character.

For some of these same Quakers are the most sanguinary of all sailors and whale hunters. They are fighting Quakers; they are Quakers with a vengeance. So there are instances among them of men, who, named with Scripture names—a singularly common feature on the island—and in childhood naturally imbibing the stately dramatic thee and thou of the Quaker idiom; still from the audacious, daring, and boundless adventure of their subsequent lives, strangely blend with these unoutgrown peculiarities, a thousand bold dashes of character, not unworthy a Scandinavian sea-king, or a poetical Pagan Roman. And when these things unite in a man of greatly superior natural force, with a globular brain and a ponderous heart . . . that man makes one in a whole nation's census—a mighty pageant creature, formed for noble tragedies. (16: 73)

With biblical images (and names) of blood and blood vengeance, with "a bold and nervous lofty language" that drenches ("imbibed") a character strangely "blended" with warrior tribes of old, the evocation of tragedies that tear to shreds men of superior force, the bloody anatomy of "heart, body, and brain" of the Hobbesian sovereign (at once natural and artificial) is compellingly joined with "a whole nation's census."[83] Undoubtedly, "he's Ahab, boy; and Ahab of old, thou knowest, was crowned king!" A vile and wicked ruler, to be sure (assuming there is another kind)—and the dogs, "did they not lick his blood?" (16: 79). Blood, then, is everywhere. Even "Ahab's harpoon had shed older blood than the Pharaohs'" (104: 457). And when he kills the whale (*if* he kills the whale), "he will dam off [his] blood, as a miller shuts his water-gate upon the stream!" (134: 556)

Ironically, stopping the flow (of blood or other fluids) is also what Ahab recognizes he is unable, and perhaps unwilling, to do. When a "bad leak" reveals that some oil caskets may have broken, Ahab commands "let it leak!" He proceeds to confirm his own condition, to affirm the lack of fluid retention that plagues his body.[84] "I'm all aleak myself," he proclaims.

> Aye! leaks in leaks! not only full of leaky casks, but those leaky casks are in a leaky ship; and that's a far worse plight than the Pequod's, man. Yet I don't stop to plug my leak; for who can find it in the deep-loaded hull; or how hope to plug it, even if found, in this life's howling gale? (109: 474)

Ahab rules and wants to rule over a circulatory system, however poorly sealed, over a body unified "according to the conventions of the mechanical sublime,"[85] with its artificial limbs ("Hold," he tells the carpenter about to remake his ivory leg, "I'll order a complete man after a desirable pattern," and he complains about his "old lost leg; the flesh and blood one, I mean. Canst thou not drive that old

Adam away?" [108: 470–71]) and its bloody members ("The crew, man, the crew! Are they not one and all with Ahab, in this matter of the whale?" [36: 164]).[86] He is their natural and artificial body, their mystical and political body. And they are all one in him, whose "wild eyes met his, as the bloodshot eyes of the prairie wolves meet the eye of their leader, ere he rushes on at their head" (36: 165). Gathering and unifying them, he is the natural and artificial man, the principle of their covenantal membership and dismemberment, order and disorder at once, binding and freeing them of all and any bond, either "moral or legal" ("Ahab was now entirely conscious that . . . he had indirectly laid himself open to the unanswerable charge of usurpation; and with perfect impunity, both moral and legal, his crew if so disposed, and to that end competent, could refuse all further obedience to him, and even violently wrest from him the command" [46: 213]). What is it then that binds them to him nonetheless? What if not "the bloody hunt"—what if not blood itself? "Will you give me as much blood as will cover this barb?" he asks of them (113: 489). Equipped with what is referred as "baptismal blood," he has long become their king and priest, and he does bind them in an "indissoluble league" (36: 166) as they drink ("Drink and pass!") from "the heavy charged flagon."[87] And do they drink! They drink the juice of life, for "so brimming life is gulped and gone" (36: 165). Akin to "the great Pope," and addressing his "sweet cardinals," Ahab "brimmed the harpoon sockets," commends "the murderous chalices" and the "fiery waters" to the church of his faithful, to his indissoluble league. And thus "the deed is done," they swear his oath and seal his covenant: "drink and swear, ye men" (it is from this, "our horrible oath," that Ishmael will try to wash his hands. Invoking the wine drawn from "fully ripe grapes," using "that inexpressible sperm" extracted from the body of the whale, Ishmael says, Pilate-like, "I washed my hands and my heart of it" [94: 416; and see also 41: 179]). "Like old wine worked anew," they have become one with him, "their hearts were bowled along" (134: 556–57).

> They were one man, not thirty. For as the one ship that held them all; though it was put together of all contrasting things—oak, and maple, and pine wood; iron and pitch, and hemp—yet all these ran into each other in the one concrete hull, which shot on its way, both balanced and directed by the long central keel; even so, all the individualities of the crew, this man's valor, that man's fear; guilt and guiltlessness, all varieties were welded into oneness, and were all directed to that fatal goal which Ahab their one lord and keel did point to. (134: 557)

"Ahab is for ever Ahab, man . . . 'Tis Ahab—his body's part" (134: 561). And "all are Ahab," as well (99: 431). He is their Christian Commonwealth, the head and heart of the Leviathan they constitute and hunt. Ahab knows it well who addressed them thus: "ye are not other men, but my arms and my legs; and so obey me" (135: 568). They are Ahab and he too is Ahab, who "integrates the crew into a glorious Christ-like body politic"[88]; "who stood before them with a crucifixion in his face" (28: 124). Or, as he himself succinctly puts it in one of his most famous, and successful, formulations, indeed, the book's very motto.[89] "Ego no baptizo te in nomine patris, sed in nomine diaboli" (113: 489).

PRACTICAL CETOLOGY (SUFFERING FOR SCIENCE)[90]

If blood governs—even as it does not exhaust—the political relations between Ahab and the sea, Ahab and the crew, and, in more ways than one, Ahab and himself, it will be obvious that it circulates as well between Ahab and Ishmael. This does not locate their relation in some alternative dimension. No distinct or privileged domain is thereby opened or charted within the larger social and political world we have been considering, but it returns us to science—no separate domain either—albeit from a different perspective. Here too, the ship remains the "laboratory" in which the "explosive economies of power" are at work—a work of dismemberment and re-memberment, a system of circulation.[91] Like Ishmael, Ahab is a scholar and a scientist. He too has "undertaken to manhandle this Leviathan." He too could have claimed that "it behooves me to approve myself omnisciently exhaustive in the enterprise; not overlooking the minutest seminal germs of his blood, and spinning out to the uttermost coil of his bowels" (104: 455). This is to say that both Ahab and Ishmael are out for blood. In the immediate, and though anatomy (and hematology) will certainly claim much of their joined attention, it is Ishmael who makes explicit his desire for a better scientific outlook—at least of things spiritual. This is not an allegory of the cave and its shadows, but it remains about science, about the knowledge of the sun, if one clouded by too many fluids. An allegory of the oyster. "Methinks that in looking at things spiritual, we are too much like oysters observing the sun through the water, and thinking that thick water the thinnest of air" (7: 37). Like Ahab, then, Ishmael is willing to donate some organs, even his body, to science, and to sacrifice his life in order to understand better "this matter of Life and Death." In fact, Ishmael says with a bare bones twist, here is my body, *hoc est corpus meum*, "take my body who will, take it I say, it is not me" (7: 37). This is consistent with what David F. Noble has called "the religion of technology," and more specifically with the developments undergone by American science at the time Melville writes.[92] The term *scientist* had just been coined in 1840, and the word *science* itself "more typically evoked a type of mental

discipline, a faculty or quality peculiar to the human mind."[93] By 1845, the emerging community of scientists—what Rebecca Herzig pertinently calls "the imagined body of science"—has its center in New England, and "Boston surpassed all other U.S. cities in numbers of scientists in residence," while the region's "scientific centers held disproportionate influence over the shape and character of research in the peripheries, as they continue to do so today."[94] The new ethos ("suffering for science") has not yet fully emerged, yet everything is as if both Ahab and Ishmael were initial prototypes, early martyrs for the cause. "Would the amputation of one's fingers or toes serve to advance knowledge, or were these efforts ultimately futile and destructive?"[95] This could have been Ahab's question, and that of Ishmael and the crew as well. ("Crack all your backbones, and bite your knives in two—that's all" says Stubb to the crew. "Take it easy," he continues, "why don't you take it easy, I say, and burst all your livers and lungs!" [48: 223]) This too is a (relative) matter of agreement, consensus, and covenant—an anatomic matter—of the kind suggested by scholars and scientists, perhaps a late consumptive and pale usher to a grammar school ("heart, body, and brain") or a "sub-sub-librarian" (xv, xvii). "Some writers describe scientific work as a contractual relationship, in which parts of the self (stomach, hands, thoughts) were temporarily bartered based on assumed returns of equal or greater value. Others described a process of deliberate disowning, a principle of forfeiture designed to distance themselves from the accumulative mindset of the 'masses.'"[96] No wonder that the figure of the scholar sometimes seems to evoke "a conception of the white male body as a machine, a collection of interchangeable parts subject to dismantling and reconstruction." Whether his "actions were to be classified as insane or admirable, degenerate or enlightened was situational, depending on the ever-changing relation between self and science."[97] This is a point that was not lost on the critics who produced the first Melville revival in the 1920s, those who "championed *Moby-Dick* as a blueprint for living within an increasingly mechanical, routinized, and bureaucratic world. They also heaped admiration upon Captain Ahab, an odd choice given the outcome of *Moby-Dick*."[98] It is a choice that makes more sense if one considers that the scientist-as-hero wins even when he loses. Ahab is also disillusioned with science, after all, although it is difficult to think that he uses the term in its contemporary sense ("Science! Curse thee, thou vain toy"). More precisely, Ahab rebels against the paradigm of Plato's allegory: the sun ("and cursed be all the things that cast man's eyes aloft to that heaven, whose live vividness but scorches him as these old eyes are even now scorched with thy light, O sun!" [118: 501]). Ahab famously maintains his faith in knowledge and science, and in technology, affirming that which he knows of fire, lightning, and, most of all, himself (119: 508). His is "the fatal pride of science."[99] A true "Prometheus," indeed (44: 202).

By insisting on the importance of blood, it is not my intent to reduce the rich wealth of scientific discourses that are at work in Melville's text. Although the quantities of blood that flow throughout are staggering—and what liquid, what fluid fails to be deployed here as a figure for blood?—mine is not a quantitative argument. Blood circulates throughout, and it imbibes the discourse of science (and of everything else really) that Melville inherits from his predecessors, beginning with Hobbes and his views on "ultimate fluidity,"[100] and onto the dissections and blood works of Harvey and Boyle. All this at a time when anatomy was fast becoming "*the* paradigm of all philosophical enterprises and was duly reflected in all branches of knowledge and artistic activity."[101] To recall that Leviathan is the blood pump, in this context, is not only to observe the sedimented effects of a history of blood that traverses the pages of *Moby-Dick*. It is to consider the extent of its distribution, the dynamic mechanisms of its circulation through numerous bodies and domains, the integrity of which is placed under interrogation, literally liquefied, under the assault of its waves.

Melville's science covers a wide array of domains, and first among them is anatomy. It is blood science or, less elegantly put, the technology of butchery.[102] "Our vocation," Ishmael admits when commenting on the whaling profession, "amounts to a butchering sort of business; and . . . when actively engaged therein, we are surrounded by all manners of defilements. Butchers we are, that is true. But butchers, also, and butchers of the bloodiest badge have been all Martial Commanders whom the world invariably delights to honor" (24: 109). By comparing whaling to war (and, indeed, to butchery), Ishmael not only highlights the dedication to blood-spilling the two professions share (both involve "bloody hunts" after all). He also argues for a certain universalism of whaling and warring, its global and epochal relevance. "This is life," life itself, and it is we, "we mortals," who, "by long toilings extracted from this world's vast bulk its small but valuable sperm; and then, with weary patience, cleansed ourselves from its defilements, and learned to live here in clean tabernacles of the soul" (98: 429). Ultimately, "we are all killers, on land and on sea; Bonapartes and Sharks included" (32: 143). The enterprise is that of life, mortal life ("this is man-killing!"), life in all its sacrificial and cleansing splendor. "Every sailor a butcher. You would have thought we were offering up ten thousand red oxen to the sea-gods" (67: 303). The universal significance of whaling is thus also a theological one, and whaling is a kind of worship. For who, after all, could forget the "bible leaves," those minced pieces of blubber which drop into the boiling pots, "fast as the sheets from a rapt orator's desk"? Who could forget the mincer, this "candidate for an archbishoprick," this "lad for a Pope" (95: 420)? Yet practical cetology is also a science. Hence, having described what he previously referred to as the work of butchers, namely, the "stripping of the body of the leviathan," Ishmael will recast that work in terms of the mounting prestige of the medical profession. He speaks here of "the beheading of the Sperm Whale," which is, he says, "a scientific anatomical feat, upon which experienced whale surgeons very much pride themselves: and not without reason" (70: 310). To belong to the community of whaling sailors is therefore to partake of no common lineage, but indeed of an aristocratic one ("they have something better than royal blood there" [24: 111]). In this, whalemen share a hematological distinction ("he fell on the hatch spouting blood like a whale" [54: 248]) with the whale itself, which is distinct and distinguished, different from other fish (Ishmael famously refuses to accept Linnaeus' opinion that whales are not, in fact, fish, for he would have thus "banished the whales from the waters" (32: 136). What then is the difference? "Lungs and warm blood; whereas, all other fish are lungless and cold blooded" (32: 137). The blood of the whale, like that of the whaleman, is a site of singularity and distinction, a shared sign of nobility. In a way, blood is the alpha and omega of the whaling enterprise. It circulates within and between mariners and whales. Blood irrigates the entire enterprise of "practical cetology."

SYSTEMS OF CONSANGUINITY (THE AESTHETICS OF REDNESS IN *MOBY-DICK*)

There is another scientific domain to Melville's science, which maintains us within the realm of anatomy and hematology while returning us to a more explicit understanding of Melville's politics. This is, of course, race science. According to Samuel Otter, Ishmael is the chief scientist here. He is the one who "confronts the alien and alluring bodies of others and joins the ethnological quest."[103] Anatomy here is divided between ethnology and phrenology (physiognomy too), and "while it may seem strange in this argument to move from human to whale anatomy, it is a move that Melville makes repeatedly in *Moby-Dick*."[104] In this context, there is another pertinent dimension of race science that is also mentioned explicitly in the book. It is part of the literary, scholarly and fictional corpus that was quickly and vastly expanding at the time and part of a long tradition of Orientalist scholarship and imagination.[105] I am referring to philology in particular, the venerable science with which Ishmael challenges his audience to a reading contest—a reading of human, animal, and textual bodies. It is a scientific challenge, and even more so, a literary one.

> Champollion deciphered the wrinkled granite hieroglyphics. But there is no Champollion to decipher the Egypt of every man's and every being's face.

Physiognomy, like every other human science, is but a passing fable. If then, Sir Williams Jones, who read in thirty languages, could not read the simplest peasant's face in its profounder and more subtle meanings, how may unlettered Ishmael hope to read the awful Chaldee of the Sperm Whale's brow? I but put that brow before you. Read it if you can. (79: 347)

Ishmael thus reiterates—as he interrogates—the standing challenge to read the body and face of every being as well as one would read an ancient text.[106] At the time, philology was precisely participating in the drive to read language as race. Yet, still closer to anatomy, it is perhaps Lewis Henry Morgan who went the furthest in finding ways of refiguring ethnology as "the continuation of philology by other means."[107] A pioneer anthropologist, Morgan was inventing the science of kinship, which can be said to have made and unmade race science, and paradoxically as having sealed the language that, we know, still governs our understanding of kinship, namely, the language of blood.

There is no question that Melville adheres to, even as he resists, the strange and pervasive, but by now fully accepted, notion that kinship and lineage are predicated on blood, that kinship is blood and blood is kinship.[108] I do not mean to suggest, therefore, that he goes against the science of his time. Having enabled us, so far, to consider the ways in which blood circulates through the bodies and domains that make or inhabit the world (the book, the ship, the sea, on the one hand, politics, science, economics, and so forth, on the other), the way blood governs its language, Melville brings us toward an interrogation of the uncanny function of the language of blood that pervades current notions of kinship. Within decades of his writing, in fact, these notions were being scientifically (and popularly) formulated and sedimented in Morgan's groundbreaking work. Expanding philology's reach, Morgan saw culture itself as possessing "the logic of pure circulation."[109] He attended to the circulatory systems of relationships, systems that, true to an older but by no means universal tradition, he called *Systems of Consanguinity and Affinity of the Human Family*, the title of his 1871 masterpiece. In this book, the product of more than twenty years of research and scholarship (he had began working with Iroquois classificatory systems in the 1840s), Morgan was seeking to show the endurance of these systems and "the stability of these forms, and their power of self-perpetuation in the streams of the blood through indefinite periods of time."[110] Suspending for now the figurative (or literal) dimension of the term *blood*, and recognizing that like a number of early theoreticians of kinship, Morgan was first of all a legal scholar who knew the determining role of law in the constitution of kinship (Morgan thus referred to "customs of the blood"), it remains the case that blood, understood as the name of the familial bond, has persisted through the emergence and disappearance of race science. Although blood acquired its *lettres de noblesse* in the science of kinship at the very same time as it did in the science of race (and not surprisingly so, as we are speaking of a scientific field that, from medicine and anatomy to philology, phrenology, and physiognomy, is governed by blood), it has yet to achieve the kind of visibility that would enable an inquiry into its history. Melville, however, or so I have been arguing, is providing us with the essentials of what such a hematography would look like.

To insist on interrogating the significance of blood in kinship is not to argue for emancipation from "ties of blood" (to argue for spirit against flesh), nor is it to revisit the nature/culture debate. Indeed, it is one thing to acknowledge that kinship and lineage are cultural artifacts and another to refer to the biological "substrate" of these artifacts as "blood." Nor is the name *blood* to be dismissed as one figure among others, which would have functioned in such manner as to mislead us into thinking that kinship is, in fact, a natural, biological matter. As a legal scholar, Morgan—and historians and anthropologists after him—understood the nature/culture division very well.[111] By repeatedly calling our attention to blood, the question that Melville puts to us is a different one. Why, he asks, is blood the persistent site—literal and figurative—of communal boundaries, whether they are racial or familial? Steeped in biblical language, Melville knew that there were alternatives.[112] He knew, for instance, that the Old Testament never once invokes the phrase "flesh and blood," that the Old Testament does not, in fact, conceive of kinship and lineage as blood. But this is a matter that goes beyond a particular vocabulary and speaks rather of the massive dissemination of blood through a number of discourses and domains, many of which preceded Melville, and all of which grew and increased at the time he was writing. And they endure after him, as does blood. Assuming then that some historical recognition of a biological substrate for kinship and lineage is called "blood" and that it has been so called for centuries (one may wonder what understanding of biology is thereby at work, but let us leave this aside—Melville interrogates science better than we here could), it is enough to acknowledge that the empirical attribution is of a changing nature through the centuries and that its particular name is hardly a universal, nor is there any necessity in extending its rule—metaphorical or otherwise—to conceptions of larger (racial or national) communities. And if blood is a name or figure, then Melville complicates its figurative dimension by making blood the figuration of a figure. Such is the blood said to run in the veins, irrigating, as we observed, an ever larger number of bodies. Its pervasive presence, moreover, could have made blood into a signifier of equality, another name for the Great Leveler (whether life or death). It is particularly striking, therefore, to be confronted with the luminous if paradoxical claim that others (aliens and animals) at once have a different kind of blood, that blood, in other words, makes a difference (rather than abolishing all differences between living, bleeding beings), but that this difference, because it is found in others (in foreign and unexpected places), warrants the abandonment—nay, the abolition—of discriminating conceptions that divide and separate between races and classes on the basis of blood.

The first being about whom this double claim is made, through a direct invocation of blood lineage, is Queequeg. "There was excellent blood in his veins— royal stuff" (12: 55). This affirmation of lineage and kinship provides the basis for a new kind of alliance, which crosses through walls of blood and of sexuality. Blood affirms and joins, circulates beyond kinship and across racial lines. Much in the same way, Ishmael pursues this argument; he expands the rule of blood by countering the claim that whalemen "have no good blood in their veins" (24: 111). They do, he insists, "they have something better than royal blood there." They have American blood, the blood of Benjamin Franklin, "all kith and kin to noble Benjamin" (24: 111). Tashtego, for his part ("an unmixed Indian from Gay Head"), is described as "an inheritor of the unvitiated blood of those proud warrior hunters" that used to people the Americas (27: 120). Blood is thereby affirmed as the union of races and classes, forms of life that are not otherwise conceived as "kith and kin." Blood is, in other words, *generalized*.

It would be an understatement to suggest that both gospel and practical cetology are about the blood of leviathan, that the sciences of Leviathan are always, if not first and foremost, about its blood, that they are governed by it. The details are provided throughout, which meticulously trace the blood flow within and without the whale's body. Hence we are told that one of the whale's peculiarities is "to have an entire non-valvular structure of the blood-vessels" and given more details still about "his whole arterial system" (81: 357). We also learn that the vitality of any creature is dependent on "a certain element, which being subsequently brought into contact with the blood imparts to the blood its vivifying principle"—"I do not think I shall err," comments Ishmael upon this, his own description, "though I may possibly use some superfluous scientific words" (85: 371). If only "all the blood in a man could be aerated with one breath"! Such capacity (the blood pump, the air pump) is unique to the whale, as "between his ribs and on each side of his spine he is supplied with a remarkable involved Cretan labyrinth of vermicelli-like vessels, which vessels, when he quits the surface, are completely distended with oxygenated blood. So that for an hour or more, a thousand fathoms in the sea, he carries a surplus stock of vitality in him, just as the camel crossing the waterless desert carries a surplus of drink for future use in its four supplementary stomachs" (85: 371). And we have already heard of Ishmael's thorough interest even in "the minutest seminal germs of his blood" (104: 455). And do not forget that "when making a passage from one feeding-ground to another, the sperm whales, guided by some infallible instinct—say, rather, secret intelligence from the Deity—mostly swim in *veins*" (44: 199).

Is this, however, the blood of kinship? I am not sure how important it is to claim that it is, but I do want to register that there are two reasons to consider that it might be the case. More precisely, the whale, by which I mean primarily the blood (which is also the sperm and oil) of the whale, is the site, it provides a view, of *another* kind of kinship, another kind of community and relation to the world. Hence the appeal: "Oh, man! Admire and model thyself after the whale! Do thou, too, remain warm among ice. Do thou, too, live in this world without being of it. Be cool at the equator; keep thy blood fluid at the Pole" (68: 307). Again, though, this is not to say that by deploying recurring images of blood-spouting whales in seas of blood and more, Melville offers an alternative to blood, as if blood was what one needed to emancipate oneself from, as if what needed to be broken were *in fact* ties of blood. Instead, Melville pours more blood and adds to its endless reservoir of literal and figurative power yet other figures. Melville, as I said, *generalizes* blood. On the one hand, kinship was never blood, Melville seems to be saying, but on the other, as that is what we call it now, it will have to do. Within its expanding circulatory systems, there are other communities, a different science of kinship, if you will, and of politics. This is most famously the case, perhaps, in the episode of "a squeeze of the hand," in which the sperm not only washes away the bond established by "our horrible oath," as we saw, but also, by way of "the gentle globules," produced the angelic picture of a community that links "my dear fellow beings," that holds in one vision if not human and animal at least humans and angels (94: 416). Within and across the bloodlines, Ishmael envisions different communities, highly ironic ones ("*Moby-Dick* projects into imaginative space a world constructed from elements of the political discourse and social tension in which Melville was entangled. There is no realistic society on the *Pequod* made coherent by relations among the characters"), he highlights and troubles the seas of blood in which we have been swimming.[113] This is the case with his marriage to Queequeg, which appears to be consummated in the blood pump itself, that is to say, in the heart ("thus, then, in our hearts' honeymoon, lay I and Queequeg—a cosy, loving pair" [10: 52]; later, Ishmael will confess to admiring Queequeg in a new outfit, "the Highland costume—a skirt and socks—in which to my eyes, at least, he appeared to uncommon advantage" [72: 319]).[114] But consider as well what could be seen as an indirect result of this union, at least a move to the next level, and to another scientific and medical domain. This time, "rather than craniometry, physiognomy, or phrenology, Queequeg performs a Caesarean operation on the head of the whale, slashing it open and delivering Tashtego."[115] Thus, "through the courage and great skill in obstetrics of Queequeg," this dangerous operation—it was, after all, a breach delivery—brings about a beautiful rebirth out of the head of the whale (78: 344).[116] In this "fatherless birth," the head stands in for the mother and, given the circumstances, Ishmael tells us, it appears to be doing fine.

> Diving after the slowly descending head, Queequeg with his keen sword had made side lunges near its bottom, so as to scuttle a large hole there; then dropping his sword, had thrust his long arm far inwards and upwards, and so hauled out our poor Tash by the head. He averred, that upon first thrusting in for him a leg was presented; but well knowing that that was not as it ought to be and might occasion great trouble;—he had thrust back the leg, and by dexterous heave and toss, had wrought a somerset upon the Indian; so that with the next trial, he came forth in the good old way—head foremost. As for the great head itself, that was doing as well as could be expected. (78: 343)

No wonder then that "midwifery should be taught in the same course with fencing and boxing, riding and rowing" (78: 344).

The final illustration of a different kind of ties that bind brings us back to Ishmael's marriage to Queequeg but gives it a very different accent. I am speaking this time of "the monkey-rope."[117] This simple apparatus, deployed for the purpose of cutting up the dead whale and loading the blubber onto the ship, binds two whalemen to each other, the first precariously standing on the whale (and thus very close to the sharks "now freshly and more keenly allured by the before pent blood which began to flow from the carcase—the rabid creatures swarmed round it like bees in a beehive" [72: 321]), the other on the ship ensuring the safety of his companion. Describing this new tie between him and Queequeg, Ishmael expands a long line of metaphors for the emerging community. He explains that "the monkey-rope was fast at both ends," which meant that "for better or for worse, we two, for the time, were wedded." Marriage, then, and again, and for better or for worse indeed, as "should poor Queequeg sink to rise no more, then both usage and honor demanded that instead of cutting the cord, it should drag me down in his wake." Having invoked their renewed marriage vows, Ishmael goes on to invoke a more expansive kinship, a new and newly intensified brotherhood. "So, then, an elongated Siamese ligature united us. Queequeg was my own inseparable twin brother" (72: 320). Like a marriage, and like the most traditional of families, which long functioned as the basic unit of production, this turns out to be a financial partnership as well, an economic merger. "I seemed distinctly to perceive that my own individuality was now merged in a joint stock company of two." More importantly, as his individuality melts into a newfound fluidity, Ishmael is gripped by a different sense of the universal human condition. "I saw that this situation of mine was the precise situation of every mortal that breathes; only, in most cases, he, one way or another, has this Siamese connexion with a plurality of other mortals" (72: 320). No blood brotherhood then, but a plural combination of affect and alliances, kinship and economic partnership. There is still blood, to be sure, the risk of its spilling ("if your banker breaks, you snap; if your apothecary by mistake sends you poison in your pills, you die"), but here it no longer governs—and certainly not rhetorically—the imagined and embodied community. Here too, irony hardly enables one to linger with some pastoral rope or hope. As the steward has prepared "a cup of tepid ginger" to comfort Queequeg now finally out of harm's reach (72: 321), he is precisely accused of malpractice in his apothecary functions. "Aye, aye, steward, cried Stubb, we'll teach you to drug a harpooner; none of your apothecary's medicine here; you want to poison us, do ye? You have got our insurances on our lives and want to murder us all, and pocket the proceeds, do ye?" (72: 322). Blood and money—at least the threat of their power—reassert themselves quickly enough. There is, at any rate, no new community. Ultimately, another ship, "in her retracing search after her missing children, only found another orphan" ("Epilogue," 573). Genealogy itself—if not necessarily blood—is defeated.[118] But much as Ishmael, while still tied to the monkey-rope, had seen "that here was a sort of interregnum in Providence" (72: 320), we may have glimpsed another science, another politics (of kinship and more), like a rope balancing above a sea of blood.

GOSPEL HEMACETOLOGY

"Looked at closely," explained Carl Schmitt, "the use of the leviathan to represent Hobbes' theory of the state is nothing other than a half-ironic literary idea born out of a fine sense of English humor."[119] The humor may have been lost (or gained) on other literary ideas. At any rate, much like blood, Leviathan certainly did become a literary idea. Like Hawthorne and his "black conceit," it came—blood came—to "pervade [Melville] through and through."[120] Commenting on Melville's anatomies, Samuel Otter perceptively shows that Leviathan also governs Melville's poetics, his writing. Otter explains how, for Melville, "ink draws on blood, as the soul is translated to paper. For ink to lie thick, the blood must be thin. Sentiment becomes a kind of lethal transfusion. Writing is represented as a parasitic activity, books as bloodsuckers. The self does not stand apart from itself and evaluate its behavior; instead, the self feeds upon itself."[121] Blood then would constitute the living source of ink. This is, of course, a common enough image but it is given the peculiar feature here of defining a kind of hydraulic relation between author and writing and between self and self. Such figures of authorial sovereignty are moreover modeled on—they are irrigated by the same "engine" as—political sovereignty, "a form of government, a form of legitimation and subordination, license and control."[122] Through the long history of debates about the centrality of head or heart, political sovereignty, in turn, was linked—by blood—to the growth of anatomy as a paradigmatic discourse and an expanding practice (incidentally, by the 1840s, "the connection between medicine and Christianity was . . . more than just a fulfillment of the requirements of Christian medical charity; it had to become a part of missionary practice").[123] The system of consanguinity, like any circulatory system, encompasses politics, religion, and medicine. It is a closed, if not a symmetric, system, much less an invulnerable one. It encompasses literature as well—if that is what it finally is—which is also suffused by the flow of blood.[124] Interrogating Hawthorne on his right to drink from his "flagon of life," Melville had illustrated the vessels through which blood flowed by invoking "the mystical language of the Eucharist," going so far as to suggest that between the two writers, everything was "as if their minds and hearts were linked by a common network of nerves and veins."[125] Flowing with blood, literature functions as a whale (the Sacred Meal) or as the world, which is to say, as a book. Filled with "the still, rich utterances of a great intellect in repose, and which sends few thoughts into circulation, except they be arterialized at his large warm lungs, and expanded in his honest heart," that book is, like Leviathan, filled with blood.[126] Attending to Melville's art, Albert Camus confirmed this anatomically precise fact when he claimed that for Melville the spiritual experience "constantly finds its blood and its flesh."[127] Clearly, "it is not the brain that can test such a man; it is only the heart."[128]

To say it again, *Moby-Dick*—and Moby Dick, "but do whales have christenings?" (54: 256)—is the Book of the Law of the Blood. But is it a Christian book? Christian art? Indeed, a "sacred text"?[129] "With what heart," in other words, "has Melville told us this story?"[130] This is a long debate, conducted in a variety of modes and positions that may bear an abbreviated revisiting. First, there is denegation ("There is no Christianity in [Father Mapple's] sermon and, indeed, very little concern anywhere in the book with anything that could be called specifically Christian"[131]; or: "[Moby Dick] is certainly not the God of orthodox or even of modernist Christianity").[132] Then, there is a growing distance or progress and escape—with mitigated success ("By 'Ishmael,' then, I mean Melville's specific encounter with Christianity, seen as flight and search"; or: "In the works preceding *Moby-Dick*, Melville dealt with the Christian religion in large part negatively, by a critique of the missionary effort; in *Moby-Dick* and the books which succeed it . . . the critique continues, but it is accompanied by an intermittent yet vital exploration of the Calvinist heritage . . . *Moby-Dick* is, in fact, an implicit critique of liberal Protestantism"; and finally, "[*Moby-Dick*] stands as a great pioneering work of comparative religion and as one of the most ambitious products of the religious imagination that American literature is likely to produce").[133] There is careful euphemism ("Now in *Moby-Dick*, a book concerned primarily with European culture, Melville allowed Queequeg to serve implicatively as the critic of that culture," or "as *Moby-Dick* presumes to practice it, literature is simply not a secular art").[134] And there is also unequivocal exultation at the outright condemnation (for Melville: "Having started with hating Christians because they were not sufficiently Christians, he proceeded to hate Christians because they were Christians"; and against Ahab: "he is a gigantic symbol of the sickness of the self, the disease of the egoist-absolutist of Christendom").[135] Finally, there is unapologetic affirmation ("Ishmael sounds like a Christian apologist intent upon discrediting the integrity of mythological and cross-cultural analogs to Christian Revelation," and: "in the first centuries, Jesus was Cetus, the Whale. And the Christians were the little fishes. Jesus, the redeemer was Cetus, Leviathan. And all the Christians all his little fishes").[136]

Do these establish *Moby-Dick* as a Christian book, then? They certainly demonstrate the persistence of a Christian question. But the matter, for now, may have to be formulated otherwise. As a matter of fact, *Moby-Dick* opens—and endures—on the very dismembered terms that have framed centuries of theological, political, and medical discourse—"heart, body, and brain" (xv) are attributed to the "pale usher" who construes the "Etymology," whereas later, Ahab's sense of self-protection is said only to "consist in his own predominating brain and heart and hand" (46: 213). The book begins again on "the long Vaticans," the books, "any book whatsoever, sacred or profane" and the claim, at once denied, that what follows should not be taken for "veritable gospel cetology." The work of a commentator, who may or may not belong "to that hopeless, sallow tribe which no wine of this world will ever warm," perhaps a bloodless tribe or one untouched by the lifeblood that wine is, *Moby-Dick* is not a Christian book. This is to say that the book's relation to Christianity—persistently inscribed through countless biblical references and most clearly by way of constant statements about and allusions to Christians and Christianity—is a determined and determining relation. Paradoxically perhaps, this means that in its negativity (it is *not* a Christian book), its opposition to, critique of, and rebellion against Christianity, as well as in its affirmation, recollection, and interpretation of Christianity, it remains through and through a Christian book. For negation "is not necessarily denial. If the negation enacted in images and simulacra is understood speculatively, it remains within an economy that is inescapably Christian."[137] From its heart, body, and brain, from the wine of this world that fills "the great Heidelburgh Tun" and more (77: 339–40),

Moby-Dick remains "Melville's most theological work."[138] It remains a Christian book. Its Christianity is in the blood.

Could it have been otherwise? In relation to what theological tradition, what political imagination and practice, what cultural and literary language, what medical discourse and what conceptions of the body—body politic and body natural—what economic system and what industry, could the book be located? In what other seas would it be swimming? That it can be read otherwise is a matter of philosophical and literary critical necessity, but that is not the question.[139] *Moby-Dick* is at once the whole and the part of a system, a circulatory system that is as closed and as opened as William Harvey's demonstrations had established. More importantly, insofar as it is a hematography, *Moby-Dick* reveals, and teaches about, the intricacies of this circulatory system. The question, then, is not whether it can be read outside of that system—whether it can "survive" without it. Rather, what should be acknowledged is that its location—as a book or a whale—is not so much determined as traversed, imbibed, and, as we have seen, governed by blood, by the circulation of blood through it, by way and through its multiple soaking of a wide array of bodies and domains, all of which—this is, again, what the book reveals—are themselves bloody. Such are the things that make Melville, Melville.[140] And the question that remains, therefore, is the question of blood.

Suggesting a "charitable" reading of a Christian history it summarizes as "impracticable," the striking pamphlet on "Chronometricals and Horologicals" quoted in *Pierre* aptly refers to that history, "the history of Christendom for the last 1800 years," as being "full of blood."[141] Why charitable? The word is Melville's, of course, but it seems to be justified because, over the evidence I have attended to in this chapter, Melville here surprisingly grants that Christianity may not be as singular as it appears—*at least with regard to its predecessors*. Such would be the question he leaves for us, at any rate: Is that history "not just as full of blood, violence, wrong, and iniquity of every kind, as any *previous* portion of the world's story?"[142]

So how are we to define blood? Are we to definite it at all? What is the nature of its circulation through theology and politics, science and literature, texts and bodies? And what is thereby asserted about "Christianity" if it is revealed as a singular domain—a body and a world (natural, social, political, and theological)—through which blood runs and flows as it never has anywhere else? First of all, and open as it is, blood unifies and integrates the different bodies and domains that form the circulatory system Melville describes: Leviathan. Second, blood engages a theological conception that is by no means isolated from other, less theological but no less Christian domains. Whatever "Christianity" is, in other words, it is much more than theology. It cannot be reduced to or exhausted by a theology (or even to a complex, diverse, and contested system of theological positions and doctrines). Third, in Melville's reading, it is not Christianity that governs blood, but blood that governs Christianity. More precisely, blood unifies Christianity, taking it, as it were, beyond itself, while maintaining (and even renewing) its relative integrity—as a distributive system of circulation. This being said, the "very veil of the Christian's deity," indeed, "the intensifying agent in things the most appalling to mankind," is very much white, "which strikes more of panic to the soul than that redness which affrights in blood" (42: 189).

Conclusion ON THE
CHRISTIAN QUESTION
(JESUS AND MONOTHEISM)

"MURDER," DERRIDA WRITES after Freud, "begins with the intention to kill. The unconscious knows no difference here between the virtual and the actual, the intention and the action (a certain Judaism also, by the way)."[1] From Oedipus to Moses, between Athens and Jerusalem, murder begins with the intention to kill. But where does it end? When is murder over and done for? How and how long does it linger? Is murder, like mourning and like analysis, terminable or interminable? If everything begins with a murder, if the past, the very foundation of law and society, the creation of a people (or of a religion), are predicated on murder, would the end of murder, the murder of all murders, spell the end of that people, the end of human society or of humanity? Or would it herald a new beginning? A new humanity? What, in other words, is *the future of murder*? And would it really apply to all and any murder? Are there different kinds, different versions or translations of murder? What would such difference, what would its disappearance, mean anyway? To what procedures of verification could it be amenable? Would it translate the exhaustion of each murderous action or the abolition of every intention to kill? Would the virtual and the actual, finally at peace and identical at last, spell the end of murderous violence? Is this the way murder ends? With a bang *and* with a whimper? Is that the future—the ends—of murder? Whatever happens, however it all ends, it is difficult to imagine that it could be pretty (but you already knew that, by now). Seriously now, the future of murder? What is that really? Is it even possible? Is it any different from the future of an illusion, indeed, from the future of a delusion?

The concluding argument I wish to offer suspends, at least in its more manifest dimensions, the question of blood and turns, as if more directly, to the Christian question. The association of blood and murder was and would have been too facile anyway, and all too general. It certainly could not exhaust the "critique of violence" with which I began. My point of departure here is in any case different and relatively straightforward, perhaps even obvious: Freud's *Moses and Monotheism* is a book about murder, and about a *catastrophic* change in the history of murder. *Wo es war.* . . . There, where murder was, Freud seems ultimately to tells us, religion shall emerge. And something else than "religion" too. Call it another scene. Religion is indisputably important for Freud, but murder—this too should be obvious—is much bigger than religion. Let us grant instead that murder frames or reframes the question of religion otherwise. Which religion? I shall proceed by asking instead: Which murder? Which history of, and for, murder? What future for it? Murder is, after all, at the center of a text most notorious perhaps for its retelling of the primal murder as well as for the analogy it makes between writing and murder. "The distortion of a text resembles a murder [*ähnlich wie bei einem Mord*]," wrote Freud in one of his felicitous formulations. "The difficulty is not in perpetrating the deed, but in getting rid of its traces."[2] The difficulty, in other words, lies in the future of murder.

Freud does not speak of just any murder of course, yet it is unclear whether one could locate with historical precision much less qualify the first murder, the murder of the primal father, with a set of particular attributes (and please remember that this is a book about Moses, "the greatest of . . . *sons*"). When and where does the murder take place exactly? Does it ever, strictly speaking, take place? What do we really know of the primordial tribes? Of the Hebrews of long ago? Is murder confined to these ancient times? "The act which turns into a trace through writing is the rejection of the founding father," explains Michel de Certeau as he signals toward the "conditions of representability" of Freud's narrative.[3] "In the text it is multiplied. . . . from Ikhnaton's erasure of the religion and the name of his father or the Egyptian people's contempt for Ikhnaton's monotheism, all the way up to the murder of Christ. The 'initial' event is basically nothing more than the name given to a series begun long before the narrative, in Egypt."[4] There is no datable event, nothing identifiable by forensic science. For Lacan, in fact, the whole thing "is introduced by Freud as a modern myth."[5] There are surely enough reasons to believe that Freud's account is meant to signify a plural and collective, indeed, a serial and universal, murder, while being at the same time, perhaps, the untimely and only roughly datable murder of one individual (as James Henry Breasted had it, whom Freud approvingly quotes, it was Akhenaten after all who "was the first individual in history").[6] From Akhenaten to Jesus, and from Oedipus to Moses, murder implicates and affects, in any case, a large part if not the whole of human-ity. It is, furthermore, collective and contagious, repeatable and repeated. "An event such as the elimination of the primal father by the company of his sons must inevi-tably have left ineradicable traces in the history of humanity; and the less it itself was recollected, the more numerous must have been the substitutes to which it gave rise."[7]

This extension—distortion and substitution, murder in translations—is no doubt one reason why the study of trauma has gravitated toward *Moses and Mono-theism*. Finding support in its complex temporality, trauma has everything to do with the tribe, the crowd, and the mass (from *Mass* to *Macht,* as Elias Canetti puts it; from mass media to mass transportation and on to mass murder). Ultimately, it can always be traced to the first murder.[8] From Oedipus to Moses, and from Moses to Freud—from *sin'ah* to *Shoah*—the murder of the first individual would also be the first "mass murder," that is, the first murder performed or (self-)inflicted, experienced (or not) by the mass, at any rate, the first trauma of the mass.[9] Put more mildly, "personal oedipal fantasy and guilt were replaced by an historic deed and group remorse."[10] The story seems transparent enough even if the original, along with its translations, is lost in the mists of historical or mythical time. This is one individual murder that, unlike Cain's (strangely forgotten, by the way), has become, as it must, a matter of collective guilt; the murder of an individual that was always already a crime for—and against—humanity. Heralding a genocide, in other (seemingly hyperbolic) words, is the condition of possibility of human society. In the beginning, then, was the future of murder, the murder *of* the mass (double genitive).[11] *In the beginning was the genocide.* Not the word nor the deed, but genocide all the same.

But "what does it mean, precisely, for history to be the history of a trauma?"[12] And how to evaluate or, again, date this hyperextension of the banality of evil to the universal roots and ends of human history? It is well known that Freud's murder story, his vision of (pre-)history, has been interpreted and reinterpreted, repeated and translated (by Freud himself), while tenaciously opposed too, dismissed by the anthropologists and by countless others. It has also served as a basis for recur-ring inquiries into the nature of Judaism and, more generally, of (monotheistic) religion. True, one might have supposed that the trauma, indeed, the traumatic beginnings of history were found primarily and first of all at one origin (just as at the end, imagine that) of a long trajectory that, I have already suggested, ineluc-tably links trauma and history, Jews and anti-Semitism—and thus the future of murder.[13] Again, the story has variants and variations, many "substitutes to which it gave rise." And Moses is not Laius, nor is he the father of the tribe. As Lacan most eloquently puts it, "What in fucking God's name [*foutre de nom de Dieu*], so to speak, does Moses have to do with Oedipus and the father of the primal horde?"[14] What kind of translations are these, in other (more polite) words?

It is of course well established, not to say obvious and manifest, that the text itself constitutes a reenactment, a translation of sorts and a "displacement from a present scene to a past or primitive one," which further "suggests analogous operations between collective representations and histories of the subject."[15] Freud was "murdering" his own father or indeed Moses himself.[16] Alternatively, he was "interpreting a present-day ritual along psychoanalytic lines to reconstruct a past traumatic event."[17] Indeed, one ritual, which Freud explicitly adopted as paradigmatic and from which he quietly admitted having derived the basic elements of his primal account, points to a distinct origin that, while recognizably specific, is no more evidently universal, nor easily universalizable. This (version of the) origin is Christian. Its ritual is the Eucharist, and the event it inevitably recalls, the passion. Here too, Freud's conviction certainly "reflects his method of working backward from the ceremony of the Christian Eucharist, which contains graphic imagery of oral incorporation in the act of communion."[18] This is hardly surprising and may even seem banal. The sources and resources upon which Freud relied, from William Robertson Smith to Ernst Sellin, were dominantly Christian scholars with a Christian outlook on the history of religions.[19] Furthermore, as Paul Vitz and Daniel Boyarin demonstrate (thereby placing under compelling interrogation the strange and tenacious reductiveness that would have Freud lacking *ambivalence* in his animus toward Christianity), Freud tended to side with Rome—"Next Easter in Rome"—the center of Christendom.[20] Robert Paul generally concurs and goes even a step further when he writes that "Freud's psychoanalytic understanding of Christianity is not, in the end, very different from the self-understanding of the New Testament authors."[21] What interests me, nevertheless, is how here and elsewhere "the standard interpretation of Sigmund Freud is that he was a thorough enemy of religion, in particular of Christianity."[22] Indeed, it seems as important to note this emphasis on a general or generic "religion" as it is to consider that the reading of Freud as anti-Christian commonly prevails. Those readers who have attended to Christian dimensions of Freud's work, when they have not dismissed him outright, have moreover felt the urge to raise objections with regard to a narrative that sees their history of salvation extended to the origins of humanity (or perhaps *first* to the Jews—again!).[23] In fact, when the building blocks of this theory (religion as guilt, religion as theophagy) were advanced by Robertson Smith, serious concerns were naturally raised. There was even a trial, legal proceedings, condemnations.[24] Meanwhile, it is the "Jewish" reception of Freud that grows, and seemingly more understandably so, for as Yosef Hayim Yerushalmi has it, "*Moses and Monotheism* remains, at its core, a deliberately Jewish book."[25]

Like others before, we may feel that we are confronted with versions of a tension whereby one finds "on the one hand, some general arguments built on particular experiences only; on the other hand, a special interpretation of these arguments." [26] The particular nature of the community (the religious tradition) that is founded and ultimately incorporated in and through the founding figure of the murdered father constitutes at one and the same time a kind of undefined universal, akin to Hobbes's state of nature, *and* a bit of an enigma among Freud and his interpreters. [27] The murder of the father is, for them, at once a universal story *and/or* a Jewish story, a general exercise in political psychology and the culmination of Freud's theses on religion (that is, on one religion at least). Yet, Guy Stroumsa describes the reading of that particular object, religion, as generally lacking in the reception of Freud's work. "If the 'Jewish' element (in its various forms) is so present in the book," Stroumsa writes, "this means, then, that Freud sees it as intimately related to the very idea of religion, or at least of monotheism. This may seem obvious, but if I am not mistaken, it does not appear to have been pointed out so far." [28] Stroumsa is mostly correct, of course, though it is partly Freud's own doing. [29] For Freud seems either to be speaking to us of a particular religion (but is it not as well a political, even racial, community?) or he is narrating anew the universal story of humankind—read: he is being antireligious. [30]

With his history of murder, Freud did more than extend his (arguably antagonistic) conception of religion. He also did more than recall the fairly ubiquitous importance of the individual founder, the prevalent role of "the foreigner as founder." [31] Freud may have intended to raise much more general questions altogether, the question of survival, for instance. [32] Otherwise put, and minor quibbles aside, Freud does not obviously appear to be asking us to reflect, in any privileged way, on a particular or on a specific kind of human community. He certainly did not restrict himself to the *religious* community—as opposed to the political or economic and, for that matter, scientific community (Freud no doubt sensed that the mass media would soon announce, or bring about, that "Freud is dead!" thereby containing as well as ensuring, for now, the future of the psychoanalytic collective). [33] Instead, Freud spoke of the Ur-tribe made up, ultimately, of the Everyman. [34] And then he also spoke of the Jews. Everything is therefore as if, from Oedipus to Moses, and from the primal tribe to the ancient Hebrews, we were presented with at least "two versions of the same subject matter in two different languages," with the transcript of a narrative "into another mode of expression, whose characters and syntactic laws it is our business to discover by comparing the original and the translation." [35] Making recognizably universal claims, Freud manifestly drew on the Christian tradition, and yet he ends up telling us most about the Jews as specific carriers of the monotheistic idea. He tells us that before they turned deicidal, the

Jews had already been patricidal—but even then *just like the rest of us* (or is it *them*? we shall come back to this).[36] Is there a distinctive difference, then, a Judeo-Christian difference? What is it that transforms and translates the history of murder (the Oedipus complex; *Totem and Taboo*), introduces and seemingly reduces it to the story of a religious tradition as *Moses and Monotheism* describes it? But for the understandable insistence now that the German title of the book is more accurate for its mention of religion (a "monotheistic religion," which, disappearing from the English title, incidentally stands in dramatic opposition to what Freud himself affirms as the very "essence," perhaps, of his own belonging), one might easily grant after all that "with *Moses*, it may not be simply a matter of religion," nor indeed of politics.[37]

Returning us to the humanity of the great man, to the universality of human finitude, Samuel Weber summarizes that "even the 'greatest' of men, the most heroic or memorable, still remains a finite being, the question of his role in constituting such a tradition is posed. This question," Weber continues, "becomes especially acute when the tradition involved is succeeded by another one that claims to be founded by a human who is the son of God."[38] Pace Weber (and, ambivalently enough, Freud himself), it is a remarkable fact that this becoming-acute did not quite come about.[39] Manifestly clear as it otherwise seems, the Christian tradition has remained as if in a state of *latency*. From Oedipus to Moses and beyond, it has rather been sidelined and deferred, displaced or translated with singular obstinacy as a *Jewish* question—or, if there is a difference again, as a religious (or antireligious) one. Between Athens and Jerusalem; from Judaism to a more general "monotheistic religion," and from Oedipus (the son) to Moses (the father), scholars have explored or refuted numerous "traces" the primal murder left and many among the founding fathers, the "substitutes to which it gave rise." Yet it is easy to see that the reception of Freud has been quite consistent in skipping over not so much the general religious (monotheistic, or even civilizational and universal) import of Freud's work, but rather the *exorbitant* centrality in it of Jesus Christ (the son "became a god himself beside the father and, actually, in place of the father"), the acutely *singular* question of Christianity and its founder.[40] And so I repeat my question: What is the future of murder? What is its origin? If the originary murder is in fact universal, does it mean that its end is as well? If it is "Jewish" (that is, "Mosaic") in some specific manner, what is there to hope for? And if it is Christian? What about the future of Christian murder? What of its origin and specificity? Is murder always the murder of the father or is it the murder of the son? But how to decide when "father and son are identical," when the father-founder of a people is primarily remembered as a son, indeed, "the greatest of its sons"?[41] Is it still religious then? Religious like any other? As I seek to apprehend the end of murder and the future of a delusion, I wish to correct a comparative imbalance and explore Freud's Christian question. I want to suggest that Freud's quest has yet to be interpreted for what it reveals of a crucial version of the history of murder, for what it tells us about Christianity *specifically*—not about Judaism or Jewish self-hatred, not about the Judeo-Christian tradition nor about anti-Semitism, and certainly not exclusively nor even primarily about religion, but first and foremost about Christianity. Diverging responses notwithstanding, secular ones too, "comparing the original and the translation" (and parsing the different versions is what awaits us still, of course), it does not seem far-fetched to suggest that, out of the (Egyptian) sources of Judaism, Freud was participating as well in the universalization, nay, the *christianization*, of human history.[42]

PART I. FREUD A CHRISTIAN ("IF JESUS WAS A JEW . . .")

But who would want to make, about Freud, so hubristically preposterous a claim here and pretend to deny a people—or is it a religion, a race, an ethnicity? a cosmopolitan ideal, perhaps—a man whom it praises among the greatest of its father-killers? Besides, that would be like robbing a text of the adoration of its devoted, and "philosemitic," audiences. Still, and with all due respect to my elders (and to the proliferation of striving studies on the son of Jakob, "the Jew-of-whatever-variety"), it has long seemed to me painfully obvious that the threads linking Freud to Jews, Judaism, and Jewishness, fascinating as they might be, are either very thin or very mysterious—let us say ambivalent at the very least, and minimally hard to read.[43] For what and where, Derrida rightly insisted, is the archive? Yosef Hayim Yerushalmi—whose exertions are themselves laudable enough, which link Freud to Judaism in a scientific manner—offers his own version of the future of murder, that is, of the future of psychoanalysis as a Jewish science. But, he himself recalls, "much will depend, of course, on how the very terms *Jewish* and *science* are to be defined."[44] Freud had certainly raised the stakes when he famously described the author of *Totem and Taboo*—with a healthy dose of denial, no doubt—as "ignorant of the language of holy writ, who is completely estranged from the religion of his fathers—as well as from every other religion—and who cannot take a share in nationalist ideals, but who has yet never repudiated his people, who feels that he is in his essential nature a Jew and who has no desire to alter that nature."[45] Freud goes on to say that he cannot put words to this "essence," thus leaving a high mark in the growing tradition that theorizes Judaism as a kind of *je ne sais quoi*.[46] But if Freud was a Christian,[47] as I have begun to hypothesize, it might be because he did manage to elaborate more successfully, and in ever so many winged words, a substantial version, albeit largely unrecognized, of "the essence of Christianity." This at least is what I will want to argue in order to raise the profile of this particular version of the history of murder. And I do not mean thereby to reiterate that Freud was following Feuerbach.[48] Nor do I mean necessarily to insist on Lacan's affectionate—and to my mind correct—accusation of "Christocentrism" on the part of Freud ("It's so close to the Christian tradition that it's really remarkable"; "it is, needless to say, odd to find this strange Christocentrism in Freud's writings. There must have been a reason for him to have slipped into it almost without realizing it").[49] In all lack of fairness, I also put aside the brilliantly unsettling display by Paul Vitz of "Sigmund Freud's Christian Unconscious" as well as John Schad's meditative exposition of "Freud's Christian Trains of Thought."[50] I truly have no desire to adjudicate on Freud's "belonging" or on his "identity" and identifications (though if I were, I would certainly elaborate on the life of Sigismund Schlomo, the son-identified, permanently rebellious, son—or on the dream of the "reddish water"; I would mention as well the rest of the remarkable evidence marshaled by Vitz regarding Freud's more covert "identification with Jesus" and its sources),[51] nor directly on the proper genre, gender, or race categorization most valid or adequate toward an understanding of Herr S. Freud—important as all those remain.[52] Incidentally, the reception of Freud's quest, its effective history, testifies to distinct headings that have been treated as either exclusive isolates or as amenable to a variably coherent integration. These headings can be summarized as "Freud and the Jewish Question" (Judaism and/or anti-Semitism, Jewish self-hatred) *or* "Freud on Religion" (Judaism and Christianity, Judeo-Christianity, and more recently Islam) *or*, in a minor key, "Freud and the Political," that is to say, the matter of the relation between the individual and group psychology.[53] Yet, as de Certeau has it in his magisterial take on Freud's *Moses*: "What is told *at the same time* about Moses, about the Jew, or about Freud cannot be reduced [*ramener*] to a single one of the *different* registers upon which is analyzed (auto-analyzed and hetero-analyzed) the production of a writing."[54] We are indeed faced with a complex transcript in which different versions overlap, a mode of expression whose characters and syntactic laws we must discover and which requires we compare the original and the translation, the one and the many. From Oedipus to Moses, which is the original, which the translation?

What concerns me corresponds to a definite displacement, a translation indeed and a transfer, a shift of critical energies away from a site of interrogation and perhaps anxiety. It belongs, in other words, to a distinct register that, incidentally (and surprisingly), de Certeau does not mention. It may therefore be of a different nature altogether. As I have been trying to explain, it has much to do with, it is in a way apposite to, the fact that Freud's reflections have carried ever further recursions, ever more sophisticated versions of the "Jewish question." Is Judaism a religion? Are Jews a nation? Are they a race? What exactly is this "essence" of Judaism to which Freud refers? Similarly, and with equal intensity, Freud's text has provoked thoughtful, and more abstract and universal, interrogations on the nature of history, democracy, sexual difference, trauma and the archive and more. Finally, it has been endlessly noted that Freud is antireligious, indeed, anti-Christian. What has *not* emerged after Freud, nor for that matter before him, not really, is a sense that Christianity is as much of an enigma, as much of a mystery as Judaism, and it is one that gains much from a recognition of Christianity's implicit and explicit role in Freud's argumentation. I speak here of investing (rather than repressing and avoiding) Christianity with the urgency of critical attention and for the need to reconsider Christianity and its uninterrogated definition as a religion. Such an inquiry would accordingly attend to the specificity, the singularity of Christianity in its manifest history, "actually existing Christianity," as it appears at the very least in Freud's text.[55] Indeed, everything remains as if Christianity were nothing but a religion, one religion among others and just like any (monotheistic) other. But is Christianity a religion, no more than a religion? Is it not perhaps a race, a new race, minimally a people, a newly imagined (political) community?[56] Maybe it is "a certain kind of character"?[57] In the winter of Huntington's discontent, is not Christianity, alternatively, a civilization?

If Freud was a Christian . . . then what? And if "Christ redeemed mankind from the burden of original sin by the sacrifice of his own life," well, would that make a difference?[58] As much or as little difference as if Moses were (really) an Egyptian and—or would it now?—if Jesus were a Jew? But perhaps Jesus was an Aryan, one of "those whom Freud called 'Christian Aryan[s].' "[59] Do we now not know, hope or wish we know, that Moses too was (un)related to that "band of Semites"?[60] Not that the latter would be "a foreign Asiatic race," God forbid, I mean, Moses.[61] Boyarin is right, of course, "Freud's *Moses and Monotheism* is best read as part of a massive socio-cultural attempt by German-speaking Jews in the nineteenth century to rewrite themselves and particularly their masculine selves as Aryans, and especially as Teutons."[62] And so two versions of the same subject matter are confronting us once again. Is this a matter of race or is it about religion? Recall that Jan Assmann's prominent contribution to the "return to Moses" treats Jesus and Christianity as a marginal nonevent, just another post on the long and murderous Mosaic road. More important, the "Mosaic distinction," the difference Moses made by bringing (Egyptian) monotheism into the world, has nothing to do with race in Assmann's rendering, only with religion. For the Mosaic distinction is, let me repeat, a religious distinction, "the distinction between true and false *in religion*."[63] But if I may insist, what does all this tell us about Christianity? What about "Jesus and mono-theism"? After all, is Freud's *Moses* anything but the narrative of an open secret? Anything but the manifest, and paradoxically implicit, exposition of the Christian tradition?[64] Consider again Samuel Weber's impeccable summary of *Moses,* which underscores with Freud's original title (*der Mann Moses*) the humanity of the founder as opposed to his divinity. (Did someone really need to be convinced? With regard to Moses?? Is there not another man—*ecce homo*—about whom "it was probably not easy . . . to distinguish the image of the man . . . from that of his God"?[65]) Consider that this "founder and leader," having been killed, "would return from the dead to redeem his murderers."[66] Ask yourself again whether he is a father or a son. Or: What is the latency of Christianity? What of its claim to a history of innocence, a history *after* murder? Is it not at all curious that Christ too was, as if by coincidence, a murdered leader who brought about the founding of "two religions" (Judaism and Christianity, Catholicism and Protestantism), that this founder too was always already two (Jesus and Paul) and that behind Freud's *Moses* there was always Jesus of course but also Paul's Moses, ultimately, a very Christian Moses?[67]

"This is the theme of Moses and Paul," Jacob Taubes masterfully explains as he tries to redirect the force of important if obvious parallels made by the Gospel between Jesus and Moses.[68] Taubes acknowledges the disputed origins of the claim that the Jews are a "Mosaic" community, the notion that "just as the Christians derive themselves from Christ so the Jews derive themselves from Moses" (33). Later it will be said that Muslims—called for the purpose Mohammedans—are worshipping their prophet, themselves mistaking (God knows by what accident or coincidence) a human prophet for a God. And who would ever do such a thing? For now, Taubes insists, it is according to Paul that it is first so, that Jews became the people of Moses—for Paul and not for Moses, who explicitly refuses and refutes such foundational belonging and ownership when "God makes the offer to destroy the people and to begin a new one with Moses." (47).[69] But the "Paul-Moses comparison is forced by Paul himself" (40). It is for Paul that "the task at hand is the establishment and legitimation of a new people of God" (28). It is Paul who "measures himself against Moses . . . and [claims that] his business is the same: the establishment of a people" (40). Ultimately, and this is Taubes' thesis, "Paul understands himself as outbidding Moses" (39). That is how "Christianity has its origin not properly in Jesus but in Paul" (40). But there are, again, two origins, that is to say, "two Moses," Jesus and Paul, if you will, Paul and Moses, Moses and Freud, the Jesus of Freud.[70] By construing Moses after Paul, at any rate, and the murder of the father after Jesus, Freud, who may have sensed "that Christ might well be a quite impossible load to bear," was raising in the most manifest manner what can hardly be called otherwise than the Christian question.[71]

PART II. IF FREUD WAS A CHRISTIAN . . .

"There on the English beach Freud is not only being stupid but stupidly Christian."[72] So much for the Christian question. But I think that what John Schad means to point out with this irreverent formulation is precisely this: that enslaved in Egypt—that is, stranded in the centers of Imperial Christendom (Vienna and London)—and looking for a people, Freud had finally a lot to say about Christianity. Theodor Herzl, that other modern Moses, was no different.[73] Like many before and after him, however, Freud did tend to understand Christianity in a restricted sense. He subsumed most of it under the general category of "religion." Or so at least on what could be called a manifest level. Persecution and the art of writing.[74] Freud was admittedly worried about upsetting Pater Schmidt and the Catholic Church with regard to his argument, going so far as to bizarrely deny the continuities and concordances between Christian anti-Semitism and Nazism, except to suggest that Germans had been poorly Christianized and that anti-Semitism was always, imagine that, the "hatred of Christians"![75] And let us not forget that in England too, Freud had ample occasions to feel isolated on that front, minimally to acknowledge that "many well-meaning strangers 'have pointed out to me the way of Christ.' "[76] True, Freud was also quite explicit that the wound he might inflict with *Moses* was first and foremost on the Jews. It would not be the first time that the author of a manifest "Jewish question" (and his readers too) would be misled into thinking that there was nothing more beyond, beneath, or beside. Yet, at that very same manifest level, has there not always been a more massive—albeit unasked, and certainly unanswered—Christian question?[77] Marx is an obvious case in point. Sartre perhaps another. It seems truly striking after all that one should be able (somehow preposterously) to insist that Marx was a Jew (and an anti-Semite to boot), to claim that Freud was too (that is, a proud "godless Jew" and/or an irreparably self-hating one), or indeed, that the twentieth century was "the Jewish century,"[78] but begin to sound like a fringe lunatic when recalling that Hobbes, Locke, and Hume, and with them the traditions of liberalism, the accelerations of capitalism, and much else of "our modernity" (Nazism included) may suffer from a lingering case of Christianity. Rather than consider what Freud says about Jews, therefore, or indeed about Judaism and anti-Semitism, it has seemed more pertinent to read an ambiguous latency and raise the possibility that we may not have access to, we may not yet know what Christianity is at all. Of course, "much will depend on what is meant" by Christianity.

Is there not enough ground, then, to raise the Christian question? I have begun to follow the pertinence of Jesus and of Christianity in reading *Moses and Monotheism*. But before Freud and after him, there have been many who have commented on one Christian aspect or another of some essential dimension of modernity. I spare you Feuerbach, Hegel, and Weber ("a thoroughgoing Christianization of the whole of life"). I leave aside the complicated cases of Nietzsche—and Bataille (whose "manuel de l'anti-chrétien" is devoted to "l'essence de l'esprit chrétien," the action of which operates "beyond priests and churches . . . sometimes even in the camp of those who believe themselves hostile to it").[79] I restrict myself to giving you the more recent highlights.[80] What Michael Allen Gillepsie calls "the theological origins of modernity," Mark C. Taylor refers to as "the protestant revolution."[81] Not necessarily following along the same, strict Hegelian lines, Karl Löwith had argued earlier that history, and its still current periodization, is really Christian.[82] Carlo Ginzburg may be beginning to agree.[83] Marcel Gauchet too, and Jean-Luc Nancy with him, think that secular modernity—the separation of religion from politics— is Christian, which is to say that, in spite of its more obvious ancient roots, Christianity is no ordinary religion: it is at the very least, and since the beginning, the religion of the end of religion, the true rise of worldly politics.[84] And though he may have quibbled on the dating, on that point or another, I do not think Ernst Kantorowicz would have fundamentally disagreed.[85] Arendt had flipped that argument around.[86] Grounding themselves in some of the same sources, Harold Berman and Pierre Legendre, who both lament our general ignorance of the matter, suggest that our entire system of law as essentially Christian, founded as it is on the synthetic work of the Canon jurists, which was imported more or less whole into the modern codes.[87] Although he never quite mentioned religion in *The Order of Things* nor sufficiently elaborated on it elsewhere in his major works, Michel Foucault did go on to substantially correct the perception that Christianity (he had reservations about the term) had little to do with modernity, indeed, with liberalism and governmentality. Incidentally, Foucault acknowledges Moses as an important figure of pastoral power, but more importantly he describes the pertinacious presence of this essential feature of the regime of modernity as fundamentally and uniquely Christian. It is the church, Foucault says, that brought about a "coagulation" of the themes, mechanisms, and institutions of pastoral power, "a type of power that I think was unknown to any other civilization."[88] Giorgio Agamben, whose own Christological inclinations are becoming increasingly evident, builds on some of these moments in Foucault's work, claiming "economic theology" as a fundamental structure of political, and religious, power and (drawing on the work of Marie-José Mondzain) the basis for an archaeology of glory, a theory and technology of the image, which governs, indeed, our very visual culture.[89] Derrida, who kept reminding us of our "globalatinization," also pointed to its manifest dimension, which he called "Christian televisualization." Derrida suggestively linked television and media to the incarnation in its Catholic and Protestant instantiations.[90]

On a different front (or not), Denise Buell, Colin Kidd, J. Kameron Carter, and Willie James Jennings have asked to rethink the proximity of race and Christianity, while the tide grows that testifies to the colonial dimensions of Christianity.[91] Peter Van der Veer gathered scholars to reflect on "the globalization of Christianity" as a broad set of conversions to modernity.[92] Earlier, Alexandre Kojève had written briefly but potently about Christianity as science, proclaiming in fact the Christian origins of modern science. So did David Noble.[93]

These are all debatable arguments, of course, not least because of the overt or covert exceptionalism, triumphalism, or, alternatively, supersessionism they (though not all) might be said to demonstrate or unwittingly reproduce. And note that most rely in one way or another on the rhetoric of "religion" (a notion that has itself been credited to Christianity by a growing number of authors), while silently contributing to undermine the circumscribed definition of this term or indeed its general applicability in the light of Christianity's singular history.[94] By recalling these arguments, I do not mean to assert that they are necessarily true or even correct, not even that they are adequate to the task they set for themselves. Is Christianity law or science? Is it race science? Is it politics or economy? Economic theology or, more restrictively, capitalism? Is it not more likely that Christianity constitutes a singular, and changing, set of divisions between realms it sometimes invents, but more often "purifies," in an always overdetermined manner?[95] For my part, I have merely meant to draw some of Christianity's contours, to elaborate on its element and provide rudiments, instruments for the measure of its expanding reach, and to join those arguing for an "anthropology of Christianity" (another heading of surprising novelty, and a field in its infancy), the posing of a question as to the nature, however diverse and changing, of Christianity.[96] For indeed, what is Christianity? What are its regions and its divisions? What are its limits and its ends? Is not Christianity a political or economic, legal or scientific, tradition as much as it is a religious one? But what can that mean? What *could* it mean to consider that Christianity is *not* a religion, by no means exclusively, not even primarily so? Am I making claims about an "essence of Christianity" then? As I conclude, I would rather propose that we begin to think of Christianity along lines parallel to the "extreme solidity," the "great force of inertia," which Foucault attributes to the prison as a complex and dynamic set of disciplinary mechanisms, technologies of subjectivation, and institutional apparatuses.[97] Or perhaps we should make use of the model of masculinity, described by Judith Surkis, "as an amalgam of a certain kind of body, a modality of desire, and a quality of mind, [that] was contingently constituted and regularly reconfigured." For while Christianity, like masculinity, was "tautologically conferred" on Christians, "its meaning remained unstable."[98] The inquiry I have attempted was at any rate guided by questions such as asked by

Mayanthi Fernando on contemporary France, namely, "how does one attend to both the inchoate quality of [Christianity] and the regulatory force of its legal and political apparatus? How does one study an object . . . that constantly posits [or alternatively denies] its own unity and coherence . . . but is in fact riven by disunity and contradiction, . . . [which] is always in the making and never entirely settled, but nonetheless has real effects on the subjects it regulates?"[99] What I wanted to show was how liquidity, "how instability, rather than undermining" Christianity "as a regulatory political and social ideal, actually lent it its force."[100]

PART III. JESUS, HIS PEOPLE, AND MONOTHEISTIC RELIGION

To summarize what I have tried to argue so far, one might offer the following formula: If Freud was a Jew, then Moses was an Egyptian. But if Freud was a Christian, then Jesus was a Jew. The obviousness of this latter version, linked to the facts of Christian history and to the ubiquity of the "foreign founder," should not detract from the attention it still deserves. De Certeau misses the mark (Judaism instead of Christianity), though he rightly points to the center of gravity of Freud's historical truth, when he writes that "everything happens as if [Freud] had mistaken one period for another, or as if he had made one the metaphor of the other. Certainly he speaks of beginnings. But he narrates in a novel about Mosaic origins what the birth of itinerant Judaism and closed scriptures during the first century of our era had been in history."[101] Freud's return, the return of Freud, has always meant a return to (the time of) Jesus and to Christianity—our "Christian unconscious," as Paul Vitz has it. Or so it should have meant. Accordingly, *Moses and Monotheism* is one version (or two?) of other textual renderings. Moses *translates* Oedipus and the primal father rather than simply repeating either of them. And then there is Jesus—that pervasive if little acknowledged translation. Or is it the original? Back to Freud, at any rate, and back to Jesus, back to murder and to its future. For, if *Moses* clearly constitutes a rewriting of *Totem and Taboo*, and if Jesus retroprospectively replaces Moses (and indeed Oedipus), there is little doubt that this substitution, this translation (the latency of Christianity), plausible as it is, is not sufficient to provide an exhaustive reading of *Moses and Monotheism*, whatever that could be. And to point out that it is suggested by Freud himself, as the quote below will confirm, does not alter the matter much. Besides, putting that substitution forward runs the risk of ignoring the fact that there is another rendering, another settling, of the Christian account, of the account of Christianity. Freud already had quite explicit things to say, in other words, about Jesus and Christianity, in that book and elsewhere as well, not all of it negative, as we saw, but more important, not all of it *religious*—if at all. And so the question that comes to mind at this point has to do with the relative place of "tradition," of the Christian tradition, in its relation to what Richard Bernstein underscores are the two central concepts of Freud's *Moses*: latency and the return of the repressed.[102] Were we to believe Freud, as a matter of fact, we would have to acknowledge that far from an original (as the thesis of universalization and christianization suggested), we are confronted here with the final chapter, the final translation of the history of murder. But both renderings are of course correct. Having been lifted to consciousness and acknowledged by Saint Paul, the founding murder is now made manifest, and to that extent brought closer to a resolution, or a cure.

> It is plausible to conjecture that remorse for the murder of Moses provided the stimulus for the wishful phantasy of the Messiah, who was to return and lead his people to redemption and the promised world-dominion. If Moses was this first Messiah, Christ became his substitute and successor [*dann ist Christus sein Ersatzmann und Nachfolger geworden*], and Paul could exclaim to the peoples with some historical justification: "Look! The Messiah has really come: he has been murdered before your eyes!" Then, too, there is a piece of historical truth in Christ's resurrection, for he was the resurrected Moses and behind him the returned primal father of the primitive horde, transfigured and, as the son, put in the place of the father.[103]

From Moses to Christ and beyond its monotheistic content, the historical truth of Christianity has to be seen as extending beyond religion, going back to—and again, translating—*the beginnings of humanity as such*. Insofar as it releases the tension of an ancient wish-phantasy while bringing about its conscious acknowledgment, it would seem truly and simultaneously to constitute the advent of a new humanity, indeed, the rise of a new man. Minimally, Christianity offers a new kind of promise, perhaps even the fulfillment of an old promise or covenant, the promise of the end of murder as the foundation of human society.[104] For at the center of Christianity's progress, there is the becoming-explicit of a figure (*figura*), the confession of murder, a confession of which the Jews—and more generally, the humanity of old—have proved incapable.[105] "It has been impossible for the Jews to join in this forward step which was implied, in spite of all its distortions, by the admission of having murdered God."[106] No wonder then that "in the history of religion—that is, as regards the return of the repressed— Christianity was an advance" (87). But murder is clearly bigger and older than religion, and the progress made by Christianity reaches, once again, far beyond such regional limits.

This too has everything to do with Jesus as substitute. Which is why we must take a closer look at the intricacies of the mechanism, the "dream-work," as it were, with which we have been struggling all along ("two versions of the same subject matter in two different languages," the need for "another mode of expression, whose characters and syntactic laws it is our business to discover by comparing the original and the translation").[107] Recall the way in which Freud had put it in *Totem and Taboo*, "an event such as the elimination of the primal father by the company of his sons must inevitably have left ineradicable traces in the history of humanity; and the less it itself was recollected, the more numerous must have been the substitutes [*Ersatzbildungen*] to which it gave rise."[108] Recall as well that Jesus is a translation for Moses, the *resurrection* of the primal father. As a matter of fact, Jesus may well be the last such substitute insofar as the event is now increasingly recollected (the more it is recollected, logic demands, the lesser the number of substitutes). Recall, finally, that Freud begins with, he finds the origin of, the primal murder in its most complete and explicit version: the story of Christ. All this is another way to point to the *condensation* here at work, another way of saying that Jesus (*alpha* and *omega*) recapitulates the history of murder, replaces the father, the murdered father, and accomplishes, *displaces* and resolves the history of murder.[109] So much, then, for the death of God (the Father).[110] But that is obviously not all Jesus substitutes for. Consider now what Freud goes on to explain as he unravels the narrative that the Christian tradition condenses and represses, namely, that "each one of the company of brothers certainly had a wish to commit the deed by himself alone and so to create an exceptional position for himself and to find a substitute for his identification with the father."[111] If the horde had a leader (and "we must in my judgment leave it undecided whether there was such a chief rebel and ringleader," says Freud), he "could be none other than the most guilty person." Is Christ the murderer then, the most guilty of murderers?[112] Much will depend on whether there was such a leader and on the difference between intention and action. But Freud is here at his best, of course.

> If there was no such ringleader, then Christ was the heir to a wishful phantasy which remained unfulfilled; if there was one, then he was his successor and his reincarnation. *But no matter whether what we have here is a phantasy or the return of a forgotten reality*, in any case the origin of the concept of a hero is to be found at this point—the hero who always rebels against his father and kills him in some shape or other.[113]

The future of murder, Freud tells us in this striking translation, is the hero, of whom Christ is the origin. More precisely, and regardless of the difference between the intention and the act of murder, between (a leaderless) phantasy and (leaderful) reality, the future of *this* murderer is that he will turn into a hero. This is an exact reversal of the story of Oedipus (and Moses), of course, where the exceptionality of the hero (the victim of a failed murder) lies less in his birth (high or low) than in his future, for the hero will here turn out to be a murderer, though an *innocent* one (unlike Jesus', Oedipus' innocence is not a viable possibility). More precisely, the murderer has turned into the innocent hero he always already was—*from the beginning.*[114] It is therefore here, in the real or phantasmic story of Christ the hero, Christ the innocent murderer, that the novelty introduced by Christianity finds its momentous source and its original character. "Christianity became a religion of the son," Freud continues, which is to say that it turned the cult of the dead father into a worship of the murdering son as innocent (87). Otherwise phrased, we witness an unprecedented transvaluation of values in the rapport to murder. "So what happens," asks Talal Asad, "if the perpetrator of death dealing dies of his own free will at the very moment of his crime? What, in other words, if crime and punishment are united?"[115] The answer, in so many words, is "life everlasting purchased by a cruel death."[116] From substitute to substitute, and from murder to murder, there is the future of murder: murder, yes, but without guilt, only innocence. Forever.

And this is not all. The genius of Paul, his "innately religious disposition" (85–86), was to bring about the very essence of an unprecedented religion, a religion like no other and therefore no religion at all. Paul knew about the rapport of the law to sin. In Freud's rendering, Paul turned around (which is to say that he invented and confirmed) the founding narrative of human society and created instead a "phantasy of atonement," a "message of redemption (*evangelium*)," and a "phantasy of redemption." As to the significance of this creation, "what was essential in it seems to have been Paul's own contribution" (85). What is this contribution precisely? "Through the idea of the redeemer, he exorcized humanity's sense of guilt" (87). With its abolition of circumcision to boot, Freud goes on, "the new religion could be a universal one, embracing all men" (87). Paul's innately religious disposition, the "advance" he brings about in the history of religion, begins at the beginning: it begins with murder, which it universalizes, and proceeds with the acknowledgment, the confession of murder.

> Irrespectively of all the approximations and preparations in the surrounding world, it was after all a Jewish man, Saul of Tarsus (who, as a Roman citizen, called himself Paul), in whose spirit the realization first emerged: "The reason we are so unhappy is that we have killed God the father." (134)

The original murder was already a translation. Derrida could not have said it better: The first time the story was iterated, narrated, was already a repetition.

The primal murder always already occurred as a Christian translation, a Christian confession. Where there was guilt, there murder shall be found; where there was abolition, there was the law. Which is to say that at the very moment it comes to consciousness and approaches its end, the murder of the father emerges as foundational. It is universalized, along with the guilt it had always already instituted. This is the end and the beginning, the alpha and the omega of the history of murder. It takes place as well at the very moment the murderer—at least one of them, one for all of them—is lionized and, most importantly, exonerated.

Is that it then? Is that the end of murder and its future?

Not quite, of course, not least because it is, Freud tells us, a phantasy and a delusion that has further import. Continuing his account of Paul and of Christianity, of the revolution and resolution thus brought about by way of innocence, Freud goes on to explain that

> it is entirely understandable that [Paul] could only grasp this piece of truth in the delusional disguise of the glad tidings: "We are freed from all guilt since one of us has sacrificed his life to absolve us." In this formula the killing of God was of course not mentioned, but a crime that had to be atoned by the sacrifice of a victim could only have been a murder. And the intermediate step between the delusion and the historical truth was provided by the assurance that the victim of the sacrifice had been God's son. (134)

Freud had earlier noted the strange collusion of historical truth and delusions. "We have long understood that a portion of forgotten truth lies hidden in delusional ideas," he had said. In fact, "the compulsive conviction which attaches to the delusion arises from this core of truth and spreads out on to the errors that wrap it round. We must grant an ingredient such as this of what may be called historical truth to the dogmas of religion as well" (84). We might ask ourselves about the universalizing gesture here again operating. But be the case as it may, we can certainly recognize the singular nature of delusion in the case of Christianity. It brings the primal murder to consciousness ("confession"), projecting and universalizing murder ("we have all killed him"), proceeds to resolve the feelings of guilt (it "exorcised humanity's sense of guilt"), and finally substitutes victim for murderer.

"How could someone guiltless of the act of murder take on himself the guilt of the murderers by allowing himself to be killed?" Freud had asked (86). His complicated answer constitutes a model of decipherment, attending as it does to the multiple mechanisms of condensation and displacement, of which the mind has shown itself capable, recognizably that is, since *The Interpretation of Dreams* at the very least. Freud restores the logic and the chronology behind his own question (first innocence, then murder, followed by the guilt of the murderers and the "punishment" of the innocent), a question that otherwise includes all the crucial elements of the event in its Christian telling as retelling: murder and sacrifice, guilt and innocence, perpetrator and victim. Properly rearranged (one might here be reminded of Levi-Strauss comparative analysis of myths), the account looks as follows: first there was murder, then there was guilt, followed by expiation, which brought about innocence (not to mention life everlasting in the resurrection). Which is to say that long before he *became* the innocent victim who was killed for the purpose of expiation, the son would turn out to have been the murderer of the father. The temporality was indeed jumbled and distorted as here it is only *after* he is punished and killed that the son becomes innocent, cleansed not just of his guilt, therefore, but of the actual murder of the father, which Freud is therefore correct in describing as "not mentioned."[117] But an event such as the elimination of the (murder of the) primal father by the (leader of) company of his sons must inevitably have left some traces in the history of humanity. There remains a translation, the good news of the exoneration of the murderer—and the purchase of eternal life— which must have affected the entire collective subject, the political community, hereby founded on the act, at once affirmed and denied, and its confession ("we have all killed him," "the son was innocent"). It is a process that turns him (them) into a victim and a hero, innocent always, a process that *catastrophically* inverts the story of Oedipus in Thebes, but also follows the quite precise terms of the account Freud gives with regard to the Christians' rapport to Jews. This is the final twist. It is also the most condensed rendering of the entire matter.

As Freud explains *twice*, the (guilty and universal) claim that "we have all killed him" is repeatedly, if surprisingly, rendered as "You killed our God," which Freud helpfully translates: "You won't admit that you murdered God" (Freud also explains, in case we forgot, that this is said of "the primal picture of God, the primal father, and his later reincarnations") (89). In the exact manner whereby the murderer became victim, then, the self-accusation turns into an accusation of the other, an accusation directed at and projected onto the other (Judas, the Jews). It becomes self-exoneration, in other words. As Freud puts the finishing (and sharpening) touch to his account of the singularity of Christianity, he ventriloquizes and recaps: " 'We did the same thing, to be sure, but we have admitted it and since then we have been absolved' " (89).

Let me join Freud, then, and reiterate this essential assertion "in its full form" and in its generalized reach, for it cannot be read enough (nor has it, really), and it cannot be confined to the matter of anti-Semitism.[118] As I said, this assertion quite literally condenses the entire trajectory of the *Moses* of Freud, all the versions of the myth plus one, and perhaps Freud's entire lifework: from Oedipus to Moses by way of the father of the primal horde ("we have all killed him"), between Moses and Jesus, from (unacknowledged) murder to (murderous) innocence: "They will not accept it as true that they murdered God, whereas we admit it and have been cleansed of that guilt" (135). Recall that the feeling of guilt—which would be present *in this very form* throughout humankind—is what must be accounted for. Freud's explanation, which has everything to do with the history of religion but goes well beyond it, illustrates the return of the repressed insofar as it is shared by humankind as a whole. Yet Christianity, which partakes of this character and provides its paradigmatic elements (from murder to totemic meal, as Robertson Smith had it; the universalization of the narrative and the Christianization of humanity), also brings about, by way of a new mytheme or narrative twist, a new humanity, a fundamental difference and a distinction that is not about the true and the false in religion, but something else entirely. Christianity, the Jesuic distinction in humanity (if I may propose this awkward rephrasing of Jan Assmann's "Mosaic distinction"), is the difference between innocence and guilt as the basis of human society, the difference *across* humanity, between the old and guilty (humans) and the new and innocent (Christians). It is indeed the advent of a new humanity. From now on, may God protect the humanity of old.

What then is the future of murder? From Oedipus to Moses, Freud could not have been clearer, even if—persecution and the art of writing, that is, murder and the distortion of writing—he has not quite been read in this way. The future of murder is innocence. In Benjaminian terms, this means that the distinction between law-instituting violence and law-preserving violence is transformed into law-abolishing violence, and then into violence-denying love. Instead of collective guilt, collective innocence. Such is the Christian dispensation, and from now on and since the beginning it constitutes at once the paradigm for, and the radically new answer to, the question: "What is man?" It is also the future of a delusion. Which I have been suggesting is not at all the same as the future of an illusion, namely, religion. It rather *supplements* the history of religions by introducing a radical rupture in the human, all-too human history it has always already taught us, a rupture that at every point of Freud's account can be seen to function as the "origin" (the origin of the myth, the origin of the hero, indeed, the origin of the primal murder). This is no simple origin, of course, no origin at all, because like all origins or beginnings, Freud is also clear that these are not locatable at a precise point in time. But this does not diminish the truth of Christianity's history, its historical truth. It moreover reveals—if also conceals—the singularity of Christianity. "Such is the movement followed during periods of latency, with the tradition that 'would like to forget'" and also remember onto others, as it were, "and that, in laboring to efface the memory of the initial murder," or rather its own foundational role in it, "betrays (reveals) what it is hiding."[119]

Are we Christians? Are we Jews? Is Freud a Christian or a Jew? And we, we who have killed him, are we Christians? Are we guilty or innocent? But of what? Much will have depended on the definition of Christianity. What I have tried to show is that Freud raised precisely this crucial question: What is Christianity? Following the history of murder, reworking its translations, Freud posed in no uncertain, but unprecedented, terms the Christian question. He rehearsed and repeated for us the history of murder that Christianity has told and variously instituted for two thousand years. Freud narrated and translated the foundation of human society and the history of humanity as the singular story of this (Christian) murder: "we have all killed him!" That is the historical truth of Christianity. Freud also made clear that, well beyond a religion, Christianity is a reinvention of humanity, a catastrophic turn in the history of murder. From this turn on, a foundational one, Christianity emerged and extended itself as a new form of human comportment, a new conception of the human collective in its rapport to murder—a multifarious act, to be sure, virtual and actual, which has for all time targeted an infinite number of victims, guilty or innocent, besides fathers or sons (recall that the Bible opens with a fratricidal, not patricidal, murder). In the covert difference between Oedipus and Moses, between Athens and Jerusalem, Freud wrote about the Jesuic translation. He showed that what Christianity has taught us is that the original is always the father (the father is the origin), the son a translation.[120] And the reverse too. Oh, and we have all killed him. Except for the innocent, who forgave and forgot—themselves.[121] Thus, the only real and significant murder, the first murder, is the murder of the father. It is the only murder, the true murder, from which we have exonerated ourselves. It is the only crime against humanity, the one of which we, we who worship the sons, are always already innocent.

A CRITIQUE OF CHRISTIANITY

What is called "Christian civilization" is none other than the ensemble of collateral effects which faith in Christ has produced on the civilizations it has encountered along the way. When His resurrection is believed in, and the possibility of the resurrection of every man in Him, everything is seen in a different way, and one acts in consequence of that, in all spheres. But a great deal of time is needed to become aware of this and make it concrete. For that reason we are, perhaps, only at the beginning of Christianity.
—RÉMI BRAGUE, "INTERVIEW"

So what is Christianity? And why insist still on identifying blood with Christianity? I have tried to make clear throughout that, neither complete nor exhaustive, this identification is nevertheless determining. Surprisingly, the singular role that blood has played, and continues to play, in the Christian imagination and in Christianity's effective history, while not quite invisible, had not been sufficiently documented and thought. It vanished under the weight of comparison and universalism, the naturalized figure of a universal blood, at a time when the difference between bloods has become increasingly sedimented and indeed universalized. It vanished under other pluralizations or periodizations, disciplinarity and dialogizations too (the alleged symmetries of the Judeo-Christian). This is why it has seemed necessary, in order to ask about Christianity, about "the essence of Christianity," as Feuerbach had it, to open a different kind of investigation into blood. Which means that to inquire after blood was another way to ask whether there is a Christian question, a concept of Christianity even, a manner whereby we have come to know, whereby we have established with any sense of certainty, what Christianity is. Certainly Christianity is named and invoked, upheld, and spread in a wide variety of instances. Like modernity, or nationalism (themselves two among its improper names), Christianity is plural and has been pluralized. Christianity, the one and the many, is globally affirmed, often defended, and sometimes even criticized (some might say "persecuted"). More often than not, however, which it to say, almost always, it is construed in the impoverished terms of a diminished "religion," or alternatively identified by way of its relegated other (Christendom, or the church, the "political" face, which Christianity, the religion, has been seen as taking in its institutional forms), that part of it which, held to scrutiny, is deemed worthy of a challenge or rebuke. But aside from the fact that such "critique" reinscribes another bloody difference between religion and politics, between individual and society, between science and religion and more, it fails to consider that Christianity ebbs and flows *between* spheres and across them, and beyond them as well. The distinction between race and religion, for instance, teaches us that it is impossible to escape the former and possible to do so with the latter. Permanence and irreparability would be the markers of race and of (modern) racism. I have sought to refute this distinction by showing that blood is the name and the form of a singular construction of identity and difference (practices of separation, segregation, and, ultimately, extermination). Enabling a broader view, blood is the name of a curious, and highly particular, identity formation, internally dynamic and artfully divided. This construction, a hematological system, carries blood (ebbing and flowing, circulating, or abruptly stopping) through all of its parts. Indeed, as we have seen, it is for Christianity and for Christianity only that blood becomes a privileged figure for parts and wholes, a figure for a collective of collectives. By the end of the process I have described, blood therefore turns out to be less the primary marker of a difference between Christians and others, nor is it the ephemeral and aberrant site of the superiority of the "white race" measured in comparative (and segregationist) terms with the dark hordes. Blood is rather an "internal" marker.

Blood (this should go without saying, but I will say it again) is by no means the *only* such marker or element. Elsewhere, I have tried to argue that the enemy is another, another crucial site where Christianity's protean integrity, historical and otherwise, can be observed and verified.[122] There are yet other markers, as there are other Christianities, and perhaps they all constitute "the subversion of Christianity."[123] But blood has flowed and risen, in overt and covert ways, we have seen, as an unavoidable element of a finite Christianity. Everything is as if with blood Christianity had unwittingly found itself in its most natural element, and there found its limits as well. For there is nothing natural about blood, and the confusion as to its literal or figurative status (a key site of difference "between bloods"), its physiologic or theological existence, is crucial to understand Christianity, to consider and reflect upon it. Christianity circulates through, over, and beyond a number of other spheres, and ultimately *as* law and culture, from economics to science, and beyond. It divides itself as, and distinguishes between, these different spheres. In Jacques Rancière's terms, Christianity might therefore be understood as a particular manner of dividing the sensible, a set of distributions, partitions, or *partages* of the world it makes and in which it operates.[124] That is how blood, or so I have argued, acquires its meanings and gains its significance. As a recurring operator and marker of these partitions, it emerges as the element or medium of Christianity. This makes blood, "the invisible medium of blood," political in a distinct sense.[125] One could say that blood *belongs* to Christianity, it defines belonging (as membership and as property) in Christianity. It marks and signals Christianity, while governing the way in which it perceives itself as lacking the solidity of essence.

Note, finally, that an answer to the all-too direct question "What is blood?" would have had to provide a way of determining how blood could come up as the site of a question, an object that is also a privileged indicator of community or indeed of inquiry. (Think of the question: What is bone? What is flesh? And ponder their equivalence, and lack thereof, with "What is blood?" Consider whether these are in any way similar questions, mere *translations* of each other? Is that which is asked about "recognized" in any comparable manner?) If I referred at times to an "analytics of sanguinity" (to be distinguished from Foucault's "symbolics of blood" and "analytics of sexuality"), it is because, again, blood is not natural, nor are the place, role, and function of its literality easily locatable, identifiable. Over against "sexuality," which has seemed silently to reinscribe a modern/premodern (and even first world/third world) divide, blood has not generated a discursive maelstrom of experts and opinions. It does not belong exclusively to the physicians, nor to the lawyers and the economists (and God knows these are all working to expand the reach of their rule). Blood is not quite an object, not a thing either. It is neither old nor new; although it is also that and more. Nor is blood a discourse that would regiment, precisely, the course of blood through the realms of human and inhuman existence. Is blood perhaps an agent or a subject? Is it an organ in a larger body? A fragment or an institution, a series of institutions? As we have seen, the "presence" of blood is pervasive. As a "metaphor" that does not relate to a literal term, whose referent is anything but granted, blood is, it should be treated as, *catachrestic*. Were it a concept, blood might be considered, minimally, an *effective* concept. But what concept would this be precisely? The argument I have advanced in this book hinges on yet another oscillation, a confusion of sorts that, as with the literal and the figurative, I have tried not to disambiguate. For the concept I have sought to engage is obviously dual at least: Blood and Christianity. Blood is that with which, and through which, Christianity becomes what it is. It flows through the familial and the social (kin and community, nation and race), the medical and the theological, the economic, the legal, and the political. After this red tide—the *liquidation* of our significant concepts—these distinctions are revealed for what they are: significant only to the extent that they articulate internal divisions.[126] Blood is the name and the thing that does and undoes the significant concepts of the Christian world, the distinctions that divide Christianity from itself: theology from medicine, finance from politics, religion from race, and so forth. It is obvious that Christianity has no essence, therefore. It does however persist as the fluidity of its transformations and the fragility of the walls of its veins, the schizophrenic division of its organs, and the innocence of its actions. After the red tide, then, what remains is the particular, and peculiar, hematology—the *hemophilia*—that is Christianity.

NOTES

PREFACE: WHY I AM SUCH A GOOD CHRISTIAN

1. More manifestly popular, the "Jewish Question" must be mentioned at the outset, if only by way of contrast. Through its iterations, all the way to the current "conflict," it has proved resilient enough, with different answers, responses, or, indeed, solutions offered with peculiar generosity and well-intended *caritas*. There have been a number of other, not strictly commensurate "questions" that elicited significant and distinct reactions, the "Negro question" and the "woman question," for instance, or the "Eastern question," and, more recently, or so it has been said, the "Muslim question." Are these metaphysical questions properly so called? Is questioning here the proper path? Nothing seems less obvious, in the case at hand, than the claim that every question, however remote, "can be asked only in such a way that the questioner as such is also there within the question" (Martin Heidegger, "What Is Metaphysics?" trans. David Farell Krell, in Heidegger, *Pathmarks*, ed. William McNeill [Cambridge: Cambridge University Press, 1998], 82). That is one reason to emulate Talal Asad, who truly knows how to turn the tables, and consider the possibility of an inquiry more pointedly focalized on the questioner or inquisitor, an inquiry torqued otherwise through the pages that follow (see, for instance, the "Polemics" section of Asad, *Genealogies of Religion: Discipline and Reasons of Power in Christianity and Islam* [Baltimore, Md.: Johns Hopkins University Press, 1993], 239–306; or Asad, *On Suicide Bombing* [New York: Columbia University Press, 2007]; and see my "The Idea of an Anthropology of Christianity," *Interventions* 11, no. 3 [2009]: 367–93; and "On the European Question," *Forum Bosnae* 55 [2012]: 13–27).

2. The phrase "the *enormous question mark* called Christianity" is Friedrich Nietzsche's ("The Anti-Christ," trans. Judith Norman, in Nietzsche, *The Anti-Christ, Ecce Homo, Twilight*

of the Idols, and Other Writings, ed. Aaron Ridley and Judith Norman [Cambridge: Cambridge University Press, 2005], 33, §36).

3. And compare with Michel Henry, who proposes to "understand the form of truth that circumscribes the domain of Christianity, the milieu in which it spreads, the air that it breathes, one might say," for the purpose of addressing the question "what do we mean by 'Christianity'?" (Michel Henry, *I Am the Truth: Toward a Philosophy of Christianity*, trans. Susan Emanuel [Stanford, Calif.: Stanford University Press, 2003], 1). Note that the word *religion* rarely appears in Henry's prose, but it does so revealingly. Henry thus identifies "decisive theses of Christianity that we must first explore if we still wish to understand a word about this kind of thought, or rather, this religion that is Christianity" (51). Bertrand Russell would not disagree, explaining why he is not a Christian, being—by way of equal opportunity criticism—"as firmly convinced that religions do harm as . . . that they are untrue" (B. Russell, *Why I Am Not a Christian and Other Essays on Religion and Related Subjects* [New York: Routledge, 2004], xxiii).

4. Nietzsche, "The Anti-Christ," 7, §8; although he significantly expands the meaning of the term and the range of its significance ("Christians are not characterized by their 'faith'" [30, §33]; "let us not underestimate the disaster that Christianity has brought even into politics!" [40, §43]) and repeatedly describes Christianity as vampiric (e.g., "Christianity was the vampire of the *imperium Romanum*" [60, §58]), Nietzsche makes clear that he directs his critique at "religion," at Christianity as a religion: "I do not want my condemnation of Christianity to lead me to be unfair to a related and—measured by the number of adherents—even more prevalent religion" (16, §20; and see 20, §23); this strict division of labor and things may explain why Nietzsche opposes, strangely enough, "philology and medicine" to Christianity (46, §47).

5. Tomoko Masuzawa, *The Invention of World Religions: Or, How European Universalism Was Preserved in the Language of Pluralism* (Chicago: University of Chicago Press, 2005).

6. "The essence of Christianity" is the expression made famous by Ludwig Feuerbach, who lingers on the theologico-anthropological difference (L. Feuerbach, *The Essence of Christianity*, trans. George Eliot [Amherst, N.Y.: Prometheus Books, 1989]) but testifies to a broader and recurring concern with the true nature of Christianity (often opposed to its historical trajectory); more recently, Brian Goldstone and Stanley Hauerwas offered a tempting alternative to the otherwise essential or institutionalized view, raising the possibility that Christendom is not what Christians have established (or were supposed to establish), that what was at stake for, say, Luke in Acts of the Apostles was a more widely conceived "call to another way of being" (Goldstone and Hauerwas, "Disciplined Seeing: Forms of Christianity and Forms of Life," *South Atlantic Quarterly* 109, no. 4 [Fall 2010]: 784). Christianity, Kavin Rowe has it, was supposed to be a "total way of life" (quoted in Goldstone and Hauerwas, "Disciplined Seeing," 770). I will be arguing that it may well have succeeded on that very front, in all its expansiveness. Importantly, Goldstone and Hauerwas explain that what they are attending to and describing cannot be seen as of yet, that it "would, in fact, no longer be recognizable to those whose lives Luke sought to narrate—that is, to Christians" (785); also see Daniel Colluciello Barber's fascinating *On Diaspora: Christianity, Religion, and Secularity* (Eugene, Ore.: Cascade Books, 2011).

7. Bruno Bosteels recently credited Leon Rozitchner for raising "the Christian Question" after Marx and for revealing the deep underlying association of religion, subjectivity, and capitalism (B. Bosteels, "On the Christian Question," *The Idea of Communism. Volume 2*, Slavoj Žižek, ed. [London: Verso, 2013], 37–55). The Christian question is indeed being raised from a different perspective and with another urgent acuity in the "Southern" or "global" context. Without quite endorsing his formulation or his use of the word *religion* (as opposed to "mere" culture), I might mention Philip Jenkins, who writes that "for anyone accustomed to living in the environment of 'Western Christianity,' the critical question must be to determine what is the authentic religious content, and what is cultural baggage. What, in short, is Christianity, and what is merely Western?" (P. Jenkins, "Christianity Moves South," in *Global Christianity: Contested Claims*, ed. Frans Wijsen and Robert Schreiter [Amsterdam: Rodopi, 2007], 32.) Indeed. But note that, settling another difference, Jenkins foregrounds the word *Christendom* as opposed to Christianity (see P. Jenkins, *The Next Christendom: The Coming of Global Christianity* [New York: Oxford University Press, 2002]), a move that goes back to Luther, at least.

8. Kojin Karatani, *Transcritique: On Kant and Marx*, trans. Sabu Kohso (Cambridge, Mass.: MIT Press, 2003), xiii; Heidegger does not quite speak, in German, of a "trinity" (the German has "Dreifache," not "Dreifaltigkeit," much less "Trinität"), yet what he refers to as a triple "relation to the world, stance, and irruption" may suggest here as well a "radical unity" that could, in turn, bring "a luminous simplicity" to the question of Christianity (Heidegger, "What Is Metaphysics?," 82–83).

9. Michel Serres, "Corruption—*The Antichrist*: A Chemistry of Sensations and Ideas," trans. Chris Bongie, in *Nietzsche in Italy*, ed. Thomas Harrison (Saratoga, Calif.: Anma Libri, 1988), 44.

10. Nietzsche understood this very well and did not restrict the matter to religion, to "the drinking of blood in Communion" (Nietzsche, "The Anti-Christ," 18, §22; the phrase "blood is the worst witness to truth" is on 53, §53); theologians, for their part, are often explicit in placing blood at the center of Christian history and Christian spirituality, see, for example, Robert J. Schreiter, *In Water and in Blood: A Spirituality of Solidarity and Hope* (Maryknoll, N.Y.: Orbis Books, 2006); on "the new atheism," see Terry Eagleton's excellent *Reason, Faith, & Revolution: Reflections on the God Debate* (New Haven: Yale University Press, 2009).

11. The literature that waxes prolific on the universality of blood seems peculiarly abundant when one relates it to the generalized understanding of blood as a confining marker of exclusive particularity (see, e.g., Bernard Seeman, *The River of Blood: The Story of Man's Blood from Magic to Science* [New York: Norton, 1961]; and Melissa L. Meyer, *Thicker Than Water: The Origins of Blood as Symbol and Ritual* [New York: Routledge, 2005]). A recent issue of the *Journal of the Royal Anthropological Institute* proposes a different, more implicit, take on blood's universality, as a generally fertile support for elaboration in specific contexts. There, "the meanings attributed to blood are neither self-evident nor stable across (or even within) different cultural and historical locations. The many meanings of blood . . . vividly attest to its polyvalent qualities and its unusual capacity for accruing layers of symbolic resonance" (Janet Carsten, "Introduction: Blood Will Out," *Journal of the Royal*

Anthropological Institute 19: S1 [May 2013] S2, special issue "Blood Will Out: Essays on Liquid Transfers and Flows," Edited by Janet Carsten).

12. I once heard Samuel Weber gloss Descartes's lonesome *cogito*, returning it to its collaborative, even collective roots (*coagitare*, agitating or shaking together).

13. Jacques Derrida, *Limited Inc.* (Evanston, Ill.: Northwestern University Press, 1988), 12.

14. See, for example, Daniel M. Gold, "First—Do No Harm," *New York Times*, September 28, 2012.

15. Pablo Neruda, "Explico algunas cosas / I Explain Some Things," trans. Mark Eisner in *The Essential Neruda*, ed. Mark Eisner (San Francisco: City Lights Books, 2004), 62–67.

16. William Connolly, *Capitalism and Christianity, American Style* (Durham, N.C.: Duke University Press, 2008), 87.

17. Carlo Ginzburg, "The Letter Kills: On Some Implications of 2 Corinthians 3:6," *History and Theory* 49 (February 2010): 71–89; and see C. Ginzburg, *Wooden Eyes: Nine Reflections on Distance*, trans. Martin Ryle and Kate Soper (New York: Columbia University Press, 2001), esp. chaps. 7 and 9.

18. Gayatri Chakravorty Spivak, *Death of a Discipline* (New York: Columbia University Press, 2003), xii.

19. Sheldon Pollock, "The Death of Sanskrit," *Comparative Studies in Society and History* 43, no. 2 (April 2001): 392–426.

20. Frank Kermode, *The Sense of an Ending: Studies in the Theory of Fiction, With a New Epilogue* (Oxford: Oxford University Press, 2000), 58.

21. Spivak, *Death of a Discipline*, 69.

22. Gaston Bachelard, *Water and Dreams: An Essay on the Imagination of Matter*, trans. Edith R. Farrell (Dallas, Tex.: Dallas Institute of Humanities and Culture, 1999).

23. Giorgio Agamben, *The Kingdom and the Glory: For a Theological Genealogy of Economy and Government (*Homo Sacer II, 2)*, trans. Lorenzo Chiesa with Matteo Mandarini (Stanford, Calif.: Stanford University Press, 2011), 4.

24. Edward W. Said, *Orientalism* (New York: Vintage, 1979), 5.

25. Spivak, *Death of a Discipline*, 16.

26. Dotan Leshem, "The Principle of Economy" [in Hebrew], in *Mafte'akh: Lexical Review of Political Thought* 4 (Fall 2011). Accessible at http://mafteakh.tau.ac.il/2011/11/07-4/.

27. Peter Szendy writes of telling and foretelling, of reading and fore-reading what is coming; he calls it "retroprospection," in his *Prophecies of Leviathan: Reading Past Melville*, trans. Gil Anidjar (New York: Fordham University Press, 2010), 29.

28. Jacques Derrida, *Resistances of Psychoanalysis*, trans. Peggy Kamuf et al. (Stanford, Calif.: Stanford University Press, 1998), 25.

29. Talal Asad, *Formations of the Secular: Christianity, Islam, Modernity* (Stanford, Calif.: Stanford University Press, 2003), 13.

30. Serres, "Corruption," 45.

31. "I have myself pronounced the judgment," writes Immanuel Kant (here appearing in his lesser-known role of censor and customs officer), "that in this kind of inquiry it is in no way allowed to hold opinions, and that anything that even looks like an hypothesis is a forbidden commodity, which should not be put up for sale even at the lowest price but

must be confiscated as soon as it is discovered" (I. Kant, *Critique of Pure Reason*, ed. and trans. Paul Guyer and Allen W. Wood [Cambridge: Cambridge University Press, 1998], 102). The parenthetical citation is from David M. Freidenreich, *Foreigners and Their Food: Constructing Otherness in Jewish, Christian, and Islamic Law* (Berkeley: University of California Press, 2011), 9.

32. *Blood Music* is the title of a novel by Greg Bear, on which see N. Katherine Hayles, *How We Became Posthuman: Virtual Bodies in Cybernetics, Literature, and Informatics* (Chicago: University of Chicago Press, 1999).

33. Joseph Valente, *Dracula's Crypt: Bram Stoker, Irishness, and the Question of Blood* (Urbana: University of Illinois Press, 2002), 11.

INTRODUCTION: RED MYTHOLOGY

1. Walter Benjamin, "Critique of Violence," trans. Edmund Jephcott, in *Selected Writings. Volume 1. 1913–1926*, ed. Marcus Bullock and Michael W. Jennings (Cambridge, Mass.: The Belknap Press of Harvard University Press, 1996), 240; *Gesammelte Schriften II.1*, ed. Rolf Tiedemann and Hermann Schweppenhäuser (Frankfurt am Main: Suhrkamp, 1974), 186; further references to the English translation will be made directly in the text, followed when pertinent with the reference to the German original (indicated by the letter G).

2. Beatrice Hanssen, *Critique of Violence: Between Poststructuralism and Critical Theory* (London and New York: Routledge, 2000), 23; for a detailed and multilayered account of the presence of war in "Critique of Violence" and a generous evaluation of Benjamin's critique, see Ariella Azoulay, "The Loss of Critique and the Critique of Violence," *Cardozo Law Review* 26 (2004–2005): 1005–1039.

3. As Dominick LaCapra puts it, "the manner in which this form of violence is bloodless remains perhaps intentionally opaque, and anything that might to some extent clarify or exemplify its meaning is absent or exiled in a manner reminiscent of the repressed image itself with respect to a presumably pure concept or to a transcendent divinity" (D. LaCapra, "Violence, Justice, and the Force of Law," *Cardozo Law Review* 11 [1989–1990]: 1072).

4. Jacques Derrida, "Force of Law," trans. Mary Quaintance, in Derrida, *Acts of Religion*, ed. Gil Anidjar (New York: Routledge, 2002), 272.

5. Stathis Gourgouris, *Does Literature Think? Literature as Theory for an Antimythical Era* (Stanford, Calif.: Stanford University Press, 2003), 82.

6. In addition to "the voice of the friend," Martin Heidegger (who had complained about "the anemic pallor of the obvious" in "What Is Metaphysics") also invoked the "voice of the blood" in his 1938 lecture course (M. Heidegger, *Logic as the Question Concerning the Essence of Language*, trans. Wanda Torres Gregory and Yvonne Unna [Albany: State University of New York Press, 2009], 127; GA 38); on the voice of the friend [*Stimme des Freundes*], see Christopher Fynsk, *Heidegger: Thought and Historicity* (Ithaca, N.Y.: Cornell University Press, 1993), 42–43; Jacques Derrida, *Politics of Friendship*, trans. George Collins (New York: Verso, 2005), 241ff.

7. By way of background (and the ignorance of blood), here are three essays I will *not* be discussing: Jürgen Habermas, "Walter Benjamin: Consciousness-Raising or Rescuing

Critique," in *Philosophical-Political Profiles*, trans. Frederick G. Lawrence (Cambridge, Mass.: MIT Press, 1985), 129–63; Alexander García Düttmann, "The Violence of Destruction," trans. Michael Shae, in *Walter Benjamin: Theoretical Questions*, ed. David S. Ferris (Stanford, Calif.: Stanford University Press, 1996), 165–84; Marc de Wilde, "Violence in the State of Exception: Reflections on Theologico-Political Motifs in Benjamin and Schmitt," in *Political Theologies: Public Religions in a Post-Secular World*, ed. Hent de Vries and Lawrence E. Sullivan (New York: Fordham University Press, 2006), 188–200.

8. Udi E. Greenberg, "Orthodox Violence: 'Critique of Violence' and Walter Benjamin's Jewish Political Theology," *History of European Ideas* 34 (2008): 325. Elina Staikou follows Derrida in arguing that "the rhetorical status of this text . . . is that of metonymy, which more than the privileging of a rhetorical figure among others, in his reading is a figure without figure, face or limit" (E. Staikou, "Force of Name: The Critique of Violence," *Parallax* 15, no. 2 [2009]: 101).

9. Giorgio Agamben, *Homo Sacer: Sovereign Power and Bare Life*, trans. Daniel Heller-Roazen (Stanford, Calif.: Stanford University Press, 1998), 63.

10. Derrida, "Force of Law," in *Acts of Religion*, 288; and see David Lloyd's persuasive iteration of Derrida's argument and of the equally troubling nature of "bloody" and "bloodless" violence (D. Lloyd, "Rage Against the Divine," *South Atlantic Quarterly* 106, no. 2 [Spring 2007]: 352).

11. Elina Staikou's alternatively compelling argument notwithstanding (see E. Staikou, "Justice's Last Word: Derrida's Post-Scriptum to Force of Law," *Derrida Today* 1, no. 2 [November 2008]: 266–90).

12. Although I find myself agreeing with Udi Greenberg on this precise point, it seems to me that he does not quite deliver on his promise to render to blood its "proper" significance (see Greenberg, "Orthodox Violence," 331–33).

13. Benjamin, "Critique of Violence," 236.

14. Foucault, *Society Must Be Defended. Lectures at the Collège de France 1975–1976*, trans. David Macey (New York: Macmillan, 2003), 47–48; Hannah Arendt credited "the anonymous author of the *Report from Iron Mountain*" with "this simple reversal," namely, that "peace is the continuation of war by other means" (H. Arendt, *On Violence* [Orlando, Fla.: Harcourt Inc., 1970], 9).

15. This narrative, which resonates with the social evolutionism dominant since Henry Sumner Maine at least and that sees in kinship ("the reality or the fiction of blood relationship") the pre-political stage of social organization (H. S. Maine, *Ancient Law: Its Connection to the History of Early Society* [Charleston, S.C.: Bibliobazaar, 2008]), can be found in Foucault as well. After proposing to turn "the expression around" and stating "that politics is war pursued by other means," Foucault goes on to explain that "a society of blood . . . where power spoke *through* blood" is what we no longer are: "we, on the other hand, are in a society of 'sex' " (Michel Foucault, *The History of Sexuality: An Introduction*, vol. 1, trans. Robert Hurley [New York: Vintage, 1990], 93, 147). This is the famous transition, indeed, transformation "from *a symbolics of blood* to *an analytics of sexuality*" (148), which Ann Stoler has eloquently and critically written about (Ann Laura Stoler, *Race and the Education of Desire: Foucault's History of Sexuality and the Colonial Order of Things*

[Durham, N.C.: Duke University Press, 1995]). Like war, politics would follow and even supersede (or sublate) blood.

16. Anselm Haverkamp, "How to Take It (and Do the Right Thing): Violence and the Mournful Mind in Benjamin's 'Critique of Violence,'" *Cardozo Law Review* 13 (1991–1992), 1166. And see Alain Brossat' qualified interrogation of "the last hours of the great dramaturgy of blood (*les dernières heures de la grande dramaturgie du sang*)" in *Drôle d'époque* 19 (Automne 2006): 29.

17. In his thoughtful engagement with Benjamin's "Critique of Violence," Gourgouris addresses the problem of naturalization in a number of pertinent ways when he writes that "to examine a social phenomenon that has achieved the status of nature means to face the work of society's imaginary. Which is to say, we must be prepared to address society's mythic domain, the interminable flux of self-representations out of which and by which society alters itself"—and fails to do so as well (Gourgouris, *Does Literature Think?*, 51). Gourgouris makes clear that this imperative applies first and foremost to the "idiomatic condition" of "what is often called 'Western culture'" (51).

18. "The biological metaphorics of 'bastardization,' a part of the 'bare life' that Benjamin emphatically avoids, contain the final trend of such a miscegenation, against which Benjamin offers defense: namely that of the fixation of bare life in scientific terminology" (Anselm Haverkamp, "Anagrammatics of Violence: The Benjaminian Ground of *Homo Sacer*" *Cardozo Law Review* 26 [2004–2005]: 1002). In an earlier essay, Haverkamp had traced Benjamin's invocation of blood to Hermann Cohen's work, making clear the ethico-juridical, as well as theological, nature of this "alternative symbolism" (Haverkamp, "How to Take It," 1169–70).

19. Greenberg delivers a pointed critique of those who take Benjamin's Jewishness for granted, although I find it surprising that he places much of the blame for this tendency on Derrida, of all people, rather than on a more likely culprit like Scholem (among a few others), as he himself recognizes (Greenberg, "Orthodox Violence," 327). Notably, Greenberg remains committed to a quite narrow form of Judeocentrism in his reading of Benjamin (Greenberg, "Orthodox Violence").

20. I should note that I am using these words, *religious* and *theological*, for convenience sake, and not to disagree with Herbert Marcuse, who importantly points out that "Benjamins Messianismus hat mit herkömmlicher Religiosität nichts zu schaffen: Schuld und Sühne sind ihm *gesellschaftliche* Kategorien" ("Nachwort," in Benjamin, *Zur Kritik der Gewalt und andere Aufsätze mit einem Nachwort von Herbert Marcuse* [Frankfurt am Main: Suhrkamp, 1965], 100–101). Recalling, as Brian Britt does, that "the two modern myths that Benjamin opposes are the myth of progress and the myth of secularization," there is no doubt that some work remains to be done on these otherwise much-taunted notions in Benjamin scholarship: "theological," "religious" and "mystical." Britt's remarks in a book that singularly calls attention to the significance of the Bible for Benjamin provide a helpful corrective on this matter as well (B. Britt, *Walter Benjamin and the Bible* [New York: Continuum, 1996], 123; and see 115–17).

21. I have tried to interrogate this and other aspects of the "story of a friendship" (as Gershom Scholem calls it) in "The Silent Voice of the Friend: Andalusī Topographies of Scholem's

Conversations (Mourning Mysticism)," in Gil Anidjar, *"Our Place in al-Andalus": Kabbalah, Philosophy, Literature in Arab Jewish Letters* (Stanford, Calif.: Stanford University Press, 2002), 102–165.

22. A striking exception is Michael Mack, "Between Kant and Kafka: Benjamin's Notion of Law," *Neophilologus* 85, no. 2 (2001): 257–72; elsewhere, Mack also demonstrates a keen sensibility to the significance of blood but strangely ignores the subject in his discussion of Benjamin. Tracy McNulty, for her part, carefully locates Benjamin's argument in its opposition to Saint Paul (McNulty, "The Commandment Against the Law: Writing and Divine Justice in Walter Benjamin's 'Critique of Violence,'" *diacritics* 37, no. 2–3 (Summer–Fall 2007): 34–60.

23. Idelbar Avelar is quite correct when he writes that "The words 'Greek' and 'Jewish' *do not appear* in Benjamin's essay in the context of mythical and divine violence, nor in any other context. Certainly, Benjamin exemplifies mythical violence with the narration of the Greek myth of Niobe. It also true that he exemplifies the nonmythic, the 'unmediated' kind of violence with a reading of the biblical story of Korah. But the leap from that to the conversion of these narratives in national or ethnic attributes" is indeed troubling (I. Avelar, *The Letter of Violence: Essays on Narrative, Ethics, and Politics* [New York: Palgrave Macmillan, 2004], 99; and see McNulty, "The Commandment," 49). As will become clear, and keeping to the general usage of these words, Benjamin's concern is, in my reading, neither with national nor ethnic attributes but with theological ones, the fragility of the distinction notwithstanding.

24. Gourgouris, *Does Literature Think?*, 82; for Beatrice Hanssen too, the "confrontation" between two forms of history in Benjamin's text takes place "between the Greek and the Judaic" (B. Hansen, *Walter Benjamin's Other History: Of Stones, Animals, Human Beings, and Angels* [Berkeley: University of California Press, 1998], 135); and whereas Mack is of the opinion that, in 1921, "Benjamin represses . . . a sense of despair at the loss of a valid Jewish tradition" (Mack, "Between Kant and Kafka," 270), Greenberg, for his part, insists that at that time at least, Benjamin's familiarity with Jewish sources was minimal at best. Nonetheless, Greenberg perceives Benjamin as intervening in an internal, Jewish dispute. My own intent is obviously not to interrogate the textual or historical accuracy of these claims. I am merely puzzled that the Jewish–Christian dispute (which obviously took many other forms than anti-Semitism) would register so weakly in readings of Benjamin.

25. Agamben, *Homo Sacer*, 66; I discuss this passage and the problem of "sacred life" at more length in "The Meaning of Life," *Critical Inquiry* 37, no. 4 (Summer 2011): 697–723.

26. Agamben, *Homo Sacer*, 67; it should probably be noted that on a number of occasions, Agamben does equate "biological life" with "blood" (see for instance *Means Without End*, where he writes that "one entered the camp as a result not of a political choice but rather of what was most private and incommunicable in oneself, that is, one's blood, one's biological body" (Agamben, *Means Without End: Notes on Politics*, trans. Vincenzo Binetti and Cesare Casarino [Minneapolis: University of Minnesota Press, 2000], 122). Moreover, given Agamben's well-known concerns (in *The Open*, for example), the focus on *human* life, to the exclusion of the animal, is also perplexing (and see Judith Butler's parallel suggestion that Benjamin's reference to "bloodless" violence "would seem to imply that it is not waged

against human bodies and human lives" [J. Butler, "Critique, Coercion, and Sacred Life in Benjamin's 'Critique of Violence,'" in *Political Theologies: Public Religions in a Post-Secular World*, ed. Hent de Vries and Lawrence E. Sullivan (New York: Fordham University Press, 2006), 201]). Elina Staikou elaborates a pertinent critique of anthropocentrism in her "Justice's Last Word."

27. Jacob Taubes refers to Benjamin's famous "Theses" as "polemical through and through," a comment that seems equally relevant here (J. Taubes, *The Political Theology of Paul*, trans. Dana Hollander [Stanford, Calif.: Stanford University Press, 2004], 70).

28. J. Taubes, "The Issue Between Judaism and Christianity: Facing up to the Unresolvable Difference," *Commentary* 16 (1953): 525–33; note that the phrase Taubes uses is "unresolvable difference." Michael Mack (whose own interest lies in "a secularized and politicized Christian theology" he calls "pseudotheology") adds the names of Georg Simmel, Sigfried Kracauer, and Franz Steiner to Taubes's list. Mack further inquires into the elements that "constitute the structural differences between the Christian and the Jewish religions" in German idealism and in its aftermath (Mack, *German Idealism and the Jew: The Inner Anti-Semitism of Philosophy and German Jewish Responses* [Chicago: University of Chicago Press, 2003], 10; and see Mack, "Between Kant and Kafka," 263).

29. Britt, *Walter Benjamin and the Bible*, 92.

30. Britt, *Walter Benjamin and the Bible*, 93.

31. Genesis 9:4, New Revised Standard Version; the King James version has "But flesh with the life thereof, which is the blood thereof, shall ye not eat"; finally, Luther: "Allein eßt das Fleisch nicht, das noch lebt in seinem Blut."

32. Leviticus 17:11; Luther: "Denn des Leibes Leben ist im Blut," but most versions agree on this rendering.

33. Compare for example how, when Shechem is said to fall in love with Dinah, the young woman he just raped, "his soul (*nafšo, anima*) was drawn to Dinah" (Genesis 34:3; Luther has "sein Herz"). Against most translations of the passages that occupy us here (all unexplained), Even-Shoshan's biblical concordance never gives "life" as a synonym for *nefeš*, a common word in the Hebrew Bible (again, when Shechem falls in love with Dinah, the text says "*wa-tidbaq nafšo*"—his soul, not his life, clung to her). I am not suggesting that "life" (for which *hayim* would be a more common term) has nothing to do with it all, only that the association between *nefeš* and "life" is at best derivative. Witness that the medieval Jewish commentaries on Genesis 9:4 know that the Hebrew prefix *be-* means either "with" or "in" so that *basar be-nafšo damo* can be read as "flesh with its soul within" (Rashi) or "flesh with its blood-soul" ("because the soul of all flesh is its blood," says Nahmanides, who thus equates the blood with the soul, not with the flesh. Note, however, that the Hebrew Bible never uses the phrase "flesh and blood" [on this last point, see Leon Morris, "The Biblical Use of the Term 'Blood,'" *Journal of Theological Studies* 3, no. 2 (October 1952): 216–26]). Ibn Ezra identifies *nefeš* with "the moving and feeling soul, that is, the body" (resonating with well-known philosophical views). E. A. Speiser proposes "whose blood is in the/its being" (*The Anchor Bible: Genesis*, Introduction, Translation, and Notes by E. A. Speiser [Garden City, N.Y.: Doubleday, 1964], 58, n. 4). André Chouraqui, one of the most important recent translators of the Bible into French, offers a parallel rendering: "la chair avec en son être son sang."

34. The debate may be said to go back to ancient Greece (Hippocrates, for instance, refers to those who "think that the man is composed of that one thing from the purging of which they saw him die. . . . They see men who are cut bleeding from the body, and so they think that blood composes the soul of a man" (Hippocrates, *On the Nature of Man*, trans. W. H. S. Jones [Loeb Classical Library IV] (Cambridge, Mass.: Harvard University Press, 1931), 18; and see Aristotle, *On the Soul*, 405b, trans. W. S. Hett [Loeb Classical Library] [Cambridge, Mass.: Harvard University Press, 1957], 28–9), but it takes a different valence in modern times, of course. It was, for instance, of significant interest to Orientalists. One could thus read William Robertson Smith's *Religion of the Semites* as a protracted attempt to "sanguify" ancient "Semites" (they, rather than the "Aryans"—their no less fictional but more powerfully incarnated cousins—would have been obsessed with blood). Robertson Smith dedicates a footnote to Genesis 9:4 and to cognates of *nafs*, which he translates as "life-blood" (W. Robertson Smith, *Religion of the Semites*, introduction by Robert Segal [New Brunswick, N.J., and London: Transaction Publishers, 2002], 40, n. 1). And consider how William Gilders's otherwise fascinating book consistently has the word "life" suspended within scare quotes, which are never accounted for (W. K. Gilders, *Blood Ritual in the Hebrew Bible: Meaning and Power* [Baltimore, Md.: Johns Hopkins University Press, 2004], esp. chap. 1: "The Identification of Blood with 'Life,'" 12–32). Of course, Gilders is following massively consensual scholarly usage. As to what the biblical concept of life or "life" is—if there is one—and how it might be read and interpreted in light of synonyms and cognates, the scholars are silent.

35. Leviticus 17:11 is also rendered consistently: "Denn die Seele des Fleisches, im Blut ist sie." The Buber–Rosenzweig translation was only published many decades later, of course, and by Buber alone, my argument being that, along with Benjamin's text, it is a manifest instance of a contestation, indeed, of a dispute—over translation, over life and its sanctity, over blood and soul.

36. Blood (and war) was the site of another Jewish–Christian struggle, articulated in the pages of Rosenzweig's work, as Michael Mack describes in detail (Mack, *German Idealism and the Jew*, chap. 8, "The Politics of Blood: Rosenzweig and Hegel," 125–35).

37. On Shylock and blood, see chap. 3 this volume, "Capital (Christians and Money)."

38. Amnon Raz-Krakotzkin strikingly describes the transformation of Jewish–Christian relations from polemics to reform and "modernization" in *The Censor, the Editor, and the Text: The Catholic Church and the Shaping of the Jewish Canon in the Sixteenth Century*, trans. Jackie Feldman (Philadelphia: University of Pennsylvania Press, 2007). Raz-Krakotzkin has long been articulating an inspiring Benjaminian reading of Jewish history in, for example, the essays gathered in *Exil et souveraineté: Judaïsme, sionisme et pensée binationale*, trans. Joëlle Marelli (Paris: La Fabrique, 2007). None of this contradicts, it rather expands, Taubes's claim, who argues that modern Jews have for the most part adopted a fundamentally Christian theological (that is, historical) perspective; and see as well, on this last point, Carlo Ginzburg, "Distance and Perspective: Two Metaphors" trans. Martin Ryle and Kate Soper in Ginzburg, *Wooden Eyes: Nine Reflections on Distance* (New York Columbia University Press, 2001), 148..

39. Britt, *Walter Benjamin and the Bible*, 80. "The Task of the Translator" is no doubt the most compelling illustration of this claim.

40. See Israel Jacob Yuval, *Two Nations in Your Womb: Perceptions of Jews and Christians in Late Antiquity and the Middle Ages*, trans. Barbara Harshav and Jonathan Chipman (Berkeley: University of California Press, 2006); Caroline Walker Bynum, *Wonderful Blood: Theology and Practice in Late Medieval Northern Germany and Beyond* (Philadelphia: University of Pennsylvania Press, 2007); David Biale, *Blood and Belief: The Circulation of a Symbol Between Jews and Christians* (Berkeley: University of California Press, 2007). I will later turn to Tomaž Mastnak's singular and highly pertinent intervention in his *Crusading Peace: Christendom, The Muslim World, and Western Political Order* (Berkeley: University of California Press, 2002), though I have begun to do so elsewhere (see next note).

41. I develop this argument in "We Have Never Been Jewish: An Essay in Asymmetric Hematology," in *Jewish Blood: Metaphor and Reality in Jewish History, Culture, and Religion*, ed. Mitchell Hart (New York and London: Routledge, 2009), 31–56.

42. LaCapra is therefore correct to point out that "there are, quite literally, many ways to kill without bloodshed, one of which was perfected by the Nazis" (LaCapra, "Violence, Justice, and the Force of Law," 1077), but the accuracy of his remark (it was after all true before the Nazis) is contingent on making Benjamin into a kind a simpleton, to whom one would have to point this out.

43. I am paraphrasing Agamben here, quoted earlier.

44. Walter Benjamin, "The Task of the Translator," trans. Harry Zohn, in *Selected Writings. Volume 1. 1913–1926*, ed. Marcus Bullock and Michael W. Jennings [Cambridge, Mass.: The Belknap Press of Harvard University Press, 1996], 253.

45. Carl von Clausewitz, *On War*, ed. and trans. Michael Howard and Peter Paret (Princeton, N.J.: Princeton University Press, 1989), 71 and 75.

46. Hannah Arendt, *Eichmann in Jerusalem: A Report on the Banality of Evil* (New York: Penguin, 1994), 269; emphasis added.

47. Talal Asad, a perspicacious reader of Benjamin and a discreetly Benjaminian anthropologist, elaborates in his work a related critique of motives and intentions; see his *On Suicide Bombing* (New York: Columbia University Press, 2007).

48. Elias Canetti, *Crowds and Power*, trans. Carol Stewart (New York: Farrar, Straus and Giroux, 1984), 467; further citations are all from this page.

49. "For Benjamin, the strike is the social, economic, and political event in which nothing happens, no work is done, nothing is produced, and nothing is planned or projected. It is the manifestation of a sociality whose effectiveness neither conforms to a paradigm from a the historical canon of politico-economic systems, nor aims at their simple recasting" (W. Hamacher, "Afformative, Strike: Benjamin's 'Critique of Violence,'" trans. Dana Hollander, in *Walter Benjamin's Philosophy: Destruction and Experience*, ed. Andrew Benjamin and Peter Osborne [London and New York: Routledge, 1994], 120–21).

50. As Rainer Nägele explains, thinking for Benjamin "is not simply a theoretical attitude, it implies positioning one's being in relation to the world." Benjamin, Nägele continues, "uses the Brechtian term *Haltung*. The word means 'attitude' or 'posture'" (R. Nägele, "Body Politics: Benjamin's Dialectical Materialism Between Brecht and the Frankfurt School," in *The Cambridge Companion to Walter Benjamin*, ed. David Ferris [Cambridge: Cambridge University Press, 2006], 162); and note that "*Haltung* and gestures are terms that are not

reducible to either body or spirit: they indicate a new definition in the relationship of these heavily charged terms" (165). Michel Foucault's "care of the self" obviously harks back to a different register but one that seems important, if not essential, to keep in mind here, for, as Nauman Naqvi reminds me, where else would Benjamin be writing from if not the rigorous demand for *askesis*?

51. Tom McCall, "Momentary Violence," in *Walter Benjamin: Theoretical Questions*, ed. David S. Ferris (Stanford, Calif.: Stanford University Press, 1996), 192; emphasis added.

52. Canetti, *Crowds and Power*, 467.

53. Taubes, "The Issue Between Judaism and Christianity," 527.

54. As Haverkamp puts it, blood "makes a difference in only one direction, and a historical difference at that" (Haverkamp, "How to Take It," 1166). Bettine Menke is more explicit: "Pure violence," she writes, that is, divine violence, "is not characterized by the Not-Blood [*das Nicht-Blut*] as symbol, but rather by the Not-Symbol" (B. Menke, "Benjamin vor dem Gesetz: Die *Kritik der Gewalt* in der Lektüre Derridas," in *Gewalt und Gerechtigkeit. Derrida–Benjamin*, ed. Anselm Haverkamp [Frankfurt am Main: Suhrkamp, 1994], 239).

55. Sigmund Freud famously pointed out what this foregrounding of the victim enables: "They will not admit that they killed God, whereas we do and are cleansed from the guilt of it" (S. Freud, *Moses and Monotheism*, trans. Katherine Jones [New York: Vintage, 1967], 176). This is how Christians can simultaneously assert that "we have all killed him" and see themselves as victims of "Christ-killers." I shall return to this matter in due course.

56. And compare Mack's account of Rosenzweig: "The state holds out the promise of immanent eternity by means of a violent transformation of the worldly into the otherworldly, as achieved by the immanent changing of the body (blood) into the body politic (conquered and accumulated land). In Rosenzweig's analysis, this idealization of war represents secularized Christian thought" (Mack, *German Idealism and the Jew*, 133).

57. For an updated rendering of this argument, see Stephen Graham, *Cities Under Siege: The New Military Urbanism* (London: Verso, 2011); incidentally, in the *Arcades Project*, Benjamin identified the police with blood, writing that "the mighty seek to secure their position with blood (police), with cunning (fashion), with magic (pomp)" (Benjamin, *The Arcades Project*, trans. Howard Eiland and Kevin McLaughlin [Cambridge, Mass.: The Belknap Press of Harvard University Press, 1999], 133).

58. In 1921, the very year he writes "Critique of Violence," Benjamin also pens the following lines: "Capitalism has developed as a parasite of Christianity in the West (this must be shown not just in the case of Calvinism, but in the other orthodox Christian churches), until it reached the point where Christianity's history is essentially that of its parasite—that is to say, of capitalism" (W. Benjamin, "Capitalism as Religion," trans. Rodney Livingstone, in *Selected Writings. Volume 1. 1913–1926*, ed. Marcus Bullock and Michael W. Jennings [Cambridge, Mass.: The Belknap Press of Harvard University Press, 1996], 289). Michael Mack importantly underscores that, in that same text, "Benjamin singles out Christianity as the only religion which is grounded in an absolute equation of life with guilt that does not allow for any form of atonement." He further "equates Christianity not only with capitalism (money), but also with law" (Mack, "Between Kant and Kafka," 259–60).

59. I have altered the translation and followed Dana Hollander's on this passage in Hamacher, "Affirmative, Strike." Hollander herself is abiding by Hamacher's argument of course: "one must distinguish between universalizability and general validity" (Hamacher, "Affirmative, Strike," 118).

60. On education such as it appears here, see Eva Geulen, "Legislating Education: Kant, Hegel, and Benjamin on 'Pedagogical Violence,'" *Cardozo Law Review* 26 (2004–2005): 943–56.

61. With this assertion, Giorgio Agamben is reflecting on Benjamin's famous statement about the state of exception, which has become the rule (G. Agamben, *State of Exception*, trans. Kevin Attell [Chicago: University of Chicago Press, 2005], 87; and see Arne de Boever's intriguing discussion in "Politics and Poetics of Divine Violence: On a Figure in Giorgio Agamben and Walter Benjamin," in *The Work of Giorgio Agamben: Law, Literature, Life*, ed. Justin Clemens, Nicholas Heron, and Alex Murray [Edinburgh: Edinburgh University Press, 2008], 82–96).

62. Eric Jacobson is alone, I think, in pointing ever so slightly toward the problem of translation here. He does so by offering "blood Gewalt," but without commenting further on this decision (E. Jacobson, *Metaphysics of the Profane: The Political Theology of Walter Benjamin and Gershom Scholem* [New York: Columbia University Press, 2003], 217; in a related manner, Tracy McNulty underscores the verb *walten* and the specific meaning it carries [McNulty, "The Commandment," 50, n. 21). It should be clear, at any rate, that "bloody violence" or "bloody power" is something else entirely than a poor translation ("Mythical violence is bloody power (*Blutgewalt*) over mere life" [250/G200]), although it seems to have been unanimously accepted. It ignores the awkwardness of the construct (hence, although Benjamin does use the adjective, the word or phrase is neither *blutig Gewalt* nor *Blutsgewalt*—as in *Blutstropfen*, drops of blood, or *Blutsbande*, ties of blood. It is rather closer to *Blutgruppe*, blood types, or to *Blutgeld*, blood money). "Bloody violence" moreover disregards the fact that Benjamin was not interested in effects (in the way state power and those who claim the *force of blood* for themselves have been). It seems therefore impossible to read here as if Benjamin was not being precise. He was writing about the power of blood and against blood violence, against "the sanctity of life" and the sovereign rule of the Sacred Blood. Benjamin was writing against Christianity.

63. Zygmunt Bauman, *Liquid Modernity* (Cambridge: Polity Press, 2000), 14; and see Iain Chambers's brilliant corrective in his "Maritime Criticism and Theoretical Shipwrecks" in *PMLA* 125, no. 3 (2010): 678–84. Adi Ophir distinguishes the modern state as "a concrete and necessary enclosure," a system of enforced enclosures (A. Ophir, "State," trans. Nick John and Natalie Melzer, in *Mafte'akh: Lexical Review of Political Thought* 2e (Winter 2011). Accessible at http://mafteakh.tau.ac.il/en/2010-01/05/).

64. The rhetoric of flow exceeds the question of power of course, though, Chambers makes clear, the two cannot be dissociated from each other. For a celebrated recasting of globalization as the increase of migratory and information flows, "the vicissitudes of international flows of technology, labor, and finance" and the decline of state power, see Arjun Appadurai, *Modernity at Large: Cultural Dimensions of Globalization* (Minneapolis: University of Minnesota Press, 1996), 41; and compare Hardt and Negri, who write of "the coming of empire" and the passing of the old system. "The boundaries *defined* by the

modern system of nation-states *were* fundamental to European colonialism and economic expansion: the territorial boundaries of the nation *delimited* the center of power from which rule was *exerted* over external foreign territories through a system of channels and barriers that alternately *facilitated* and *obstructed* the flows of production and circulation" (Michael Hardt and Toni Negri, *Empire* [Cambridge, Mass.: Harvard University Press, 2000], xii; emphases added to underscore the past tense); for a perspective that highlights the importance of circulation in the body of power, see Jose Gil, *Metamorphoses of the Body*, trans. Stephen Muecke (Minneapolis: University of Minnesota Press, 1998).

65. Benjamin Lee and Edward LiPuma, "Cultures of Circulation," *Public Culture* 14, no. 1 (2002): 191–213.

66. Foucault, *Discipline and Punish: The Birth of the Prison*, trans. Alan Sheridan (New York: Vintage, 1995), 198; and see "*Society Must Be Defended." Lectures at the College de France 1975–76*, trans. David Macey (New York: Picador, 2003), 27; many among his readers have adopted Foucault's notion of "capillary power" and popularized it. Hans Sluga pushes the implicit imagery that concerns me here when he writes that Foucault "sees power as circulating through the entire body of society," assuming "that it flows sometimes in large currents and sometimes invisibly through the social capillaries" (H. Sluga, "Foucault's Encounter with Heidegger and Nietzsche," in *The Cambridge Companion to Foucault*, ed. Gary Gutting [Cambridge: Cambridge University Press, 2005], 232). Wendy Brown describes how "contemporary critical theory has attuned us to modalities of power radically at odds with either the symbolic or literal prophylactic of walls. We have learned," Brown continues, "to keep our eye on power's discursive dross, its noncentralized habitus, its noncommodifiable operation and its deterritorialization," on "power's spatial mobility" and "its disciplinary or networked qualities, its rhizomatic, irrigating, or circulatory movements, its light and vaporous qualities" (W. Brown, *Walled States, Waning Sovereignty* [New York: Zone Books, 2010], 80–81). Walls, and particularly the new walls, "have been compared to dams insofar as they are built to regulate, rather than impede flows" (103; and see the proliferation of flows Brown invokes [98]). The origins of the term *capillary*, and its significance, have not attracted critical attention however, though see Judith Surkis's discussion of "social capillarity" and its sources in demographics (J. Surkis, *Sexing the Citizen: Morality and Masculinity in France, 1870–1920* [Ithaca, N.Y.: Cornell University Press, 2006], 117–20) and Hervé Le Bras on the importance of hydraulics and hydrology as metaphorical reserves for demographics (H. Le Bras, *Le sol et le sang* [Paris: L'aube, 1994], 35). Antonio Gramsci had also invoked the "capillary" form, leading Adam Morton to refer to him as "a paramount theorist of capillary power" (A. D. Morton, *Unravelling Gramsci: Hegemony and Passive Revolution in the Global Political Economy* [London: Pluto, 2007], 92).

67. N. Katherine Hayles, *How We Became Posthuman: Virtual Bodies in Cybernetics, Literature, and Informatics* (Chicago: University of Chicago Press, 1999), xi.

68. Mark C. Taylor, *After God* (Chicago: The University of Chicago Press, 2007), 313.

69. "The Sea Is History" is the title of a famous poem by Derek Walcott, quoted and perceptively discussed by Ian Baucom, *Specters of the Atlantic: Finance Capital, Slavery, and the Philosophy of History* (Durham, N.C.: Duke University Press, 2005), 309ff. Note that

Baucom refrains from deploying (and celebrating) figures of circulation as much as figures of exchange and accumulation, sedimentation.

70. Friedrich Nietzsche, *The Gay Science*, trans. Josefine Nauckhoff (Cambridge: Cambridge University Press, 2001), book III, section 124.

71. Todd Presner, *Mobile Modernity: Germans, Jews, Trains* (New York: Columbia University Press, 2007). Echoing Foucault on the heterotopic importance of the ship, Presner is also concerned with vessels at sea and finds inspiration in Paul Gilroy's *Black Atlantic*—indeed, Gilroy underscores the mobility of the (slave) ship, but much less the embrace of free flows (P. Gilroy, *The Black Atlantic: Modernity and Double Consciousness* [Cambridge, Mass.: Harvard University Press, 1993], 4, 16–17). "Modernity at Sea" is the title of Cesare Casarino's meticulous book (C. Casarino, *Modernity at Sea: Melville, Marx, Conrad in Crisis* [Minneapolis: University of Minnesota Press, 2002]).

72. Carl Schmitt, *Theory of the Partisan: A Commentary/Remark on the Concept of the Political*, trans. A. C. Goodson (East Lansing: Michigan State University, 2004), 49.

73. Alexander R. Galloway and Eugene Thacker, *The Exploit: A Theory of Networks* (Minneapolis: University of Minnesota Press, 2007), 26.

74. Carl Schmitt, *The Nomos of the Earth in the International Law of the Jus Publicum Europaeum*, trans. G. L. Ulmen (New York: Telos Press, 2006), 43.

75. Bauman, *Liquid Modernity*, 119–20.

76. Schmitt, *Nomos*, 37–38.

77. Schmitt, *Nomos*, 97.

78. Quoted in Schmitt, *Nomos*, 285.

79. Harry Schmidtgall, "Zur Rezeption von Harveys Blutkreislaufmodell in der englischen Wirtschaftstheorie des 17. Jahrhunderts: Ein Beitrag zum Einfluß der Naturwissenschaften auf die Ökonomie," *Sudhoffs Archiv: Zeitschrift für Wissenschaftsgeschichte* 57, no. 4 (1973): 416–30; Joseph Vogl, "Ökonomie und Zirkulation um 1800," *Weimarer Beiträge* 43 (1997): 69–78.

80. Michel Foucault, *The Order of Things: An Archaeology of the Human Sciences* (London: Routledge, 2002), 179; and see S. Todd Lowry, "The Archaeology of the Circulation Concept in Economic Theory," *Journal of the History of Ideas* 35, no. 3 (July–September 1974): 429–44.

81. Marx, *Grundrisse*, 187.

82. On the "antinomy" of circulation, see Karatani, *Transcritique*, 224.

83. And see Casarino, *Modernity at Sea*, esp. 84–85.

84. Mark C. Taylor, *The Moment of Complexity: Emerging Network Culture* (Chicago: University of Chicago Press, 2003), 91.

85. Kieran Healy refers to this moment in Marx and puts it in the context of blood donation and collection (K. Healy, *Last Best Gifts: Altruism and the Market for Human Blood and Organs* [Chicago: University of Chicago Press, 2006], 4–5).

86. Karl Marx, *Capital*, vol. 1 ("The General Formula for Capital"), in *The Marx Engels Reader*, ed. Robert C. Tucker (New York: W. W. Norton & Co., 1978), 333.

87. Kaushik Sunder Rajan, *Biocapital: The Constitution of Postgenomic Life* (Durham, N.C.: Duke University Press, 2006); I should make clear that Rajan does not participate in the

rhetoric of free flow, something that should underscore the possibility of alternatives. Timothy Mitchell most eloquently describes how "the economy" (a recent notion, the history of which Mitchell traces) "depends upon, and helps establish, boundaries between the monetary and the nonmonetary, national and foreign, consumption and investment, public and private, nature and technology, tangible and intangible, owner and nonowner, and many more" (T. Mitchell, *Rule of Experts: Egypt, Techno-Politics, Modernity* [Berkeley: University of California Press, 2002], 9). By asking about boundaries and their making, Mitchell is not merely offering a different perspective. He demonstrates that the rhetoric of flow and circulation is *contingent*.

88. Taylor, *Moment of Complexity*, 231; in *About Religion*, Taylor describes how transformations of the economic system lead to a situation in which "signs are left to float freely on a sea that has no shore," a diagnostic that is of obvious pertinence for my own reflections in what follows (Taylor, *About Religion: Economies of Faith in Virtual Culture* [Chicago: University of Chicago Press, 1999], 11).

89. Brown, *Walled States*, 103; and compare Elizabeth Grosz, who writes that "the state functions to grid and organize, to hierarchize and coordinate the activities of and for the city and its state-produced correlate, the country(side). These are the site(s) for chaotic, deregulated, and unregulatable flows" (E. Grosz, *Space, Time, and Perversion: Essays on the Politics of Bodies* [London: Routledge, 1995], 107).

90. Italo Calvino, "Blood, Sea" in *t zero*, trans. William Weaver (Orlando, Fla.: Harcourt, Inc., 1969), 39. "Blood, Sea [*Il sangue, il mare*]" is part of Calvino's "Cosmicomics" series. Cf. Calvino, *Tutte le cosmicomiche*, a cura di Claudio Milanini (Milano: Oscar Mondadori, 2002), 185–95.

91. Calvino, "Blood, Sea," 39–40/I185.

92. Edmund Burke spoke of "the chosen race and sons of England," of those "in whose veins the blood of freedom circulates" (quoted in Domenico Losurdo, *Liberalism: A Counter-History*, trans. Gregory Elliott [London: Verso, 2011], 54). There is much in Losurdo to suggest that the history of liberalism constitutes an elaborate chapter of the history of blood, an appraisal that is confirmed by John Rogers, *The Matter of Revolution: Science, Poetry, and Politics in the Age of Milton* (Ithaca, N.Y.: Cornell University Press, 1996).

93. "O our poor nobility of blood!" (Dante, *Paradisio*, XVI).

94. Calvino, "Blood, Sea," 47.

95. Werner Hamacher, *pleroma—Reading in Hegel* (Stanford, Calif.: Stanford University Press, 1998), 237.

96. Greg Bear, *Blood Music* (New York: Ace Books, 1985), 189.

97. "The postmodern economic simulacrum" writes David Wills, "the system of exchange that seems to be posited on purer and purer flow, an always more fluid abstraction from the solidity of the commodity, simply occludes its own reliance on a play between solid and fluid forms" (D. Wills, *Prosthesis* [Stanford, Calif.: Stanford University Press, 1995], 81). I join Wills in asking about the role and function of this occlusion, on the dominance of the "positing" of flow.

98. I found Bernard Harcourt's account particularly compelling (B. E. Harcourt, *The Illusion of Free Markets: Punishment and the Myth of Natural Order* [Cambridge, Mass.: Harvard

University Press, 2011]), but see also the work of David Garland, Keally McBride, Angela Davis, Marie Gottschalk, and Loïc Wacquant.

99. Taylor, *Moment of Complexity*, 42–43.

100. Calvino, "Blood, Sea," 47/I192.

101. Emerson, quoted in Taylor, *After God*, 313.

102. Jonathan Miller, *The Body in Question* (London: Jonathan Cape, 1978), 216.

103. Arlette Farge, "Présentation," in *Affaires de sang*, ed. Arlette Farge (Paris: Imago, 1988), 13.

104. Mark C. Taylor, *Mystic Bones* (Chicago: University of Chicago Press, 2007), 31.

105. G. W. F. Hegel, *Phenomenology of Spirit*, trans. A. V. Miller (Oxford: Oxford University Press, 1977), 208.

106. Piero Camporesi, *Juice of Life: The Symbolic and Magic Significance of Blood*, trans. Robert R. Barr (New York: Continuum, 1995), 17.

107. Foucault, *Discipline and Punish*, 16.

108. Michel Foucault, *The History of Sexuality. Vol. 1*, trans. Robert Hurley (New York: Vintage Books, 1990), 147.

109. Michel Foucault, *The History of Sexuality. Vol. 1*, 148–49; Dominique Laporte agrees, though, for him, there are other factors or indeed elements involved in "the transition from a blood society to a society of 'health, progeny, race, survival of the species, vitality of the social body'" (D. Laporte, *History of Shit*, trans. Nadia Benabid and Rodolphe El-Khoury [Cambridge, Mass.: MIT Press, 2000], 82; quoting Foucault); and compare, for another version of this narrative independent of Foucault's periodization, Susan Mizruchi's assertion that "where a traditional kinship system stresses blood identity, a modern capitalist might stress 'merit' or industry" (S. L. Mizruchi, *The Science of Sacrifice: American Literature and Modern Social Theory* [Princeton, N.J.: Princeton University Press, 1998], 27).

110. See Uli Linke, *Blood and Nation: The European Aesthetics of Race* (Philadelphia: University of Pennsylvania Press, 1999), and see Carolyn Walker Bynum, *Wonderful Blood: Theology and Practice in Late Medieval Northern Germany and Beyond* (Philadelphia: University of Pennsylvania Press, 2007) and Bettina Bildhauer, *Medieval Blood* (Cardiff: University of Wales Press, 2006).

111. Douglas Starr, *Blood: An Epic History of Medicine and Commerce* (New York: Harper Collins, 2002), xv; Healy, *Last Best Gifts*, esp. 43–69.

112. Donna J. Haraway, *Modest_Witness@Second_Millenium. FemaleMan©_Meets_OncoMouse™: Feminism and Technoscience* (New York: Routledge, 1997), 237; and see also, for a particular and enduring illustration, Michael G. Kenny, "A Question of Blood, Race, and Politics," *Journal of the History of Medicine and Allied Sciences* 61, no. 4 (October 2006): 456–91.

113. See, for example, *Blood: Art, Power, Politics, and Pathology*, ed. James M. Bradburne (Munich and London: Prestel Verlag, 2002).

114. Samuel Weber, *Targets of Opportunity: On the Militarization of Thinking* (New York: Fordham University Press, 2005), vii.

115. Paul Goodman, *Of One Blood: Abolitionism and the Origins of Racial Equality* (Berkeley: University of California Press, 1998); Susan Gillman, *Blood Talk: American Race Melodrama and the Culture of the Occult* (Chicago: University of Chicago Press, 2003).

116. Gilman, *Blood Talk*, 70.

117. Calvino, "Blood, Sea," 48.

118. James M. Bradburne, "Perspectives on Art, Power, Politics, and Pathology," in *Blood: Art, Power, Politics, and Pathology*, 11.

119. Calvino, "Blood, Sea," 49.

120. For Shakespeare's blood, see David S. Berkeley, *Blood Will Tell in Shakespeare's Plays* (*Graduate Studies Texas Tech University* 28 [January 1984]) and D. S. Berkeley, "Shakespeare's *Severall Degrees in Bloud*," in *Shakespeare's Theories of Blood, Character, and Class: A Festschrift in Honor of David Shelley Berkeley*, ed. Peter C. Rollins and Alan Smith (New York: Peter Lang, 2001), 7; and see Stephen Greenblatt, who articulates his notion of "the circulation of social energy" in and around Shakespeare, strangely doing so without crediting either Harvey or Marx (Greenblatt, *Shakespearean Negotiations*, 1–20); and see chap. 3 this volume ("Capital: Christians and Money"). On Marlowe, see Lowell Gallagher, "Faustus' Blood and the (Messianic) Question of Ethics," *ELH* 73 (2006): 1–29; on Dante, see Jeremy Tambling, "Monstrous Tyranny, Men of Blood: Dante and 'Inferno' XII," *The Modern Language Review* 98, no. 4 (October 2003): 881–97.

121. Adam Smith, *The Theory of Moral Sentiments*, ed. David D. Raphael and Alec L. Macfie (Indianapolis: Liberty Fund, 1984), 222 (V.ii.I.10). I am grateful to Martin Harries for this reference.

122. Friedrich Nietzsche's *Zarathustra* quoted in Babette E. Babich, *Words in Blood, Like Flowers: Philosophy and Poetry, Music and Eros in Hölderlin, Nietzsche, and Heidegger* (Albany: State University of New York Press, 2006), vii.

123. Benedict de Spinoza, "Correspondence," in *On the Improvement of the Understanding. The Ethics. Correspondence*, trans. R. H. M. Elwes (New York: Dover Publications, 1955), 291 (Letter XV [XXXII], dated November 20, 1665); I return to Spinoza's worm in chap. 2 this volume.

124. Hegel, *Phenomenology*, 100; see Werner Hamacher, *pleroma—Reading in Hegel*, trans. Nichlas Walker and Simon Jarvis (Stanford, Calif.: Stanford University Press, 1998), 244–46; and Markus Semm, *Der Springende Punkt in Hegels System* (München: Klaus Boer Verlag, 1994), 17–70.

125. Taylor, *After God*, 312.

126. Thomas Hobbes, *Leviathan*, ed. Richard Tuck (Cambridge: Cambridge University Press), chap. 24, 174–75.

127. Jonathan Miller, *The Body in Question* (London: Jonathan Cape, 1978), 216.

128. Giambattista Vico, *On the Study Methods of Our Time*, trans. Elio Gianturco (Ithaca, N.Y.: Cornell University Press, 1990), 6.

129. Circe Sturm, *Blood Politics: Race, Culture, and Identity in the Cherokee Nation of Oklahoma* (Berkeley: University of California Press, 2002), 2.

130. F. J. Davis, *Who Is Black? One Nation's Definition* (University Park: Pennsylvania State University Press, 2001); Anne Norton, *Bloodrites of the Post-Structuralists: Words, Flesh, and Revolution* (New York: Routledge, 2002).

131. Norton, *Bloodrites*, 10.

132. Elizabeth Grosz, *Volatile Bodies: Toward a Corporeal Feminism* (Bloomington: Indiana University Press, 1994), 204, quoting Iris Young.

133. Peggy McCracken, *The Curse of Eve, the Wound of the Hero: Blood, Gender, and Medieval Literature* (Philadelphia: University of Pennsylvania Press, 2003), 116.

134. Derrida, "Force of Law," trans. Mary Quaintance, in *Acts of Religion*, ed. Gil Anidjar (New York: Routledge, 2002), 292; and see Donna Haraway's proximate assertions in Haraway, *Modest_Witness*, 134 and 265.

135. Starr, *Blood*.

136. Karl Marx, *Capital: A Critique of Political Economy. Volume 1*, trans. Ben Fowkes (New York: Penguin, 1990), 367; Richard M. Titmuss, *The Gift Relationship: From Human Blood to Social Policy* (New York: The New Press, 1997); Rajan, *Biocapital*; Healy, *Last Best Gifts*; Lesley A. Sharp, *Strange Harvest: Organ Transplants, Denatured Bodies, and the Transformed Self* (Berkeley: University of California Press, 2006).

137. Catherine Waldby and Robert Mitchell, *Tissue Economies: Blood, Organs, and Cell Lines in Late Capitalism* (Durham, N.C.: Duke University Press, 2006), 183; and see Annemarie Mol and John Law, "Regions, Networks and Fluids: Anaemia and Social Topology," *Social Studies of Science* 24 (1994): 641–71.

138. Waldby, 108; see also Jacob Copeman, *Veins of Devotion: Blood Donation and Religious Experience in North India* (New Brunswick, N.J.: Rutgers University Press, 2009) and see, for a general, critical perspective, Vandana Shiva, *Biopiracy: The Plunder of Nature and Knowledge* (Cambridge, Mass.: South End Press, 1997).

139. Latour, *Pandora's Box*, 80; Cormac McCarthy, *Blood Meridian: Or the Evening Redness in the West* (New York: Vintage, 1992).

140. *Selected Prose of T.S. Eliot*, ed. Frank Kermode (New York: Farrar, Straus and Giroux, 1975), 130.

141. Calvino, "Blood, Sea," 49.

142. Galeano, *We Say No*, 251.

143. Calvino, "Blood, Sea," 44.

1. NATION (JESUS' KIN)

1. Peter Fitzpatrick, *Modernism and the Grounds of Law* (Cambridge: Cambridge University Press, 2001), 17.

2. Roberto Esposito, *Communitas: The Origin and Destiny of Community*, trans. Timothy Campbell (Stanford, Calif.: Stanford University Press, 2010), 5; further references appear parenthetically in the text.

3. This is not to be confused with sacrifice or with self-sacrifice, where an excess of substance is presupposed, which is not to say that, as Reiko Ohnuma demonstrates, there is not much to learn from a contrast with the Buddhist tradition of "giving away the body" (R. Ohnuma, *Heads, Eyes, Flesh, and Blood: Giving Away the Body in Indian Buddhist Literature* [New York: Columbia University Press, 2007]).

4. Paul W. Kahn, *Putting Liberalism in Its Place* (Princeton, N.J.: Princeton University Press, 2005), 9.

5. Claude Lefort, *Democracy and Political Theory*, trans. David Macey (Cambridge: Polity, 1988), 213–55.

6. Benedict Anderson, *Imagined Communities: Reflections on the Origins and Spread of Nationalism* (London: Verso, 1991), 13.

7. On the papal revolution, see Eugen Rosenstock-Huessy, *Out of Revolution: Autobiography of Western Man* (Providence, R.I.: Berg, 1993 [1938]); and, in Rosenstock-Huessy's footsteps, Harold J. Berman, *Law and Revolution: The Formation of the Western Legal Tradition* (Cambridge, Mass.: Harvard University Press, 1983); see as well Gerd Tellenbach, *Church, State, and Christian Society at the Time of the Investiture Contest*, trans. R. F. Bennett (Oxford: Basil Blackwell, 1948).

8. On "early techniques of mass social operations," see José Antonio Maravall, *Culture of the Baroque: Analysis of a Historical Structure*, trans. Terry Cochran (Minneapolis: University of Minnesota Press, 1986), 14; for a compelling demonstration of medieval art and church architecture as means of information and propaganda, see Claudio Lange, *Der nackte Feind: Anti-Islam in der Romanischen Kunst* (Berlin: Parthas Verlag, 2004); on "one body, one flesh," see Henri de Lubac, *Corpus Mysticum: The Eucharist and the Church in the Middle Ages*, trans. Gemma Simmonds et al. (Notre Dame, Ind.: University of Notre Dame Press, 2006), 168–86.

9. On Christian discipline in the Middle Ages, see Talal Asad's essential work in *Genealogies of Religion: Discipline and Reasons of Power in Christianity and Islam* (Baltimore, Md.: Johns Hopkins University Press, 1993), esp. chaps. 3 and 4.

10. Claude Meillassoux, *Mythes et limites de l'anthropologie: Le sang et les mots* (Lausanne: Editions Page Deux, 2001), 49; and see Janet Carsten, *After Kinship* (Cambridge: Cambridge University Press, 2004). David d'Avray notes the accuracy of Jack Goody's observation to the effect that "the northern and southern sides of the Mediterranean have rather similar social structures when set against those of sub-Saharan society, but that the strict consanguinity prohibition on the Christian, European side, north of the Mediterranean, differentiates it both from the southern Arab side and from the ancient civilizations of the Mediterranean" (D. L. d'Avray, "Peter Damian, Consanguinity and Church Property," in *Intellectual Life in the Middle Ages: Essays Presented to Margaret Gibbon*, ed. Lesley Smith and Benedicta Ward [London: The Hambledon Press, 1992], 75; quoting Goody, *The Development of the Family and Marriage in Europe* [Cambridge: Cambridge University Press, 1983]).

11. Richard Southern hesitates less, though the challenge is to understand what he precisely means: "Between the eleventh and the thirteenth centuries there is no nobility of blood" (R. W. Southern, *The Making of the Middle Ages* [New Haven, Conn.: Yale University Press, 1953], 110); on the nobility, blood, and periodization, see Kathleen Biddick, "The Cut of Genealogy: Pedagogy in the Blood," *Journal of Medieval and Early Modern Studies* 30, no. 3 (Fall 2000): 449–62; R. Howard Bloch writes of the emergence of a "biopolitics of lineage," "a growing consciousness of blood relations in distinction to those by marriage," and an "increased emphasis upon time and blood." The nobility, he continues, became "synonymous with race (*sanguine nobilitatis*)" (R. Howard Bloch, *Etymologies and Genealogies: A Literary Anthropology of the French Middle Ages* [Chicago: University of Chicago Press, 1983], 69–70; and see Zrinka Stahuljak, *Bloodless Genealogies of the French Middle Ages: Translatio, Kinship, and Metaphor* (Gainesville: University Press of Florida, 2005).

12. As I will have occasion to repeat, the identification of blood as *primarily* a physiologic or biological, "natural" substance is particularly puzzling when considering the "sympathetic constellation" it constitutes, its otherwise ubiquitous and pervasive status as a "symbol." As Jacques Le Goff puts it in a proximate context, "A handsome man has a red skin because one feels the palpitation of the blood flowing underneath, a principle of nobility as of impurity, but in any case a basic principle. But how does one disentangle the concrete from the abstract in this taste for blood?" (J. Le Goff, *Medieval Civilization 400–1500*, trans. Julia Barrow [Oxford: Blackwell, 1988], 335). Rarer is the attempt to read blood (and more generally the body) in terms of "narrative *mythos*" and "organizing metaphors" (see, e.g., Gabrielle M. Spiegel, "Genealogy: Form and Function in Medieval Historical Narrative," *History and Theory* 22, no. 1 [February 1983]: 43–53; Sarah Beckwith, *Christ's Body: Identity, Culture, and Society in Late Medieval Writings* [London: Routledge, 1993]; Stahuljak, *Bloodless Genealogies of the French Middle Ages*); finally, a more sustained attention to a wider rhetorical range of which blood is an essential element can be found in Louis Marin, *Food for Thought*, trans. Mette Hjort (Baltimore, Md.: Johns Hopkins University Press, 1989).

13. The argument is famously advanced by Bruno Latour in *We Have Never Been Modern*, trans. Catherine Porter (Cambridge, Mass.: Harvard University Press, 1993), but see, more proximately, Andrew Colin Gow's brilliant " 'Sanguis naturalis' and 'sang de miracle': Ancient Medicine, 'Superstition,' and the Metaphysics of Mediaeval Healing Miracles," *Sudhoffs Archiv fuer Geschichte der Medizin und der Naturwissenschaften* 87, no. 2 (2003): 129–58.

14. "Instead of setting up an asymmetry, instead of distributing science to Boyle and political theory to Hobbes," Latour explains after the authors of *Leviathan and the Air-Pump*, we must come to see that both science and politics are, as it were, shared among them (Latour, *We Have Never Been Modern*, 16–17). That is why Latour speaks of a comparative and symmetric anthropology (the French subtitle of his book is "an essay in symmetric anthropology"). But I am trying to show that blood becomes the site of a distribution, that there emerges a difference within and between bloods that establishes asymmetries which may or may not be undone. I hold on, therefore, to some reservations with regard to the periodization or leveling Latour adheres to; note that "certain basic physiological concepts and associated therapeutic methods—notably humoral theory and the practice of bloodletting to get rid of bad humors—had a continuous life extending from Greek antiquity into the nineteenth century" (Nancy Siraisi, *Medieval and Early Renaissance Medicine: An Introduction to Knowledge and Practice* [Chicago: University of Chicago Press, 1990], 97).

15. In order to supplement A. J. Gurevich's "categories of medieval culture" (A. J. Gurevich, *Categories of Medieval Culture*, trans. G. L. Campbell [London: Routledge and Kegan Paul, 1985]), I humbly borrow my section title from Joan W. Scott's groundbreaking essay, "Gender: A Useful Category of Analysis," in Scott, *Gender and the Politics of History* (New York: Columbia University Press, 1988), 28–50; my attempt to follow in her footsteps is obviously not meant to be as exhaustive and far-reaching, but it is intended to suggest the potential of a perspectival shift that involves many a historical object. The phrase "eucharistic matrix" is Louis Marin's, in his *Food for Thought*, for example, 12, 161.

16. Miri Rubin, *Corpus Christi: The Eucharist in Late Medieval Culture* (Cambridge: Cambridge University Press, 1991), 1; and see for a different and comprehensive perspective, which also marks the Eucharist's centrality, Regina Mara Schwartz, *Sacramental Poetics at the Dawn of Secularism: When God Left the World* [Stanford, Calif.: Stanford University Press, 2008]. Carolyn Walker Bynum has been both instrumental to and critical of the wealth of studies dedicated to the Eucharist and its effects ("Recent work seems to find the Eucharist everywhere," C. Walker Bynum, "The Blood of Christ in the Later Middle Ages," *Church History* 71, no. 4 [December 2002], 686). She has also done much to expand the significance of blood beyond eucharistic practices, something that hardly diminishes Rubin's point (see, among Bynum's books, *Wonderful Blood: Theology and Practice in Late Medieval Northern Germany and Beyond* [Philadelphia: University of Pennsylvania Press, 2007]).

17. Edward Peters, *Inquisition* (Berkeley: University of California Press, 1989), 1; as Bartolomé Bennassar points out, the Inquisition *was* a myth, it operated as a myth and by means of it, using "this formidable instrument of political and social integration; this powerful instrument in the hands of the Church and those of the state, by way of which one body was molded from the diversity of the Spanish masses" (B. Bennassar, *L'Inquisition espagnole, XVe-XIXe siècles* (Paris: Hachette, 2009), 283.

18. Ernst Robert Curtius, *European Literature and the Latin Middle Ages*, trans. Willard R. Trask (New York: Harper, 1963), 542; the "lateness" and "exceptionality" of Spain and the Spanish Empire, its exclusion too, are still debated of course; see, for example, Donald E. Worcester, "Historical and Cultural Sources of Spanish Resistance to Change," *Journal of Inter-American Studies* 6, no. 2 (April 1964): 173–80, or more recently Jorge Cañizares-Esguerra, *Nature, Empire, and Nation: Explorations of the History of Science in the Iberian World* (Stanford, Calif.: Stanford University Press, 2006).

19. Tomaž Mastnak, *Crusading Peace: Christendom, the Muslim World, and Western Political Order* (Berkeley: University of California Press, 2002); more on this later.

20. Albert A. Sicroff writes of "une révolution sociale" in his *Les controverses des status de "pureté de sang" en Espagne du XVe au XVIIe siècles* (Paris: Didier, 1960), 95.

21. Rubin, *Corpus Christi,* 347; and see Henri de Lubac, *Corpus Mysticum*; Ernst Kantorowicz, *The King's Two Bodies: A Study in Mediaeval Political Theology* (Princeton, N.J.: Princeton University Press, 1997).

22. Scholars do see the *limpieza de sangre* as a form of "race thinking," as Irene Silverblatt calls it (I. Silverblatt, *Modern Inquisitions: Peru and the Colonial Origins of the Civilized World* [Durham, N.C.: Duke University Press, 2004]), but locate it within a Hispanic, not particularly Christian, genealogy or they associate it with a "Semitic" one, referring to those whom "sixteenth-century Spain glorified as being most unsullied by the urban contagion of Semitic blood" (Barbara Fuchs, *Mimesis and Empire: The New World, Islam, and European Identities* [Cambridge: Cambridge University Press, 2004], 112). The notion that, more generally, the blood of Christians could be the subject of investment, desire, or envy, that it could become something worthy of acquisition (indeed, a property) and therefore of protection and preservation is, of course, at the center of the "blood libel" and of the history of anti-Semitism. The implication—that Christians have a different

blood, even a pure blood—seems to be of a different order; it raises, at any rate, another set of questions. Thankfully, Denise Kimber Buell has opened a path that would enable these questions to be asked in her groundbreaking *Why This New Race: Ethnic Reasoning in Early Christianity* (New York: Columbia University Press, 2005); as Buell writes in a later essay, there were those for whom "Jesus' blood not only makes it possible to become Christian but is explicitly interpreted as begetting or birthing a people linked by faith *and* ancestry—an understanding produced and reinforced through communal rituals, especially the eucharist" (D. K. Buell, "Early Christian Universalism and Modern Forms of Racism," in *The Origins of Racism in the West*, ed. Miriam Eliav-Feldon, Benjamin Isaac, and Joseph Ziegler [Cambridge: Cambridge University Press, 2009], 112). Typically enough, there is no other mention of the Eucharist in this collection.

23. Benjamin Isaac, *The Invention of Racism in Classical Antiquity* (Princeton, N.J.: Princeton University Press, 2004), and see Denise Eileen McCoskey's excellent review: "Naming the Fault in Question: Theorizing Racism among the Greeks and Romans," in *International Journal of the Classical Tradition* 13, no. 2 (Fall 2006): 243–67.

24. Piero Camporesi, *Juice of Life: The Symbolic and Magic Significance of Blood*, trans. Robert R. Barr (New York: Continuum, 1995), 27.

25. Biddick, "The Cut of Genealogy," 449–51.

26. An essential interrogation of periodization and its function in producing "the silenced space of Spanish/Latin America and Amerindian contributions to universal history and to postcolonial theorizing" can be found in Walter D. Mignolo, *The Darker Side of the Renaissance: Literacy, Territoriality, and Colonization* (Ann Arbor: University of Michigan Press, 1995), xi; engaged in similar efforts, Irene Silverblatt seeks to have the Spanish empire admitted into bureaucratic modernity and the rise of the banality of evil (as Hannah Arendt famously called it), a proto-national achievement toward the rise of the modern nation-state (Silverblatt, *Modern Inquisitions*).

27. R. W. Southern, *The Making of the Middle Ages* (New Haven, Conn.: Yale University Press, 1961).

28. Kathleen Davis, *Periodization and Sovereignty: How Ideas of Feudalism and Secularization Govern the Politics of Time* (Philadelphia: University of Pennsylvania Press, 2008), 80.

29. And consider that "the role which the medieval Church allotted to kingship was that of the secular arm, which carried out the commands of the priestly order, and polluted itself in the place of the Church by using physical force and violence and spilling the blood of which the Church washed its hands" (Jacques Le Goff, *Medieval Civilization*, 271). As Georges Bataille writes, "Killing is not the only way to regain sovereign life, but sovereignty is always linked to a denial of the sentiments that death controls. Sovereignty requires the strength to violate the prohibition against killing" (G. Bataille, *The Accursed Share: An Essay on General Economy*, trans. Robert Hurley [New York: Zone Books, 1993], vol. 2 and 3, 220).

30. Although theorists of sovereignty have not lingered on that particular aspect, Michel Foucault importantly elaborated on the association between sovereignty and blood. One might also think of other sites of political reflection, of tyranny, for instance, and the motif of the "men of blood," and so forth; see, for example, Jeremy Tambling, "Monstrous Tyranny, Men of Blood: Dante and 'Inferno' XII," *The Modern Language Review* 98, no. 4

(October 2003): 881–97; on sovereignty and historical legitimacy, see *The Legitimacy of the Middle Ages: On the Unwritten History of Theory*, ed. Andrew Cole and D. Vance Smith (Durham, N.C.: Duke University Press, 2010). Mahmood Mamdani describes the treatment of state boundaries into "boundaries of knowledge, thereby turning political into epistemological boundaries," an insight that must be profitably applied to historical periods and their boundaries (M. Mamdani, *When Victims Become Killers: Colonialism, Nativism, and the Genocide in Rwanda* [Princeton, N.J.: Princeton University Press, 2001], xii).

31. Norbert Elias, *The Civilizing Process: The History of Manners and State Formation and Civilization*, trans. Edmund Jephcott (Oxford: Blackwell, 1994); on the Eucharist and the secularization narrative, see C. J. Gordon, "Bread God, Blood God: Wonderhosts and Early Encounters with Secularization," *Genre* 44, no. 2 (Summer 2011): 105–128.

32. F. Tönnies, *Community and Civil Society*, trans. Jose Harris and Margaret Hollis (Cambridge: Cambridge University Press, 2001), 27.

33. Bettina Bildhauer, *Medieval Blood* (Cardiff: University of Wales Press, 2006); this remarkable book teaches everything one needs to know about medieval blood, which it takes as a point of entry to a better understanding of medieval bodies. Bildhauer demonstrates that, in addition to its association with Jews, "blood was of concern across discourses like medicine, philosophy, Christian devotion and theology, courtly fiction and law" (13).

34. Peggy McCracken, *The Curse of Eve, the Wound of the Hero: Blood, Gender, and Medieval Literature* (Philadelphia: University of Pennsylvania Press, 2003).

35. Carolyn Dinshaw, *Getting Medieval: Sexualities and Communities: Pre- and Postmodern* (Durham, N.C.: Duke University Press, 1999).

36. One could of course argue, along with Chris Knight, that it is a blessing and not a curse. In this case too, it bespeaks our *distant* past, the origins of culture (C. Knight, *Blood Relations: Menstruation and the Origins of Culture* [New Haven, Conn.: Yale University Press, 1991]), but for a different account of periodization, civilization, and racial hierarchies in relation to menstruation, see Ashwini Tambe, "Climate, Race Science and the Age of Consent in the League of Nations," *Theory, Culture and Society* 28, no. 2 (March 2011): 109–130.

37. Marc Bloch, *Les rois thaumaturges* (Paris: Gallimard, 1983); physicians were also recasting themselves as healers after Christ, with blood—and the purification of the blood—as a primary (and esoteric) source of their healing power (see Joseph Ziegler, *Medicine and Religion c. 1300: The Case of Arnau de Vilanova* [Oxford: Clarendon Press, 1998], 146, 154–55); for more on blood in the context of medieval medicine and the Christian rapport to Jews, see Gow, " 'Sanguis naturalis' and 'sang de miracle.' "

38. Christine Caldwell Ames, *Righteous Persecution: Inquisition, Dominicans, and Christianity in the Middle Ages* (Philadelphia: University of Pennsylvania Press, 2009), 7; and see William T. Cavanaugh, "Eucharistic Sacrifice and the Social Imagination in Early Modern Europe," *Journal of Medieval and Early Modern Studies* 31, no. 3 (Fall 2001): 585–605.

39. It has been evident for some time that neither the Eucharist nor obviously the Inquisition can be treated independently of Christian anti-Semitism (or anti-Judaism, or Judeophobia, or whatever one might want to call it). Now, whether he was correct on the specifics, Benzion Netanyahu did remind us that anti-Semitism may thrive where no Jews are found and must

therefore be understood, as it were, on its own terms (a Sartrean argument of sorts). I tend to agree with him on that particular point, even as I recognize the contributions made, the not quite collateral damage, which both the Eucharist and the Inquisition inflicted on Jews and others. Accordingly, the association of Jews and blood in the Christian imagination is pervasive, and it is by now often mentioned, as is the fact that the dispute between Judaism and Christianity has been conducted over blood; see Israel Jacob Yuval, *Two Nations in Your Womb: Perceptions of Jews and Christians in Late Antiquity*, trans. Barbara Harshav and Jonathan Chipman (Berkeley: University of California Press, 2006); David Biale, *Blood and Belief: The Circulation of a Symbol between Jews and Christians* (Berkeley: University of California Press, 2007); and see also Claudine Fabre-Vassas, *The Singular Beast: Jews, Christians, and the Pig,* trans. Carol Volk (New York: Columbia University Press, 1997). I insist here on the importance of a singular and reflexive formation of Christianity, as it were prior to its "others," the relative independence and integrity it achieves as a community of blood that precedes, historically and logically, the construction of and relation to Jews and/ as others. Blood, in other words, had to become the site of a (pure, internal) difference, however fictive.

40. More on this later. The "blood hyphen," which I loosely borrow from Leo Steinberg, is the trickle of blood emerging from Christ's wound, represented as flowing against the laws of gravity (the body is laid down), toward his genitals, thus linking crucifixion and circumcision (L. Steinberg, *The Sexuality of Christ in Renaissance Art and in Modern Oblivion* [Chicago: University of Chicago Press, 1996], 168–71).

41. Barbara Fuchs, *Mimesis and Empire: The New World, Islam, and European Identities* (Cambridge: Cambridge University Press, 2004), 162.

42. R. I. Moore, *The Formation of a Persecuting Society: Authority and Deviance in Western Europe 950–1250* (Oxford: Blackwell, 2007); none of the numerous books and anthologies I have consulted that theorize and historicize racism and recognize the importance of blood in its many incarnations ever mention the pure blood of Jesus Christ. However, the contribution of Christianity to, minimally its co-incidence with, racism and anti-Semitism is not really in doubt (but see next note).

43. Henry Charles Lea, "Ethical Values in History" (The President's address to the American Historical Association, December 29, 1903), *The American Historical Review* 9, no. 2 (January 1904): 234, 236; and see Edward Peters, "Henry Charles Lea: Jurisprudence and Civilization," *Digital Proceedings of the Lawrence J. Schoenberg Symposium on Manuscript Studies in the Digital Age* volume 2 (2010), issue 1, article 2. Accessible at http://repository .upenn.edu/ljsproceedings/vol2/iss1/2. Morgan's version is as follows: "The cruelty inherent in the heart of man, which civilization and Christianity have softened without eradicating, still betrays the savage origin of mankind" (Lewis Henry Morgan, *Ancient Society or Researches in the Lines of Human Progress from Savagery through Barbarism to Civilization* [New York: Henry Holt, 1877], 505; Thomas Trautmann writes that "it is no accident that of the inventors of kinship Morgan was a practicing lawyer," a scholar of Roman law, as well as an ambivalent Christian (T. R. Trautmann, *Lewis Henry Morgan and the Invention of Kinship* [Berkeley: University of California Press, 1987], 39, 63ff.); Morgan's concern with "communities of blood" and with the "purity of blood" is inscribed on every page of

his *Systems of Consanguinity and the Affinity of the Human Family* (Lincoln: University of Nebraska Press, 1997); and see Gillian Feeley-Harnik, " 'Communities of Blood': The Natural History of Kinship in Nineteenth-Century America," *Comparative Studies in Society and History* 41, no. 2 (April 1999): 215–62.

44. In his fundamental study of universalism, the seemingly benign belief that "all men are brothers," Marc Shell shows the paradoxes and exclusionary logics at work within Christian universalism. By shifting the perspective slightly, from universal kinship to the community of blood, I offer no corrective, but merely a footnote to Shell's sweeping demonstration (Marc Shell, *Children of the Earth: Literature, Politics, and Nationhood* (New York: Oxford University Press, 1993).

45. Recall that there were alternatives to this notion that blood was a property of a community, the site of difference between collectives. According to A. J. Gurevich, blood could be seen as a different element, not as a site of communal difference, or the private property of anyone. It linked world and creature, part of "the microcosm [which] was conceived in the form of man, who could be understood only within the framework, of the parallelism between the 'small' and the 'great' universe. This theme, which is found in the ancient East and in classical Greece, enjoyed enormous popularity in the Middle Ages, especially from the twelfth century onwards. The elements of the human body were identical, it was held, with the elements forming the universe. Man's flesh was of the earth, his blood of water, his breath of air and his warmth of fire" (A. J. Gurevich, *Categories of Medieval Culture*, 57; and see Jacques Le Goff, *Medieval Civilization*, 138).

46. See the argument conducted throughout the pages of *Queer Iberia: Sexualities, Cultures, and Crossings from the Middle Ages to the Renaissance,* ed. Josiah Blackmore and Gregory S. Hutcheson (Durham, N.C.: Duke University Press, 1999).

47. A detailed discussion of "social disciplining" (a term suggested by Gerhard Oestrich and informed by Michel Foucault and Norbert Elias) can be found in Philip S. Gorski's *The Disciplinary Revolution: Calvinism and the Rise of the State in Early Modern Europe* (Chicago: University of Chicago Press, 2003).

48. The pervasiveness of blood attributed to the "Religion of the Semites" is most obvious in William Robertson Smith, *Religion of the Semites* (New Brunswick, NJ: Transaction Publishers, 2002 [1894]), but as we shall repeatedly see, it is hardly unique to him. David Biale interprets it as, quite precisely, Judeo-Christian (D. Biale, *Blood and Belief: The Circulation of a Symbol Between Jews and Christians* [Berkeley: University of California Press, 2007]). I have no real disagreement, nor do I claim the exhaustive expertise of eminent scholars who have preceded me and on whom I rely in my own, highly abbreviated, rendering. My reservations have to do with the lack of evidence that would support the claim that "blood stands for life," the equation of blood with kinship, and ultimately the notion that blood is the substance of the community. To suspend these uninterrogated presuppositions is to catch sight of a very different entryway into a reading of blood in the Bible. It is also, as we shall repeatedly see, to conceive otherwise of the Jewish–Christian divide.

49. Dennis J. McCarthy, "The Symbolism of Blood and Sacrifice," *Journal of Biblical Literature* 88, no. 2 (June 1969): 166–76; and by the same author, "Further Notes on the Symbolism

of Blood and Sacrifice," *Journal of Biblical Literature* 92, no. 2 (June 1973): 205–210; see also Nancy Jay, *Throughout Your Generations Forever: Sacrifice, Religion, and Paternity* (Chicago: University of Chicago Press, 1992); William K. Gilders, *Blood Ritual in the Hebrew Bible: Meaning and Power* (Baltimore, Md.: Johns Hopkins University Press, 2004); although it is not easy to disentangle gender from the matter of sacrifice, the blood of menstruation has garnered a well-deserved attention of its own; see Charlotte Elisheva Fonrobert, *Menstrual Purity: Rabbinic and Christian Reconstructions of Biblical Gender* (Stanford, Calif.: Stanford University Press, 2000); Evyattar Marienberg, *Niddah: Lorsque les juifs conceptualisent la menstruation* (Paris: Belles Lettres, 2003); Ruth Tsoffar, *The Stains of Culture: An Ethno-Reading of Karaite Jewish Women* (Detroit, Mich.: Wayne State University Press, 2006).

50. Jay, *Throughout Your Generations Forever*, 150; for a different view on modern society and its voluntary associations, not to mention inclinations toward sacrificial blood spilling, see Paul W. Kahn, *Sacred Violence: Torture, Terror, and Sovereignty* (Ann Arbor: Michigan University Press, 2008).

51. L. Morris, "The Biblical Use of the Term 'Blood,' " in *The Journal of Theological Studies* III, no. 2 (October 1952): 216–26. Morris points out that the phrase "flesh and blood" only appears in the New Testament (223), an observation that has remained surprisingly unheeded; for more on the anthropological study of the Bible and its failures, see Howard Eilberg-Schwartz, *The Savage in Judaism: An Anthropology of Israelite Religion and Ancient Judaism* (Bloomington: Indiana University Press, 1990); and see also *Sangue e Antropologia Biblica* (Roma: Centro Studi Sanguis Christi, 1980).

52. There is, of course, a covenant of blood in the Old Testament, but it cannot be mistaken for the blood of the community. It is, first of all, spilled blood, and literally the blood *of* the covenant (see, e.g., Exodus 24:6–8); and see Lawrence A. Hoffman, *Covenant of Blood: Circumcision and Gender in Rabbinic Judaism* (Chicago: University of Chicago Press, 1996), although a random search for books with "blood covenant" in their title is inherently instructive.

53. In the context of his argument against Américo Castro on the historical sources of the Statutes on the Purity of Blood, Benzion Netanyahu already explained that "in ancient Hebrew, 'blood' did not serve to indicate 'race' or racial continuity; the term used for this purpose in Hebrew was not 'blood,' but 'seed' " (B. Netanyahu, *Toward the Inquisition: Essays on Jewish and Converso History in Late Medieval Spain* [Ithaca, N.Y., and London: Cornell University Press, 1997], 3; Netanyahu underscores "bone and flesh" as well and adds that " 'blood,' it seems, did not signify any ethnic or racial relationship for the Hebrews," 204, n. 11). With the centrality of seed in biblical genealogical thought, it may be relevant to mention that the "idea of semen stored away in the bones, without any sequence involving processing of the blood, is found in the Sumerian and Egyptian civilizations," hence the preoccupation with the ancestor's bones (Francoise Héritier-Augé, "Semen and Blood: Some Ancient Theories Concerning Their Genesis and Relationship," in *Fragments for a History of the Human Body*, ed. Michel Feher (New York: Zone Books, 1989), vol. 3, 169). Furthermore, "the bones live on and remain attached by a kind of umbilical cord to the localized family or to the ethnic group" (170, quoting Elena Cassin).

54. Writing about medieval Europe, E. Champeaux argues that even in the case of *consanguinitas*, the understanding of kin is based primarily on fraternity and only secondarily on cross-generational relations (from parents to children, and so forth). Recalling, perhaps, Antigone (and most certainly Hegel's Antigone), although not explicitly so, Champeaux illustrates his argument with numerous instances in which a brother or a sister is privileged over a spouse or a parent. As in early nomadic tribes, Champeaux continues, kin is first of all lateral and contemporary: "La parenté se développe en collatérale, elle n'existe véritablement que chez des contemporains, et c'est une conception qui nous fait remonter très haut, à une famille nomade et militaire de combattants du même ban" (E. Champeaux, "*Jus Sanguinis*. Trois façons de calculer la parenté au Moyen Âge," *Revue historique de droit français et étranger*, Quatrième série, Douzième année [1933]: 249). Later, Champeaux will argue that this illuminates the practice of Levirate marriage among the Israelites, which privileges the brother over all other relations. It is, moreover, this narrow definition of "blood kinship" that explains the medieval practice of limiting both genealogical trees, *arbores consanguinitatis* (which only appear in the second half of the twelfth century), as well as marriage interdictions on the basis of blood such as were first legislated by the Lateran Council (253–54 and 272). As we will see, and as Champeaux already documents, major shifts are taking place in the Christian understanding of blood and blood relations between the twelfth and fourteenth centuries in Europe. At a different level of rhetoric and metaphoricity (the tree), this is also the argument made by Christiane Klapisch-Zuber in *L'ombre des ancêtres: Essai sur l'imaginaire médiéval de la parenté* (Paris: Fayard, 2000).

55. The Rabbinic tradition understands and maintains this conception of flesh as a sign of contiguity and contemporaneity, indeed of intimacy, rather than as a marker of lineage and continuity between generations. "Rav Yosef cited a tannaitic tradition: "Flesh: this means the intimacy of the flesh, namely that he should not behave with her in the manner of the Persians who make love while dressed" (TB, Ketubot 48a, quoted in Daniel Boyarin, *Carnal Israel: Reading Sex in Talmudic Culture* [Berkeley: University of California Press, 1995], 48).

56. This is Amos Funkenstein's argument in *Perceptions of Jewish History* (Berkeley: University of California Press, 1993), 11–12.

57. Howard Eilberg-Schwartz, *The Savage in Judaism: An Anthropology of Israelite Religion and Ancient Judaism* (Bloomington: Indiana University Press, 1990), 164ff. In a later account of kinship and genealogical conceptions in the Hebrew Bible, Eilberg-Schwartz will hardly mention blood. Rather, he shows that lineage—that is to say, rhetorically, symbolically, or ritually reinscribed lineage—is located in the semen or "seed" of the father. Distinct from the Greek model, however, if only because of a complete lack of evidence, seed is not blood (H. Eilberg-Schwartz, "The Father, the Phallus, and the Seminal Word: Dilemmas of Patrilineality in Ancient Judaism," *Gender, Kinship, Power: A Comparative and Interdisciplinary History*, ed. Mary Jo Maynes et al. [New York and London: Routledge, 1996).

58. See, for example, *Henoch* 30 (February 2008): 329–65 (special issue on "Blood and the Boundaries of Jewish and Christian Identities in Late Antiquity," ed. Ra'anan S. Boustan and Annette Yoshiko Reed).

59. Daniel Boyarin, "The Bartered Word: Midrash and Symbolic Economy," in *Commentaries—Kommentare [Aporemata: Kritische Studien zur Philologiegeschichte*, ed. Glenn W. Most (Göttingen: Vandenhoeck & Ruprecht, 1999), 44, commenting on the Babylonian Talmud, Tractate *Nidda* 30a; for a discussion of an equally Galenic, and quite similar description by the tenth century 'Ali ibn al-'Abbas al-Majusi, see Danielle Jacquart and Claude Thomasset, *Sexuality and Medicine in the Middle Ages*, trans. Matthew Adamson (Cambridge: Polity Press, 1988), 71–72.

60. Charlotte Elisheva Fonrobert, *Menstrual Purity: Rabbinic and Christian Reconstructions of Biblical Gender* (Stanford, Calif.: Stanford University Press, 2000), 109.

61. Morris, "Biblical Use," and see A. Caquot's review of "H. Christ. *Blutvergiessen im Alten Testament*," *Revue de l'histoire des religions* 196, no. 1 (1979): 93–94

62. Morris also asserts that the association between blood and life is not a simple one, arguing that "life" in this context is often closer to, and even synonymous with, death. Moreover, although the link between blood and life is well established, there is no ground to claim that either genealogy or reproduction is governed by blood. In fact, precisely because blood is equated with the life of creatures, blood should be thought of as the great equalizer—like death—rather than as a site or mark of distinction and separation (Morris, "Biblical Use," 219).

63. Incidentally, "Luther holds that when Jesus says, 'this is my blood of the covenant, which is poured out' (Matthew 26:28), Jesus is referring to the primary element of a testament or last will, namely his impending death" (Matthew Levering, *Sacrifice and Community: Jewish Offering and Christian Eucharist* [Malden, Mass.: Blackwell, 2005], 12).

64. Paul still curses those who oppose him by claiming that their blood is on their heads (Acts 18:6).

65. Eilberg-Schwartz, *The Savage*, 179; Eilberg-Schwartz adds that blood is gendered, that there is a distinction between male and female blood. Clearly, Eilberg-Schwartz's emphasis on a gendered analysis is essential to any understanding of an analytics or poetics of blood, but as he himself suggests by discussing a wider range of bodily fluids, the question is whether one can speak of different kinds of bloods or of different modes of blood functioning. By describing, for instance, how menstrual blood is at times deployed as "a metaphor for murder" (Ezekiel 36:17–18), Eilberg-Schwartz underscores that it is what happens to the blood, the change in its location, that may be determining (181ff., 187ff.). This, again, is not said to diminish the patriarchal dimension of the Bible, but to raise the question of what it means (or doesn't) regarding blood.

66. Eilberg-Schwartz, *The Savage*, 147. Eilberg-Schwartz also shows implicitly that the sacrificial or apotropaic use of blood is predicated upon the leveling nature of blood: As long as it is in its place, blood is blood, in any creature. It can only acquire value, and even meaning, once it begins to flow outward.

67. Even atonement is massively linked to blood insofar as it means death, rather than life (Morris, "Biblical Use," 221–22). Atonement also occurs by putting someone(s) to death (e.g., 2 Samuel 21:3ff.). "The question of whether the meaning of 'sacrifice' for the ancient Israelites is found in the death or in the blood lies outside the scope of our investigation," writes Matthew Levering. "For our purposes, it suffices to note that if the blood of Christ

sanctifies, purifies, or expiates, then it is the death of Christ, his free giving up of his life, that does these things"—this is important to bear in mind for our discussion of later developments (Levering, *Sacrifice and Community*, 51, n. 4).

68. But see, for a critical discussion, Biale, *Blood and Belief*, 31ff.

69. The contested matter of "purity" in the Hebrew Bible has generated an inordinate amount of discussion. However one understands it, the biblical lexicon inscribes important distinctions between purity and sanctity, to mention one important cluster on the issue. It is therefore surprising (and, I think, misleading) that "purity" is sometimes used quite loosely, producing associations that are, to say the least, historically dubious. In the context of an extended discussion of blood purity and impurity (focusing, for the most part, on menstrual blood—a blood that is emphatically "out of place"), Eilberg-Schwartz thus proceeds to address "the concern about the purity of Israelite lineage" (190). Such widening of the field of blood significance—making the ancient Israelites into potential proto-Nazis—can only be understood if kinship is thought to establish a bloodline (although there is quite a conceptual distance to cover before reaching the notion that the bloodline would thus be rendered impure as a result of sexual intercourse!), but this is not the biblical view. Or consider that in his argument about the *limpieza de sangre*, Jean-Paul Zuñiga also collapses biblical conceptions of purity with genealogy and blood kinship, recalling, perhaps, those "Semitic" origins of which there are other famous examples. Interestingly enough, Zuñiga goes on to point to the different "spirit" that would be found in the New Testament. The purity of blood, allegedly foreign to Christianity, would thus reveal "la contamination des idéaux du christianisme par des valeurs foncièrement différentes." An *impure* Christianity? (J. P. Zuñiga, "La voix du sang," 429–30). To be sure, one encounters equally careless conflations of ancient practice with modern, juridico-scientific racism all the time. I shall have more to say about all this in chap. 4, "Odysseus' Blood."

70. Uli Linke's meticulous research into Northern European sources of blood symbolism fails to produce any notion of "pure blood" prior to a sixteenth-century translation of the celebrated Spanish text by Fernando de Rojas, *La Celestina*. On the basis of this translation and further associations of blood, blossoms, and flowers, blood came to be "suggestive of both sexual potency and victimization, [and] assumed connotations of purity, innocence, and the absence of defilement" (U. Linke, *Blood and Nation: The European Aesthetics of Race* [Philadelphia: University of Pennsylvania Press, 1999], 47). It is doubtful that this chain of association, and foremost among them, purity, could be found independent of Christian conceptions. Even notions of linguistic purity are traced no further than the seventeenth century (51ff.).

71. David Biale disagrees, although the supporting argument he brings seems to me to show the exact opposite: "So the blood of childbirth should also be associated with the creation of new life, rather than with death. As Tikva Frymer-Kensky puts it: 'The person who has experienced birth has been at the boundaries of life/non-life'" (Biale, *Blood and Belief*, 34).

72. I am explicitly at odds with Eilberg-Schwartz, who, relying on anthropological knowledge, asserts that the blood of circumcision often symbolizes the continuity of (patrilineal) lineage. There is a telling moment in Eilberg-Schwartz's discussion in *The Savage in Judaism*, where he asserts that the blood of circumcision is spilled ("he is brought into the

covenant when his own male blood is spilled. His blood is clean, unifying, and symbolic of God's covenant," 174), but fails to provide any proof text, biblical or other, to support that assertion. Later, Eilberg-Schwartz will restate his unfounded argument in an even more troubling way and write that "circumcision *and by extension blood from the male organ*, is symbolic of patrilineal descent" (181). If it is historically accurate to situate the Bible in anthropological lore, surely the way it differs from this lore, notably around the figure of blood (and its absence), must be taken into account. Whatever physiologic understanding was at work in these notions, at any rate, the figural addition *supplements* (in the Derridean sense) what should never have needed addition or confirmation in the first place. If circumcision is "a kind of blood brotherhood" (Eilberg-Schwartz, *The Savage*, 162), then brotherhood, and indeed kinship, is clearly *not* located in the blood. Whether this is tied to the alleged certainty or uncertainty of paternity and maternity is, in this context, moot. One can, of course, agree with Eilberg-Schwartz on the view that circumcision becomes a site of (a highly gendered) genealogical continuity. Yet, it is not the only such site, nor should one ignore that blood rarely figures in biblical accounts of circumcision (the prominent exception being Exodus 4, where blood is spilled in order to *establish* a covenant, rather than seen as its carrier in the body).

73. "By the proper use of blood, Israel becomes a 'blood community,' that is, a community constituted through its sacrificial relationship to its God. Here, the meaning of 'blood community' is very far from what it was to become in the age of modern nationalism, namely, a nation based on common racial origins," and on blood, I would add, as property and substance, as a site of difference and differentiation between communities (Biale, *Blood and Belief*, 42–43).

74. Petar Ramadanovic, "Antigone's Kind: The Way of Blood in Psychoanalysis," *Umbr(a): A Journal of the Unconscious* (2004) 173; and see also Nicole Loraux, "La guerre dans la famille," *CLIO, Histoire, Femmes et Sociétés* 5 (1997), esp. 30–33.

75. I do not mean to suggest that murder has not showed itself to be an essential element of fraternity, only that fraternity cannot be reduced to it, much as kinship cannot be reduced to blood, neither as origin nor as ground. Incidentally, the book of Genesis has God refer twice to Abel's blood when castigating Cain. Each time, Abel's blood is referred to as "your brother's blood." There is not the slightest suggestion that this blood could be the same blood as Cain's, indeed, that the brothers would be "sharing" blood in any way.

76. Nicole Loraux seems to oscillate when she describes the blood of kinship along with the blood of murder with one Greek phrase: "with *haima homaimon* (the murder of a consanguine relative; literally, blood of the same blood)" (N. Loraux, "La guerre dans la famille," 26). A few lines later, Loraux explains that "*haima* is the name of spilled blood" (27), which testifies to a specific "kind" of kinship (*phylon*, "a semantic specter that goes from 'race' to 'tribe' via lineage and all the forms of the group insofar as it thinks its closure as a natural given"), *emphylion haima* (27). She then makes explicit the impossibility of disentangling blood from murder in the Greek texts (30–32). Ultimately, however, Loraux translates *syngeneia*—the result of a common *genos*—as *consanguinitas*, "kinship by blood, in other words, the most natural of all relations, which need not be codified in order to be lived in the immediacy of daily existence" (49, and see 54, n. 108, and 61). Blood is fully

naturalized, it is *made* natural, against all evidence—and *not* by "the Greeks"—whoever they were.

77. Stahuljak, *Bloodless Genealogies of the French Middle Ages*, 13.

78. Peter Biller, *The Measure of Multitude: Population in Medieval Thought* (Oxford: Oxford University Press, 2000), 155.

79. Giulia Sissa, "Subtle Bodies," trans. Genevieve Lloyd, in *Fragments for a History of the Human Body*, ed. Michel Feher (New York: Zone Books, 1989) vol. 3, 140; in the same volume, Françoise Héritier-Augé elaborates on "Semen and Blood: Some Ancient Theories Concerning Their Genesis and Relationship," trans. Tina Jolas, 159–75; finally, for a discussion of the debate about and the late (namely, medieval) qualified acceptance of hematogenic views, see Jacquart and Thomasset, *Sexuality and Medicine*. Pomata also alludes to that long debate in "Blood Ties and Semen Ties: Consanguinity and Agnation in Roman Law," in *Gender, Kinship, Power: A Comparative and Interdisciplinary History*, ed. Mary Jo Maynes et al. (New York and London: Routledge, 1996), 43–64.

80. Thomas Laqueur, *Making Sex: Body and Gender from the Greeks to Freud* (Cambridge, Mass.: Harvard University Press, 1990), 41.

81. Laqueur, *Making Sex*, 42; quoting Aristotle's *Generation of Animals*. Laqueur is relying on Sissa's impressive reading of Aristotle in her "Subtle Bodies," mentioned earlier. Sissa explains that for Aristotle, the semen has nothing to do with blood or with any other matter. To the extent that it affects matter, semen does so by dissolving and evaporating. Like "fig juice that sets and curdles milk . . . it does not remain as a part of the bulk that is set and curdled" (Sissa, "Subtle Bodies," 140; quoting Aristotle). Semen, as opposed to blood, is neither part nor whole. Again, I return to the matter of "Greek blood" in chap. 4 ("Odysseus' Blood").

82. Joan Cadden, *Meanings of Sex Difference in the Middle Ages: Medicine, Science, and Culture* (Cambridge: Cambridge University Press, 1993), 79. To be sure, since Aristotle, the mother's blood was taken to constitute the matter "formed" by the male sperm, but this conception, to the extent that it was accepted, does not appear to have imparted a sense that the maternal bond could be called a *blood* relation. Peggy McCracken underscores the matter when she recalls that throughout medieval literature, there is no explicit reference to the mother's blood as the blood of lineage. Only between father and child is there "all one blood" (McCracken, *The Curse of Eve, the Wound of the Hero*, 55). The "value of the mother's blood" is in question indeed insofar as the blood of parturition is neither described nor conceptualized as the blood of lineage (78), and see also Stahuljak, *Bloodless Genealogies of the French Middle Ages*.

83. On heredity and its contingent, but not necessarily contested, connection to blood, see *Heredity Produced: At the Crossroads of Biology, Politics, and Culture, 1500–1870*, ed. Staffan Müller-Wille and Hans-Jörg Rheinberger (Cambridge, Mass.: MIT Press, 2007), and *L'hérédité entre Moyen Âge et Époque moderne. Perspectives historiques*, ed. Maaike van der Lugt and Charles de Miramon (Firenze: Sismel—Edizioni del Galluzzo, 2008); on the "shared substance" of kinship as an uninterrogated assumption, see Janet Carsten, *After Kinship* (Cambridge: Cambridge University Press, 2004), chap. 5 ("Uses and Abuses of Substance").

84. Nancy Siraisi, *Medieval and Early Renaissance Medicine*, 91.

85. It is the paucity of a critical reflection that distinguishes between blood and kinship, blood and community (familial or ethnic), that makes me skeptical of the otherwise massive description of Greek kinship as "blood-based" even in the work of those who are overturning so many of our assumptions about ethnicity, race, and religion (e.g., Nicole Loraux; and see Denise Kimber Buell, *Why This New Race: Ethnic Reasoning in Early Christianity* [New York: Columbia University Press, 2005], 37–38).

86. I have argued elsewhere that the Christian contribution to the "meaning of life," and most importantly to the notion that life is sacred, has been vastly overlooked (Gil Anidjar, "The Meaning of Life," *Critical Inquiry* 37, no. 4 [Summer 2011], 697–723).

87. Eilberg-Schwartz, *The Savage*, 200, but see Buell, *Why This New Race*, and Caroline Johnson Hodge, *If Sons, Then Heirs: A Study of Kinship and Ethnicity in the Letters of Paul* (Oxford: Oxford University Press, 2007).

88. A similar gesture, albeit void of blood, is made by Jesus himself in the gospels, where it is other Christians who become kin rather than one's existing family, which must be abandoned. As for the distinct understanding of "flesh and blood," as well as the repetitive inscription of Jesus' blood in its significance, it does not necessarily contradict Morris's assertion that "in both the Old and New Testaments the blood signifies essentially the death" (Morris, "Biblical Use," 227), but it registers more of a shift between the two corpuses than Morris here allows.

89. In my limited understanding, I am here guided by Daniel Boyarin, *A Radical Jew: Paul and the Politics of Identity* (Berkeley: University of California Press, 1994).

90. Eilberg-Schwartz, *The Savage*, 205; and cf. Mark 5:25–34. Note, however, that in Acts, blood is reinscribed as something that even Gentiles should abstain from, much as fornication and the pollution of idols, among other things (Acts 15:20).

91. Xavier-Léon Dufour, *Le partage du pain eucharistique selon le Nouveau Testament* (Paris: Seuil, 1982), 168ff.

92. A few verses down, Paul will assert that the cup is offered by Jesus "in remembrance" of him, reasserting the spiritual meaning of the blood (and see also Hebrews 9:20–24). The partaking turns ominous (and will cause much anxiety in the future practice of the Eucharist) when Paul writes that one must be worthy of it. Otherwise, one is participating in the death of Christ, "guilty of the body and blood of the Lord" (1 Corinthians 11:25–27).

93. Camporesi, *Juice of Life*, 54, 102.

94. Bynum, *Wonderful Blood*, 258; I take Bynum to be exemplary not only because of the thoroughness and erudition of her work, but also because, among the most recent studies, hers embraces a particularly wide range of novel approaches to the question of blood in general and of blood in Christianity in particular.

95. As I pointed out earlier, Bynum herself did much to contribute to that growth (see in particular her *Holy Feast and Holy Fast: The Religious Significance of Food to Medieval Women* [Berkeley: University of California Press, 1987], as did Miri Rubin, who is credited with the idea for the striking exhibit (later, the book) *Blood: Art, Power, Politics, and Pathology*, ed. James M. Bradburne (Munich and London: Prestel, 2001).

96. Bynum, *Wonderful Blood*, xvii; Bynum later writes: "I have not in my book attempted to consider secular literature" (271, n. 114).

97. See Talal Asad, *Genealogies of Religion: Discipline and Reasons of Power in Christianity and Islam* (Baltimore, Md.: Johns Hopkins University Press, 1993), and see my discussion of Asad's contribution to a more critical understanding of Christianity as "religion" (Gil Anidjar, "The Idea of an Anthropology of Christianity," *Interventions* 11, no. 3 [2009], 367–93).

98. On the association of marriage with the Eucharist (and the Eucharist as marriage of the church with Christ), see David d'Avray, *Medieval Marriage: Symbolism and Society* (Oxford: Oxford University Press, 2005), and see John Witte Jr., *From Sacrament to Contract: Marriage, Religion, and Law in the Western Tradition* (Louisville, Ky.: Westminster John Knox Press, 1997); and note that "the secular marriage metaphor . . . became rather popular in the later Middle Ages when, under the impact of juristic analogies and corporational doctrines, the image of the Prince's marriage to his *corpus mysticum*—that is, to the *corpus mysticum* of his state—appeared to be constitutionally meaningful" (Kantorowicz, *The King's Two Bodies*, 212).

99. Bynum, *Wonderful Blood*, 139; quoting Adelheid Langmann.

100. Consider by way of comparison how for Avicenna, the body was generated from all four humors, and not primarily from blood, which is only one of the humors (Siraisi, *Medieval and Early Renaissance Medicine*, 106).

101. Augustine, *Confessions*, quoted in de Lubac, *Corpus Mysticum*, 178.

102. de Lubac, *Corpus Mysticum*, 178.

103. As we saw, the blood of circumcision does make a covenant and by extension can be said to *produce* community. It is predicated on a distinction between male and female, but it is not what distinguishes between the community and its others. Besides, in this case, blood is not the primal ground but rather a derivative *substitute* for the "natural" connection between mother and child (see Eilberg-Schwartz, *The Savage in Judaism*, 162–94; and see Hoffman, *Covenant of Blood*).

104. I am of course referring to Mary Douglas, *Purity and Danger: An Analysis of the Concepts of Pollution and Taboo* (London and New York: Ark Paperbacks, 1984).

105. Pomata, "Blood Ties," 44–45; and see Klaus Schreiner, "Consanguinitas—Verwandschaft als Strukturprinzip religiöser Gemeinschafts- und Verfassungsbildung in Kirche und Mönchtum des Mittelalters," in *Beiträge zu Geschichte und Struktur der Mittelalterlichen Germania Sacra*, ed. Irene Crusius (Göttingen: Vandenhoeck & Ruprecht, 1989), 176–305; Frank Roumy, "La naissance de la notion canonique de *consanguinitas* et sa réception dans le droit civil," in *L'hérédité entre Moyen Âge et Époque moderne: Perspectives historiques*, ed. Maaike van der Lugt and Charles de Miramon (Firenze: Sismel-Edizioni del Galluzzo, 2008), 41–66.

106. Pomata, "Blood Ties," 51.

107. Pomata, "Blood Ties," 52; on the endurance, and waning, of Galenic conceptions, see also Nanci G. Siraisi, *History, Medicine, and the Traditions of Renaissance Learning* (Ann Arbor: University of Michigan Press, 2007), and Andrea Carlino, *Books of the Body: Anatomical Ritual and Renaissance Learning*, trans. John Tedeschi and Anne C. Tedeschi (Chicago: University of Chicago Press, 1999).

108. In *Wonderful Blood*, Bynum describes the endurance and shifts of the gendered dimension of blood, of "blood as engendering and gendered" (Bynum, *Wonderful Blood*, 159). Hence "the fact that blood as kinship or descent is relatively rare in [medieval] texts is significant and lends support to recent arguments that older scholarship overemphasized lineage in the later Middle Ages" (157). Perhaps, but not so blood. More than significant, therefore, and indeed "crucial" is the fact that "the blood from which the individual is constituted is gendered female; the body *is* the mother's blood" (158).

109. Pomata, "Blood Ties," 59.

110. Blake Leyerle, "Blood is Seed," *Journal of Religion* 81, no. 1 (January 2001): 26–48; Leyerle mentions how Tertullian draws on and argues with "Jewish rites and thought," embryology, theology and soteriology, genealogy and kinship, indeed, "Christian kinship" (although by this, indeed by blood, Tertullian presumably "understands a spiritual rather than physical filiation" [41]).

111. José Antonio Maravall describes such a configuration, a "coinciding dependency," with regard to a given historical situation (Maravall, *The Culture of the Baroque*, 11).

112. "The 'next of kin' (*proximus*) is so called because of closeness (*proximitas*) of blood. 'Bloodrelatives' (*consanguineus*) are so called because they are conceived from one blood (*sanguis*), that is, from one seed of a father.... However, 'maternal brothers' (*germanus*) are those issuing from the same mother (*genetrix*) and not, as many say, from the same seed (*germen*); only the latter are called *fratres*" (*The Etymologies of Isidore of Seville*, Stephen A. Barney, W. J. Lewis, J. A. Beach, Oliver Berghof, with the collaboration of Muriel Hall [Cambridge: Cambridge University Press, 2006], IX.vi.7, 208); for later developments, see Harold J. Berman, *Law and Revolution: The Formation of the Western Legal Tradition* (Cambridge, Mass.: Harvard University Press, 1983).

113. Dominique Barthélemy, "Kinship," trans. Arthur Goldhammer in *A History of Private Life: Revelations of the Medieval World*, ed. Georges Duby (Cambridge, Mass.: The Belknap Press of Harvard University Press, 1988), 124; Barthélemy and others have taken issue with the periodization of medieval practices of kinship and lineage that was proposed by historians such as Marc Bloch, Georges Duby, and others. It should be obvious that I am not arguing that there was (or was not) a revolution or a renaissance, only that blood spread across numerous "domains" and collectives in Western Christendom.

114. Pomata, "Blood Ties," 59–60; and see E. Champeaux, "*Jus Sanguinis*. Trois façons de calculer la parenté au Moyen Âge," *Revue historique de droit français et étranger*, Quatrième série, Douzième année (1933): 241–90; Jack Goody, *The Development of the Family and Marriage in Europe* (Cambridge: Cambridge University Press, 1983), 56ff.; on Isidore in this context, see Laqueur, *Making Sex*, 55–56.

115. Stefan Müller-Wille and Hans-Jörg Rheinberger, "Heredity—The Formation of an Epistemic Space," in *Heredity Produced: At the Crossroads of Biology, Politics, and Culture, 1500–1870*, ed. Staffan Müller-Wille and Hans-Jörg Rheinberger (Cambridge, Mass.: MIT Press, 2007), 12; and see Clara Pinto-Correia, *The Ovary of Eve: Egg and Sperm and Preformation* (Chicago: University of Chicago Press, 1997).

116. Champeaux, "*Jus Sanguinis*," 263. The notion of "flesh" (in *unitas carnis*) had, like biblical bones, an expiration date and did not signify the genealogical link as such, only

contemporaries (270); and see Duby, who underscores "the relatively restricted field of family consciousness." "The memory of ancestors," he goes on to explain, "is short" (Georges Duby, *La société chevaleresque: Hommes et structures du Moyen Âge* (Paris: Flammarion, 1988), 147.

117. Before Ernst Kantorowicz, Henri de Lubac meticulously documented this transformation in his magisterial *Corpus Mysticum,* recently translated into English as *Corpus Mysticum: The Eucharist and the Church in the Middle Ages,* trans. Gemma Simmonds et al. (Notre Dame, Ind.: Notre Dame University Press, 2006), but published in French in 1949 as *Corpus Mysticum: L'eucharistie et l'Église au Moyen Âge* (Paris: Aubier, 1949) (incidentally, the very phrase "mystical body [*corpus mysticum*]" only dates from the fourteenth century); for a summary of Lubac on this particular point, see Kantorowicz, *The King's Two Bodies,* 196; the transformation is explicitly linked to the debates around and evolving practices of the Eucharist.

118. Champeaux, "*Jus Sanguinis,*" 284. The notion of "royal blood" also emerges at this time, along with the conception of a blood nobility; see Kantorowicz, *The King's Two Bodies,* 330ff., and Beaune, *Naissance de la Nation France,* 216–25; and see also Joseph Morsel, "Inventing a Social Category: The Sociogenesis of the Nobility at the End of the Middle Ages," trans. Pamela Selwyn in *Ordering Medieval Society: Perspectives on Intellectual and Practical Modes of Shaping Social Relations,* ed. Bernhard Jussen, (Philadelphia: University of Pennsylvania Press, 2001), 200–240; for more on the nobility, see Georges Duby, *Qu'est-ce que la société féodale?* (Paris: Flammarion, 2002); Philippe Contamine, *La noblesse au Moyen Âge. XIe-XVe siècles* (Paris: Presses Universitaires de France, 1976); *Nobilitas: Funktion und Repräsentation des Adels in Alteuropa,* ed. Otto Gerhard Oexle and Werner Paravicini (Göttingen: Vandenhoeck & Ruprecht, 1997); Constance Brittain Bouchard, "*Those of My Blood*": *Constructing Noble Families in Medieval Francia* (Philadelphia: University of Pennsylvania Press, 2002); André Devyver, *Le sang épuré: Les préjugés de race chez les gentilshommes français de l'Ancien Régime (1560–1720)* (Bruxelles: Editions de l'université de Bruxelles, 1973). As can be gathered from these works, the nature, meaning, and dating of the nobility in the Middle Ages and beyond is a complex problem the resolution of which has not quite brought about consensus. The lexicon of blood is, however, pervasive in the scholarly literature, even if less compelling in the sources themselves. There is no ground to doubt that that lexicon was adopted between the eleventh and the thirteenth centuries, which makes that development a part of a wider and slow transformation that the Church negotiated, a transformation that was theological and political as well as social and juridical—ultimately, hematological. It is that very transformation or rather the factors that signal toward it that I seek to draw out.

119. Vassalage and adoption should of course be taken into account as well in this context, if and when they are articulated in (or in relation to) a language of blood; see, for example, Dominique Barthélemy, "Kinship," trans. Arthur Goldhammer in *A History of Private Life: Revelations of the Medieval World,* ed. Georges Duby (Cambridge, Mass.: The Belknap Press of Harvard University Press, 1988); Bernhard Jussen, *Spiritual Kinship as Social Practice: Godparenthood and Adoption in the Early Middle Ages,* trans. Pamela Selwyn (Newark, Del.: University of Delaware Press; London and Cranbury, N.J.: Associated University

Presses, 2000); and Kristin Elizabeth Gager, *Blood Ties and Fictive Ties: Adoption and Family Life in Early Modern France* (Princeton, N.J.: Princeton University Press, 1996).

120. Maravall, *The Culture of the Baroque*, 11; James Casey points out how, in the Iberian Peninsula, "the sheer proliferation of these investigations of ancestry, covering both *hidalguía* and *limpieza*, gave a new twist to the old concern with establishing one's background in a racially mixed society" (J. Casey, *Early Modern Spain: A Social History* [London: Routledge, 1999], 141).

121. Benjamin Keen, "The Black Legend Revisited: Assumptions and Realities," *The Hispanic American Historical Review* 49, no. 4 (November 1969): 703.

122. Fuchs, *Mimesis and Empire*, 69, 99.

123. Margaret R. Greer, Walter D. Mignolo, and Maureen Quilligan, "Introduction," in *Rereading the Black Legend: The Discourses of Religious and Racial Difference in the Renaissance Empires*, ed. M.R. Greer, W.D. Mignolo, and M. Quilligan (Chicago: University of Chicago Press, 2007), 1.

124. Bynum, *Wonderful Blood*; and see *Le sang au Moyen Âge*, ed. Marcel Faure (Montpellier: Publications de l'Université Paul-Valéry Montpellier III / Cahiers du C.R.I.S.I.M.A. 4, 1999).

125. In a section entitled "the future" (of Inquisition scholarship), Jean-Pierre Dedieu and René Millar Carvacho assert with a degree of uncertainty that "l'Inquisition sort de son ghetto," that "elle n'est plus une institution marginale de pays excentrés se livrant à des activités en marge du courant principal de l'histoire européenne" (J.-P. Dedieu and R. Millar Carvacho, "Entre histoire et mémoire. L'Inquisition à l'époque moderne: Dix ans d'historiographie," *Annales: Histoire, Sciences Sociales* 57, no. 2 [Mars–Avril 2002]: 368–69).

126. For an elaborate argument on the internal and geographical differences of "the" Spanish Inquisition, see William Monter, *Frontiers of Heresy: The Spanish Inquisition from the Basque Lands to Sicily* (Cambridge: Cambridge University Press, 1990).

127. With regard to the *limpieza de sangre*, I can only attend to some of the vast literature available. As I have already pointed out, however, studies of medieval blood generally leave the *limpieza* out. It is hardly more mentioned in the wider context of "blood studies." Consider, for example, the work of Caroline Walker Bynum, who has otherwise done so much to advance our understanding of blood worship, and to whom I repeatedly return, or the collection of conference papers entitled *Le sang au moyen âge* where no mention is made of the *limpieza*. Or consider the extensive Italian collections of essays edited by Francesco Vattioni in the series "sangue e antropologia," where *limpieza* is equally absent. In fact, I have found only one, and therefore all the more remarkable, if brief, exception. While insisting on the importance of maintaining "an awareness of the vast regional differences in devotional styles and representational habits," Miri Rubin nonetheless alludes to *limpieza* as one of the important sites in the "circulation" of blood throughout Christian Europe in the Middle Ages. "In Spain," she writes, "blood came to be the carrier of identity, an indelible attribute of religious and ethnic adherence, which was supported by the concept of limpid, pure blood (*limpieza de sangre*)" (Miri Rubin, "Blood: Sacrifice and Redemption in Christian Iconography," in *Blood: Art, Power, Politics, and Pathology*, ed. James M. Bradburne [Munich and London: Prestel, 2001], 97–98).

128. Max Sebastián Hering Torres, "'Limpieza de Sangre'¿Racismo en la Edad Moderna?" *Tiempos Modernos* 9 (2003–2004): 1–16; for an excellent historical account, see María Elena Martínez, *Genealogical Fictions: Limpieza de Sangre, Religion, and Gender in Colonial Mexico* (Stanford, Calif.: Stanford University Press, 2008), who traces the Iberian precedents of a practice that persisted through many transformations in the Americas. The date 1449 is often given as the earliest date for the statutes. It has been placed under interrogation by I. S. Révah, on the basis of earlier documents. Arbitrary as it is, the date serves here no more than a rhetorical role in an attempt to explore a larger process of historical transformation and focalization (I. S. Révah, "La controverse sur les statuts de pureté du sang: Un document inédit," *Bulletin hispanique* LXXIII [1971]: 263–306).

129. Yosef Hayim Yerushalmi has perhaps made the most forceful argument for an inclusion of the statutes in the history of modern, biological racism. Yerushalmi goes, however, further, in claiming that within European Christian culture, physical traits were attributed to Jews, traits that were often considered permanent and immutable. He thus proposes that the opposition between religious and secular be reconsidered in the case of the history of racism, as racism coexisted with religion. In this long history, the statutes represent nonetheless a beginning, the coagulation of previous inchoate currents. (Y. H. Yerushalmi, "Assimilation et antisémitisme racial: le modèle ibérique et le modèle allemand," trans. Cyril Aslanoff in Yerushalmi, *Sefardica: Essais sur l'histoire des Juifs, des marranes & des nouveaux-chrétiens d'origine hispano-portugaise* [Paris: Chandeigne, 1998]: 255–92).

130. I quote from what is indisputably one of the most thoughtful and erudite among recent accounts of the events leading to 1492 and to everything that goes under the heading of "the Spanish Inquisition" (David Nirenberg, "Conversion, Sex, and Segregation: Jews and Christians in Medieval Spain," *American Historical Review* 107, no. 4 (October 2002): respectively 1073, 1076, 1077, 1085, 1087–88, 1091).

131. Nirenberg, "Conversion, Sex, and Segregation," 1093.

132. As a more recent article on the *limpieza* impeccably and unhesitatingly puts it: "Racism is a secular phenomenon, contingent on the truth monopoly of the 'scientific experience' and displacing theology as an authoritative power [*Rassismus ist eine säkulare Erscheinung, die sich auf ein Wahrheitsmonopol der 'wissenschaftlichen Erfahrung' beruft und die Theologie als autoritative Kraft verdrängt*]" (Max Sebastián Hering Torres, "'Limpieza de Sangre'—Rassismus in der Vormoderne?" in *Wiener Zeitschrift zur Geschichte der Neuzeit* 3, no. 1 [2003]: 22). Hering Torres makes it clear that what is at stake is the specific concept of "race" one deploys, and he poses the choice in no uncertain terms: either theology or science ("Welche theologischen oder gegebenenfalls naturwissenschaftlichen Ansätze fundierten dieses Denken?" 25). One constructs an absolute break whereby the only connection between religion and science, between *limpieza* and racism, is a "lack of evidence as to historical causality" ("... da bislang keine Hinweise auf historische Kausalketten zwischen 'limpieza'-Doktrin und modernen Rassismus gefunden werden konnten," 35). It should be clear that my purpose is not to adjudicate on the "proper" concept of racism, but only to indicate the way in which the historical object "limpieza," whether included or excluded in the history of racism, is constituted as *exception* (excluded or included).

133. Ann Laura Stoler, *Race and the Education of Desire: Foucault's* History of Sexuality *and the Colonial Order of Things* (Durham, N.C., and London: Duke University Press, 1995), 37, n. 51.

134. Stoler, *Race*, 37, quoting Collette Guillaumin.

135. Stoler, *Race*, 41, 50.

136. Stoler, *Race*, 51–52, quoting Deborah Root and Verena Stolcke; emphasis added.

137. Compare Charles Amiel's argument that "le sang pur, en Espagne, n'est pas le 'sang bleu'—à la différence de l'Ancien Régime français, où le 'sang épuré' sera l'apanage de la noblesse" (C. Amiel, "La 'pureté de sang' en Espagne," *Etudes inter-ethniques* 6 [1983]: 29). Amiel does acknowledge that the Toledo statutes were established "en pleine rébellion populaire armée contre l'autorité royale" (30), later affirming that the people made "de la pureté du sang sa noblesse à lui" (41). Amiel even describes the stance of the opposition to the statutes as articulated around the question of nobility (33) and goes on to address the matter of the *libros verdes*, documenting the "impurity" of the nobility's blood due to alliances with Jews and/or *conversos*. Yet, the division between the theological and the political (and by extension between religion and race) is complete: "L'argumentation s'est écartée du débat théologique ou juridique pour dégénérer en une polémique antisémite grossière" (32). Toward his conclusion, it is the temporal division between religion and race, origin and history, that is asserted: "L'exclusion a pu être dictée au début par un zèle religieux . . . Puis, étant donné la dilution de la judéité et l'effacement du judaïsme, ce racisme à motivation religieuse a été relayé par un racisme à fondement biologique" (40). Finally, the uncertainty as to this temporality cannot cancel the fundamental analytical distinction *as* conjunction, "la conjonction de ces racismes religieux, biologique et classiste—successifs ou simultanés" (41). For a rare exception to this narrative, see Adeline Rucquoi, "Etre noble en Espagne aux XIVe-XVIe siècles," in *Nobilitas: Funktion und Repräsentation des Adels in Alteuropa*, ed. Otto Gerhard Oexle and Werner Paravicini (Göttingen: Vandenhoek & Ruprecht, 1997), 273–98. Rucquoi not only links the discourse of the nobility's blood to the *limpieza* but also argues for the link, in blood discourse, between Spanish and French nobility (the same French nobility that is otherwise credited with having initiated a blood-based, racial and racist "class" discourse. In Spain, Rucquoi writes, "noblesse et pureté de sang vont donc aussi de pair" (296). Rucquoi explicitly accounts for the nobility's concern with blood by way of the *conversos* (as well as of the Jews and the blood of Christ). Although lineage was perhaps already understood in blood terms, the governing logic to the nobility's constitution is never the logic of blood, prior, that is, to the fourteenth and fifteenth centuries. It is only henceforth that one can speak of a new concept of nobility in which antiquity itself is being refigured in order to assert a "natural" rather than "civil" right of nobility. Interestingly enough, Rucquoi also argues that this change will lead to an increasing confusion between "theological nobility" and "political nobility." Being noble and being Christian will come to mean the very same thing (288ff.).

138. Benedict Anderson, *Imagined Communities: Reflections on the Origin and Spread of Nationalism* (London and New York: Verso, 1991), 149. One should perhaps underscore the fact that historians of racism have been less eager to protest the lack of rigor or the "anachronism" of a claim that locates a nonscientific racism in sixteenth-century France. On

another note, the most puzzling assertion that a racial concern with purity of blood began with the aristocracy may have been made by the foremost expert on the Spanish Inquisition, Henry Kamen himself. In a chapter on "the ruling elite" of early modern Europe, Kamen asserts that the role of the state in creating nobles and "gentlemen" provoked a defensive reaction on the part of the older nobility. By the sixteenth century, "a number of writers in Flanders, France and Italy [*sic*—not in Spain!] reacted against the parvenus and reaffirmed that the hereditary elite were the true aristocrats." This and apparently nothing else but "this created a new emphasis, which was to last into the eighteenth century, on origins and 'race.' Nobility could only be transmitted by heredity: nobility, it has been commented, was seminal fluid." I could not find in this book any reference to the Statutes on the Purity of Blood (Henry Kamen, *Early Modern European Society* [London and New York: Routledge, 2000], 71; incidentally, Kamen refers his readers to the same French scholars whom Foucault may have read, and who explicitly informed Stoler's work [252, n. 3]). I should mention that the book is a revised version of Kamen's earlier work, entitled *The Iron Century*. In this 1971 book, Kamen did not yet think that there was anything new about the assertion of "good lineage." This was rather a "traditionalist position." What was new was the approach of the parvenus. Although we get no closer to "religion" or to the New Christians, we may here recognize that both "Old" and "New" are quite novel, indeed, radically novel figurations (Henry Kamen, *The Iron Century: Social Change in Europe, 1550–1660* [New York: Praeger Publishers, 1971], 130). For different arguments on the "invention of the nobility," including a new emphasis on descent (in any case, a development contemporary with the Statutes on the Purity of Blood), see Joseph Morsel, "Inventing a Social Category: The Sociogenesis of the Nobility at the End of the Middle Ages," in *Ordering Medieval Society: Perspectives on Intellectual and Practical Modes of Shaping Social Relations*, ed. Bernhard Jussen, (Philadelphia: University of Pennsylvania Press, 2001), 200–240; and see also *La noblesse au moyen âge*, ed. Philippe Contamine (Paris: Presses Universitaires de France, 1976). As Philippe Contamine shows in his introduction, the scarce evidence hardly allows sustaining Marc Bloch's assertion regarding a transmission of nobility by way of blood (19–21). Worse, the evidence that is adduced as to the importance of genealogy is unconvincing because no reference to blood is found in it (28).

139. Giorgio Agamben, *Sovereign Power and Bare Life*, trans. Daniel Heller-Roazen (Stanford, Calif.: Stanford University Press, 1998], 129). Agamben is right in directing us toward a history of blood in Roman culture and in Roman law, but the assertion that these two juridical categories were part of the Roman legal apparatus is close to baseless. What does appear, at any rate, is difficult to compare or to consider as antecedent. Thus, Adolf Berger, in his *Encyclopedic Dictionary of Roman Law*, does include entries for both *ius sanguinis* and *ius solis*. The first, found in the Justinian corpus, is about inheritance between father and son and is said to be impervious to civil law. The second (*ius solis*) has to do with the legal status of a piece of land (A. Berger, *Encyclopedic Dictionary of Roman Law* [Philadelphia: American Philosophical Society, 1953], 533). I thank Christophe Guilmoto and Christopher S. Mackay for their help in clarifying this matter.

140. Although he does not use the phrase "theologico-political," Kamen provides a compelling description of the way the Spanish Inquisition was of a "peculiar dual nature," indeed, quite

precisely a theologico-political institution. A constant site of tension between jurisdictions and powers, the Inquisition "represented both pope and king." In 1503, Queen Isabella "confirmed the dual jurisdiction of the Holy Office, saying that 'the one jurisdiction aids and complements the other, so that justice may be done in the service of God'" (Kamen, *The Spanish Inquisition*, 164–65).

141. Sicroff, *Les controverses*, 28.

142. This "secularizing" bias regarding racism is shared by an overwhelming number of scholars. Etienne Balibar, for example, who underscores the theological debts of the idea of the nation, nonetheless writes that "l'antijudaïsme théologique a été transposé en exclusion généalogique fondée sur la 'pureté du sang'" (E. Balibar and Immanuel Wallerstein, *Race, Nation, Classe: Les identités ambiguës* [Paris: La découverte, 1997], 75). Later, and following the analyses of Léon Poliakov, it is a social and political unification that the statute will be said to serve (278). And see also David Nirenberg, "Conversion, Sex, and Segregation: Jews and Christians in Medieval Spain," *American Historical Review* 107, no. 4 [October 2002]: 1066). Benzion Netanyahu, who considers "religious or spiritual" issues to be "supportive factors" rather than "determining" ones, insists on the racism of the Inquisition, but hardly sees in it a beginning, of course, as anti-Semitism is simply perennial (B. Netanyahu, *The Origins of the Inquisition in Fifteenth-Century Spain* [New York: New York Review of Books, 2001], 75). Typical of Netanyahu's perspective is the assertion that "so much stress has been laid by most historians on religion as the prime cause" for the opposition of Spanish cities to their Jews that the record needs to be corrected (this will not prevent him elsewhere to argue that rabbinic rulings alone will enable us to decide whether *conversos* were, in fact, Jews as the Inquisition claimed) (82). Netanyahu refers to the notion of purity of blood as a case of "discrimination against the converts on purely [*sic*] racial grounds" (272). In 1449, he writes further, "the issue of Marranism as a question of race exploded in the midst of a political storm" (281). In spite of all evidence against this clarity, Netanyahu sees definite boundaries between religion, politics, and the social (the latter being, throughout, the main and "determining" factor for an understanding of the Inquisition. Not quite a Marxist, Netanyahu would nonetheless fit quite well in the tradition of "vulgar" Marxist historians). Commenting on the first Statutes on the Purity of Blood, he writes that "just as in the first stage of the rebellion the persecution of the conversos had assumed a new form when it passed from political to religious lines, it now changed its form again when it passed from religious to social lines" (327). Finally, Jerome Friedman, who rightly underscores the importance of looking past the Reformation for a thorough analysis of modern racism, downplays the religious dimension of the purity of blood statutes. These were, in fact, formulated within an atmosphere of "religious fanaticism," but they provided "the foundation for a secular, biological conception of Jews." Overall, it is as if religion— consistently construed as an earlier, distinct, and restricted domain—"hardly ever played a role at all" (Jerome Friedman, "Jewish Conversion, the Spanish Pure Blood Laws and Reformation: A Revisionist View of Racial and Religious Antisemitism," *The Sixteenth Century Journal* 18, no. 1 [Spring 1987]: 26–27). The opposition between religion and race, between religious motives and circumstances and social ones, and, finally, between religion and politics governs the entirety of the scholarship I am aware of concerning the

limpieza de sangre (I began to articulate this argument in broader terms in my *Semites: Race, Religion, Literature* [Stanford, Calif.: Stanford University Press, 2008]).

143. For an exemplary and related interrogation of the division between religion and politics in early modern times, see Ines G. Zupanov, *Disputed Mission: Jesuit Experiments and Brahmanical Knowledge in Seventeenth-Century India* (New Delhi: Oxford University Press, 2001). Zupanov reminds us that the history of colonialism is the history of Christian Europe—and therefore that the history of racism is always already theological. "The separation of the political and the religious spheres initiated the reorganization of the medieval epistemic grid encompassing India" (100), she writes, and further shows how a Jesuit missionary could approach and document Hindu culture by way of a "distinction between the civil and the religious" (98) and finally combine "the rhetoric and textual authority usually associated with the Indianist/Orientalist disciplines which were to emerge in the 18th century" (127–28). Zupanov thus begins "to trace the tangled lineage of the colonial and post-colonial discursive practices" and attempts "to connect the early Jesuit controversy between Nobili and Fernandes [to whom Zupanov's book is dedicated— G.A.] to the constitution of European 'scientific' discourses" (143). Rather than think of two epochs of Western cultural history (the Middle Ages, early modern and modern discipline and knowledge) "as mutually disjointed and discontinuous constellations of knowledge," she proposes to consider "how larger, seemingly discrete discourses depended on innumerable local negotiations and dialogues and evolved through ruptures, temporary redefinition, dissociation, adaptation, imposed silences, and oblivion" (144–45).

144. Henry Kamen has argued that the Inquisition and, more importantly for us here, the Statutes on the Purity of Blood were perhaps less important, had less effect on the masses than centuries of mythologization repeatedly suggested. If anything, Kamen writes, "the central issue was power: race or religion was secondary" (H. Kamen, "Limpieza and the Ghost of Americo Castro: Racism as a Tool of Literary Analysis," in *Hispanic Review* 64, no. 1 [Winter 1996]: 20). Arguing from a different perspective, Linda Martz explores the fact that the statutes, even when accepted by institutions, were rarely implemented (L. Martz, "Implementation of Pure-Blood Statutes in Sixteenth-Century Toledo," in *Iberia and Beyond: Hispanic Jews Between Cultures*, ed. Bernard Cooperman [Newark: University of Delaware Press, 1998], 245–71). The question, it seems to me, is not whether the Inquisition directly affected a massive amount of people in their daily life but rather whether it participated in reshaping the way in which they related to each other and how; whether it refigured the communities to which they saw themselves as belonging. Kamen is of course well aware of the dynamics of "social disciplining" deployed by the Inquisition (of which denunciation was a major mechanism) (see H. Kamen, *The Spanish Inquisition: A Historical Revision* [New Haven, Conn.: Yale University Press, 1997], 176ff., 239ff.); and see *Inquisition et pouvoir*, ed. Gabriel Audisio (Aix-en-Provence: Publications de l'université de Provence, 2004).

145. Geoffrey Galt Harpham made a compelling argument regarding the modernity of the Inquisition by pointing out the congruences between Inquisition and Enlightenment (G. G. Harpham, "So . . . What *Is* Enlightenment? An Inquisition into Modernity," *Critical Inquiry* 20 [Spring 1994]: 524–56); more recently, Nathan Wachtel made a parallel claim,

with the significant difference that the "modernity of the Inquisition" would be partial. It is not modernity at large that it announces, but within it the rise of totalitarian regimes (N. Wachtel, *La logique des bûchers* [Paris: Seuil, 2009]).

146. As Deborah Root puts it, "the inquisitorial machine" extended "policing to the entire community" and surveillance "was transformed into internal or self-policing by all Christians" (D. Root, "Speaking Christian: Orthodoxy and Difference in Sixteenth-Century Spain," *Representations* 23 [Summer 1988]: 129). In his discussion of religious discipline and the modern state, however, Gorski typically ignores Spain and Catholicism (as well as, strangely enough, England). For a partial corrective, see Henry Kamen's discussion of "social discipline and marginality" in his *Early Modern European Society* (but the whole book is relevant to the issue), and see William V. Hudon, "Religion and Society in Early Modern Italy: Old Questions, New Insights," *American Historical Review* 101, no. 3 (June 1996): 783–804, and see also John O'Malley, *Trent and All That: Renaming Catholicism in the Early Modern Era* (Cambridge, Mass.: Harvard University Press, 2000); also relevant, although it too ignores Spain, is R. Po-Chia Hsia, *Social Discipline in the Reformation: Central Europe 1550–1750* (London and New York: Routledge, 1989). Hsia, an expert on the blood libel, does refer to the importance of a "blood cult" throughout Europe but does not invoke ritual murder here, nor, when he does, does he recall the purity of blood issue (see R. Po-Chia Hsia, *Trent 1475: Stories of a Ritual Murder Trial* [New Haven, Conn.: Yale University Press, 1991]). Max Weinreich discusses "political biology" in the Nazi context in his *Hitler's Professors: The Part of Scholarship in Germany's Crimes Against the Jewish People* (New Haven, Conn.: Yale University Press, 1999), 27ff.

147. My understanding of Walter Benjamin's statement, as of much else in this chapter, is indebted to Amnon Raz-Krakotzkin, whose work on historiography as a theologico-political question has long been guided by Benjamin's historical theses and a theorization of the exception. It should be noted, in this context, that the exceptionalism of Spain is formally and historically constituted along the same lines as the hermetic limits of modern racism, the singularity of Nazi Germany, and, finally, the exceptionalism of Jewish victimhood. Dynamic (not to say, dishonest) conceptions of "contextualization" serve in different ways as one "contextualizes" the Holocaust as a Jewish event by decontextualizing it from its other victims. Alternatively, one contextualizes Nazi Germany in the singular history of blood racialism—a history in which Spain and Germany would be the two exceptional subjects—and does so while decontextualizing these two "countries" from the history of Christian Europe (not to mention, the history of colonialism and its genocides).

148. The theoretical model on these issues I learn from Amos Funkenstein, who writes of a deeply related matter that "the separation of science from religion may have been as often demanded as it was violated" (A. Funkenstein, *Theology and the Scientific Imagination* [Princeton, N.J.: Princeton University Press, 1986], 9). "Do the categories of continuity and change still have a heuristic value?" Funkenstein asks, answering that "the 'new' often consists not in the invention of new categories or new figures of thought, but rather in a surprising employment of existing ones" (14); it is thus often the case that "the transition from the old to the new theory was a case of radicalization of already present possibilities of interpretation" (18). Arguing that, temporarily at least, science *became* theology, taking

over specific objects of inquiry that had earlier been reserved for professional theologians, Funkenstein refers to secularization as a kind of popularization, even a democratization: "theological discussions were carried on by laymen" (4) at a time when one witnessed a "rising number of educated laymen, as a reading public, as authors, and as teachers. . . . Theology became 'secularized' in many parts of Europe in the original sense of the word: appropriated by laymen" (5). As we will see, such popularization, what one could call the popularization of blood (the appropriation of a theology and cult of blood by laymen, as well as the emergence of a notion of community—the people—*as* blood) was increasingly taking over medieval consciousness, doctrine, and science. Be it the church, a class, or a nation, blood became the community, and the community became blood. While working on these issues, I have also found useful Balibar's notion of a "historical articulation," operative most significantly, between racism and nationalism. Balibar writes of the necessary relation that links racism to nationalism, both of which contribute to the production of "fictitious ethnicity." The difference between nationalism and racism is *necessary* to both. Each is contingent on the other in order to function. They can be distinguished, in other words, but not separated. At least not at this historical juncture. Historical markings notwithstanding, I am attempting to make a similar argument as to the relations of race and religion (E. Balibar, "Racisme et nationalisme," in E. Balibar and I. Wallerstein, *Race, Nation, Classe: Les identités ambiguës* [Paris: La découverte, 1997], 71–72).

149. Following again the work of Raz-Krakotzkin on Christian and Jewish censorship in the sixteenth century, I have begun to argue elsewhere that race and religion (as the contentious terms we know them to be in modernity) emerge at the same time rather than in temporal succession (A. Raz-Krakotzkin, *The Censor, the Editor, and the Text: The Catholic Church and the Shaping of the Jewish Canon in the Sixteenth Century*, trans. Jackie Feldman [Philadelphia: University of Pennsylvania Press, 2007]). Whatever religion "was" (if it was), what has come to be called "religion" is co-extensive with what has come to be called "race" (see Anidjar, *Semites*, esp. chap. 1). There is, however, an empirical dimension to my assertion that religion is contemporary with race, one that should have drawn more attention. Henry Kamen asserts that in sixteenth-century Spain, the problem was not whether "religion" had been perverted, but whether Christianity had come into existence at all prior to that time, prior that is to the colonization of the New World. Rather, "in many parts of Spain it could be doubted whether there was any true religion at all. . . . Over much of Spain Christianity was still only a veneer" (Henry Kamen, *The Spanish Inquisition*, 255–56). In a striking testimony, a Jesuit reports about certain villagers that "many live in caves, without priests or sacraments; so ignorant that some cannot make the sign of the cross; in their dress and way of life very like Indians" (quoted in Kamen, 258). Hence, during the sixteenth and seventeenth centuries, the Holy Office "dedicated itself in great measure to disciplining the Old Christian population" (260). As I am arguing, it is these "Old Christians" that are, in fact, the paradigmatic *New* Christians.

150. Tomás Cerdán de Tallada, for instance, makes quite clear that this spiritual union is produced from above. Much as Christ had "brought together Jew and Gentile in a single faith," he it is as well "who unites his followers in a single Body" (cf. Ronald W. Truman,

Spanish Treatises on Government, Society, and Religion in the Time of Philip II: The 'de regimine principium' and Associated Traditions [Leiden: Brill, 1949], 190 and 190, n. 2). In his 1449 bull, Pope Nicolas V had already written the following: "Sicut enim corpus unum est et membra multa habet, omnia autem membra corporis cum sint multa, unum tamen corpus sunt, ita et spiritus" (the text of this bull is reproduced in V. Beltrán de Heredia, "Las bulas de Nicolás V acerca de los conversos de Castilla," *Sefarad* XXI, no. 1 [1961]: 41).

151. And compare Henri de Lubac's formulation, regarding the earlier comprehension of the Eucharist as a ritual in which operation and action, indeed "confection," are primary (H. de Lubac, *Corpus mysticum*, 47–66, and see also 70 and 98; and see de Certeau, *Fable mystique*, 112 and 112, n. 15). The ritual is moreover temporally oriented, toward both past and, more importantly for us here, future: it is past insofar as it recalled the Passion of Christ and the two Testaments; it announces the future, as the ritual, as well as the mass in its entirety, constitutes a promise and an anticipation, a figure for a future yet to come. The Eucharist, then, "a pour fin de nous conduire 'ad unitatis societatem,'" "l'achèvement futur du grand Corps" (H. de Lubac, *Corpus mysticum*, 81). There is never any doubt that unity is achieved rather than given, produced rather than assumed. *Through* the Eucharist then, and necessarily dependent upon it, the church is made one, and its members are joined (100, 112). "L'Eucharistie *fait* l'Église" (104; emphasis in original).

152. Michel de Certeau locates in the thirteenth century a shift whereby "la réforme *in capite* (à la tête)" is followed by "une réforme *in membris*, une thérapeutique des 'membres'" (de Certeau, *Fable mystique*, 115). The vacuum that ensues announces the final decapitation. In other words, the empty seat is made possible because the sovereign is no longer the head. Sovereignty becomes the heart, as we shall see.

153. Claude Lefort, *Democracy and Political Theory*, trans. David Macey (Cambridge: Polity, 1988), 232; as Lefort explains, "the body of the king . . . also represents its head" (251). Indeed, "whilst a single body is defined both as the body of a person and as the body of a community, the head remains the symbol of a transcendence that can never be effaced" (253; translation modified).

154. Lefort, *Democracy*, 239; Lefort goes on to quote Michelet, who explains that blood had to remain invisible because it signified eternal life: "If, when that head was struck, even a single drop of blood flowed, that was proof of life; people began to believe once more that it was a living head; royalty had come back to life" (246).

155. On this meeting, see Netanyahu, *Origins*, 324ff. and 351ff. For the text of the statutes, from which I quote here, see Eloy Benito Ruano, *Toledo en el siglo XV: Vida política* (Madrid: Consejo Superior de Investigaciones Científicas, 1961), 191–96.

156. "After all, the very claim of the Church to be a new dispensation introduced a shift of values both in the classical world and among the converted Germanic tribes of the Middle Ages. 'New' was to both mentalities a suspicious attribute: only the old was a mark of quality and authenticity. The classical political term for a dangerous revolutionary was *homo rerum novarum cupidus*; in the legal consciousness of the early Middle Ages, only old law (*altes Recht*) was good law (*gutes Recht*), and Pope Gregory VII shocked his imperial adversaries when he claimed his right to establish new laws (*novas leges condere*)" (Amos Funkenstein, *Perceptions of Jewish History* [Berkeley: University of California Press, 1993], 317). The

view that Spain was the land of the elect, that Spaniards are the *newly* chosen people while insisting on its antiquity, can be compared to England's parallel claim to being the "New Israel" as part of the Christian renewal then taking place (on Spain as the chosen people, see *Les problèmes de l'exclusion en Espagne (XVIe-XVII2 siècles): Idéologie et discours*, ed. Augustin Redondo [Paris: La Sorbonne, 1983], 17ff.).

157. B. Netanyahu, *Origins*, 382.

158. The cannibalistic dimension of the Eucharist, as well as the modes of identification it sustained (carried, for example, by incorporation, figurative and material); the rich web of gratification and frustration generated by the interruption of the drinking of the wine in the sacrament – all have received wide attention at the hands of philosophers (Hamacher, by way of Hegel), historians (Miri Rubin), psychoanalysts (Julia Kristeva), anthropologists (Alan Dundes), and cultural critics (Uli Linke). I return to it in chap. 5, "Bleeding and Melancholia."

159. "The Church as the mystical body of Christ—and that means: Christian society as composed of all the faithful, past, future, and present, actual and potential—might appear to the historian so typically mediaeval a concept, and one so traditional, that he would easily be inclined to forget how relatively new that notion was when Boniface VIII [1235–1303] probed its strength and efficiency by using it as a weapon ... the concept of the Church as *corpus Christi*, of course, goes back to St. Paul; but the term *corpus mysticum* has no biblical tradition and is less ancient than might be expected. It first came into prominence in Carolingian times and gained some importance in the course of the controversy about the Eucharist" (Kantorowicz, *The King's Two Bodies*, 195ff.). This controversy, which took place in the ninth century and continued, if in different forms, all the way to the fourteenth, is traced and documented in detail in Miri Rubin, *Corpus Christi*. Rubin demonstrates the extensive dissemination of blood and blood imagery throughout Western Christendom, as well as the increased association of the Jews with the Eucharist (as witnesses or desecrators and symbolic and not so symbolic murderers) in medieval narratives, representations, and rumorological circles. It should be noted again that, keeping with a long historiographical tradition, Rubin has very little to say specifically about Spain, which is not to say, of course, that her descriptions do not correspond to Iberian society, as can be inferred from numerous sources. One illustration among many: The Archbishop of Toledo at the time the statutes were established was building a major argument on the case of ritual murder by Jews upon the *Niño de la Guardia*, rumors about whom had been widely circulating for fifty years prior to 1449 (cf. Sicroff, *Les controverses*, 107, cf. also 168–69). The feast of *Corpus Christi*, "the first time that a universal feast was founded by a pope," was recognized in 1264, although the success of its spread was not finalized until the fourteenth century (Rubin, *Corpus Christi*, 176, 181). For a recent exemplary attempt to rethink early modern Catholicism while massively ignoring Spain, see John W. O'Malley, *Trent and All That: Renaming Catholicism in the Early Modern Era* (Cambridge, Mass.: Harvard University Press, 2000). The insularity of national boundaries in the scholarly discussion of the Inquisition was recently lamented by Jean-Pierre Dedieu and René Millar Carvacho, "Entre histoire et mémoire: L'inquisition à l'époque moderne: dix ans d'historiographie," in *Annales: Histoire, Science sociales* 57, no. 2 (Mars–Avril 2002): 349–72.

160. Miri Rubin explains that "the pain of the Passion, the most exalted pain, was powerfully linked to the spilling and loss of blood. And the blood-merchants *par excellence*, both past and present, were the Jews. They were said to drain the bodies of little boys and girls whom they killed (sometimes in crucifixion, sometimes also circumcised), using every possible cut and incision to drain the blood. This blood was said to be needed for a variety of applications; medical, cosmetic, ritual and magical. . . . Blood and body parts were part of a vast economy of salvation, a sort of symbolic cannibalism between generations which died for each other, and who all hoped to be saved through a single exemplary immolation" (Miri Rubin, "The Person in the Form: Medieval Challenges to Bodily 'Order,'" in *Framing Medieval Bodies*, ed. Sarah Kay and Miri Rubin [Manchester: Manchester University Press, 1994], 114–15). There is extensive scholarship on all these "attributes" of the Jews, their dissemination and effects, and their historicity. Most of the attention has been granted to the "blood libel," that is, accusations of ritual murder perpetrated by Jews on the body of Christians, children or adults (on which see, for example, R. Po-chia Hsia, *The Myth of Ritual Murder* [New Haven, Conn.: Yale University Press, 1988]). One should also mention legends according to which Jews were sprayed with Jesus' own blood at the crucifixion, that they suffer from blood flux and menstruate, that Jewish children are born with the right hand full of blood, and so forth (Josette Riandiere la Roche, "Du discours d'exclusion des Juifs: Antijudaïsme ou antisémitisme?" in *Les problèmes de l'exclusion en Espagne (XVIe-XVIIe siècles): Idéologie et discours* [Paris: Sorbonne, 1983], 64).

161. Lee Palmer Wandel, *The Eucharist in the Reformation: Incarnation and Liturgy* (Cambridge: Cambridge University Press, 2006), 46.

162. As one instance among many, Joseph Ziegler attends to medieval medicine and to statements that, not necessarily in accordance with either Aristotle or Galen, much less church doctrine, nevertheless assert an undeniable consensus on the blood of Christ that "seed was involved in the Virgin's conception—namely, her own. As the factor responsible for the formation of the body of Christ it was the purest of its kind, since it originated in her blood which is the purest and most essential of all humors in any living creature" (J. Ziegler, *Medicine and Religion*, 173).

163. As Piero Camporesi writes, "it is in this society, in which blood is thick with magical significations, mystical claims, pharmacological prodigies, alchemical dreams (the artificial man, the *homunculus*, is born of putrefied sperm, and feeds on blood) that the torments of Christ, along with the cult of his body and blood, becomes a collective *passio*—all but an epidemic of morbidity, a murky disease of the soul (*animi passiones* were the imbalances and disturbances of the humoral equilibrium) mirroring the simultaneous horror of and attraction for the wanton destruction of life symbolized in the Blood that was spilled by the rejection perpetrated by the human being upon the Creator of all that lives and moves, through the refusal to look for one's identity in the blood of the Man-God" (Camporesi, *Juice of Life*, 54). It is remarkable that Camporesi reads this *passio* less as a reservoir of hatred directed at enemies of Christ, but rather as "a sullen, unsatisfied desire for suicide, for a rejection of life, creation, and love" (55)—passion for blood as a site and sign of self-hatred.

164. Even the more sophisticated discussions of the *limpieza de sangre* can only hold the distinction between lineage and blood—"material" or "metaphorical"—for so long (see,

e.g., Michel Jonin, "De la pureté de foi vers la pureté de sang. Les ambiguités orthodoxes d'un plaidoyer *pro converso*," in *L'hérédité entre Moyen Âge et Époque moderne. Perspectives historiques*, ed. Maaike van der Lugt and Charles de Miramon [Firenze: Sismel—Edizioni del Galluzzo, 2008], 83–102).

165. David Nirenberg, "Conversion, Sex, and Segregation," 1092. Nirenberg phrases the novelty as moving from sex to reproduction ("the worries of St. Vincent's generation [Vicente Ferrer, a major and active missionary of the fourteenth century] were sexual, but they had little to do with reproduction, and even less to do with race," 1091). Doing so, however, he leaves unproblematized the equation of lineage with blood. Nirenberg thus refers quite matter of factly to the theological scandal that articulates itself with the statutes, treating it as a marginal oddity that would later grow. "Some," he writes, "went so far as to see this insincerity [of the *conversos*] as a product of nature. Baptism could not alter the fact that the Jews' blood was corrupted by millennia of mixture and debasement, indelibly saturated with a hatred of everything Christian. Hence purity of blood laws were needed to bar the descendants of converts from any position of power or privilege, and 'natural Christians'" (1078). Aside from his reinscription of "nature" where one should see theology (Nirenberg argues for an understanding based on a kind of pre-religious, "social" logic; he also insists on "translating" the phrase "Old Christian" into "Natural Christian"), Nirenberg appears to have forgotten that by 1391 it was Western Christendom as a whole (rather than some irrational Spaniards) that, in practices of and related to the Eucharist, had come to consider Christian blood to be substantially distinct from Jewish blood, while the former was deemed vulnerable to the latter.

166. Sicroff, *Les controverses*, 31.

167. Juan Arce de Otalora, *De nobilitate et immunitatis Hispaniae*, quoted in Henry Méchoulan, *Le sang de l'autre ou l'honneur de Dieu: Indiens, juifs et morisques au Siècle d'Or* (Paris: Fayard, 1979), 126. Méchoulan explains that the "infection" will be transmitted to other bodily fluids such as sperm and milk. Hence, he documents a number of cases in which the lineage of wet nurses was scrutinized in order to establish their "purity of blood" and, by extension, of breast milk (11, 141). Méchoulan relates the Spanish obsession with the purity of blood not to the European-wide embrace of the Eucharist but to the specific devotion to Mary and to the Immaculate Conception widely found in the Iberian Peninsula (140). Holding here to a no less rigorous notion of Spanish exceptionalism, Marc Shell does see a link with Christ and his blood, but it is one he attributes to the "old law code" of "Gothic Christians" and to the "old Arian heresy" according to which "kinship in Christ does not fully transcend consanguinity" and "spiritual religion is not all that matters: blood counts" (Marc Shell, *Children of the Earth: Literature, Politics, and Nationhood* [New York and Oxford: Oxford University Press, 1993], 27). Shell uniquely recognizes the role of Christianity in the constitution of community as a community of kin—the entire book is an argument against its pervasiveness and dangerous consequences—but he considers the allegiance to blood to be distinct and, apparently, exceptional (on the same page, Shell's only illustrations of this literal concern for blood are Spain, an unidentified "upper class" in the eighteenth century, Nazi Germany, and fascist Italy and Spain). In this specific context, by relegating the Eucharist to no more than a historical footnote, Shell misses what should have become, it seems to me, an essential part of his argument (166–67, 197).

168. I. S. Révah writes of "le caractère foncièrement antichrétien des statuts de pureté du sang," thus buttressing their secular dimension, but missing their novel theological ground (Révah, "La controverse," 265). Compare Sicroff for a less oppositional rhetoric of transformation that theological discourse underwent (Sicroff, *Les controverses*, 38). The theological paradox was that given the forced nature of most conversions, one could have dismissed the validity of baptism in this case (see Josette Riandiere la Roche, "Du discours d'exclusion des Juifs: Antijudaïsme ou antisémitisme?" in *Les problèmes de l'exclusion en Espagne (XVIe-XVIIe siècles): Idéologie et discours* [Paris: Sorbonne, 1983]). Henry Kamen, however, explains that "the standard reply" to the argument on the lack of efficacy of the sacraments was simple. "The mere fact that the Jews had *chosen* baptism as an alternative to death or exile meant that they had exercised the right of free choice: there was therefore no compulsion, and the sacrament was valid" (H. Kamen, *The Spanish Inquisition: A Historical Revision* [New Haven, Conn.: Yale University Press, 1997], 70; and see also Sicroff, *Les controverses*, 38). The claim regarding impure, Jewish blood entailed, again, a conception that saw in it the interruption of the cleansing, purifying power of baptismal waters.

169. Edward Peters, *Inquisition* (New York: Free Press, 1988), 84–85.

170. Maravall, *Culture of the Baroque*, 133.

171. Kamen, *The Spanish Inquisition*, 254.

172. Miriam Bodian, *Hebrews of the Portuguese Nation: Conversos and Community in Early Modern Amsterdam* (Bloomington: Indiana University Press, 1997), 86.

173. Yosef Kaplan, "The Self-Definition of the Sephardic Jews of Western Europe and Their Relation to the Alien and the Stranger," in *Crisis and Creativity in the Sephardic World 1391–1648*, ed. Benjamin R. Gampel (New York: Columbia University Press, 1997), 125.

174. Isaac Cardoso, *Las Excelencias de los Hebreos,* quoted in Yosef Kaplan, "Political Concepts in the World of the Portuguese Jews of Amsterdam during the Seventeenth Century: The Problem of Exclusion and the Boundaries of Self-Identity," in *Menasseh Ben Israel and His World*, ed. Yosef Kaplan et al. (Leiden: E.J. Brill, 1989), 53; and see also Yosef Kaplan, *An Alternative Path to Modernity: The Sephardi Diaspora in Western Europe* (Leiden: E.J. Brill, 2000), for more discussion of these issues.

175. Menasseh ben Israel, *Esperanza de Israel*, quoted in Kaplan, "Self-Definition," 128.

176. Gordon Weiner argues that "there emerged such a level of hostility on the part of wealthy Sephardic Jews towards their poorer Ashkenazic brethren in the Northern European urban centers that the term 'Jewish anti-Semitism' is not an overstatement" (G. M. Weiner, "Sephardic Philo- and Anti-Semitism in the Early Modern Era: The Jewish Adoption of Christian Attitudes," in *Jewish Christians and Christian Jews: From the Renaissance to the Enlightenment*, ed. Richard H. Popkin and Gordon M. Weiner (Dordrecht: Kluwer, 1994), 189.

177. Sicroff, *Les controverses,* 73, n. 42.

178. Sicroff, *Les controverses*, 75.

179. Uli Linke, *Blood and Nation: The European Aesthetics of Race* (Philadelphia: University of Pennsylvania Press, 1999), 133.

180. Miri Rubin, *Gentile Tales: The Narrative Assault on Late Medieval Jews* (New Haven, Conn.: Yale University Press, 1999), 27–28; the chapter from which I quote is entitled "From Jewish Boy to Bleeding Host."

181. Caroline Walker Bynum, "The Blood of Christ in the Later Middle Ages," *Church History* 71, no. 4 (December 2002): 688. Bynum's work, impressive as it is, is also a remarkable example of the disciplinary borders isolating Spain from the rest of Europe. Hence, underscoring the dissolving and fragmenting aspects of blood symbolism in Christian Europe and focusing most specifically on Germany, France, and England, Bynum simply ignores the relevance of Spain for a thinking of "blood cult," never mentioning the peculiar chapter in the history of blood that occupies us here. Ironically, Bynum does recall, in a footnote, that "blood can, of course, have denotations of community, especially in a family or racial sense . . ." (708, n. 77). The reader who may expect a reference to what some have called "the birth of modern racism" (namely, medieval Spain) will be disappointed. Bynum continues: ". . . as the rhetoric of National Socialism makes clear."

182. A. Sicroff, *Les controverses*, 41.

183. "Dicit esse aliqua que christus non posset purgare suo sanguine et tam profunas scelerum suorum pristinorum uniri corporibus ac animis cicatrices, ut medicina illius attenuari nequeant. Quid aliud agit nisi ut christus frustra mortuus sit" (*Defensorium*, quoted in Sicroff, 51, n. 92). Transubstantiation of the infinite into the finite, the Eucharist was, by definition, if one may put it that way, finite. Hence its vulnerability (and sacrificability—for nothing—not just its sacredness), which, along with that of the body of Christ and of the Christian (child), was constantly recalled and replayed in Christian communities by way of accusations of desecration and ritual murder, most often attributed to Jews (but also to women, criminals, and heretics). In the debates surrounding the Statutes on the Purity of Blood, the accusation was made on both sides that the opponent was "dividing" the body of Christ and the church (cf., for example, Alonso de Oropesa's *Lunem ad revelationem gentium*, discussed in Sicroff, *Les controverses*, 72 and 176).

184. Henry Kamen, *The Spanish Inquisition: A Historical Revision* (New Haven, Conn.: Yale University Press, 1997), 34; and see also Sicroff, *Les controverses*, 61; it is the same Nicolas V who issued on January 8, 1455, the bull entitled *Romanus Pontifex*, in which he granted to the King of Portugal the right of conquest. This bull is considered by some one of the earliest instances of papal authorizations announcing and enabling the conquest of the New World (www.nativeweb.org/pages/legal/indig-romanus-pontifex.html).

185. Kate Langdon Forhan, "Introduction," to Christine de Pizan, *The Book of the Body Politic* (Cambridge: Cambridge University Press, 1994), xx; see also *Représentation, Pouvoir et Royauté à la fin du moyen âge*, ed. Joël Blanchard (Paris: Picard, 1995), esp. 154ff.; and see Philippe Buc, *L'ambiguité du Livre: Prince, pouvoir et peuple dans les commentaires de la bible* (Paris: Beauchesne, 1994)

186. Amos Funkenstein's argument regarding the "abstract" turn from a metaphorical to a conceptual and functional understanding of the state, occurring at the same time as Dante's radical separation of humanity and Christianity, his claim for an "earthly paradise," may thus be understood as a becoming-immanent of the community (*Theology*, 268, 270). By claiming (incidentally about the Romans) that "as a corporate body, as a people, they embody the monarchical virtues," Dante announces the end of a hierarchy in which the sovereign is not only necessarily above the community, but simply necessary to ensure its unity. What is "perhaps the earliest example of a secular theology" signals (or perhaps only promises)

the end of transcendence (271). For a detailed argument regarding parallel changes in papal sovereignty, changes that involved a well-theorized *limitation* of sovereignty as well as the end of transcendence, see Paolo Prodi, *The Papal Prince, One Body and Two Souls: The Papal Monarchy in Early Modern Europe*, trans. Susan Haskins (Cambridge: Cambridge University Press, 1987). In a different perspective, Geoffrey Galt Harpham has suggested, if somehow ironically, for an understanding of the Inquisition as "democratizing" ("Some of the condemnations of the Inquisition sound, to enlightened ears, like antidemocratic whining," 547). And see Armand Arriaza's exposition of a 1622 argument to the effect that "if one insists on considering nobility to be a biologically-transmitted quality, then one really cannot stop retracing one's own lineage at the first forebear to hold noble status no matter how far back one's genealogy might go. . . . One must continue tracing the lineage back to its very beginning... [and] since Adam and Eve held noble status, all human beings can claim to have 'noble blood' " (A. Arriaza, "Adam's Noble Children: An Early Modern Theorist's Concept of Human Nobility," *Journal of the History of Ideas* 55, no. 3 [July 1994]: 386–87).

187. Christine de Pizan, *The Book of the Body Politic,* ed. Kate Langdon Forhan (Cambridge: Cambridge University Press, 1994), 4.

188. This is not to say that there were no alternative modes of conceiving and practicing the collective bond, of course. Bernhard Jussen documents an important facet of such alternatives at the level of the family in his *Spiritual Kinship as Social Practice: Godparenthood and Adoption in the Early Middle Ages*, trans. Pamela Selwyn (Newark: University of Delaware Press, 2000).

189. Tzvetan Todorov famously linked the "two" 1492s in his *The Conquest of America: The Question of the Other*, trans. Richard Howard (Norman: University of Oklahoma Press, 1999), but a more extensive discussion of *both* Europe and the Americas can be found in the earlier Méchoulan, *Le sang de l'autre*, especially the chapter on "Les indiens"; and see María Elena Martínez, *Genealogical Fictions: Limpieza de Sangre, Religion, and Gender in Colonial Mexico* (Stanford, Calif.: Stanford University Press, 2008) as well as the collection of essays edited by Mary E. Giles, *Women in the Inquisition: Spain and the New World* (Baltimore, Md.: Johns Hopkins University Press, 1999).

190. On the Spaniards as "marranos," see Sicroff, *Les controverses*, 130, 191; on the Portuguese, see Nathan Wachtel, *La foi du souvenir: Labyrinthes marranes* (Paris: Seuil, 2001), 27; and see also Mirian Bodian, *Hebrews of the Portuguese Nation*, 13.

191. See Méchoulan, *Le sang de l'autre*, 151. Méchoulan also mentions how the French Franciscan Henri Mauroy, who strenuously opposed the Statutes on the Purity of Blood, nonetheless adopted the language of race ("Honorez la race des Hébreux!" 170) and deployed a medical lexicon of contamination and of disease control against Spain (171).

192. Kamen, *The Spanish Inquisition*, 245; the bibliographic material on the Jesuits and their significance is, of course, enormous. One particularly useful discussion in a different but highly pertinent context can be found in Rivka Feldhay, *Galileo and the Church: Political Inquisition or Critical Dialogue?* (Cambridge: Cambridge University Press, 1995). Feldhay engages the "modernity" of the Jesuits (110); and see of course Robert O'Malley, *The First Jesuits* (Cambridge, Mass.: Harvard University Press, 1993) and *The Jesuits: Cultures,*

Sciences, and the Arts, 1540–1773, ed. Robert O'Malley et al. (Toronto: University of Toronto Press, 1999).

193. Friedman, "Jewish Conversion," 23.

194. Kamen, *The Spanish Inquisition,* 245.

195. "La préoccupation de pureté de sang était d'origine plébéienne et elle allait prendre le caractère d'une révolution sociale, dans laquelle, sous prétexte de 'pureté de sang,' on contesterait les positions et les privilèges dont les nobles jouissaient au nom de leur noblesse" (A. Sicroff, *Les controverses,* 95). Mauricio Damián Rivero reaffirmed this consensus when he wrote that "the Castilian populace were not only active in the persecution of *conversos,* but were often the catalysts for such persecutions" (M. D. Rivero, review of Juan Hernández Franco Murcia's *Cultura y limpieza de sangre en la España moderna* in *Sixteenth Century Journal* 29, no. 3 [1998]: 922).

196. Antonio Dominguez Ortiz, *The Golden Age of Spain: 1516–1659,* trans. James Casey (New York: Basic Books, 1971), 219.

197. See Armand Arriaza, "Adam's Noble Children: An Early Modern Theorist's Concept of Human Nobility," *Journal of the History of Ideas* 55, no. 3 (July 1994): 385–404.

198. José Antonio Maravall has made an elaborate argument about "the first modern revolution," which takes place at the beginning of the sixteenth century in Castille (J. Maravall, *Las comunidades de Castilla: Una primera revolucíon moderna* [Madrid: Revista de Occidente, 1963]).

199. Quoted in Kamen, *The Spanish Inquisition,* 248; and see also Sicroff, *Les controverses,* 195, 203, 210ff., 290–97. Early in his book, Sicroff explains that doubts on the purity of blood plagued virtually everyone, especially the nobility ("personne ne pouvait être sûr de n'avoir pas de 'tache' juive, doute sensible surtout chez les nobles") (A. Sicroff, *Les controverses,* 40, 189).

200. The complex web of relations linking Jews to the king and to the nobles is documented in painstaking detail by Netanyahu, *The Origins.* The 1449 statutes themselves were immediately perceived to constitute an attack on the nobility. An early response argued against them that "it is well known that old and recent alliances by marriage have been made by a great number of Spanish nobles. The Spanish nobility thus associated itself with a large diversity of lineages, as has always been the case everywhere in the world" (quoted in Sicroff, *Les controverses,* 125). It was well understood that the entire nobility of Spain had been "implicated" in marriage alliances with *conversos.* The famous *libros verdes* would repeatedly document that fact, often in an attempt to demonstrate the ridicule of anyone claiming purity of blood (217–18). An interesting illustration of the association between Jews and nobility occurs in Don Alonso de Cartagena's *Defensorium,* mentioned earlier, in which the author (who, once again, *opposed* the Statutes on the Purity of Blood) must clarify that "all Jews cannot claim a noble status since no nation is entirely made up of nobles" (A. Sicroff, *Les controverses,* 50).

201. A. Sicroff, *Les controverses,* 101.

202. A. Sicroff, *Les controverses,* 106, 115, and 133; interestingly enough, even the opposition to Silíceo deployed an argument on the true nature of nobility, the claim being that nobility is not, in fact, "natural," but rather granted by God to individuals: "true nobility is

implanted in the true Christian, whether he is of Gentile, Jewish, or Negro origin" (Sicroff, *Les controverses*, 104). On Silíceo, see also Kamen, *The Spanish Inquisition*, 159ff., 236ff.; Netanyahu, *The Origins*, 1064ff., 1161ff.

2. STATE (THE VAMPIRE STATE)

1. Benedict de Spinoza, "Correspondence," in *On the Improvement of the Understanding. The Ethics. Correspondence*, trans. R. H. M. Elwes (New York: Dover Publications, 1955), 291 (Letter XV [XXXII], dated November 20, 1665); *Spinoza Opere*, ed. Carl Gebhard (Heidelberg: Carl Winters Universitätsbuchhandlung, 1924), vol. 4, 171–74. All citations are from this letter. I am grateful to Teresa Vilarós for having directed me toward "Spinoza's worm."

2. Amos Funkenstein, *Theology and the Scientific Imagination From the Middle Ages to the Seventeenth Century* (Princeton, N.J.: Princeton University Press, 1986), 281.

3. John Locke, "The Fundamental Political Constitution of Carolina" [1669], in *Political Essays*, ed. Mark Goldie (Cambridge: Cambridge University Press, 1997), 164; in his 1690 *Two Treatises*, Locke elaborates on the right of a man "to inherit the property of another, because he is of kin to him, and is known to be of his blood" ("First Treatise" in John Locke, *Two Treatises of Government and A Letter Concerning Toleration*, ed. Ian Shapiro [New Haven, Conn.: Yale University Press, 2003], 63). In a wonderful lecture on "The Property of the Dead," Wendy Brown recently discussed the liberalism of Locke, the fact that he enshrines property in filiation (which he clearly locates in the blood). Raising the question of the just conqueror in the "Second Treatise," Locke argues that he has absolute power, power over life and death. Locke insists, however, that absolute power cannot truly *interrupt* blood, for "the father, by his miscarriages and violence, can forfeit but his own life, but involves not his children in his guilt or destruction. His goods, which nature, that willeth the preservation of all mankind as much as is possible, hath made to belong to the children to keep them from perishing, do still continue to belong to his children" (63). Locke, who earlier opposes the idea that "absolute power purifies men's blood" (139), also asserts that it gives not "a right and title to their possessions," no right over the dead's *stuff* (181). In this scheme, property is private but not quite individual (commenting on Locke's property, Roberto Esposito writes of "the duration of possession for a temporality that goes well beyond the personal life to whose preservation it is also ordered . . . the proprietary paradigm's immunitary procedure is able to preserve life only by enclosing it in an orbit that is destined to drain it of its vital element" [R. Esposito, *Bíos: Biopolitics and Philosophy*, trans. Timothy Campbell (Minneapolis: University of Minnesota Press, 2008), 69]). Property runs, but it also stays, in the blood.

4. Martin D. Yaffe, "Body and the Body Politic in Spinoza's *Theologico-Political Treatise*," in *Piety, Peace, and the Freedom to Philosophize*, ed. Paul J. Bagley (Dordrecht: Kluwer Academic Publishers, 1999), 159–87.

5. See William Harvey, *The Works of William Harvey*, trans. Robert Willis (Philadelphia: University of Pennsylvania Press, 1989). Spinoza opens his letter with a reference to Robert Boyle, whose connection to Harvey is well known (see, e.g., Robert G. Frank Jr., *Harvey*

and the Oxford Physiologists: Scientific Ideas and Social Interaction [Berkeley: University of California Press, 1980]).

6. Spinoza, "Correspondence," 292.

7. *Dictionnaire de l'Académie françoise* (1694), quoted in Kristin Elizabeth Gager, *Blood Ties and Fictive Ties: Adoption and Family Life in Early Modern France* (Princeton, N.J.: Princeton University Press, 1996), 17.

8. In contemporary Israel, among other places, and testifying to the endurance of conceptions of blood as community belonging, "it is not surprising . . . to find some Israeli Karaite leaders arguing for their community's legitimacy and for the personal status of individual Karaites by advocating the use of 'blood tests' to 'prove' their ethnic purity, as if to say, 'Our blood has been clean for thousands of years. . . . No foreign blood entered us. . . . We did not mix with the *goyim* [gentiles]'" (Ruth Tsoffar, *The Stains of Culture: An Ethno-Reading of Karaite Jewish Women* [Detroit, Mich.: Wayne State University Press, 2006], 56). For a benign rendering of the relation between nationalism, racism, blood, and "imagined communities," see Benedict Anderson, *Imagined Communities: Reflections on the Origin and Spread of Nationalism* (London: Verso, 1991), 141–54; for a more extended discussion, see Etienne Balibar and Immanuel Wallerstein, *Race, Nation, Class: Ambiguous Identities* (London: Verso, 1992).

9. Franz Rosenzweig, *Der Stern der Erlösung* (Frankfurt am Main: Suhrkamp, 1988), 331–32; Rosenzweig does not have to be construed as a racist, if only because blood, as a figure for the community, precedes and exceeds "race thinking"—and it is not less troubling for that. Beginning with the equation of blood and procreation, as I will argue, it may in fact be more pervasive (see Haggai Dagan, "The Motif of Blood and Procreation in Franz Rosenzweig," *AJS Review* 26, no. 2 [2002]: 241–49). In his groundbreaking work, Marc Shell explains that "the boundary of the Christian 'nation' became no more than race and genealogy, shorthand reports of which gave Spaniards easy access to a breederlike knowledge of who was in the *Germania* and who wasn't. Blood now defined the nation: national kinship was literalized as consanguineous and consanguinity itself was upheld as ascertainable" (M. Shell, *Children of the Earth: Literature, Politics, and Nationhood* [New York: Oxford University Press, 1993], 29), but as Shell goes on to demonstrate, and as I am trying to elaborate in the previous chapter and throughout, Spain too is hardly exceptional.

10. And compare: "The blood, while circulating in the vessels, appears to the eye to be a homogeneous mass; but when it is passing in vessels so small as almost to separate its visible parts, and is viewed in a microscope, there is no appearance but that of globules moving in the vessels." (John Hunter, *A treatise on the blood, inflammation, and gun-shot wounds, by the late John Hunter. To which is prefixed, A short account of the author's life, by his brother-in-law, Everard Home.* London, 1794, p. 15. Based on information from *English Short Title Catalogue. Eighteenth Century Collections Online.* Gale Group. Accessible at http://galenet.galegroup.com.arugula.cc.columbia.edu:2048/servlet/ECCO.) Hunter goes on to make the original claim that blood is itself a living organ, a whole of sorts.

11. I am obviously not suggesting that group distinctions exclusively come about on the basis of blood, only that this particular and pervasive "figure" has a specific conceptual and historical reach that must be recognized, reflected upon, and thereby evaluated, on its own terms—as a whole, as it were.

12. "Jewish blood" is a privileged example often (and erroneously) taken to hark back to biblical conceptions (on which more later). One illustration among too many of the unhistorical complacency ruling the field of inquiry: "It is well known that the books of Ezra and Nehemiah are concerned, among other things, with mixed marriages and *the purity of blood of the Jewish community*" (John Rogerson, "Structural Anthropology and the Old Testament," *Bulletin of the School of Oriental and African Studies* 33, no. 3 [1970]: 497). Neither blood-based distinctions nor the idea of blood purity would be anything new, or so we are led to believe.

13. "Blood is characterized as that which animates the flesh," explains William Gilders, which is why the Hebrew "*benafsho damo* [flesh with its life, its blood]" of Genesis 9:4 should not be translated as "*with* its lifeblood," which suggests "that a specific type of blood is at issue." Rather, blood and life are equated, Gilders insists, they are one and the same. "Blood really *is* life," and *not* a symbol of it. Whatever the explanation for this statement, it does show blood to be equalizing, not as a principle of differentiation or distinction (W. K. Gilders, *Blood Ritual in the Hebrew Bible: Meaning and Power* [Baltimore, Md.: Johns Hopkins University Press, 2004], 17–18). Following Gilders, I have less investment in the general import of this equation than in its significance as an instance that supports a nondifferentiating conception of blood.

14. Each of the terms invoked here, beginning with "family," could be (and, in fact, has often been) problematized, historically and otherwise. In my discussion, the designation of the group (and even its contours) is however less important than the place and function of blood in its description and/or constitution.

15. C. McCarthy, *Blood Meridian or the Evening Redness in the West* (New York: Vintage, 1985).

16. I earlier began to explain that blood is better understood as an element. But by "blood is not a concept" I mean something else, namely, that blood has not been subjected to philosophical or theoretical inquiry or to formal analysis, nor has it been reflectively assigned to a particular field or sphere or examined for its apparent failure to keep within the limits of such confinement. Thus, blood visibly operates today as a physiologic, medical, and economic and marketable object, and though it seems to have broad import elsewhere, it has not emerged as an abstract or general notion upon which rulers, jurists, or political philosophers work or reflect, institute or institutionalize, in the way they have worked and reflected on, institutionalized (or tried to), for instance, sovereignty, representation, justice, and democracy. Put differently, on the face of things, blood may or may not belong "originally" to medicine and to anthropology, but it has not been claimed by philosophy or by politics, nor, it seems, should it.

17. Martin Luther, quoted in Sheldon S. Wolin, *Politics and Vision: Continuity and Innovation in Western Political Thought* (Princeton, N.J.: Princeton University Press, 2004), 142.

18. Denis Diderot, quoted in Sankar Muthu, *Enlightenment Against Empire* (Princeton, N.J.: Princeton University Press, 2003), 109.

19. Alain Brossat, "Les dernières heures de la grande dramaturgie du sang?" in *Drôle d'époque* 19 (Automne 2006): 29; more assertive, Pheng Cheah declares that "the decolonizing nation is not an archaic throwback to traditional forms of community based on the blind

ties of blood and kinship" (P. Cheah, *Spectral Nationality: Passages of Freedom from Kant to Postcolonial Literatures of Liberation* (New York: Columbia University Press, 2003), 382.

20. G. W. F. Hegel, *Phenomenology of Spirit*, trans. A. V. Miller (Oxford: Oxford University Press, 1977). The full passage in the section called "Consciousness" reads as follows: "This simple infinity, or the absolute Notion, may be called the simple essence of life, the soul of the world, the universal blood, whose omnipresence is neither disturbed nor interrupted by any difference, but rather is itself every difference, as also their supersession; it pulsates within itself but does not move, inwardly vibrates, yet is at rest. It is self-identical, for the differences are tautological; they are differences that are none" (100).

21. For instance, blood does not register in Quentin Skinner's *Foundations of Modern Political Thought*, vol. 1 and 2 (Cambridge: Cambridge University Press, 1978), nor does it appear in *Rethinking the Foundations of Modern Political Thought*, ed. Annabel Brett and James Tully with Holly Hamilton-Bleakley (Cambridge: Cambridge University Press, 2006).

22. Jean-Pierre Baud writes a unique, albeit brief history of the juridical nature of blood, which he traces back to the Old Testament (Greece is not mentioned), by way of Roman law and the notion of *person* ("la plus remarquable création juridique de la civilisation romaine"), and the tradition of blood donation that links Jesus Christ to military and civilian blood banks. Baud fails to comment on the phrase "flesh and blood" nor does he engage with kinship or with "jus sanguinis." One can only speculate as to whether Baud might have reconsidered his statement that blood—and even the body—disappeared from law (the person, Baud suggestively writes, *substitutes* for blood), that since the abandonment of blood vengeance, "le juriste ne se préoccupait plus beaucoup du sang," or that sensitive to an older sacrality "il refusa donc de nommer le sang" (Jean-Pierre Baud, "La nature juridique du sang," *Terrain* 56 [Mars 2011]: 90–105; and see, for one small corrective focus on criminal justice, Marie-Sylvie Dupont-Bouchat et Xavier Rousseaux, "Le prix du sang: Sang et justice du XIVe au XVIIIe siècle," in *Affaires de sang*, ed. Arlette Farge [Paris: Imago, 1988], 43–72).

23. Spinoza, "Correspondence," 291.

24. I cite Norman O. Brown's "Filthy Lucre," in Brown, *Life Against Death: The Psychoanalytic Meaning of History* (Middletown, Conn.: Wesleyan University Press, 1985), 234.

25. As I mentioned earlier, I am recasting Carl Schmitt's famous formulation: "all significant concepts of the modern theory of the state are secularized theological concepts not only because of their historical development—in which they were transferred from theology to the theory of the state, whereby, for example, the omnipotent God became the omnipotent lawgiver—but also because of their systematic structure, the recognition of which is necessary for a sociological consideration of these concepts" (C. Schmitt, *Political Theology: Four Chapters on the Concept of Sovereignty*, trans. George Schwab [Chicago: University of Chicago Press, 2005], 36).

26. Daniel Defoe, *The Compleat English Gentleman*, quoted in J. C. D. Clark, *English Society 1660–1832: Religion, Ideology and Politics During the Ancien Regime* (Cambridge: Cambridge University Press, 2000), 229.

27. I quote from Elise Lemire's important work on race in America because it is exemplary in the conciseness, precision, and exhaustiveness of its account of "the rhetoric of blood"

(E. Lemire, *"Miscegenation": Making Race in America* (Philadelphia: University of Pennsylvania Press, 2002), 36–37.

28. Gail Kern Paster, *The Body Embarrassed: Drama and the Disciplines of Shame in Early Modern England* (Ithaca, N.Y.: Cornell University Press, 1993), 69.

29. Acts of the Apostles 17:26; neither Greek nor Latin uses the word *blood*. For an account of the success of the phrase, see Paul Goodman, *Of One Blood: Abolitionism and the Origins of Racial Equality* (Berkeley: University of California Press, 1998).

30. Anton-Hermann Chroust, "The Corporate Idea and the Body Politic in the Middle Ages," *The Review of Politics* 9, no. 4 (October 1947): 430. Marc Shell probably went the farthest in exploring the consequences of this equality of blood with regard to kinship in Christianity, "the interconnection of Christian kinship and nationhood" (M. Shell, *Children of the Earth: Literature, Politics, and Nationhood* [Oxford: Oxford University Press, 1993], 60), while Uli Linke extends the argument to the entirety of Indo-European history (U. Linke, *Blood and Nation: The European Aesthetics of Race* [Philadelphia: University of Pennsylvania Press, 1999]).

31. Ludwig Feuerbach, *The Essence of Christianity*, trans. George Eliot (Amherst, Mass.: Prometheus Books, 1989), 146; it might be relevant to note, with Janet Carsten, that "Ethnographic data from different areas in South Asia have produced rather different versions of indigenous notions of personhood, including those in which body and 'spirit,' or blood and 'spirit,' are separately derived" (J. Carsten, *After Kinship* [Cambridge: Cambridge University Press, 2004], 118).

32. On the "savage slot," see M.-R. Trouillot, "Anthropology and the Savage Slot: The Poetics and Politics of Otherness," in *Recapturing Anthropology: Working in the Present*, ed. Richard G. Fox (Santa Fe, N.Mex.: School of American Research Press, 1991), 17–44; on the concept of "anthropotheism," see Stefanos Geroulanos, *An Atheism That Is Not Humanist Emerges in French Thought* (Stanford, Calif.: Stanford University Press, 2010); on Renan, see Benzion Netanyahu, "Américo Castro and His View of the Origins of the *Pureza de Sangre*," *Proceedings of the American Academy for Jewish Research* 46/47 (1928–29/1978–79), part 2 (1979–1980): 397–457.

33. Aristotle, *The Politics*, trans. Benjamin Jowett (Mineola, NY: Dover Publications, 2000) 1252b, 27.

34. This argument is no more than a footnote to Jacques Derrida's *Politics of Friendship*, trans. George Collins (New York: Verso, 1997).

35. Henry James Sumner Maine, *Ancient Law: Its Connection to the History of Early Society*, Introduction by J. H. Morgan (Charleston, N.C.: BiblioBazaar, 2008), 99; of course, as Karuna Mantena explains, blood kinship is a fiction (Maine says "assumption") but it is taken to be a universal fiction (K. Mantena, *Alibis of Empire: Henry Maine and the Ends of Liberal Imperialism* [Princeton, N.J.: Princeton University Press, 2010], 79; and see Carol Pateman, *The Sexual Contract* [Stanford, Calif.: Stanford University Press, 1998], 27); one could refer to Ferdinand Tönnies as well (F. Tönnies, *Community and Civil Society*, trans. Jose Harris and Margaret Hollis [Cambridge: Cambridge University Press, 2001]).

36. Donna J. Haraway, *Modest_Witness@Second_Millenium. FemaleMan©_Meets_OncoMouse™: Feminism and Technoscience* (New York: Routledge, 1997), 265.

37. Alys Eve Weinbaum, *Wayward Reproductions: Genealogies of Race and Nation in Transatlantic Modern Thought* (Durham, N.C.: Duke University Press, 2004), 5.

38. Peter Wade, ed., *Race, Ethnicity and Nation: Perspectives from Kinship and Genetics* (New York: Berghahn Books, 2009), 1; and see Lemire, "*Miscegenation*."

39. Brackette F. Williams, "Classification Systems Revisited: Kinship, Caste, Race, and Nationality as the Flow of Blood and the Spread of Rights," in *Naturalizing Power: Essays in Feminist Cultural Analysis*, ed. Sylvia Yanagisako and Carol Delaney (New York: Routledge, 1995), 201.

40. Enric Porqueres i Gené, "Kinship Language and the Dynamics of Race," in *Race, Ethnicity and Nation*, 127; here too, Marc Shell's *Children of the Earth* is a notable exception.

41. Porqueres i Gené, "Kinship Language," 127; Christiane Klapisch-Zuber acknowledges and documents the particular "manière dont l'Occident s'est représenté la parenté et la filiation," "les outils mentaux et graphiques dont l'Occident chrétien a disposé," though she focuses on the arboreal rather than the hematological (C. Klapisch-Zuber, *L'ombre des ancêtres. Essai sur l'imaginaire médiéval de la parenté* [Paris: Fayard, 2000], 14, 19). The two are of course related (26–28, 97); but Klapisch-Zuber seems to suggest that the representations (such as the tree) are all figures *of* consanguinity (242, 249).

42. Émile Benveniste, *Le vocabulaire des institutions indo-européennes* (Paris: Minuit, 1969), volume 1 being the most relevant with regard to kinship (*parenté*).

43. Michel Foucault, *Sécurité, Territoire, Population* (Cours au Collège de France, 1977–1978) (Paris: Hautes Études/Gallimard/Seuil, 2004). Incidentally, Foucault there expresses reservation regarding the use of the word *Christianity*, but he quickly gets over it. He is thus unambiguous in his description of "a religion that claims in that manner to a daily government of men in their real life [*dans leur vie réelle*] under the pretext of their salvation and on the scale of humanity as a whole, that is the Church and we have no other such example in the history of societies. . . . The Christian religion as the Christian Church, this pastoral power was no doubt transformed over the course of fifteen centuries of history. No doubt it was displaced, dislocated, transformed, and integrated into different shapes, but at bottom it was never truly abolished" (151–52).

44. Foucault, *The History of Sexuality, Volume 1: An Introduction*, trans. Robert Hurley (New York: Pantheon, 1978), 148; earlier, and in a different register, Foucault had written of "the shift from a criminality of blood to a criminality of fraud" (Foucault, *Discipline and Punish: The Birth of the Prison*, trans. Alan Sheridan [New York: Vintage, 1995], 77); for a summary of the debate over periodization (and blood), see Kathleen Biddick, "The Cut of Genealogy: Pedagogy in the Blood," *Journal of Medieval and Early Modern Studies* 30, no. 3 (Fall 2000): 449–62.

45. Stoler, *Race and the Education of Desire*, 51.

46. Jean-Pierre Baud is mostly interested in the contemporary status of blood (thing or commodity), blood donation and blood transfusion. For him the importance of blood in Christianity (Baud writes of a "hématologie sacrée") is exhaustively found in a "mystique du don," a gift mysticism, which figures Jesus as the first blood donor (Baud, "La nature juridique," 95).

47. Jacques Rancière, *On the Shores of Politics*, trans. Liz Heron (London: Verso, 1995). 88.

48. Adriana Cavarero, *Stately Bodies: Literature, Philosophy, and the Question of Gender*, trans. Robert de Lucca and Deanna Shemek (Ann Arbor: University of Michigan Press, 2002), 113.

49. Jonathan Gil Harris, *Sick Economies: Drama, Mercantilism, and Disease in Shakespeare's England* (Philadelphia: University of Pennsylvania Press, 2004), 167; Hobbes, *Leviathan*, ed. Richard Tuck (Cambridge: Cambridge University Press, 1996), chap. 24, 174.

50. On Zwingli's "combination of money, blood, and the sale of bodies," see Valentin Groebner, *Liquid Assets, Dangerous Gifts: Presents and Politics at the End of the Middle Ages*, trans. Pamela E. Selwyn (Philadelphia: University of Pennsylvania Press, 2002), 105 and 149.

51. David Hume, "Of Pride and Humility of Animals," in *Treatise of Human Nature*, book II, section 12; "It is apparent," writes David Warren Sabean, "that dividing property among all the children regardless of sex, models the flow of property in a parallel manner to the way theologians modeled the flow of blood or substance" (D. W. Sabean, "From Clan to Kindred: Kinship and the Circulation of Property in Premodern and Modern Europe," in *Heredity Produced: At the Crossroads of Biology, Politics, and Culture, 1500–1870*, ed. Staffan Müller-Wille and Hans-Jörg Rheinberger [Cambridge, Mass.: MIT Press, 2007], 42); on the relation between "consanguinity" and property in the history of the church and the medieval West, see J. Goody, *The Development of the Family and Marriage in Europe* (Cambridge: Cambridge University Press, 1983).

52. Catherine Waldby and Robert Mitchell, *Tissue Economies: Blood, Organs, and Cell Lines in Late Capitalism* (Durham, N.C.: Duke University Press, 2006), 4; "the gift of blood," they continue, " is historically associated wit the constitution of a community-minded citizenry and a resilient nation" (9).

53. Foucault, *Discipline and Punish*, 216.

54. As Paul Kahn writes, "the distinction between citizen and noncitizen is the fundamental inequality of political life. This inequality is defined both geographically and historically. The dual sources of this political inequality are represented explicitly in the dual sources of citizenship at birth: bloodline and geography, or *ius sanguinis* and *ius soli*. . . . Our political communities, even our liberal communities, are overwhelmingly founded on 'blood and soil' " (P. W. Kahn, *Putting Liberalism in its Place* [Princeton, N.J.: Princeton University Press, 2005], 44–45). On *jus sanguinis* in modern Europe, see Rogers Brubaker, *Citizenship and Nationhood in France and Germany* (Cambridge, Mass.: Harvard University Press, 1992), and see Peter Sahlins, *Unnaturally French: Foreign Citizens in the Old Regime and After* (Ithaca, N.Y.: Cornell University Press, 2004); and see next note.

55. Gianna Pomata, "Blood Ties and Semen Ties: Consanguinity and Agnation in Roman Law," in *Gender, Kinship, Power: A Comparative and Interdisciplinary History*, ed. Mary Jo Maynes et al. [New York and London: Routledge, 1996), 43–64; E. Champeaux, "*Jus Sanguinis*. Trois façons de calculer la parenté au Moyen Âge," *Revue historique de droit français et étranger* (1933): 241–90; Anne Lefebvre-Teillard, "Ius sanguinis: L'émergence d'un principe (Éléments d'histoire de la nationalité française)," *Revue critique de droit international privé* 82, no. 2 (1993): 223–50; Frank Roumy, "La naissance de la notion canonique de *consanguinitas* et sa réception dans le droit civil," in *L'hérédité entre Moyen Âge et Époque moderne*, ed. Maaike van der Lugt and Charles de Miramon (Firenze: Sismel—Edizioni del Galluzzo / Micrologus Library, 2008), 41–66.

56. Needless to say, blood ties were always fictive ties, as the practice of adoption would easily demonstrate; see, for example, Kristin Elizabeth Gager, *Blood Ties and Fictive Ties: Adoption and Family Life in Early Modern France* (Princeton, N.J.: Princeton University Press, 1996), and see Zrinka Stahuljak, *Bloodless Genealogies of the French Middle Ages: Translatio, Kinship, and Metaphor* (Gainesville: University Press of Florida, 2005).

57. Claude Meillassoux, *Mythes et limites de l'anthropologie: Le sang et les mots* (Lausanne: Editions Page Deux, 2001).

58. Philip S. Gorski, *The Disciplinary Revolution: Calvinism and the Rise of the State in Early Modern Europe* (Chicago: University of Chicago Press, 2003). As I mentioned earlier, Gorski entirely ignores plausible Catholic precedents.

59. de Lubac, *Corpus Mysticum*, 250; a narrative that follows a proximate periodization, with blood as a central element, can be found in Colette Beaune, *Naissance de la Nation France* (Paris: Gallimard, 1985).

60. Quoted in Caroline Walker Bynum, *Wonderful Blood: Theology and Practice in Late Medieval Northern Germany and Beyond* (Philadelphia: University of Pennsylvania Press, 2007), 139.

61. Ernst H. Kantorowicz, *The King's Two Bodies: A Study in Mediaeval Political Theology* (Princeton, N.J.: Princeton University Press, 1997), 331; emphasis added; and see Beaune, *Naissance de la nation France*, 216–25; Beaune refers to an early version of the one-drop rule when she refers to the novel idea, in fourteenth-century France, that "le royaume passe à tout héritier mâle, même très éloigné, qui a dans les veines une goutte du sang des rois" (222).

62. Kantorowicz acknowledges the existence of "a race promoted by Christ from the very beginnings of the Christian faith, a most holy royal house to which God had granted a heavenly oil for the anointment of its kings," yet for him, such "a royal stock [was] endowed with miraculous gifts the like of which not even the Church could claim" (333). He is, in other words, thinking about Christianity, but for him, "the idea of a specially refined soul, 'subtle and noble,' and infused in the blood of princes" is neither Aristotelian nor Stoic. It is "reminiscent rather of the Hermetic tenet concerning the creation of the souls of kings, but it seems doubtful that this doctrine was known at that time" (332).

63. "At least once a year, the vast majority of Christians in the Middle Ages had an immediate and personal experience of anthropophagy. In swallowing a consecrated wafer that did not merely represent the body of Christ, but was the body of Christ, the medieval believer not only partook of human and divine flesh, but was incorporated into a community of theophagists for whom theophagy was a central and fundamental aspect of the church" (Merrall Llewelyn Price, *Consuming Passions: The Uses of Cannibalism in Late Medieval and Early Modern Europe* [New York: Routledge, 2003], 26); and see Beate Fricke, "Jesus Wept! On the History of Anthropophagy in Christianity. A New Reading of a Miniature in the Gospel Book of Otto III," *Res. Journal of Anthropology and Aesthetics* 59/60 (2011): 192–205.

64. Esposito, *Communitas*, 5–7; writing of the French Middle Ages, R. Howard Bloch explains that "property, like blood, flows downward in a straight line" (R. Howard Bloch, *Etymologies and Genealogies: A Literary Anthropology of the French Middle Ages* [Chicago: University of Chicago Press, 1983], 85).

65. William Shakespeare, *The Merchant of Venice*, ed. Jay L. Hallo (Oxford: Oxford University Press, 1994), 4.1.111–112.

66. Randall Lesaffer, "Peace Treaties from Lodi to Westphalia," in *Peace Treaties and International Law in European History from the Late Middle Ages to World War One*, ed. R. Lesaffer (Cambridge: Cambridge University Press, 2004), 29.

67. Benedict Anderson, *Imagined Communities: Reflections on the Origin and Spread of Nationalism* (London: Verso, 1991), 145; see Marc Shell's implicit answer to Anderson on the question "is there a nationalism without racism?" in Shell, *Children of the Earth*, 179ff. I would ask differently, namely, whether nationalism, as it is conceived in Christian Europe, could exist without blood?

68. See Uday Mehta, "Kinship and Friendship: Two Conceptions of Political Action," unpublished paper; John Rogers, *The Matter of Revolution: Science, Poetry, and Politics in the Age of Milton* (Ithaca, N.Y.: Cornell University Press, 1996), and see Norman O. Brown's discussion of liberty and fraternity in *Love's Body* (Berkeley: University of California Press, 1966), as well as Shell, *Children of the Earth*. Michael Rogin explores the (blood) connections between liberalism and paternalism, primitive accumulation and Indian removal (Michael Paul Rogin, *Fathers and Children: Andrew Jackson and the Subjugation of the American Indian* [New York: Vintage, 1976]). Paul Kahn attends to the illiberal aspects of the liberal state in *Sacred Violence: Torture, Terror, and Sovereignty* (Ann Arbor: University of Michigan Press, 2008).

69. Ian Shapiro, "Introduction: Reading Locke Today," in John Locke, *Two Treatises of Government and a Letter Concerning Toleration,* edited and with an introduction by Ian Shapiro (New Haven, Conn.: Yale University Press, 2003), xii; Victor Nuovo mentions that "the preface to Boyle's *Memoirs for the Natural History of Humane Blood* (1684) is addressed to Locke" (V. Nuovo, *Christianity, Antiquity, and Enlightenment. Interpretations of Locke* [Dordrecht: Springer, 2010], 107, n. 9).

70. Locke, *Two Treatises*, 67; Locke wonders about the relevance of blood quantum in succession and inheritance (70) and perhaps seeks to demonstrate the linguistic quality of blood as well when he asks, about inheritance still, "whether a sister by the half-blood, before a brother's daughter by the whole blood" could be more deserving (76).

71. James Q. Whitman, *The Origins of Reasonable Doubt: Theological Roots of the Criminal Trial* (New Haven, Conn.: Yale University Press, 2008); Jean-Jacques Rousseau, "Discourse on the Origin and the Foundations of Inequality Among Men," in *The Discourses and Other Early Political Writings*, ed. Victor Gourevitch (Cambridge: Cambridge University Press, 1997), 118; Edmund Burke berated the French assembly on their high regard for Rousseau, "His blood they transfuse into their minds," he had written, "and into their manners."

72. Daniel J. Kevles, *In the Name of Eugenics: Genetics and the Uses of Human Heredity* (Berkeley: University of California Press, 1985).

73. Eric A. Feldman and Ronald Bayer, eds., *Blood Feuds: AIDS, Blood, and the Politics of Medical Disaster* (New York: Oxford University Press, 1998).

74. Edmund Burke, *Reflections on the Revolution in France*, ed. Frank M. Turner (New Haven, Conn.: Yale University Press, 2003), 30.

75. Auden, "Vespers," quoted in Norman O. Brown, *Love's Body* (Berkeley: University of California Press, 1966), 27.

76. David M. Schneider, *American Kinship: A Cultural Account* (Chicago: University of Chicago Press, 1980); and see also Schneider's *A Critique of the Study of Kinship* (Ann Arbor: University of Michigan Press, 1984).

77. It is because "the United States of America and the Republic of France stand out uniquely in the modern world as states with . . . a conception of citizenship based on place of birth rather than on ethnic or 'blood' ties" that I insist on the non-paradigmatic and unexceptional (Norman Ravitch, "Your People, My People; Your God, My God: French and American Troubles Over Citizenship," *The French Review* 70, no. 4 [March 1997]: 515). But this only appears paradoxical if one ignores the determining role and function of blood in, say, kinship or property in the modern state at large.

78. Kathleen Davis, *Periodization and Sovereignty: How Ideas of Feudalism and Secularization Govern the Politics of Time* (Philadelphia: University of Pennsylvania Press, 2008); further references in the body of the text.

79. A glance at Blackstone suffices to recognize that feudalism too is another bloody concept, that blood plays, in other words, an essential role in its elaboration (see "Rights of Things— Title by Descent," in Sir William Blackstone, *Commentaries on the Laws of England*, ed. Hardcastle Browne (St. Paul: West Publishing, 1897), e.g., 275, 279, 285.

80. Cited in Charles Leslie Wayper, *Political Thought* (New York: Philosophical Library, 1954), ix.

81. This phrase and much of what follows is inspired by the work of Claude Meillassoux, *Mythes et limites de l'anthropologie: Le sang et les mots* (Lausanne: Editions Page Deux, 2001). There is a measure of irony in seemingly reinstituting a strict distinction between word and thing, although I would not want to claim that it is my own doing. Still, I assume the responsibility, for the sake of argument and to highlight, if not resolve, a number of problems with blood—not merely a *thing*, of course, and even less *one* thing.

82. Raymond Williams, *Culture and Society. 1780–1950* (New York: Columbia University Press, 1983); Norbert Elias, *The Civilizing Process*, trans. Edmund Jephcott (Oxford: Blackwell, 1994).

83. Leo Marx, "Technology: The Emergence of a Hazardous Concept," *Social Research* 64, no. 3 (Fall 1997): 965–88.

84. Williams, *Culture and Society*, xvii. I heed Marylin Strathern's distinction between "invention" and "discovery," although she makes clear that both share in the rhetoric of the new (M. Strathern, *Kinship*, 34).

85. I have been inspired here by Timothy Mitchell's most trenchant interrogation of "human agency" in the humanities and social sciences in his *Rule of Experts: Egypt, Techno-Politics, Modernity* (Berkeley: University of California Press, 2002).

86. For one pertinent example among many, see Janet Adelman, "Her Father's Blood: Race, Conversion, and Nation in *The Merchant of Venice*," *Representations* 81 (Winter 2003): 4–30.

87. Bruno Latour, *We Have Never Been Modern*, trans. Catherine Porter (Cambridge, Mass.: Harvard University Press, 1993).

88. Latour, *We Have Never Been Modern*, 7; translation slightly modified.

89. Funkenstein, *Theology*, esp. 277–89; as I indicated above, Funkenstein also discusses Spinoza in this context.

90. Funkenstein, *Theology*, 298.

91. On the pervasiveness of a rhetoric of labor, production, and action, see Foucault, *Histoire de la folie à l'âge classique* (Paris: Gallimard, 1972), esp. part III, chaps. 2 and 3; and see Werner Hamacher, "Afformative, Strike: Benjamin's 'Critique of Violence,' " trans. Dana Hollander, in *Walter Benjamin's Philosophy: Destruction and Experience*, ed. Andrew Benjamin and Peter Osborne (London and New York: Routledge, 1994), 110–38; and see Avital Ronell, *Stupidity* (Urbana: University of Illinois Press, 2002).

92. Among many examples, see Jean-Paul Roux, *Le sang. Mythes, symboles et réalités* (Paris: Fayard, 1988); Piero Camporesi, *Juice of Life: The Symbolic and Magic Significance of Blood*, trans. Robert R. Barr (New York: Continuum, 1995); Douglas Starr, *Blood: An Epic History of Medicine and Commerce* (New York: Harper Collins, 2002); Uli Linke, *Blood and Nation: The European Aesthetics of Race* (Philadelphia: University of Pennsylvania Press, 1999); Miri Rubin, *Corpus Christi*. More directly about the Jews, see Lawrence A. Hoffman, *Covenant of Blood: Circumcision and Gender in Rabbinic Judaism* (Chicago: University of Chicago Press, 1996); Charlotte Fonrobert, *Menstrual Purity: Rabbinic and Christian Reconstructions of Biblical Gender* (Stanford, Calif.: Stanford University Press, 2000); Claudine Fabre-Vassas, *The Singular Beast: Jews, Christians, and the Pig*, trans. Carol Volk (New York: Columbia University Press, 1997); Israel Jacob Yuval, *Two Nations in Your Womb: Perceptions of Jews and Christians in Late Antiquity and the Middle Ages*, trans. Barbara Harshav and Jonathan Chipman (Berkeley: University of California Press, 2006); Carolyn Walker Bynum, *Wonderful Blood: Theology and Practice in Late Medieval Northern Germany and Beyond* (Philadelphia: University of Pennsylvania Press, 2007); D. Biale, *Blood and Belief: The Circulation of a Symbol Between Jews and Christians* (Berkeley: University of California Press, 2007).

93. For a forceful and pertinent formulation of the operation of the fact/interpretation distinction within historical discourse, see Marc Nichanian, *The Historiographic Perversion*, trans. Gil Anidjar (New York: Columbia University Press, 2009); a more contained reinscription of the fact/fiction distinction in the case of blood is succinctly described by Marc Shell: "The commonplace Western view is that kinship by consanguinity is primary or real kinship. Anthropologists and sociologists usually have lumped together all other kinds as pseudo-kinship (or kinship by extension), which they then divide into subcategories such as figurative, fictive, artificial, and ritual." There is, Shell continues, "a still unresolved debate about whether kinship is essentially a matter of biology . . . or sociology" (M. Shell, *The End of Kinship: 'Measure for Measure,' Incest and the Ideal of Universal Siblinghood* [Baltimore, Md.: Johns Hopkins University Press, 1988], 4). Elsewhere, Shell moves the question to verifiability, explaining further that "the standard of consanguinity assumes that literal kinship resides in the blood, *which may or may not be the case*, and also that blood kinship is sometimes undeniably ascertainable and therefore 'not a fiction,' which is not the case" (M. Shell, *Children of the Earth*, 98). My own question remains: What is it that made blood the *name* of biology and the *figure* of the nonfictive? What is it that maintains it as the name of, we would now know, a pervasive fiction?

94. Latour, *We Have Never Been Modern*, 7.

95. Frederick Engels, *The Origin of the Family, Private Property, and the State in the Light of the Researches of Lewis H. Morgan*, edited with an introduction by Eleanor Burke Leacock (New York: International Publishers, 1972), 102–103; and see how Françoise Héritier, historical anthropologist, opens her important study by stating that "the study of kinship is that of the relations that unite human beings by way of ties grounded in consanguinity and affinity" (F. Héritiér, *L'exercice de la parenté* [Paris: Seuil, 1981], 13).

96. David M. Schneider, *A Critique of the Study of Kinship* (Ann Arbor: University of Michigan Press, 1984), 53. Elsewhere Schneider summarizes the common view: "Kinship is the blood relationship, the fact of shared biogenetic substance" (D. Schneider, *American Kinship: A Cultural Account* [Chicago: University of Chicago Press, 1980], 107). The distinction between fact and idea is mapped onto nature and culture and reproduces Lewis Henry Morgan's separation of blood from language (see note 99).

97. For the classic formulation, see Anderson, *Imagined Communities*.

98. Schneider, *A Critique*, 167.

99. It might be important to linger on the remarkable fact that Emile Benveniste, who reviewed the vocabulary of kinship among many Indo-European institutions, never attends to "blood" as a lexical term, an element of the vocabulary he circumscribes to be explored or analyzed. Equally remarkable is Marc Shell, whose work is no less essential, and indeed equally accepting of the notion of "familial consanguinity" as a given, if one that is "ultimately unknowable" (Shell, *Children of the Earth*, vii and 5). In a similar manner, alerted to the complexity and finitude of kinship classifications and designations by way of philological concerns, Lewis Henry Morgan had affirmed and buttressed the distinction between "blood" and "language." Morgan defined "systems of consanguinity" as "founded upon a community of blood." He was concerned with "the classification of nations upon the basis of affinity of blood" and he never interrogated the linguistic or physiologic ground of "consanguinity" (L. H. Morgan, *Systems of Consanguinity and Affinity of the Human Family* [Lincoln: University of Nebraska Press, 1997 [1870], 8–10).

100. Marshall Sahlins makes a parallel argument, strangely exonerating anthropologists ("when sociobiologists use the term 'kinship' and mean by that 'blood' connections") offering birth as an alternative that must also be reconsidered ("in cultural practice it is birth [and not blood] that serves as the metaphor of kinship, not kinship as the expression of birth" (M. Sahlins, *The Use and Abuse of Biology: An Anthropological Critique of Sociobiology* [Ann Arbor: University of Michigan Press, 1976], 58).

101. Meillassoux, *Mythes et limites*, 49.

102. The problem goes further, as Latour recognizes: it is that the very distinction and distribution between nature and culture, the biological and the social, are not universal, minimally, they follow different mappings and divisions.

103. Daniel Boyarin, "The Bartered Word: Midrash and Symbolic Economy," in *Commentaries— Kommentare [Aporemata: Kritische Studien zur Philologiegeschichte]*, ed. Glenn W. Most (Göttingen: Vandenhoeck & Ruprecht, 1999), 44, commenting on the Babylonian Talmud, Tractate *Nidda* 30a; the passage, and its Galenic parallels, is also mentioned by Joseph Needham, *A History of Embryology* (Cambridge: Cambridge University Press, 1959), 78.

104. Fonrobert, *Menstrual Purity*, 109.

105. As Elizabeth Povinelli describes the effect of the work of lawyers and anthropologists (among others) on Australian aborigines, "the spiritual and material relationship that Aboriginal men and women had to land, to the dead, and to the unborn was reduced *in the last instance* to the heterosexual reproduction of blood, *symbolically* narrowed and demarcated by the patrilineal totem" (E. A. Povinelli, *The Cunning of Recognition: Indigenous Alterities and the Making of Australian Multiculturalism* [Durham, N.C.: Duke University Press, 2002], 209). Addressing conceptions of kinship (and the different realms it covers when "translated"), the anthropologist acknowledges that this is "what we summarize as blood" (248). One can therefore ask who or what speaks when the historian writes about medieval times that "if a man married a woman of higher station, the blood of his lineage could be irrigated by that of kings, princes, and counts. This periodic infusion of good blood not only rejuvenated the family's nobility but ensured the cohesion of the dominant class" (Dominique Barthélemy, "Kinship," trans. Arthur Goldhammer, in *A History of Private Life: Revelations of the Medieval World*, ed. Georges Duby [Cambridge, Mass.: The Belknap Press of Harvard University Press, 1988], 120).

106. As I reiterate a number of times throughout this book, race science, or the medical ground for the establishment of the "bio-political" diagnosed by Foucault and others, is a latecomer among the various conditions that rendered bio-power possible—and real (see, e.g., Jonathan Marks, "Blood Will Tell (Won't It?): A Century of Molecular Discourse in Anthropological Systematics," *American Journal of Physical Anthropology* 94 (1994): 59–79.

107. Even an astute historian of race might thus reduce blood to biology rather than recognize biology as a limited moment in a much larger *hematology* (see Arlette Jouanna, *Ordre social. Mythes et hiérarchies dans la France du XVIe siècle* [Paris: Hachette, 1977], e.g., 42).

108. As M. Schrenk points out, "hematology is the scientific teachings on blood," it is a tradition that consists in the study of blood—blood as "empirical fact," as it were (M. Schrenk, "Blultkulte und Blutsymbolik," in *Einführung in die Geschichte der Hämatologie*, ed. K. G. v. Boroviczény et al. [Stuttgart: Georg Thieme Verlag, 1974], 1). I take the term in a wider sense, which would include the history of hematology, everything that would account for the "genesis and development" of blood as a fact—empirical, scientific, and more (see Ludwig Fleck, *Genesis and Development of a Scientific Fact*, trans. Fred Bradley and Thaddeus J. Trenn (Chicago: University of Chicago Press, 1979). Fleck's book is another essential moment in the history of blood, most particularly of "syphilitic blood." It describes the simultaneous generalization and specialization that increasingly frames the concept of blood as the operation of "socio-cogitative forces" (23) and enables us to understand hematology as the fabric of which Latour speaks, at the historical development of blood as one among "somewhat hazy proto-ideas" about which Fleck explains that they "existed long before any scientific proofs were available and were supported in different ways throughout the intervening period until they received a modern expression" (24). I thank Mario Biagioli for directing me to Fleck's work.

109. "The history of words," Samuel Weber writes, "is rarely simple or transparent." Indeed, "it is almost always symptomatic, which is to say, significant, though often in a dissimulating mode" (S. Weber, *Targets of Opportunity: On the Militarization of Thinking* [New York:

Fordham University Press, 2005], vii). If "blood" is a word, even if it is merely a word, we would have to follow Weber's advice and ask about the hematologization or perhaps simply about the bloodiness of thinking.

110. Documenting the place of Native Americans in the American imagination, Renée Bergland asks: "Why must America write itself as haunted?" As will become apparent, there are many reasons to borrow her pointed line of interrogation and extend it to blood (R. L. Bergland, *The National Uncanny: Indian Ghosts and American Subjects* [Hanover, N.H.: University Press of New England, 2000], 4).

111. Susan E. Lederer, *Flesh and Blood: Organ Transplantation and Blood Transfusion in Twentieth-Century America* (Oxford: Oxford University Press, 2008), xiii; and see Orlando Patterson, *Rituals of Blood: Consequences of Slavery in Two American Centuries* (Washington, D.C.: Civitas, 1998) and Carolyn Marvin and David W. Ingle, *Blood Sacrifice and the Nation: Totem Rituals and the American Flag* (Cambridge: Cambridge University Press, 1999).

112. I quote from J. Kēhaulani Kauanui, *Hawaiian Blood: Colonialism and the Politics of Sovereignty and Indigeneity* (Durham, N.C.: Duke University Press, 2008), 7, and see Sally Engle Merry, *Colonizing Hawai'i: The Cultural Power of Law* (Princeton, N.J.: Princeton University Press, 1999); for an excellent review and analysis of the issue with regard to Native Americans, see Circe Sturm, *Blood Politics: Race, Culture, and Identity in the Cherokee Nation of Oklahoma* (Berkeley: University of California Press, 2002), and see for a comparative approach, Ariella J. Gross, *What Blood Won't Tell: A History of Race on Trial in America* (Cambridge, Mass.: Harvard University Press, 1998). Gross reminds us that "in establishing its dominance over a subject people, the U.S. government introduced the notion of blood quantum to divide those who were considered too incompetent to sell or transfer their land from those who would not receive legal protection; that notion of 'blood' then took on a life of its own to separate once united peoples along the lines of white and black, pure and mixed" (179).

113. I return to the "one-drop rule" in more detail later in the chapter.

114. J. Kēhaulani Kauanui discusses the typical manner in which F. James Davis, in his otherwise groundbreaking book on the one-drop rule, "completely neglects to mention the use of blood quantum laws to define Hawaiianness" (*Hawaiian Blood*, 21). Circe Sturm, for her part, attends to the complex history of black slavery among Native Americans, but mentions the one-drop rule only in passing (*Blood Politics*, 70 and 105).

115. "The ultimate insignificance of ethnicity and race," writes Colin Kidd quite representatively, "surfaces in the New Testament. Acts 17:26 sets out a clear statement of the unity of humankind" (Colin Kidd, *The Forging of Races: Race and Scripture in the Protestant Atlantic World* [Cambridge: Cambridge University Press, 2006], 20); Kidd elaborates on the possibility of holding profoundly racist positions together with a commitment to that verse (38). Elise Lemire documents the centrality of blood, and blood mixing, in abolitionist discourse. Whether this meant "a physical injection of blood" or other forms of "mixture," the role and significance of blood was a matter of shared concerns (E. Lemire, *"Miscegenation": Making Race in America* [Philadelphia: University of Pennsylvania Press, 2002], 129); and see also Kenneth N. Addison, *"We Hold These Truths to Be Self-Evident..." An Interdisciplinary*

Analysis of the Roots of Racism and Slavery in America (Lanham, Md.: University Press of America, 2009), 274; Susan Gillman, *Blood Talk: American Race Melodrama and the Culture of the Occult* [Chicago: University of Chicago Press, 2003], 46).

116. Paul Goodman, *Of One Blood: Abolitionism and the Origins of Racial Equality* (Berkeley: University of California Press, 1998); Patterson, *Rituals of Blood*.

117. Susan Gillman, *Blood Talk: American Race Melodrama and the Culture of the Occult* (Chicago: University of Chicago Press, 2003).

118. Paul F. Campos, *Jurismania: The Madness of American Law* (Oxford: Oxford University Press, 1998).

119. James Q. Whitman, *The Origins of Reasonable Doubt: Theological Roots of the Criminal Trial* (New Haven, Conn.: Yale University Press, 2008), see, e.g., 126.

120. And see also William Blackstone, *Commentaries on the Laws of England*, ed. Hardcastle Browne (St. Paul, Minn.: West Publishing, 1897), 195, 287; Colin Dayan expands on the "corruption of blood" and on the significance of blood in relation to property and slavery in *The Law is a White Dog: How Legal Rituals Make and Unmake Persons* (Princeton: Princeton University Press, 2011) 44–53.

121. With the phrase "the sanguinary empire," Keally McBride refers to the practices of punishment inscribed in the laws of the United States and in its history (K. McBride, *Punishment and Political Order* [Ann Arbor: University of Michigan Press, 2007], 81–102); Richard Slotkin, *Redemption Through Violence: The Mythology of the American Frontier, 1600–1860* (Norman: University of Oklahoma Press, 1973); James Q. Whitman, *Harsh Justice: Criminal Punishment and the Widening Divide Between America and Europe* (Oxford: Oxford University Press, 2003); Austin Sarat, ed., *The Killing State: Capital Punishment in Law, Politics, and Culture* (Oxford: Oxford University Press, 1999).

122. Robert Cover, *Narrative, Violence, and the Law*, 102; Cover later adds that "some interpretations are writ in blood and run with a warranty of blood as part of their validating force" (146).

123. Eva Saks, "Representing Miscegenation Law," in *Interracialism: Black-White Intermarriage in American History, Literature, and Law*, ed. Werner Sollors (Oxford: Oxford University Press, 2000), 67–68.

124. Abraham Lincoln, "Address Before the Young Men's Lyceum" (1838), quoted in Russ Castronovo, *Fathering the Nation: American Genealogies of Slavery and Freedom* (Berkeley: University of California Press, 1995), 1; Castronovo's is in many ways a muted meditation on "the curses and blessings of blood" in America (224–25); Susan Mizruchi suggests that for Lincoln at that time, "the obligation to preside over an internal bloodbath widely classified as 'national atonement' must have seemed a prophetic fulfillment" (S. L. Mizruchi, *The Science of Sacrifice: American Literature and Modern Social Theory* [Princeton, N.J.: Princeton University Press, 1998], 363); and Priscilla Wald documents a later development, namely, the events surrounding Lincoln's 1850 Repeal Speech, and the debate with Senator Stephen Douglas, who himself had invoked "the purity of the blood" as an American ideal. In his rejoinder, Wald argues, Lincoln "replaces 'blood ties' with an 'electric cord' of shared political beliefs" (P. Wald, *Constituting Americans: Cultural Anxiety and Narrative Form* (Durham, N.C.: Duke University Press, 1995), 58–59.

125. Alys Eve Weinbaum, *Wayward Reproductions: Genealogies of Race and Nation in Transatlantic Modern Thought* (Durham, N.C.: Duke University Press, 2004), 5.

126. Michael Paul Rogin, *Fathers and Children: Andrew Jackson and the Subjugation of the American Indian* (New York: Vintage, 1976), and see Russ Castronovo, *Fathering the Nation: American Genealogies of Slavery and Freedom* (Berkeley: University of California Press, 1995).

127. David M. Schneider, *American Kinship: A Cultural Account* (Chicago: University of Chicago Press, 1980), 91 and 111; and see Lewis Henry Morgan, *Systems of Consanguinity and Affinity of the Human Family* (Lincoln: University of Nebraska Press, 1997 [1866]); Gillian Feeley-Harnik, "'Communities of Blood': The Natural History of Kinship in Nineteenth-Century America," *Comparative Studies in Society and History* 41, no. 2 (April 1999): 215–62; as well as Feeley-Harnik, "The Ethnography of Creation: Lewis Henry Morgan and the American Beaver," in *Relative Values: Reconfiguring Kinship Studies*, ed. Sarah Franklin and Susan McKinnon (Durham, N.C.: Duke University Press, 2001), 54–84; and see Kath Weston, "Kinship, Controversy, and the Sharing of Substance: The Race/Class Politics of Blood Transfusion" in the same volume, 147–74.

128. Keith Wailoo, *Drawing Blood: Technology and Disease Identity in Twentieth-Century America* (Baltimore, Md.: Johns Hopkins University Press, 1997), 163; Jeanne Linden and Celso Bianco, *Blood-Safety and Surveillance* (New York and Basel: Marcel Dekker, 2001).

129. Wailoo, *Drawing Blood*, 6 and 85.

130. Bruno Latour, *Pandora's Hope: Essays on the Reality of Science Studies* (Cambridge, Mass.: Harvard University Press, 1999), 80; , Latour first published this book in English, with an American publisher. It was translated into French a few years later.

131. Ludwik Fleck, *Genesis and Development of a Scientific Fact*, trans. Fred Bradley and Thaddeus J. Trenn (Chicago: University of Chicago Press, 1989).

132. Melbourne Tapper, *In the Blood: Sickle Cell Anemia and the Politics of Race* (Philadelphia: University of Pennsylvania Press, 1999).

133. Michael Sappol, *A Traffic of Dead Bodies: Anatomy and Embodied Social Identity in Nineteenth Century America* (Princeton, N.J.: Princeton University Press, 2002), and see Ruth Richardson, *Death, Dissection, and the Destitute* (London: Phoenix Press, 2001); see also Whitt, *Science, Colonialism* (see references there); Harriet A. Washington, *Medical Apartheid: The Dark History of Medical Experimentation on Black Americans from Colonial Times to the Present* (New York: Harlem Moon, 2006); and see Castronovo's contribution, discussing the hygienic restriction of masturbation for the harm it does to the blood (R. Castronovo, *Necro Citizenship: Death, Eroticism, and the Public Sphere in The Nineteenth-Century United States* [Durham, N.C.: Duke University Press, 2001], 266, n. 18).

134. Quoted in Alexandra Minna Stern, *Eugenic Nation: Faults and Frontiers of Better Breeding in Modern America* (Berkeley: University of California Press, 2005), 84.

135. Peggy Pascoe, *What Comes Naturally: Miscegenation Law and the Making of Race in America* (Oxford: Oxford University Press, 2009), 138.

136. Wailoo, *Drawing Blood*, 196 and 190.

137. Lederer, *Flesh and Blood*, xii.

138. Paul A. Kramer, *The Blood of Government: Race, Empire, the United States, and the Philippines* (Chapel Hill: University of North Carolina Press, 2006).

139. Richard Hofstadter, *The Paranoid Style in American Politics and Other Essays* (New York: Vintage, 2008), 3–4.

140. Tocqueville, *Democracy in America*, see 887 note c.

141. Tocqueville, travel note from January 3, 1832, in *Democracy*, 547 note a, and see 573 and 581; In the 1830s, Charles de Beaumont was traveling with Tocqueville and he wondered about seating arrangements in American theaters. He was informed, he says, "that the dignity of the white blood demanded these distinctions" (quoted in Morone, *Hellfire Nation*, 119).

142. *Democracy*, 497; emphasis added. As one commentator has it, "Tocqueville's allusions to the barriers between civilized and uncivilized are couched in terms of skin color and blood, whiteness and redness, or if not redness, of a darkish color, visibly, and therefore, it would seem, intrinsically different and separate" (Harvey Mitchell, *America After Tocqueville: Democracy Against Difference* [Cambridge: Cambridge University Press, 2004], 80).

143. Drew Gilpin Faust, *This Republic of Suffering: Death and the American Civil War* (New York: Alfred A. Knopf, 2008), 3.

144. Kern Paster, *The Body Embarrassed*, 66.

145. John Adams, "On the British Constitution," quoted in Bailyn, *The Ideological Origins of the American Revolution*, 68; I suppose that I mean to provide here a recapitulation, albeit truncated, of Catherine Holland's study of the body in the American political imagination, while questioning the privileging of the figurative (C. A. Holland, *The Body Politic: Foundings, Citizenship, and Difference in the American Political Imagination* [New York: Routledge, 2001]).

146. I. Bernard Cohen, "Harrington and Harvey: A Theory of the State Based on the New Physiology," *Journal of the History of Ideas* 55, no. 2 (April 1994): 197–98.

147. *The Federalist*, November 30, 1787, in Hamilton, Madison, and Jay, *The Federalist with Letters of "Brutus*," ed. Terrence Ball (Cambridge: Cambridge University Press, 2004), 63.

148. Thomas Paine, *The Complete Writings*, ed. Philip S. Foner (New York: Citadel Press, 1945), vol. 2, 15 and 464.

149. Paine, *Complete Writings*, vol. 1, 400, and see vol. 2, 200 and 387n21.

150. John Quincy Adams, quoted in Rogin, *Fathers and Children*, 105.

151. Bartlett, *Wrong on Race*, 125.

152. "President Barack Obama's Inaugural Address," January 20, 2009. Accessible at www .whitehouse.gov/blog/inaugural-address/.

153. Drew Gilpin Faust cites this phrase from a 1864 letter by a Confederate soldier who considers the opportunity given him and his brothers-in-arms confronting "some nasty blue Yankees" to "take still more that of your own hearts take that with what you have already drunk" (D. G. Faust, *This Republic of Suffering*, 36).

154. Ian Baucom, *Specters of the Atlantic: Finance Capital, Slavery, and the Philosophy of History* (Durham, N.C.: Duke University Press, 2005); John T. Irwin, *American Hieroglyphics: The Symbol of the Egyptian Hieroglyphics in the American Renaissance* (Baltimore, Md.: Johns Hopkins University Press, 1980); John T. Coleman, *Vicious: Wolves and Men in America* (New Haven, Conn.: Yale University Press, 2004); Cesare Casarino, *Modernity at Sea: Melville, Marx, Conrad in Crisis* (Minneapolis: University of Minnesota Press, 2002); Carl Schmitt, *Nomos of the Earth*; Gerald Horne, *The White Pacific: U.S. Imperialism and*

Black Slavery in the South Seas After the Civil War (Honolulu: University of Hawai'i Press, 2007); Anders Stephanson, *Manifest Destiny: American Expansionism and the Empire of Right* (New York: Hill and Wang, 1995); Richard Drinnon, *Facing West: The Metaphysics of Indian-Hating and Empire-Building* (Norman: University of Oklahoma Press, 1997); Susan L. Mizruchi, *The Science of Sacrifice: American Literature and Modern Social Theory* (Princeton, N.J.: Princeton University Press, 1998); Michael H. Hunt, *The American Ascendency: How the United States Gained and Wielded Global Dominance* (Chapel Hill: University of North Carolina Press, 2007).

155. Bloch, *Visionary Republic*, 87.

156. Kath Weston, "Kinship, Controversy, and the Sharing of Substance," 147; and compare Benedict Anderson's assertion that "The dreams of racism actually have their origin in ideologies of class, rather than in those of nation: above all in claims to divinity among rulers and to 'blue' or 'white' blood and 'breeding' among aristocracies" (B. Anderson, *Imagined Communities: Reflections on the Origin and Spread of Nationalism* [London: Verso, 1991], 149).

157. Kidd, *Forging of the Races*, 233.

158. Kidd, *Forging of the Races*, 50ff.; Jean Gaulmier, "Poison dans les veines. Note sur le thème du sang chez Gobineau," *Romantisme* 11, no. 31 (1981): 197–208; and see Susannah Heschel, *The Aryan Jesus: Christian Theologians and the Bible in Nazi Germany* (Princeton, N.J.: Princeton University Press, 2008).

159. Ruth H. Bloch, *Visionary Republic: Millennial Themes in American Thought, 1756–1800* (Cambridge: Cambridge University Press, 1985), 43; Rebecca M. Herzig, *Suffering for Science: Reason and Sacrifice in Modern America* (New Brunswick, N.J.: Rutgers University Press, 2005); Richard M. Titmuss, *The Gift Relationship: From Human Blood to Social Policy* (New York: The New Press, 1997); Catherine Waldby and Robert Mitchell, *Tissue Economies: Blood, Organs, and Cell Lines in Late Capitalism* (Durham, N.C.: Duke University Press, 2006); Kieran Healy, *Last Best Gifts*.

160. Titmuss, *The Gift Relationship*, 219.

161. Michael Davidson, "Strange Blood: Hemophobia and the Unexplored Boundaries of Queer Nation," in *Beyond the Binary: Reconstructing Cultural Identity in a Multicultural Context*, ed. Timothy B. Powell (New Brunswick, N.J.: Rutgers University Press, 1999), 39–60; and see Wailoo, *Drawing Blood*, for a specific focus on hematology.

162. Henry A. Giroux, "Zombie Politics and Other Late Modern Monstrosities in the Age of Disposability." Accessible at www.truth-out.org/111709Giroux. I thank Tanya Erzen for referring me to this essay; and see David McNally, *Monsters of the Market: Zombies, Vampires and Global Capitalism* (Leiden: Brill, 2011).

163. Seth-Grahame Smith, *Abraham Lincoln: Vampire Hunter* (New York: Grand Central Publishing, 2010), now a major motion picture, a prequel of sorts to Steven Spielberg's serial Christology; but see as well Steven Shaviro, *The Cinematic Body* (Minneapolis: University of Minnesota Press, 1993), esp. chap. 2; Rob Latham, *Consuming Youth: Vampires, Cyborgs, and the Culture of Consumption* (Chicago: University of Chicago Press, 2002); Laurence A. Rickels, *The Vampire Lectures* (Minneapolis: University of Minnesota Press, 1999).

164. Henry David Thoreau, *Walden and Other Writings* (New York: The Modern Library, 2000), 385; Thoreau will later rephrase, perhaps correct, this statement, and assert that "friendship is not so kind as it is imagined; it has not much human blood in it" (400).

165. "By their very language the spokesmen of Manifest Destiny evinced as early as 1845 a hunger that could be satisfied fully only in war. So palpable were their desires that Channing, according to one of the Stockbridge Sedgwicks, felt impelled, shortly before his death, to insist '*We must not give this people a taste for blood!*'" (Alan Heimert, "Moby-Dick and American Political Symbolism," *American Quarterly* 15, no. 4 [Winter 1963]: 507). As Benjamin explained, however, war is not naturally bloody. Nor is there anything natural about war. Consider, as one example among myriads, that "northern clergyman and theologian Horace Bushnell celebrated northern victory" and *compared* war to bleeding. "Bleeding, he asserted, was necessary to God's expansive—and expensive—purposes for America, and 'in this blood our unity is cemented and forever sanctified.'" That may be why he had earlier asserted that "like Christianity, history 'must feed itself on blood'"(D. F. Gilpin, *This Republic of Suffering*, 189–90).

166. Cormac McCarthy, *Blood Meridian Or the Evening Redness in the West* (New York: Vintage, 1992).

167. Mark C. Taylor, *Mystic Bones* (Chicago: University of Chicago Press, 2007), and see Jean-Clet Martin's proposal to conduct an "anatomy of the Middle Ages" by way of ossuaries, a book that notably, if not necessarily paradoxically, is guided by a concern with "fluxes" (J.-C. Martin, *Ossuaires: Anatomie du Moyen Âge roman* [Paris: Payot, 1995]).

168. Mark C. Taylor, *Field Notes from Elsewhere: Reflections on Dying and Living* (New York: Columbia University Press, 2009), 51–54.

169. Mark C. Taylor, *Confidence Games: Money and Markets in a World Without Redemption* (Chicago: University of Chicago Press, 2004), 67; I take this up again in the next chapter.

170. Saidiya V. Hartman, *Scenes of Subjection: Terror, Slavery, and Self-Making in Nineteenth Century America* (New York and Oxford: Oxford University Press, 1997), 133, 130.

171. Lederer, *Flesh and Blood*, xii; and see Waldby and Mitchell, *Tissue Economies*, 36.

172. Jonathan Gil Harris, *Sick Economies: Drama, Mercantilism, and Disease in Shakespeare's England* (Philadelphia: University of Pennsylvania Press, 2004). I attend to some of the links between blood and money in chap. 3.

173. Alan Hyde, *Bodies of Law* (Princeton, N.J.: Princeton University Press, 1997), 60.

174. Avital Ronell, *Finitude's Score*.

175. Matthew D. Lassiter and Joseph Crespino, eds., *The Myth of Southern Exceptionalism* (Oxford: Oxford University Press, 2010), focuses on the American South; for a more extended treatment, geographic and other, see María deGuzmán, *Spain's Long Shadow: The Black Legend, Off-Whiteness, and Anglo-American Empire* (Minneapolis: University of Minnesota Press, 2005) and *Rereading the Black Legend: The Discourses of Religious and Racial Difference in the Renaissance Empires*, ed. Margaret R. Greer, Walter D. Mignolo, and Maureen Quilligan (Chicago: University of Chicago Press, 2007).

176. Anne Norton, *Bloodrites of the Post-Structuralists: Words, Flesh, and Revolution* (New York: Routledge, 2002); and see Biale, *Blood and Belief*; Hart, *Jewish Blood*.

177. Caroline Walker Bynum, "The Blood of Christ in the Later Middle Ages," *Church History* 71, no. 4 (December 2002): 686; and see David Aers, "New Historicism and the Eucharist," *Journal of Medieval and Early Modern Studies* 33, no. 2 (Spring 2003): 241–59.

178. Keith Wailoo, *Drawing Blood*, 187 and 171.

179. Benny Hinn, *The Blood: Its Power from Genesis to Jesus to You* (Orlando, Fla.: Creation House, 1993); Billye Brym, *The Blood and the Glory* (Tulsa, Okla.: Harrison House, 1995); Brian Vickers, *Jesus' Blood and Righteousness: Paul's Theology of Imputation* (Wheaton, Ill.: Crossway Books, 2006).

180. Tuveson, *Redeemer Nation: The Idea of America's Millennial Role* (Chicago: University of Chicago Press, 1968).

181. James A. Morone, *Hellfire Nation: The Politics of Sin in American History* (New Haven, Conn.: Yale University Press, 2001), 12.

182. Francis Jennings, *The Creation of America: Through Revolution to Empire* (Cambridge: Cambridge University Press, 2000), 289.

183. See Melissa L. Meyer, *Thicker than Water: The Origins of Blood as Symbol and Ritual* (New York: Routledge, 2005).

184. On the "symbolics of blood" and the "analytics of sexuality," see Foucault, *The History of Sexuality, vol. 1: An Introduction*, trans. Robert Hurley (New York: Pantheon, 1978), 148 and passim.

185. In modern Western societies, writes Gayle Rubin, sexuality is "burdened with an excess of significance." My argument is that this is true of blood as well, before and after sexuality (Gayle Rubin, "Thinking Sex: Notes for a Radical Theory of the Politics of Sexuality," in *Pleasure and Danger: Exploring Female Sexuality*, ed. Carole S. Vance, [London: Routledge, 1984], 279). This is one reason why I have steered clear of the links between blood and sex—another layer of obviousness—which pervade our visual and televisual field, and for which vampires provide a privileged focalization.

186. For a recent instance of this discourse of exception, which includes (but is also often restricted to) Nazi Germany, apartheid South Africa, and the segregated United States, see Fay Botham's otherwise compelling study, *Almighty God Created the Races: Christianity, Interracial Marriage, and American Law* (Chapel Hill: University of North Carolina Press, 2009), 51; for a suggestive and wider casting of the net, see Guillaume Aubert, " 'The Blood of France': Race and Purity of Blood in the French Atlantic World," *The William and Mary Quarterly* 61, no. 3 (July 2004): 439–78.

187. I borrow the phrase "the vampire state" from Jonathan H. Frimpong-Ansah, *The Vampire State in Africa: The Political Economy of Decline in Ghana* (Trenton, N.J.: Africa World Press, 1992), and see Tomislav Longinovic, *Vampires Like Us: Writing Down 'The Serbs'* (Belgrade: Belgrade Circle, 2005), Dragan Kujundzic, "vEmpire, Glocalization, and the Melancholia of the Sovereign," *The Comparatist* 29 (May 2005): 82–100. For more on the state in this particular perspective, see Fernando Coronil, *The Magical State: Nature, Money, and Modernity in Venezuela* (Chicago: University of Chicago Press, 1997), Austin Sarat, ed., *The Killing State: Capital Punishment in Law, Politics, and Culture* (Oxford: Oxford University Press, 1999); David Theo Goldberg, *The Racial State* (Oxford: Blackwell, 2002); Mark Neocleous, *Imagining the State* (Maidenhead, U.K.: Open University Press,

2003); Suzanne Mettler evokes the interesting figure of "the submerged state" (S. Mettler, "Reconstituting the Submerged State: The Challenges of Social Policy Reform in the Obama Era," *Perspectives on Politics* 8, no. 3 [September 2010]: 803–824).

188. Hofstadter, *Paranoid Style*, 7.

189. Hofstadter, *Paranoid Style*, 6.

190. Mitchell, *America After Tocqueville*, 193, n. 13.

191. See Daniel J. Sharfstein, "Crossing the Color Line: Racial Migration and the One-Drop Rule, 1600–1860," *Vanderbilt University Law School Public Law and Legal Theory, Working Paper Number 08-30* (accessible at ssrn.com/abstract=1124999), 592–656, who comes the closest, but I could find no equivalent, by a legal scholar, or even a professional historian, that would compare with Paul Spruhan's "A Legal History of Blood Quantum in Federal Indian Law to 1935" (*South Dakota Law Review* 51 [2006]: 1–50); and note that some of the otherwise relevant founding studies are altogether missing any account of the rule. A. Leon Higginbotham Jr., *In the Matter of Color: Race and the American Legal Process* (Oxford: Oxford University Press, 1978), for instance, never explicitly mentions the one-drop rule. Scott Malcomson's bizarrely egalitarian rendering of race relations in America obviously refers to the rule in its title, but only mentions it explicitly very late in the volume (S. Malcomson, *One Drop of Blood: The American Misadventure of Race* [New York: Farrar, Straus and Giroux, 2000], 356).

192. Ariella Gross, *What Blood Won't Tell*, 297.

193. Sharfstein, "Crossing the Color Line," 595–96; Ariella Gross is most thorough in tracing some of the older deployment of blood and describing "the relatively recent history of 'blood' as a factor in the determination of citizenship, and its association with policies that destroyed indigenous peoples' land base" (Gross, *What Blood Won't Tell*, 210).

194. Sharfstein, "Crossing the Color Line," 596.

195. George M. Fredrikson, *Racism: A Short History* (Princeton, N.J.: Princeton University Press, 2002), 124.

196. F. J. Davis, *Who Is Black? One Nation's Definition* (University Park: Pennsylvania State University Press, 2001), 5.

197. Sturm, *Blood Politics*, 78; Sturm also notes that, to this day, "the federal government through the Bureau of Indian Affairs continues to use blood quantum as both a metaphor and measure of 'Indian' identity to manage tribal enrollments and determine eligibility for social services" (2); and see also Pauline Turner Strong and Barrik Van Winkle, " 'Indian Blood': Reflections on the Reckoning and Refiguring of Native North American Identity," *Cultural Anthropology* 11, no. 4, Resisting Identities (November 1996): 547–76.

198. Here is a succinct and accurate summary of the difference between bloods: "Although people must show only the slightest trace of 'black blood' to be forced (with or without their consent) into the category 'African American,' modern American Indians must formally produce strong evidence of often rather substantial amounts of 'Indian blood' to be allowed entry into the corresponding racial category. The regnant racial definitions applied to Indians are simply quite different than those that have applied (and continue to apply) to blacks. Modern Americans, as Native American studies professor Jack Forbes puts the matter, 'are always finding "blacks" (even if they look rather un-African), and . . .

are always losing "Indians" ' " (Eva Marie Garroutte, "The Racial Formation of American Indians: Negotiating Legitimate Identities Within Tribal and Federal Law," *American Indian Quarterly* 25, no. 2 [Spring 2001], 231); what ensued, of course, are all the expected and unexpected effects of a 'divide and rule' situation (see, e.g., Ariella Gross, *What Blood Won't Tell*, 128, 141ff.; and see Rogin, *Fathers and Children*, 125); alternatively, there could emerge singular "problems," that is, collective identities that are contested across existing divisions. Such is the case of the Lumbee Indians (Karen I. Blu, *The Lumbee Problem: The Making of an American Indian People* [Lincoln: University of Nebraska Press, 1980]).

199. "Blood quantum enshrines racial purity as the ideal for authentic American Indian identity" writes Chadwick Allen (C. Allen, "Blood (and) Memory," *American Literature* 71, no. 1 [March 1999]: 96). I am claiming that the one-drop rule operates in a similar, if also distinct, manner for African Americans, and for white folks too.

200. Frank W Sweet, *Legal History of the Color Line: The Rise and Triumph of the One-Drop Rule* (Palm Coast, Fla.: Backintyme, 2005), 171; this dense and compelling book is the closest we have to an exhaustive history of the one-drop rule in American history; on Virginia, see as well A. Leon Higginbotham Jr. and Barbara K. Kopytoff, "Racial Purity and Interracial Sex in the Law of Colonial and Antebellum Virginia," *Georgia Law Journal* 77 (1988–1989): 1967–2030; and see Paul Finkelman, "The Crime of Color," *Tulane Law Review* 67 (1992–1993): 2063–2112; for more on the "legal construction of race" in the United States, see Ian Haney-López, *White By Law: The Legal Construction of Race*, Revised and updated edition (New York: New York University Press, 2006), and Ariella Gross, *What Blood Won't Tell*; Gross also mentions the 1705 Virginia law (114).

201. Pascoe, *What Comes Naturally*, 7; Pascoe seems broadly in agreement with Frank Sweet, whom she does not mention; and compare: "such modern definitions of identity based on blood quantum closely reflect nineteenth- and early-twentieth-century theories of race introduced into indigenous cultures by Euro-Americans. These understood blood as quite literally the vehicle for the transmission of cultural characteristics" (Garroutte, "The Racial Formation of American Indians," 225).

202. Virginia R. Domínguez, *White by Definition: Social Classification in Creole Louisiana* (New Brunswick, N.J.: Rutgers University Press, 1986), 89.

203. Indeed, it may depend what is meant by "blood." Minimally, as Joyce E. Chaplin reminds us, "if race in modern times signifies a fixed set of bodily traits, purportedly specific to national or ethnic groups and transmitted through procreation, it was not a coherent hypothesis in the early modern period" (J. E. Chaplin, "Natural Philosophy and an Early Racial Idiom in North America: Comparing English and Indian Bodies," in *The William and Mary Quarterly*, third series, 54, no. 1 [January 1997]: 230); for a pertinent account of the narrowness—and persistence—of racial thought, see Walter Benn Michaels, "The No-Drop Rule," *Critical Inquiry* 20, no. 4 (Summer 1994): 758–69; a further compendium of thoughtful reflections on the issue can be found in *The German Invention of Race*, ed. Sara Eigen and Mark Larrimore (Albany: State University of New York Press, 2006).

204. Addison, *We Hold These Truths*, 188.

205. Kidd, *Forging of Races*, 8; as Felicity Nussbaum writes, "these kinds of gradation of complexion in the wider eighteenth-century world complicate and transform the

calibrations more familiar to students of the greater Caribbean—including Moreau de Saint-Méry's elaborate classification of degrees of black ancestry based on fractions of 'blood' transmitted through seven generations—and extend well beyond the increasingly rigid categorizations of early anthropology to sketch out an intricate racial atlas" (F. A. Nussbaum, "Between 'Oriental' and 'Blacks So Called,' 1688–1788," in *The Postcolonial Enlightenment: Eighteenth-Century Colonialism and Postcolonial Theory*, ed. Daniel Carey and Lynn Festa [Oxford: Oxford University Press, 2009], 144).

206. Ignatiev, *How the Irish Became White*, 97.

207. Race science obviously had much to say about blood, as did—to the extent that the two can be distinguished—medicine, but it seems that blood, which had never been the *exclusive* object of medical discourse, followed multiple and semi-independent paths of entry into the emerging scientific discourse and practice. Law and anthropology, nosology and phrenology, as it were, thickened blood's existing significance, elaborating on the older idea of a difference *between bloods,* but without becoming, not for a long time, a distinct hematology (recall that blood tests are a late nineteenth-century practice). The omnipresence of blood, its silent rule, is thus never thematized as such, as the documents assembled by Hammonds and Herzig show (*The Nature of Difference: Sciences of Race in the United States from Jefferson to Genomics*, ed. Evelynn M. Hammonds and Rebecca M. Herzig [Cambridge, Mass.: MIT Press, 2008]); for a more recent take on medicine and blood, as it were, *after* race science, see Melbourne Tapper, *In the Blood: Sickle Cell Anemia and the Politics of Race* (Philadelphia: University of Pennsylvania Press, 1999).

208. Winthrop D. Jordan, *White Over Black: American Attitudes Toward the Negro, 1550–1812* (Baltimore, Md.: Penguin Books, 1969), 165ff.

209. Herodotus, *Histories* 8.144, on which see Rosalind Thomas, "Ethnicity, Genealogy, and Hellenism in Herodotus," in *Ancient Perceptions of Greek Ethnicity*, ed. Irad Malkin (Cambridge, Mass.: Center for Hellenic Studies / Harvard University Press, 2001), 213–33; I attempt a different interpretation of "Greek blood" in chap. 4.

210. Ivan Hannaford, *Race: The History of an Idea in the West* (Baltimore, Md.: Johns Hopkins University Press, 1996), 10.

211. Américo Castro, as summarized by Hannaford, *Race*, 149.

212. Robert J. C. Young, *The Idea of English Ethnicity* (Oxford: Blackwell Publishing, 2008), 50; the argument for the novelty of race and of notions of hybridity is elaborated most fully by Young in *Colonial Desire: Hybridity in Theory, Culture, and Race* (London: Routledge, 1995).

213. The innumerable connections between Spain and the Americas with regard to the comportment and treatment of "others" are meticulously documented and elaborated by Jonathan Schorsch in his *Jews and Blacks in the Early Modern World* (Cambridge: Cambridge University Press, 2004); and see Schorsch's exhilarating *Swimming the Christian Atlantic: Judeoconversos, Afroiberians, and Amerindians in the Seventeenth Century* (Leiden: Brill, 2009).

214. Henry Goldschmitt, "Introduction," in *Race, Nation, and Religion in the Americas*, ed. Henry Goldschmitt and Elizabeth McAlister (Oxford: Oxford University Press, 2004), 13 (emphasis added); the one-drop rule is mentioned twice in this collection, without any explicit link made with the Statutes on the Purity of Blood (181, 202, n. 6).

215. Stoler, *Race and the Education of Desire*; Etienne Balibar and Immanuel Wallerstein, *Race, Nation, Class: Ambiguous Identities* (London and New York: Verso, 1991), 52, 208; David Brion Davis, *Inhuman Bondage: The Rise and Fall of Slavery in the New World* (Oxford: Oxford University Press, 2006); Irene Silverblatt insists that "race thinking took several, coeval shapes and that race thinking's duplicity lay in the ways its different manifestations went unrecognized and became intertwined" (Silverblatt, *Modern Inquisitions*, 120); earlier, she refers to "the colonial confusions over race and religion" (108).

216. Ronald Sanders, *Lost Tribes and Promised Lands: The Origins of American Racism* (Boston: Little, Brown and Company, 1978).

217. María Elena Martínez, *Genealogical Fictions: Limpieza de Sangre, Religion, and Gender in Colonial Mexico* (Stanford, Calif.: Stanford University Press, 2008), 40.

218. Barbara Fuchs, *Mimesis and Empire: The New World, Islam, and European Identities* (Cambridge: Cambridge University Press, 2001), 10, 93; and see also María deGuzmán, *Spain's Long Shadow: The Black Legend, Off-Whiteness, and Anglo-American Empire* (Minneapolis: University of Minnesota Press, 2005), esp. 115–19, 133; strangely enough, in her own efforts to counter the Black Legend, Irene Silverblatt makes her case for the modernity of the Inquisition by having the Spanish empire foreshadow the one-drop rule. More precisely, she writes that Peruvian "Inquisitors followed something like the 'one drop of blood' rule in their dealings with New Christians" (Silverblatt, *Modern Inquisitions*, 124).

219. Frank Sweet makes the compelling argument that the one-drop rule was in fact deployed independent of slavery, that the notion of "invisible blackness" only makes sense when slavery's mode of control and domination are absent (Sweet, *Legal History of the Color Line*).

220. María Elena Martínez gives an exemplary account of the significance of the Spanish purity of blood statutes in Mexico, but although she hints at the potential comparison, not to mention direct connections, she does not discuss the northern history of blood (M. E. Martínez, *Genealogical Fictions: Limpieza de Sangre, Religion, and Gender in Colonial Mexico* [Stanford, Calif.: Stanford University Press, 2008]); and see also Claudio Lomnitz, *Deep Mexico, Silent Mexico: An Anthropology of Nationalism* (Minneapolis: University of Minnesota Press, 2001).

221. See, for example, James H. Sweet, "The Iberian Roots of American Racist Thought," *The William and Mary Quarterly*, third series, 54, no. 1 (January 1997): 143–66.

222. It is this very distinction that María Elena Martínez is intent on undoing, identifying "race" in a premodern context. Though I have tried to engage the matter from a different perspectives (in *Semites*), I tend to agree with her argument, but only wonder whether the "recognition" that race and religion are coextensive should not lead to a further interrogation of historical or geographic boundaries, which otherwise seem to isolate or segregate this configuration from potential analogues. Thus, Martínez has nothing to say about Anglo America, for example (which, some might still try to argue, is not so far from Mexico—see David J. Weber, *The Spanish Frontier in North America* [New Haven, Conn.: Yale University Press, 2009]—but the walls are getting higher); for distinct but related projects see Denise Kimber Buell, *Why This New Race: Ethnic Reasoning in Early*

Christianity (New York: Columbia University Press, 2005), and Tracy Fessenden, *Culture and Redemption: Religion, The Secular, and American Literature* (Princeton, N.J.: Princeton University Press, 2007).

223. Consider, for instance, how evoking "the idea of fixed racial or 'blood' categories" in the context of Native American memory "distressingly echoes," according to Chadwick Allen, "Nazi racialist belief" rather than the very American history of blood quantum (or racialist doctrine, law, and science) Allen cogently goes on to discuss (Chadwick Allen, "Blood (and) Memory," *American Literature* 71, no. 1 [March 1999]: 95; and recall C. Walker Bynum, "The Blood of Christ in the Later Middle Ages," *Church History* 71, no. 4 [December 2002]: 708, n. 77).

224. It is in this sense, I think, that Ralph Peters writes of "blood borders," while helping us along toward an essential—nay, world-historical—categorization of the world according to American foreign policy: "winners" and "losers" (Ralph Peters, "Blood Borders: How a Better Middle East Would Look," *Armed Forces Journal* [2006]. Accessible at www .armedforcesjournal.com/2006/06/1833899).

225. Susan Gillman, *Blood Talk: American Race Melodrama and the Culture of the Occult* (Chicago: University of Chicago Press, 2003). One could of course argue that there is also a persistent *absence* of blood talk, even where one would expect it. Thus, Paul Goodman's *Of One Blood: Abolitionism and the Origins of Racial Equality* (Berkeley: University of California Press, 1998), which places blood—one blood—at the source and center of a social and political movement, does not spend anytime on, well, blood.

226. Sir Henry James Sumner Maine, *Ancient Law: Its Connection to the History of Early Society* (Charleston, S.C.: Bibliobazaar, 2008), 52, 99.

227. Balibar and Wallerstein, *Race, Nation, Class*, 100.

228. Michel Foucault, *The Birth of Biopolitics. Lectures at the College de France, 1978–79*, trans. Graham Burchell (New York: Palgrave Macmillan, 2008), 34.

229. Charles Sumner, the Massachusetts statesman, referred to slavery—which he staunchly opposed—as a "bloody flower" blooming "everywhere in sight" (quoted in Richard Franklin Bensel, *Yankee Leviathan: The Origins of Central State Authority in America, 1859–1877* [Cambridge: Cambridge University Press, 1990], 20, n. 3).

230. David Brion Davis, *The Problem of Slavery*.

231. "The tide of change continued to erode the soil of freedom from beneath the feet of African colonists when Massachusetts became the first colony to give statutory recognition to slavery in 1641, with Connecticut following in 1650" (Addison, *We Hold These Truths*, 244).

232. See the excellent survey of these debates in the work of Denise Eileen McCoskey, and see Denise Buell, *Why This New Race*, and *The Origins of Racism in the West*.

233. See, for example, *Mixed Race America and the Law: A Reader*, ed. Kevin R. Johnson (New York: New York University Press, 2003).

234. For a concise and effective critique of the shortcomings of the category of "bad science," see Nadia Abu el-Haj, *Facts on the Ground: Archaeological Practice and Territorial Self-Fashioning in Israeli Society* (Chicago: Chicago University Press, 2001), 8–9.

235. Cover, *Narrative, Violence, and the Law*, 102; Whitman, *The Origins of Reasonable Doubt*.

236. Peter Goodrich, *Oedipus Lex: Psychoanalysis, History, Law* (Berkeley: University of California Press, 1995), 79.

237. Sir William Blackstone, *Commentaries on the Laws of England*, ed. Hardcastle Browne (St. Paul, Minn.: West Publishing, 1897), 732.

238. Otto von Gierke, *Natural Law and the Theory of Society*, trans. Ernest Barker (Cambridge: Cambridge University Press, 1934), 226; earlier Gierke had complained that "the sovereignty of the State of which Grotius writes never becomes anything more than a bloodless category" (56). Sovereignty, like law, is or should be bloody.

239. Pierre Legendre, *Lecons IV: L'inestimable objet de la transmission: Études sur le principe généalogique en Occident* (Paris: Fayard, 2004), e.g., 146, 154, 282.

240. Christine Caldwell Ames, *Righteous Persecution: Inquisition, Dominicans, and Christianity in the Middle Ages* (Philadelphia: University of Pennsylvania Press, 2009); for a more extended discussion of the specifically legal aspects of the Inquisition, see Edward Peters, *Inquisition* (Berkeley: University of California Press, 1989). Geoffrey Galt Harpham argues that the Inquisition was a fundamentally modern, rather than "medieval" (in the sense of backward and bloody), institution (G. G. Harpham, "So . . . What *Is* Enlightenment: An Inquisition into Modernity," *Critical Inquiry* 20, no. 3 [Spring 1994]: 524–56), and see *Rereading the Black Legend: The Discourses of Religious and Racial Difference in the Renaissance Empires*, ed. Margaret R. Greer, Walter D. Mignolo, and Maureen Quilligan (Chicago: University of Chicago Press, 2007).

241. Often a signifier of the archaic, blood stays behind as well in the work of historians of law. David Cohen explains that "historians of Greek law have not investigated the place of law in the broader agonistic context of Athenian society . . . they generally assume that by the classical era Athens had long before made the 'transition' to another 'stage' of legal development, marked by the displacement of blood feud by the rule of law" (David Cohen, *Law, Violence, and Community in Classical Athens* [Cambridge: Cambridge University Press, 1993], 196).

242. Danielle S. Allen, *The World of Prometheus: The Politics of Punishing in Democratic Athens* (Princeton, N.J.: Princeton University Press, 2000), 3; for further illustration, consider Hans Kelsen: "it seems that blood revenge is the earliest socially organized sanction" (H. Kelsen, *General Theory of Law and State*, trans. Anders Wedberg [Cambridge, Mass.: Harvard University Press, 1949], 17), or note the basic agreement here of the Marxist legal theorist Evgeny B. Pashukanis, who writes that "historically, the origin of criminal law is associated with the custom of blood vengeance" (E. Pashukanis, *General Theory of Law and Marxism*, trans. Barbara Einhorn [New Brunswick, N.J.: Transaction Publishers, 2007], 168).

243. Randall Lesaffer, "Peace Treaties from Lodi to Westphalia," in *Peace Treaties and International Law in European History from the Late Middle Ages to World War One*, ed. R. Lesaffer (Cambridge: Cambridge University Press, 2004), 29.

244. "No real blood runs in the veins of the cognitive subject that Locke, Hume, and Kant constructed," complained Dilthey, quoted in Hans-Georg Gadamer, *Truth and Method*, trans. Joel Weinsheimer and Donald G. Marshall (London: Continuum, 2004), 238; wishing to "give flesh and blood to the law," Colin Dayan shows this is a problematic

take (*The Law Is a White Dog*, 254); she particularly underscores the role of blood in the unmaking of the slave as a legal person (53–54); and see Rick Mohr, "Flesh and the Person," University of Wollongong, Faculty of Law, 2008 (accessible at Research Online, http://ro.uow.edu.au/lawpapers/41), and Ngaire Naffine, *Law's Meaning of Life: Philosophy, Religion, Darwin, and the Legal Person* (Oxford: Hart Publishing, 2009). Does it make a difference whether the "person"—assuming this could be deemed a universal concept (see Mauss and the literature on the person)—is understood as "flesh and blood" or as "flesh and bones" (as the Hebrew Bible signals the individual) or as "bone" alone (Cai Hua, *Society Without Fathers*)? Does it matter whether law is produced in relation to a medical discourse that sees the body as full (too full) of blood or as balanced (Kuriyama, *The Expressiveness of the Body*)? Does blood make a difference? The question is misleading because it is the very fact that blood and difference are articulated together that marks the contours of the very "field" I am aiming to trace.

245. Rogin, *Fathers and Children*, 101.

246. Susan Gilman, *Blood Talk*, 46.

247. *The Revised Code of the Laws of Virginia* (Richmond, Va.: Thomas Ritchie, 1819), 357; and see Sir William Blackstone, *Commentaries on the Laws of England*, ed. Hardcastle Browne (St. Paul, Minn.: West Publishing, 1897), where the phrase "inheritable blood" and versions of blood quantum are deployed repeatedly ("Half-blood cannot inherit," 279).

248. See again Blackstone, *Commentaries*.

249. Goodrich, *Oedipus Lex*, 132.

250. W. J. Jennings, *The Christian Imagination: Theology and the Origins of Race* (New Haven: Yale University Press, 2010), see also Kameron Carter, *Race: A Theological Account*; Orlando Patterson, *Rituals of Blood: Consequences of Slavery in Two American Centuries* (Washington, D.C.: Civitas/Counterpoint, 1998); Goldschmitt and McAlister, *Race, Nation, and Religion in the Americas;* Buell, *Why This New Race;*.

251. For a general treatment of the state, see *States and Citizens*, ed. Quentin Skinner and Bo Strath (Cambridge: Cambridge University Press, 2003), and see *States of Imagination: Ethnographic Explorations of the Postcolonial State*, ed. Thomas Blom Hansen and Finn Stepputat (Durham, N.C.: Duke University Press, 2001), and *The Anthropology of the State: A Reader*, ed. Aradhana Sharma and Akhil Gupta (Oxford: Blackwell Publishing, 2006); for a summary of Foucault on "political anatomy" see Francois Ewald, "Anatomie et Corps Politiques," *Critique* 31 (1975), reprinted in *Michel Foucault: Critical Assessments*, vol. 5, ed. Barry Smart (London: Routledge, 1995), 3–33.

252. Wendy Brown, *Walled States, Waning Sovereignty* (New York: Zone Books, 2010), 21; Brown insists throughout on the importance of "flows," something that may, as it were, *fuse* or *liquefy* her reference to an earlier time, when "settled and intact state sovereignty" did not require visible signs. Whether it is the case that, prior to its waning, sovereignty "produces bounded national composition and order without hyperbolic border militarization and barricading—it orders through its structuring and ubiquitous presence, through the charisma of sovereignty, and above all, through the *fusion* of nation, state, and sovereign" (118; emphasis added). One might be encouraged here to think of the sovereignty of blood, of sovereignty as blood.

253. *Contemporary States of Emergency: The Politics of Military and Humanitarian Interventions*, ed. Didier Fassin and Mariella Pandolfi (New York: Zone Books, 2010).

254. Quoted in Nancy Ruttenburg, *Democratic Personality: Popular Views and the Trial of American Authorship* (Stanford, Calif.: Stanford University Press, 1998), 63.

255. Quoted in Matthew Frye Jacobson, *Whiteness of a Different Color: European Immigrants and the Alchemy of Race* (Cambridge, Mass.: Harvard University Press, 1998), 177 (the language of "degeneration" reflects the prevalent anti-Spanish sentiment of the time, while the *limpieza* argument is once again turned on its head); and see Addison, who comments: "Despite the fact that Sewall had directed an antislavery polemic against Saffin, the two men did agree on one central issue, which was the potential that the "extravasate blood" of African aliens would taint the body politic and possibly the bloodline of the colony if left unchecked" (Addison, *We Hold These Truths*, 245).

256. "Is Slavery Christian?" Incidentally, the *Oxford English Dictionary* approximates the first use of the word *extravasate* around 1663–1676, which makes Sir Robert Boyle's 1684 concern with "extravasated" blood a fairly original instance (see Kern Paster, *The Body Embarrassed*, 67), and Sewall's use almost contemporary with it. I need to reiterate that this excluded inclusion is not exceptional, nor is it exceptionally American. As Laporte describes it in his discussion of race, class, and "all those things tied to a vile and earthly trade (money, blood, sex) . . . the State is understood as pure and inviolable, as capable of purifying the most repulsive things— even money—through the touch of its divine hand" (D. Laporte, *History of Shit*, trans. Nadia Benabid and Rodolphe El-Khoury [Cambridge, Mass.: MIT Press, 2000], 40). The state is, in other words, as "disinclined to dirty itself with either the blood of Christ or the shit of commerce" (58), which is to say that it maintains an essential relation to both. There is more to be said about money and commerce, about which in the next chapter.

257. George M. Fredrickson, *White Supremacy: A Comparative Study in American and South African History* (Oxford: Oxford University Press, 1981), 126; Fredrickson is also commenting on Sewall's statement about the "extravasat blood" of the body politic.

258. George Lawson, *Politica Sacra et Civilis*, ed. Conal Condren (Cambridge: Cambridge University Press, 1992), 252.

259. Timothy Mitchell, "The Limits of the State: Beyond Statist Approaches and Their Critics," *American Political Science Review* 85, no. 1 (March 1991): 77; and see responses to Mitchell by John Bendix, Bertell Ollman, and Bartholomew H. Sparrow, "Going Beyond the State?" in *American Political Science Review* 86, no. 4 (December 1992): 1007–1021.

260. Ashis Nandy, *The Romance of the State and the Fate of Dissent in the Tropics* (Delhi: Oxford University Press, 2003), 7.

261. Nandy, *The Romance of the State*, 7; a different phrasing of this argument can be found in Sudipta Kaviraj, "On the Enchantment of the State: Indian Thought on the Role of the State in the Narrative of Modernity," *European Journal of Sociology* 46, no. 2 (2005): 263–96; more recently, see the argument made by Paul Kahn on the sovereign state and its deployment of violence in *Political Theology: Four New Chapters on the Concept of Sovereignty* (New York: Columbia University Press, 2011).

262. Karen Ho, *Liquidated: An Ethnography of Wall Street* (Durham, N.C.: Duke University Press, 2009), 11.

263. See, for example, Charles Lewis Wayper, *Political Thought* (New York: Philosophical Library, 1954), and see Jacques Rancière, *On the Shores of Politics*, trans. Liz Heron (London: Verso, 1995.

264. Sarah Beckwith, *Christ's Body: Identity, Culture, and Society in Late Medieval Writings* (London: Routledge, 1993); it is an interesting fact in itself that in spite of Kantorowicz's work, numerous histories of the body politic ignore Paul's contribution or the role played by Christ's body. Consider how Adriana Cavarero's impeccably succinct history of the body politic excludes the body of Christ but includes the following acknowledgment: "Although the bodily metaphor is generally called 'organic' or 'organological,' the idea of a body made of organs is absent among the Greeks and probably begins in the Middle Ages" (A. Cavarero, *Stately Bodies: Literature, Philosophy, and the Question of Gender*, trans. Robert de Lucca and Deanna Shemek (Ann Arbor: University of Michigan Press, 2002), 106; and compare Tilman Struve, "Der Staat als Funktion des *corpus Christi*," in Struve, *Die Entwicklung der organologischen Staatsauffassung im Mittelalter* (Stuttgart: Anton Hiesermann, 1978), 87–97; and Hale, *Body Politic*, 28ff.

265. Samuel Mintz rightly, and not untypically, insists on the metaphorical in his reading of Hobbes, granting no more than "imaginative truth" to its efficacy, whereas I am arguing for the instability of the metaphorical in its relation to the literal, indeed, to the political (S. I. Mintz, "Leviathan as Metaphor," *Hobbes Studies* II [1989]: 9).

266. Dante, *Monarchy*, ed. Prue Shaw (Cambridge: Cambridge University Press, 1996), 55. I am in agreement with John Bendix here who, in his answer to Timothy Mitchell, insists on the importance of law in the institutions of the state and toward its understanding. Unlike Bendix, who asserts that he is "neither sanguine about the state nor convinced that the state is an association like other social groups," I see in the emergence of blood in law and in the state a crucial and defining feature (Bendix et al., "Going Beyond the State?" 1007). Bendix concludes by quoting Jacob Burckhardt on the state as the "guardian of law" that prevents "blood feuds" (1010).

267. Shigehisa Kuriyama, *The Expressiveness of the Body and the Divergence of Greek and Chinese Medicine* (New York: Zone Books, 2002), 208.

268. Kuriyama, *The Expressiveness of the Body*, 214; and see Kern Paster, *The Body Embarrassed*, 74–78.

269. Frank Roumy, "La naissance de la notion canonique de *consanguinitas* et sa réception dans le droit civil," in *L'hérédité entre Moyen Âge et Époque moderne: Perspectives historiques*, ed. Maaike van der Lugt and Charles de Miramon (Firenze: Sismel-Edizioni del Galluzzo, 2008), 41–66; there is, I think, a larger, equally indisputable, argument at work here (or perhaps a "thicker" one) than the version proposed by Alain Boureau, to the effect that scholastic thought has "largely created, under the form of the Republican state [*l'État-république*] what would become the nation-state [*l'État-nation*]" (A. Boureau, *La religion de l'État: La construction de la République étatique dans le discours théologique de l'Occident médiéval (1250–1350). La raison scholastique I* [Paris: Les Belles Lettres, 2008], 179), and compare the chronology proposed by Thomas Ertman in his *Birth of Leviathan: Building States and Regimes in Medieval and Early Modern Europe* (Cambridge: Cambridge University Press, 1997).

270. John Bossy, "Blood and Baptism: Kinship, Community, and Christianity in Western Europe from the Fourteenth to the Seventeenth Centuries," in *Sanctity and Secularity: The Church and the World (Papers Read at the Eleventh Summer Meeting and the Twelfth Winter Meeting of the Ecclesiastical History Society)*, ed. Derek Baker (New York: Harper and Row, 1973), 129; I refer here to Philip S. Gorski's argument in *The Disciplinary Revolution: Calvinism and the Rise of the State in Early Modern Europe*, but I wish to extend the argument and consider the "papal revolution," which includes the renewal of Roman law, the "liberty of the church," and the institution of the sacraments, and among them, the Eucharist and its dissemination throughout Western Christendom.

271. Bettina Bildhauer, *Medieval Blood* (Cardiff: University of Wales Press, 2006), 15.

272. Blood thus adds a significant layer to Agamben's argument about "the kingdom and the glory," the theological and the economic (Agamben, *The Kingdom and the Glory*).

273. "The terminological change by which the consecrated host became the *corpus naturale* and the social body of the Church became the *corpus mysticum*, coincided with that moment in the history of Western thought when the doctrines of corporational and organic structure of society began to pervade anew the political theories of the West and to mold most significantly and decisively the political thinking in the high and late Middle Ages. It was in that period—to mention only the classical example—that John of Salisbury wrote those famous chapters of his *Policraticus* in which he compared, under the guise of Plutarch, the commonweal with the organism of the human body, a simile popular also among the jurists" (E. Kantorowicz, *The King's Two Bodies*, 199).

274. Dietmar Peil comes close in his *Untersuchungen zur Staats- und Herrschaftsmetaphorik in literarischen Zeugnissen von der Antike bis zur Gegenwart* (München: Wilhelm Fink Verlag, 1983), where he makes passing references to blood and to the heart (see, e.g., 331) or in *Der Streit der Glieder mit dem Magen* (Frankfurt am Main: Peter Lang, 1985), which is devoted to the reception of Menenius Agrippa's fable. L. Barkan also covers quite extensive ground in *Nature's Work of Art: The Human Body as Image of the World* (New Haven, Conn.: Yale University Press, 1975), esp. 61–115. For specific studies of medieval usage of the figure, see Kantorowicz, *The King's Two Bodies*, and Tilman Struve, *Die Entwicklung der Organlogischen Staatsauffassung im Mittelalter* (Stuttgart: Anton Hiersemann, 1978); see also J. Le Goff, "Head or Heart? The Political Use of Body Metaphors in the Middle Ages," in *Fragments for a History of the Human Body: Part Three*, ed. Michel Feher et al. (New York 1989), 12–26; and Jacques Le Goff and Nicolas Truong, *Une histoire du corps au Moyen Âge* (Paris: Liana Levi, 2003); and see M. C. Pouchelle, *Corps et chirurgie à l'apogée du moyen-âge* (Paris: Flammarion, 1983), all of which testify, more or less explicitly, to the importance of blood in the imagination, the final "dominance" of the heart over the conception of the sovereign as *caput rei publicae*, but without remarking on the discrepancy with political representations.

275. M. Douglas, *Purity and Danger: An Analysis of the Concepts of Pollution and Taboo* (London: Routledge, 1966); J. Schlanger, *Critique des totalités organiques* (Paris: Vrin, 1971); David George Hale, *The Body Politic: A Political Metaphor in Renaissance English Literature* (The Hague: Mouton, 1971); L. Barkan, *Nature's Work of Art*; Tilman Struve, "The Importance of the Organism in the Political Theory of John of Salisbury," in *The*

World of John of Salisbury, ed. Michael Wilks (Oxford: Basil Blackwell / The Ecclesiastical History Society, 1984), 303–317; Adriana Cavarero, *Stately Bodies: Literature, Philosophy, and the Question of Gender*, trans. Robert de Lucca and Deanna Shemek (Ann Arbor: University of Michigan Press, 2002); Charles Leslie Wayper, *Political Thought* (New York: Philosophical Library, 1954); Jonathan Gil Harris, *Sick Economies: Drama, Mercantilism, and Disease in Shakespeare's England* (Philadelphia: University of Pennsylvania Press, 2004).

276. See, for example, Antoine de Baecque's masterful *Body Politic: Corporeal Metaphor in Revolutionary France 1770–1800*, trans. Charlotte Mandell (Stanford, Calif.: Stanford University Press, 1997); and see *From the Royal to the Republican Body: Incorporating the Political in Seventeenth- and Eighteenth-Century France*, ed. Sara E. Melzer and Kathryn Norberg (Berkeley: University of California Press, 1998); *The Body in Parts: Fantasies of Corporeality in Early Modern Europe*, ed. David Hillman and Carla Mazzio (New York: Routledge, 1997); see as well, M. Neocleous, *Imagining the State*; Sergio Bertelli, *The King's Body: Sacred Rituals of Power in Medieval and Early Modern Europe*, trans. R. Burr Litchfield (University Park: Pennsylvania State University Press, 2001); Jonathan M. Hess, *Reconstituting the Body Politic: Enlightenment, Public Culture, and the Invention of Aesthetic Autonomy* (Detroit, Mich.: Wayne State University Press, 1999); Pheng Cheah, *Spectral Nationality: Passages of Freedom from Kant to Postcolonial Literatures of Liberation* (New York: Columbia University Press, 2003); *Le corps comme métaphore dans l'Espagne des XVIe et XVIIe siècles*, ed. Augustin Redondo (Paris: Presses de la Sorbonne Nouvelle, 1992); Mary Poovey, *Making a Social Body: British Cultural Formation 1830–1864* (Chicago: University of Chicago Press, 1995).

277. John Rogers, *The Matter of Revolution: Science, Poetry, and Politics in the Age of Milton* (Ithaca, N.Y.: Cornell University Press, 1996), 23; writing of baroque culture in Europe, José Antonio Maravall explains how a "general principle" was "accepted by everyone: 'Everybody's soul is the only movement.' The discovery of the circulation of blood, which was coetaneous with baroque culture, confirmed this general law that ruled everywhere . . . from science to morality, everything spoke to baroque individuals about this universal law of movement" (J. A. Maravall, *Culture of the Baroque: Analysis of a Historical Structure*, trans. Terry Cochran [Minneapolis: University of Minnesota Press, 1986], 176).

278. Marc Shell traces the alliance between the Roman sources of liberal thought (the word *liber*, Shell points out, means both "free" and "son") and the Christian notion of kinship and fraternity. This alliance, Shell writes, "is significant for understanding the development of the ideology of nationalism in modern secular Christendom" (M. Shell, *Children of the Earth*, 139). The very "development of a liberal state" finds its origins therein, Shell goes on to assert, a liberal state that is "not only . . . a conglomeration of acquisitive individuals, but also . . . a polis of *liberi*—free and equal brothers and sisters"—in blood (145–46).

279. Q. Skinner, "From the State of Princes to the Person of the State," in Skinner, *Visions of Politics. Volume 2: Renaissance Values* (Cambridge: Cambridge University Press, 2002), 368–413; and see also Skinner, "Hobbes and the Purely Artificial Person of the State," in Skinner, *Visions of Politics. Volume 3: Hobbes and Civil Science* (Cambridge: Cambridge University Press, 2002), 177–208.

280. Andreas Musolff, "Political Metaphor and *Bodies Politic*," in *Perspectives in Politics and Discourse*, ed. Urszula Okulska and Piotr Cap (Amsterdam: John Benjamins Publishing Company, 2010), 23–42. I should note that setting aside the striking figurations found in Petrarch's "Italia Mia" or Shakespeare's spectacular *Coriolanus*, John Fortescue (inspired like Dante by Aristotle) offers a singular contrast for this absence in his *On the Laws and Governance of England*, though whether this constitutes an exception to the rule or changes the rule instead could only be determined if blood moved to the center of a more extensive inquiry. It seems at any rate that blood is taken by Fortescue as a matter of course (a nourishing matter, true to the reigning medical conceptions I explore in chap. 4), thus underscoring the puzzling absence of blood elsewhere in the political tradition (Sir John Fortescue, *On the Laws and Governance of England*, ed. Shelley Lockwood [Cambridge: Cambridge University Press, 1997], esp. chap. XIII; and see John O'Neill's *Five Bodies: The Human Shape of Modern Society* [Ithaca, N.Y.: Cornell University Press, 1985], 75–76, who places Fortescue at the center of his reflections on the body politic); on Coriolanus as a "thing of blood," see James Kuzner, "Unbuilding the City: Coriolanus and the Birth of Republican Rome," *Shakespeare Quarterly* 58, no. 2 (2007): 174–99, and see Hale, *The Body Politic*, 96–107; on Petrarch, see Margaret Brose, "Petrarch's Beloved Body: 'Italia Mia,' " in *Feminist Approaches to the Body in Medieval Literature*, ed. Linda Lomperis and Sarah Stanbury (Philadelphia: University of Pennsylvania Press, 1993), 1–20.

281. C. Beaune, *Naissance de la nation France* (Paris: Gallimard, 1985), 216; the transformation of blood into a governing term for lineage, and for sacred lineage, which Beaune links to the "culte du sang du Christ" (223), can be witnessed elsewhere, in Machiavelli, for example, who typically substitutes "blood" where Livy's Latin had "birth" (N. Machiavelli, *Discourses on Livy*, trans. Harvey C. Mansfield and Nathan Tarcov [Chicago: University of Chicago Press, 1994], 121, n. 2).

282. James Longrigg explains, "the theory of *pros to kenoumenon akolouthia*—the *horror vacui*" was derived from Strato by Erasistratus, whose theory of disease had as its main cause "*plethora*, i.e., the flooding of the veins with a superfluity of blood engendered by an excessive intake of nourishment" (J. Longrigg, *Greek Rational Medicine: Philosophy and Medicine from Alcmaeon to the Alexandrians* [New York: Routledge, 1993], 215–16; and see Peter Brain, *Galen on Bloodletting: A Study of the Origins, Development, and Validity of His Opinions, with a Translation of the Three Works* [Cambridge: Cambridge University Press, 1986], 11); on "consumption," which "usually refers to the burning up of the humors, the wasting of the body, and specific ills of the blood," see J. Gil Harris, *Sick Economies*, 165, and chap. 7 as a whole ("Consumption and Consumption"). And see Shigehisa Kuriyama, *The Expressiveness of the Body and the Divergence of Greek and Chinese Medicine* (New York: Zone Books, 2002).

283. See C. W. Bynum, *Holy Feast and Holy Fast: The Religious Significance of Food to Medieval Women* (Berkeley: University of California Press,1987), and see also, in a different perspective, M. G. Grossel, " 'Le calice suave de la passion': Images et appréhension de l'Eucharistie chez quelques mystiques mediévales," in *Le sang au moyen-âge*, ed. M. Faure (Montpellier: Publications de l'université de Montpellier, 1999), 415–32.

284. On this new understanding see de Lubac, *Corpus mysticum*.

285. Cary Nederman writes that "the most obvious illustration of John's understanding of politics as a fundamentally secular enterprise stems from his famed use of organic imagery both to identify and to describe the cooperation between the functional parts of the public body" (Cary J. Nederman, "Aristotelianism and the Origins of 'Political Science' in the Twelfth Century," *Journal of the History of Ideas* 52, no. 2 [April–June 1991]: 191). Whether or not this is the case, it would certainly seem to force a recognition that blood must be treated separately, as a theological marker. "The validity of a secular political realm" would at any rate be dependent on the absence, or invisibility, of blood (192; and see Cary J. Nederman, "The Physiological Significance of the Organic Metaphor in John of Salisbury's *Policraticus*," *History of Political Thought* 8 [1987]: 211–23; for a different approach to the matter of the secular in this context, see Anton-Hermann Chroust, "The Corporate Idea and the Body Politic in the Middle Ages," *The Review of Politics* 9, no. 4 [October 1947]: 423–52).

286. By speaking of the long centuries hereby hastily summarized as a "moment," I mean to recall Kantorowicz's description of the same period with this very term: "The terminological change by which the consecrated host became the *corpus naturale* and the social body of the Church became the *corpus mysticum*, coincided with that moment in the history of western thought when the doctrines of corporational and organic structure of society began to pervade anew the political theories of the West and to mold most significantly and decisively the political thinking in the high and late Middle Ages" (Kantorowicz, *The King's Two Bodies*, 199).

287. In highlighting the bloodlessness of this person, I am not claiming that Hobbes had nothing to say about blood. Quite the contrary, I seek to indicate some of the structural reasons that could make the good friend of William Harvey erase blood from relevance when speaking of the body politic "proper." Put another way, I argue that the importance of blood can only be determined here by examining where, and how, it continues to flow.

288. Skinner, "From the State," 387.

289. Skinner, "From the State," 389–90.

290. Skinner, "From the State," 394.

291. Skinner, "From the State," 394.

292. Skinner, "Hobbes and the Purely Artificial," 198.

293. Skinner, "Hobbes and the Purely Artificial," 204. I leave aside the theological dimensions that Hobbes maintains in different ways throughout *Leviathan* and that lead A. L. Angoulvent to emphasize that Hobbes's system has a "statut hybride politico-religieux" (A. L. Angoulvent, *Hobbes ou la crise de l'état baroque* [Paris: Presses Universitaires de France, 1992], 145).

294. Skinner, "Hobbes and the Purely Artificial," 201.

295. Skinner, "From the State," 398.

296. Skinner, "From the State," 399; quoting Hobbes, *Leviathan*, chap. 31.

297. Skinner, "Hobbes and the Purely Artificial," 206.

298. Quentin Skinner first pointed out to me that Hobbes does discuss blood and its circulation, if quite belatedly so, in chap. 24 of *Leviathan*. As we will see, Hobbes identifies blood with money and commerce, the effect of which he describes as the "sanguification of the

commonwealth." Judging by his closeness to Harvey, Hobbes was initiating a larger trend, which identifies blood with the "matter of revolution" (as John Rogers has it). As Foucault and others have discussed, this coincides with the elaboration of political economy by mercantilists and Physiocrats. Rogers, *The Matter of Revolution*; Gallagher, *The Body Economic*; Schabas, *The Natural Origins of Economics*; Foucault, *Birth of Biopolitics*; Cheah, *Spectral Nationality*.

299. Steven Shapin and Simon Shaffer, *Leviathan and the Air-Pump: Hobbes, Boyle, and the Experimental Life* (Princeton, N.J.: Princeton University Press, 1985). I write "seals and begins" because the very terms of historiographic discourse reiterate a logic of periodization that is nothing less than problematic. Guided by other histories of science, and before Shapin and Shaffer, Marie-Christine Pouchelle locates in the fourteenth-century surgeon Henri de Mondeville the emergence of a new and distinct discipline that figures or refigures a multiplicity of bodies (physical and political, physical or political) and the discourses that rule over them. Her argument, published two years before *Leviathan and the Air-Pump*, announces much of that later book (M. C. Pouchelle, *Corps et Chirurgie à l'apogée du moyen-âge* (Paris: Flammarion, 1983); see also Kathleen Davis, *Periodization and Sovereignty: How Ideas of Feudalism and Secularization Govern the Politics of Time* (Philadelphia: University of Pennsylvania Press, 2008).

300. Michel Foucault, *Security, Territory, Population: Lectures at the College de France*, trans. Graham Burchell (New York: Picador, 2007), 49; and see S. Todd Lowry, "The Archaeology of the Circulation Concept in Economic Theory," *Journal of the History of Ideas* 35, no. 3 (July–September 1974): 429–44. Mary Poovey credits William Petty's *Anatomy of Ireland* for being "one seventeenth century revision of the medieval 'body politick.'" In Poovey's view, the eighteenth century "adapted Petty's idea that money and goods should be allowed to circulate as freely as blood.... At midcentury, this image was elaborated when François Quesnay and the other Physiocrats sought a way to explain the law-governed, natural domain that we call the economy" (M. Poovey, *Making a Social Body: British Cultural Formation, 1830–1864* (Chicago: University of Chicago Press, 1995). On "wounded" or "injured" sovereignty (*la souveraineté blessée*), see Foucault, *Discipline and Punish*, 48.

301. Thomas Hobbes, *Leviathan*, ed. Richard Tuck (Cambridge: Cambridge University Press), chap. 24, 174–75.

302. Michael O'Malley, "Specie and Species: Race and the Money Question in Nineteenth-Century America," *The American Historical Review* 99, no. 2 (April 1994): 372.

303. Rob Latham, *Consuming Youth: Vampires, Cyborgs, and the Culture of Consumption* (Chicago: University of Chicago Press, 2002).

304. Ariella Gross mentions how "Justice Antonin Scalia, in a 1995 case restricting affirmative action in government contracts, conflates 'blood' and 'skin color' as biological facts that are socially, culturally, politically, and legally irrelevant" (Gross, *What Blood Won't Tell*, 299).

305. Gross, *What Blood Won't Tell*, 10.

306. One example among all too many should suffice. Referring to U.S. miscegenation laws, Eva Saks writes that "it frequently lacked external physical referents: the crime that it defined and punished was a crime of 'blood,' *a metaphor that miscegenation law itself helped to invent and promote*. The central criminal element of miscegenation was a difference

in blood, which *existed only as a figure of speech.* . . . The legal, semiotic discourse of miscegenation was not mimetic; it did not describe visible material objects but instead provided signs of representation, like 'blood' " (Eva Saks, "Representing Miscegenation Law," in *Interracialism: Black-White Intermarriage in American History, Literature, and Law,* ed. Werner Sollors (Oxford: Oxford University Press, 2000), 63.

307. Compare Daniel J. Sharfstein, "The Secret History of Race in the United States," *The Yale Law Journal* 112, no. 6 (April 2003): 1473–509.

308. Indeed, it hardly seems negligible that, as Rosalind Thomas points out, Herodotus' so-called definition of Greekness is placed in the mouth of the Athenians as they are out for blood, bent on blood revenge, in fact. It is to this blood in common, it seems, rather than to some purported "ethnic" identity (based on blood as metonymic marker of all such identities!!) that Herodotus' report points (R. Thomas, "Ethnicity, Genealogy, and Hellenism in Herodotus," in *Ancient Perceptions of Greek Ethnicity,* ed. Irad Malkin [Cambridge, Mass.: Harvard University Press, 2001], esp. 214–15). Claudia Barracchi's remarks, though made in another, albeit proximate, context, are quite pertinent here: "It is essential to notice how, in the passage quoted, the profound difficulty of the distinction between same and other is at once announced and covered over. Socrates does not attribute to the *helleneikon genos* the qualities of *oikeiotes* and *suggeneia,* while defining *to barbarikou (hoi barbaroi,* not even a *genoi,* just an indefinite, disparate multitude) as *ethneion* and *allotrion.* Rather, it is the Greek *genos* that is *oikeion* and *suggenes* (in relation to itself) but, *at the same time,* also *ethneion* and *allotrion* (in relation to the barbarians). Rigorously speaking, then, it is the Greek kind that is *both* the same and different, familiar and foreign—in different respects. The difference between the same and the different appears to be internal to the same" (Baracchi, *Of Myth, Life, and War in Plato's* Republic [Bloomington: Indiana University Press, 2002], 174, n. 21).

309. By sidelining medicine at this late point, I hope I will not be understood as diminishing the importance of blood in medical discourse, practice, and development, much less to refute—as if it were possible—the relation between medicine and the state (I am quite convinced by the importance of inquiries such as those conducted by Paul Starr, *The Social Transformation of American Medicine: The Rise of a Sovereign Profession and the Making of a Vast Industry* [New York: Basic Books, 1982], Peter Baldwin in *Contagion and the State in Europe, 1830–1930* [Cambridge: Cambridge University Press, 2004], or Starr in *Blood and Medicine*). I seek, once again, to torque the frame of attention and locate the bloods of medicine within a larger hematology.

310. Harold J. Berman, *Law and Revolution: The Formation of the Western Legal Tradition* (Cambridge, Mass.: Harvard University Press, 1983), 42; Berman found much inspiration in the work of Eugen Rosenstock-Huessy, who coined the phrase "Papal Revolution" in his *Out of Revolution: Autobiography of Western Man* (Providence, R.I.: Berg, 1993 [1938]); Colin Morris calls it, more conventionally, "the Papal Reform" (C. Morris, *The Papal Monarchy: The Western Church from 1050 to 1250* (Oxford: Clarendon Press, 1989).

311. Gerd Tellenbach, *Church, State, and Christian Society at the Time of the Investiture Contest,* trans. R. F. Bennett (Oxford: Basil Blackwell, 1948), 111; and see Joseph R. Strayer, *On the Medieval Origins of the Modern State* (Princeton, N.J.: Princeton University Press, 1970).

312. I quote and draw from R. F. Bennett's "Introduction" to Tellenbach, *Church, State*, viii–ix.

313. Berman, *Law and Revolution*, 51; Tellenbach refers to this "idea of the unity of all Christian people" as including the whole church and "all believers, living and dead" (Tellenbach, *Church, State*, 81 and 81, n. 1).

314. I write "largely ignored" because the numerous reviews of this important and otherwise well-received book have not attended to it, nor do recent studies of blood in the Middle Ages register what is in my judgment a groundbreaking contribution (among many others Mastnak made).

315. Tomaz Mastnak, *Crusading Peace: Christendom, the Muslim World, and Western Political Order* (Berkeley: University of California Press, 2002), 16.

316. On the *filioque* controversy, see Berman, *Law and Revolution*, 105, 178ff., and 581, n. 26.

317. Mastnak, *Crusading*, 37–38. Earlier, "around 861, Pope Nicholas I had declared that soldiers of this world (*milites seculi*) were distinct from the soldiers of the Church (*milites ecclesiae*), so it was not becoming to the soldiers of the Church to fight worldly battles (*saeculo militare*) in which blood would necessarily be shed" (22–23).

318. Alexander II, quoted in Mastnak, *Crusading*, 21.

319. Raymond of Aguilers, quoted in Mastnak, *Crusading*, 60–61.

320. Bernard Hamilton, reviewing *Crusading Peace: Christendom, the Muslim World, and Western Political Order* in *The American Historical Review* 108, no. 4 (October 2003): 1204.

321. John of Salisbury, *Policraticus*, ed. Cary J. Nederman (Cambridge: Cambridge University Press, 1990), 173; and see Mastnak, *Crusading Peace*, 154; for a brilliant discussion of "men of blood," see Jeremy Tambling, "Monstrous Tyranny, Men of Blood: Dante and 'Inferno' XII," *The Modern Language Review* 98, no. 4 (October 2003): 881–897.

322. Bernard of Clairvaux, quoted in Mastnak, *Crusading Peace*, 169.

323. William Shakespeare, *The Merchant of Venice*, ed. Jay L. Hallo (Oxford: Oxford University Press, 1994), 4.1.111–112.

324. Finkelman, "The Crime of Color," 2072.

3. CAPITAL (CHRISTIANS AND MONEY)

1. Karl Marx and Frederick Engels, "Manifesto of the Communist Party," in *The Marx-Engels Reader*, 2nd ed., ed. Robert C. Tucker (New York: Norton, 1978), 476.

2. Jacques Derrida, *Specters of Marx: The State of the Debt, the Work of Mourning, and the New International*, trans. Peggy Kamuf (New York: Routledge, 1994).

3. Michel Serres, "Corruption—*The Antichrist*: A Chemistry of Sensations and Ideas," trans. Chris Bongie, in *Nietzsche in Italy*, ed. Thomas Harrison (Saratoga, Calif.: Anma Libri, 1988), 34; the phrase "chains of metamorphoses" appears on p. 44.

4. Serres, "Corruption," 34.

5. Gilles Deleuze and Félix Guattari, *A Thousand Plateaux: Capitalism and Schizophrenia*, trans. Brian Massumi (Minneapolis: University of Minnesota Press, 1987), 109.

6. Marshall Berman, *All That Is Solid Melts into Air: The Experience of Modernity* (New York: Penguin, 1988).

7. Karen Ho, *Liquidated: An Ethnography of Wall Street* (Durham, N.C.: Duke University Press, 2009).

8. Albert Hirschman proposed to renew the inquiry into "the spirit of capitalism" by attending to the role and value attributed to "commerce and other forms of money-making" (A. O. Hirschman, *The Passions and the Interests: Political Arguments for Capitalism Before Its Triumph* [Princeton, N.J.: Princeton University Press, 1977], 9).

9. *Goethe's Faust*, trans. Walter Kaufmann (New York: Anchor, 1990), 117; William E. Connolly, *Capitalism and Christianity, American Style* (Durham, N.C.: Duke University Press, 2008), chap. 1.

10. Zygmunt Bauman, *Liquid Modernity* (Cambridge: Polity, 2000), 3.

11. Marx and Engels, "Manifesto," 476; Connolly, *Capitalism and Christianity*, 17, 19.

12. In the scholarly literature, images of liquidity, figures of circulation are seen as one set among many fleeting rhetorical resources, mostly confined to eighteenth-century Physiocrats and their contemporaries, with lingering effects on the Victorian imagination (see *Natural Images in Economic Thought: "Markets Read in Tooth and Claw,"* ed. Philip Mirowski [Cambridge: Cambridge University Press, 1994], and see Margaret Schabas, *The Natural Origins of Economics* [Chicago: University of Chicago Press, 2005]).

13. J. K. Gibson-Graham, *The End of Capitalism (As We Knew It): A Feminist Critique of Political Economy* (Minnesota: University of Minnesota Press, 2006), 135–36; Niall Ferguson waxes and spins positive on the idea when he writes that "markets are efficient, meaning that the movement of stock prices cannot be predicted; they are continuous, frictionless and completely liquid" (N. Ferguson, *The Ascent of Money: A Financial History of the World* [New York: Penguin, 2008], 327).

14. Karl Marx, "Speech at the Anniversary of the *People's Paper*," *The Marx-Engels Reader*, 578.

15. Marx, "Speech," 577.

16. See Jennifer Bajorek, *Counterfeit Capital: Poetic Labor and Revolutionary Irony* (Stanford, Calif.: Stanford University Press, 2009), 4; and see M. Neil Browne and J. Kevin Quinn, "Dominant Economic Metaphors and the Postmodern Subversion of the Subject," in *The New Economic Criticism: Studies at the Intersection of Literature and Economics*, ed. Martha Woodmansee and Mark Osteen (New York: Routledge, 1999), 113–28, and see as well *Metaphors of Economy*, ed. Nicole Bracker and Stefan Herbrechter (Amsterdam: Rodopi, 2005), and Catherine Packham, "The Physiology of Political Economy: Vitalism and Adam Smith's 'Wealth of Nations,'" *Journal of the History of Ideas* 63, no. 3 (July 2002): 465–81.

17. Timothy Mitchell, "Carbon Democracy," *Economy and Society* 38, no. 3 (August 2009): 413; and see Mitchell, *Carbon Democracy: Political Power in the Age of Oil* (London: Verso, 2011).

18. Mitchell, "Carbon Democracy," 415; Connolly ties "the volatility of capitalism" to the limits of fossil fuels that Max Weber had envisaged (Connolly, *Capitalism and Christianity*, 19).

19. *Glasgow Citizen*, quoted in Timothy L. Alborn, "Economic Man, Economic Machine: Images of Circulation in the Victorian Money Market," in *Natural Images in Economic Thought*, 186.

20. Norman O. Brown, *Apocalypse and/or Metamorphosis* (Berkeley: University of California Press, 1991), 187.

21. Henry A. Giroux, "Zombie Politics and Other Late Modern Monstrosities in the Age of Disposability." Accessible at www.truth-out.org/111709Giroux; Jean Comaroff and John Comaroff, "Alien-Nation: Zombies, Immigrants, and Millennial Capitalism," *South Atlantic Quarterly* 101, no. 4 (Fall 2002): 779–805; and see Rob Latham, *Consuming Youth: Vampires, Cyborgs, and the Culture of Consumption* (Chicago: University of Chicago Press, 2002); Jon Stratton provides an overview of the current popularity of zombies (without connection to Marx) in "Zombie Trouble: Zombie Texts, Bare Life, and Displaced People," *European Journal of Cultural Studies* 14, no. 3 (2011): 265–81; and see David McNally, *Monsters of the Market: Zombies, Vampires, and Global Capitalism* (Leiden: Brill, 2011).

22. Laurence A. Rickels, *The Vampire Lectures* (Minneapolis: University of Minnesota Press, 1999), 222.

23. Nicole Shukin, *Animal Capital: Rendering Life in Biopolitical Times* (Minneapolis: University of Minnesota Press, 2009), 21–22, 40; emphasis added.

24. For an extensive discussion of literature and political economy, see *The New Economic Criticism: Studies at the Intersection of Literature and Economics*, ed. Martha Woodmansee and Mark Osteen (New York: Routledge, 1999); Catherine Gallagher, *The Body Economic: Life, Death, and Sensation in Political Economy and the Victorian Novel* (Princeton, N.J.: Princeton University Press, 2006), and Mary Poovey, *Genres of the Credit Economy: Mediating Value in Eighteenth- and Nineteenth-Century Britain* (Chicago: University of Chicago Press, 2008).

25. Indeed, at some stages of the critique of political economy, economic life was not supposed to remain abstract: "the political economists have abstracted value, severed it from flesh and blood. "The true veins of wealth," Ruskin writes, "are purple—and not in Rock but in Flesh.... [T]he final outcome and consummation of all wealth is in the producing as many as possible fullbreathed, bright-eyed, and happy-hearted human creatures'" (Gallagher, *The Body Economic*, 88, quoting Ruskin).

26. Shukin, *Animal Capital*, 23.

27. Shukin, *Animal Capital*, 5.

28. G. W. F. Hegel, *Phenomenology of Spirit*, trans. A. V. Miller (Oxford: Oxford University Press, 1977), 212; and note that for William Harvey, "the material substance constitutive of blood is indistinguishable from rational spirit" (John Rogers, *The Matter of Revolution: Science, Poetry, and Politics in the Age of Milton* [Ithaca, N.Y.: Cornell University Press, 1996], 11), but the connection between blood and thought is an ancient one (see next chapter).

29. Hegel, *Phenomenology*, 100; in anticipation of the argument I will go on to propose on the association of blood and money, it might be useful to consider Georg Simmel's elaborations on money clearly written with Hegel in mind: "Money is the symbol in the empirical world of *the inconceivable unity of being*, out of which the world, in all its breadth, diversity, energy and reality, flows. ... And this being, however empty and abstract its *pure notion* may be, appears as *the warm stream of life*, flowing into the schemata of concepts of things, allowing them to blossom and unfold their very essence, no matter how diverse or antagonistic their content and attitude may be" (G. Simmel, *The Philosophy of Money*, trans. Tom Bottomore, David Frisby, and Kaethe Mengelberg [New York: Routledge, 2004], 503–504; emphases added).

30. McNally, *Monsters of the Market*, 138.

31. Mark C. Taylor, *Confidence Games: Money and Markets in a World Without Redemption* (Chicago: University of Chicago Press, 2004), 67. In a posthumously published set of fragments, Walter Benjamin—whose argument on "capitalism as religion" provides an essential impetus for this chapter—had located "Wergeld" or blood money as a crucial site of inquiry concerning "the links between myth and money" (W. Benjamin, "Capitalism as Religion," trans. Rodney Livingstone, in *Selected Writings vol. 1, 1913–1926*, ed. Marcus Bullock and Michael Jennings [Cambridge, Mass.: The Belknap Press of Harvard University Press, 1996], 290, and see Werner Hamacher, "Guilt History: Benjamin's Sketch 'Capitalism as Religion'" in *diacritics* 32, no. 3–4 [Fall/Winter 2002]: 81–106, and Giorgio Agamben, *Profanations*, trans. Jeff Fort [New York: Zone Books, 2007]). Philip Goodchild for his part writes that "the association between money and blood derives from the Gospel of Matthew" (P. Goodchild, *The Theology of Money* [Durham, N.C.: Duke University Press, 2009], 225). Marx himself oscillated on the matter, opposing, in the *Grundrisse*, the spurious "analogy" ("To compare money with blood—the term circulation gave occasion for this—is about as correct as Menenius Agrippa's comparison between the patricians and the stomach" [Marx, *Grundrisse*, trans. Martin Nicolaus (New York: Vintage, 1973), 181; and see S. S. Prawer, *Karl Marx and World Literature* (Oxford: Oxford University Press, 1978), 291–92]).

32. I do not know if he was the first, but Robert H. Nelson had proposed the phrase "economic theology" in his *Economics as Religion from Samuelson to Chicago and Beyond* (University Park: Pennsylvania State University Press, 2001), xviii; Nelson is careful to distinguish his work from "the economic study of religion" and implicitly, I would add, from the religious study of economics. The title and the phrase "economic theology" rather suggest that it is indeed a matter of treating economics *as* religion. And see also R. H. Nelson, *Reaching for Heaven on Earth: The Theological Meaning of Economics* (Lanham, Md.: Rowman and Littlefield, 1991) as well as A. M. C. Waterman, *Political Economy and Christian Theology Since the Enlightenment: Essays in Intellectual History* (New York: Palgrave Macmillan, 2004). My use of the phrase here does not claim the same reach, much less the distinct and impressive terrain staked for it by Giorgio Agamben, which mostly stays away from the modern domain of economics (G. Agamben, *The Kingdom and the Glory: For a Theological Genealogy of Economy and Government*, trans. Lorenzo Chiesa [with Matteo Mandarini] [Stanford, Calif.: Stanford University Press, 2011]). It is merely meant to highlight one particular vector in the long history to which Nelson and Agamben dedicate their work.

33. T. Harv Ecker, *Secrets of the Millionaire Mind* (New York: Harper Business, 2005), 94; quoted in Barbara Ehrenreich, *Bright-Sided: How Positive Thinking Is Undermining America* (New York: Metropolitan, 2009), 93; a more scholarly version would no doubt go like this: "A world without money would be worse, much worse, than our present world. It is wrong to think (as Shakespeare's Antonio did) of all lenders of money as mere leeches, sucking the life's blood out of unfortunate debtors" (N. Ferguson, *The Ascent of Money*, 63).

34. Max Weber, *The Protestant Ethic and the Spirit of Capitalism*, trans. Talcott Parsons (New York and London: Routledge, 2001), 18, 33; Weber's question was revisited by Albert Hirschman in *Passions and the Interests*, and see Boltanski and Chiapello, who write that

"whereas the first spirit of capitalism gave more than its due to an ethic of saving, and the second to an ethic of work and competence, the new spirit is marked by a change in terms of the relation to both money and work" (Luc Boltanski and Eve Chiapello, *The New Spirit of Capitalism*, trans. Gregory Elliot [London: Verso, 2007], 151). On the mediation, indeed, formation of value and the naturalization of money, with no direct reference to blood (or to Christianity), see Mary Poovey's magisterial *Genres of the Credit Economy: Mediating Value in Eighteenth- and Nineteenth-Century Britain* (Chicago: University of Chicago Press, 2008); Marcel Hénaff provides a concise, and somehow tame, summary of the changes undergone by money since the early modern period. It is, he writes, the "transformation of money from immoral agent to neutral instrument" (M. Hénaff, *The Price of Truth: Gift, Money, and Philosophy*, trans. Jean-Louis Morhange [Stanford, Calif.: Stanford University Press, 2010], 16). But the changes marked by the history of usury, indeed, with regard to the church's relation to money, must be mitigated and refigured along a more graded continuum (see Robert B. Ekelund Jr., Robert F. Herbert, Robert D. Tollison, Gary M. Anderson, and Audrey B. Davidson, *Sacred Trust: The Medieval Church as an Economic Firm* [New York: Oxford University Press, 1996], see esp. chap. 6, "How the Church Gained from Usury and Exchange Doctrines," 113–30).

35. Immanuel Kant, "Perpetual Peace," quoted in Egidius Berns, "European Surrogate," in *The Cultural Diversity of European Unity: Findings, Explanations and Reflections from the European Values Study*, ed. Wilhelmus A. Arts, Jacques A. Hagenaars, and Loek Halman (Leiden: Brill, 2003), 456. Berns elaborates on the links between economy and credit, economy and faith, in his "L'Euro et le politique," in *L'argent: Croyance, mesure, speculation*, ed. Marcel Drach (Paris: La Découverte, 2004), 249–57; and see also Jean-Joseph Goux, *Les monnayeurs du langage* (Paris: Galilée, 1984), and Bernard Stiegler, *Mécréance et discrédit. 1. La décadence des démocraties industrielles* (Paris: Galilée, 2004). For a broader, contextual discussion of the separation of politics and economics, see Norbert Elias, *The Civilizing Process 2. State Formation and Civilization*, trans. Edmund Jephcott (Oxford: Blackwell, 1994), 380ff, and see next notes.

36. Immanuel Kant, "Perpetual Peace: A Philosophical Sketch," trans. H. S. Reiss, in Kant, *Political Writings*, ed. H. S. Reiss (Cambridge: Cambridge University Press, 1991), 114; on the genealogy of the opposition of war and commerce ("le doux commerce"), of "the spirit of commerce" and "the spirit of conquest," or of "modern economy" and "the folly of despotism," see Hirschman, *The Passions*, 79–80, 85, and passim. Hirschman underscores as well that the consensus was not absolute. Commerce, in other words, might also be "characterized as 'perpetual combat' by Colbert and as 'a kind of warfare' by Sir Josiah Child" (79).

37. Bernard E. Harcourt, *The Illusion of Free Markets: Punishment and the Myth of Natural Order* (Cambridge, Mass.: Harvard University Press, 2010), 36. I should mention that, for Harcourt, "hydraulic metaphors are passé" (39), and he may very well be right; as he is to point out that "each new iteration of these ideas also changes, however slightly, the relationship between economy and punishment" (39). But what seems to persist, for quite a while now, is blood, and indeed the very terms of the relationship Harcourt attends to, the possibility of "a longer view of the relationship between economy and punishment"

(44). Strengthened by Harcourt's own vector of inquiry ("to explore how the acceptance of those beliefs—beliefs in natural order and legal despotism—affects our contemporary social distributions" [49]), I propose to translate his "economy and punishment" quite banally, into "economy and religion."

38. William Shakespeare, *The Merchant of Venice*, ed. Jay L. Hallo (Oxford: Oxford University Press, 1994), 3.1.37–38. I return to Shakespeare's play and to the economic enemy in the later part of this chapter.

39. A fuller bibliography, and a distinct perspective from the one offered here, may be found in Robert H. Nelson's work, and see Taylor, *Confidence Games*, as well as Philip Goodchild, *Capitalism and Religion: The Price of Piety* (New York: Routledge, 2002), and Nimi Wariboko, *God and Money: A Theology of Money in a Globalizing World* (Lanham, Md.: Lexington Books, 2008), and see Mary-Jane Rubenstein, "Capital Shares: The Way Back into the With of Christianity," *Political Theology* 11, no. 1 (2010): 103–119; Poovey's general point stands, of course, regarding the far-reaching process of generic and disciplinary differentiation whereby literature and political economy, for instance, came to occupy distinct positions and play different functions. By attending to "religion" or indeed to Christianity, I am not arguing for the importance of a distinct or indeed other discipline or genre, however, but trying to access an earlier stage of this process, if not quite an undifferentiated one (see Poovey, *Genres of the Credit Economy*, e.g., 237). One could think along the lines of Connolly's "capitalist axiomatic" (borrowed from Deleuze and Guattari), which binds a number of elements, some immediately recognizable as belonging to capitalism, others less so (the educational system, science and technology, state policy, an ethos) (Connolly, *Capitalism and Christianity*, 10–12, 22). If it is true that "capitalism forms with a general axiomatic of decoded flows" (Deleuze and Guattari, *Thousand Plateaux*, 453), I am venturing toward a slight reformulation, an account of something like a "Christian axiomatics," perhaps.

40. The Gospel According to Mark, 12:13–17.

41. Karl Marx, "On the Jewish Question," trans. Rodney Livingstone and Gregor Benton, in *Early Writings*, ed. Lucio Colletti (London: Penguin Books, 1975), 237; to put it another way, Shylock "is thoroughly integrated into the Venetian economy" (Michael Ferber, "The Ideology of *The Merchant of Venice*," *English Literary Renaissance* 20 [1990]: 459).

42. Kojin Karatani, *Transcritique: On Kant and Marx*, trans. Sabu Kohso (Cambridge, Mass.: MIT Press, 2003), 140; and see Taylor, *Confidence Games*, 106; and see also Jean-François Lyotard, *Économie libidinale* (Paris: Minuit, 1974); Michael Taussig, *The Devil and Commodity Fetishism in South America* (Chapel Hill: University of North Carolina Press, 1980). Tawney's phrase is found in his *Religion and the Rise of Capitalism: A Historical Study* (New York: Harcourt, Brace & Co., 1952), 36.

43. Walter Benjamin explains that "the religious structure of capitalism" does not amount merely to what Max Weber describes as "a formation conditioned by religion." Rather, it is an "essentially religious phenomenon." (Benjamin, "Capitalism as Religion," 288). Georges Bataille more famously wrote of "la détermination religieuse de l'économie . . . elle définit la religion" (G. Bataille, *La part maudite* [Paris: Minuit, 1967], 156). Pierre Klossowski proposed another vector to follow by returning to Sade and arguing that money constitutes

the incarnate exchange of bodies, a function he locates primarily in the effect of numbers and which he calls "une fonction évidente de *transsubstantiation*" (P. Klossowski, *La monnaie vivante* [Paris: Payot et Rivages, 1997], 64).

44. Karl Marx, *Capital: A Critique of Political Economy*, vol. 1, trans. Ben Fowkes (New York: Penguin Books, 1990), 181, n. 4.

45. Connolly, *Capitalism and Christianity*, 21; on the singular importance of "the religious" as spectral and otherwise for Marx, see Derrida, *Spectres de Marx* (e.g., 232ff, 252, 264); on Christ in particular, see 229ff. Throughout his work, and since "Différance," at least Derrida has underscored the significance and inescapability of "economy" (see, e.g., Derrida, *Positions*, trans. Alan Bass [Chicago: University of Chicago Press, 1981], 8). And see also Derrida, "Du 'sans prix' ou le 'juste prix' de la transaction," in *Comment penser l'argent*, 386–401, and "Autour des écrits de Jacques Derrida sur l'argent," in *L'argent: Croyance, mesure, spéculation*, 201–232; Derrida elaborates on the generalized logic of faith and credit in his "Faith and Knowledge: The Two Sources of 'Religion' at the Limits of Reason Alone," trans. Samuel Weber, in Derrida, *Acts of Religion*, ed. Gil Anidjar (New York: Routledge, 2002).

46. Ferber, "The Ideology," 440.

47. Ferber, "The Ideology," 441; one might invoke Ferber's own comment on the construction of "inconsistencies and paradoxes" in Shakespeare (431) as opposed to what he calls the "contradictions," "compromises," and "layers of hypocrisy" of Christianity (440–41), or even "the tension between the worldly and otherworldly dimensions of Christianity" (442). Thus, when he writes of "the inconsistencies and paradoxes that have been turned up, however, often seem arbitrary, either because they are not folded back into a general assessment of the play or, more important, because they are not traced to the ideas and practices of Shakespeare's historical moment" (431), Ferber seems to disregard the possibility that the very same argument could be made about Christianity, "one version of Christian[ity]" (460), or something else than a "two-term" Christianity (463) in its historical development.

48. Werner Hamacher, "The Right to Have Rights (Four-and-a-Half Remarks)," in *And Justice for All? The Claims of Human Rights*, ed. Ian Balfour and Eduardo Cadava, A Special Issue of *South Atlantic Quarterly* 103, no. 2/3 (Spring/Summer 2004): 345, quoting Marx on the Jewish question. And compare how Agamben, commenting on Benjamin's "Capitalism as Religion," at once describes the particular confusion of human and divine, sacred and profane in Christianity (Agamben, *Profanations*, 80) thus underscoring Benjamin's focus, and reverts back, as it were, to "religion." Thus, when it comes to capitalism, Agamben writes that it "generalizes in every domain the structure of separation that defines *religion*" (81; emphasis added). Against Benjamin's logic of the parasite, Agamben follows a logic of separation and of distinctions between secularization and profanation, between transubstantiation and consumption (of the host), between this sacrificial, individual consumption and the self-sacrifice of modern tourism. Yet, this is precisely the fragile but victorious logic whereby Christianity ensured the survival of a religious system that should have brought about the collapse of the very distinctions it upholds and its ensuing transformation into its "parasite"—not its distinct opposite—namely, capitalism.

49. León Rozitchner, *La Cosa y la Cruz. Cristianismo y Capitalism (En torno a las Confesiones de san Agustín)* (Buenos Aires: Editorial Losada, 1996).

50. Connolly, *Capitalism and Christianity*, 31; beside Connolly, I am thinking here of Linda Kintz and Bethany Moreton who all show, in an essential manner, the enduring legacy and presence of a Christianity that must be more broadly conceived in historical and indeed "axiomatic" terms. Philip Goodchild, mentioned earlier, expands our historical and theological horizons, as does *The Marketplace of Christianity*, Robert B. Ekelund Jr., Robert F. Herbert, and Robert D. Tollison (Cambridge, Mass.: MIT Press, 2006).

51. Charles Baudelaire, from his notebooks, quoted in Bajorek, *Counterfeit Capital*, 5; I substitute "capitalist spirit" for Baudelaire's "republican spirit" and "capitalism" for his "democracy." Baudelaire knew something about blood and about melancholy consumers: "In love I've sought an hour's oblivion but / love to me is a pallet stuffed with pins / that drains away my blood for whores to drink" (C. Baudelaire, "The Fountain of Blood," in *Les fleurs du mal*, trans. Richard Howard [Boston: David Godine, 1982], 131).

52. J. Derrida, "Faith and Knowledge." In a proximate context, Anthony Waterman points out that "An 'internal' intellectual-historiographic account of the replacement of the rhetoric of Christian theology by that of political economy has yet to be produced; though an economist has lately suggested that modern economics is actually the current manifestation of Western religion and is the lawful heir of a putatively defunct Christianity" (A. M. C. Waterman, *Political Economy and Christian Theology Since the Enlightenment: Essays in Intellectual History* (New York: Palgrave Macmillan, 2004), 5; Waterman is referring to Robert H. Nelson and to his *Reaching for Heaven on Earth*.

53. I therefore agree with Michael Ferber that "Weber's and Shakespeare's spirits of capitalism … differ as much as their Christian ethics. Shakespeare would separate mercantile capital from finance capital and attribute to the former not only the Christian virtues but the virtues of the aristocracy" (448). The question—a family quarrel, to some extent—is whether one could say that only one of these "spirits" is, in fact, Christian, and for what purpose, with what analytic purchase.

54. W. Benjamin, "Capitalism as Religion," 289.

55. "Marx's views on the subject of money are relevant as they uncannily express what Shakespeare dramatically suggested centuries earlier. To paraphrase Kenneth Muir, Shakespeare may or may not have been a proleptic Marxist, but Marx was certainly a Shakespearean" (Peter F. Grav, *Shakespeare and the Economic Imperative: "What's aught but as 'tis valued?"* [New York: Routledge, 2008], 6).

56. All quotations in this section are from Moses Hess, "Über das Geldwesen [On the Essence of Money]," in M. Hess, *Philosophische und Sozialistische Schriften 1837–1850*, ed. Auguste Cornu and Wolfgang Mönke (Berlin: Akademie-Verlag, 1961), 345; my translation.

57. Karl Marx, *Capital: A Critique of Political Economy*, vol. 1, trans. Ben Fowkes (New York: Penguin Books, 1990), 172.

58. Connolly, *Capitalism and Christianity*, 9.

59. Taylor, *Confidence Games*, 67; and see also Marc Shell, "L'art en tant qu'argent en tant qu'art," in *Comment penser l'argent*, ed. Roger-Pol Droit (Paris: Le Monde Editions, 1992), 103–128.

60. Marc Shell, *Money, Language, and Thought: Literary and Philosophical Economies from the Medieval to the Modern Era* (Baltimore, Md.: Johns Hopkins University Press, 1993), 1, 3.

61. Valentin Groebner, *Liquid Assets, Dangerous Gifts: Presents and Politics at the End of the Middle Ages*, trans. Pamela E. Selwyn (Philadelphia: University of Pennsylvania Press, 2002), 22; and further: "Gifts were, first of all, represented as liquids. When the word *geschenckt* appears in the register, something was usually flowing, and when the bestowed objects were not literally fluid but were gratuities (the German word means 'drink-money'), cups, or drinking vessels filled with money, they were still presented as liquid, with an explicit or implicit reference to wine, the ritual political liquid of the late Middle Ages par excellence" (64).

62. On Harvey, see Rogers, *The Matter of Revolution*; on Luther and "filthy lucre," see Norman O. Brown, *Life Against Death: The Psychoanalytical Meaning of History* (Middletown, Conn.: Wesleyan University Press, 1985), 234–304; and see Karen Ho, *Liquidated: An Ethnography of Wall Street* (Durham, N.C.: Duke University Press, 2009); the association between money and blood (the blood of Christ in particular) seems to me to enfold that of money and shit (the divine kind as well). It is at any rate outlined—"where shit was, so gold shall be"—in some (sparse but graphically convincing) detail by Dominique Laporte in his *History of Shit*, trans. Nadia Benabid and Rodolphe El-Khoury (Cambridge, Mass.: MIT Press, 2000), 38, and see 58, 79, 82, 110, and it relates, in properly psychoanalytical fashion, to the vampire state and its "sphincterial training of the social body" (66). Laporte insists that he writes of the "Christian West," of capitalism (and colonialism) throughout, and he goes on to explain that "the distribution of wealth according to each person's needs marks an increasingly public and antiseptic social exchange. The subject finds himself in the restrained posture of a force-fed goose, literally stuffed by the State that shits in his mouth," and simultaneously sucks his blood (66).

63. Shell, *Money, Language, and Thought*, 40, n. 43.

64. I mean here to affirm and expand the relation between "race and money" brilliantly explored by Michael O'Malley in his "Specie and Species: Race and the Money Question in Nineteenth-Century America," *American Historical Review* 99, no. 2 (April 1994): 369–95; O'Malley considers the central role of blood in this argument (372, 381–82).

65. This is the argument I elaborate in the previous chapter, "The Vampire State."

66. Throughout his inspiring study, Mark Taylor insists on the importance of immanence as a major site of the transformation upon which modern economics depends (Taylor, *Confidence Games*, e.g., 84, 89, 98, 101ff.), and see also Benjamin, "Capitalism as Religion," 289. Commenting as well on Benjamin's unpublished essay, Samuel Weber underscores the "biologization of God" and "pure immanence." Weber thus describes a process that is "in principle infinite and yet immanent" in which money, rather than labor, emerges as "the salient trait of the capitalist cult-religion" (S. Weber, *Targets of Opportunity: On the Militarization of Thinking* [New York: Fordham University Press, 2005], 117–23).

67. In *La bourse et la vie*, Jacques Le Goff associates "tabou du sang" with "tabou de l'argent" in a narrative of exclusion that culminates around, or upon, the Jews (J. Le Goff, *La bourse et la vie: Économie et religion au Moyen Âge*, in Le Goff, *Un autre Moyen Âge* (Paris: Gallimard / Quarto, 1999], 1293). That *The Merchant of Venice* stands at the cusp of the transvaluation

of money (parallel to the transvaluation of blood that had occurred earlier) is evident in Michael Ferber's remark that "as the universal medium of exchange and the means of the communication or circulation of wealth, money reduces the moral question to simple terms: hoarding or free circulating, too much or too little, greed or generosity. Money is isomorphic to a one-commodity economy and mates well with the single spiritual commodity of love or friendship" (Ferber, "The Ideology," 453).

68. Marx, "Speech," 577.

69. On the Eucharist, see Miri Rubin, *Corpus Christi: The Eucharist in Late Medieval Culture* (Cambridge: Cambridge University Press, 1991), and see also Carolyn Walker Bynum on the blood cult. On the history of the blood libel, see R. Po-Chia Hsia. On Jews and money in medieval culture, see, among many others, Joseph Shatzmiller, *Shylock Reconsidered: Jews, Moneylending, and Medieval Society* (Berkeley: University of California Press, 1990), and Jacques Le Goff, *La bourse et la vie*. Le Goff points to the configuration linking the Eucharist to anti-Judaism and to economic conceptions on p. 1285. Finally, Benjamin Nelson wrote a history of the idea of usury that demonstrates that Christians were thinking (about) money "with" the Jews, as it were (B. N. Nelson, *The Idea of Usury: From Tribal Brotherhood to Universal Otherhood* [Princeton, N.J.: Princeton University Press, 1949]).

70. Nevertheless it is also the case that "surprisingly, given the centrality of economic themes in modern anti-Semitism, as well as the very real economic crises that affected much of European Jewry, historians have tended to approach Jewish economic discourse in an indirect fashion, at best" (D. J. Penslar, *Shylock's Children: Economics and Jewish Identity in Modern Europe* [Berkeley: University of California Press, 2001], 2). I am suggesting that the same can be said as well of Christian economic discourse, evidence to the contrary notwithstanding. Incidentally, in spite of his title, Penslar has little to say about Shakespeare's play.

71. This title, which I offer, only partly in jest—considering the number of books addressing, quite seriously, the matter of "Jews and money" (see next note)—could have served as a subheading of Bartolomé Clavero's impressive study *Antidora. Anthropología católica de la economía moderna* (Milan: Dott. A. Giuffre Editore, 1991) translated into French under the title *La grâce du don. Anthropologie catholique de l'économie moderne*. Trad. Jean-Frédéric Schaub. Préface de Jacques le Goff (Paris: Albin Michel, 1996).

72. I have mentioned a few, but the number of books and treatises dealing with Jews and money is really too large to include here, and though not all of them document negativity (some even go so far as to suggest that it is a good thing that Jews are associated with money), they render conspicuous the absence of a similar study that would take Christians as their object. For a sample of studies with bibliographic information, see *Les Juifs et l'économique: miroirs et mirages*, ed. Chantal Benayoun et al. (Toulouse: Presses Universitaires du Mirail, 1992); Jacques Attali, *Les Juifs, le monde et l'argent. Histoire économique du peuple juif* (Paris: Fayard, 2002); Edouard Valdman, *Jews and Money: Towards a Metaphysics of Money*, trans. Margaret Flynn (Rockville, Md.: Schreiber Publishing, 2000); Yuri Slezkine, *The Jewish Century* (Princeton, N.J.: Princeton University Press, 2004); and see Kirill Postoutenko, "Wandering as Circulation: Dostoevsky and Marx on the 'Jewish Question,'" in *The Economy in Jewish History: New Perspectives on the Interrelationship Between Ethnicity and*

Economic Life, ed. Gideon Reuveni and Sarah Wobick-Segev (Oxford: Berghahn Books, 2010), 43–61. For a reminder of "the ability of Christian thought to generate Judaism 'out of its own entrails,'" see David Nirenberg, "Shakespeare's Jewish Questions," *Renaissance Drama* 38 (2010): 79.

73. Jacques Derrida, "What Is a 'Relevant' Translation?" trans. Lawrence Venuti, *Critical Inquiry* 27, no. 2 (Winter 2001): 186.

74. For an overview of Shakespeare on blood, see *Shakespeare's Theories of Blood, Character, and Class: A Festschrift in Honor of David Shelley Berkeley*, ed. Peter C. Rollins and Alan Smith (New York: Peter Lang, 2001), and particularly David S. Berkeley's essay, "Shakespeare's *Severall Degrees in Bloud*," 7–18; and see also Gail Kern Paster, "Laudable Blood: Bleeding, Difference, and Humoral Embarrassment," in Kern Paster, *The Body Embarrassed*, 64–112.

75. Amos Funkenstein, *Theology and the Scientific Imagination from the Middle Ages to the Seventeenth Century* (Princeton, N.J.: Princeton University Press, 1986).

76. *The Works of William Harvey*, 30–31. No matter how momentous the discovery, it is important to recall that its scientific validity was not, in fact, established by Harvey. As his biographer Robert Willis puts it, Harvey "left the doctrine of the circulation as an inference or induction only, not as a sensible demonstration. He adduced certain circumstances, and quoted various anatomical facts which made a continuous transit of the blood from the arteries into the veins, from the veins into the arteries, a necessary consequence; but he never saw this transit; his idea of the way in which it was accomplished was even defective" (R. Willis, *The Life of William Harvey*, in *The Works of William Harvey*, edited and translated by Robert Willis (Philadelphia: University of Pennsylvania Press, 1989), xli. It is hardly insignificant to note, moreover, that, in spite of initial resistance, Harvey enjoyed a rare privilege. He is one of the few discoverers who "in his lifetime had the high satisfaction of witnessing his discovery generally received, and inculcated as a canon in most of the medical schools of Europe; he is, therefore, one of the few—his friend Thomas Hobbes says, he was the only one within his knowledge—'Solus quod sciam,' who lived to see the new doctrine which he had promulgated victorious over opposition, and established in public opinion" (lii).

77. *The Works of William Harvey*, 3–4; emphasis added. See also where Harvey compares the heart to the sun or "heart of the world" and to a "household divinity" (47) and where he likens the heart to the prince of a kingdom (83). Willis also points out that Harvey's formal education at Cambridge University was in logic and divinity, not physics or medicine. Harvey, in whom "the religious sentiments appear to have been active" (lxxviii), clearly secularizes (or rather, immanentizes) the divine prime mover by incarnating it in the heart of man, while conclusively settling medical and political disputes over the centrality of heart versus liver, and head versus heart, as seats of sovereign governance; on that debate, see Jacques Le Goff, "Head or Heart? The Political Use of Body Metaphors in the Middle Ages," in *Fragments for a History of the Human Body: Part Three*, ed. Michel Feher et al. (New York: Zone Books, 1989), 12–26.

78. See Paul P. Christensen, "Hobbes and the Physiological Origins of Economic Science," *History of Political Economy* 21, no. 4 (1989): 689–709.

79. R. Willis, *The Life of William Harvey*, in *The Works of William Harvey*, xvii.

80. Thomas Hobbes, *Leviathan*, ed. Richard Tuck (Cambridge: Cambridge University Press, 1996), chap. 24, "Of the Nutrition, and Procreation of a Common-wealth," 174–175; Goodchild makes a note of Hobbes's contribution in *Theology of Money*, 227 and 265, n. 7.

81. For an illuminating reading of Hobbes on the seas, that is to say, on the surface of Melville's *Moby-Dick*, see Peter Szendy, *Prophecies of Leviathan: Reading Past Melville*, trans. Gil Anidjar (New York: Fordham University Press, 2010). The phrase "Leviathan is the text" is, of course, Melville's, commented by Szendy; and see chap. 6 this volume, "Leviathan and the Blood-Pump."

82. John Law quoted in Frederick C. Green, *Eighteenth-Century France: Six Essays* (New York: Frederick Ungar Publishing, 1964), 7; and see, for earlier antecedents, Jonathan Gil Harris, *Sick Economies*, 143–46. For a biography of Law, see Janet Gleeson, *Millionaire: The Philanderer, Gambler, and Duelist Who Invented Modern Finance* (New York: Simon & Schuster, 1999); for more on Law and the mercantilists, and their contribution to the history of money, particularly the importance of circulation in the production of wealth, see Eli F. Hecksher, *Mercantilism*, trans. Mendel Shapiro (London: George Allen & Unwin Ltd, 1934) (I am grateful to Partha Chatterjee for directing me to Hecksher's work). Earlier, Quesnay had already pictured the kingdom as a closed system within which commodities circulate as blood in the body (see V. Foley, "An Origin of the *Tableau Économique*," *History of Political Economy* 5, no. 1 [1973]: 121–50, and Paul P. Christensen, "Fire, Motion, and Productivity: The Proto-Energetics of Nature and Economy in Francois Quesnay," in *Natural Images in Economic Thought*, 249–88). Turgot, another Physiocrat, followed suit. Montesquieu, a contemporary of Law, seems to have thought that "honor" used to be the blood of the state ("Honor," he wrote, "reigns in monarchies; there it gives life to the whole body politic, to the laws, and even to the virtues" [Montesquieu, *Spirit of the Laws*, trans. Anne M. Cohler et al. [Cambridge: Cambridge University Press, 1989], book 3, chap. 8, 28).

83. E. F. Hecksher, *Mercantilism*, vol. 2, 216. Hecksher suggests that the transformation with regard to money and circulation found its origins in the Middle Ages, but he does not account for its sources or larger theologico-economic significance except when he refers to the mercantilists' "idolatry of money" as an unconscious idea, as part of "unconscious elements" that "provided a halo of significance to the terms gold, silver, and money, which is not exhausted by the functions consciously ascribed to them" (261). For a thorough inquiry into the early modern uptake of Galenic medicine in political economy, see Jonathan Gil Harris, *Sick Economies: Drama, Mercantilism, and Disease in Shakespeare's England* (Philadelphia: University of Pennsylvania Press, 2004); for a reconsideration of the medieval church's economic roles and practices, see Robert B. Ekelund Jr., Robert F. Herbert, Robert D. Tollison, Gary M. Anderson, and Audrey B. Davidson, *Sacred Trust: The Medieval Church as an Economic Firm* (New York: Oxford University Press, 1996).

84. Timothy Mitchell reframes this event and proposes a more pointed description. "When European banks requested payment for their dollars in gold," Mitchell writes, "the US defaulted. Described as 'the abandoning of the gold standard,' it amounted to a declaration of bankruptcy by the US government" (Mitchell, "Carbon Democracy," 419).

85. Shakespeare, *The Merchant of Venice*, 1.3.21–24.

86. At the center of Marcel Mauss's *Essai sur le don* are inscribed the associations of the religious and the economic, but more importantly for now, the practice of "prestations totales de type agonistique" (M. Mauss, *Sociologie et anthropologie* [Paris: Quadrige/PUF, 1995], 153). Mauss insists throughout on the agonistic dimension of exchange.

87. Carl Schmitt, *The Concept of the Political*, trans. George Schwab (Chicago: University of Chicago Press, 1996), 29. On Schmitt's omission of the theological in the concept of the enemy, see Jacob Taubes, *The Political Theology of Paul*, trans. Dana Hollander (Stanford, Calif.: Stanford University Press, 2003), and see my *The Jew, the Arab: A History of the Enemy* (Stanford, Calif.: Stanford University Press, 2003).

88. Schmitt, *The Concept of the Political*, 28.

89. Schmitt, *The Concept of the Political*, 79; emphasis added.

90. Schmitt, *The Concept of the Political*, 78.

91. Schmitt, *The Concept of the Political*, 79.

92. Schmitt strikingly writes of an evolution toward "oceanic culture," beginning with the discovery of the Americas (C. Schmitt, *Land und Meer* [Stuttgart: Klett-Cotta, 1993], 23). It led to a "planetary space revolution [*eine planetarische Raumrevolution*]" (54), and it was "the first authentic" revolution in world history, "without comparison" (64). I have commented on this gradual but momentous "liquefaction" of space in Schmitt's work in my "Terror Rights" in *CR: The New Centennial Review* 4, no. 3 (Winter 2004) [Special issue on Carl Schmitt's *Theory of the Partisan*]: 35–69. As I indicated earlier, Gilles Deleuze and Félix Guattari have underscored the importance of flux and flow— and their interruption—toward an understanding of capitalism in *L'Anti-Oedipe: Capitalisme et schizophrénie* (Paris: Minuit, 1972). Calling attention to William Gaddis's 1955 *The Recognitions* and to the figure of blood banks in this novel, Mark Taylor goes on to highlight the larger phenomenon in which "referents that once provided secure foundations for thought and action are 'liquefied' and begin to circulate freely" (Taylor, *Confidence Games*, 25).

93. Mark Netzloff, "The Lead Casket: Capital, Mercantilism, and *The Merchant of Venice*," in *Money and the Age of Shakespeare: Essays in New Economic Criticism*, ed. Linda Woodbridge (New York: Palgrave, 2003), 171.

94. Ferber, "The Ideology," 435.

95. Lars Engle, "'Thrift is Blessing': Exchange and Explanation in *The Merchant of Venice*," *Shakespeare Quarterly* 37, no. 1 (Spring 1986): 26.

96. Schmitt describes Venice's half-millennium dominion over the sea, as well as the ceremony of these *sposalizio del mare* in *Land und Meer*, 20–21.

97. Shakespeare, *The Merchant of Venice*, 1.1.8–14. Further references to the play will be made parenthetically in the body of the text.

98. Curiously, the index in Jay Hallo's edition refers only to two instances of the word *blood* in the play. Money barely appears either, except once as "moneys" and once as "money-bags."

99. In the next scene, Portia will recall the warm liquid as exceeding the bounds of the law, thus prefiguring her later Christian lesson to Shylock: "The brain may devise laws / for the blood; but a hot temper leaps o'er a cold decree" (1.2.17–20).

100. Shylock is, of course, black, that is, jet to Jessica's fair, ivory flesh (3.1.36–39).

101. Walter Cohen, "*The Merchant of Venice* and the Possibilities of Historical Criticism," *ELH* 49, no. 4 (Winter 1982): 766.

102. Gail Kern Paster, *The Body Embarrassed: Drama and the Disciplines of Shame in Early Modern England* (Ithaca, N.Y.: Cornell University Press, 1993), 85.

103. Ferber comments that "Salario elaborates on how different the two fleshes and the two bloods are" (Ferber, "The Ideology," 463, n. 48); François-Xavier Gleyzon provides the most explicit rendering of the difference by scrupulously following the trail leading "from circumcision to the Eucharist" (F.-X. Gleyzon, "Opening the Sacred Body or the Profaned Host in *The Merchant of Venice*," forthcoming).

104. Kern Paster, *The Body Embarrassed*, 85.

105. As Netzloff comments, Bassanio's "status as a gentleman . . . is dependent on a supply of capital to keep that bloodstream circulating. . . . [He] adjudicates his value in terms of a circulating body of capital that is represented, not embodied, by the letter indicating Antonio's losses. This disembodied paper, similar in form to credit or a bill of exchange, is nonetheless likened to Antonio's body, and depicted as bleeding capital in the form of lost 'ventures' and shipwrecks" (Netzloff, "The Lead Casket," 165).

106. Patricia Parker, "Cutting Both Ways: Bloodletting, Castration/Circumcision, and the 'Lancelet' of The Merchant of Venice," *Alternative Shakespeares 3*, ed. Diana Henderson (New York: Routledge, 2007), 95–118; Parker draws a broader picture of cutting and bloodletting instruments through the play, beginning with the wordplay on Lancelot / lancelet.

107. Although he does not mention Harvey, Ferber notes that "Shakespeare was probably unaware of the doctrine of the 'velocity of circulation,' according to which a growth in the rate of circulation of money is a growth in the amount of money" (Ferber, "The Ideology," 454). Sigurd Burckhardt had described *The Merchant of Venice* as "a play about circularity and circulation" (S. Burckhardt, *Shakespearean Meanings* [Princeton, N.J.: Princeton University Press, 1968], 210). John Rogers suggests that Harvey may have been influenced by Shakespeare, among others (Rogers, *The Matter of Revolution*, 24), whereas Jonathan Gil Harris reports Ernest Gillman's suggestion that Harvey "remapped the global voyages of the great circumnavigators" (quoted in Harris, *Sick Economies*, 162).

108. Netzloff, "The Lead Casket," 168.

109. Karl Marx, "On the Jewish Question," trans. Rodney Livingstone and Gregor Benton, in Marx, *Early Writings*, ed. Lucio Colletti (London: Penguin Books, 1975), 237.

110. On Marx and *The Merchant of Venice*, see Walter Cohen, "The Merchant of Venice," 772–73. Cohen importantly writes that "by the end of the trial scene most of the Christian characters have fairly settled accounts with Shylock. The trouble is that Christianity has not" (773). Attending to the somehow neglected critique of Christianity in Shakespeare's play, René Girard argues that "the main object of satire is not Shylock the Jew. But Shylock is rehabilitated only to the extent that the Christians are even worse than he is and that the "honesty" of his vices makes him almost a refreshing figure compared to the sanctimonious ferocity of the other Venetians" (R. Girard, "'To Entrap the Wisest': A Reading of *The Merchant of Venice*," in *Literature and Society*, ed. Edward W. Said [Baltimore, Md.: Johns Hopkins University Press / The English Institute, 1980], 107); David Nirenberg

joins in on the downplaying of Shakespeare's anti-Semitism, highlighting the critique of capitalism as well as, in a paradoxically titled essay, what seems really a "Christian question" in Shakespeare (D. Nirenberg, "Shakespeare's Jewish Questions," *Renaissance Drama* 38 [2010]: 77–113).

111. R. H. Tawney, *Religion and the Rise of Capitalism*, 84.

112. Max Weber, *The Protestant Ethic and the Spirit of Capitalism*, trans. Talcott Parsons (New York and London: Routledge, 2001), 18. Weber nonetheless returns a number of times to the "devotion to the calling of making money" (33) and to the "conception of money-making as an end in itself" (34). For a thorough discussion of Marx and ensuing misreadings with regard to work versus exchange, see Karatani, *Transcritique*.

113. Tawney, *Religion and the Rise of Capitalism*, xii.

114. "Ce que le politique n'a pas su accomplir, à savoir ce rapport souverain de la société à elle-même, l'économisation de la société y parvient, car elle totalise la société sans extériorité. Elle organise la société dans un mouvement circulaire où toute dépense est calculée en vue d'un retour qui maintient la circularité du mouvement" (Egidius Berns, "L'Euro et le politique," in *L'argent: Croyance, mesure, spéculation*, 252).

PART TWO. HEMATOLOGIES

1. Michel Foucault, *The Archaeology of Knowledge*, trans. A. M. Sheridan Smith (New York: Routledge, 1989), 10.

4. ODYSSEUS' BLOOD

1. Erich Auerbach, "Odysseus' Scar," in Auerbach, *Mimesis: The Representation of Reality in Western Literature*, trans. Willard Trask (Princeton, N.J.: Princeton University Press, 2003), 3–23 / "Die Narbe des Odysseus," *Mimesis. Dargestellte Wirklichkeit in der abendländischen Literatur* (Bern: A. Francke AG. Verlag, 1946), 7–30; further references will be made parenthetically in the text, with the letter G for the German pagination. In this section, I acknowledge being guided in no small part by James Porter's recent study, in which he writes the following: "Not for nothing did Auerbach wish for his essay to be remembered—literally scarred—by the word *scar* (*Narbe*) in the title, signaling a wound, a trauma, and a stigma, but also its concealment and its hardened (if not healed) condition" (James I. Porter, "Auerbach and the Judaizing of Philology," *Critical Inquiry* 35 [Autumn 2008]: 131).

2. It should be obvious that by "Homer himself" (and later by "the Greeks") I do not mean to refer to a historical figure. I follow Auerbach instead, described, once again, by Porter: "By *Homer* and what we would call the *Homeric tradition* Auerbach means us to understand first Homer and next the Greek mentality that Homer embodies and then eventually passes on to Rome and into later antiquity, *as this was understood in modernity*" (Porter, "Auerbach," 127); and see also Gregory Nagy, *Homeric Questions* (Austin: University of Texas Press, 1996), esp. chap. 3.

3. "For all that he may underestimate the background they constitute and the shadow cast by the very obliqueness of their allusive representation," writes Laura Slatkin, "Auerbach

himself clearly perceives that the continuous integration of mythological passages *supplementing* (although they appear to delay) the poem's narrative progress must be appreciated as the reflection, on the level of style, of a distinctive way of seeing and comprehending epic personages and events *in their totality*" (Laura M. Slatkin, *The Power of Thetis: Allusion and Interpretation in the* Iliad [Berkeley: University of California Press, 1991], 115; emphasis added). Slatkin is obviously referring, as I do after her, to the logic of the "supplement" theorized by Jacques Derrida.

4. Moses I. Finley, *The World of Odysseus* (New York: New York Review of Books, 2002), 121.

5. Plato, *The Republic*, trans. Paul Shorey (Cambridge, Mass.: Harvard University Press, 1935), 537a. On the "lettuce war" among classicists, which was apparently started by Marcel Détienne, see the dossier compiled in *Antiquities (Postwar French Thought, volume III)*, ed. Nicole Loraux, Gregory Nagy, and Laura Slatkin (New York: New Press, 2001), 176–94. "It is a kind of plant," explains Détienne, "whose nature suggests we make an inventory of the various humors to define the relations between lactation, menstruation, production of seed, the body (feminine and masculine), and the mechanics of vital fluid" (190). Much of this is of interest to me in what follows, and note that just a few lines below, Détienne transitions seamlessly to the fact that "the blood of Adonis gives birth to the anemone," the blood flower.

6. Borrowing Nagy's title phrase (G. Nagy, *Homeric Questions*). It should already be pointed out, however, that blood does not exactly stand at the center of scholarly attention. An important collection of critical essays on Homer, which includes Auerbach's, does no more than mention blood a handful of times (*Homer: A Collection of Critical Essays*, ed. George Steiner and Robert Fagles [Englewood Cliffs, N.J.: Prentice-Hall, 1962]).

7. M. Furth does argue that for Anaxagoras, "the whole world is Blood," but the claim entails that "the whole world is also Boar," so I leave it cautiously aside (M. Furth, "A 'Philosophical Hero?' Anaxagoras and the Eleatics," *Oxford Studies in Ancient Philosophy* 9 (1991): 113, n. 27).

8. Verity Harte thoughtfully engages the matter of parts and whole in Plato as an entry point to composition (V. Harte, *Plato on Parts and Wholes: The Metaphysics of Structure* (Oxford: Oxford University Press, 2002). My concern, however, is with the plausible wholes, if there are such, to which blood relates, with which it enters into a composition. Whether blood is at all a part, and of what, is of course no less important, but it is secondary to the question of where, in what sort of whole, one should look for it.

9. "It is important," writes Gregory Nagy, "to stress the explicit role of religion in the very function of epic. For purposes of this presentation, a minimalist working definition of religion will suffice: let us consider it for the moment as simply the interaction of myth and ritual. I propose further to specify "religion" in terms of *cult*, which I define for the moment as *a set of practices combining elements of ritual as well as myth*" (Nagy, *Homeric Questions,* 47). John Peradotto, for his part, reminds us that "early Greek society is not the only place where it is often difficult to find the lines that divide poet from holy man, seer, and prophet, and where there is something like a cult of divinely inspiring Muses. It is no accident that the greatest storyteller in the *Odyssey*, Odysseus himself, has maternal uncles, sons of the arch-trickster Autolycus, whose powers of song go so far beyond simple

persuasion, instruction, or entertainment that they are able to cause the blood in a wound to congeal by their incantations (19.457), a power richly documented in a variety of cultures" (J. Peradotto, *Man in the Middle Voice: Name and Narration in the Odyssey* [Princeton, N.J.: Princeton University Press, 1990], 28). I return to this episode later.

10. As Vassilis Lambropoulos writes, "although he argues that the two works express opposite worldviews and dictate different readings, [Auerbach] uses for both the approach derived from the second. He does not read Homer against the Bible, as he claims, but rather reads Homer through the Bible: his is a Biblical treatment" (V. Lambropoulos, *The Rise of Eurocentrism: Anatomy of Interpretation* [Princeton, N.J.: Princeton University Press, 1993], 5; for a similar, if more positive, argument about Auerbach's "Judaizing" take, see Porter, "Auerbach"). And yet, the indispensable literary categories deployed by Auerbach are emphatically "epic" and "tragic." One could perhaps wonder, therefore, whether these, which insistently serve as comparative terms found on both sides of the divide, might not provide for a reversal of the argument in favor of the Greeks, as it were (Auerbach, *Mimesis*, 22). In my own reading, at any rate, the Bible seems minimally to function as the "fraught background" that would be missing from the manifest luminosity of the Greek text—and vice versa.

11. Auerbach was no doubt aware of Hegel's remarks on "the absolute Notion," "the simple essence of life, the soul of the world, the universal blood," which I have already quoted (G. W. F. Hegel, *Phenomenology of Spirit*, trans. A. V. Miller (Oxford: Oxford University Press, 1977), 100.

12. Stathis Gourgouris reviews some of the essential literature and offers a striking reading of Homer (and Kafka) in "The Gesture of the Sirens," chap. 4 of *Does Literature Think? Literature as Theory for an Antimythical Era* (Stanford, Calif.: Stanford University Press, 2003), 161–97.

13. A. L. Peck, "Preface," in Aristotle, *Generation of Animals* (Cambridge: Harvard University Press/Loeb Classical Library, 1942), xlix; a later note will explain that "part does not necessarily imply a limb" (44); commenting on Aristotle, Claudia Baracchi explains that "*Morion* (meaning 'piece,' 'portion,' 'constituent,' 'member,' 'part' in the broadest sense) is the term Aristotle mostly employs ... to refer to the partitions of the soul." She goes on to suggest that whether parts are separable or inseparable, distinct or aspects of the same whole, may or may not be of importance (C. Baracchi, *Aristotle's Ethics as First Philosophy* [Cambridge: Cambridge University Press, 2008], 174, n. 34). For an extended discussion of Aristotle and followers on the difference between organs with distinguished (*anhomoiomerous*) parts and tissues and fluids in which parts are not discernible (*homoiomerous*), see Sylvia Berryman, "Necessitation and Explanation in Philoponus' Aristotelian Physics," in *Metaphysics, Soul, and Ethics in Ancient Thought. Themes from the Work of Richard Sorabji*, ed. Ricardo Salles (Oxford: Oxford University Press, 2005), 65–79.

14. Porter, "Auerbach," 115; later on Porter explains that "resemblances [of the Homeric world] to the current situation in Nazi Germany are all too evident in Auerbach's eyes" (135).

15. Most famous in this context is Karl Popper on Plato, evoking "blood and soil" in Popper, *The Open Society and Its Enemies, Vol. I, The Spell of Plato* (Princeton, N.J., 1966), 151–53; and see George B. Walsh, "The Rhetoric of Birthright and Race in Euripides' *Ion*," *Hermes*

106, no. 2 (1978): 309. More recently, there are those who make clear that one is to make no difference between ancient perceptions and modern racial ones: "One may quickly dismiss the Herodotean category of blood relationships as irrelevant to the modern study of ethnicity; not even a very sentimental Hellenist would want to insist on racial purity and continuity on those terms" (Katerina Zacharia, "Herodotus' Four Markers of Greek Identity," in *Hellenisms: Culture, Identity, and Ethnicity from Antiquity to Modernity*, ed. K. Zacharia [Aldershot: Ashgate, 2008], 34, and see in the same volume 132–33). Marcel Détienne, who offers a telling description of Athenian politics ("Clustering around the first-born from an idealized bloodless mythology, the Athenians postured as pure autochthonous beings, confident that they had been polluted by no drop of foreign blood" [M. Détienne, *The Greeks and Us: A Comparative Anthropology of Ancient Greece*, trans. Janet Lloyd (Cambridge: Polity, 2007), 80]), also posits everything that must be unthought, the very possibility of "de-nationalizing all national histories," all nationalisms, as hinging on the sign of autochthony, on "pure blood" and "national" difference from Athens to Paris (M. Détienne, *Comment être autochtone: Du pur Athénien au Français raciné* [Paris: Seuil, 2003]); and see the strenuous argument against the appropriation of Athens and its "discriminating policies" by the far-right in France in Loraux, *Born of the Earth: Myth and Politics in Athens*, trans. Selina Stewart (Ithaca, N.Y.: Cornell University Press, 2000), esp. 125–42. Interrogations of blood in racial discourse (is it really in the blood?) have yet to reach kinship, in other words.

16. Walsh, "The Rhetoric of Birthright," 301; before citing Walsh approvingly, Josiah Ober comments that "The myth of Athenian autochthony, despite the fact that even in historical times exogeny had been legal, allowed all Athenians to regard themselves as pure-blooded and thus, by definition, of well-born ancestry" (J. Ober, *Mass and Elite in Democratic Athens: Rhetoric, Ideology, and the Power of the People* [Princeton, N.J.: Princeton University Press, 1989], 262).

17. It is, of course, well accepted that blood is, in ancient Greece, the site of difference between human and divine, as well as between men and women (Helen King, *Hippocrates' Woman: Reading the Female Body in Ancient Greece* [London and New York: Routledge, 1998], 91–92). As King puts it, "blood and sacrifice thus separate humans from gods, and men from women" (94; and see Froma I. Zeitlin, "La politique d'éros," *Mètis. Anthropologie des mondes grecs anciens* 3, no. 1 [1988], 231–59). I seek to further solicit these insights, as well as a remark made by Pierre Chantraine that, when it comes to meaning and use, there are two "categories" for blood, one for "expressive and poetic language," and one for "the technical vocabulary of scholars and physicians" (P. Chantraine, *Dictionnaire Étymologique de la langue grecque. Histoire des mots* [Paris: Klincksieck, 1968], vol. 1, 34).

18. Nicole Loraux's extraordinary book is also about invisibility and a paradoxical forgetting, the forgetting—in memory and remembrance—of civil war and of blood (N. Loraux, *La cité divisée. L'oubli dans la mémoire d'Athènes* [Paris: Payot, 1997]). Loraux's reflections on the city and on its divisions cannot be separated from her reflections on blood (see most obviously her "La guerre dans la famille," *CLIO* 5 [1997]: 21–62) and see *La tragédie d'Athènes. La politique entre l'ombre et l'utopie* (Paris: Seuil, 2005).

19. Jan Kott, *The Eating of the Gods: An Interpretation of Greek Tragedy*, trans. Boleslaw Taborski and Edward J. Czerwinski (Evanston, Ill.: Northwestern University Press, 1987), 170; Kott is reading Sophocles' *Philoctetes*, itself a reading of Homer, which casts Odysseus in a different light. "Sophocles knew Homer by heart," though admittedly "he interpreted him in a dark light" (126). Kott explains how "the wound that does not heal is a *figura* and a sign" (167). So is, it seems, a wound that does.

20. Homer, *Odyssey,* trans. A. T. Murray, rev. George E. Dimock (Cambridge, Mass., Harvard University Press, 1995), book 19, 474–75.

21. Homer, *Odyssey,* book 19, 445–54.

22. Nagy, *Homeric Questions*, 18 and 133ff. "Signs tell stories," writes Tom McCall, with whom I do not find myself in complete agreement as to the narrative location of the blood. The scar of Odysseus tells one too. It "encapsulates the whole story of this first boyhood adventure, blood or bloodshed, which [Walter] Benjamin would have tell us the story of a certain mythical transformation: how a singular act of violence, making a singular bloody mark upon a (momentary, singular) body, magically transubstantiates its own evanescent act into an indelible mark, thereby memorializing that act with the psychological scars of trauma and the lasting inscriptions of bodily scars" (Tom McCall, "Momentary Violence," in *Walter Benjamin: Theoretical Questions*, ed. David S. Ferris [Stanford, Calif.: Stanford University Press, 1996], 192).

23. François Hartog, *The Mirror of Herodotus: The Representation of the Other in the Writing of History*, trans. Janet Lloyd (Berkeley: University of California Press, 1988), 181; for a discussion of the relations (of proximity or opposition) between hunting and sacrifice, see Pierre Vidal-Naquet, "Hunting and Sacrifice in Aeschylus' *Oresteia*," in Jean-Pierre Vernant and Pierre Vidal-Naquet, *Myth and Tragedy in Ancient Greece*, trans. Janet Lloyd (New York: Zone Books, 1990), 141–59.

24. Nicole Loraux, "La main d'Antigone," *Mètis. Anthropologie des mondes grecs anciens* 1, no. 2 (1986): 189.

25. Jean-Louis Durand explains how, in ancient graphic representations, "the deed that actually drenches the blade and altar in blood is never pictured. Whenever the throat is shown hewn by the sword, the sacrificial meaning has departed from the image" (J.-L. Durand, "Greek Animals: Toward a Typology of Edible Bodies," trans. Paula Wissing, in Marcel Détienne and Jean-Pierre Vernant, *The Cuisine of Sacrifice Among the Greeks* [Chicago: University of Chicago Press, 1989], 91). Durand immediately points out that the same representational repugnance does not apply to human blood, in contrast with the practice of the tragic stage. As he goes on to evoke "the gaping throat" that "speaks of nothing more than the fact of the animal's death, a death that is mysterious and incomprehensible and refers only to itself" (91), one notes strange resonances with Auerbach.

26. Auerbach, *Mimesis*, 5.

27. Hartog, *Mirror of Herodotus*, 182; Laura Slatkin puts the matter beautifully when she writes the following: "In the continuously reversible shift of emphasis from explicit to implicit meaning, how does the poet activate the implicit? For an audience to whom this fundamental compositional resource is foreign or to whom the myths in their essential multivalence, flexibility, and systematicity are unfamiliar, the task of hearing as Homer's

audience did requires the apparently paradoxical task of listening for what is unspoken" (Slatkin, *Power of Thetis*, xvi).

28. Robert Renehan, who insists that the practice is a combination of "rational" medicine (the bandage) and magical rite (the charm or incantation), writes here of "the natural flow of the Greek of lines 456–58, which clearly describe two distinct, but related, acts, namely the skillful bandaging of the wound and the checking of the bleeding by an incantation" (R. Renehan, "The Staunching of Odysseus' Blood: The Healing Power of Magic," *The American Journal of Philology* 113, no. 1 [Spring 1992]: 2); and see Emile Benveniste, "The Medical Tradition of the Indo-Europeans," trans. Arthur Goldhammer, in *Antiquities (Postwar French Thought, volume III)*, esp. 424–25.

29. Homer, *Odyssey*, 19: 455–62.

30. Walter Burkert, *Greek Religion*, trans. John Raffan (Cambridge, Mass.: Harvard University Press, 1985), 59–60.

31. Pierre Vidal-Naquet, *The Black Hunter: Forms of Thought and Forms of Society in the Greek World*, trans. Andrew Szegedy-Maszak (Baltimore, Md.: Johns Hopkins University Press, 1986), 20.

32. John Heath reads this scene in an intriguing manner, questioning the actuality of this need for blood and the "witlessness" of the dead (J. Heath, *The Talking Greeks: Speech, Animals, and the Other in Homer, Aeschylus, and Plato* [Cambridge: Cambridge University Press, 2005], 57–60).

33. Homer, *Odyssey*, book 11, 48–50; further references in this section are to book 11, by line number.

34. Max Horkheimer and Theodor W. Adorno, "Odysseus or Myth and Enlightenment," trans. Edmund Jephcott, in *Dialectic of Enlightenment: Philosophical Fragments*, ed. Gunzelin Schmid Noerr (Stanford, Calif.: Stanford University Press, 2002), 41.

35. The phrase "patriarchal hardness" is Horkheimer and Adorno's in "Odysseus or Myth and Enlightenment," 59.

36. David M. Schneider, *A Critique of the Study of Kinship* (Ann Arbor: University of Michigan Press, 1984).

37. Although no doubt French-inflected, Jacqueline de Romilly's insistence on the "laicity" of Greek law is quite typical of the general "theologico-political" divide generally regulating the field of classics: Greek "religion" is not Greek "politics," and democracy was a secular project from its glorious origins onward. The role blood plays in this persistent narrative can hardly be gainsaid (J. de Romilly, *La loi dans la pensée grecque* [Paris: Les Belles Lettres, 2006]). Which is why Stanley Rosen's formulation works equally well: "Citizenship is determined by political function, not bloodlines" (S. Rosen, *Plato's Republic: A Study* [New Haven, Conn.: Yale University Press, 2005], 184).

38. G. E. R. Lloyd, *Disciplines in the Making: Cross-Cultural Perspectives on Elites, Learning, and Innovation* (Oxford: Oxford University Press, 2009).

39. Jean-Pierre Vernant, *Myth and Society in Ancient Greece*, trans. Janet Lloyd (New York: Zone Books, 1988), 149; and see Burkert, already mentioned, as well as the representative approach in Th. C. W. Oudemans and A. P. M. H. Lardinois, *Tragic Ambiguity: Anthropology, Philosophy, and Sophocles' Antigone* (Leiden: Brill, 1987).

40. See the informative, if bloodless, *Rethinking Revolutions Through Ancient Greece*, ed. Simon Goldhill and Robin Osborne (Cambridge: Cambridge University Press, 2006); my friend Stathis Gourgouris alerts me to the question of historical limits with regard to the significance of blood, an intriguing and not unlikely possibility that requires a measured assessment of blood of the kind I am precisely arguing for (even if I cannot hope to bring it about and answer this and other important questions).

41. "Thus, blood and violence lurk fascinatingly at the very heart of religion," writes Walter Burkert in *Homo Necans: The Anthropology of Ancient Greek Sacrificial Ritual and Myth*, trans. Peter Bing (Berkeley: University of California Press, 1983), 2; for some of the difficulties associated with the term *religion* in the ancient Greek context, see Jean Rudhardt, "Sur la possibilité de comprendre une religion antique," *Numen* 11, no. 3 (September 1964): 189–211. Paul Veyne remarks on a "balkanization of the symbolic field," which "reflected in each mind" would correspond to "a sectarian politics of alliance" may not be the most felicitous image, if one actually thinks about the Balkans, but it might apply nonetheless, for a large number of reasons (P. Veyne, "Social Diversity of Beliefs and Mental Balkanization," trans. Paula Wissing, in *Antiquities (Postwar French Thought, volume III)*, 203).

42. Michel Briand "Sur AIMONA ΘHPHΣ (*Iliade* E, 49)," *Metis* 12, no. 1 (1997): 129–60; I cite from p. 138; and see also Hermann Koller, "Αἷμα," *Glotta. Zeitschrift für griechische und lateinische Sprache* 14 (1967): 149–55; Koller writes, right at the outset of his study, that "bei Homer 'Blutsaft' ist Träger des *genos* . . . oder bedeutet gelegentlich 'Blutvergießen'" (149). Note that the constellation of "race, ethnicity, and nation" and its relation to "the key discourse of human relatedness through corporeal substance and nature—that is, kinship" was recently said to be "still rather little-explored" in modern or classical studies (Peter Wade, "Race, Ethnicity, and Nation: Perspectives from Kinship and Genetics," in *Race, Ethnicity, and Nation: Perspectives from Kinship and Genetics*, ed. Peter Wade [New York: Berghahn Books, 2007], 1).

43. I borrow the phrase "rituals of blood" from Orlando Patterson, *Rituals of Blood: Consequences of Slavery in Two American Centuries* (Washington, D.C.: Civitas, 1998). Walter Burkert's *Homo Necans* attends to such familiar "rituals of blood," murder and sacrifice, in ancient Greece. With these common associations, blood—or the preoccupation with it—fails to emerge as a problem.

44. As one scholar puts it, albeit overstating the case a bit: "A consensus seems to exist among scholars of ancient Israel and the Hebrew Bible that blood was of little importance in Greek religion, and that where it did play a role, it had only a dark and chthonic meaning utterly different from its significance in ancient Israel" (Stanley Stowers, "On the Comparison of Blood in Greek and Israelite Ritual," in *Hesed ve-Emet: Studies in Honor of Ernest S. Frerichs*, ed. Jodi Magness and Seymour Gitin [Atlanta, Ga.: Scholars Press, 1988], 179); note however that Stowers, like Nancy Jay, from whom he draws inspiration, focuses on "religion"; see Nancy Jay, *Throughout Your Generations Forever: Sacrifice, Religion, and Paternity* (Chicago: University of Chicago Press, 1992).

45. See, for example, Dennis J. McCarthy, "The Symbolism of Blood and Sacrifice," *Journal of Biblical Literature* 88, no. 2 (June 1969): 166–76; and "Further Notes on the Symbolism

of Blood and Sacrifice," *Journal of Biblical Literature* 92, no. 2 (June 1973): 205–210. I too overstate the case, no doubt (see, e.g., the even-handed distribution of essays in *Sangue e antropologia biblica* of the Centro Studi Sanguis Christi [Roma: Pia Unione Preziosissimo Sangue, 1981]), yet the contrast I draw is secondary to the argument I seek to make, namely, that we lack a map of the "field" of blood in ancient Greece (from worship to politics, from medicine to tragedy), and minimally so because it remains fragmented; at most because there are substantial reflective lacunae with regard to the matter of kinship and politics, which will occupy me principally in what follows.

46. For Robertson Smith, it was of course "both races," namely Aryans and Semites, that had "a political system based on the principle of kinship," in which the community was "held together by the tie of blood, the only social bond which then had absolute and undisputed strength, being enforced by the law of blood revenge" (W. Robertson Smith, *Religion of the Semites* [New Brunswick, N.J., and London: Transaction Publishers, 2002], 32). But whereas Aryans left this allegiance to blood rapidly behind, "the independent evolution of Semitic society was arrested at an early stage" (33). I am by no means suggesting that a concern with blood is or could be confined to "Athens and Jerusalem," only that one encounters in this dual context a constant oscillation between universal preoccupation and particular obsession, without much effort devoted to mapping out the contour of the semantic and rhetorical range covered by blood in each of the given areas.

47. Jean-Paul Roux, *Le sang. Mythes, symboles et réalités* (Paris: Fayard, 1988), 19. For this historian of blood, "one could write a history of blood in Judeo-Christianity or in Hinduism. One cannot do so for the whole of humanity since it has not lived the same adventure" (25).

48. Starr, *Blood*, xiv.

49. I borrow the phrase from Philippe Moreau, who maps out the difficulty of the task in the case of ancient Rome in "Sangs romains. Taxinomie du sang dans la Rome ancienne," in *Penser et représenter le corps dans l'Antiquité*, sous la direction de F. Prost et J. Wilgaux (Rennes: Presses Universitaires de Rennes, 2006), 319–32.

50. Friedrich Nietzsche, *The Birth of Tragedy and Other Writings*, ed. Raymond Guess and Ronald Speirs, trans. Ronald Speirs (Cambridge: Cambridge University Press, 1999), 39 and 50; there is of course much blood in Nietzsche, but I have not found explicit mention of it in relation even to those Greeks whose "veins [were] taut with hatred or the arrogance of triumph" (Nietzsche, "Homer on Competition," trans. Carol Diethe, in *On the Genealogy of Morality*, ed. Keith Ansell-Pearson [Cambridge: Cambridge University Press, 1994], 188).

51. This is obviously not meant as a critique of the recent scholarship, much of which is impressively covered and expanded upon in Mitchell Hart's collection, *Jewish Blood: Reality and Metaphor in History, Religion, and Culture* (London and New York: Routledge, 2008); for an excellent study of blood in the Hebrew Bible, with an extensive bibliography, see William K. Gilders, *Blood Ritual in the Hebrew Bible: Meaning and Power* (Baltimore, Md.: Johns Hopkins University Press, 2004). In these, there is nothing comparable to Jonathan Hall's elaborate apologetic discussion on the origins of blood rhetoric in modern, classical scholarship. Hall is at pain to reinstate the relevance of blood (albeit in the fairly restricted

sense of "descent" and "ethnicity"), while clearing it from "the heinous consequences of the ethnic theories of the previous 150 years" (Jonathan M. Hall, *Ethnic Identity in Greek Antiquity* [Cambridge: Cambridge University Press, 1997], 13).

52. Nicole Loraux, "On the Race of Women and Some of Its Tribes," in Loraux, *Children of Athena: Athenian Ideas About Citizenship and the Division Between the Sexes*, trans. Caroline Levine (Princeton, N.J.: Princeton University Press, 1994), 72–110; and see, for the dissymmetry, Helen King's unavoidable demonstration in *Hippocrates' Woman*, but see also Chris Knight, *Blood Relations: Menstruation and the Origins of Culture* (New Haven, Conn.: Yale University Press, 1991).

53. Auerbach, *Mimesis*, 17.

54. Paradoxically, Mary Douglas's pointed critique of the enduring biases of Robertson Smith did not prod her to consider the evidence from ancient Greece (see M. Douglas, *Purity and Danger: An Analysis of the Concepts of Pollution and Taboo* [London and New York: Routledge, 1984] and *Natural Symbols: Explorations in Cosmology* [London and New York: Routledge, 2003]); and see for an anthropology (and restricted hematology) of the Bible, Howard Eilberg-Schwartz, *The Savage in Judaism: An Anthropology of Israelite Religion and Ancient Judaism* (Bloomington: Indiana University Press, 1990).

55. I put the word "biology" in scare quotes in order to indicate the potential anachronism (a point I develop in "The Meaning of Life," *Critical Inquiry* 37, no. 4 [Summer 2001]: 697–723). As to the importance of Greek medicine, in a comparative context, it has of course not gone unrecognized. And rightly so. Consider, for example, that "the word αἷμα is among the one hundred most frequently used words in the [Hippocratic] corpus" (Duminil, *Le sang*, 205, n. 1). Greek medicine naturally occupies a great deal more space than the Bible in historical treatments of hematology (see, e.g., *Einführung in die Geschichte der Hämatologie*, ed. K.-G. v. Boroviczény, H. Schipperges, and E. Seidler [Stuttgart: Georg Thieme Verlag, 1974], esp. 17–25, with a brief paragraph on the Old Testament, and the "extraordinary [außerordentliche] meaning" of blood in it [19]). But more on medicine later on.

56. Hall, *Ethnic Identity*, 10, referring to "social evolutionism, . . . environmental determinism and consanguinity." On the significance and complexity of genealogy, see Molly Broadbent, *Studies in Greek Genealogy* (Leiden: E.J. Brill, 1968).

57. Irad Malkin, "Introduction," *Ancient Perceptions of Greek Ethnicity*, ed. I. Malkin (Cambridge, Mass.: Harvard University Press / Center for Hellenic Studies, 2001), 10.

58. Robertson Smith knew this, of course (cf. *Religion of the Semites*, 274), but fails to grant it significance.

59. L. Morris, "The Biblical Use of the Term 'Blood,'" *Journal of Theological Studies* 3, no. 2 (October 1952): 216–26; the ancient Hebrews are, of course, hardly alone in this; compare, for instance, Evans-Pritchard's famous description: "The Zande does not regard kinship as a community of blood, and hence there is no idea of artificially creating bonds of kinship by transfusion of blood. I cannot recall a single occasion during my residence in Zandeland on which I heard kinship spoken of in terms of blood. Azande speak of members of the same clan as having sprung from the same seed, but the filiation is not spoken of as one of blood" (E. E. Evans-Pritchard, "Zande Blood-Brotherhood," *Africa: Journal of the International African Institute* 6, no. 4 [October 1933]: 397).

60. As I argued in the introduction, the persistence of this translation of Leviticus 17, where the original Hebrew, earlier rendered as *psyche* or *anima*, is translated as "life" is nothing less than remarkable. And it is of a piece with entirely baseless claims that, perpetuated by scholars, construe Jewishness "as vouchsafed by the blood passed from mother to child" (Ra'anan Boustan and Annette Yoshiko Reed, "Introduction to the Theme-Issue: Blood and the Boundaries of Jewish and Christian Identity in Late Antiquity" *Henoch: Studies in Judaism and Christianity from Second Temple to Late Antiquity* 30 [2008/2]: 230). Neither the biblical text nor rabbinical embryological theories (nor Greek and Roman ones either) ever supported the notion that blood is the carrier of identity and kinship, much less of heredity in the ancient world. I return to this matter, with regard to ancient Greek medicine, later.

61. Compare with Yan Thomas's remarks, a model for the general direction of my own inquiry: "In Roman law a child who has been conceived but not yet born is called a *venter*.... The word's usage is specific. First of all, it does not refer to any kind of organic entity. *Partus* is the word used for embryo . . . but no legal value is added to the obstetrical meaning: the *partus* is that to which the woman must give birth (*pario*). *Venter*, on the contrary, refers to nothing outside of law" (Y. Thomas, "The *Venter*: Maternal Body, Paternal Right," trans. Florent Heintz, in *Antiquities (Postwar French Thought, volume III)*, 292).

62. David Biale, *Blood and Belief: The Circulation of a Symbol Between Jews and Christians* (Berkeley: University of California Press, 2007), 10; to be sure, Biale does underscore the proximity between the Israelites and the Greeks, which is why he expresses reservations about Stowers's argument (221, n. 58). My argument has to do with the scope and range of the comparison, the epistemological fields and regions of being it engages.

63. Auerbach, *Mimesis*, 7.

64. Auerbach, *Mimesis*, 17/G22.

65. Homer, *Iliad* 16: 300 (Odysseus to Telemachos).

66. I quote from Jean-Pierre Vernant's *Myth and Society in Ancient Greece*, trans. Janet Lloyd (New York: Zone Books, 1988), 249; Vernant is here commenting on "the reason of myth" by way of Lévi-Strauss on Oedipus.

67. In fact, as Hermann Koller points out, "Greek does not know a word for blood that is Indo-German." (H. Koller, "Αἷμα," 149).

68. See J. Jouanna and P. Demond, "Le sens d'ἰχώρ chez Homère (*Iliade* V, v. 340 et 416) et Eschyle (*Agamemnon*, v. 1480) en relation avec les emplois du mot dans la *Collection Hippocratique*," *Revue des études anciennes* 83, no. 3–4 (1981): 197–209.

69. Homer, *Iliad*, trans. A. T. Murray (Cambridge: Mass.: Harvard University Press, 1924), book 6, 211.

70. Page duBois is neither confining "metaphors of the female body" to dead cemeteries nor trying to revive a different reservoir of such metaphors (P. duBois, *Sowing the Body: Psychoanalysis and Ancient Representations of Women* (Chicago: University of Chicago Press, 1988). She considers metaphor in its structural and historical relation to metonymy (34–36), and "the politics of metaphor" (63–64), but stays away, for the most part, from blood (though see 70).

71. Aristotle, *The Politics and the Constitution of Athens*, ed. Stephen Everson (Cambridge: Cambridge University Press, 1996), 12–13. I purposefully refer exclusively to the English translation for now.

72. Aristotle, *The Politics*, 13; emphasis added.

73. Henry James Sumner Maine, *Ancient Law: Its Connection to the History of Early Society*, Introduction by J. H. Morgan (Charleston, N.C.: BiblioBazaar, 2008), 99. Often a signifier of the archaic, blood also stays behind in the work of other historians, as David Cohen explains: "Historians of Greek law have not investigated the place of law in the broader agonistic context of Athenian society . . . they generally assume that by the classical era Athens had long before made the 'transition' to another 'stage' of legal development, marked by the displacement of blood feud by the rule of law" (David Cohen, *Law, Violence, and Community in Classical Athens* [Cambridge: Cambridge University Press, 1993], 196). For David Grene, to take another example, "the definitive departure from the earlier forms of government in Athens is the ending of the blood brotherhoods as the significant unit in political association" (D. Grene, *Greek Political Theory: The Image of Man in Thucydides and Plato* [Chicago: University of Chicago Press, 1965], 35).

74. In his *Politics and Society in Ancient Greece*, Nicholas F. Jones seems quite fond of the expression (Westport, Conn.: Praeger, 2008), e.g., 23–24, 126.

75. H. Phelps Gates, "The Kinship Terminology of Homeric Greek," *Indiana University Publications in Anthropology and Linguistics. Supplement to International Journal of American Linguistics* 37, no. 4 (October 1971): 2.

76. "The word *ethos*," writes Claudia Baracchi, "signifies precisely disposition, character in the sense of psychological configuration, and hence comportment, the way in which one bears oneself. However, the semantic range of the term exceeds this determination and signals that it must be situated in the broader context of custom, of shared usage, and even understood in the archaic sense of the accustomed place where the living (animals, plants, or otherwise) find their haunt or abode" (Baracchi, *Aristotle's Ethics*, 53). On this last aspect, Paul Demont adds that "*ethos* is one of the points which should be scrutinized in order to study the differences between animals. Let us first pose the question at a general level. There are physiognomic observations in Aristotle, which trace the relationship between non-uniform parts of the body, such as the nose, the forehead, the eyes, or the heart, and a given character. Such a character is mainly specific to a class of animals, but it may also serve to distinguish some types and even some individuals in the class. Uniform parts of the body, such as humours, and of course, blood, may also contribute to the understanding of character" (P. Demont, "About Philosophy and Humoral Medicine," in *Hippocrates in Context, Papers Read at the XIth International Hippocrates Colloquium University of Newcastle upon Tyne. 27–31 August 2002*, ed. Philip J. Van der Eijk [Leiden: Brill, 2005], 282).

77. E. Benveniste, *Le vocabulaire des institutions indo-européennes. 1. Économie, parenté, société* (Paris: Minuit, 1969), 9.

78. Pierre Vidal-Naquet asks this question in a pertinent context, as if commenting on Benveniste (P. Vidal-Naquet, "The Black Hunter Revisited," in *Antiquities (Postwar French Thought, volume III)*, 90). A few pages earlier, Vidal-Naquet had written that "of course, an

institution is much less visible than an epic figure. The more familiar the institution is to the audience, the less it will be nominated" (87).

79. Benveniste famously took a stand against this position, with regard to the cognates of the word *phrater* (*Le vocabulaire*, 212–14), and see the critique by Jean-Louis Perpillou, who argues that blood is, in fact, the basis for a proper understanding (J. L. Perpillou, "Frères de sang ou frères de culte," *Studi Micenei ed Egeo-Anatoloci* XXV [1984]: 205–220).

80. Édouard Will, "Syngeneia, Oikeiotès, Philia," *Revue de philologie, de littérature et d'histoire anciennes*, ser. 3, 69, no. 2 (1995): 299–325.

81. Claude Meillassoux, *Mythes et limites de l'anthropologie. Le sang et les mots* (Lausanne: Editions Page Deux, 2001). Throughout this chapter, I am once again indebted to the work of Meillassoux. I should also mention the essential contribution to these issues made by Marc Shell, particularly in *Children of the Earth: Literature, Politics, and Nationhood* (Oxford: Oxford University Press, 1993), as well as Enric Porqueres i Gené, who acknowledges the singularity and pervasiveness of blood discourse and its effect on contemporary theories of kinship (see his contribution to *Race, Ethnicity, and Nation*, 125–44). One more thing, which should already be clear: Although related to "biology as ideology," the "ideology of consanguinity" is something distinct, simply because it focuses on the peculiar significance of blood, let us say for now, as a figure (cf. Richard C. Lewontin, *Biology as Ideology: The Doctrine of DNA* [New York: HarperPerennial, 1991]).

82. There are exceptions, of course, most notably Uli Linke, who amassed a wealth of sources and resources pertaining to blood, beginning with Indo-European linguistics. Attuned to historical depth, and even more so to Nazism, Linke does not spend much time on the Greeks or on the Bible, but she most definitely brought blood into the foreground; see U. Linke, *Blood and Nation: The European Aesthetics of Race* (Philadelphia: University of Pennsylvania Press, 1999); and see as well the universalizing musings of Melissa L. Meyer, *Thicker than Water: The Origins of Blood as Symbol and Ritual* (New York and London: Routledge, 2005).

83. "It is necessary to realize . . . that in classical Athens (where the evidence is reasonably detailed) there are four overlapping kinship terminologies associated with different contexts: the terms of address and intimate reference used in the home, terms of common public reference, precise terms used in legal contexts, and poetic terms . . . The Athenian of the classical period was expected to use and understand, in different contexts, kinship terminologies which differed not only in vocabulary but also in structure" (S. C. Humphreys, *Anthropology and the Greeks* [London: Routledge and Kegan Paul, 1978], 205–206).

84. Studies of kinship terminology, including the doyen of the field, Emile Benveniste, use and abuse the lexicon of blood, while perfectly aware of the vagueness of its referent (minimally, agnatic vs. cognatic). It is after all remarkable that blood and its, well, cognates are at no point recognized as a category or a *terminus technicus*, much less as an "institution;" and see Benveniste's discussion of *pater* and *phrater* and cognates, where Benveniste repeatedly invokes "blood" and "consanguinity" (E. Benveniste, *Le vocabulaire des institutions indo-européennes. 1. Économie, parenté, société* [Paris: Minuit, 1969]). Similar gestures can be found in H. Phelps Gates, "The Kinship Terminology of Homeric Greek"—otherwise

most thorough, Phelps uses the term *consanguineous* quite profusely and in a technical sense, yet he quickly refers to blood (*haíma*), almost in passing, as an "abstract" or "general" term in the Greek sources (32); and see also M. Miller, "Greek Kinship Terminology," *The Journal of Hellenic Studies* 73 (1953): 46–52; Munro S. Edmonson, "Kinship Terms and Kinship Concepts," *American Anthropologist* 59, no. 3 (June 1957): 393–433 and response by John Andromedas, "Greek Kinship Terms in Everyday Use," *American Anthropologist* n.s. 59, no. 6 (December 1957): 1086–1088 (blood being entirely absent from these last items); Oswald Szemerényi, "Das Griechische Verwandtschaftsnamensystem vor dem Hintergrund des Indogermanischen Systems," *Hermes* 105, no. 4 (1977): 385–405; Ian Morris, "The Gortyn Code and Greek Kinship," *Greek, Roman, and Byzantine Studies* 31, no. 3 (Fall 1990): 233–54; Paul Friedrich, "Proto-Indo-European Kinship" *Ethnology* 5, no. 1 (January 1966): 1–36; Adrian Pârvulescu, "Blood and IE. Kinship Terminology," *Indogermanische Forschungen* 94 (1989): 67–88, which is particularly interesting because it seeks to demonstrate that blood terminology was originally the most general, later becoming more specialized to particular relationships (Pârvulescu does not comment on the more recent return of that generalized use, much less its dating); and see also Sergey Kullanda, "Indo-European 'Kinship Terms' Revisited," *Current Anthropology* 43, no. 1 (2002): 89–111.

85. See Sergey Kullanda, "Indo-European 'Kinship Terms' Revisited," 93 and 93, n. 24.

86. Briand, "Sur AIMONA," 138.

87. Aside from a brief mention or two of "blood brotherhood," W. K. Lacey's classic study stays strikingly clear from the rhetoric of blood (W. K. Lacey, *The Family in Classical Greece* [Ithaca, N.Y.: Cornell University Press, 1968]); Sarah Humphreys also omits any explicit references to blood in *Anthropology and the Greeks* (London: Routledge and Kegan Paul, 1978), an absence most glaring in her discussion of kinship (193–208).

88. The *Cambridge History of Greek and Roman Political Thought* (ed. Christopher Rowe and Malcom Schofield [Cambridge: Cambridge University Press, 2005]) makes no mention of blood either, while *A Guide to Greek Thought: Major Figures and Trends* (ed. Jacques Brunschwig and Geoffrey E. R. Lloyd, trans. Catherine Porter et al. [Cambridge, Mass.: The Belknap Press of Harvard University Press, 2003]) barely refers to blood at all, and the same goes for Paul Cartledge's account, in *The Greeks: A Portrait of Self and Others* (Oxford: Oxford University Press, 2002). In *The Greeks and Their Gods*, William Guthrie relates "the laws of Drako about murder and homicide" to "Delphic ideas of *miasma* and its purification," as well as to "the beginnings of Athenian democracy, according to Aristotle's statement that when Kleisthenes introduced his artificially constructed *phylae* to replace the old organization based on blood-relationship he called them after heroes" (W. K. C. Guthrie, *The Greeks and Their Gods* [Boston: Beacon Press, 1955], 185, referring to Aristotle, *Athenian Constitution*, trans. H. Rackham [Cambridge, Mass.: Harvard University Press / London: William Heinemann, 1938], XXI, 6).

89. I continue to confine myself in this section to the matter of kinship, a question that is far from antiquarian when it comes to Greece (see, e.g., Michael Herzfeld, "Interpreting Kinship Terminology: The Problem of Patriliny in Rural Greece," *Anthropological Quarterly* 56, no. 4 (October 1983): 157–66; Juliet Du Boulay, "The Blood: Symbolic Relationships

Between Descent, Marriage, Incest Prohibitions, and Spiritual Kinship in Greece" *Man*, n.s. 19, no. 4 [December 1984]: 533–56; Roger Just, "Triumph of the Ethnos," in *History and Ethnicity*, ed. Elizabeth Tonkin, Maryon McDonald, and Malcolm Chapman [London: Routledge, 1989]: 71–88).

90. D. Roussel, *Tribu et cité. Études sur les groupes sociaux dans les cités grecques aux époques archaïque et classique* (Paris: Annales littéraires de l'université de Besançon / Les belles lettres, 1976), 4; and see the more recent, magisterial study of *The Family in Greek History* by Cynthia B. Patterson (Cambridge, Mass.: Harvard University Press, 1998), as well as the critical review of the scholarly literature on *genos/gens* and cognates in C. J. Smith, *The Roman Clan: The* Gens *from Ancient Ideology to Modern Anthropology* (Cambridge: Cambridge University Press, 2006).

91. Numa Denis Fustel de Coulanges, *The Ancient City: A Study on the Religion, Laws, and Institutions of Greece and Rome*, trans. Willard Small (Kitchener, Ontario: Batoche Books, 2001), 97.

92. M. Miller, "Greek Kinship Terminology," *The Journal of Hellenic Studies* 73 (1953): 52; a few years later, Wesley Thompson conducts his own study of kinship terminology and concludes that "the same terms which apply to relatives by blood also apply to relatives by adoption" (W. E. Thompson, "Attic Kinship Terminology," *The Journal of Hellenic Studies* 91 [1971]: 112). It goes without saying that here too the term *blood* is not included in the terminology under interrogation.

93. Walter Donlan, *The Aristocratic Ideal and Selected Papers* (Wauconda, Ill.: Bolchazy-Carducci Publishers, 1999), 49; "pride of blood," Donlan explains, would only appear later (63), and one can bring up numerous examples, clear statements "that blood does not determine good or bad behavior" (137).

94. R. J. Littman, *Kinship and Politics in Athens 600–400 B.C.* (New York: Peter Lang, 1990), 7. Note that it is "consanguinity" that would be culturally determined, not kinship; nature, as it were, and not culture. Gianna Pomata and Frank Roumy have made quite manifest the anachronisms to which the term *consanguinity* has been subjected, as has Claude Meillassoux.

95. Daniel Ogden, "Bastardy and Fatherlessness in Ancient Greece," in *Growing Up Fatherless in Antiquity*, ed. Sabine R. Hübner and David Ratzan (Cambridge: Cambridge University Press, 2009), 107; please note the scare quotes, that, more often than I care to count, place blood in a suspended state that remains unexplained.

96. Catherine Morgan, *Early Greek States Beyond the Polis* (London and New York: Routledge, 2003), 15; Morgan is in fact critical of the pervasiveness of "kinship" references, yet here she is not disagreeing on the substance, as it were, behind the term.

97. Giulia Sissa, "La famille dans la cité grecque (V-IVe siècle avant J.C.)," in *Histoire de la famille 1. Mondes lointains, mondes anciens*, sous la direction de André Burguière, Christiane Klapisch-Zuber, Martine Segalen, Françoise Zonabend (Paris: Armand Colin, 1986), 173; Sissa might have been invoking Simon Goldhill's reference to Athens as a "city of words" or to a famous book on Greek iconography entitled *La cité des images* (on these references, see Vidal-Naquet, "The Black Hunter Revisited," 90).

98. Homer, *Iliad*, 19: 100–105; does it matter that the question of divine blood (which most scholars refer to as *ichor*, though the text here does say *aima*) is a vexed one? For a concise

discussion, see Giulia Sissa and Marcel Detienne, *The Daily Life of the Greek Gods*, trans. Janet Lloyd (Stanford, Calif.: Stanford University Press, 2000), esp. 29–33 ("Immortal Blood in Context").

99. Aristotle, *Politics*, trans. H. Rackham (Cambridge, Mass.: Harvard University Press / London: William Heinemann, 1944), 1262a.

100. And compare Alcinous' question to Odysseus: "Did some kinsman of yours fall before Ilium, some good, true man, your daughter's husband or your wife's father, *such as are nearest to one after one's own kin and blood [meth' haímá te kaì génos autôn]*?" (Homer, *Odyssey*, 8: 580–83; emphases added). As Uli Linke, Tom Laqueur, Nancy Jay, and others have made clear, it is of course not possible to elude the question of sexual difference when it comes to blood.

101. Aristotle, *The Nicomachean Ethics*, 1161b, trans. H. Rackham (Cambridge, Mass.: Harvard University Press / London: William Heinemann, 1962), VIII.xii.3; there is of course much to be said about Aristotle and blood with regard to medicine, something to which I return later on.

102. Maine, *Ancient Law*, 99.

103. Aristotle, *Politics*, 1252b; translation altered following Bourriot's argument.

104. F. Bourriot, *Recherches sur la nature du Genos. Étude d'histoire sociale athénienne—périodes archaïque et classique* (Paris: Librairie Honoré Champion, 1976), 663–78; and see the detailed discussion by Hans Derks, who cogently writes that "it always remains worthwhile to look under γαλα and derivations in the relevant dictionaries, etc. This does not mean that the question of the use of milk in consumption, cult or medicine is solved. Far from that" (H. Derks, "A Note on ΟΜΟΓΑΛΑΚΤΕΣ in Aristotle's ΠΟΛΙΤΙΚΑ," *Dialogues d'histoire ancienne* 21, no. 2 [1995]: 28). How much more so for blood.

105. For an intriguing measure of the distribution of friends and family in the entire Greek tragic corpus, see Elizabeth S. Belfiore, *Murder Among Friends: Violation of Philia in Greek Tragedy* (New York and Oxford: Oxford University Press, 2000).

106. "Here is the origin of the European, 'Western' sense of distinctiveness," writes Anthony Pagden (A. Pagden, *Worlds at War: The 2,500-Year Struggle Between East and West* [New York: Random House, 2008], 6). Within the field of classical studies, the sheer frequency of the reference to Herodotus' admittedly weighty "definition" is, I think, quite striking: an entire volume dedicated to "Greek ethnicity" revolves around it, or, as the introduction to the book puts it, "we can acknowledge ancient articulations of ethnicity as authentic, especially when these appear in essentialist terms of primordial blood kinship" (Irad Malkin, "Introduction," *Ancient Perceptions of Greek Ethnicity*, I. Malkin, ed. [Cambridge, Mass.: Harvard University Press / Center for Hellenic Studies, 2001], 5). It is as if, against all the critiques of naturalism and biologism (always affirmed and reiterated, of course, e.g., 53–54), one nonetheless had to gravitate toward blood or better yet, "blood." And see Hall, *Ethnic Identity* and his *Hellenicity: Between Ethnicity and Culture* (Chicago: University of Chicago Press, 2002), where the historical trajectory traced is, as in Maine, an "emancipation" from blood, from ethnicity to culture; for critical remarks, see Margalit Finkelberg, *Greeks and Pre-Greeks: Aegean Prehistory and Greek Heroic Tradition* (Cambridge: Cambridge University Press, 2005), esp. 16–23. It should also be mentioned

that Herodotus uses forms of the word *homaimos* on other occasions, for example, 5: 49 ("*andres homaimones*"), and see also 1: 151.

107. See Nicole Loraux, "La main d'Antigone," 178, and Loraux, "La guerre dans la famille," *CLIO* 5 (1997): 21–62; and see Briand, "Sur AIMONA," 139 and 139, n. 33; see as well Jasper Griffin, "Herodotus and Tragedy," in *The Cambridge Companion to Herodotus*, ed. Carolyn Dewald and John Marincola (Cambridge: Cambridge University Press, 2006), 46–59.

108. Plato, *Laws*, trans. R. G. Bury [Cambridge, Mass.: Harvard University Press / London: William Heinemann, 1967), 729c; *Republic*, trans. Paul Shorey (Cambridge: Mass.: Harvard University Press / London: William Heinemann, 1969), 565e–566a.

109. Plato, *The Sophist*, trans. Harold N. Fowler (Cambridge, Mass.: Harvard University Press / London: William Heinemann, 1921), 268c–d; Plato is quoting Homer, *Iliad*, 6: 211.

110. Nicole Loraux, "La guerre dans la famille," *CLIO* 5 (1997): 25.

111. According to Jérôme Wilgaux, the term *homaimoi*, and by extension, the understanding that blood is what is shared among kin, was still a topic of debate in twelfth-century Byzantium: Whereas many considered blood that which was shared exclusively by brothers and sisters, Wilgaux explains, the scholar Michel Italikos "shows on the contrary that *homaimoi* can be used to designate . . . the entirety of kin [*l'ensemble des parents*], insofar as they precisely 'share the same blood' " (J. Wilgaux, "Corps et parenté en Grèce ancienne," in *Penser et représenter le corps dans l'Antiquité*, sous la direction de F. Prost et J. Wilgaux [Rennes: Presses Universitaires de Rennes, 2006], 342–43). Wilgaux fails to comment on the fact that the ground of that "demonstration" does not seem to be available from the sources accessible to us, at least none that he quotes or that I have found.

112. Plato, *Symposium*, trans. Harold N. Fowler (Cambridge, Mass.: Harvard University Press / London: William Heinemann, 1925), 207d–e.

113. Plato, *Theaetetus*, trans. Harold N. Fowler (Cambridge, Mass.: Harvard University Press / London: William Heinemann, 1921), 174e–175b; and note, of course, that contrary to some translations, the word *blood* never appears in this passage.

114. See, for example, Barry S. Strauss's intriguing critique of "familialism" in *Fathers and Sons in Athens: Ideology and Society in the Era of the Peloponnesian War* (London: Routledge, 1993).

115. In his *Panegyricus*, Isocrates alludes to a claim that recalls and departs from Herodotus' famous passage: "the title Hellenes is applied rather to those who share our culture than to those who share a common blood"—but here too the term *blood* does not appear in the Greek, only "common origin [*koinês physeos*]" (Isocrates, "Panegyricus," trans. George Norlin, in *Isocrates* (Cambridge, Mass.: Harvard University Press / London: William Heinemann, 1980), 4: 50; Jonathan Hall discusses this passage and placidly renders the phrase by "common biological inheritance" in his *Hellenicity*, 209.

116. Robert Parker describes how oracles too are absent from jurisdiction. There are few exceptions, but they are unusual, Parker says, referring to one such case in Sparta. But "what is a society without blood-tests to do," he asks, "when the purity of the queen mother come into doubt?" (R. Parker, "Greek States and Greek Oracles," in *Oxford Readings in Greek Religion*, ed. Richard Buxton [Oxford: Oxford University Press, 2000], 91).

117. Aside from David Cohen's *Law, Violence, and Community in Classical Athens* (mentioned earlier and which highlights "blood vengeance" and the blood feud), I have consulted Illias

Arnaoutoglou, *Ancient Greek Laws: A Sourcebook* (London and New York: Routledge, 1998); A. R. W. Harrison, *The Law of Athens. Volume 1: The Family and Property* (Indianapolis, Ind.: Hackett Publishing Co., 1998); *The Cambridge Companion to Ancient Greek Law*, ed. Michael Gagarin and David Cohen (Cambridge: Cambridge University Press, 2005); Edward M. Harris, *Democracy and the Rule of Law in Classical Athens: Essays on Law, Society, and Politics* (Cambridge: Cambridge University Press, 2006); L. Foxhall and A. D. E. Lewis, *Greek Law in Its Political Setting: Justifications Not Justice* (Oxford: Clarendon Press, 1996); Cheryl Anne Cox, "Sibling Relationships in Classical Athens: Brother-Sister Ties," *Journal of Family History* 13, no. 4 (1988); Vincent Farenga, *Citizen and Self in Ancient Greece: Individuals Performing Justice and the Law* (Cambridge: Cambridge University Press, 2006); Adriann Lanni, *Law and Justice in the Courts of Classical Athens* (Cambridge: Cambridge University Press, 2006); Christopher Carey, *Trials from Classical Athens* (London: Routledge, 1997); *Greek Historical Inscriptions. 404–323BC*, ed. P. J. Rhodes and Robin Osborne (Oxford: Oxford University Press, 2003); and Eran Lupu, *Greek Sacred Law. A Collection of New Documents (NGSL)* (Leiden: Brill, 2005); a slightly different picture can be found in Victoria Wohl's *Law's Cosmos: Juridical Discourse in Athenian Forensic Oratory* (Cambridge: Cambridge University Press, 2010).

118. The phrase *dikê homaimôn* appears mostly in tragedies, "where there is a play on words on the theme of consanguinity on the one hand and the blood actually spilled on the other" (Pierre Vidal-Naquet, "The Shield of the Heroes," in Jean-Pierre Vernant and Pierre Vidal-Naquet, *Myth and Tragedy in Ancient Greece*, 296). It is in this tragic context that it is mostly discussed by scholars. As Vidal Naquet points out, there are a number of translations for the phrase, most referring to "kinship" (482, n. 70); see also H. D. Cameron, "The Debt to Earth in the Seven Against Thebes," *Transactions and Proceedings of the American Philological Association* 95 (1964): 1–8, and Karsten Wilkens, "ΔΙΚΗ ΟΜΑΙΜΩΝ? Zu Aischylos Sieben 415," *Hermes* 97, no. 1 (1969): 117–21.

119. Denise Eileen McCoskey offers, I think, the most sophisticated account of these debates, and though I explore a different route here, I am hoping to be joining her efforts in doing so; by way of a rich entry point see McCoskey's "Naming the Fault in Question: Theorizing Racism Among the Greeks and Romans," *International Journal of the Classical Tradition* 13, no. 2 (Fall 2006): 243–67.

120. Plato, *Menexenus*, trans. W. R. M. Lamb (Cambridge, Mass.: Harvard University Press / London: William Heinemann, 1925), 245d; I quote the French translation from Nicole Loraux, *Né de la terre. Mythe et politique à Athènes* (Paris: Seuil, 1996), 37; Loraux is careful to correct potential misunderstandings; she soon explains that none of Plato's words should be taken as having to do with "any politics of racial discrimination" (37); a similar (if more historically sweeping) gesture, which seeks to cleanse blood from racial overtones, is made by Ivan Hannaford, who writes: "In Greece and Rome the organizing idea of race was absent so long as the political idea flourished to reconcile the volatile blood relationship (kinship) found in family, tribe, and clan, with the wider demands of the community" (I. Hannaford, *Race: The History of an Idea in the West* [Washington, D.C.: Woodrow Wilson Center Press / Baltimore, Md.: Johns Hopkins University Press, 1996], 14; and see Jonathan Hall's reading of the *Menexenus* passage in *Hellenicity*, 214–17 [next note]).

121. Hall, *Hellenicity*, 191; and see also his *Ethnic Identity*, where Hall explains with much assurance that "consanguinity refers to a notion of kinship that uses blood as a metaphor. Again, this is to be found in antiquity: Homer uses the word 'blood' (*haima*) to express kin relationships, and Herodotus enumerates blood as one of the criteria of Hellenic identity" (7).

122. Like the medical literature, the blood of tragedies has, of course, attracted much attention, if not always directly, but see Vernant and Vidal-Naquet, *Myth and Tragedy*, as well as the extensive work of Nicole Loraux, already mentioned, and, for example, Barbara Hughes Fowler, "The Creatures and the Blood," *Illinois Classical Studies* 16, no. 1–2 (1991): 85–100; and Petar Ramadanovic, "Antigone's Kind: The Way of Blood in Psychoanalysis," *UMBR(a): A Journal of the Unconscious* (2004): 161–81.

123. The Lidell–Scott lexicon has v. αιμα; I. "blood," "of anything like blood," "with collat. meaning of spirit, courage," II. "bloodshed, murder," and III. "blood relationship, kin" and finally "concrete, of a person" (Henry George Liddell and Robert Scott, *A Greek-English Lexicon*, revised and augmented throughout by Sir Henry Stuart Jones, with the assistance of. Roderick McKenzie [Oxford: Clarendon Press, 1940]).

124. I am guided here by Derrida's persistent interrogation of metaphor (and concept), and particularly in what he proposed as a text that was first published in a volume dedicated to Jean-Pierre Vernant. The final version of that text by Derrida is available in French as *Khôra* (Paris: Galilée, 1993) and in English, trans. Ian McLeod, in Derrida, *On the Name*, ed. Thomas Dutoit (Stanford, Calif.: Stanford University Press, 1995).

125. Charles Malamoud's account of Benveniste's method might help here, which explains that the study of the vocabulary of institutions requires that one isolates "the *signification* of words from their *designation*. To study the designation of a word is to study its referent, that is, the reality to which it refers. By contrast, to grasp the signification of a word, one must examine its place in the vocabulary as a whole" (C. Malamoud, "The Work of Emile Benveniste: A Linguistic Analysis of Indo-European Institutions," trans. Arthur Goldhammer, in *Antiquities (Postwar French Thought, volume III)*, 436). It would be preposterous, of course, to make any comparison between the work of Benveniste and what I am trying to do here, which consists merely in mapping out the significance (and signification) of (the word) blood.

126. I borrow this expression from Charles Mopsik, *Les grands textes de la cabale. Les rites qui font Dieu. Pratiques religieuses et efficacité théurgique dans la cabale des origines au milieu du XVIIIe siècle* (Paris: Verdier, 1993). But rites and what Florence Gherchanoc calls "pratiques de sociabilité" are, in ancient Greece, constitutive quite precisely of what continues to be called "blood" and "consanguinity," namely, filiation. There is a "creation" of filiation, a making of the child that leaves to birth no more than a minor (rather than a determining) function, if any (F. Gherchanoc, "Le lien filial dans l'Athènes classique: Pratiques et acteurs de sa reconnaissance," *Mètis. Anthropologie des mondes grecs anciens* 13, no. 1 [1998]: 313–44). More on this later.

127. Hall, *Hellenicity*, 172–228; for the universal aspect, see Irad Malkin's assertion that "the notion of kinship is obviously central to perceptions—ancient and modern—of ethnicity. 'Having the same blood' (*homaimon*) seems to be a universal aspect" (Malkin, "Preface,"

in *Ancient Perceptions of Greek Ethnicity*, 10). The Bible or the Na of China would then be cast as a "particularist" exception, I suppose: "for the Na, *ong* (bone) is traditionally considered the carrier of hereditary and racial characteristics. It comes from the mother and is an immutable principle" (Cai Hua, *A Society Without Fathers or Husbands: The Na of China*, trans. Asti Hustvedt [New York: Zone Books, 2001], 120). Not wanting to be left out, perhaps, Hua goes on to add: "In this study, I use the word *blood* for *ong* and *consanguineal relatives* for *ong hing*" (121).

128. Rosalind Thomas, "Ethnicity, Genealogy, and Hellenism in Herodotus," in *Ancient Perceptions of Greek Ethnicity*, 217.

129. Jérôme Wilgaux, "Corps et parenté en Grèce ancienne," in *Penser et représenter le corps dans l'Antiquité*, sous la direction de Francis Prost et Jérôme Wilgaux (Rennes: Presses Universitaires de Rennes, 2006), 337; one could of course invoke countless more examples from the scholarly literature.

130. Focusing, as she herself puts it, on "real, red, fluid blood as the foundation for further metaphoric expressions," Melissa Meyer also argues that "people have widely associated blood with lineage. . . . Attributing to blood the ability to transmit or reflect the essence of the family, clan, lineage, people, nation, race, or ethnic group stemmed *logically* from the widespread association of blood with life and fertility" (M. L. Meyer, *Thicker than Water: The Origins of Blood as Symbol and Ritual* [New York: Routledge, 2005], 8; emphasis added).

131. Without being too reductive or even endorsing a persistent exceptionalism, there seems to be room to wonder about the innovation or even mere specificity that seems otherwise attributed to German romanticism and Nazi ideology. After all, and true to illustrations cited earlier, everything is as if the origin of democracy was also the origin of the fascism of "blood and soil."

132. C. J. Smith, *The Roman Clan: The Gens from Ancient Ideology to Modern Anthropology* (Cambridge: Cambridge University Press, 2006), 120; Smith is here commenting on the work of Roussel and Bourriot.

133. Lloyd explains that "'Greek science' is here used . . . merely as a shorthand expression to refer to certain ideas and theories in the ancient writers and it does not presuppose any particular view concerning the status of these ideas and theories on the part of the ancient writers themselves" (G. E. R. Lloyd, *Early Greek Science: Thales to Aristotle* [New York: W.W. Norton & Co., 1970], xiii).

134. Plato, *Phaedo*, trans. Harold North Fowler (Cambridge, Mass.: Harvard University Press, 1914), 96b; Empedocles had asserted that "thought is blood around the heart" (cited in Longrigg, *Greek Rational Medicine*, 76). Jonathan Barnes clarifies: "Empedocles does not say that it is the blood which thinks; nor does he say that the heart, or the heart's blood, is the *sole* organ or instrument of thought; the heart is of pre-eminent importance, but it is only the place where 'especially' we think" (J. Barnes, *The Presocratic Philosophers* (London: Routledge, 1982). In his wake, perhaps, many ancient physicians held that too much blood (too much thought?) led to epilepsy or even madness. Marie-Paule Duminil discusses at more length "the role attributed to blood in psychical and intellectual phenomena, which is probably one of the most important questions that

medicine and anthropology have raised in Antiquity" (Duminil, *Le sang*, 235 and 241ff.). One treatise locates "human reason" in the left ventricle, in fact (246), while others distribute psychical phenomena between the heart and the brain (306). Incidentally, Aristotle did see a connection between blood and intelligence, but Empedocles is better known for his singular opposition to blood sacrifice.

135. Aristotle, *On the Soul*, translated by W. S. Hett (Cambridge, Mass.: Harvard University Press, 1957), 403a–403b; and, for the second citation, G. E. R. Lloyd, *Science, Folklore and Ideology: Studies in the Life Sciences in Ancient Greece* (Cambridge: Cambridge University Press, 1983), 22; Lloyd later explains that Aristotle held those animals in highest esteem "whose blood is hot and at the same time thin and pure, for that is good both for courage and for intelligence." Aristotle is referring to human beings here. "Yet," Lloyd continues, "how precisely the 'purity' and the 'thinness' of the blood are to be determined is not explained" (33). So much for "blood purity," that beloved expression of historians of ethnicity. For a discussion of Aristotle on blood and sensation, see Longrigg, *Greek Rational Medicine*, 173–74.

136. Erna Lesky, *Die Zeugungs- und Vererbungslehren der Antike und ihr Nachwirken (Abhandlunken der Geistes- und Sozialwissenschaftlichen Klasse)*, 19; Jacquard and Thomasset explain that "thanks to the work of Erna Lesky, there are few obscurities left as regards these [embryological and heredity] theories, and the three Greek doctrines, as well as their principal representatives are well known" (Danielle Jacquart and Claude Thomasset, *Sexuality and Medicine in the Middle Ages*, trans. Matthew Adamson [Princeton, N.J.: Princeton University Press, 1988], 53).

137. Joseph Needham, *A History of Embryology* (New York: Abelard-Schuman, 1959), 28.

138. Jacquart and Thomasset, *Sexuality and Medicine*, 72 (quoting the tenth-century Galenist 'Ali ibn al-'Abbas al-Majusi); for a citation of the Talmud, see Needham, *History of Embryology*, 78, and see Daniel Boyarin, *Sparks of the Logos: Essays in Rabbinic Hermeneutics* (Leiden: Brill, 2003), 142–43.

139. Thomas Laqueur, *Making Sex: Body and Gender from the Greeks to Freud* (Cambridge, Mass.: Harvard University Press, 1990); on which see Katharine Park and Robert A. Nye, "Destiny is Anatomy," *The New Republic* 204, no. 7 (February 18, 1991): 53–57.

140. Jacquart and Thomasset, *Sexuality and Medicine*, 53.

141. The view that blood and kinship are one and the same dominates in the tragedies, of course, and yet, Apollo's famous declaration gives pause that "the mother of what is called her child is not its parent, but only the nurse of the newly implanted germ" (Aeschylus, *Eumenides*, trans. Herbert Weir Smyth [Cambridge, Mass.: Harvard University Press, 1926], 658–59). It cannot be glossed, as Jean-Pierre Vernant proposes, with "maternal blood can never run in the veins of the son" (J.-P. Vernant, *Myth and Thought Among the Greeks*, trans. H. Piat [London: Routledge and Kegan Paul, 1983], 134). There is no necessary relation, at any rate, between the one-seed theory and hematogenesis.

142. Even with regard to humoral theory, Aristotle's hematocentrism did not become hegemonic until the Middle Ages (see Nancy Siraisi, *Medieval and Early Renaissance Medicine: An Introduction to Knowledge and Practice* [Chicago: University of Chicago Press, 1990], 105ff).

143. See Paola Manuli and Mario Vegetti, *Cuore, sangue et cervello. Biologia e antropologia nel pensiero antico* (Milano: Episteme Editrice, 1977), chap. V: "Il cardio-emocentrismo di Aristotele," 113–56.

144. Aristotle, *Generation of Animals*, trans. A. L. Peck (Cambridge, Mass.: Harvard University Press, 1942), 726b, 727a; it should be recalled that this is a view that is completely absent from the Hippocratic corpus, as is the view that the heart has anything to do with the formation of blood (Duminil, *Le sang*, 163, 239).

145. Aristotle, *Generation of Animals*, 729a.

146. Aristotle, *Generation of Animals*, 767b.

147. Jean-Baptiste Bonnard, "Il paraît en effet que les fils ressemblent à leurs pères," in *Penser et représenter le corps dans l'Antiquité*, sous la direction de Francis Prost et Jérôme Wilgaux (Rennes: Presses Universitaires de Rennes, 2006), 318; and see Laura Slatkin, "Genre and Generation in the Odyssey," *Mètis. Anthropologie des mondes grecs anciens* 1, no. 2 (1986): 259–268.

148. Aristotle, *Generation of Animals*, 729a.

149. Giulia Sissa, "Subtle Bodies," 137; emphasis added; Needham lists this conception as one of Aristotle's "three big mistakes," referring first of all to the view "that the male supplies nothing tangible to the female in the process of fertilization. To say that the semen gave the 'form' to the inchoate 'matter' of the menstrual blood was equivalent to saying that the seminal fluid carried nothing in it but simply an immaterial breath along with it" (Needham, *History of Embryology*, 55); for an account that typically misses the issue and invents, by way of a solution, a distinction between two kinds of blood, "nutritive blood" and "honest-to-god semen," see John M. Cooper, *Knowledge, Nature, and the Good: Essays on Ancient Philosophy* (Princeton, N.J.: Princeton University Press, 2004), 177.

150. Not that persistence, whether or not it has anything to do with matter, is an easy, well, matter; see Frank A. Lewis, "Form and Matter," in *A Companion to Aristotle*, ed. Georgios Anagnostopoulos (Chichester: Blackwell, 2009), esp. 181–82.

151. Aristotle, *Generation of Animals*, 729a.

152. Aristotle, *Generation of Animals*, 751b; Ann Hanson also remarks that in post-Hippocratic medicine, "blood is less in evidence," and, when it comes to "women's biological nature," at least, the dominant view "downplays blood and bleeding" (Ann Ellis Hanson, "The Medical Writers' Woman," in *Before Sexuality: The Construction of Erotic Experience in the Ancient Greek World*, ed. David M. Halperin, John J. Winkler, and Froma I. Zeitlin [Princeton, N.J.: Princeton University Press, 1990], 331–32).

153. Sissa, "Subtle Bodies," 137; it might be interesting to note that for another, much later Aristotelian, "the male semen contributed neither form nor matter to the egg, but was only the provider of the energizing essence through which the egg became fertile and fit to engender an embryo." For William Harvey (being described here), "this happened by a kind of contagion, effluvium, intangible penetration, seminal aura, or essence. Having performed this subtle office, the male semen either escaped from the body, dissolved, or turned into vapor and vanished" (Clara Pinto-Correia, *The Ovary of Eve: Egg and Sperm and Preformation* [Chicago: University of Chicago Press, 1997], 110).

154. Aristotle, *Generation of Animals*, 729b; arguably, one could still discern a materialism of sorts, and many have, but the important point, I think, is that however one understands the site or agency of form, be it blood or air, it is explicitly not something that remains, not what is transmitted, in other words. And note that earlier, Aristotle asserted that material links are not necessary to understand hereditary resemblance, as "children resemble their remoter ancestors, from whom nothing has been drawn for the semen," much less from other body parts (722a).

155. Duminil, *Le sang*, 318; there are of course questions as to what this precisely means when considering that the heart, rather than the belly or the liver, is the center and origin (*arche*) of Aristotle's understanding (320), but they are not pertinent to my argument.

156. Plato, *Timaeus*, trans. W. R. M. Lamb (Cambridge, Mass.: Harvard University Press / London: William Heinemann, 1925), 80d–81b; James Longrigg comments at length on this passage in his *Greek Rational Medicine: Philosophy and Medicine from Alcmaeon to the Alexandrians* (London and New York: Routledge, 1993), 135ff.

157. Longrigg, *Greek Rational Medicine*, 112, and see 173ff. or Helen King, "Food and Blood in Hippokratic Gynaecology," in *Food in Antiquity*, ed. J. Wilkins, D. Harvey, and M. Dobson (Exeter: University of Exeter Press, 1995), 351–58; and see also Shigehisa Kuriyama, *The Expressiveness of the Body and the Divergence of Greek and Chinese Medicine* (New York: Zone Books, 2002), chap. 5 ("Blood and Life"), and Philip J. van der Eijk, *Medicine and Philosophy in Classical Antiquity: Doctors and Philosophers on Nature, Soul, Health, and Disease* [Cambridge: Cambridge University Press, 2005], e.g., 153, n. 54); for more examples, drawn from very different anthropological material, see Janet Carsten, *After Kinship* (Cambridge: Cambridge University Press, 2004).

158. The episode we considered earlier, where Odysseus feeds blood to the dead, should make it clear that blood is not "life," for blood does not revive the dead, merely nourishes them: "Even after they have drunk the blood, the souls of the dead remain physically insubstantial, unable to embrace, much less affect, those who are still alive" (Sarah Iles Johnston, *Restless Dead: Encounters Between the Living and the Dead in Ancient Greece* [Berkeley: University of California Press, 1999], 8). And consider how funerary rites included animal sacrifice, how, as with Odysseus, "the blood was meant to feed the dead, and could even be used to summon the (*psychê* of the) dead from the grave" (Josine H. Blok, "Solon's Funerary Laws: Questions of Authenticity and Function," in *Solon of Athens: New Historical and Philological Approaches*, ed. J. H. Blok and A. P. M. H. Lardinois [Leiden: Brill, 2006], 237).

159. Longrigg, *Greek Rational Medicine*, 74, quoting Friedrich Solmsen, "Tissues and the Soul," *Philosophical Review* 59 (1950): 454.

160. Longrigg, *Greek Rational Medicine*, 75; and see Nancy Siraisi, *Medieval and Early Renaissance Medicine: An Introduction to Knowledge and Practice* (Chicago: University of Chicago Press, 1990).

161. King, *Hippocrates' Woman*, 51, and later: "Since the origin of blood is food, more food means more blood" (72). King elaborates on the argument that there is, in Greek medicine, a profound link between sacrificial blood and menstrual blood, and beyond that between medicine, cooking, and sacrifice (88–98). Put another way, "like sacrificial ritual,

Hippocratic gynaecology is about ensuring blood is shed at the proper times and in the proper ways" (99).

162. Aristotle, *Generation of Animals*, 766a.

163. Michael Boylan, "The Digestive and 'Circulatory' Systems in Aristotle's Biology," *Journal of the History of Biology* 15, no. 1 (Spring 1982): 115; and see also the fine analyses of Aristotelian intricacies by Serge Margel, "Les nourritures de l'âme. Essai sur la fonction nutritive et séminale dans la biologie d'Aristote," *Revue des études grecques* 108, no. 1 (1995): 91–106. Note as well that upon conception, for Aristotle, "it is the heart which is immediately formed and in turn forms the blood. The blood and other uniform parts then fashion the other organs of the body" (M. Boylan, "The Galenic and Hippocratic Challenges to Aristotle's Conception Theory," *Journal of the History of Biology* 17, no. 1 [Spring 1984]: 98). Blood is, in a particular way, derivative.

164. Aristotle, *Generation of Animals*, 726b; I quoted this passage earlier, of course, but without underscoring the essential point about food or nourishment.

165. Marie-Paule Duminil, *Le sang, les vaisseaux, le coeur dans la collection hippocratique. Anatomie et physiologie* (Paris: Les Belles Lettres, 1983), 150.

166. It is the nourishing faculty of blood, Longrigg explains, that leads Aristotle to discard his own earlier view of blood as a part endowed with perception and sensation (Longrigg, *Greek Rational Medicine*, 174).

167. More precisely, perhaps, to the extent that it has anything to do with blood, kinship is food before it is lineage.

168. See Marcel Détienne and Jean-Pierre Vernant, *The Cuisine of Sacrifice Among the Greeks*, trans. Paula Wissing (Chicago: University of Chicago Press, 1989), and Vernant's own contribution to that volume in particular (21–86), where he describes, for example, the division of food as the site of distinction between gods, humans, and animals (37–38), corresponding to different modes of comportment of the races (in Hesiod's sense of the term) (49). David Freidenreich explores the role of food in "constructing otherness" and identity (D. M. Freidenreich, *Foreigners and Their Food: Constructing Otherness in Jewish, Christian, and Islamic Law* [Berkeley: University of California Press, 2011]).

169. Longrigg, *Greek Rational Medicine*, 208.

170. See J. Jouanna and P. Demond, "Le sens d'ἰχώρ chez Homere (*Iliade* V, v. 340 et 416) et Eschyle (*Agamemnon*, v. 1480) en relation avec les emplois du mot dans la *Collection Hippocratique*," *Revue des études anciennes* 83, no. 3–4 (1981): 197–209; but see for a sharp critique, Pierre Judet de la Combe, "Remarks on Aeschylus's Homer," in *Antiquities (Postwar French Thought, volume III)*, 384–394. For the medical understanding of *ichor*, see Duminil, *Le sang*, 164ff.

171. Homer, *Iliad*, trans. A. T. Murray (Cambridge: Mass.: Harvard University Press, 1924), book 5, 340–342.

172. Recall that the term *homogalaktes* has been interpreted as "co-uterine," whereas more anthropologically informed analyses contend that milk is a different kind of shared substance, at the expected center of the diet of pastoral societies (see note 105 earlier). Indo-European philologists might have caught this one. The Urdu (and Persian) word *hamshir* is the precise equivalent of *homogalaktes* and refers to those who become "brothers"

as the result of drinking from the same cup of milk (I thank Nauman Naqvi for sharing this precious information with me); for an extended discussion of shared substances and "milk kinship," see Corinne Fortier, "Blood, Sperm, and the Embryo in Sunni Islam and in Mauritania: Milk Kinship, Descent, and Medically Assisted Procreation," *Body and Society* 13, no. 3 (2007): 15–36.

173. Detienne, "Culinary Practices and the Spirit of Sacrifice," in *The Cuisine of Sacrifice Among the Greeks*, 3, referring to *Histories* II: 41.

174. Heleen Sancisi-Weerdenburg comments on these passages of the *Histories* where eating habits are not only compared but where they function as "part of *Greek* ethnic boundary-marking practices" (H. Sancisi-Weerdenburg, "Yaunâ by the Sea and Across the Sea," in *Ancient Perceptions of Greek Ethnicity*, 339). And Page duBois expounds on "the analogy between intercourse and cooking," which precisely reverses the logic of ground/figure that I have attended to throughout (P. duBois, *Sowing the Body: Psychoanalysis and Ancient Representations of Women* [Chicago: University of Chicago Press, 1984], 123ff.).

175. Stanley K. Stowers, "Greeks Who Sacrifice and Those Who Do Not: Toward an Anthropology of Greek Religion," in *The Social World of the First Christians: Essays in Honor of Wayne A. Meeks*, ed. L. Michael White and O. Larry Yarbrough (Minneapolis, Minn.: Fortress Press, 1995), 307; see also duBois, *Sowing the Body*, esp. chap. 6 ("Oven"), 110–129.

176. "The Greeks," writes Stowers, who relies on a well-established if mistaken reading of Aristotle (301ff.), "used blood to think about procreation and about the manipulation of procreation" (329). I have shown that such was not the case, but this diminishes neither the importance of blood nor the centrality of sexual difference. Nor does it take away from Stowers's main point as to sacrifice's significance and its extent.

177. Baracchi, *Aristotle's Ethics*, 109.

178. Jean Rudhardt elaborates a striking argument about this word and its cognates, invoked in the context of paternal recognition and adoption, extending its range to the numerous (in fact, never quite completed) rites that make a child a member of the *oikos* and later the phratry. "The verb *poiesthai* signifies properly a creation," a series of acts and gestures—the rites—that could be said to "sediment" the belonging of the legitimate child (J. Rudhardt, "La reconnaissance de la paternité: sa nature et sa portée dans la société athénienne: sur un discours de Démosthène," *Museum Helveticum* 19 [1962]: 39–64; citation from p. 56); see Gherchanoc, "Le lien filial," and for more general remarks, Baracchi, *Aristotle's Ethics*, 115 and 183–87.

179. Jean-Pierre Vernant, *Myth and Society*, 134; Baracchi extends Vernant's account and explains that "precisely in its orientation, sense, and non-indifference, life (and most notably human life) demands to be situated in an environment exceeding the human. It implies a context neither merely human-made nor merely based on the arbitrariness of human self-assertion. Of their own accord, the meaning and direction found in life necessitate and reveal a plot in which the human is implicated, while being neither the author nor the source of it. The task, then, involves acknowledging the broader fabric of sense into which the human is woven, which provides the limits and direction orienting human life" (Baracchi, *Aristotle's Ethics*, 239–40).

180. Vernant's teacher, Louis Gernet, highlights the parallel between wine and blood on the one hand and milk and honey on the other. Although he too confines his remark to the cultic domain, he describes "the notion of a quality [*vertu*] immanent to blood, and particularly so in its pre-contractual significance . . . we would say that the effects of blood are not only of a subjective order—concerning the participants as such—but objective—which is to say that they are exercised beyond them [*en dehors d'eux*]" (L. Gernet, *Anthropologie de la Grèce antique* [Paris: François Maspero, 1968], 210).

181. Baracchi, *Aristotle's Ethics*, 240.

182. Baracchi, *Aristotle's Ethics*, 309; for a pertinent account of the profound interrogation with regard to "our" Greekness, such as took place on the French scholarly scene, see Miriam Leonard, *Athens in Paris: Ancient Greece and the Political in Post-War French Thought* (Oxford: Oxford University Press, 2005).

5. BLEEDING AND MELANCHOLIA

1. In an earlier rendering, this chapter bore a different title: "Trust No One: On the Vicissitudes of Christian Melancholia." I had meant to follow a vector linking Max Weber's "Protestant Ethic" to the work of the melancholic spirit. Weber writes of English Puritan literature and of its "warnings against any trust in the aid of friendship of men" (M. Weber, *The Protestant Ethic and the Spirit of Capitalism*, trans. Talcott Parsons [London and New York: Routledge, 2001], 62). On that same page of the American translation, Weber goes on to ponder what links this warning to another, still current, American proverb of sorts, "trust no one."

2. Sigmund Freud, "Mourning and Melancholia," trans. Joan Riviere and James Strachey, in *The Standard Edition of the Complete Psychological Works of Sigmund Freud*, ed. J. Strachey (London: The Hogarth Press and the Institute of Psycho-Analysis, 1957), vol. XIV, 253; *Gesammelte Werke* (Frankfurt am Main: Fischer Taschenbuch Verlag, 1999), Bd. X, 439; further references to this essay will be made in the body of the text, with English pagination first, followed by the German (G).

3. On "melancholy and the act," see Slavoj Žižek's essay by that title in *Critical Inquiry* 26, no. 4 (Summer 2000): 657–81. There is little sense in disagreeing (or for that matter, agreeing) with Žižek. In what follows, I only wonder about the distinction he makes between postcolonial melancholia (such as he attacks it) and Christianity (whatever one apologetically identifies as its perverse and/or perverted core).

4. Ian Chambers, *Mediterranean Crossings: The Politics of an Interrupted Modernity* (Durham, N.C.: Duke University Press, 2008), 55; Chambers is speaking of music here, but also of memory and of "discontinuous histories," of an instrument that has "blood in the strings" (55).

5. The texts collected by Jennifer Radden repeatedly demonstrate that the theory of humors often gave blood a prominent status (*The Nature of Melancholy from Aristotle to Kristeva*, ed. J. Radden [Oxford: Oxford University Press, 2000], e.g., 61–68; 79–85). However, only "medieval physiology . . . reduced all bodily fluids to blood" (Gail Kern Paster, *The Body Embarrassed: Drama and the Disciplines of Shame in Early Modern England* [Ithaca, N.Y.: Cornell University Press, 1993], 107).

6. See the moving and inspiring account by Amy Hollywood of the configuration that links melancholia, lovesickness, and the theological imagination (A. Hollywood, "Acute Melancholia," *Harvard Theological Review* 99, no. 4 [October 2006]: 381–406); incidentally, Corey D. B. Walker, has recently elaborated suggestively on "the wound of theology" by recalling Adorno's "wound of reason." This is not without pertinence, obviously (Peter Goodwin Heltzel and Corey D. B. Walker, "The Wound of Political Theology: A Prolegomenon to a Research Agenda," *Political Theology* 9, no. 2 [2008]: 252–55).

7. Rebecca Comay, "The Sickness of Tradition: Between Melancholia and Fetishism," in *Walter Benjamin and History*, ed. Andrew Benjamin (London and New York: Continuum, 2005), 88–89; and see Comay, *Mourning Sickness: Hegel and the French Revolution* (Stanford, Calif.: Stanford University Press, 2011).

8. Laurence Rickels refers to Freud's January 1895 letter to Fliess, in which "the inward turn of the melancholic psychic apparatus comes into focus as an 'indrawing process' or 'internal bleeding' which, 'in a manner analogous to pain,' 'operates like a wound'" (L. Rickels, *Aberrations of Mourning: Writing on German Crypts* [Detroit, Mich.: Wayne State University Press, 1988], 27).

9. It should become increasingly relevant to note that Bram Stoker has Jonathan Harker evoke similar references and figures. "This diary seems horribly like the beginning of the 'Arabian Nights,' for everything has to break off at cock-crow—or like the ghost of Hamlet's father" (Bram Stoker, *Dracula*, ed. John Paul Riquelme [Boston: Bedford/St. Martin's, 2002], 54; cf. also 60).

10. David Scott, *Conscripts of Modernity: The Tragedy of Colonial Enlightenment* (Durham, N.C.: Duke University Press, 2004), 163.

11. Rickels describes "the economy of melancholia" in terms of "a war economy of stored, rationed, and synthesized resources that must close ranks around every reserve, push back the specter of disappearance of all fuel or energy, and go for the total victory that in turn can only recuperate everything in infinite recycling" (Laurence A. Rickels, *The Vampire Lectures* [Minneapolis: University of Minnesota Press, 1999], xvi). I am more than indebted to this extraordinary book, which lays out the terrain for any attempt, mine included, at engaging with any rigor the stiff figure of these "melancholic cannibals" that are vampires.

12. Comay, "The Sickness of Tradition," 94.

13. Karl Marx, *Capital: A Critique of Political Economy*, trans. Ben Fowkes (New York: Penguin/NLR, 1990), vol. 1, 367 ("Day-Work and Night-Work, The Shift-System"); I have mentioned some of the literature on vampirism and capitalism, but for a more sustained discussion of political economy in Stoker's *Dracula*, see Gail Turley Houston, *From Dickens to Dracula: Gothic, Economics, and Victorian Fiction* (Cambridge: Cambridge University Press, 2005); Houston considers Dracula as a figure of the corporation (his "amalgamated corporate personality" [126]), indeed of the corporate state; she considers the displacement of the corporate imagery from the state to the banking system. She elaborates on Dracula's association with money and "the lifeblood of commerce" (118) and on the motif of circulation.

14. Rickels, *Aberrations*, 141.

15. Joan Copjec, "Vampires, Breast-Feeding, and Anxiety" *October* 58 (1991): 33; and see also, in a different context, Ruth Tsoffar, "'A Land that Devours its People': Mizrahi Writing from the Gut," *Body and Society* 12, no. 2 (2006): 25–55. I owe much of my understanding of cannibalism to Tsoffar.

16. Stoker, *Dracula*, 305.

17. Stoker, *Dracula*, 317.

18. On the "deceiving demons," see the selection from Johann Weyer (1562) *Of Deceiving Demons* in *The Nature of Melancholy*, 97–105.

19. Pierre Fédida, "Le cannibale mélancolique," *Nouvelle Revue de Psychanalyse* 6 (Automne 1972) ("Destins du cannibalisme"): 123–27. Following the work done in this issue of *NRP*, Giorgio Agamben underscored the importance of the links between cannibalism and melancholia (G. Agamben, *Stanzas: Word and Phantasm in Western Culture*, trans. Ronald L. Martinez [Minneapolis: University of Minnesota Press, 1993], 21, n. 2). Maggie Kilgour further points out that "the cannibalistic Saturn is both ruler of the Golden Age and also god of melancholy" (M. Kilgour, "The Function of Cannibalism at the Present Time," in *Cannibalism and the Colonial World*, ed. Francis Barker, Peter Hulme, and Margaret Iversen [Cambridge: Cambridge University Press, 1998], 247). She had elaborated on this Saturnine dimension in *From Communion to Cannibalism: An Anatomy of Metaphors of Incorporation* (Princeton, N.J.: Princeton University Press, 1990), esp. chap. 4.

20. Tomislav Z. Longinović, *Vampires Like US: Writing Down "the Serbs"* (Belgrade: Belgrade Circle, 2005), and see now Longinović, *Vampire Nation: Violence as Cultural Imaginary* (Durham, N.C.: Duke University Press, 2011).

21. Rickels, *Vampire Lectures*, 56.

22. Rickels, *Aberrations*, 141.

23. Stoker, *Dracula*, 245.

24. Christopher Herbert, "Vampire Religion," *Representations* 79, no. 1 (Summer 2002): 100–121; Stephen Arata has been credited with having launched a postcolonial reading of Bram Stoker's *Dracula*, interestingly enough by contrasting (not opposing) a growing concern with history with early psychoanalytically inclined readings of the novel; see Stephen D. Arata, "The Occidental Tourist: *Dracula* and the Anxiety of Reverse Colonization," *Victorian Studies* 33, no. 4 (1990): 621–45. Joseph Valente, for his part, writes of "the metrocolonial vampire" while staying away from melancholia and from the title's promise to provide, perhaps, a cryptology or cryptonymy (J. Valente, *Dracula's Crypt: Bram Stoker, Irishness, and the Question of Blood* [Urbana: University of Illinois Press, 2002], esp. chap. 3).

25. Longinovic, *Vampires like US*, 46; and see *Balkan as Metaphor: Between Globalization and Fragmentation*, ed. Dušan I. Bjelic and Obrad Savić (Cambridge, Mass.: MIT Press, 2002).

26. Stoker, *Dracula*, 184 and 320.

27. Luise White, *Speaking with Vampires: Rumor and History in Colonial Africa* (Berkeley: University of California Press, 2000), 44; White explains her concern early on by asserting that "there are many obvious reasons why Africans might have thought that colonial powers took precious substances from African bodies" (18).

28. Luis García-Ballester, "Introduction," in *Practical Medicine from Salermo to the Black Death*, ed. García-Ballester et al. (Cambridge: Cambridge University Press, 1994), 11; and

see Danielle Jacquart and Claude Thomasset, *Sexuality and Medicine in the Middle Ages*, trans. Matthew Adamson (Princeton, N.J.: Princeton University Press, 1988), 54ff; as well as *The Nature of Melancholy*.

29. "De melancolia nigra et canina" is a phrase Agamben quotes from a medieval tractate by Vincent de Beauvais (Agamben, *Stanzas*, 17).

30. Stoker, *Dracula*, 115.

31. Quoted in Sven Lindqvist, *Exterminate All the Brutes*, trans. Joan Tate (New York: New Press, 1996), 140; *Dracula* should most obviously be read in the context of the literary production, fantasies of mass extermination, described in exquisitely painful details by Lindqvist in this book as well as in his *History of Bombing*, trans. Linda Haverty Rugg (New York: New Press, 2000).

32. M. Ficino, *De Amore*, quoted in Agamben, *Stanzas*, 17.

33. "They say much of blood and bloom," says Van Helsing (Stoker, *Dracula*, 314–15).

34. Žižek, "Melancholy and the Act," 663.

35. There is, of course, nothing incidental about the association between blood and love in the Western Christian medical tradition; see Joseph Ziegler, *Medicine and Religion c. 1300: The Case of Arnau de Vilanova* (Oxford: Clarendon Press, 1998).

36. R. Comay, "The Sickness of Tradition," 94.

37. On *Dracula* as "that perennially misjudged heroic epic of the final victory of technological media," see Friedrich Kittler, *Gramophone, Film, Typewriter*, trans. Geoffrey Winthrop-Young and Michael Wutz (Stanford, Calif.: Stanford University Press, 1999), 86; Rickels elaborates further in *Vampire Lectures*.

38. Hildegard von Bingen, *Causae et Curae*, quoted in Agamben, *Stanzas*, 16.

39. See Arata on history versus psychoanalysis in *Dracula* in Arata, "The Occidental Tourist."

40. Longinovic, *Vampires Like US*, 34.

41. The work of the Mitscherlichs, which inspired Paul Gilroy, does point to an important, if rarer, understanding of melancholia under the heading of group psychology (see P. Gilroy, *Postcolonial Melancholia* [New York: Columbia University Press, 2005], esp. 98ff., and see also Ranjana Khanna, *Dark Continents: Psychoanalysis and Colonialism* [Durham, N.C.: Duke University Press, 2004], esp. chap. 4, "Colonial Melancholy"). Judith Butler offers an important psycho-social precedent with the notion that "gender identification is a kind of melancholia" (J. Butler, *Gender Trouble: Feminism and the Subversion of Identity* [New York: Routledge, 1990], 63; and see "Melancholy Gender/Refused Identification," in Butler, *The Psychic Life of Power: Theories in Subjection* [Stanford, Calif.: Stanford University Press, 1997], 132–59).

42. Rickels, *Vampire Lectures*, 77; and see of course Freud, *The Ego and the Id*, where Freud makes the explicit link between identification and cannibalism (S. Freud, *The Ego and the Id*, trans. Joan Riviere [New York: W.W. Norton & Company, 1962], 19, n. 2.

43. Butler, *Psychic Life*, 167.

44. Friedrich Kittler, "Dracula's Legacy," trans. William S. Davis, in *Literature, Media, Information Systems*, ed. John Johnston (Amsterdam: OPA/G+B Arts, 1997), 57.

45. Elias Canetti, *Crowds and Power*, trans. Carol Stewart (New York: Farrar, Straus and Giroux, 1984), 467; earlier, Canetti had explained the logic around which "lamenting

packs" are formed, and where "we find wounds and blood," along with "the tendency to prolong the passion." Canetti further writes that "the dead man has died for the sake of the people who mourn him . . . he was their savior. His preciousness is stressed in every possible way. . . . His death is not recognized by the mourners. They want him alive again. . . . The living try to hold him back . . . and strive to keep him. . . . Most of them perhaps do not divine that, while they feed their bodies, they also feed the darkness within themselves" (144–45). The "core" of the religion, in other words, "remains the same: it is the lament" (144). Focusing on Greek Orthodox practices, Neni Panourgía provides a striking account of the way in which Christ's death is lived again and again, how Christ lives and dies again during Holy Week (N. Panourgía, *Fragments of Death, Fables of Identity: An Athenian Anthropography* [Madison: University of Wisconsin Press, 1995], 151–58).

46. William Robertson Smith, *The Religion of the Semites* (New Brunswick, N.J., and London: Transaction Publishers, 2002), 226–27.

47. Preserved Smith, *A Short History of Christian Theophagy* (Chicago and London: The Open Court Publishing Co., 1922); Werner Hamacher, *pleroma—Reading in Hegel*, trans. Nicholas Walker and Simon Jarvis (Stanford, Calif.: Stanford University Press, 1998); and see Luise White's discussion of Thomas Fox-Pitt, colonial administrator, and his 1953 unpublished essay, "Cannibalism and Christianity" (White, *Speaking with Vampires*, 189ff.).

48. Louis Marin, *Food for Thought*, trans. Mette Hjort (Baltimore, Md.: Johns Hopkins University Press, 1989; the phrase "eucharistic matrix," which I mentioned earlier, appears on p. 161; incidentally, the book ends on a discussion of "the king's unhappy body" (237), the king as "melancholic figure" (239), with reference to Louis XIV's physician and to Walter Benjamin's claim that "the king is the paradigm of the melancholic figure" (240), a Christological figure too. And see for medieval antecedents and illuminating elaborations, Merrall Llewelyn Price, *Consuming Passions: The Uses of Cannibalism in Late Medieval and Early Modern Europe* (New York: Routledge, 2003), and Heather Blurton, *Cannibalism in High Medieval English Literature* (New York: Palgrave, 2007).

49. Joseph S. Bierman, "*Dracula*: Prolonged Childhood Illness, and the Oral Triad," *American Imago* 29, no. 2 (Summer 1972): 186.

50. Maggie Kilgour, *From Communion to Cannibalism*, 5; "he does not care for solid things," said Nietzsche about Jesus (Nietzsche, "The Anti-Christ," 29, §32).

51. Judith Butler, *Gender Trouble*, 61.

52. Fédida, "Le cannibale mélancolique," 127.

53. Rickels, *Vampire Lectures*, 116.

54. Norman O. Brown, *Life Against Death: The Psychoanalytical Meaning of History* (Middletown, Conn.: Wesleyan University Press, 1959), 252; as I suggested earlier, the association of money and blood, which Brown does not directly explore, seems to me quite relevant here. "Money is human guilt with the dross refined away till it is a pure crystal of self-punishment; but it remains filthy because it remains guilt" (266). Blood shares the symbolic range that extends from the purity of crystal to the filth of guilt.

55. G. Obeyesekere, *Cannibal Talk: The Man-Eating Myth and Human Sacrifice in the South Seas* (Berkeley: University of California Press, 2005), 261; Maggie Kilgour does recognize

the "potential for cannibalism in the sacrament of the Eucharist," but she goes on to say that "it becomes difficult to say precisely *who* is eating *whom*" (Kilgour, *Communion to Cannibalism*, 13). Christianity could therefore be read along Girardian lines as the sacrifice of sacrifice, the cannibalization of cannibalism. Kilgour herself suggests another reading, or indeed the next step in that difficult reading, when she quotes the survivors of the 1972 plane crash that became the basis for the bestseller (and movie) *Alive*. "If Jesus, in the Last Supper, offered his body and blood to all the disciples, he was giving us to understand that we must do the same . . . what we did was really Christian. We went back to the very source of Christianity . . . we swallowed little bits of flesh with the feeling that God demanded it of us. We felt like Christians" (quoted in Kilgour, 149).

56. C. Herbert, "Vampire Religion," 110; although he uniquely, and substantially, contributes to a reading that is otherwise rare by engaging *Dracula* and Christianity, Herbert seems to waver when he writes that "vampirism and Christianity *may* coincide" (111; emphasis added). Clearly, it is the very proximity left open (like a gaping wound, as it were) between vampirism and Christianity that constitutes the unequivocal contribution made by Stocker.

57. As Miri Rubin succinctly puts it, "by the year 1300 a narrative had developed in Europe that included a sequence wherein a Jew acquired the consecrated host and abused it. According to it the blood gushed forth from the 'abused' Host as the most visible sign of the outrage that the Jews were alleged to have perpetrated" (M. Rubin, "Blood: Sacrifice and Redemption in Christian Iconography," in *Blood: Art, Power, Politics, and Pathology*, ed. James M. Bradburne [Munich, London, New York: Prestel, 2001], 93). Rubin continues and describes how "the late thirteenth century witnessed the growth of cults based on the belief that Jews required Christian blood for the completion of the Passover rituals. . . . Thus every year a Christian boy was said to have been sought and killed by a Jewish community, and the blood was shared with other Jews" (95–96).

58. R. Po-Chia Hsia, *Trent 1475: Stories of a Ritual Murder Trial* (New Haven, Conn.: Yale University Press, 1992), 89; many historians of anti-Judaism and anti-Semitism have pointed out the connection between eucharistic practice, accusations of ritual murder, and cannibalistic use of Christian blood by Jews; see Blurton, *Cannibalism,* who notably shows the extension of the projective practice onto Mongols as well.

59. Rubin phrases this projection in terms of a resonance of desires "the lust for blood imputed to the Jew echoed the desire for the blood of Salvation in the Christian" (M. Rubin, "Blood," 97).

60. Sarah Beckwith, *Christ's Body: Identity, Culture, and Society in Late Medieval Writings* (London and New York: Routledge, 1993), 42.

61. Stoker, *Dracula*, 143.

62. Stoker, *Dracula*, 285.

63. Kilgour, *From Communion to Cannibalism*, 173.

64. Beckwith, *Christ's Body*, 59; and see Hollywood, "Acute Melancholia," as well as her "'That Glorious Slit': Irigaray and the Medieval Devotion to Christ's Side Wound," in *Luce Irigaray and Premodern Culture: Thresholds of History*, ed. Theresa Krier and Elizabeth D. Harvey (New York: Routledge, 2004), 105–125.

65. Rickels, *Aberrations*, 319; on Jesus as Mother see Caroline Walker Bynum, *Jesus as Mother: Studies in the Spirituality of the High Middle Ages* (Berkeley: University of California Press, 1984). Like Rickels, Julia Kristeva underscores the way in which, in melancholia, "Freudian theory detects everywhere the same *impossible mourning for the maternal object*" (J. Kristeva, *Black Sun: Depression and Melancholia*, trans. Leon S. Roudiez [New York: Columbia University Press, 1989], 9). It should be added, however, that though she has more to say than most about the persistence of the Christian question, Kristeva is quite clear in confessing to having earlier "assumed depressed persons to be atheistic—deprived of meaning, deprived of values" (14).

66. Rickels, *Aberrations*, 319.

67. Stoker, *Dracula*, 296.

68. Ian Chambers, *Mediterranean Crossings: The Politics of an Interrupted Modernity* (Durham, N.C.: Duke University Press, 2008), 138.

69. Hadewijch, quoted in Caroline Walker Bynum, *Fragmentation and Redemption: Essays on Gender and the Human Body in Medieval Religion* (New York: Zone Books, 1991), 173; and see Hollywood, "That Glorious Slit" for similar, graphic descriptions of Angela of Foligno and others (e.g., 106, 112); there are other, earlier instances that link melancholia and lovesickness (an older association) with the blood of Christ (an original Christian invention) mentioned in Hollywood's "Acute Melancholia" (e.g., 388, 392).

70. The Monk of Farne, quoted in Bynum, *Fragmentation*, 159.

71. I cite the Wesleys' hymns from Herbert, "Vampire Religion," 116; for more on John Wesley, consider his sermons, where he demonstrates his blood expertise, among other ways, by explaining that the forbidden fruit "seems to have contained a juice, the particles of which were apt to cleave to whatever they touched. Some of these, being received into the human body, might adhere to the inner coats of the finer vessels; to which again other particles that before floated loose in the blood, continually joining, would naturally lay a foundation for numberless disorders in all parts of the machine" (*John Wesley's Sermons: An Anthology*, ed. Albert C. Outler and Richard P. Heitzenrater [Nashville: Abingdon Press, 1991], 17); for more on Methodism and blood in the American context, see Morris L. Davis, *The Methodist Unification: Christianity and the Politics of Race in the Jim Crow Era* (New York: New York University Press, 2008).

72. Catherine of Sienna, quoted in Piero Camporesi, *Juice of Life: The Symbolic and Magic Significance of Blood*, trans. Robert R. Barr (New York: Continuum, 1995), 73–74.

73. Stoker, *Dracula*, 243.

74. Friedrich Nietzsche, *The Gay Science*, trans. Josefine Nauckhoff (Cambridge: Cambridge University Press, 2001), 237 ("Why We Are Not Idealists").

75. Kristeva is the one exception I have found, who refers to Benjamin's remarks on Christianity (Kristeva, *Black Sun*, 101–103).

76. Walter Benjamin, *Origin of the German Tragic Drama*, trans. John Osborne (London: NLB/Verso, 1985), 139/G317.

77. G. W. F. Hegel, *Phenomenology of Spirit*, trans. A. V. Miller (Oxford: Oxford University Press, 1977), 100; *Phänomenologie des Geistes* (Frankfurt am Main: Ullstein Materialen, 1983), 102.

78. Stoker, *Dracula*, 337.

79. G. W. F. Hegel, "The Spirit of Christianity," in *Early Theological Writings*, trans. T. M. Knox (Philadelphia: University of Pennsylvania Press, 1971), 252; *Werke 1: Frühe Schriften* (Frankfurt am Main: Suhrkamp, 1971), 369.

80. Sigmund Freud, *Moses and Monotheism*, trans. Katherine Jones (New York: Vintage, 1967), 115; Hannah Arendt puts it differently but pertinently: "Where all are guilty, no one is; confessions of collective guilt are the best possible safeguards against the discovery of culprits, and the very magnitude of the crime the best excuse for doing nothing" (H. Arendt, *On Violence* [Orlando, Fla.: Harcourt, Inc., 1970], 65). Then again, some may still put some good-willed, and well-intended, efforts into finding *alternative* culprits.

81. Khanna, *Dark Continents*, 65.

82. Kristeva, *Black Sun*, 71; in this final section, I am following, if with a slightly different inflection, in the footsteps of Kristeva's intermittent discussion of Christianity throughout *Black Sun* (e.g., "Holbein's Dead Christ," 105–138).

83. Rickels aptly summarizes some of the effects of this extraordinary assertion (Matthew 8:22; Luke 9:60), resurrection, and the drinking of blood. "Vampire stories remind us that the work of mourning is always the work of representation in mourning. To bury the dead is also to represent the dead. And all the difficulties we have representing death go hand in hand, hand in teeth, with the problem of disposing of the dead, burying them, putting them to rest" (Rickels, *Vampire Lectures*, 205). For an instructive, philological reading of the biblical verse and its difficulties, see Byron R. McCane, " 'Let the Dead Bury Their Own Dead': Secondary Burial and *Matt* 8:21–22," *The Harvard Theological Review* 83, no. 1 (January 1990): 31–43.

84. "The uncovering of *Christian morality* is an event without equal," writes Nietzsche, "a real catastrophe. . . . Everything that has been called 'truth' so far is recognized as the most harmful, treacherous, subterranean form of lie; the holy pretext of 'improving' humanity is recognized as the ruse to *suck the blood* out of life itself, to make it anaemic. Morality as *vampirism* . . ." (Nietzsche, "Ecce Homo," trans. Judith Norman, in *The Anti-Christ, Ecce Homo, Twilight of the Idols, and Other Writings*, ed. Aaron Ridley [Cambridge: Cambridge University Press, 2005], 150).

85. I borrow this formulation from Pierre Fédida who writes of the "fantasmatic ability to relate to the object and to keep it alive as lost object [*de le maintenir vivant comme objet perdu*]" (Fédida, "Le cannibale mélancolique," 126).

86. Rickels, *Vampire Lectures*, 56.

87. Stoker, *Dracula*, 327.

88. Rickels, *Vampire Lectures*, 203.

89. Stoker, *Dracula*, 242.

90. Kittler, "Dracula's Legacy," 62.

91. Giorgio Agamben, "Benjamin and the Demonic," trans. Daniel Heller-Roazen, in Agamben, *Potentialities: Collected Essays in Philosophy* (Stanford, Calif.: Stanford University Press, 1999), 141–42; Agamben goes on to cite Benjamin's description of Giotto's Cupid as "a demon of wantonness with a bat's wings and claws" (141), agreeing that "in Klee's painting, the angel's feet certainly bring to mind a bird of prey" (142).

Having recalled the bat, Agamben seems to forget his own lesson (see later) when he disputes the possibility that the angel might be "a melancholy figure" (144). Agamben does not comment on the angel's teeth. He does go on to write, a few pages down, that "the new angel, who makes his appearance at the point at which origin and destruction meet, is therefore a destructive figure whom the claws of 'Agesilaus Santander' suit well. Yet he is not a demonic figure but rather 'the messenger of a more real humanism'" (151; quoting Benjamin). Still, Agamben adds, "this is not to say that we are confronted here by a pure and simple liquidation of the past. (The two metaphors of the origin show their difference here, 'redemption' being a final, absolving payment and 'liquidation' being a transformation into available funds.)" (154).

92. Martin Harries, *Forgetting Lot's Wife: On Destructive Spectatorship* (New York: Fordham University Press, 2007), 100; commenting on Klee, Benjamin, and Anselm Kiefer, Harries addresses the "problems in reading the figure of the angel" (99), the difficulty in understanding "the association of the angel with destruction" (100).

93. Agamben, *Stanzas*, 27, n. 6.

94. Copjec, "Vampires," 38.

95. Stoker, *Dracula*, 126.

6. LEVIATHAN AND THE BLOOD PUMP

1. The epigraphs for this chapter are, first, Francis Hopkinson, quoted in Michael Sappol, *A Traffic of Dead Bodies: Anatomy and Embodied Social Identity in Nineteenth-Century America* (Princeton, N.J.: Princeton University Press, 2002), 46; as Sappol describes, Hopkinson (1737–1791) "was an eminent figure, a signer of the Declaration of Independence, friend and correspondent of Benjamin Franklin and Thomas Jefferson, designer of the American flag, inventor, judge, composer, poet and wit" (44). The poem, "An Oration Which Might Have Been Delivered to the Students in Anatomy on the Late Rupture Between the Two Schools in This City," was published in 1789. The second is Saint Evremond, hand-copied on a flyleaf of his New Testament and Psalms by Herman Melville, as reported by William Braswell, *Melville's Religious Thought* (New York: Pageant Books, 1959), 23.

2. Steven Shapin and Simon Schaffer, *Leviathan and the Air-Pump: Hobbes, Boyle, and the Experimental Life* (Princeton, N.J.: Princeton University Press, 1985).

3. Peter Szendy, *Prophecies of Leviathan: Reading Past Melville*, trans. Gil Anidjar (New York: Fordham University Press, 2010), 90; my tentative reading of Melville is indebted to Szendy's rigorous book.

4. As Alan Heimert wrote, "in the process of canonizing Herman Melville as a major American writer, critics have generally failed to touch on the specific political context of his works" (A. Heimert, "Moby-Dick and American Political Symbolism," *American Quarterly* 15, no. 4 (Winter 1963): 498. This is no longer as true as it was in 1963, though in a forthcoming collection of essays on Melville and political theory, Jason Frank can still make the general point that Melville's "work is left out of anthologies of American political thought, overlooked on syllabi, and very rarely engaged in professional research" (J. Frank,

"Introduction: American Tragedy: Herman Melville's Political Thought," in *A Political Companion to Herman Melville*, ed. Jason Frank [Lexington: University Press of Kentucky, 2013]).

5. Daniel Eleazar makes the following cryptic remark (cryptic because isolated and unexplored), which seems nonetheless essential toward an assessment of Melville's contribution to American political thought, indeed, toward an assessment of American political thought at large: "It seems that Melville is more sympathetic to Hobbes than he is to Locke" (D. J. Eleazar, *Covenant and Constitutionalism: The Great Frontier and the Matrix of Federal Democracy* [New Brunswick, N.J.: Transaction Publishers, 1998], 155).

6. Maurice Blanchot, "The Secret of Melville," in *Faux Pas*, trans. Charlotte Mandel (Stanford, Calif.: Stanford University Press, 2001), 239; the book obviously exceeds as well the bounds of any *human* experience, as Philip Armstrong importantly demonstrates (P. Armstrong, "What Animals Mean, in *Moby-Dick*, For Example," *Textual Practice* 19, no. 1 [2005]: 93–111).

7. Susan Mizruchi comments on the significance of blood in Melville, though she associates it mostly with the sphere of sacrifice, confining it therein and focusing, perhaps as a result, on *Billy Budd* ("Melville also sees sacrifice as expressing the human need for protection, considered as both a universal and a political concern. Probably the most vivid hint of this is the narrative preoccupation with blood. Blood in *Billy Budd* is about inheritances and legacies, about inspiration, warning, and safety, and about ceremonial give and take" [S. L. Mizruchi, *The Science of Sacrifice: American Literature and Modern Social Theory* [Princeton, N.J.: Princeton University Press, 1998], 175).

8. I quote from the early reviews of the book reproduced in *Moby-Dick as Doubloon: Essays and Extracts (1851–1970)*, ed. Hershel Parker and Harrison Hayford (New York: W.W. Norton & Co., 1970), 10, 22, 86. The first remark on classification is dated 1938, cited on p. 179; more recently, John Lardas Modern aptly described the book as "written in a variety of dialects and genres—from Shakespearian prosody, Swiftian wit, and the argot of whaling to frontier adventure and the reasonable parables of natural science" (J. Lardas Modern, *Secularism in Antebellum America: Reference to Ghosts, Protestant Subcultures, Machines, and Their Metaphors; Featuring Discussions of Mass Media,* Moby-Dick, *Spirituality, Phrenology, Anthropology, Sing Sing State Penitentiary, and Sex with the New Motive Power* [Chicago: University of Chicago Press, 2011], xv).

9. For the "thematics of form," see Edgar A. Dryden, *Melville's Thematics of Form: The Great Art of Telling the Truth* (Baltimore, Md.: Johns Hopkins Press, 1968); the final citation is from James Duban, *Melville's Major Fiction: Politics, Theology, and Imagination* (Dekalb: Northern Illinois University Press, 1983), 85.

10. Christopher Norris, "Literary Theory, Science, and Philosophy of Science," in *The Cambridge History of Literary Criticism, vol. 9,* ed. Christa Knellwolf and Christopher Norris (Cambridge: Cambridge University Press, 2001), 401–417.

11. Although I will not keep the phrase, I propose "asymmetric cartography" as a borrowing from Bruno Latour's "symmetric anthropology" (the untranslated French subtitle of Latour, *We Have Never Been Modern*, trans. Catherine Porter [Cambridge, Mass.: Harvard University Press, 1993]). Describing Latour's project, Dominique Pestre argues that it

seeks to account for a different, mutual production and transformation of the social and of the scientific, and beyond that, for the emergence of "a new—and collective—reading of *things*" (D. Pestre, *Introduction aux Science Studies* [Paris: La Découverte, 2006], 47).

12. On the figure of the "bloody heart" in Melville's family history, and by way of commentary on Melville's famous "I stand for the heart," see Michael Paul Rogin, *Subversive Genealogy: The Politics and Art of Herman Melville* (Berkeley: University of California Press, 1983), 57–59, 75.

13. C. L. R. James, *Mariners, Renegades, and Castaways: The Story of Herman Melville and the World We Live In* (Hanover, N.H.: University Press of New England, 2001), 124.

14. Eduardo Cadava, *Emerson and the Climates of History* (Stanford, Calif.: Stanford University Press, 1997), 3; Cadava aims to restore "the historical element" of Emerson's writing, and with it the "meaning of America" such as it is deployed in figures of rhetoric (9, 11). Cadava goes on to show that, for Emerson, "the force of political language ... depends on 'figurative expressions'" (71). The meaning of the word *figurative* is what is at stake throughout, for "natural metaphors," for example, "take on specific historical, political, theological, and literary connotations." They "are not merely tropes but also principles of articulation among language, politics, and history" (51–52).

15. Herman Melville, *Moby-Dick; Or The Whale* (Evanston and Chicago, Ill.: Northwestern University Press and The Newberry Library, 1988), 1: 4 and 7. All ensuing references will be made directly in the text, with chapter number followed by page number.

16. Alexis de Tocqueville, *Democracy in America*, trans. Harvey C. Mansfield and Delba Winthrop (Chicago: University of Chicago Press, 2000), 6–7.

17. Giles Gunn, *The Interpretation of Otherness: Literature, Religion, and the American Imagination* (New York: Oxford University Press, 1979), 5; Michael Rogin opens his discussion of Melville on Tocqueville's reflections on politics and literature (Rogin, *Subversive Genealogy*, 15–23); Tocqueville discusses American and democratic literature in *Democracy in America*, 428ff.; Melville himself made the connection between politics and literature to lament their disjunction (Herman Melville, "Hawthorne and His Mosses," in *The Piazza Tales and Other Prose Pieces, 1839–1860* [Evanston, Ill.: Northwestern University Press and The Newberry Library, 1987], 248).

18. Edward W. Said, *Reflections on Exile and Other Essays* (Cambridge, Mass.: Harvard University Press, 2000), 358–59; and see Tim Deines "Re-marking the Ultra-transcendental in *Moby-Dick,*" *symplokē* 18, no. 1–2 (2010): 261–79.

19. Said, *Reflections*, 359.

20. Charles Olson, *Call Me Ishmael* (Baltimore, Md., and London: Johns Hopkins University Press, 1997), 102; this anti-Christian line of reading is pursued most systematically, and most persuasively, by Lawrence Thompson in *Melville's Quarrel with God* (Princeton, N.J.: Princeton University Press, 1952); the book involves a meticulous documentation of the ways in which Christianity "surrounded" Melville, how it remained, as it were, in his blood.

21. Sophia Hawthorne is quoted in James McIntosh, "The Mariner's Multiple Quest," in *New Essays on Moby-Dick*, ed. Richard H. Brodhead (Cambridge: Cambridge University Press, 1986), 23; on the "Book of the Law of the Blood," see Olson, *Call Me Ishmael*, 85; for a reading of prophecy in Melville, see E. M. Forster, *Aspects of the Novel* (New York:

Harcourt, Brace & World, 1927), 181–212, and Rowland A. Sherill, *The Prophetic Melville: Experience, Transcendence, and Tragedy* (Athens, Ga.: University of Georgia Press, 1979). For an extended discussion of prophecy as a literary structure, see Szendy, *Prophecies*. T. Walter Herbert sees Melville as one of the well-recognized "prophets" of the secularization of "Western consciousness" (T. Walter Herbert Jr., *Moby-Dick and Calvinism: A World Dismantled* [New Brunswick, N.J.: Rutgers University Press, 1977], ix); Cesare Casarino, for his part, refers to Melville as being "the Judas Iscariot of the world of whaling" (C. Casarino, *Modernity at Sea: Melville, Marx, Conrad in Crisis* [Minneapolis: University of Minnesota Press, 2002], 82).

22. This is how Hobbes himself was known, as Carl Schmitt reports (C. Schmitt, *The Leviathan in the State Theory of Thomas Hobbes: Meaning and Failure of a Political Symbol*, trans. George Schwab and Erna Hilfstein [Westport, Conn.: Greenwood Press, 1996], 5).

23. Olson, *Call Me Ishmael*; the phrase "blood and oil" appears in *Moby-Dick*, 98: 428; the phrase "Golgotha of the heart" is William Faulkner's in *The Merill Studies in Moby-Dick*, ed. Howard P. Vincent (Columbus, Ohio: Charles E. Merill, 1969), 162.

24. For a history and analysis of the American whaling industry, linking technology and capital in particular, see Lance E. Davis, Robert E. Gallman, and Karin Gleiter, *In Pursuit of Leviathan: Technology, Institutions, Productivity, and Profits in American Whaling, 1816–1906* (Chicago: University of Chicago Press, 1997); for a pertinent analysis of the history of oil and its relation to American foreign policy, see Timothy Mitchell, *Carbon Democracy: Political Power in the Age of Oil* (London and New York: Verso, 2011).

25. E. Drake quoted in Kevin Phillips, *American Theocracy: The Peril and Politics of Radical Religion, Oil, and Borrowed Money in the 21st Century* (New York: Viking, 2006), 9.

26. Phillips, *American Theocracy*, 9; and see also Alfred W. Crosby, *Children of the Sun: A History of Humanity's Unappeasable Appetite for Energy* (New York: W.W. Norton & Co., 2006), 85–92.

27. Robert Zoellner, *The Salt-Sea Mastodon: A Reading of Moby-Dick* (Berkeley: University of California Press, 1973), 112.

28. "Ahab mirrors the voracious conquistador of the Spanish Black Legend," writes Antonio Barrenechea in his "Conquistadors, Monsters, and Maps: *Moby-Dick* in a New World Context," *Comparative American Studies* 7, no. 1 (March 2009): 23.

29. The phrase "mariners, and renegades and castaways," which provided C. L. R. James with his title, is found in *Moby-Dick*, 26: 117; I borrow the phrase "labor as flood" (and much else) from Casarino, *Modernity at Sea*, 115; incidentally, in his description of "the period from 1760 to 1880" as "the anatomical era in American medicine," Michael Sappol also explains that sailors were a choice target for dissection (which usually provided itself by means of grave robbery). "It is also likely," he adds, that many of them were nonwhite—as any reader of *Moby-Dick* knows, the antebellum sailing ship was a multiracial workplace—and this perhaps also made them safer targets for body-snatching activities" (Sappol, *Traffic of Dead Bodies*, 75, 116).

30. Eduardo Cadava, "The Guano of History," in *Cities Without Citizens*, ed. Eduardo Cadava and Aaron Levy (Philadelphia: Slought Books, 2003), 161–62.

31. Quoted in James, *Mariners*, 78.

32. Casarino, *Modernity at Sea*, 4.

33. Constance Classen, "The Odor of the Other: Olfactory Symbolism and Cultural Categories," *Ethos* 20, no. 2 (June 1992): 133–66.

34. Donna Haraway pointed out that "the air-pump was a technology of gender at the heart of scientific knowledge. It was the general absence, not the occasional presence, of women...that gendered the experimental way of life in a particular way" (D. Haraway, *Modest_Witness@ Second_Millennium. FemaleMan©_Meets_OncoMouse™: Feminism and Technoscience* [New York: Routledge, 1997], 28), and she is even more correct when it comes to the blood pump, something I am taking the risk of blatantly reinscribing here and throughout. On the vexed question of "Melville and women," and more generally on sexual difference in Melville, see Robyn Wiegman, "Melville's Geography of Gender," in *Herman Melville: A Collection of Critical Essays*, ed. Myra Jehlen (Englewood Cliffs, N.J.: Prentice Hall, 1994), 187–98; for a review of the discussion see Jennifer M. Wing, "Defining Women in *Moby-Dick*," in *Misogynism in Literature: Any Place, Any Time*, ed. Britta Zangen (Frankfurt am Main: Peter Lang, 2004), and the extensive *Melville and Women*, ed. Elizabeth Schultz and Haskell Springer (Kent, Ohio: Kent State University Press, 2006); on the related masculinity see David Leverenz, *Manhood and the American Renaissance* (Ithaca, N.Y.: Cornell University Press, 1989), and Philip Armstrong, "'Leviathan is a Skein of Networks': Translations of Nature and Culture in *Moby-Dick*," *ELH* 71, no. 4 (2004): 1039–1063.

35. Wai-chee Dimock, *Empire for Liberty: Melville and the Poetics of Individualism* (Princeton, N.J.: Princeton University Press, 1989), chap. 4 ("Blaming the Victim").

36. Heimert, "Moby-Dick and American Political Symbolism," 533; for singular contributions and extensive critical discussions of Melville and politics, see Michael Paul Rogin, *Subversive Genealogy*; Wai-chee Dimock, *Empire for Liberty: Melville and the Politics of Individualism* (Princeton, N.J.: Princeton University Press, 1989); William V. Spanos, *The Errant Art of Moby-Dick: The Canon, the Cold War, and the Struggle for American Studies* (Durham, N.C.: Duke University Press, 1995); Nancy Fredricks, *Melville's Art of Democracy* (Athens, Ga., and London: University of Georgia Press, 1995).

37. Arnold Rampersad, "Melville and Race," in *Herman Melville: A Collection of Critical Essays*, ed. Myra Jehlen (Englewood Cliffs, N.J.: Prentice Hall, 1994), 173.

38. D. H. Lawrence, "Herman Melville's 'Moby Dick,'" in *Critical Essays on Herman Melville's Moby-Dick*, ed. Brian Higgins and Hershel Parker (New York: G. K. Hall, 1992), 209.

39. Henry Nash Smith, "The Image of Society in *Moby-Dick*," in *Moby-Dick: Centennial Essays*, ed. Tyrus Hillway and Luther S. Mansfield (Dallas, Tex.: Southern Methodist University Press, 1953), 59–75; Smith mentions "homo homini lupus" as ancient wisdom, which it is, and makes no reference to Hobbes (67). Catherine Zuckert argues that Melville is among a group of American authors who were "seeking the grounds on which a just community might be founded" (C. H. Zuckert, *Natural Right and the American Imagination: Political Philosophy in Novel Form* [Savage, Md.: Rowman & Littlefield, 1999], 1).

40. Sharon Cameron, *The Corporeal Self: Allegories of the Body in Melville and Hawthorne* (New York: Columbia University Press, 1991), 4.

41. As Bainard Cowan puts it, "to remember (and re-member) the dismembered" is the task of allegory, a task most eloquently described by Walter Benjamin (B. Cowan, *Exiled Waters:*

Moby-Dick and the Crisis of Allegory [Baton Route: Louisiana State University Press, 1982], 10). Cowan traces the "association between body and text" to Paul (19) and goes on to document its Christian history, such as it is redeployed by Melville.

42. Cameron, *Corporeal Self*, vii, 7.

43. Cameron, *Corporeal Self*, 24, 32.

44. Thomas Hobbes, *Leviathan*, ed. Richard Tuck (Cambridge: Cambridge University Press, 1996), XXIV, 174; and see Shapin and Schaffer, *Leviathan and the Air-Pump*, who dedicate their entire study to that debate and its significance, and see Latour, *We Have Never Been Modern*, 15–48; Armstrong takes matters further in his "Leviathan is a Skein of Networks."

45. On "science's blood flow," see Bruno Latour, *Pandora's Hope: Essays on the Reality of Science Studies* (Cambridge, Mass.: Harvard University Press, 1999), 80–112; on responses to Hobbes's *Leviathan*, see Samuel Mintz, *The Hunting of Leviathan: Seventeenth-Century Reactions to the Materialism and Moral Philosophy of Thomas Hobbes* (Cambridge: Cambridge University Press, 1962). On Hobbes and Harvey, see Shapin and Schaffer, *Leviathan*; and see also J. W. N. Watkins, *Hobbes's System of Ideas: A Study in the Political Significance of Philosophical Theories* (London: Hutchinson University Library, 1973); Thomas A. Spragens Jr., *The Politics of Motion: The World of Thomas Hobbes* (Lexington: University Press of Kentucky, 1973); Martin A. Bertman, *Body and Cause in Hobbes: Natural and Political* (Wakefield, N.H.: Longwood Academic, 1991).

46. Melville, *Moby-Dick*, xvii ("Extracts"); Branka Arsić demonstrates a parallel and rich importance of the circulation of blood in "Bartleby" (B. Arsic, *Passive Constitutions or 7½ Times Bartleby* [Stanford, Calif.: Stanford University Press, 2007], esp. 34–38).

47. William Harvey, *An Anatomical Disquisition on the Motion of the Heart and Blood in Animals*, in *The Works of William Harvey*, trans. Robert Willis, M.D. (Philadelphia: University of Pennsylvania Press, 1989), 78.

48. Roger French, "Harvey in Holland: Circulation and the Calvinists," in *The Medical Revolution of the Seventeenth Century*, ed. Roger French and Andrew Wear (Cambridge: Cambridge University Press, 1989), 86; French makes clear that the theological stakes were very high, whereas I have argued that Harvey's own discovery is to be seen as an instance of what Amos Funkenstein has called "secular theology" (A. Funkenstein, *Theology and the Scientific Imagination from the Middle Ages to the Seventeenth Century* [Princeton, N.J.: Princeton University Press, 1986].

49. Lisa Jardine, *Ingenious Pursuits: Building the Scientific Revolution* (New York: Anchor Books, 1999), 114; incidentally, as he "demonstrated his famous air pump," Boyle is also said to have turned "a piece of roasted mutton into pure blood, which was very rare" (Samuel Pepys, quoted in John Rogers, *The Matter of Revolution: Science, Poetry, and Politics in the Age of Milton* [Ithaca, N.Y.: Cornell University Press, 1996], 179).

50. Noel Malcolm writes that Hobbes "performed dissections with William Petty" (N. Malcolm, *Aspects of Hobbes* (Oxford: Oxford University Press, 2002), 320. A member of numerous clubs of "the Oxford Physiologists," Petty also worked with Boyle on dissections and collaborative study (Robert G. Frank Jr., *Harvey and the Oxford Physiologists: Scientific Ideas and Social Interaction* [Berkeley: University of California Press, 1980], 95).

51. Frank, *Harvey and the Oxford Physiologists*, xiv.

52. Jardine, *Ingenious Pursuit*, 114; and see also Frank, *Harvey*, esp. 140–63.

53. Thomas Hobbes, *Elements of Philosophy; The First Section, Concerning Body*, in *The English Works of Thomas Hobbes of Malmesbury*, ed. Sir William Molesworth (Darmstadt: Scientia Verlga Aalen, 1962 [1839]), vol. I, viii.

54. Watkins, *Hobbes's System*, 69; and see 31, 41.

55. See Quentin Skinner, *Visions of Politics. Volume III: Hobbes and Civil Science* (Cambridge: Cambridge University Press, 2002). Skinner elaborates on the relation to Harvey's anatomy in his *Reason and Rhetoric in the Philosophy of Hobbes* (Cambridge: Cambridge University Press, 1996), esp. 215, 263–64, 328.

56. Hobbes, *Leviathan*, XXIV, 175; see also Samantha Frost, "Reading the Body: Hobbes, Body Politics, and the Vocation of Political Theory," in *Vocations of Political Theory*, ed. Jason A. Frank and John Tambornino (Minneapolis: University of Minnesota Press, 2000), 263–83.

57. Watkins, *Hobbes's System*, 75; and see Hobbes, *Elements of Philosophy*, 392; for an account that has the head as the source, see Hobbes, *Human Nature*, in *The English Works of Thomas Hobbes*, vol. IV, 31.

58. Carolyn Porter, "Call Me Ishmael, or How to Make Double-Talk Speak," in *New Essays on Moby-Dick*, ed. Richard H. Brodhead (Cambridge: Cambridge University Press, 1986), 100.

59. D. H. Lawrence, "Herman Melville's 'Moby Dick,'" in *Critical Essays on Herman Melville's Moby-Dick*, ed. Brian Higgins and Hershel Parker (New York: G. K. Hall & Co., 1992), 198; Szendy provides a rare discussion of Melville's conversation with Hobbes in his *Prophecies*; and see Agnès Derail, "Melville's Leviathan: *Moby-Dick; or, the Whale* and the Body Politic," in *L'Imaginaire-Melville: A French Point of View*, ed. Viola Sachs (Saint-Denis: Presses universitaires de Vincennes, 1992), 23–31; as well as Julian Markels, *Melville and the Politics of Identity: From King Lear to Moby-Dick* (Urbana: University of Illinois Press, 1993); Eyal Peretz briefly testifies to the fact that "*Moby-Dick* is a critical reading of Hobbes's *Leviathan*" (E. Peretz, *Literature, Disaster, and the Enigma of Power: A Reading of 'Moby Dick'* [Stanford, Calif.: Stanford University Press, 2003], 162, n. 59), and John Lardas Modern says it "may be seen as a rewriting of Thomas Hobbes's *Leviathan*" (Modern, *Secularism*, xxiv). Notably (or perhaps symptomatically), Hobbes barely registers as a significant source in Merton Sealts's description of Melville's library and readings (Merton M. Sealts Jr., *Melville's Reading* [University of South Carolina, 1988]); William Braswell reports that Melville "praised Hobbes's style, calling him a 'paragon of perspicuity,' and wrote of Hobbes's 'mental habits' as though he knew a good deal about them" (W. Braswell, *Melville's Religious Thought* (New York: Pageant Books, 1959), 14.

60. Sappol, *Traffic of Dead Bodies*; the connection with Melville, mentioned earlier, is made on p. 116, but Harvey, Hunter, Paley, and Melville's acquaintance, Oliver Wendell Holmes, are present throughout; and see Samuel Otter, *Melville's Anatomies* (Berkeley: University of California Press, 1999); John Hunter, "the distinguished eighteenth century medical man, whose careful dissection of whales . . . laid the groundwork for scientific whale anatomy," is also the author of *A Treatise on Blood*, where argument is made regarding the blood as a living organ (Howard P. Vincent, *The Trying-Out of Moby-Dick* [Carbondale: Southern Illinois University Press, 1949], 218).

61. Lewis Mumford saw in science "the element that makes the difference," which "separates [Melville] completely from the poets of that day" (L. Mumford, "Moby-Dick," in *Critical Essays*, 405), and see Richard Dean Smith, *Melville's Science. "Devilish Tantalization of the Gods!"* (New York: Garland Publishing, 1993), and more directly related to medicine, by the same author, *Melville's Complaint: Doctors and Medicine in the Art of Herman Melville* (New York: Garland Publishing, 1991).

62. Melville, "Hawthorne and His Mosses," 243.

63. Quoted in Eduardo Cadava, "The Guano of History," in *Cities Without Citizens*, ed. Eduardo Cadava and Aaron Levy (Philadelphia: Slought Books, 2003), 148. As Rebecca Herzig pointed out to me, my use of the word *technology* is an anachronism (see Leo Marx, "Technology: The Emergence of a Hazardous Concept," *Social Research* 64, no. 3 [Fall 1997]: 965–89). Herzig also indicates that Melville participates in the elaboration of a concept (the word *technology* in its modern sense only appears in 1829) that was still in the process of being articulated. As she writes, "Melville so effectively conveys that sense of force beyond our control or comprehension even before the language of 'technology' was available to him. And, after reading your piece, I see that he does that through that extended metaphor of blood: a fluid, circulatory system of governance. . . . It allows him to place agency/causality in a 'system' (rather than in discrete individuals or institutions) without resorting to the regular abstractions. The sovereign rule (as you say) of Blood rather than Capital or (as we would say) Technology" (personal communication, April 12, 2007).

64. William V. Spanos, *The Errant Art of Moby-Dick*, 5; Spanos is not speaking about blood here, but I hope to show that by invoking him in that way, I remain true to his intent, particularly when considering his critique of a "vestigial—untheorized—nationalism" in the study of Melville (25) or the links between the different "sites of American knowledge production (the discourse on 'cetology'), economic production (the *Pequod* as factory) and sociopolitics (the *Pequod* as the state)" (47).

65. Szendy compellingly unfolds the lines and pages of this equation (Szendy, *Prophecies*, 40–47).

66. Northrop Frye, *Anatomy of Criticism: Four Essays* (Princeton, N.J.: Princeton University Press, 1957), 308ff. Frye's suggestion was taken up by Samuel Otter who extends it by describing Melville as performing "anatomies of anatomies" (Otter, *Melville's Anatomies*, 6 and 102).

67. Herman Melville, *Pierre; Or The Ambiguities* (Evanston and Chicago, Ill.: Northwestern University Press, 1971), 304. Andrew Delbanco, whose rendering I am using here, invokes this passage as testimony of the way in which Melville looked "back at his labors on *Moby-Dick*" (A. Delbanco, *Melville, His World and Work* [New York: Alfred A. Knopf, 2005], 146).

68. James, *Mariners*, 107, 119.

69. Describing "a transition from Christian to evolutionary notions of the 'chain of being,' which simultaneously broke down received divisions between the human and the animal," Philip Armstrong interrogates the direction of the process and suggests it moves *toward* cannibalism as well (P. Armstrong, "'Leviathan is a Skein of Networks': Translations of

Nature and Culture in *Moby-Dick*," *ELH* 71, no. 4 [2004]: 1040, 1049, 1051; and see Geoffrey Sanborn, *The Sign of the Cannibal: Melville and the Making of a Postcolonial Reader* [Durham, N.C.: Duke University Press, 1998]).

70. 1 Kings 17:1 and 7.

71. 1 Kings 18:43.

72. 1 Kings 19:10 and 14; and see Job 1:15, 17, 19; quoted in "Epilogue," *Moby-Dick*, 573.

73. 1 Kings 22:37–38.

74. "Captain Ahab—Dylan calls him '*Ay*-rab,' no doubt in tribute to Ray Stevens's 1962 hit 'Ahab, the Arab,' pronounced "Ay-rab'" (Greil Marcus, *Like a Rolling Stone: Bob Dylan at the Crossroads* [New York: PublicAffairs, 2005], 63; the reference is to "Bob Dylan's 115th Dream" in his 1965 *Bringing It All Back Home*); on the significance of the desert and wilderness—"whether of land or of sea—in Melville, see Nathalia Wright, *Melville's Use of the Bible* (New York: Octagon Books, 1980), 48ff.

75. Carl Schmitt, *The* Nomos *of the Earth in the International Law of the* Jus Publicum Europaeum, trans. G. L. Ulmen (New York: Telos Press, 2006); Catherine Zuckert briefly evokes the connection between Melville and Hobbes on the precise matter of "loose-fish" and "fast-fish" (Zuckert, *Natural Right*, 102). She otherwise finds that "Melville's stance is more Rousseauian" (100); Michael Rogin describes in detail Melville's personal relation to a major figure of the law, namely, Judge Lemuel Shaw, "chief justice of the Massachusetts Supreme Court . . . the embodiment of the law . . . his decisions decisively shaped the histories both of American slavery and of Melville's fiction" (Rogin, *Subversive Genealogy*, 10).

76. Szendy elaborates on the figure of the reader as "fast-fish" and "loose-fish" in *Prophecies*, esp. 53–55.

77. D. Graham Burnett has shown, in a different way, that "the case" of "leviathan" is at the center of a configuration that involves law, science, economics, and politics: "when Leviathan is the text, the case is altered" (D. G. Burnett, *Trying Leviathan: The Nineteenth-Century New York Court Case That Put the Whale on Trial and Challenged the Order of Nature* [Princeton, N.J.: Princeton University Press, 2007], vii; quoting *Moby-Dick* in the book's epigraph). "There is no documentary evidence," Burnett writes, "establishing that Melville was familiar with *Maurice v. Judd* [the case to which Burnett's book is dedicated], but it is hard to imagine that he could have missed it" (107). Although *Moby-Dick* is marginal to the book as a whole, many of the issues raised by Burnett gain traction from it and are in fact resonating through it.

78. Commenting on what she sees as Ahab's representative American individualism, Susan McWilliams does not mention Hobbes either, but she writes that "the grand threat of an *isolato* culture is that when the individuals within it act, they tend to act with a kind of brutality that is self-denying and ultimately self-destroying" (S. McWilliams, "Ahab, American," *Review of Politics* 74 [2012]: 238). For intimations of the Christological, see Paul Brodtkorb Jr., *Ishmael's White World: A Phenomenological Reading of* Moby-Dick (New Haven, Conn.: Yale University Press, 1965), esp. 75–76; "Ahab, one might say, has taken upon himself the suffering of mankind" (Braswell, *Melville's Religious Thought*, 66; or again: "Melville defines Ahab as both god-like and ungodly, included in Christendom's

census, yet alien" (William Hamilton, *Melville and the Gods* [Chico, Calif.: Scholars Press, 1985], 49); Susan Mizruchi, for her part, argues that "Ahab is himself an inflamed offering" (S. L. Mizruchi, *The Science of Sacrifice: American Literature and Modern Social Theory* [Princeton, N.J.: Princeton University Press, 1998], 141). Interestingly enough, a Christological reading is implicitly reinforced by noting, with Eyal Peretz, that "like the whale, Ahab bleeds continuously to death, but unlike the whale, his bleeding is prolonged into an entire life. *The human, like the whale, bleeds to death, but human bleeding becomes an entire life-time*" (Peretz, *Literature, Disaster*, 136–38, n. 3 and n. 5); for a parallel discussion regarding Bartleby, see Branka Arsić, *Passive Constitutions*, 174, n. 49.

79. As Edward Said notes, the figure of sovereignty that is Ahab corresponds to the American empire. Indeed, "whereas other empires control land, America seeks sovereignty over water, and whereas other seamen use the oceans as a way from one landfall to another or as a site on which to do what they do on land (plunder, for instance), only the Americans, and the Nantucketer in particular, live on and derive a living from the sea" (E. Said, *Reflections on Exile*, 363). Ahab is "a convincing example of the new imperialism [Melville] ascribes to the United States" (368).

80. Zoellner, *The Salt-Sea Mastodon*, 68.

81. Casarino, *Modernity at Sea*, 9; Schmitt points out that in its mythological import, Leviathan also appears as a huge mechanism of which the modern warship is "the most complete image." The state and the whale are figures of "the technically perfect mechanism of a big ship in the hands of an absolute authority who determines its course" (Schmitt, *Leviathan in the State Theory*, 50).

82. Hamilton, *Melville and the Gods*, 57; Alexis de Tocqueville, *Democracy in America*, 278.

83. As he notes the relation between Harvey and Hobbes (and the importance of understanding that there was, as of yet, no opposition between "mechanism" and "organism"), Carl Schmitt underscores the importance of the *machina*, of the *automaton*, and ultimately the *homme-machine* as "the mechanization of the human body," a kind of cyborg at the origin of the modern conception of the state. "The state," he writes, "is body and soul, a *homo artificialis*, and, as such, a machine. It is a manmade product. Its material and maker, *material et artifex*, machine and engineer, are one and the same, namely, men" (Schmitt, *Leviathan in the State Theory*, 34, and see 41 and 91–100). Implicitly questioning the Hobbesian reading (not to mention the Cold War one, which saw in Ahab the perfect totalitarian leader), Catherine Zuckert argues that Ahab "represents an emphatically democratic hero who has risen on the basis of his own deeds and talents, not so much to high social or political position as to nobility of soul" (Zuckert, *Natural Rights*, 106).

84. On the leaking body of Ahab and its relation to rhetoric, see Doran Larson, "Of Blood and Words: Ahab's Rhetorical Body," *Modern Language Studies* 25, no. 2 (Spring 1995): 18–33. Larson's title promises a more extensive discussion of blood but only attends to a limited number of hematological instances.

85. Bryan Wolf, "When Is a Painting Most Like a Whale?: Ishmael, *Moby-Dick*, and the Sublime," in *New Essays on Moby-Dick*, ed. Richard H. Brodhead (Cambridge: Cambridge University Press, 1986), 143; and see Rogin, *Subversive Genealogy*, 138; Rogin refers in this context to "one body in Christ" and to Hobbes (139–40).

86. "Ahab's obsession," writes Michael Rogin, "unifies a society fragmented by human claims to power. The whaling industry disintegrated leviathans, but it could not restore wholeness to the world. Ahab creates, from leviathan's natural body, the *Pequod*'s organic, communal, social body" (Rogin, *Subversive Genealogy*, 128). It is not irrelevant, of course, to note that one of the crew at least is said to have "live blood," which "would not spoil like bottled ale," although he too (namely, Starbuck) is "a Quaker by descent" (XXVI, 115).

87. In his mythological reading, H. Bruce Franklin describes Ahab as "a priest-king-god" as well as a "ruler of the infernal regions," and finally as "Christ to Moby Dick as Leviathan" (H. Bruce Franklin, *The Wake of the Gods: Melville's Mythology* [Stanford, Calif.: Stanford University Press, 1963], 74 and 98); for Russ Castronovo, this is "political vampirism" (R. Castronovo, *Fathering the Nation: American Genealogies of Slavery and Freedom* [Berkeley: University of California Press, 1995], 100): Ahab is a "mad priest" and the crew "responds uniformly to the ritual, drinking together as one body" (93); Richard Slotkin sees here and elsewhere an instance of "the cannibal Eucharist" (R. Slotkin, "*Moby-Dick*: The American National Epic," in *Twentieth-Century Interpretations of Moby-Dick*, ed. Michael T. Gilmore [Englewood Cliffs, N.J.: Prentice Hall, 1977], 19–20); Graham Burnett refers to "rites of blooding and consumption" (Burnett, *Trying Leviathan*, 128).

88. Derail, "Melville's Leviathan," 26.

89. As Melville wrote to Hawthorne on June 29, 1851, "this is the book's motto (the secret one)—Ego non baptiso te in nomine—but make out the rest yourself" (Herman Melville, *Correspondence* [Evanston, Ill.: Northwestern University Press and The Newberry Library, 1993], 196). Henry A. Murray famously borrows the phrase for his title but does not have much to say about it specifically (H. A. Murray, "In Nomine Diaboli," in *Moby-Dick: Centennial Essays*, 3–22).

90. The phrase "practical cetology" appears in *Moby*-Dick, 74: 329; I borrow this section subtitle from Rebecca M. Herzig's *Suffering for Science: Reason and Sacrifice in Modern America* (New Brunswick, N.J.: Rutgers University Press, 2005). Having been slowly guided into the history of science by Amos Funkenstein and by Dominique Pestre, I am here particularly indebted to Herzig for convincing me of the importance of its approaches on the question of blood, as well as on my reading of *Moby-Dick*. Incidentally, Herzig makes clear that "suffering *for* science" was always about causing pain as well. Sappol joins her in putting this in the specifically medical, anatomical context, "the necessity of causing pain and the ability to heal through procedures that caused pain, were part of the vocabulary of curative authority" (Sappol, *Traffic of Dead Bodies*, 59).

91. On the invention of the laboratory as a new social space, see Shapin and Schaffer, *Leviathan and the Air-Pump*, 57ff.; on the ship (and the sea narrative) as a "laboratory," see Casarino, *Modernity at Sea*, 9, 33, 38; on circulation, again see Casarino, *Modernity at Sea*, 84ff.; John Lardas Modern also comments on the importance of circulation in Melville and elsewhere (Lardas Modern, *Secularism in Antebellum America*, e.g., 33, 51, 196).

92. David F. Noble, *The Religion of Technology: The Divinity of Man and the Spirit of Invention* (New York: Penguin Books, 1999).

93. On *scientist*, see Smith, *Melville's Science*, xv; on *science*, see Herzig, *Suffering for Science*, 42; Herzig dates the word *scientist* to 1834 (45).

94. Herzig, *Suffering for Science*, 7; the phrase "the imagined body of science" appears on p. 22 and throughout.

95. Herzig, *Suffering for Science*, 46.

96. Herzig, *Suffering for Science*, 46.

97. Herzig, *Suffering for Science*, 95–96; on Ahab's "Faustian compulsion," his embodying "the thrust of Western man for ultimate knowledge and power," as well as the specific and "paradoxical affinity between Ahab and the mechanistic view of life," see Leo Marx, *The Machine in the Garden: Technology and the Pastoral Idea in America* (New York: Oxford University Press, 1964), 293, 299.

98. John Lardas, "Deus in Machina Movet: Religion in the Age of Technological Reproducibility," *Method and Theory in the Study of Religion* 18 (2006): 16.

99. Smith, *Melville's Science*, 144.

100. On Hobbes and "ultimate fluidity," see Shapin and Schaffer, *Leviathan and the Air-Pump*, 115–25; for a specific discussion of blood in Hobbes, again see Shapin and Schaffer, *Leviathan and the Air-Pump*, 95, and in relation to Harvey (ignoring, however, the matter of "sanguification"), 127. Branka Arsić has a beautiful note on "various liquids and juices" in Melville's *Typee* (B. Arsić, *Passive Constitutions*, 186, n. 14).

101. Emily-Jane Cohen, quoted in Sappol, *Traffic in Dead Bodies*, 49; Sappol goes on to describe how in 1841, a medical professor "lauded anatomy as the medical discipline that was the 'most legitimately deserving the name of a science.' Outside the profession, the same sentiment prevailed: an 1850 Boston paper praised anatomy as 'one of the most scientific of all scientific subjects' " (55). The genealogical links to Harvey and Boyle were explicit (56).

102. As Siegfried Gideon refers to it, the technology of butchery would soon become the massive "mechanization of death" in the modern slaughterhouses (see S. Gideon, *Mechanization Takes Command: A Contribution to Anonymous History* (Oxford: Oxford University Press, 1948), esp. 209–246.

103. Otter, *Melville's Anatomies*, 101.

104. Otter, *Melville's Anatomies*, 132.

105. Edward Said, *Orientalism* (New York: Vintage, 1979), and more specifically, Dorothee Metlitsky Finkelstein, *Melville's Orienda* (New Haven, Conn.: Yale University Press, 1961), and for the later works, Hilton Obenzinger, *American Palestine: Melville, Twain, and the Holy Land Mania* (Princeton, N.J.: Princeton University Press, 1999); and see also Malini Johar Schueller, *U.S. Orientalisms: Race, Nation, and Gender in Literature, 1790–1890* (Ann Arbor: University of Michigan Press, 2001), as well as Timothy Marr's discussion of "American Islamicism" (T. Marr, *The Cultural Roots of American Islamicism* [Cambridge: Cambridge University Press, 2006], esp. chap. 5). In these last two books, Melville is shown to have played a key role in those traditions.

106. Gabriele Schwab, from whom I borrow the subtitle of this section, elaborates on the importance of the face as one of the central features of the "aesthetics of blankness in *Moby-Dick*" (G. Schwab, *Subjects Without Selves: Transitional Texts in Modern Fiction* [Cambridge, Mass.: Harvard University Press, 1994], 49–71); on philology and blood, see F. Max Müller's remarks, quoted by Tomoko Masuzawa, to the effect that "Arian blood" circulates in the languages of the Indian subcontinent (T. Masuzawa, *The Invention*

of World Religions: Or , How European Universalism Was Preserved in the Language of Pluralism [Chicago: University of Chicago Press, 2005], 239).

107. Thomas R. Trautmann, *Lewis Henry Morgan and the Invention of Kinship* (Berkeley: University of California Press, 1987), 6; Morgan was the inspiration beyond Frederick Engels, *The Origin of the Family, Private Property and the State In the Light of the Researches of Lewis H. Morgan*, ed. Eleanor Burke Leacock (New York: International Publishers, 1972).

108. On the specific changes in the history of the family—Melville's being one particular illustration—see Michael Rogin, *Subversive Genealogy*; on Melville's desire "to transcend kinship," see Dimock, *Empire for Liberty*, 140ff.; what kinship is or would be is hardly clarified thereby, although Dimock's reference later to Herman Humphrey and his notion of the family as "a little state, or empire within itself" does evoke the specific history of blood that occupies us here (158–59).

109. Lardas Modern, *Secularism in Antebellum America*, 226, but the whole chapter on Morgan is essential reading (183–238).

110. Quoted in Trautmann, *Lewis Henry Morgan*, 8.

111. As we have seen in previous chapters, blood continues to rule the discourse of kinship even as the importance (or even relevance) of biology is interrogated. Thus Marshall Sahlins uses the term, at times suspending it within quotation marks, at other times without such marks (M. Sahlins, *The Use and Abuse of Biology: An Anthropological Critique of Sociobiology* [Ann Arbor: University of Michigan Press, 1976], 42, 58). David M. Schneider interrogates the primacy of biology, even its relevance ("why has kinship been defined in terms of the relations that arise out of the process of human sexual reproduction?" he repeatedly asks) but never asks about the *language* of blood: why has kinship been defined *in some societies* as a matter of blood? Why not bones, for example? Or even "spirit"? (D. M. Schneider, *A Critique of the Study of Kinship* [Ann Arbor: University of Michigan Press, 1984], 175.)

112. For the most recent and thorough discussion of Melville and the Bible, see Ilana Pardes, *Melville's Bibles* (Berkeley: University of California Press, 2008).

113. Rogin, *Subversive Genealogy*, 107.

114. I should point out that I am not attributing any redemptive or even subversive dimension to the recasting of relations such as it takes place here and elsewhere. I fully agree with Leo Bersani that homoeroticism and other forms of "new relations that are being tested" in *Moby-Dick* are "socially unthreatening" (Leo Bersani, *The Culture of Redemption* [Cambridge, Mass.: Harvard University Press, 1990], 147). I am simply trying to draw attention to the manner in which "the oxymoronic impasse of democracy" is also traversed by blood (149).

115. Otter, *Melville's Anatomies*, 152.

116. Sappol explains that the term *obstetrics* supplanted *man-midwifery* in the 1820s, at the end of a long process whereby physicians "eventually supplanted the midwife" (Sappol, *Traffic in Dead Bodies*, 61ff).

117. For a more extended discussion of images of "lines and ropes" in *Moby-Dick*, see Gunn, *Interpretation of Otherness*, 165ff.; Rita Bode elaborates on the maternal dimension of such lines and cords in " 'Suckled by the Sea': The Maternal in *Moby-Dick*," in *Melville and*

Women, ed. Elizabeth Schultz and Haskell Springer (Kent, Ohio: Kent State University Press, 2006), 194–95.

118. Dimock, *Empire for Liberty*, 139; Spanos identifies this "ontological orphanage" as a positive contribution of Melville's writing (Spanos, *Errant Art*, 161 and 155).

119. Schmitt, *Leviathan in the State Theory*, 94.

120. Melville, "Hawthorne and His Mosses," 243.

121. Otter, *Melville's Anatomies*, 249; Otter is commenting on *Pierre* but invokes the passage I have quoted earlier, which critics have read as reflecting Melville's sentiments about *Moby-Dick*.

122. Wai-chee Dimock, *Empire for Liberty*, 10; on the heart as "engine," see William Paley, *Natural Theology or Evidence of the Existence and Attributes of the Deity, Collected from the Appearances of Nature*, ed. Matthew D. Eddy and David Knight (Oxford: Oxford University Press, 2006), 82.

123. Sappol, *Traffic in Dead Bodies*, 187; on the head and heart debate, see Jacques Le Goff, "Head or Heart? The Political Use of Body Metaphors in the Middle Ages," in *Fragments for a History of the Human Body, Part Three*, ed. Michel Feher, Ramona Naddaff, and Nadia Tazi (New York: Zone Books, 1989), 13–26; and Scott Manning Stevens, "Sacred Heart and Secular Brain," in *The Body in Parts: Fantasies of Corporeality in Early Modern Europe*, ed. David Hillman and Carla Mazzio (New York: Routledge, 1997), 263–82.

124. It may be possible to argue that within the "exiled waters" described by Bainard Cowan as a rhetorical and literary issue, there is a measure of blood. Cowan suggests this when he invokes the circulatory system of "American criticism," which "has had to ignore increasingly the vast network of texts and structures that interlock to form the heart of *Moby-Dick*" (Cowan, *Exiled Waters*, 5); for an interrogation of the notion of literature in Melville, see Peretz, *Literature, Disaster*; Peretz elaborates on the book's "bleeding sentences" (71).

125. Delbanco, *Melville*, 137.

126. Melville, "Hawthorne and His Mosses," 245.

127. Albert Camus, "Melville: Un créateur de mythes," in *Moby-Dick as Doubloon*, 249.

128. Melville, "Hawthorne and His Mosses," 244.

129. Lawrence Buell, "*Moby-Dick* as Sacred Text," in *New Essays on Moby-Dick*, 53–72; and see also in the same volume T. Walter Herbert, "Calvinist Earthquake: *Moby-Dick* and Religious Tradition," 109–140.

130. John T. Irwin, *American Hieroglyphics: The Symbol of the Egyptian Hieroglyphics in the American Renaissance* (Baltimore, Md.: Johns Hopkins University Press, 1983), 344.

131. Geoffrey Stone, "The Blasphemy in *Moby-Dick*," in *Moby-Dick as Doubloon*, 195.

132. Newton Arvin, "The Whale," in *Moby-Dick as Doubloon*, 223.

133. Hamilton, *Melville and the Gods*, 1; "Critical Extracts" (Ann Douglas), in *Ahab*, ed. Harold Bloom (New York: Chelsea House Publishers, 1991), 42–43; Lawrence Buell, "*Moby-Dick* as Sacred Text," 69.

134. Vincent, *The Trying-Out of Moby-Dick*, 78; Richard H. Brodhead, "Trying All Things: An Introduction to *Moby-Dick*," in *New Essays on Moby-Dick*, ed. R. H. Brodhead (Cambridge: Cambridge University Press, 1986), 5.

135. Thompson, *Melville's Quarrel with God*, 423; "Critical Extracts" (James Baird), in *Ahab*, 27.

136. Duban, *Melville's Major Fiction*, 148; D. H. Lawrence, "Herman Melville's 'Moby Dick,'" 210.

137. Mark C. Taylor, *About Religion: Economies of Faith in Virtual Culture* (Chicago: University of Chicago Press, 1999), 26.

138. Taylor, *About Religion*, 4; and compare Loren Baritz's assertion that Melville's work is "so purely American because of the depths of his rejection of America" (quoted in Sacvan Bercovitch, *The American Jeremiad* [Madison: University of Wisconsin Press, 1978], 194); for Walter Herbert, "Melville challenged the theocentric scheme by working within its own terms" (Herbert, *Moby-Dick and Calvinism*, 9).

139. Timothy Marr's compelling discussion of "Melville's Literary Islamism" comes to mind here, as does Bruce Franklin's account of "Melville's Mythology," but the matter far exceeds a *religious* tradition (or traditions), as it demands a reconsideration of the very meaning of the term *Christianity*—as a matter of blood.

140. Speaking of "the blackness in Hawthorne," which fixes and fascinates him, this blackness that "furnishes the infinite obscure of his back-ground," Melville invokes Shakespeare as well. The blackness, along with other things, "these are the things that make Shakespeare, Shakespeare" (Melville, "Hawthorne and His Mosses," 244).

141. Herman Melville, *Pierre; Or The Ambiguities* (Evanston and Chicago, Ill.: Northwestern University Press, 1971), 215.

142. Melville, *Pierre*, 215 (emphasis added).

CONCLUSION: ON THE CHRISTIAN QUESTION (JESUS AND MONOTHEISM)

1. Jacques Derrida, *Archive Fever: A Freudian Impression*, trans. Eric Prenowitz (Chicago: University of Chicago Press, 1996), 65–66; translation altered.

2. Sigmund Freud, *Moses and Monotheism*, trans. James Strachey, *The Standard Edition of the Complete Psychological Works of Sigmund Freud, volume XXIII (1937–1939)* (London: The Hogarth Press and the Institute of Psychoanalysis, 1964), 42; after the established convention, I will refer to the *Standard Edition* with the abbreviation *SE*, followed by the volume number and page.

3. "Conditions of representability" are described by Freud as part of the "dream-work" in *The Interpretation of Dreams* (S. Freud, *The Interpretation of Dreams*, trans. James Strachey, *SE V*, 338ff.). Ilse Grubrich-Simitis proposes to read *Moses and Monotheism* as "a kind of daydream" in her *Early Freud and Late Freud: Reading Anew* Studies on Hysteria *and* Moses and Monotheism, trans. Philip Slotkin (New York: Routledge, 1997), 50.

4. Michel de Certeau, *The Writing of History*, trans. Tom Conley (New York: Columbia University Press, 1988), 325.

5. Jacques Lacan, *The Ethics of Psychoanalysis 1959–1960 (The Seminar of Jacques Lacan, Book VII)*, trans. Dennis Porter (New York: W.W. Norton & Co., 1997), 143; like any other myth, Lacan goes on to say, "it doesn't explain anything." And later, "The myth of the murder of the father is the myth of a time for which God is dead. But if for us God is dead, it is because he always has been dead, and that's what Freud says. He has never been the father except in the mythology of the son" (177).

6. Freud, *Moses*, 20, n. 1; quoting J. H. Breasted, *A History of Egypt from the Earliest Times to the Persian Conquest* (New York: Charles Scribner's Sons, 1905). Samuel Weber comments and expands that "Freud introduces the hero of his novel by quoting Breasted, one of his scholarly sources, to the effect that Moses was 'the first individual in human history'" (S. Weber, *Targets of Opportunity: On the Militarization of Thinking* [New York: Fordham University Press, 2005], 71).

7. Sigmund Freud, *Totem and Taboo*, trans. James Strachey, in *SE XIII (1913–1914)*, 154.

8. I am referring to the German title of Elias Canetti's *Crowds and Power*, trans. Carol Stewart (New York: Continuum, 1981).

9. Whereas Freud "robs" the Jews of their founder, Jan Assmann generously "grants" them their murderous foundation. A different kind of universalist, Assmann elaborates on Freud to tell the story of how "hate came into the world," together with what he calls "the Mosaic distinction" ("the distinction between true and false in religion" and a "murderous distinction" as he describes it). Assmann finds confirmation of this momentous event in the Babylonian Talmud, which glosses the name *Sinai* (the mountain) with the word *sin'ah* (hate). "To be sure," Assmann proceeds to acknowledge that this may amount to "holding the victims responsible for their fate," but he strenuously rejects accusations of anti-Semitism. True, "the Jews murdered by the Nazis were not asked whether they professed faith in Judaism. But this should not blind us to the nature of faith, nor prevent us from seeing how inseparably this category is bound up with the Mosaic distinction" (J. Assmann, *The Price of Monotheism*, trans. Robert Savage [Stanford, Calif.: Stanford University Press, 2010], 21; the phrase "murderous distinction," which refers to the Mosaic distinction, first appears in Assmann, *Moses the Egyptian: The Memory of Egypt in Western Monotheism* [Cambridge, Mass.: Harvard University Press, 1997], 6).

10. Harold P. Blum, "Freud and the Figure of Moses: The Moses of Freud," in *Reading Freud's Reading*, ed. Sander L. Gilman, Jutta Birmele, Jay Geller, and Valerie D. Greenberg (New York: New York University Press, 1994), 121; placing Freud in the tradition that posits a foreign founder for the political community, Bonnie Honig cites Rousseau on the great souls, "the few great cosmopolitan souls, who surmount the imaginary barriers that separate peoples and who, following the example of the sovereign Being who created them, *include the whole human race in their benevolence*" (Rousseau, *Social Contract*, in Honig, *Democracy and the Foreigner* [Princeton, N.J.: Princeton University Press, 2001], 14).

11. As Mahmood Mamdani makes clear, the identification of mass murder, of genocide, is inextricable from its historicity, from the problem of temporality, its ranges and its paradoxes: "It is killing with intent to eliminate an entire group of people—a race, for example—that is genocide. Those who prioritize knowing over doing assume that genocide is the name of a consequence, and not its context or cause. But how do we decipher 'intent' except by focusing on *both* context and consequence? The connection between the two is the only clue to naming an action" (M. Mamdani, *Saviors and Survivors: Darfur, Politics, and the War on Terror* [New York: Pantheon, 2009], 3).

12. Cathy Caruth, *Unclaimed Experience: Trauma, Narrative, and History* (Baltimore, Md.: Johns Hopkins University Press, 1996), 15.

13. For a brilliant rendering of *Moses'* contemporary—and murderous—futures within the confines of a Jewish question ("Jewish guilt"), see James Schamus, "Next Year in *Munich*: Zionism, Masculinity, and Diaspora in Spielberg's Epic," *Representations* 100, no. 1 (Fall 2007): 53–66.

14. Jacques Lacan, *The Other Side of Psychoanalysis (The Seminar of Jacques Lacan. Book XVII)*, trans. Russell Grigg (New York: W.W. Norton & Co., 2007), 117, translation slightly altered; earlier, Lacan describes the story of the murder of the primal father as "exactly the contrary" of the myth of Oedipus (114).

15. Michel de Certeau, "Psychoanalysis and Its History," trans. Brian Massumi, in de Certeau, *Heterologies: Discourse on the Other* (Minneapolis: University of Minnesota Press, 1986), 9.

16. de Certeau, *Writing of History*, 327, referring to a number of interpretations that go in this direction, beginning with David Bakan, *Sigmund Freud and the Jewish Mystical Tradition* (Princeton, N.J.: D. Van Nostrand Company, 1958). De Certeau himself insists on Freud's ambivalence, suggesting with Otto Rank that "the 'founding father' of psychoanalysis" might have been defending paternal authority (de Certeau, *Writing of History*, 327).

17. Robert A. Paul, *Moses and Civilization: The Meaning Behind Freud's Myth* (New Haven, Conn.: Yale University Press, 1996), 7; Paul approves and argues for the correctness of Freud's account, as long as we recognize that it refers to a "great mythic narrative." "That is, if we look at the Christian Mass and its related beliefs and practices as enactments of a great mythic narrative, then we may ask whether we can interpret the ritual, and the story of the Passion it dramatizes, as the fruition of an earlier deed—not, however, an event that has occurred earlier in *history* but rather an event that occurs earlier *in the mythic narrative itself*" (11). How does history become the history of trauma, then? It does not, according to Paul. Instead, myth must be conceived as the myth of trauma.

18. Paul, *Moses and Civilization*, 120.

19. On the Christian origins of the comparative study of religion, see Maurice Olender, *The Languages of Paradise: Race, Religion, and Philology in the Nineteenth Century*, trans. Arthur Goldhammer (Cambridge, Mass.: Harvard University Press, 1992); Serge Margel, *Superstition: L'anthropologie du religieux en terre de chrétienté* (Paris: Galilée, 2005); Tomoko Masuzawa, *The Invention of World Religions: Or, How European Universalism Was Preserved in the Language of Pluralism* (Chicago: University of Chicago Press, 2005).

20. "Next Easter in Rome" is Freud's suggested closing to a 1900 letter to Fliess (Paul C. Vitz, *Sigmund Freud's Christian Unconscious* [Grand Rapids, Mich.: Eerdmans, 1993], 73; Vitz elaborates on the peculiar importance of Easter for Freud). "Freud's ambivalence toward Christianity" is discussed by Michael Mack in *German Idealism and the Jew: The Inner Anti-Semitism of Philosophy and German-Jewish Responses* (Chicago: University of Chicago Press, 2003), 138.

21. Paul, *Moses and Civilization*, 208; Vitz, for his part, asserts that "an orthodox Christian would agree with Freud" (*Sigmund Freud's Christian Unconscious*, 170).

22. Vitz, *Sigmund Freud's Christian Unconscious*, 1; and see R. S. Lee, *Freud and Christianity* (Harmondsworth: Penguin Books, 1967).

23. Even committed Christians who feel positively inclined toward psychoanalysis take at their point of departure the discord that opposes it to Christianity (see, e.g., B. G. Sanders,

Christianity After Freud: An Interpretation of the Christian Experience in the Light of Psycho-Analytic Theory [London: Geoffrey Bles, 1949]; Françoise Dolto, *L'évangile au risque de la psychanalyse* [Paris: Seuil, 1980]). Jan Assmann opposes Freud's "simplistic outsider's perspective" to an "insider perspective," according to which "it must be said that Christianity is primarily and fundamentally distinguished by a principle that could no more aptly be characterized than with Freud's phrase, 'progress in intellectuality'" (Assmann, *The Price of Monotheism*, 100–101); then again, Freud may have been ironically (and contradictorily) making use of Christian clichés, topoi, and archetypal formulas (ibid.). Needless to say, the only operative conception of Christianity throughout is that it is a religion. Obviously.

24. William Robertson Smith, *Religion of the Semites* (New Brunswick, N.J.: Transaction Publishers, 2002), and see Paul, *Moses and Civilization*, 121.

25. Yosef Hayim Yerushalmi, *Freud's Moses: Judaism Terminable and Interminable* (New Haven, Conn.: Yale University Press, 1991), 2; for a striking extension of the argument see Schamus, "Next Year in *Munich.*" Jacob Taubes, whose "prolegomena to these passages in Freud" I am duly following (J. Taubes, *The Political Theology of Paul*, trans. Dana Hollander [Stanford, Calif.: Stanford University Press, 2004], 94), had characteristically noted that "most interpreters who connect A with A think to themselves, the Jew, what's his name? Sigmund Freud, what makes more sense than that he sees his own reflection in Moses! Nothing of the sort" (89). Two recent studies of "Freud's Jewish Body," of his "Jewish question," are excellent illustrations and provide comprehensive summaries of the issue. They are: Jay Geller, *On Freud's Jewish Body: Mitigating Circumcisions* (New York: Fordham University Press, 2007), and Eliza Slavet, *Racial Fever: Freud and the Jewish Question* (New York: Fordham University Press, 2009), and see *The Jewish World of Sigmund Freud: Essays on Cultural Roots and the Problem of Religious Identity*, ed. Arnold D. Richards (Jefferson, N.C.: McFarland, 2010)

26. de Certeau, "The Freudian Novel: History and Literature," in de Certeau, *Heterologies*, 19.

27. "Something is even more troubling," writes Nicole Loraux with regard to Freud's *Moses* and its applicability across categorical (and regional) borders: "if only religious phenomena— in this case, Jewish monotheistic religion—can accurately be described as having first 'undergone the fate of being repressed,' what will we find in *Moses and Monotheism* when we focus on politics rather than religion, and when, moreover, the politics is *Greek?*" (N. Loraux, *The Divided City: On Memory and Forgetting in Ancient Athens*, trans. Corinne Pache and Jeff Fort [New York: Zone Books, 2006], 77.)

28. G. G. Stroumsa, "Myth into Novel: The Late Freud on Early Religion," in *New Perspectives on Freud's "Moses and Monotheism,"* ed. Ruth Ginsburg and Ilana Pardes (Tübingen: Max Niemeyer, 2006), 206.

29. It is the least of Freud's concerns, Lacan says with regard to the "moral experience" around which *Moses* is centered, "to call it religious, since it tends to universalize it, and yet he does formulate it in the very terms by which the properly Judeo-Christian religious experience historically developed and formulated it" (J. Lacan, "Discours aux Catholiques," in Lacan, *Le triomphe de la religion* [Paris: Seuil, 2005], 37). With regard to the reception of Freud as an intervention in the field of "religion," Stroumsa may have overstated the case (see next note).

30. "What science is worth, for Freud, is first of all as a bulwark against the religious illusion" (Jean-Luc Nancy, *L'adoration (Déconstruction du christianisme, 2)* [Paris: Galilée, 2010], 143). Richard J. Bernstein makes a most forceful argument for considering both Freud's "Jewish question" and the universality of his "religious" concerns (Richard J. Bernstein, *Freud and the Legacy of Moses* [Cambridge: Cambridge University Press, 1998]), and see also Philip Rieff, who underscores "Freud's claim to encompass impartially . . . the entire historical variety of religion" while directing its most heavy and accurate critique, Rieff says, at Christianity (P. Rieff, *The Jew of Culture: Freud, Moses, and Modernity*, ed. Arnold M. Eisen and Gideon Lewis Kraus [Charlottesville: University of Virginia Press, 2008], 34). I am of course not disputing Freud's "animus," as Rieff calls it, against Christianity, but I do wonder about a range, minimally a more ambivalent set of emotions with regard to a broader and more refined conception of Christianity in its singularity. The point seems lost as well in R. Z. Friedman's otherwise illuminating "Freud's Religion: Oedipus and Moses," *Religious Studies* 34, no. 2 (May 1998): 135–49.

31. Honig, *Democracy and the Foreigner*, 15; I already quoted de Certeau who explains that "the act which turns into a trace through writing is the rejection of the founding father" (de Certeau, *Writing of History*, 325). Honig's argument is that "the figure of the foreign-founder may be a way of managing some paradoxes of democratic founding, such as the alienness of the law" (7); she recalls that his foreignness means that "the founder must leave" (23), and there are many ways for him (or her) to do so, many stories about his (or her) departure, literal or figurative. Honig remains notably agnostic on whether such narratives are at all necessary to any founding—political, rather than religious, founding—in her account (and see as well B. Honig, "Declarations of Independence: Arendt and Derrida on the Problem of Founding a Republic," *American Political Science Review* 85, no. 1 (March 1991): 97–113; and, for a proximate reading of *Totem and Taboo* as a narrative of the founding of law, which may well be identical to religion, see Peter Fitzpatrick, *Modernism and the Grounds of Law* [Cambridge: Cambridge University Press, 2001]).

32. Grubrich-Simitis explains that "while working on *Moses and Monotheism,* Freud himself was concerned with the matter of the survival of psychoanalysis" (Grubrich-Simitis, *Early Freud and Late Freud*, 10); Bernstein locates the matter (and the matter of survival) in another, if equally particular, locale: "if I were asked," he writes, "while standing on one foot, to say what *The Man Moses and the Monotheistic Religion* is about, I would not hesitate to say it is about hope and the promise of Jewish survival" (Bernstein, *Freud and the Legacy of Moses*, 116); Cathy Caruth, finally, argues that reading *Moses* will reveal "the full complexity of the problem of survival at the heart of human experience" (Caruth, *Unclaimed Experience*, 58).

33. On the nature of the psychoanalytic collective in its *rapport sans rapport* to Freud, see Samuel Lézé's brilliant *L'autorité des psychanalystes* (Paris: Presses Universitaires de France, 2010).

34. As Paul Vitz strikingly puts it, "Freud can be viewed as a brilliant psychologist of fallen human nature, who showed us, with Oedipus, that the Anti-Christ is Everyman" (Vitz, *Christian Unconscious*, 170).

35. Freud, *Interpretation of Dreams*, 276.

36. Robert Paul adds regicide to the list (Paul, *Moses and Civilization*, 210). No wonder Lou Andreas-Salomé ever so gently threw back at Freud his own claim that he was relying on "a non-Jewish scholar" (Freud was referring to Ernst Sellin). As she writes her reply, Andreas-Salomé cites Freud to Freud and fills in the blanks: "the fact that you enlist in your cause a 'non-Jewish scholar,' who already discussed the Moses question *from the historical and Christian point of view*, is surely in your favor" (I cite from the 1935 exchange between Freud and Andreas-Salomé reproduced in Bernstein, *Freud and the Legacy of Moses*, 117–18; emphasis added). It should not be too hard to see Freud as "raising" the Jews to the level of the Christian manly man (Boyarin)—"we too are capable of killing the father!"—or indeed as participating in the extraction of Jews (i.e., Semites) from the arid race and the accursed group of "people without mythology": Semites as Aryans. This is the famous debate that opposed Goldziher to Renan (see Maurice Olender, *Languages of Paradise: Race, Religion, and Philology in the Nineteenth Century*, trans. Arthur Goldhammer [Cambridge, Mass.: Harvard University Press, 1992], esp. chap. 8, "Semites as Aryans," and see Marc Nichanian, *Mourning Philology: Art and Religion at the Margins of the Ottoman Empire*, trans. G. M. Goshgarian [New York: Fordham University Press, 2014]).

37. Philippe Lacoue-Labarthe and Jean-Luc Nancy, "La panique politique," trans. Céline Surprenant, in Lacoue-Labarthe and Nancy, *Retreating the Political*, ed. Simon Sparks (New York: Routledge, 1997), 21; Gayatri Spivak goes further, and away, from religion when she writes about *Moses and Monotheism* that "transcendental imperialism by this Freudian account is a Jewish game accidentally practised by the British" (G. C. Spivak, "Psychoanalysis in Left Field and Fieldworking: Examples to Fit the Title," in *Speculations After Freud: Psychoanalysis, Philosophy, and Culture*, ed. Sonu Shamdasani and Michael Münchow [New York: Routledge, 1994], 60).

38. Weber, *Targets of Opportunity*, 72.

39. "The obvious connection of this with the destiny of the founder of a later religion does not concern us here," says Freud, who will of course contradict himself later (Freud, *Moses*, 35–36).

40. Freud, *Moses*, 135; and see de Certeau on the centrality of terms like *replace* and *taking the place* in the book (*Writing of History*, 326). Kenneth Reinhard is undoubtedly correct when he argues that, at one level of the text, "Freud's narrative seems to take up the typological accounts of interpretation and history inaugurated by Saint Paul and fulfilled in Hegel, in which history entails the translation and fulfillment of the past—the Hebrew Bible becomes the 'Old Testament' which always already pointed at the New Dispensation that vitiates its laws" (K. Reinhard, "Lacan and Monotheism: Psychoanalysis and the Traversal of Cultural Fantasy," *Jouvert: A Journal of Postcolonial Studies* 3, no. 1–2 [1999]: §21). What this says about "religion"—and about Christianity—is what concerns me.

41. Paul, *Moses and Civilization*, 129; Freud famously uses the phrase "the greatest of its sons" in the opening line of *Moses and Monotheism*; and see, more generally, *The Dead Father: A Psychoanalytic Inquiry*, ed. Lila J. Kalinich and Stuart W. Taylor (London: Routledge, 2009).

42. As much as he resists his own insight, as much as he recognizes the paucity of Freud's manifest views on "the great religions," insisting on the incompatibility of "psychoanalysis

and religion," Philip Rieff must admit that at the center of Freud's argument, there is "the same great event," which is followed by "attempts to appease the sense of guilt" (P. Rieff, *The Jew of Culture: Freud, Moses, and Modernity*, ed. Arnold M. Eisen and Gideon Lewis Kraus [Charlottesville: University of Virginia Press, 2008], 53). This is precisely "the conception," and the moment, "at which psychoanalysis meets Christianity back-to-back, so speak. . . . Freud's meaning and that of Christianity are indeed close but," adds Rieff as if to reassure himself, "completely at odds" (55). Earlier, Rieff described the way in which "what the religious think of as a moral evil . . . [Freud] discusses as entirely natural" (52). Freud naturalizes, indeed, universalizes Christian morality by way of a narrative that perceives all "religions" as based on the same social ground, for it is a universal "society" and not only "religion" that was and is "now based on complicity in the common crime" (Freud, *Totem and Taboo*, 145). That Freud sought to "remedy" this situation otherwise hardly diminishes the specificity of the shared ground. However, exonerating Judaism, as Rieff reads Freud, changes little of the restricted understanding of the Christian conception here at work as "religious."

43. Hard to read indeed. After "Heidegger's Jewish followers," is it not time perhaps to hear of Freud's Christian followers? (See *Heidegger's Jewish Followers*, ed. Samuel Fleischacker [Pittsburgh, Pa.: Duquesne University Press, 2008].) Would *that* make any difference? There is, at any rate, a veritable cottage industry that testifies to a (mostly) Judeophilic obsession, and it is hardly limited to Jews. Commenting, one would think, on another time and on another place, Ronald Schechter writes of "the emphasis on the apparent future of the Jewish question in the postrevolutionary age, and the corresponding need to cast retrospective judgments on those who previously addressed the Jewish question." But, Schechter continues, these have "occluded what would otherwise seem surprising: the bizarre preoccupation of French commentators with a tiny and weak minority. The disjunction between the attention to the Jews and their 'objective' importance calls for an explanation. In 1789 there were at most forty thousand Jews in the kingdom, roughly one-fifth of 1 percent of the total population. Living literally as well as figuratively on the periphery of France, most were poor, many desperately so, and together they were correspondingly lacking in political power and social prestige" (R. Schechter, *Obstinate Hebrews: Representations of Jews in France, 1715–1815* [Berkeley: University of California Press, 2003], 7). Incidentally, Schechter attends to the period when "Egyptomania," so identified by Assmann, is at its height.

44. Yerushalmi, *Freud's Moses*, 100; Derrida devotes much of *Archive Fever* to a meditation on what is implied in this futurity, and more generally to what such privileging of Judaism might mean after Freud; see my "Zionist Fever (Mal de Sionisme)," in *Living Together: Jacques Derrida's Communities of Violence and Peace*, ed. Elisabeth Weber (New York: Fordham University Press, 2013) 45–58.

45. Freud, *Totem and Taboo*, xiv ("Preface to the Hebrew Translation").

46. As she endorses the view that, along with Viennese Jewry, Freud "adopted universalism as a specifically Jewish dream of freedom and justice which was the task of the Jews in general, and psychoanalysis in particular, to disseminate across the globe," Jacqueline Rose asserts that "Freud believed . . . that it was the task of Jewish particularity to *universalize* itself"

(J. Rose, "Response to Edward Said," in Edward W. Said, *Freud and the Non-European* [London and New York: Verso with The Freud Museum, 2003], 72; to be sure, this is a Jewish particularity that has shed "the trappings of linguistic, religious and national identity," or most of them (71). There is a long list of monikers to invoke here from "the non-Jewish Jew" to the "imaginary Jew" and beyond (see, e.g., Judith Butler, *Parting Ways: Jewishness and the Critique of Zionism* [New York: Columbia University Press, 2012], 28–30). Could the Christians—the "secular Christians," the "non-Christian Christians" too—please stand up?

47. Bakan, who inquires into Jewish antinomianism, writes that "through the image of Moses, as he develops it in his *Moses and Monotheism*, Freud becomes a Gentile psychologically as he makes a Gentile of Moses" (Bakan, *Sigmund Freud*, 148); Edward Said favors the attribute "European" and rightly asserts that "Freud's was a Eurocentric view of culture," adding: "and why should it not be?" (Said, *Freud and the Non-European*, 16).

48. Ludwig Feuerbach, *The Essence of Christianity*, trans. George Eliot (New York: Prometheus Books, 1989); Feuerbach is of course famous for having revived the theory of "projection" whereby the divine is a reflection of human self-image, however distorted: theology is anthropology, man is God, but then God is dead, and all that.

49. Lacan, *Ethics of Psychoanalysis*, 174, 176.

50. Vitz, *Sigmund Freud's Christian Unconscious*; John Schad, *Queer Fish: Christian Unreason from Darwin to Derrida* (Brighton: Sussex Academic Press, 2004).

51. See Vitz, *Sigmund Freud's Christian Unconscious*, 20; on the identification with Jesus, see 69, 87, 140; Vitz underscores Freud's ambivalence as well, when he discusses his identification with the Anti-Christ, see 158–66; and see Vitz's intriguing chart of Christ as Anti-Oedipus (169).

52. With regard to genre, Kenneth Reinhard shifts our attention away from the oft-repeated matter of the "historical novel" and proposes an alternative technical term also used by Freud, namely, "construction"—an untimely intervention, "a patently fictional narrative that is meant not to interpret [western culture's] desire but to get at the cause of its desire, to encounter and refigure the *fantasy* that is at its core, *its fantasy of origins*" (K. Reinhard, "Lacan and Monotheism," §23; Reinhard insists on reinscribing the "religious" reading of Freud's *Moses* [§27]). As to gender and race (along with Judaism and Orientalism), the most compelling treatment can be found in Daniel Boyarin, *Unheroic Conduct: The Rise of Heterosexuality and the Invention of the Jewish Man* (Berkeley: University of California Press, 1997), and, more recently, Dušan I. Bjelić, *Normalizing the Balkans: Geopolitics of Psychoanalysis and Psychiatry* (Farnham: Ashgate, 2011).

53. As I mentioned, Guy Stroumsa commented on the curious and near exclusive focus on Judaism in the reception of Freud's *Moses*, as if Freud did not have much to say about religion conceived generally (Stroumsa, "Myth into Novel," in *New Perspectives on Freud's "Moses and Monotheism,"* 203–216). There is little room to disagree, but for the lingering sense that Moses continues to be perceived throughout as a *religious* figure, and Judaism as the paradigmatic "monotheism" (if it gets really bad, Islam gets foregrounded as well). By way of an alternative, Lacoue-Labarthe and Nancy offer, to my mind, a most rigorous reading of "Freud and the political." On psychoanalysis and Islam, see *Umbr(a)* (2009), special issue on Islam.

54. De Certeau, *The Writing of History*, 313; translation slightly altered.

55. Daniel Colluciello Barber cites and applies this fabulous phrase and discusses its uses and limits toward a consideration "the differential tension that resides in the concept of Christianity" in *On Diaspora: Christianity, Religion, and Secularity* (Eugene, Ore.: Cascade Books, 2011), xii, 120.

56. Denise Kimber Buell, *Why This New Race: Ethnic Reasoning in Early Christianity* (New York: Columbia University Press, 2005).

57. Rieff suggests that Freud defines Jewishness "more fundamentally, in terms of a certain kind of character rather than by adherence to a specific creed" (Rieff, *The Jew of Culture*, 35).

58. Freud, *Totem and Taboo*, 153; Freud goes on to say that "*we are driven to conclude* that the sin was a murder." It is Robert Paul who underscores, later explaining that if Freud could do that, if "on the basis of the Christian myth," he could reconstruct "the underlying myth of the primal horde," then "it seems probable that everyone else can too, albeit perhaps unconsciously" (Paul, *Moses and Civilization*, 7 and 173).

59. Schad, *Queer Fish*, 62.

60. Freud was a big admirer of Ernest Renan, who was an early proponent of the thesis that Jesus was not a Semite, but an Aryan, a foreign founder that should have made it to the top of the list. Like Renan, Freud could also be said to have tried "to wrest Christianity from the clutches of Semitic monotheism" (Olender, *Languages of Paradise*, 69) and see Susannah Heschel, *The Aryan Jesus: Christian Theologians and the Bible in Nazi Germany* (Princeton, N.J.: Princeton University Press, 2008). One can also turn the pattern around and claim the founding father/murdered son as a Semite or even an Arab-Jew.

61. Freud, *Moses*, 116.

62. Boyarin, *Unheroic Conduct*, 246; I agree with Edward Said, of course, that Freud is not quite as bad as Gobineau, though he is very close to Renan, closer than Said allows (Said, *Freud and the Non-European*, 16); and compare Schamus's reading of Spielberg's own "family romance" by way of *E.T.* and *Munich*'s Avner as "perfect Zionists" (Schamus, "Next Year in *Munich*," 64). Schamus does invoke the compelling reading of *E.T.* by Frank Tomasulo as a full-blown Christology, which recasts Jesus, and Christianity, in the central role (F. P. Tomasulo, "The Gospel According to Spielberg in *E.T.: The Extra-Terrestrial*," *Quarterly Review of Film and Video* 18, no. 3 [2001]: 273–182).

63. Assmann, *Moses the Egyptian*, 1; emphasis added; in spite of multiple hints and allusions to Nazism, I could find no reference to the question of race or to racism in this book, nor in its sequel, *The Price of Monotheism*.

64. David Lloyd calls attention to "a triangle of identifications" and recalls that, for Freud, "it is not the Moses of the Bible that Michelangelo has portrayed" (D. Lloyd, "Rage Against the Divine," *South Atlantic Quarterly* 106, no. 2 [Spring 2007]: 360–61); it is not too far-fetched to suggest that the same can be said about Freud's own portrayal, and Lloyd does precisely that when he writes that "the motive that Freud attributes to Michelangelo is then his own, the attempt to depict Moses as *a reproachless adult, a higher being, an* übermensch" (363; emphasis added).

65. Freud, *Moses*, 109.

66. Weber, *Targets of Opportunity*, 77; as Robert Paul explicates, "despite having been killed, that same person must go on to survive, having by his death erased the universal guilt

for the primal crime. . . . The execution and miraculous resurrection of Jesus fulfills these conditions" (Paul, *Moses and Civilization*, 77).

67. And consider that since Paul, Luther, and Hobbes, the—hardly marginal—Christian question may well have been, as Joshua Mitchell has it, "Who Was Moses, Who Was Christ?" (J. Mitchell, "Luther and Hobbes on the Question: Who Was Moses, Who Was Christ?" *The Journal of Politics* 53, no. 3 [August 1991]: 676–700.)

68. Taubes, *The Political Theology of Paul*, 39; on Jesus and Moses, see Paul, *Moses and Civilization*, chap. 10.

69. "The Lord said to Moses, 'I have seen this people, how stiff-necked they are. Now let me alone, so that my wrath may burn hot against them and I may consume them; and of you I will make a great nation.' But Moses implored the Lord his God . . ." (Exodus 32:9–11); since the flood at least, it does appear that God was always the first to advocate the genocidal option: a different history of trauma, perhaps. Yet there is one God, but perhaps more than one origin.

70. Boyarin refers to a " 'personality split' within Moses and likewise the Jewish people. Each of the 'religious' categories which Freud projects is, like Rome, split and doubled. Judaism is not identical with itself, and neither is Christianity" (Boyarin, *Unheroic Conduct*, 267–68).

71. Schad, *Queer Fish*, 54; Assmann illustrates the precise temporality of the matter: "Paul the Jew bridges the opposition between Jews and Christians in the same way as Moses the Egyptian did in the religious controversies of the Age of Enlightenment" (Assmann, *Moses the Egyptian*, 11).

72. Schad, *Queer Fish*, 74; compare with Bakan's claim that "Freud's assertions make the Jews the butt of the greatest joke in history; and thereby achieve for them also the greatest gain in history, freedom from persecution. It converts them from threatening to comical and stupid characters" (Bakan, *Sigmund Freud*, 156).

73. On Freud and Herzl, and Moses, see Boyarin, *Unheroic Conduct*, 221–70.

74. Bakan proposed early on to read Freud in light of Leo Strauss's famous argument; see Bakan, *Sigmund Freud*, 142, and see L. Strauss, *Persecution and the Art of Writing* (Chicago: University of Chicago Press, 1988 [1952]); as Boyarin puts it: "While still in the killing field of the 'evil harvest,' Freud perceives the violence of civilization. Safe, however, among 'the great[est] ruling power among the white nations,' " Freud reaches "a kind of insight, all the more powerful for its being disguised in the texts. This disguise is not, on this reading, mystification but 'persecution and the art of writing.' " (Boyarin, *Unheroic Conduct*, 269).

75. Freud, *Moses*, 91; and see Schad, *Queer Fish*, 51. On Pater Schmidt, see Vitz, *Sigmund Freud's Christian Unconscious*, 197–99, and see Yerushalmi's disparaging comments in *Freud's Moses*, 120, n. 24. Curiously, Yerushalmi has nothing to say about Vitz's main thesis, based as it is in a somehow larger archive than the "discovery" on which Yerushalmi grounds himself. Freud's final statement on anti-Semitism, to the effect that he forgot what Christian had written a critique of anti-Semitism, in effect, a critique of Christianity, is well worth pondering as a corrective (Freud, "A Comment on Anti-Semitism," trans. James Strachey, *SE XXIII*, 289–93). Boris Groys revives the argument on the collusion of anti-Semitism and anti-Christianism in his *Introduction to Antiphilosophy*, trans. David Fernbach (New York: Verso, 2012), 105–130.

76. Schad, *Queer Fish*, 65.

77. Vitz mentions Jacques Maritain's 1939 *A Christian Looks at the Jewish Question* and states that what "Freud said on the 'Jewish question' [is] exactly what Maritain had said: It is as if he were speaking, like Maritain, from within the logic of the Christian position, and not as a Jewish 'outsider'" (Vitz, *Christian Unconscious*, 203).

78. Yuri Slezkine, *The Jewish Century* (Princeton, N.J.: Princeton University Press, 2004).

79. Georges Bataille, "Manuel de l'Anti-Chrétien," in *Oeuvres complètes II (Écrits posthumes 1922–1940)* (Paris: Gallimard, 1970), 377–78; in the outline of this unfinished manual, Bataille mentions current events as reasons to "confront Christianity directly and not fascism" (387).

80. Max Weber, *The Protestant Ethic and the Spirit of Capitalism*, trans. Talcott Parsons (New York: Routledge, 1992), 77.

81. M. A. Gillespie, *The Theological Origins of Modernity* (Chicago: University of Chicago Press, 2008); Mark C. Taylor, *After God* (Chicago: The University of Chicago Press, 2007).

82. Karl Löwith, *Meaning in History* (Chicago: University of Chicago Press, 1949), and see Kathleen Davis, *Periodization and Sovereignty: How Ideas of Feudalism and Secularization Govern the Politics of Time* (Philadelphia: University of Pennsylvania Press, 2008).

83. "The phrase '*verus Israel*' (the true Israel), inasmuch as it is the self-definition of Christianity, is also the matrix of the conception of historical truth that remains—and here I deliberately use an all-embracing term—our own" (Carlo Ginzburg, *Wooden Eyes: Nine Reflections on Distance*, trans. Martin Ryle and Kate Soper [New York: Columbia University Press, 2001], 155; in his "Secularism, the Christian Ambivalence Toward the Jews and the Notion of Exile" [forthcoming], Amnon Raz-Krakotzkin alerts us to the significance of Ginzburg's argument).

84. Marcel Gauchet, *The Disenchantment of the World: A Political History of Religion*, trans. Oscar Burge (Princeton, N.J.: Princeton University Press, 1999); Jean-Luc Nancy, *Dis-Enclosure: The Deconstruction of Christianity*, trans. Bettina Bergo et al. (New York: Fordham University Press, 2008); and see, for an illuminating survey, Ward Blanton, *Displacing Christian Origins: Philosophy, Secularity, and the New Testament* (Chicago: University of Chicago Press, 2007).

85. Ernst H. Kantorowicz, *The King's Two Bodies: A Study in Mediaeval Political Theology* (Princeton, N.J.: Princeton University Press, 1997).

86. For Arendt, Christianity spelled the end of worldly politics; see my "The Meaning of Life," *Critical Inquiry* 37, no. 4 (Summer 2011): 697–723.

87. Harold J. Berman, *Law and Revolution: The Formation of the Western Legal Tradition* (Cambridge, Mass.: Harvard University Press, 1983); Legendre's work spans many volumes, but consider for starters, *L'inestimable objet de la transmission (Étude sur le principe généalogique en Occident)* (Paris: Fayard, 2004).

88. Michel Foucault, *Security, Territory, Population: Lectures at the College de France 1977–1978*, trans. Graham Burchell (New York: Picador, 2009), 130.

89. Giorgio Agamben, *The Kingdom and the Glory: For a Theological Genealogy of Economy and Government*, trans. Lorenzo Chiesa and Matteo Mandarini (Stanford, Calif.: Stanford University Press, 2011), 91; Marie-José Mondzain, *Image, Icon, Economy: The Byzantine*

Origins of the Contemporary Imaginary, trans. Rico Franses (Stanford, Calif.: Stanford University Press, 2005); and see also, on the image, Georges Didi-Huberman, *L'image ouverte: Motifs de l'incarnation dans les arts visuels* (Paris: Gallimard, 2007); in the footsteps of Erich Auerbach, Jacques Rancière extends the incarnation argument to literature, which turns out to be Christian as well (J. Rancière, *The Flesh of Words: The Politics of Writing*, trans. Charlotte Mandell [Stanford, Calif.: Stanford University Press, 2004]). More typical, Didi-Huberman is ambivalent about the Christianity of his argument, and note that the word *Christian* is in any case absent from the title, although none of the works leaves any doubt as to what the object of inquiry is or what the archive upon which it depends.

90. Jacques Derrida, "Above All, No Journalists!" Trans. Samuel Weber, in *Religion and Media*, ed. Hent de Vries and Samuel Weber (Stanford, Calif.: Stanford University Press, 2001).

91. Denise Kimber Buell, *Why This New Race: Ethnic Reasoning in Early Christianity* (New York: Columbia University Press, 2005); Colin Kidd, *The Forging of Races: Race and Scripture in the Protestant Atlantic World, 1600–2000* (Cambridge: Cambridge University Press, 2006); J. Kameron Carter, *Race: A Theological Account* (Oxford: Oxford University Press, 2008); Willie James Jennings, *The Christian Imagination: Theology and the Origins of Race* (New Haven, Conn.: Yale University Press, 2010).

92. *Conversion to Modernities: The Globalization of Christianity*, ed. Peter van der Veer (New York: Routledge, 1996).

93. Alexandre Kojève, "L' origine chrétienne de la science moderne," *Mélanges Alexandre Koyré II (L'aventure de l'esprit)* (Paris: Herman, 1964), 295–306; David F. Noble, *The Religion of Technology: The Divinity of Man and the Spirit of Invention* (New York: Penguin Books, 1999).

94. Margel and Masuzawa were mentioned earlier, but see of course Talal Asad, *Genealogies of Religion: Discipline and Reasons of Power in Christianity and Islam* (Baltimore, Md.: Johns Hopkins University Press, 1993). Guy G. Stroumsa, *A New Science: The Discovery of Religion in the Age of Reason* (Cambridge, Mass.: Harvard University Press, 2010) offers a milder version of the argument and refers to a "discovery" of religion rather than to its invention, suggesting perhaps that religions are natural objects that, like America, awaited their discovery by the Christian West.

95. Bruno Latour writes of "practices of purification" as creating "entirely distinct ontological zones" in *We Have Never Been Modern*, trans. Catherine Porter (Cambridge, Mass.: Harvard University Press, 1993), 10–11

96. See Joel Robbins, "What is a Christian? Notes Toward an Anthropology of Christianity," *Religion* 33 (2003): 191–99; Joel Robbins, *Becoming Sinners: Christianity and Moral Torment in a Papua New Guinea Society* (Berkeley: University of California Press, 2004); and see *The Anthropology of Christianity*, ed. Fenella Canell (Durham, N.C.: Duke University Press, 2006); as well, among a number of other works, Webb Keane, *Christian Moderns: Freedom and Fetish in the Mission Encounter* (Berkeley: University of California Press, 2007); Simon Coleman, *The Globalization of Charismatic Christianity* (Cambridge: Cambridge University Press, 2007); commenting on the work of Talal Asad, I have tried to engage the issue in "The Idea of an Anthropology of Christianity," *Interventions* 11, no. 3 (2009): 367–93.

97. Michel Foucault, *Discipline and Punish: The Birth of the Prison*, trans. Alan Sheridan (New York: Vintage, 1995), 305; to remain with the elemental means of course to recall the liquidity that has preoccupied me throughout and that delineates but the contours of a much larger edifice, however changing.

98. Judith Surkis, *Sexing the Citizen: Morality and Masculinity in France, 1870–1920* (Ithaca, N.Y.: Cornell University Press, 2006), 8.

99. Mayanthi L. Fernando, *The Republic Unsettled: Islam, Secularism, and the Future of France*, forthcoming from Duke University Press; I substitute the word *Christianity* for Fernando's *France*.

100. Surkis, *Sexing the Citizen*, 8.

101. de Certeau, *Writing*, 320.

102. It may be important to point out that if tradition is the advent and preservation of law as the enduring will of the murdered father, then Christianity is not quite a tradition either: after all, the father is and is not murdered, that is to say, first, that Christians are innocent of his murder, and second, God (the father and the son) lives. He lives! The resurrection is the ultimate institutionalization of the future of murder as innocence.

103. Freud, *Moses*, 88–89.

104. René Girard, *Violence and the Sacred*, trans. Patrick Gregory (Baltimore, Md.: Johns Hopkins University Press, 1977).

105. The classic statement on the Christian *figura* is found in Erich Auerbach, "Figura," trans. Ralph Mannheim, in Auerbach, *Scenes from the Drama of European Literature* (Minneapolis: University of Minnesota Press, 1984), 11–76.

106. Freud, *Moses,* 135.

107. Freud, *Interpretation of Dreams*, 276.

108. Freud, *Totem and Taboo*, 154; Erich Fromm does not mention Moses, but he elaborates on some of the important substitutions of Jesus and father, which he understands as social and historical (E. Fromm, *The Dogma of Christ and Other Essays on Religion, Psychology, and Culture* (New York: Holt, Rhinehart and Winston, 1963).

109. I follow Freud's cue in describing the death of God on the cross as the death (and therefore murder) of the Father. In a recent rendering, "The death of God is 'good news' because God is no longer regarded from the point of view of a sacerdotal faith as the transcendent Other, alienated from the world, an object of religious worship, a Father and Judge infinitely distant from the world, but through the kenotic realization of death is experienced now by a prophetic faith as increasingly incarnate in our very midst as the 'flesh,' or active embodiment, or actual eventfulness of the world" (Lissa McCullough, "Historical Introduction," in *Thinking Through the Death of God: A Critical Companion to Thomas J.J. Altizer*, ed. L. McCullough and Brian Schroeder [Albany: State University of New York Press, 2004], xvii).

110. There is also the murder of the son, minimally his suicide, in Talal Asad's telling version, "God's only begotten son gave his life willingly and deliberately in order to redeem mankind: the supreme sacrifice. Although he did not murder himself, he devised that he should be cruelly killed. . . . In fact, Christ's indirect suicide—his public torture— constitutes a paradox: it is at once a loving gift and a model of unjust suffering" (T. Asad, *On Suicide Bombing* [New York: Columbia University Press, 2007], 84).

111. Freud, *Moses*, 86.

112. In his attempt to vindicate Freud ("Freud was right to see that one can 'reconstruct' the myth of the primal horde from the myth and narrative performed in the Christian communion"), Robert Paul surprisingly goes in the opposite direction, suggesting that "it is Moses himself who is the perpetrator of the primal deed" (Paul, *Moses and Civilization*, 13, 215). The murdered father is always a murdering son! To be sure, my conclusion stays very close to Paul's, who clearly states that "Christ's sacrifice . . . undoes the deed that gave rise to both the guilt and the Law" (212) and that Jesus, "having first played the martyred victim, reigns as innocent heir and new legitimate ruler" (215). Yet, for Paul, this seems to be a mere "transformation of the myth of Moses and the Exodus" (194), and there is no significant difference between seeing the cycle as a delusion or as truth (208–209). Freudian enough, but then Christian too.

113. Freud, *Moses*, 86.

114. "Jesus as the Anti-Oedipus" is the argument presented by Paul Vitz, who writes that "Jesus provides the model for the negation—in fact, for the canceling out or removal—of the Oedipal structure" (Vitz, *Sigmund Freud's Christian Unconscious*, 168). Vitz underscores "love and obedience," whereas I see something quite different in the nature of "the new man" (169). Vitz, it might be clear by now, reads *Moses* as the book in which Freud "produced some of his most unequivocally pro-Christian remarks" (202); and compare Bakan for whom "making Moses an Egyptian, Freud absolves himself and the Jews of the guilt associated with the murder-thought. Killing Moses-as-an-Egyptian is simply killing a member of the group which first persecuted the Jews" (Bakan, *Sigmund Freud*, 168).

115. Asad, *On Suicide Bombing*, 90.

116. Asad, *On Suicide Bombing*, 85; Asad elaborates on the endurance of the structure whereby the crucifixion continues to represent "the truth of violence" in a secular age. "In popular visual narratives (film, television, etc.), the male hero often undergoes severe physical punishment or torture at the hands of ruthless men, but his acute suffering is the very vindication of truth. The audience suffers with him and anticipates a healing. This replays a modern secular crucifixion story in which the truth of the lonely figure is sustained by his willingness to suffer in mind and in body, to undergo unbearable pain and ecstasy that can become through sympathy an exquisite part of the spectator's own sensibility" (86).

117. "Freud appears not to have understood that in Christianity the Son does not replace the Father," writes Vitz (170) in a gesture reminiscent of Yerushalmi's disclaimer to the effect that "if Moses had actually been killed by our forefathers, not only would the murder not have been repressed but—on the contrary—it would have been remembered and recorded" (Yerushalmi, *Freud's Moses*, 85; and see Derrida, *Archive Fever*, 64–67). It is as if, for Vitz, God did not die on the cross! But note that "setting aside Freud's curious interpretation of Jesus as replacing the father, we can certainly see that he probably did understand much of the essential message of Christianity" (170).

118. That Freud conceals his critique of Christianity behind an account of anti-Semitism should not be surprising. Although he seemed explicitly to exonerate Christianity from anti-Semitism (a "pagan" remainder), putting more smoke in the eyes of his readers by equating the hatred of Jews with the hatred of Christians, Freud leaves little doubt that

he understood quite precisely the nature of Christianity and its discontent, its singularity. Here too, Freud ventriloquizes: "But we profess a religion of love. We ought to love even our enemies as ourselves" (Freud, "A Comment on Anti-Semitism," 291). I say that Freud ventriloquizes rather than cites from the mouths of Christians because, following Ernst Jones, the consensus is that this "remarkable confession," in the first person plural and allegedly made by "someone who was not a Jew" (292), is, as James Strachey puts it, "in fact by Freud himself" (289; and see Yerushalmi, *Freud's Moses*, 128, n. 54).

119. de Certeau, *Writing of History*, 325.

120. Commenting on this oft-spoken difference between the New Testament and the Old, Marianne Thompson describes "the relative infrequency of the term 'Father' for God" in the latter, which does "contrast sharply with the regular use of the term in the New Testament" (M. M. Thompson, *The Promise of the Father: Jesus and God in the New Testament* [Louisville, Ky.: Westminster John Knox Press, 2000], 39). Thompson insists that there are continuities, but she also makes clear that in the Old Testament, the reference to God as father has little to do with "the relationship of the individual to God, nor is the relationship between Father and children to be understood primarily hierarchically. God's Fatherhood relates primarily to the corporate entity of Israel, and that framework implies the obligation of the children to each other" (47). My intention is not that one should endorse "fraternity" (murderous or otherwise) instead—Carole Pateman, Marc Shell, and Jacques Derrida have provided significant warnings thereabout. I mean merely to underscore a measure of difference in founding narratives or structuring events.

121. Michael Mack promisingly opens his discussion of Freud with the question of "Christian innocence," but he anchors it mostly to anti-Semitism and enlightenment (Mack, *German Idealism and the Jew*, 136–42.

122. Gil Anidjar, *The Jew, the Arab: A History of the Enemy* (Stanford, Calif.: Stanford University Press, 2003).

123. Jacques Ellul, *The Subversion of Christianity*, trans. Geoffrey W. Bromiley (Eugene, Ore.: Wipf & Stock, 2011).

124. Jacques Rancière writes of "the distribution of the sensible [*partage du sensible*]" in J. Rancière, *The Politics of Aesthetics*, trans. Gabriel Rockhill (New York: Continuum, 2004), 7.

125. W. J. T. Mitchell, *Seeing Through Race* (Cambridge, Mass.: Harvard University Press, 2012), 24.

126. Ward Blanton locates the "liquidation of religion" in the aftermath of *Moby-Dick* (W. Blanton, *True Religion* [Malden, Mass.: Blackwell, 2003], 115–17).

INDEX